FORMULAS FOR CALCULATING DAMAGES

Second Edition

MARK S. GURALNICK

Cover design by Tony Nuccio/ABA Publishing.

Printed in the United States of America

23 22 21 20 19 5 4 3 2 1

Contents

Acknowledgments .... **xi**

Introduction .... **xiii**

Chapter 1
Overview **1**
1.1. Why Use Formulas? 1
1.2. How to Use Formulas 3
1.3. When to Use Formulas 5

Chapter 2
The 10 Basic Rules **9**
2.1. Rule 1: Due Diligence 9
2.2. Rule 2: Assumptions 10
2.3. Rule 3: Reliability and Verifiability 12
2.4. Rule 4: Risk of Change 13
2.5. Rule 5: Timing is Everything 15
2.6. Rule 6: Money Moves 17
2.7. Rule 7: Formula Value versus Settlement Value 18
2.8. Rule 8: Hidden and Missing Numbers 19
2.9. Rule 9: Fraud and Irregularities 20
2.10. Rule 10: Show Me the Money First 21

Chapter 3
Strategies and Myths **23**
3.1. The Past and the Future 23
3.2. Faulty Trend Spotting 25
3.3. Footnotes and Attachments 26
3.4. Volatility and Smoothing Techniques 29
3.5. Creative Accounting 30
3.6. Off-Balance Sheet Liabilities 33
3.7. Earnings and Consumption Myths 34
3.8. Silly Shortcuts and Ridiculous Rules of Thumb 35
3.9. Experts and Formulas 37
3.10. Free Data on the Internet 39

Chapter 4
Speed Math, Estimation, and Memorization 45
4.1. Math with No Hands 45
4.2. Finding the Complement 46
4.3. High-Speed Addition 47
4.4. High Speed Subtraction 49
4.5. Rounding and Reversing 50
4.6. High-Speed Multiplication 52
4.7. High-Speed Division 56
4.8. Rapid Squaring 60
4.9. Shortcutting and Double-Checking 62
4.10 Percentage Power 67
4.11 Estimation Techniques 69
4.12. Memorization Strategies 73

Chapter 5
The Basic Formulas 81
5.1. Time Value of Money 81
5.2. Future Value 83
5.3. Future Value of an Uneven Cash Flow 85
5.4. Present Value 87
5.5. Net Present Value 89
5.6. Present Value of an Annuity 93
5.7. Present Value of a Perpetuity 94
5.8. Central Tendency 96
5.9. Moving Averages 102
5.10 Arithmetic Mean versus Geometric Mean 107
5.11. The Breakeven Formula 111

Chapter 6
Calculating Interest 115
6.1. Simple Interest 115
6.2. Compound Interest 117
6.3. Principal, Rate, and Time 119
6.4. Real and Nominal Interest Rate 120
6.5. Periodic Interest Rate 122
6.6. Effective Interest Rate 123

Chapter 7
Determining Probability 125
7.1. Single Event Probability 125
7.2. Multiple Event Probability 127

7.3. Dependent Events .131
7.4. Mutually Exclusive Events .133

Chapter 8
Rates of Return .135
8.1. The Basic Calculation .135
7.2. Return on Investment .136
8.3. Simple Annualized Return on Investment .138
8.4. Compound Annual Growth Rate .138
8.5. Cash Flow Method .140
8.6. Expected Rate of Return .141
8.7. Return on Equity .143
8.8. Return on Assets .144
8.9. Net Worth .146
8.10. Book Value .147
8.11. Internal Rate of Return .148
8.12. Net Terminal Value .151

Chapter 9
Helpful Financial Ratios .155
9.1. Earnings Per Share .155
9.2. Price-to-Earnings Ratio .157
9.3. Debt-to-Equity Ratio .159
9.4. Quick Balance Sheet Math .161
9.5. Dividend Yield .162
9.6. Earnings Yield .163
9.7. Quick Ratio .164
9.8. Interest Coverage Ratio .166
9.9. Price-to-Book Ratio .168
9.10. Inventory Turnover .169
9.11. Accounts Receivable Turnover .171
9.12. Accounts Payable Turnover .173
9.13. Current Asset Turnover .174
9.14. Current Ratio .175
9.15. Capitalization Rate .176
9.16. Benefit-Cost Ratio .177

Chapter 10
Handy Numerical Rules .181
10.1. Rule of 72 .181
10.2. Rule of 70 .182

10.3. Rule of 69.3 183
10.4. Rule of 78 184

Chapter 11
Personal Injury and Wrongful Death Damages 189

Lost Earnings 189

11.1. Putting the Basic Formulas to Work 189
11.2. Future Earnings Loss 190
11.3. Work Expectancy 194
11.4. Offset Approaches 200
11.5. Putting a Quick Value on a Case 204

Lost Fringe Benefits 205

11.6. Calculating Lost Benefits 205
11.7. Stock Options 211
11.8. Social Security Benefits 214

Damage Reducers 215

11.9. Estimating Personal Consumption 215
11.10. Estimating Taxes 218

Other Losses 219

11.11. Lost Household Services 219
11.12. Lost Advice, Counsel, and Companionship 222
11.13. Hedonic Damages 223
11.14. Emotional Distress 225
11.15. Pain and Suffering 229

Chapter 12
Business Damages 235
12.1. Determining the Best Formula 235
12.2. Sources of Information 238
12.3. Dissecting Financial Statements 243
12.4. What's *Not* in the Financial Statements 259
12.5. Forms 10-K, 10-Q, and 8-K 262
12.6. Applying Net Worth 272
12.7. Applying Shareholders' Equity 274
12.8. Applying EPS 276
12.9. Applying the P/E Ratio 280
12.10. Applying Rates of Return 285
12.11. Liquidity versus Indebtedness 290
12.12. Profit Margins 292

12.13. Devising Your Own Specific Business Ratios 295
12.14. Dealing with Professional Practices and Small Businesses 301

Chapter 13
Employment Law Damages 313
13.1. Statutory Damages Framework 313
13.2. Front Pay 316
13.3. Back Pay 321
13.4. Nonpecuniary Losses 329
13.5. Liquidated Damages 330
13.6. Punitive Damages 334
13.7. Prejudgment Interest 339

Chapter 14
Real Estate Damages 343
14.1. Origin of Property Damage Claims 343
14.2. Sales Comparison Approach 344
14.3. Cost Approach 348
14.4. Direct Income Capitalization Approach 351
14.5. Discounted Cash Flow Approach 357
14.6. Rental Loss Formulas 361
14.7. Income Loss Formulas 365

Chapter 15
Environmental Damages 373
15.1. Methods of Valuation 373
15.2. Change in Value 377
15.3. Restoration Costs 378
15.4. Replacement Costs 384
15.5. Hedonic Pricing Method 389
15.6. Travel Cost Method 391
15.7. Contingent Valuation Method 393
15.8. Total Economic Value 394

Chapter 16
Bankruptcy Risk 399
16.1. Bankruptcy Ratios 399
16.2. Working Capital to Total Assets 402
16.3. Retained Earnings to Total Assets 404
16.4. EBIT to Total Assets 407
16.5. Equity to Debt 408

16.6. Sales to Total Assets .410
16.7. Z-score Bankruptcy Prediction Formula .412
16.8. Cash Flow Ratios .414

Chapter 17
Intellectual Property Damages .423

[Patents] .423

Lost Profits .423

17.1. Conceptual Framework .423
17.2. Lost Sales .426
17.3. Price Erosion .430
17.4. Combined Losses .431
17.5. Future Lost Profits .433
17.6. Accelerated Entry Damages .434

Royalties .436

17.7. Reasonable Royalty .436
17.8. Analytical Approach .439
17.9. Weighted Average Cost of Capital .440

[Trademarks] .444

Valuation Methods .444

17.10. Overview .444
17.11. DCF Approach .446
17.12. NTV Approach .448
17.13. Replacement Cost Method .450
17.14. Market Comparables Method .453

Estimation Models and Rules of Thumb .455

17.15. Profit Split Methods .455
17.16. Premium Pricing Method .457
17.17. Scale Comparison Method .459
17.18. Return on Assets Employed .460
17.19. Shortcuts and Rules of Thumb .463
17.20. Other Techniques and Considerations .465

[Copyrights] .468

Statutory Damage Schemes .468

17.21. Actual Damages Plus Profits 468
17.22. Statutory Damages 471
17.23. Punitive Damages 473

Infringer's Accounting Methods 474

17.24. Full Absorption Costing 474
17.25. Variable Costing 475

Chapter 18
Family Law Formulas 479

Time Value Calculations 479

18.1. Division of Assets 479
18.2. Alimony and Spousal Support 486
18.3. Assessing Interest 490

Ratio Analysis 491

18.4. Debt-to-Asset Ratio 491
18.5. Liquid Assets to Take-Home Pay Ratio 495
18.6. Take-Home Pay to Debt-Service Ratio 498
18.7. Liquid Assets to Current Liabilities 501

Valuation Formulas 502

18.8. Actual Cash Value 502
18.9. Home Affordability Tests 503
18.10. Adequacy of Life Insurance 514

Other Useful Devices 516

18.11. Break-Even Analysis 516
18.12. Gross and Net Analysis 518
18.13. Wilcox's Prediction Formula 524
18.14. Pressing vs. Patient Liabilities 526

Chapter 19
Admiralty and Aviation Law Damages 529
19.1. Scope 529

Admiralty Law 531

19.2. Legal Framework for Admiralty Cases 531
19.3. Damages Available 536
19.4. Calculating Damages 539

Aviation Law *552*

19.5. Legal Framework for Aviation Cases 552
19.6. Damages Available 558

Chapter 20
Forensic Experts **571**
20.1. When to Retain an Expert 571
20.2. Educational Credentials 573
20.3. Certifications and Designations 578
20.4. Top 25 Rules for Using Financial Experts 595
20.5. Objections to Expert Testimony 602
20.6. Scientific Validity and Reliability 607

Tables
Worklife Expectancy 198
Mortality Tables 613
Day of the Year Tables 614

Index **617**

About the Author **635**

Acknowledgements

I wish to extend my gratitude to the many attorneys, professors, accountants, and economists who shared thoughts with me concerning the manner in which damages are calculated, negotiated, and decided in our court system. Those informal comments, frustrations, and suggestions first prompted me to write an article for a bar association newsletter entitled "Twenty Formulas Every Family Lawyer Should Know." Once the idea took root, however, it blossomed into a larger project that examined how losses are calculated in a variety of legal specialties.

I owe a debt of gratitude to John Palmer, Executive Editor at ABA Publishing, who took the initiative to reincarnate this book into this larger, more up-to-date volume. John diligently navigated the process to producing a top-notch second edition. His management and efficiency steered the course, allowing us to collaborate in a collegial and productive manner.

My sincere thanks also go to Erin Nevius, former executive editor of ABA Publishing. Erin responded favorably to my proposal for a book on this subject, and maintained faith in me, even as I missed deadlines and became sidetracked by the day-to-day practice of law. Erin's patience, guidance, and initiative shaped this project into the book you now hold in your hands.

I'm also grateful to Tim Brandhorst at ABA Publishing, who first glimpsed my written proposal and passed it on to Erin.

I also wish to express my sincere appreciation to all of the editors and publishing professionals who work behind the scenes at the ABA, tending to the unglamorous task of formatting, designing, packaging, and distributing a book. Your expertise and diligence transformed my manuscript into a tangible and appealing product.

I would be remiss if I did not also thank my former classmates at Columbia University and at London Business School, where I earned dual MBAs. I first learned many of the formulas in this book some years ago, as I labored all night in New York or London, sequestered in classrooms, hotels, and pubs with members of my study group, Olivier

Do Ngoc, Maxwell Federbush, and Federica Bietta. Those early days were an awakening to a lawyer who habitually steered clear of all things mathematical, and I thank my study partners for their compassion and guidance.

MSG

Introduction

Numbers are scary. They have a mystifying language of their own—*binomial, exponent, logarithm, quotient*—and they tend to confound us as they get larger and larger. *What is the negative square root of 16? What is the highest prime number greater than 900 and less than 1,000?* If you stopped taking math in high school, you might find such questions bewildering.

Yet not all numbers require the expertise of a mathematician or the specialized skills of an accountant, a statistician, or an economist. Simple arithmetic and a basic knowledge of algebra can lead to many useful discoveries. Particularly for lawyers, who spend more time mastering the peculiarities of language than of numbers, a trip down mathematical memory lane may provide some wonderful insights and helpful techniques for practicing law.

This book is meant to improve legal practice. It provides a variety of formulas that can be applied to thousands of case scenarios. The formulas can be used to estimate the value of a case informally, to negotiate or mediate settlements, or to prove damages in the course of a trial. While many of the discussions that follow deal with the calculation of damages or the estimation of losses, the formulas that fill these pages can be exploited to serve many useful purposes: deciding whether to accept or reject a case, whether to hire an employee or retain a contractor, whether to sell or not sell a business, to name a few.

Of course, there is no substitute for a forensic financial expert when it comes to complex litigation such as substantial tort cases, class actions, high-income divorces, and disputes over the value of a business. Still, this book will enable attorneys to add a dose of precision lawyering to their case work-ups, their settlement demands, and their presentations to mediators, arbitrators, judges, and juries. Even where expert witnesses are retained, this book will assist lawyers in preparing the experts, understanding their methodologies, and cross-examining the opposing experts. For those lawyers who make arbitrary settlement demands or offers without any technical support for the numbers in dispute, this volume should be a game-changer.

The book is divided into 20 chapters. The first ten chapters address the basic rules and strategies and introduce the most fundamental formulas. Important threshold concepts, like calculating interest and measuring probability, are discussed, and the key rates of return and financial ratios are outlined. The last ten chapters of the book introduce and apply various formulas to the major practice specialties: personal injury and wrongful death, business cases, employment law, real estate, environmental law, bankruptcy, intellectual property, family law, and admiralty and aviation law. The last chapter provides a detailed examination of the retention of forensic experts and the top rules for using them strategically.

No attempt is made here to provide the level of technical training or the depth of analysis that would accompany the teaching of such formulas in a graduate business or accounting program. Rather, the book is meant for practicing attorneys who want to understand how a formula works, what it does, and how it can assist them to address, resolve, or value a case. While it can be read cover to cover, the book can also be consulted frequently as a reference source for busy practitioners: *What was that formula for calculating lost fringe benefits?* (See Chapter 11). *How much money should we offer today to avoid a long-term alimony obligation?* (See Chapter 18).

Achieving mathematical literacy is an admirable goal unto itself. This book does not promise such results. Still, if the use of well-recognized formulas serves to professionalize the practice of law, to bolster the quality of advice provided to our clients, and to generate a more responsibly and skillfully presented case for damages, then we will have advanced the legal profession in a meaningful way while cross-fertilizing the fields of law, accounting, economics, and statistics.

Mark S. Guralnick

Chapter 1

Overview

1.1. Why Use Formulas?

What's the value of a human life, a broken marriage, a stolen copyright, a contaminated water system, or a sexually harassed office worker? How much is the case worth?

And . . .

Should we take the case? Should we settle now or hold out longer? Will it be worth more or less if we delay settlement negotiations? If we go to trial, what offsets or enhancements should the judgment include? When, if ever, will the business break even?

All of these questions have answers. They are answers that can be expressed in mathematical terms and then used to calculate damages. In some cases, these answers can be established scientifically using precise formulas that are universally accepted among financial and accounting experts. In other cases, the answers can be deduced from formulas that provide insight and guidance, if not scientific certainty, about a particular case.

For some lawyers, the most basic tools—averaging, compounding interest, determining probabilities—will prove tremendously helpful in evaluating the strength of a case, or positioning oneself for settlement talks or mediation sessions. For others, the more advanced devices, such as calculating the compound annual growth rate or using a debt-to-equity ratio, may accelerate settlement discussions or assist the trier of fact in fixing damages in a particular case.

While there are many reasons why formulas are helpful, there are also many reasons why they are necessary. At the outset, formulas can guide lawyers and law firms toward making important *intake* decisions:

1. Should we take the case? Will the cost justify the expense?
2. What kind of retainer agreement should we offer the client in view of the projected value of the case?
3. How extensive/expensive will the pretrial discovery process be, in order for us to gather the information necessary to apply a particular formula?

Formulas can also assist lawyers in determining whether to resolve a case informally before filing suit or going to trial:

1. Will the cost of litigation substantially erode the value of the case?
2. Is the evidence necessary to prove a particular formula admissible in this particular court, or should we apply our formulas outside of court, as a negotiating device only?
3. How long will litigation take? Will the time value of money reduce the ultimate benefit to be achieved?

Formulas can tell a lawyer what pretrial discovery to conduct, which questions to ask, and which documents to demand in production prior to trial. For example, in a wrongful death action, the court will want to see admissible evidence of the decedent's work expectancy. Thus, it may be necessary to obtain proper work expectancy tables from a reliable government source, and to determine whether the court can take judicial notice of such records. In a real estate case, it may be necessary to obtain architectural plans, appraisals, land use regulations, site plans, termite reports, leases, loans, escrow and closing documents, and title reports, some or all of which may provide the raw data necessary to run the formulas.

Formulas can also provide a necessary platform for demanding a settlement figure or rejecting such a demand. They may channel the course of negotiations in a mediation or a judicially supervised settlement conference. In a complex divorce case, for example, formulas will allow the attorney to calculate quickly the cash flow to a dependent spouse, to offer alternatives to permanent alimony, and to demand the proper amount of life insurance coverage. In an employment discrimination case, the attorney will be able to apply appropriate formulas to demand the proper damages for lost benefits, bonuses, and salary upgrades.

In smaller cases, which do not justify the retention of expensive expert witnesses, knowing how to use formulas strategically can boost the value of the case and provide a defense against arbitrary and baseless offers and demands.

Perhaps the most important reason to use formulas is to conduct one's representation ethically and thoroughly. By documenting the efforts to valuate a case, a loss, a business transaction, or other event, attorneys can demonstrate their due diligence. They can apply math and science to a process that is often aimless or misdirected. Formulas may, in fact, keep lawyers out of trouble by helping them to prove the positions they've taken and the recommendations they've made to clients.

1.2. How to Use Formulas

The first rule of using formulas is to use them secretly—that is, privately—until you know the results. In most cases, attorneys are not required to apply particular formulas to a damages calculation. In fact, negotiations often proceed quite unscientifically: plaintiff makes a high demand, defendant counters with a low offer, followed by a more realistic demand, then a more realistic offer, and so forth. In many law firms, the valuation of a case may be tied to the latest jury verdict research showing the amounts that juries awarded in other, similar cases. Such research is not always comparable or realistic. Other law firms keep track of trends in their local courthouses, developing a settlement range in particular cases that is consistent with the history of juries in their particular locales. All of these approaches are acceptable, but none of them should be considered exclusively.

Formulas can be used both as private decision-making tools (privileged attorney work product) and as published negotiating or litigating tools. They should never be used arbitrarily or haphazardly. They should not be overused, or used too hastily, or without sufficient determination of the underlying figures. Where the circumstances are highly complex, or the positions asserted require specialized expertise and experience, attorneys should engage financial experts to explain and justify the use of a particular formula.

As a private decision-making tool, the formulas provided in this book supply a reference guide for problem-solving and analytical measurement. Attorneys should explore the formulas, the ratios, the shortcuts, and other techniques discussed in these pages as part of the early case work-up and brainstorming process. Running the numbers through a few different formulas, and hypothesizing about how the evidence might alter the results, can focus the case acutely on the target issues and the primary discovery questions that lie ahead. Applying the formulas can also tell attorneys what the client or the adversary is worth: simple net-worth calculations or turnover ratios can offer immediate clues about the financial stability of an individual or a business entity.

Formulas should be used to avoid "shooting from the hip." Settlement offers pitched in the hallway of a courthouse or in the caucus of a mediation session should not be plucked out of thin air. Rather, they should be calculated on a calculator, scratched out on a notepad, and identified as a particular formula—a net present value, a periodic interest rate, a multiple event probability, or a price-to-earnings ratio, as the case may be. By using formulas to fix a more precise monetary amount, attorneys can simultaneously argue their positions mathematically, justify their demands or defenses ethically, and professionalize the negotiating process.

Plaintiffs' attorneys who deal with difficult insurance carriers may find that formulas can help them settle a case for policy limits rather than superficially threatening bad faith litigation. Indeed, rather than dispatching boilerplate letters to insurance companies warning them of the risk of a bad faith claim, attorneys can lay out formulaic calculations to explain why tendering the policy limits would be highly justified in the circumstances. Such letters are likely to be treated as far more persuasive than the boilerplate warning letters used by some attorneys.

Formulas should not be used, however, whenever they will destroy a tactical advantage between the parties or their attorneys. Where a weak opponent has failed to do his homework, or an insurance claims adjuster has initiated discussions with far too high an opening figure, attorneys should never cling to formulas blindly. After all, the objective of an advocate is to represent his client's interests zealously, and that may require him to act upon a strategic advantage that occurs from time to time. In such cases, a formula, calculated privately, may help an attorney appreciate how good a deal awaits him because of his weakened opponent's position.

Formulas should not be arbitrarily shared with clients inasmuch as they may do more harm than good. They may mislead clients about the value of a potential claim, or the legitimacy of a particular formula for determining value. Formulas, considered in a vacuum, do not take into consideration the many other reasons why a lawyer may recommend settlement at a particular value or at a particular moment in time. In the case of unsophisticated clients, the results of a formula calculation, prematurely shared with them, may cause them, unrealistically, to fixate on a certain damages figure, frustrating the lawyer's efforts to settle the case. Yet when negotiations are successful, a formula may provide a useful device for selling the client on the settlement. Showing a client how a formula adopts the facts of his case may reveal to him how the proffered settlement is consistent with, or perhaps greater than, the mathematical value of his loss.

1.3. When to Use Formulas

Formulas should be used whenever a decision can be informed by data. If a business loses money based on a trade violation by a competing business, how do we calculate that loss? Is it as simple as averaging past profits? What if the historical profits for the business have fluctuated over time? The answer? Apply a moving averages formula.

Should a client invest $100,000 if the result will bring $200,000 in one year? Or should the client invest $200,000 to litigate a related issue that will likely pay damages of $400,000 three years from now? Which alternative makes more sense? The answer? Conduct a net present value comparison.

Or, your client tells you that he wants to make a deal involving a parcel of commercial real estate, but only if two events occur first. There's a 50% chance of the first event occurring, and a 65% chance of the second event occurring. How can you assess the likelihood that *both events* will occur first in order to move forward with the real estate deal? The answer? Perform a multiple events probability calculation.

In each case, the question includes certain data, numbers, percentages, figures, or dollar amounts. Because a formula requires one or more mathematical factors, the questions posed must include numbers in some form or another. Whenever such data or numbers exist, the question may find an answer in a formula.

Exactly when to use a formula is a personal choice. When to reveal a formula is a strategic decision. Formulas can be used at virtually every stage of legal representation, from the case intake process, through the pretrial discovery and settlement phases, and in the evidence presentation and legal argument stages of the litigation. They can be explained and displayed in pretrial memoranda, arbitration and mediation summaries, trial briefs, and on the board at trial. They can be applied retrospectively to evaluate whether the disposition of the case (i.e., the final judgment) was statistically favorable or cost beneficial. Whether a formula should be *revealed,* or *relied upon*, at any of these stages, however, is a strategic decision.

Attorneys should not rely on formulas before the discovery necessary to complete the formula has been fully conducted. Revealing a formula before all of the data is gathered may tip your adversary as to the importance of a missing factor, or how that factor can dramatically alter the perceived value of the case. It is better, then, to gather all of the data from reliable documents and testimony, and then use the data—as if it were admissions under oath—to build an irrefutable formula.

Let's assume, for example, that a business dispute has focused on the question of how quickly a particular producer of consumer goods turns over its inventory. The formula for inventory turnover, discussed in Section 8.10, requires us to first calculate the "cost of goods sold." In order to determine the cost of goods sold, we must know the company's beginning inventory, the amount of inventory it purchased thereafter, and the inventory presently remaining. Until we conduct discovery on each of these values and obtain reliable data for each value, we should not reveal the inventory turnover formula as one of our bargaining tools.

Consider another example. Your client is a dependent wife in a divorce case. Her husband claims that he has far too many credit card bills to be able to pay the amount of spousal support that you are demanding on behalf of your client. A helpful formula is the take-home pay-to-debt-service ratio, through which you can determine the relationship between the husband's net earnings and his bill-paying obligations. (See Section 17.11.) You should not, however, disclose this formula or attempt to demonstrate its logic, until you've reviewed the husband's pay stubs to establish his take-home pay and you've obtained his admission that he has no credit card debt beyond the several accounts he specifically identified on his financial affidavit. Obtain the credit card statements with a request for production directed to the husband or a subpoena served on the credit card companies. Once you have irrefutable dollar amounts, the take-home pay-to-debt-service ratio can prove extremely helpful as a bargaining device or a litigation tool.

In some cases, it may be more strategically advantageous to invoke a formula only at trial, and only *after* the evidence has concluded. After both parties have presented their evidence, and it is time to deliver a closing argument (or to submit a written summation), the attorney may argue in favor of the competent evidence available for the court's consideration.

He may argue that, based on the testimony and documentary evidence, the court should now determine the value of a particular loss or gain, or of a particular asset or liability. He may argue that a particular formula is best suited to determining the value in question, and he may demonstrate for the court how the formula can be populated with the figures adduced at trial and admitted into evidence. As counsel makes his summation, he can argue for a particular judgment based on a value established by applying the appropriate formula to the evidence at trial.

Chapter 2

The 10 Basic Rules

Risky, ambiguous, unreliable. These are some of the most common words used to describe formulas that are applied hastily to settle a case. In practice, a formula is only as valid as the data used to support it, the timing in which it is applied, and the circumstances under which it is introduced. The information generated by the formula does not guarantee a perfect settlement, and indeed a formula can backfire if certain conditions do not exist, or if they cease to exist. With this is mind, attorneys should follow the 10 rules below as a foundation for using formulas effectively to calculate damages.

2.1. Rule 1. Due Diligence

Without targeted information-gathering, attorneys will find it extremely difficult, if not impossible, to apply many of the useful formulas discussed in this book. Some formulas are simple mathematical calculations, but others require due diligence, the process of asking questions, reading reports, investigating leads, conducting research, and verifying data.

In a real estate case, for example, a formula based on fair market value is only reliable if the market data is accurate and the method used to determine fair market value is trustworthy. In a business valuation case, the valuation formula can be rendered invalid by the failure to discover the company's technology license agreements or a list of executory contracts with suppliers. In a wrongful death case, a formula based on the loss of the decedent's household services could be undermined by a failure to determine the decedent's self-consumption of such services.

What does this mean for attorneys? It means that they must conduct pretrial discovery and prefiling investigations with an eye on the ultimate formulas to be applied. All reasonable sources must be consulted in order to gather the best data and the most up-to-date, verifiable, and reliable information. Attorneys must undertake every effort to find the right numbers. They must ask targeted questions in interrogatories and depositions.

Where appropriate, subpoenas should be issued to obtain documents from third parties to validate interest rates, tax rates, earnings histories, wage loss data, and other financial specifics. Private investigators, law clerks, and paralegals must be supervised carefully to ensure that they corroborate the information that will form the basis for the formulas to be applied. An error or a gap in information-gathering could render a formula inaccurate or incomplete.

Due diligence in calculating damages also requires reliance upon objective and factual sources. Thus, an attorney cannot expect to calculate future pension benefits to a spouse based on her husband's unverified representation of the future monthly payout from his retirement account. Only a certified statement from the pension plan administrator, applying recognized actuarial standards, would be trustworthy in such a case. Similarly, in a patent infringement case, an attorney would not expect to apply the so-called "25 percent rule" which allocates one-fourth of the infringer's operating profit to the patent holder, without objectively measuring the operating profit or verifying the royalty rate by using another recognized method.

Doing one's homework to gather accurate base figures, tying the data to pretrial discovery and other admissible evidence, and confirming the objective validity of the information will make a persuasive argument for applying formulas to achieve the most beneficial results.

2.2. Rule 2. Assumptions

Every mathematical attempt to calculate damages rests on certain facts and assumptions about the plaintiff or about the defendant. Most personal facts can be established through basic pretrial discovery devices.

These include such facts as the party's date of birth, gender, date of accident or loss, educational achievement, and reported income. Other facts fall into a category of generally accepted or recognized facts because they are based on public data sources. These include tax rates, prime rates, interest rates, minimum wage rates, cost-of-living tables, and the consumer price index.

Yet facts get fuzzier as we try to interpret ambiguous events or forecast future losses. Establishing an injury victim's future earning capacity, predicting a college freshman's total future higher education costs, or estimating the cost of raising a child are all based on assumptions about what may or may not happen in the future. They depend on projections about whether certain behaviors will remain constant (would the college freshman take four years to finish his degree or perhaps five years?). They are founded on assumptions about economic events (would the injury victim's employer have remained in business for the rest of the victim's work life?).

Assumptions, therefore, are a necessary part of formula-building. But if they are not shared by all parties, and clearly articulated, then the formulas will be built on a faulty or uncertain foundation. For example, assumptions about the future unemployment rate, the change in the inflation rate, or the growth rate for the commercial construction industry are ultimately subjective and are not necessarily shared uniformly among all experts. Where a formula is built on such assumptions, it is vulnerable to attack. Where an expert witness relies on flawed assumptions to apply a formula and draw a conclusion, his testimony may be impeached at trial.

The role of the attorney is, therefore, multidimensional: In all cases, the attorney must ascertain the assumptions upon which the formula will be based. Where a formula will be adopted, by consent, to determine the amount of damages in a case to be settled, the underlying assumptions should be expressed in a signed stipulation between counsel or otherwise agreed upon in a settlement document. Where a formula will be offered at trial as a method for determining damages, the court should be asked to take judicial notice of as many facts as will support the assumptions upon which the formula will be based. Where the assumptions are not shared, the formulas are intrinsically unsound and must be abandoned.

2.3. Rule 3. Reliability and Verifiability

Numbers do not occur naturally; they exist as outputs from a variety of inputs, many of which are often controlled and engineered. Financial information reported by private businesses may satisfy the auditor's compliance checklist but may nevertheless be unreliable if the business owners controlled the timing, the method, and the manner in which they made certain sales or acquisitions. In an environmental case, baseline data about when hazardous chemicals first started flowing into an estuary may be drawn—unreliably—through a variety of inconsistent data-collection methods used over a period of years. In a personal injury case, a loss of earnings may be measured only by what appears on one year's tax returns, giving no consideration to the victim's capacity to delay the reporting of earnings until a month later when a new tax year begins.

All of these strategies may be perfectly legal and yet may produce unreliable figures for use in calculating damages. A corporation may manipulate its current profits by increasing the amount of its reserves. It may choose to defer the writing off of uncollectible bad loans to increase its apparent profits. It may continue to accrue interest income on bad loans as a further method to mischaracterize its profits. Individual litigants are similarly capable of manipulating the system: debtors in bankruptcy court listing dormant debts or overstating contingent liabilities; wrongful termination claimants refusing to look for work; divorcing spouses over-estimating the value of property subject to distribution.

In some cases, unreliable or unverified data can be ferreted out by experts who know the rules, such as accountants who detect departures from generally accepted accounting principles (GAAP) or attorneys who specialize in compliance under the Sarbanes-Oxley Act. In other cases, however, it will be necessary to test the reliability of information by asking fundamental questions, conducting pretrial discovery to reconstruct timelines and transactions, spotting trends and patterns, and questioning any behavior that is inconsistent with prior practice.

The integrity of any formula used to calculate damages is based on the reliability of the figures that feed the formula. The figures must be drawn from verifiable data and they must arise from circumstances that are reasonable and rational in view of all attending circumstances.

2.4. Rule 4. Risk of Change

Not all figures are static or constant. Numbers used to calculate formulas at any particular moment in time could change if they depend on interest rates, market fluctuations, consumer behavior, social or economic trends, or government regulations. Therefore, any formula used to establish damages in a civil action must take into consideration the period of time over which the damages will be paid as well as the status of the data supporting the formulas amid prevailing circumstances.

From a technical perspective, information is inherently outdated unless it is applied seconds after it is generated. For example, a corporation's annual report is a reflection of history: the minute it is published, the corporation has moved into a new accounting period, and the data may have changed. Income statements, cash-flow statements, and balance sheets may appear to be fixed in time when viewed on paper or on a computer screen but, in fact, such financial statements are dynamic and constantly changing. Because of the risk that the underlying figures have changed, or that they will continue to change before damages can be paid, every effort should be exerted to obtain the most recent data, and to remain alert for patterns or trends that might invalidate the data.

Numbers can change, for example, if there is any modification in the accounting method or information-reporting schemes used to generate financial data. Reporting earnings or expenses on an accrual basis is much different from reporting on a cash basis, and a midstream switch between these two accounting methods could materially alter the numbers.

Changing the way a company reports inventory can likewise offset the bottom line. Does it count inventory monthly, semiannually, annually? Does it maintain the same records every time, and when and how does it report the results on its books? Prior accounting practices may be instructive too. A company that routinely tinkers with the amount of accumulated depreciation it reports or frequently modifies executive compensation packages may require greater scrutiny before accepting any guarantees about its future financial trends. A small business in which the owner mixes and matches personal and corporate assets is similarly suspect, such as where one finds a personal automobile on the company books or purported business travel expenses that were actually incurred for a family vacation.

Rapid growth by a corporation is suspect; so, too, are sudden or extreme losses over a short period of time. Significant changes in pricing, sales techniques, or purchasing habits may require greater analysis. A high degree of volatility from one year to the next makes trend-spotting difficult and could suggest unpredictable changes in the future. Any settlement that involves a long-term or structured payout is inherently susceptible to changing circumstances simply because of the passage of time. In all of these cases, lawyers should conduct a risk analysis and consider trends, patterns, and timelines. They should ask the following questions:

- What could possibly change between now and the time this settlement is fully satisfied?
- Should this formula include a mathematical or statistical factor that takes into consideration an evolving change or a possible change in value?
- Should the payout period be reduced to minimize the risk of change over time?
- Should there be additional language in the settlement agreement to provide for different terms in the event of any significant change, or if any of the foundation data is modified by changing circumstances?
- Are the numbers used in the current formulas up to date, and were they generated using consistent and reliable methods?
- Are there any macroeconomic circumstances or external factors that suggest a high risk of change (such as a rapidly fluctuating interest rate; a pending class action lawsuit; or an international labor, terrorism, or banking crisis that could adversely impact the numbers)?

It may be appropriate in certain cases to memorialize in writing a set of assumptions about the risk of change. A calculation, for example, may be based on the assumption that a price of goods does not exceed a certain point, or that a tax rate or interest rate remains within certain parameters. Indeed, the only fail-safe method to account for the risk of change is to account for it, in writing, as part of the case settlement terms. Where the risk of change is substantial, or the possibility exists that the payment terms could be modified by ambiguous circumstances, it may be necessary to combine due diligence in the investigative stage, expert skill in the formula-building stage, and smart draftsmanship in the agreement-writing stage.

2.5. Rule 5. Timing is Everything

Investors abide by the credo that "timing is everything" because they know that every index, market development, news item, or worthy rumor could justify a decision to buy or sell from one moment to the next. Yet not every piece of financial information can be updated as quickly as the stock market. In business litigation, tort claims, divorces, and many other kinds of cases, it is often difficult to know when to settle a case. At what moment in time can the best leverage be applied? When will the defendant be most vulnerable to attack? Most amenable to settlement? Most likely to reach an agreement on beneficial terms? While the answers to these questions will vary from case to case, it is important to keep an eye on the timing of settlement negotiations or courtroom proceedings to maximize the value of the formulas being used.

One can manipulate the results generated by a formula by raising or lowering the value of certain time-sensitive factors in the formula. For example, if a formula requires an interest rate, the final result can be manipulated by raising or lowering the rate. Thus, in a market in which interest rates change every six months, it would make sense to expedite or to delay the introduction of the formula, by speeding up or slowing down settlement negotiations or trial dates, in order to capture the desired rate.

Consider, for example, the formula for determining the present value of money to be paid in five years (discussed in Part 4). If $1,000 is to be paid in five years at a certain interest rate, how much should be paid today to buy out the obligation early? The answer would vary depending on the interest rate at any given moment in time. At 4%, the buyout figure would be $821.69 today, but at 5%, the figure would be $783.70 today. Timing thus becomes important if the prevailing interest rate (or the basis for determining the interest rate) will change during the pendency of the litigation or during the course of settlement negotiations.

Suppose, for example, that a public company's risk and volatility tend to fluctuate over time, and measuring this risk is important to determine when to resolve a legal claim against (or on behalf of) the company. One way to measure the risk is to calculate the beta, which is a technical number obtained through regression analysis (discussed in Part 11). By definition, beta equals 1, which equals the overall risk of investing in a large market such as a stock exchange. A particular company's beta is that company's risk or volatility compared with the entire market. For example, on June 18, 2010, Citigroup, Inc. was reported on Yahoo! Finance as having a beta of 2.69. As such, Citigroup could be said to have been 2.69 times more risky or more volatile than the overall market—at that point in time.

But what about other points in time? If a company's beta is a factor in a financial calculation—for example, a formula to determine the rate of return on investing in that company—it would be valuable to know how the beta is calculated and how it changes over time. A beta that falls below 1.0 means that the company (or an investment in the company) would be less volatile than the overall market, and this could be a significant consideration, particularly for a conservative negotiator. By contrast, a risk-taker might be willing to strike a deal with a higher beta investment, banking on the hope that greater returns on the investment will materialize without any adverse consequences.

Timing is also important in making deals in nonbusiness litigation. In a divorce case, for example, an employed spouse may be entitled to exercise certain stock options after a certain period of active service with the same employer. In many states, however, stock options cannot be easily distributed between spouses where they have not yet vested, or where the employed spouse has not yet achieved the right to exercise those options. In determining the value of the marital estate, the nonemployee spouse may wish to time her calculation of assets until the stock options are vested and exercisable (if possible). In the same vein, the nonemployee spouse would be well-advised to determine the value of such options at the point in time when the employer is reporting its best performance.

In cases involving depletion of natural resources, environmental torts, and damages to real property, formulas used to calculate damages can be offset by the development or amendment of enforcement regulations. The same can be said of employment discrimination cases that often exist within an extensive regulatory framework. In all of these civil actions, regulations that prescribe the right to damages, attorneys' fees, and interest rates should be consulted, along with pending legislation or rule-making proceedings at the administrative level that could result in regulatory changes. Overlooking a new or pending regulation that improves a plaintiff's right of recovery could lead to an ill-timed settlement based on an outdated formula and could expose an attorney to claims of professional negligence.

2.6. Rule 6. Money Moves

Because money can be converted from cash to negotiable instruments to securities to real and personal property and back to cash again, documents that reflect a certain monetary value can be misleading. The liquid assets reflected on a financial statement could, in fact, reflect cash on hand only at the time of publishing the statement. Money can be moved from person to person, from entity to entity, from one form to another, from one country to another, and through one or more forms of legal instruments and devices (such a multigeneration trusts). Thus, a basic rule in calculating damages is to preserve the assets from which the damages will be paid.

Assume, for example, that a formula is based on uneven cash payments over five years: $200,000 in year 1, $300,000 in year 2, $400,000 in year 3, and $500,000 in both years 4 and 5. The total value of the payments over five years is $1.9 million. The party obligated to make the payments could be persuaded to pay a discounted amount today instead of $1.9 million over five years. Such an agreement would ensure payment before time passes and circumstances change. An insurance policy or a bond could be purchased to guarantee payment over five years. A provision can be included in the settlement agreement that provides for the transfer of property or of legal rights upon a default in payment.

For even greater protection, the party entitled to the payment could obtain injunctive relief to prevent dissipation or diversion of the assets in question. Because money can be freely moved, converted, and transferred after a settlement is reached, it may be necessary to obtain restraints against the transfer of money while a settlement remains in payment status. In the alternative, an agreement could provide for the establishment of a trust to secure the funds and to prevent the funds from being commingled with the obligor's other monetary assets. An agreement could also provide that certain earmarked funds will not be transferred, invested, reassigned, or otherwise moved without the signatures of two or more parties, until the full settlement is paid.

2.7. Rule 7. Formula Value versus Settlement Value

Financial and mathematical formulas are extremely helpful in providing information that can be used in settling a case or in rendering a judgment. However, the values obtained by using formulas are not necessarily the best settlement values, nor are they necessarily the most equitable values on which to base a final judgment. With any case, the best settlement value is the greatest amount the plaintiff can possibly recover, or the least amount the defendant can possibly pay, under all of the existing circumstances. So, while formulas can provide a reliable factual basis for calculating damages, they are not—and should not be presumed to be—the final measure of the best settlement value in every case.

Indeed, it may be appropriate in some cases to use formulas privately, as a form of attorney work product, rather than as a negotiation or litigation strategy shared with one's adversary. A formula may reveal a lesser value than anticipated, or it may rely on assumptions that cannot be sustained. No formula can substitute for the judgment of experienced counsel in evaluating the risks and vulnerabilities of the parties, the strengths and weaknesses of the attorneys, the temperament and culture of local courts and juries, or the perceptions and predispositions about settlement value.

In other cases, a formula may produce a result that is much better than anticipated. The formula may, in fact, become the key negotiating tool and the principal device through which a settlement figure is reached. A value generated by a formula is not, however, a fair market value, or an equitable value, or a maximum settlement value. For this reason, formula values must be considered in the context of the entire case, weighing all important factors and considerations. If a better settlement can be achieved by emphasizing other factors and circumstances, then blind allegiance to a formula would be a disservice to the client.

2.8. Rule 8. Hidden and Missing Numbers

A financial affidavit supplied by a spouse in a divorce case lists all but one of her current bank accounts. A balance sheet provided by a corporate defendant in pretrial discovery fails to mention a pending lawsuit that could lead to large losses. A tax return submitted by a plaintiff in a wrongful termination case contains no Schedule C (Profit or Loss Statement) for his part-time landscaping business. The missing information in each case may have been deliberately excluded, or it may be buried in footnotes, in attachments, or in vague or inconspicuous references. Hidden and missing financial information presents problems for lawyers who use formulas. In addition to invalidating the figures used to calculate the formulas, the absence of all of the available financial information may impair the attorney's ability to choose the appropriate formulas.

Only a scrupulous and investigative approach to information gathering, and a careful reading of all available documents and reports, will minimize the risk of error based on hidden or missing numbers. When a financial statement is supplied by a corporation, all reasonable inquiries must be made to determine if the corporation is failing to report any off-balance sheet liabilities or contingent risks (such as a pending lawsuit). Relying on a balance sheet without inquiring about unreported long-term obligations or contingent liabilities is a potentially dangerous practice.

Attorneys should also take a broad, longitudinal view of accounting records, looking for fraudulent and tactical accounting schemes. For example, a business that seeks to portray itself as being conservative could take a large, one-time charge to adjust its balance sheet, thus reducing its costs in future years. This so-called "big bath" technique can produce increased future earnings which might be misunderstood without reference back to the large one-time clean-up charge. Another technique, characterized as "cookie jar reserves," is the aggressive accrual of current operating expenses in an effort to reduce future operating expenses.

Hidden information also can be found in a company's annual report. The notes section that follows the company's financial statements is often rich with details that illuminate the meaning of the numbers. For example, a note on "consolidation" may reveal which of several interrelated companies or subsidiaries is covered by the data reported in the annual report. A note about inventory will likely reveal how the company values its inventory, that is, by purchase price, resale price, or otherwise. A note on amortization usually reveals the rate at which buildings, furniture, equipment, and other assets are depreciated over time. Of particular interest is any note on long-term debt, which generally specifies the long-term debt obligations of the company, stating due dates on principal, interest rates on loans, and related detail.

2.9. Rule 9. Fraud and Irregularities

A husband in a divorce case reports a diminished income from his family-owned business as his employer (his own father) diverts a portion of his earnings to a special savings account or instead pays him excessive reimbursements for travel expenses in lieu of a full salary. A restaurant partnership defers some of its current-year revenues to next year in an attempt to portray itself as less profitable. A building contractor makes unnecessary purchases of raw materials long before they're needed, and accelerates its future expenses as current-year expenses, in order to cast itself as more debt-ridden and less profitable. Manipulating how and when revenues and expenses are reported, and deferring or diverting how income is received, are common, albeit potentially fraudulent, techniques to mischaracterize the current financial status of individual and business litigants.

Vigilant attorneys are always on the lookout for deferred income, accelerated expenses, and other unorthodox transactions. They question any sales and purchases that seem ill-timed or unusually high-valued. Is the sale fictitious? Is it a legitimate sale that was carried out or recognized early for accounting purposes? Have items been shipped to customers who didn't order the items, so that the sales could be recorded on the books? Have sales been booked while items haven't yet been shipped to customers? Has the company neglected to account for returned goods?

Spotting irregularities is an important function for counsel before building formulas based on financial data. Suspiciously constant increases in sales and profits can be as questionable as unusually erratic spikes in financial data. Thus, it is important to ask questions to learn the acceptable buying and selling parameters for a business or the spending trends and patterns of a family or of an individual client.

In dealing with business transactions, personal relationships matter. Attorneys will want to inquire with whom the corporate client, or the individual client, does business. To whom are the goods being sold? With whom is the financial transaction being undertaken? High-risk, undisclosed, and suspect relationships between buyers and sellers and parties to business transactions can undermine the integrity of the financial data, thus rendering formulas a useless academic exercise.

In dealing with matrimonial disputes, attorneys should apply the same level of fraud-alert sensitivity. A spouse may defer his earnings by making a private arrangement with his employer. Or he may request excessive payroll deductions for deferred income, insurance, and retirement plans. Unnecessary or undisclosed company loans and payroll deductions to repay credit union advances may also raise red flags.

Combing through financial records in search of irregularities is a useful practice to safeguard against unreliable data in the creation of formulas. By searching for fraudulent transactions and manipulated accounting entries, attorneys can ferret out the real numbers to be used in formula-building, and in so doing, expose the misdeeds of their adversaries.

2.10. Rule 10. Show Me the Money First

There's no reason to determine the future value of damages or to agree to a structured settlement payout if the party agreeing to make the payments is a high credit risk or has a history of nonliquid assets. While the formula for calculating the future payments may be unassailable, the process is ill-advised unless the obligor can first show you the money.

Thus, the advice: don't enter into a deal that requires a future payout unless you are satisfied that the party obligated to make the payments has the money to pay you.

To proceed cautiously, then, attorneys should look at balance sheets, consider capital resources, and examine how the obligated party pays its debts. They should scrutinize balance sheets for the value and the nature of the assets and liabilities. For example, a company that overvalues its goodwill as an independent asset with material value may be overstating its level of solvency. Contingent assets and contingent liabilities (such as a suspected lawsuit which a company anticipates will be filed against its principals) also require close scrutiny.

The capital structure of the company should also be examined. In other words, what are the values and sources of the company's operating funds? To determine if a company's capital structure is adequate to pay the damages or the settlement agreed upon, counsel should consider the company's line of credit and its credit rating. Financial ratios, many of which are discussed in Part 8, may help attorneys evaluate the adequacy of capital.

Whether a company has enough money to pay a settlement can also be inferred by the way it pays its existing debts when they come due. Examining cash flow statements or running an accounts payable turnover formula (Section 8.12) may provide additional guidance. A careful analysis will also inquire into the amount of cash on hand reported by the company over time, its free cash flows earned during the applicable time period, and the company's borrowing ability over time.

Chapter 3

Strategies and Myths

3.1. The Past and the Future

In building formulas, attorneys and their experts will frequently be called on to predict the future. Choosing an interest rate to calculate future value and forecasting sales to predict market share are examples of this process. Of course, none of us has a crystal ball to tell us what the interest rate, prime rate, tax rate, inflation rate, exchange rate, or more specific index rates will be in the future. So how do we predict the future?

The most reliable answer is to understand the past thoroughly. Indeed, past performance is the best indicator of future results, but this is not intended to be a superficial statement. Understanding past performance can require a significant investment of time and research. It may require extensive discovery about a corporation's performance, or an individual litigant's investment history, buying and spending patterns, and credit status. Still, thinking about past performance can assist attorneys in discrediting adversaries and their experts who rely on inadequate data and faulty assumptions in predicting the future.

So, for example, if a dispute involves the future of a business enterprise, a thorough examination of its past sales, earnings, inventory, overhead, accounts receivable, and accounts payable would assist us in gauging its financial trajectory in the future. If a husband in a divorce case proposes to invest certain money to generate a college fund for the children in the years to come, a detailed study of his investment history and his credit profile may provide insight into his ability to obtain a particular interest rate on the future investment.

Smart litigators and negotiators cannot afford to ignore the past. Because there is no absolute formula for choosing future interest rates or inflation rates, these uncertainties must be determined from the best information available about the past. Some general rules have thus evolved: a long-term trend presents a better picture of the past than a short-term trend. Moreover, some fluctuations (some volatility) may be ordinary, and should not be automatically assumed to be evidence of an upturn or a downturn. Ultimately, it is best to take a broad view of the business, or of the individual, under consideration, and to spot as many long-term trends or patterns as possible.

While a fundamental investigation of past performance is the key to predicting future trends and index rates, there are some generally accepted shortcuts which attorneys and experts may choose to follow reliably and efficiently. For example, mortgage interest rates are based on mortgage-backed securities or mortgage bonds. Pinning future mortgage interest rates to these measures, in order to build a formula, would not be incorrect, assuming that a proper trend could be established. The question always boils down to reliability. Thus, tracking the 10-year Treasury note would not be a good method for predicting future mortgage interest rates since the Treasury note sometimes trends in the opposite direction from mortgage bonds.

A full-blown macroeconomic analysis could also be undertaken, but this exercise would be far too complex and time-consuming for most cases. Economists can use specialized forecasting models, such as a *yield curve,* to predict U.S. recessions and other economic activity. Knowing such information may provide insight into inflation and interest rate trends, but any such analysis is susceptible to scientific challenge on many levels.

In the end, it is a judgment call. How much information to gather, and what research to conduct, in order to pick a future interest rate is a decision that will have to be made on a case-by-case basis. It is a very important decision, however. An unscrupulous attorney who agrees to a 4% interest rate in calculating the future value of $1 million to be paid in five years will have made a $60,000 mistake in judgment if the interest rate should have been 5%. (For Future Value, see Section 4.2.) Even when the resources available for investigation are limited, attorneys should view the choice of interest rates, inflation rates, and other such rates as vulnerable to attack. They should advocate the rates that will best protect their clients' interests and that can be most clearly attributed to reliable industry markers and tied to past performance trends and patterns.

3.2. Faulty Trend Spotting

Although it is important to consider movements and patterns in evaluating the past performance of an entity or an individual, attorneys should not be hasty in assuming that a trend exists. To avoid faulty trend-spotting, the following guidelines may be helpful:

- **Look for repetitive events over extended periods of time.** A single spike in the data does not necessarily signal a change in direction or a change in performance. There may, indeed, be a valid explanation for an anomalous entry in the data. Even several repetitive spikes or departures in the pattern of data may suggest a short-term aberration without indicating a trend. Yet, if an event or change appears to occur repeatedly, and over an extended period of time, it is more likely to be validated as a trend.
- **Cross-check using other indicators.** An apparent trend can be further validated by reference to several cross-checking methods. Assume, for example, that a business entity claims that it is suffering tremendous financial hardship and heading toward insolvency. Perhaps a review of its inventory levels, and the rate at which it turns over its inventory, supports this conclusion. But is that enough? By testing other theories, one can perform a defensible cross-check. For example, what are the accounts receivable and accounts payable levels over time? What is the company's interest coverage ratio or its debt-to-equity ratio over time? (See Part 8 for a look at a variety of helpful ratios.)
- **Always ask for the most recent data.** While trends require a starting point somewhere in the past, they should run forward in time until the latest moment at which data has been collected. There's no sense in basing a decision, or choosing a

mathematical factor in a formula, using year-old data, unless that's the most recent data available. If data is published quarterly or monthly, the most recent reports should be examined. Otherwise, a trend that seemed evident in last year's data, and may have reversed itself in recent months, will go undetected.

- **Moderate high-value patterns over time.** Avoid the assumption that a company's high revenues or an individual's good fortune will last forever, and that positive outcomes will trend forward infinitely in such a pattern. Because all trends level out over time, it is reasonable to assume that a business reporting high revenue increases over a pattern of years would not—and statistically could not—do so forever. Such data may need to be tempered and adjusted down to more reasonable figures as time marches forward.

Trying to spot financial trends is a valuable practice is sizing up a business entity or an individual, but it ought to be conducted thoroughly and patiently. Good research may provide useful arguments to counsel, for or against certain assumptions in crafting formulas to calculate damages.

3.3. Footnotes and Attachments

In preparing to use formulas strategically, it is important to consider *all of the information* that supports the financial disclosures from which the data will be pulled. Annual reports, SEC filings, and other financial records filed by corporations are all summaries of data, and the numbers alone do not tell the entire story. Financial affidavits, income and expense forms, and other financial documents submitted in civil and matrimonial cases likewise capture only resulting numbers—the data entries resulting from a mathematical process or a data-reporting procedure. As such, attorneys must scrutinize footnotes, endnotes, prefaces, preambles, exhibits, and other attachments, in order to learn more about how the numbers were determined, how the data was gathered, what the data includes or excludes, and what adjustments may have been made. Without taking these additional steps, the data may be intrinsically unreliable or incomparable with other data.

Scouring financial reports and disclosures for additional information can be a highly productive exercise. Not only do such reports and disclosures often plainly disclose valuable information about the data, they may also reveal other valuable information about the business or the individual in question. For example, the 2009 Annual Report of ExxonMobil Corporation consists of 48 pages, but the first full financial statement does not appear until page 38. The introductory pages are rich with information about the company's initiatives and activities. A Summary of Accounting Policies and Practices, which appears on page 37, advises that ExxonMobil is defending a number of pending lawsuits and tax disputes and provides a source for further information about these claims. The 2009 Annual Report for Starbucks is likewise rich with data and narrative information about the corporation. Some 47 exhibits are attached to the Starbucks Annual Report, including various SEC forms 10-Q and 8-K and other agreements and certifications. Such annual reports also contain footnotes or endnotes that provide greater insight into the meaning of the numbers. For example, the Notes section of the 2006 Annual Report for American Express Corporation contains the following narrative sections:

Note 1. Summary of Significant Accounting Policies
Note 2. Discontinued Operations
Note 3. Investments
Note 4. Loans
Note 5. Securitized Loans
Note 6. Variable Interest Entities
Note 7. Goodwill and Other Intangible Assets
Note 8. Short and Long-Term Debt and Borrowing Agreements
Note 9. Common and Preferred Shares
Note 10. Derivative and Hedging Activities
Note 11. Guarantees and Certain Off-Balance Sheet Items
Note 12. Contingencies
Note 13. Fair Values of Financial Instruments
Note 14. Significant Credit Concentrations
Note 15. Stock Plans
Note 16. Retirement Plans
Note 17. Income Taxes

Note 18. Earnings per Common Share (EPS)
Note 19. Reportable Operating Segments and Geographic Operations
Note 20. Quarterly Financial Data (Unaudited)
Note 21. Restructuring Charges

Each Note provides valuable information which, depending on the circumstances of a particular case, could render certain data suspect or incompatible. The notes attached to the Annual Report also provide extensive references to important legal events and accounting assumptions that underlie the figures. Note 1, for example, includes subheadings entitled (a) Acquisitions and Divestitures; (b) Principles of Consolidation; (c) Foreign Currency; (d) Net Revenues; (e) Expenses; (f) Balance Sheet; and (g) Recently Issued Accounting Standards. Most of these subheadings, in turn, contain numerous subsections, detailing everything from derivative financial instruments and hedging activities to goodwill and other intangible assets.

Like annual reports, financial records required to be filed with courts in particular kinds of cases should also be scrutinized from top to bottom. The most useful information is often buried in footnotes and attachments and ought not to be ignored. For example, in a New Jersey divorce or domestic relations case, in which alimony, child support, or property distribution are under consideration, the parties are required to file a Case Information Statement, a form spanning approximately 10 pages and outlining each party's earned and unearned income, assets, short-term and long-term debts, and obligations. Eleven attachments are required:

1. A full and complete copy of your last federal and state income tax returns with all schedules and attachments
2. Your last calendar year's W-2 statements, 1099s, and K-1 statements
3. Your three most recent pay stubs
4. Bonus information including, but not limited to, percentage overrides, timing of payments, etc; the last three statements of such bonuses, commissions, etc.
5. Your most recent corporate benefits statement or a summary thereof showing the nature, amount, and status of retirement

plans, savings plans, income deferral plans, insurance benefits, etc.

6. Affidavit of Insurance Coverage
7. List of all prior/pending family actions involving support, custody, or domestic violence, with the docket number, county, state, and the disposition reached. Attach copies of all existing orders in effect
8. Details of each wage execution
9. Schedule of payments made for a spouse and/or children not reflected in the Case Information Statement
10. Any agreements between the parties
11. Child Support Guidelines Worksheet, as applicable, based upon available information

Attorneys who encounter such forms are duty-bound to demand compliance with all required attachments and to inspect each of the attachments for useful information. If a litigant has been involved in a prior divorce (or for that matter, a prior bankruptcy, business sale or purchase, receivership, etc.), the scrupulous attorney should request his financial submissions from the earlier cases as well. Unusually simple financial statements may suggest a lack of disclosure or inadequate explanation for the disclosures provided. Unusually complex financial statements may be warning signs of unorthodox accounting practices. Only by demanding production of all of the supporting information and investing the time to study that information can attorneys rest assured that their calculations will survive attack.

3.4. Volatility and Smoothing Techniques

If the risk of an investment is at issue, then volatility is an important measure to be considered. For example, if the price of a share of stock changes dramatically, in both directions, over a short period of time, it is considered more volatile and therefore a riskier investment. If the stock's value fluctuates steadily over a more extended period of time, it will be considered less volatile and thus less risky. While the term *volatility* is largely used to measure returns on a given investment, security, or market index, the concept of volatility can be extended to many practical scenarios.

Consider, for example, a dental practice that is being valuated as part of a breakup between partners. Financial reports prepared for the dental practice over 15 years reveal extreme deviations from year to year, making it difficult to extrapolate a trend. The volatile financial patterns in the dental practice may reflect changes in accounting procedures (and/or in the choice of accountants); they may reflect other policy choices by the dentists themselves; or they may suggest a high degree of manipulation of the data and tinkering with the books.

To minimize the appearance of volatility, business owners often apply *smoothing techniques* to their books. Smoothing refers to accounting strategies, which are usually completely legal, that are aimed at leveling off certain figures in order to minimize the appearance of volatility and to maximize the appearance of steady, predictable growth. For example, a dental practice that experiences a high-revenue year could defer the receipt and reporting of certain income until a subsequent year that is expected to be a lower-revenue period. Conversely, it could delay the recognition of certain expenses from one period to another period when new patient charges and insurance reimbursements are expected to increase.

Understanding the revenue-generating scheme of a business and its bill-paying habits can be very helpful in ascertaining whether its financial reports have been smoothed to reflect a steady, less volatile income pattern. Volatility means risk, and excessive smoothing may simply mask high volatility. Therefore, attorneys must inquire as to how a business enterprise works, what policies and procedures it follows, and how much managerial discretion is exercised in the reporting of revenue and expenses.

If a business owner or manager has complete freedom as to *when* to record sales or expenses, that freedom may be exercised strategically to smooth the numbers from period to period. The greater the level of discretion in choosing when to record sales and expenses, the greater the likelihood that volatile patterns are being hidden by smoothing techniques.

3.5. Creative Accounting

Creative accounting consists of making adjustments on the books to produce a desired image. Whether the party in question is a business entity or an individual, creative accounting techniques can be employed to alter and manipulate the financial results in order to portray the party as being more or less solvent, more or less creditworthy, more or less profitable, or more or less volatile. Here are some of the more common adjustments:

Improper Recognition of Revenue

Under the accrual method of accounting, revenues can be reported in the year the sales are made or the services are rendered but before any cash is actually paid. The same is true for costs and expenses: they can be reported on the books when they are billed, which may not be the same as when they are actually paid. Accountants can therefore recognize income in December from a sale, the bill for which is not actually paid until January (a new year). Had the company actually received payment at the moment that it made the sale, the revenue would have been simultaneously received and reported. Yet when the payment will be forthcoming in the future (for example, within 30 days), the accountant retains the power as to when to record the sale. That power, exercised creatively, can give the impression that a company was more or less profitable during a particular reporting period.

A business can engage in such front-end loading of revenue by a number of internal procedural maneuvers designed to get the earnings onto the books as quickly as possible. For example, earnings can be recorded (a) before a contract is signed; (b) before an actual order for goods has been placed; (c) before the terms of payment or of delivery have been agreed upon; and/or (d) before goods are actually shipped. A company may assume that an order will be placed by a customer based on past ordering practices, and thereupon count the order as having been placed and the revenue as having been earned. Even more dishonestly, sales and services may be provided to a company's subsidiaries and affiliates and recorded immediately as having generated earnings, even if the related companies are under no present obligation to make payment.

Yet another technique for overstating earnings is to take immediate credit for overpayments, prepayments, retainers, and deposits. Whenever a party receives money in advance, it can update its books to reflect the receipt of those funds, and in so doing inflate the actual financial status of the company or individual at that moment in time.

Thus, for example, if a business overpays a supplier or prepays for a future delivery, those overpayments or prepayments can be reported as current earnings. Similarly, if a business remits a deposit, a retainer, or a down payment to a supplier or a service provider, these payments are all intended to forge a transactional relationship that will take place in the future—yet the funds may be reported immediately as if they were current earnings.

In some cases, a company may apply creative accounting techniques to *reduce* its earnings. For example, if a company earns more than necessary to prove its current-year profitability, it may attempt to set up a "reserves" account to hold the excess profits until the future when actual earnings are not so high. It then releases the reserves to raise its revenue level in a future period, allowing it to mislead shareholders and investors into believing that its profit has steadily trended upward over time. Holding such "unearned revenues" in reserve is a dangerous and misleading practice: while it permits a company to smooth out its earnings over time, it does so by misleading others about the actual earning pattern of the company.

Improper Recognition of Expenses

Costs and expenses can likewise be incurred in one accounting period, while they are not paid until another period. For example, a purchasing manager places an order for office supplies in December and records the cost contemporaneously with the order. The invoice from the office supplies vendor does not arrive until January. Under an accrual accounting system, nothing stops the bookkeeper from entering the cost of the purchase on the books in January anytime before the invoice arrives, thus delaying the debt until the next accounting period. Manipulating when costs and expenses are reported allows a company (or an individual litigant) to control the appearance of profitability or indebtedness.

A corporation may also attempt to preserve the appearance of profitability by burying or redesignating debt under misleading accounting categories. By improperly recording the amount of debt, or classifying debt as something else, a corporation can deceive its shareholders and prospective investors.

A company or an individual party can also reverse the deception. By claiming expenses now rather than later, a corporation or an individual can give the appearance of much greater indebtedness or insolvency—a timeworn tactic for breadwinner spouses trying to minimize their liability in divorce court or debtors trying to meet certain thresholds in bankruptcy court. For example, a husband who runs a retail store subject to equitable distribution in a matrimonial proceeding may attempt to *beef up* his expenses during the valuation period by prepaying future expenses or recognizing debts long before they're actually incurred or due, in order to minimize the amount of equity available for his wife. By improperly recognizing expenses prematurely, the husband is able to distort his indebtedness to his ultimate advantage.

3.6. Off-Balance Sheet Liabilities

The fact that "off-balance sheet liabilities" are recognized as a common category is itself an anomaly. After all, a balance sheet is supposed to be a summary of *all* of a company's assets and liabilities. Yet the financial reporting industry widely acknowledges that certain liabilities will be excluded from the financial statement. As such, attorneys must make a diligent inquiry as to the existence of, and the nature of, all off-balance sheet liabilities.

By diverting certain liabilities from the financial statements to an off-sheet status, a company is able to artificially inflate its profits and trick its investors into believing it has less debt. The essence of the process is to report assets without recognizing any offsetting liabilities. A company may thus appear to be more creditworthy and may fool lenders into overestimating its assets versus its liabilities.

Not every off-balance sheet liability is unlawful: the accounting industry largely acknowledges the relegation of long-term leases and purchasing agreements to this category. Under conventional accounting rules, leases should be capitalized in certain cases. This means that the lease would be recognized as if it were a purchase, making both the lease asset and the lease liability reportable. The lease asset would thus be depreciated over time and the lease liability would be amortized as payments are made. If the lease is not capitalized, however, it is treated as an operating lease, meaning no asset or liability is recorded.

Contingent liabilities, such as pending lawsuits, are also generally excluded from balance sheets. Because such liabilities are contingent on a certain set of conditions occurring, they are not recognized as reportable liabilities until the conditions actually arise. Still, an attorney may wish to know whether a target defendant is already facing a substantial claim for damages from other pending litigation—and looking at the numbers on the financial statements may provide no insight.

Executory contracts, by which a company has promised to make a payment at a future date, are also a common form of off-balance sheet liability. While such contracts may be legally binding, they are not technically classifiable as liabilities when the contracts are signed, but rather only when the benefits are received. Thus, they may be pushed to an off-balance sheet status.

Most troubling are the more creative off-balance sheet devices used to hide debt or hold debt while the assets generated through the debt are reported on the balance sheets. For example, assume that a company sells subprime mortgage securities and reports the proceeds from these sales as assets. If it fails also to report the financial obligations tied to these sales, then it has materially misled investors as to its actual profit margin. Government regulators have, of course, become increasingly rigorous in their enforcement of such violations and have mandated increased disclosures in recent years. Still, new financial products and management devices continue to emerge, and it is important to inquire meticulously about all possible off-balance sheet liabilities.

3.7. The Earnings and Consumption Myths

When we attempt to calculate an injury victim's future earnings, we inherently make an assumption: everyone's earnings grow at the same rate. We also assume that wage growth occurs at a constant rate. These are flawed assumptions, particularly when applied to the net discount rate discussed in Section 11.2. In fact, experienced employees and older employees tend to earn more than inexperienced and younger employees.

Consider, for example, two employees working at the same job, who are simultaneously injured and rendered permanently disabled on April 1, 2019. The first employee had been employed in 2017 and had received two annual pay raises by the date of the accident. The second employee, by contrast, had been hired on March 5, 2019, and had less than one month on the job at the time of the accident. If we apply the myth that earnings grow at the same rate for everybody, then we are disregarding the value of the first employee's experience and assuming inaccurately that wage growth for the two victims would have been identical.

The net discount rate is applied on the theory that discount rates in general are overstated because wages will continue to grow over time. A net discount rate thus attempts to adjust the discount rate by expressing the discount rate in terms of a growth rate. Yet, if we maintain the myth that everyone's earnings grow at the same rate, we are inherently invalidating the net discount rate too. Adjusting for this problem may require more intricate calculations or the assistance of an expert witness.

In the same vein, we make faulty assumptions about consumption when we attempt to adjust a victim's income by deducting the value of his personal subsistence and maintenance costs. In addition to assuming that all people consume at the same rate, or that the rate of consumption is constant over time, we also mistakenly assume that the wage earner is the only person spending his money for consumption. In fact, a wage earner's spouse and minor children are also likely to consume the income.

In a wrongful death case, where consumption is subtracted from the decedent's earnings in order to calculate a total economic loss, as illustrated in Section 19.7, the formula is actually incomplete because it does not account for income sources or consumption rates *after retirement.* The formula is thus technically flawed insofar as consumption is presumed to terminate when the decedent would have retired.

3.8. Silly Shortcuts and Ridiculous Rules of Thumb

Busy attorneys, like busy managers and accountants, often succumb to the popularity of mathematical shortcuts and rules of thumb instead of applying recognized formulas as discussed in this book. Falling prey to this practice is dangerous, however, and should be avoided as a general practice. Following are some of the most inadvisable shortcuts and rules of thumb.

Fives Times Earnings

One method for placing a value on a business is to multiply its earnings times five. The 5E myth may produce credible results, but it is technically inaccurate. Proponents of this approach claim that lenders historically grant loans to small businesses for no more than five years, and that business investors and buyers generally expect a return on investment within five years.

Business valuation, however, is not so simplistic an analysis: the value of a business implies calculations that account for the time value of money. Forecasting cash flows is an uncertain process, and it may be necessary to adjust for premiums and discounts. Interest rates and capitalization rates must be accurately fixed. Comparable values of similar businesses may also provide important market benchmarks.

Forward Multiples

Doubling or tripling annual revenues is another sloppy way to place a value on a business. This procedure has gained popularity in the past as a valuation method, especially for small firms and professional practices, but it is neither consistent nor scientific. By using a multiple of revenues (or book value), one can predict the value of a business enterprise, but it will likely be a shallow prediction. In fact, such *forward multiples* are not true forecasting formulas. They tell us nothing about future cash flow, or the difference between one kind of industry and another.

Asset Approaches

A straight asset approach to valuing a business involves calculating the sum of the value of all of the company's assets. A book value approach measures assets based on what they originally cost, but in most cases, this kind of historical data is meaningless. A fair market value approach considers the net value of assets based on what they're worth today to a willing buyer. A liquidation value approach calculates the total value of the business assets as if they were to be immediately auctioned as part of a company-wide liquidation.

All of these asset approaches are flawed because they don't tell us anything about the intangible value of the company. What is the company's good name worth? Its goodwill? Its future earnings capacity? Present assets, no matter how they are valued, don't tell us anything about the value of a company's client lists or the projection for repeat business based on the reputation and experience of the enterprise.

Market Approaches

One could compare a business to similar businesses and thereby estimate its value. Much as a real estate appraiser looks at comparable home sales, one could consider the market value of similar businesses, and then draw the comparison. This approach usually prompts valuators to make adjustments and corrections for perceived differences between the businesses under comparison.

The process is both superficial and artificial. Businesses cannot logically be valued by a transparent match game played with purportedly similar businesses. A much deeper evaluation needs to be conducted, in which a variety of factors are explored, including the nature of the business, its product market, its book value and industry position, its capital structure, management style and performance history, its credit and loan status, its competition and its competitive advantages, and its revenue and earnings history.

Past Losses versus Future Profits

It is also a myth that companies that fail to turn a profit are valueless or otherwise bad investments. While historical performance can be an important measure of future results, a business may report losses for an extended period of years before ever turning profitable. It is the likelihood of future cash flow, not the history of indebtedness, which drives the question.

Especially in the case of innovative industry-leading start-ups, methodological projections of future cash flow are far better valuation devices than reliance on reported losses.

3.9. Experts and Formulas

Not every case requires or justifies retaining an expert witness. In some cases, liability is in doubt. In other cases, the amount of provable damages is quite low, or the insurance policy limits are minimal. In still other cases, the amount of damages is fixed by contract or statute, and the proofs are not complicated.

In larger, more complex legal actions, where the determination of damages is elusive or controversial, and where the amount of insurance coverage is substantial, it is important to develop a *theory of damages* and to engage an expert witness who can develop, explain, and articulate the theory in meaningful terms. A theory of damages, conceived and tested early in a case, will provide attorneys with meaningful positions in responding to pretrial discovery, in preparing for mediations and arbitrations, and ultimately in drawing on expert testimony at trial. (See Chapter 18 for a discussion of how to choose the right expert, and related expert witness issues.)

Damages experts are often overlooked by attorneys who are preoccupied with liability issues. Where they are used, damages experts are frequently retained as an afterthought, or as a final act in the pretrial discovery process. Yet, because such experts can assist attorneys in crafting a theory of damages from the outset of the litigation, they should be consulted and utilized at a much earlier prefiling stage of case development.

Using formulas to calculate damages initially may, in fact, prompt some attorneys to search for a particular kind of expert. In a business dissolution dispute, for example, an attorney may find that by running several formulas—return on investment, return on equity, return on assets, compound annual growth rate—he can develop a theory of the case built around the economic direction of the business in question. Fine-tuning this theory, and refining the formulas, may be the work of an expert witness who can then assist the attorney in targeting the necessary information through certain depositions and document requests.

Similarly, in an employment discrimination case, a series of formulas applied to retirement payouts may unveil an age discrimination issue in which younger workers are favored under an employer's pension plan, and in so doing, may call for the retention of an actuary or taxation expert.

Experts can also tell an attorney why one formula is better than another as an indicator of a particular value in dispute. Where there are disputes over the quality or reliability of data to be applied in particular formulas, an expert may be able to guide attorneys as to how to authenticate the data, test its reliability, and defend challenges to the numbers. A good damages expert can also advise attorneys about the findings of rebuttal experts—why their data is flawed, their formulas are ill-suited, or their conclusions are based on faulty assumptions.

In large, multifaceted cases, an expert retained early in the prefiling phase may also advise counsel as to what additional experts or specialists would be helpful in building the case for damages. For example, a forensic economist, retained at the outset of a personal injury case, may recommend a functional capacity expert to provide core data or information about the plaintiff's ability to perform his occupation, or a psychologist to provide psychometric test results about the plaintiff's emotional state and to thereby project the length of time to recovery.

3.10. Free Data on the Internet

The Internet is overflowing with free data that can be helpful in building formulas. Stock quotes, pricing information, market fluctuations, interest rates, tax rates, and exchange rates—these are just a few of the figures that can be plucked from the cybersphere. As with any online resources, however, web-based data compilers should be studied critically before assuming the integrity of their information. Attorneys should exercise great care to ensure the reliability of the data they pull from the Internet, and to question whether the data sources are owned or sponsored by biased or interested parties. Second-hand sources, such as bloggers quoting what they read elsewhere, should be ignored; publicly written and loosely edited sources like Wikipedia should be double-checked and verified through other sources.

For off-the-cuff rapid formula building, or for informal negotiations, a quick survey of useful websites may provide the missing data needed to estimate damages in a particular case. Below, in several categories, are some of the more reliable sources of free data and useful information on the Internet.

Government Financial Websites

Bureau of Economic Analysis	www.bea.gov/industry/
Census Information	www.census.gov
Child Care Tax Credits	www.irs.gov/newsroom/claiming-the-child-and-dependent-care-tax-credit
Earned Income Tax Credit	www.irs.gov/credits-deductions/individuals/earned-income-tax-credit
Employee Benefits Security Administration	www.dol.gov/ebsa/
FannieMae	www.fanniemae.com
Federal Accounting Standards Advisory Board	www.fasab.gov
Federal Deposit Insurance Corporation	www.fdic.gov

Federal Reserve Rates	www.federalreserve.gov
Federal Retiree Benefits	www.opm.gov/retire/retire_employees.asp
Federal Statistics	www.fedstats.gov
Financial Management Service	www.fms.treas.gov/index.html
Government Accountability Office	www.gao.gov
Government Benefits	www.benefits.gov/benefits/benefit-finder
Medicaid	www.cms.gov/home/medicaid.asp
Medicare	www.medicare.gov/default.aspx
My Money.Gov	www.mymoney.gov
Pension Benefit Guaranty Corporation	www.pbgc.gov
Savings Bonds	www.savingsbonds.gov
Securities and Exchange Commission	www.sec.gov
Social Security	www.ssa.gov
State Statistics	www.fedstats.gov/qf/
State Statistical Abstracts	www.census.gov/compendia/statab/st_abstracts.html
Statistical Abstracts of the U.S.	www.census.gov/compendia/statab/
Supplemental Security Income (SSI)	www.ssa.gov/pubs/11000.html
Treasury Department	www.ustreas.gov
Unemployment Insurance	www.dol.gov/dol/topic/unemployment-insurance/index.htm
Wages by Area and Occupation	www.bls.gov/bls/blswage.htm

Investor Websites

Adjustable Rate Mortgage Index Rates	www.hsh.com/idxhst.html
American Association of Individual Investors	www.investware.com/aaii.stm
Currency Exchange Rates	www.exchangerate.com
Federal Prime Rate	www.fedprimerate.com
Financial Forecast Center	www.forecasts.org

Financial Planning Association	www.fpanet.org
Foreign Exchange Rates	www.cnnfn.com/markets/currencies.html
Future Source	www.futuresource.com
Treasury and other Government Bond Rates	http://www.bloomberg.com/markets/rates-bonds/government-bonds/us/
Investopedia	www.investopedia.com
Morningstar	www.morningstar.com
Motley Fool	www.fool.com
National Futures Association	www.nfa-futures.org
Online Investor	www.theonlineinvestor.com
Raging Bull	www.ragingbull.com
Quote.com	www.quote.com
Zacks Investment Research	www.zacks.com

Domestic Exchanges

American Stock Exchange	www.amex.com
Chicago Board of Options Exchange	www.cboe.com
Chicago Stock Exchange	www.chx.com
Chicago Mercantile Exchange	www.cme.com
Intercontinental Exchange	www.theice.com
NASDAQ	www.nasdaq.com
New York Board of Trade	*See Intercontinental Exchange above.*
New York Stock Exchange	www.nyse.com
Philadelphia Stock Exchange	www.phlx.com

Foreign Exchanges

Deutsche Boerse (Germany)	www.deutsche-boerse.com
Hong Kong Stock Exchange	www.hkex.com.hk
London Stock Exchange	www.londonstockexchange.com
National Stock Exchange of India	www.nse-india.com
Shanghai Stock Exchange	www.sse.com.cn
SIX Swiss Exchange	www.six-swiss-exchange.com
Tokyo Stock Exchange	www.tse.or.jp
Toronto Stock Exchange	www.tmx.com

Credit and Investment Rating Services

A.M. Best Company	www.ambest.com
Bankrate	www.bankrate.com/rates/safe-sound/bank-ratings-search.aspx
DBRS, Ltd.	www.dbrs.com
Equifax	www.equifax.com
Experian	www.experian.com
Moody's	www.moodys.com
Rating and Investment Information, Inc.	www.r-i.co.jp/eng/
Standard & Poor's	www.standardandpoors.com
TransUnion	www.transunion.com

Wage and Salary Data

Economic Research Institute	www.eri-salary-survey.com
Real-time Salary Data	www.payscale.com
Salary Information	www.salary.com
Salary Surveys	www.salaryexpert.com
	www.wageweb.com

Financial News Sources

Bloomberg	www.bloomberg.com
Business Week	www.businessweek.com
Business Wire	www.businesswire.com
CEO Express	www.ceoexpress.com
CNBC	www.cnbc.com
CNN Money	www.money.cnn.com
Financial News	www.financialnews.com
Financial Times	www.ft.com
Forbes	www.forbes.com
Fortune	www.fortune.com
Investment News	www.investmentnews.com
Investors Business Daily	www.investors.com
Kiplinger	www.kiplinger.com
Market Watch	www.marketwatch.com
MSN Money	www.money.msn.com
MSNBC	www.msnbc.msn.com
Reuters	www.reuters.com

Seeking Alpha	www.seekingalpha.com
Smart Money	www.smartmoney.com
The Street	www.thestreet.com
This is Money	www.thisismoney.com
Topix	www.topix.com/business/financial-services
USA Today Money	http://www.usatoday.com/money/default.htm
Wall State Journal	www.wallstreetjournal.com
Yahoo! Business News	biz.yahoo.com
Yahoo! Finance	www.finance.yahoo.com

Chapter 4

Speed Math, Estimation, and Memorization

4.1. Math with No Hands

Imagine the attorney who has memorized a key formula and is prepared to demonstrate his mathematical prowess when . . . he cannot locate or recollect the numbers that will be used in the formula. He sifts through his notes, searches his file, and riffles his loose papers trying to find the important numbers that will be plugged into the formula. Valuable time is lost, and, in the end, the calculation may appear much less impressive.

Wouldn't it be better if the attorney could repeat the essential numbers to be used in the formula, without consulting his notes? Wouldn't he appear more in control of the process if the numbers came flowing back to his memory? In fact, where appearances count, such as before a judge or a jury, or in the throes of a strategic negotiation, wouldn't it seem important to recall the essential numbers quickly and seamlessly?

Solving math problems in one's head and memorizing numbers along the way are important skills. Indeed, mathematicians have developed many shortcuts and high-speed techniques to allow us to perform calculations in our heads, without using a calculator, a cell phone app, or pencil and paper. We can perform addition, subtraction, multiplication and division swiftly and accurately in our heads—literally, math with no hands—and we can memorize large complex numbers along the way.

Of course, nothing comes without practice, and the mental math techniques and shortcuts discussed in this chapter will require some practice. By the end of this chapter, you should be able to determine 93% of 350; estimate the square root of 75; and memorize and add 4,676, 5,391 and 8,042, all in a matter of seconds—with your hands tied behind your back.

4.2. Finding the Complement

To develop your speed math skills, the first step is to adopt the habit of finding the *complement* of numbers that you are adding or subtracting in your head. The *complement* is the number that you must add to any number to arrive at a third number. Usually, the third number is 10, but when dealing with calculations involving larger figures, the third number may be, for example, 100 or 1,000. As you will see in the examples that follow, finding the complement provides a shortcut for adding and subtracting numbers, quickly and accurately.

Let's start with some very basic examples:

Number	+	Complement	Equals
4		6	10
8		2	10
78		22	100
33		67	100
255		745	1,000
727		273	1,000

Calculating the complement is simple when we're dealing with smaller numbers. Thus, we all know that the complement of 4 is 6. But how can we quickly determine the complement of a larger number such as 727. The answer is, proceeding from left to right, to determine what number added to each digit will increase that digit to a sum of 9 (except for the last digit, which must total 10). So, we break down 727 to three numbers: 7 and 2 and 7, as follows:

Number	+	Complement	Equals	Explanation
7	+	2	9	The complement of the first number on the left must bring the total to 9.
2	+	7	9	The complement of the second number must also bring the total to 9.
7	+	3	10	The complement of the last number (to the right) must bring the total to 10.

As shown above, the number 727 produces the complement 273. What we have done rapidly in our heads is to dissect 727 by looking at the 7, the 2, and the 7, and asking (1) what number will increase the first 7 to a 9, (2) what number will increase the 2 to a 9, and (3) what number will increase the final 7 to a 10 (because the last number to the right must equal 10). Calculating the complement quickly will prove to be a useful skill in performing other mental mathematical shortcuts as discussed in the sections that follow.

Understanding complements is also a handy method for performing high-speed arithmetic problems on the spot. For example, a cashier charges \$34.76 for a purchase, and you hand him a \$100 bill. *How much should you expect to receive in change?* Begin again by working left to right and determining what the complement of each individual number is. Remember that each number, plus its complement, must total 9, except for the last number, which must total 10. In seconds, you should be able to arrive at the answers: 6, 5, 2, 4. The change that the cashier gives you is \$65.24.

4.3. High-Speed Addition

It is easy to appear mathematically proficient when the numbers are easy to add. We all know, for example, that 6,000 plus 6,000 equals 12,000. The question is no more complicated than 6 + 6 = 12. The zeros add nothing to the puzzle. Likewise, we know that \$3,000,000 plus \$2,000,000 equals \$5,000,000. Making the figures even larger or adding a dollar sign does not complicate the problem. It's still simple arithmetic: 3 + 2 = 5.

What happens when the numbers get more confusing and more cumbersome?

Let's consider some case scenarios. In the heat of negotiations over a contract to repay several loans, a party suggests that the debtor would repay Loan No. 1 over 63 months, and then at the conclusion of that period, pay Loan No. 2 over the next 28 months. The debtor's attorney wants to quickly determine when the debtor will be debt free if he accepts the deal (thus, 63 + 28). Or, in a jury trial over an employment law dispute, the plaintiff's attorney finds herself in the middle of cross-examination over the employer's assessment of eligible accrued vacation time, sick leave, and paid time-off days, and needs to quickly add the numbers 79 and 76 on the spot. Or, in a divorce mediation, the wife's attorney asks for $883 in child support plus $466 in alimony, and the husband and his attorney want to quickly determine the sum of these two figures.

Without a calculator or a cell phone app, how quickly can you solve any of these addition problems?

63 + 28 (the loan contract example)
34 + 47
79 + 76 (the employment law jury trial example)
419 + 278
883 + 466 (the divorce mediation example)

To conquer these addition problems swiftly, you must break down the second number into bite-size addable pieces. In the first example, 63 + 28, the second number (28) can be broken down into 20 and 8. We can easily add 63 + 20, which equals 83. Now all we need to do is add 8. The answer comes quickly now, 83 + 8 = 91.

In the second example, 34 + 47, the second number (47) breaks down into 40 and 7. Thus, 34 + 40 = 74. Then, 74 + 7 = 81.

In the third example, 79 + 76, we break down 76 into 70 + 6. The addition then becomes 79 + 70 which is 149. Then 149 + 6 = 155.

When we move onto three-digit numbers, the second number needs to be broken down in several stages. So, in the fourth example above, 419 + 278, we break down 278 initially to 200 and 78. First, we calculate 419 + 200 = 619. Next, what is 619 + 78? Let's break down 78 into 70 and 8. So, 619 + 70 = 689. And finally, 689 + 8 = 697.

In the fifth example above, 883 + 466, we break down 466 initially into 400 and 66. Then, we rapidly perform the following mental calculations:

883 + 400	=	1,283
66 (= 60 + 6)		
1,283 + 60	=	1,343
1,343 + 6	=	1,349

Unlike the right-to-left logic that has been taught for many years in schools, in which students have been trained to stack numbers in column form and add them vertically from right to left and to carry two-digit numbers to the column to the left, the speed-math techniques discussed here apply a *left-to-right logic,* and are designed to avoid pencil and paper (or calculator and cell phone). These techniques are designed to encourage extemporaneous mental calculations performed quickly.

4.4. High-Speed Subtraction

Subtracting difficult numbers on the fly can be mastered using the same high-speed techniques as we explored in the high-speed addition section above.

Assume, for example, in a loan repayment negotiation, the lender agreed to reduce a 63-month loan term by 28 months. Thus, we want to know, quickly, what is 63 minus 28. Attack the problem initially by breaking down the second number (28) into two numbers, 20 and 8. Then, in your head, perform the first calculation: 63 – 20 = 43. Next, calculate 43 – 8, which is 35. *And that's the answer:* 63 – 28 = 35.

In the middle of a trial, you need to subtract 19 from 88, and there's no time to spare. The formula is 88 – 19, which translates into 88 – (10 + 9). First, perform the easy calculation: 88 – 10 = 78. Then, proceed to the second calculation: 78 – 9 = 69. Therefore, 88 – 19 = 69.

In a child custody case, the mother's attorney alleges that an estranged father has not seen his son for 555 days. The father's attorney says that 238 of those days should not be counted against him because he was actively engaged in the military service for that period of time. His attorney thus seeks to determine the *actual period of estrangement* by calculating the difference: 555 – 238. He should begin by breaking down the second number, 238, into three numbers, 200, 30, and 8. Here are the quick mental calculations:

555 – 200 = 355
355 – 30 = 325
325 – 8 = 317

In a matter of seconds, the father's attorney should have the answer: 555 – 238 = 317.

Not counting his military service, the child's father appears to have been actually estranged from the child for 317 days.

4.5. Rounding and Reversing

One of the fastest techniques for high-speed addition and subtraction is to round up complex numbers and then reverse the mathematical function. This process, in fact, may prove faster and easier than the techniques discussed above. Let's revisit the same equations we used in Sections 4.3 and 4.4. In Section 4.3, we looked at the following equations:

63 + 28
34 + 47
79 + 76
419 + 278
883 + 466

Instead of breaking down the second number, this time let's round up the second number (keeping in mind the difference between the actual number and the rounded-up number).

Original Equation	Rounded Up	= Total	Reversal	=	Final Total
63 + 28	63 + 30	= 93	–2	=	91
34 + 47	34 + 50	= 84	–3	=	81
79 + 76	79 + 80	= 159	–4	=	155
419 + 278	419 + 300	= 719	–22	=	697
883 + 466	883 + 500	= 1,383	–34	=	1,349

In the first example above, 63 + 28, the process was accelerated by rounding 28 up to 30. By doing so, we were able to quickly and easily add 63 to 30 to arrive at the answer of 93. But this answer is too high because we rounded 28 up by 2. So, we need to *reverse* functions and subtract 2 from the answer: 93 – 2, which equals 91, and that's our final total.

When dealing with three-digit numbers, the amount to be subtracted in the final calculation can present a problem if the final subtraction problem is, itself, a difficult one to perform. In the fifth example above, 883 + 466, we see that rounding 466 up to 500 requires us to subtract 34 in the final calculation. This is somewhat difficult to do, on the fly. *How can we make this calculation faster?* One way to accelerate the process is to round up the first number instead of the second number. So, for example, you might try this approach:

Original Equation	Rounded Up	= Total	Reversal	=	Final Total
883 + 466	900 + 466	= 1,366	– 17	=	1,349

Another approach is to round up both the first and the second number, and to round each of them up to smaller numbers, if possible. So, for example, 883 would be rounded up to 900, and 466 would be rounded up to 470. The rounded-up figures, 900 and 470, can be easily added together, but now the difference between both rounded-up figures must be added together and subtracted from the total. Let's examine the details:

Original Equation	Rounded Up	= Total	Reversal	=	Final Total
883 + 466	900 + 470	= 1,370	– 21*	=	1,349

* 21 includes 17 from the rounded-up figure of 900, and 4 from the rounded-up figure of 470.

In Section 4.4 above, we examined the equation 63 – 28 = 35 and how to break it down for a high-speed calculation. We can solve the same equation by applying a rounding-up technique. Step one is round up the second number (28) to 30. Then do the math: 63 – 30 = 33. Next, simply reverse the function and instead of subtracting, *add* back 2, representing the amount by which you rounded up the second number. Thus: 33 + 2 = 35, and that's your final answer.

You may also recall the example in Section 4.4 involving the estranged father and the calculation for the period of estrangement. The equation was 555 – 238. Instead of breaking down 238 as demonstrated in Section 4.4, let's round up 238 to 250 (which is an increase of 12). Now let's do the math using the rounded-up figure: 555 – 250 = 305. This is much easier to calculate quickly in one's head. Our answer, 305, must now be *increased* by the amount that we rounded up the second figure (12). So, 305 + 12 = 317.

4.6. High-Speed Multiplication

The process for performing high-speed multiplication, like high-speed addition and subtraction, begins with learning how to break down an equation into smaller parts. So, for example, we can solve simple problems such as 6 x 50 because our brain simplifies the equation to 6 x 5 and adds a zero at the end. Thus, 6 x 5 = 30, and with the zero on the end, we can simply visualize this answer in an instant: 6 x 50 = 300.

The problem becomes somewhat hairier when it's 6 x 54. Now, we must break it down. So, quickly in our heads, we can split this into two smaller calculations: 6 x 50 = 300, plus 6 x 4 = 24. Therefore, 6 x 54 = 300 + 24 = 324.

Let's try a few more:

76 x 7
49 x 5
8 x 67

Your answers to the problems above should be 532, 245, and 536, respectively. But how did you do the math? In the first case, you should have split 76 in 70 and 6 and performed two quick operations: 7 x 70 = 490 and 7 x 6 = 42. So, 76 x 7 = 490 + 42 = 532. Similarly, with the second problem, 49 x 5, you should have split 49 into 40 and 9. Thus, 40 x 5 = 200 and 9 x 5 = 45. Then, 200 + 45 = 245. The third problem, 8 x 67, requires us to look at the second number (67) to break down. We solve it as follows: 8 x 60 = 480, plus 8 x 7 = 56. Then 480 + 56 becomes an addition problem which we break down further: 480 + 50 = 530 and 530 + 6 produces the final answer: 536.

We can rapidly multiply even larger numbers using the same breakdown technique. Find the answer to this problem: 674 x 3. You should now immediately process this problem as three smaller calculations: 600 x 3 plus 70 x 3 plus 4 x 3. Here's the math:

674 x 3
600 x 3 = 1,800   70 x 3 = 210   4 x 3 = 12
1,800 + 210 + 12 = 2,022

With a little practice, you can quickly, mentally, split most numbers into smaller numbers and perform such rapid operations in your head without reaching for a calculator.

Rounding Up for Further Speed

Rounding up, as discussed in Section 4.5 above, will also serve as an accelerator when performing multiplication operations. So, for example, observe the problem above, 49 x 5. While you certainly could have solved that problem by breaking down 49 into 40 and 9, you might solve it faster by rounding 49 up to 50. The problem then becomes quite simple: 50 x 5 = 250. However, since we rounded up by 1, we must follow up with some *reversal* operation to perfect the calculation. In this case, we simply multiply 1 x 5 = 5. We subtract 5 from 250 which equals 245, the final answer.

Using rounding, how would you solve these problems at high speed?

86 x 4
47 x 6

In the first problem, 86 x 4 becomes 90 x 4, which equals 360. Then, because 86 was rounded up by 4, we must multiply 4 x 4 and subtract that product from 360. Thus, 360 – 16 = 344. In the second problem, 47 x 6, we round up 47 to 50. Then, 50 x 6 = 300. And, 3 x 6 = 18. So, 300 – 18 = 282.

Using Complements for Further Speed

By rounding up and using complements, we can further catalyze the multiplication process. Assume, for example, that a storage facility sues a customer for overdue storage fees. The monthly storage fee is $696, including taxes. The parties are mediating their dispute in small claims court when the customer's attorney offers to settle the case for 9 payments of $696. The storage facility's attorney wants the money in one lump sum payment. How much exactly is 9 x 696?

First, by rounding, we turn the question into 9 x 700 = 6,300, and 9 x 4 = 36. So, we are left with the simple subtraction problem 6,300 – 36. But, on the fly, as we're negotiating, such a simple problem can still slow us down because we are preprogrammed to think from right to left and to stack the figures vertically in our heads in order to perform old-fashioned arithmetic.

Instead, use complements to accelerate the process. *What is the complement of 36?* The answer is 64. Since we know that 6,300 – 36 will equal six thousand two hundred *and something,* finding the complement provides the missing piece of information: 6,300 – 36 = 6,264.

Handling Multiple Zeros

Sometimes, a multiplication problem is quite easy, but it appears overwhelming because it involves large numbers containing multiple zeros. For example, 16,000 x 9,000. Or worse yet, 1,850,000 x 3,000. The trick to solving these problems with lightning speed is simple: Remove all of the zeros, then add the exact same amount of zeros back to the answer.

So, for example, 16,000 x 9,000 becomes the super-simple multiplication problem 16 × 9, which is 144. Remember, you could solve this instantly by breaking down 16 into 10 and 6 (thus, 9 x 10 = 90 and 9 x 6 = 54; 90 + 54 = 144). Or you could round up one of the numbers. For example, 16 x 10 = 160. Then subtract 1 x 16 or simply 16. The result is: 160 – 16 = 144. Once you know that the answer is 144, then you must add back all of the removed zeros from both sides of the equation—six zeros altogether. The answer is 144 million (16,000 x 9,000 = 144,000,000).

In the second example above, 1,850,000 x 3,000, the math is no more complicated than 185 x 3. So, 3 x 100 = 300 and 3 x 80 = 240 and 3 x 5 = 15. Then, by adding, we get 300 + 240 + 15 = 555. Now, add back all seven zeros in the equation to get the final answer: 5,550,000,000.

Halving and Doubling

Another technique for multiplying large numbers is the halving and doubling method. This works when at least one of the numbers is even. Consider the problem 20 x 3,411. Simply cut the even number (20) in half, and the problem becomes very simple: 10 x 3,411 = 34,110.

Now, double it: 34,110 x 2 = 68,220. Halving and doubling offers another quick approach to performing multiplication problems that may appear difficult at first glance.

Try another: 136 x 40. By halving 40 to 20, we can do the math quickly in our heads: 20 x 136 is calculated as 2 x 136 or 272, then add back the zero (from the 20) to yield a result of 2,720. Now we must double the result: 2 x 2,720 = 5,440. Done in a flash: 136 x 40 = 5,440.

You could have attacked this problem yet another way, perhaps faster, using the halving and doubling method. You could cut 40 in half *twice,* but that means you would need to double your final result *twice.* So, 40 cut in half twice gives us a new multiplier of 10. Then, 10 x 136 is easy math: 1,360. Now we must double 1,360 twice (which is another way of saying multiply it by 4). So, 1,360 x 2 = 2,720 x 2 = 5,440. Or, if you prefer, 1,360 x 4 = 4,000 + 1,200 + 240 = 5,440.

Multiplying Numbers Ending in 5

A variation of the halving and doubling technique can be applied when multiplying numbers ending in 5. What's 44 x 25? The high-speed shortcut is to double the number ending in 5, and then halve the other number. So, 25 becomes 50 (doubled), and 44 becomes 22 (halved). In fact, 44 x 25 is mathematically the same as 22 x 50. It's easier for us to mentally calculate 22 x 50. The answer is 20 x 50 + 2 x 50 or 1,000 + 100 which equals 1,100. Thus, 44 x 25 = 1,100.

Try another one: What is 82 x 35? First, we double 35 to get 70. Then we halve 82 to get 41. Our new problem is thus 41 x 70. We can solve that quickly in our heads: 40 x 70 = 2800 *and* 1 x 70 = 70. Then, 2800 + 70 = 2,870. In fact, 82 x 35 = 41 x 70 = 2,870.

This technique gets a bit trickier when the first number being multiplied is an odd number. Consider, for example, 17 x 45. We can easily double 45 to get 90. But we cannot easily halve 17 without making the problem more time consuming. The answer is to treat 17 as 16 (an even number that can be easily halved), while remembering that we reduced it by 1. What we actually did is reduce the entire equation by 1 x 45. Therefore, we will need to add 45 to whatever answer we get. So let's approach 17 x 45 as being 16 x 45 (with 45 owed at the end). Double 45 to get 90 and halve 16 to get 8. Do the math: 8 x 90 = 720. Then add back the 45: 720 + 45 = 765. Indeed, 17 x 45 = 765.

4.7. High-Speed Division

The starting point for high-speed division is to look at the number being divided. This number is known in mathematics as the *dividend.* Look at the last number in the dividend. Is it even or odd? What number divides into it? Will that number, the *divisor,* go perfectly into the dividend, or will there be a *remainder*? We know from our elementary school years that 10 divided by 5 equals 2 and 9 divided by 3 equals 3. When we encounter a problem such as 9 divided by 4, we can quickly compute in our heads that the divisor (4) will divide into 9 two times, but no more than two times, and it won't give us perfectly whole numbers. That is, 4 x 2 = 8. So, we know that 9 divided by 4 produces a result, known as a *quotient,* of 2, with a *remainder* of 1.

Fortunately, division is based on a series of rules that can be quickly memorized in order to determine which divisors go into which dividends equally. The table below summarizes those rules:

DIVISOR	SAMPLE EQUATION	THE RULE
2	6,894 ÷ 2 = 3,447	A number is divisible by 2 if it ends with 0, 2, 4, 6, or 8. Thus, 6,894 ends with 4 and can be divided by 2.
3	5,943 ÷ 3 = 1,981	A number is divisible by 3 if the sum of all of the digits is evenly divisible by 3. With the dividend, 5,943, we add 5 + 9 + 4 + 3 = 21. Because 21 is evenly divisible by 3, the number 5,943 is also divisible by 3.
4	7,628 ÷ 4 = 1,907	A number is divisible by 4 if it ends in 00 or the last two digits are divisible by 4. So, 100 and 1,300 are both divisible by 4. So is the dividend 7,628 because the last two digits (28) are divisible by 4.

5	950 ÷ 5 = 190	A number is divisible by 5 if it ends in either 0 or 5. Therefore, 950 is divisible by 5, and so is 955.
6	3,078 ÷ 6 = 513	A number is divisible by 6 if it is divisible by both 2 and 3. Here, the dividend 3,078 is divisible by 2 because it ends with 8. It is also divisible by 3 because the sum its digits (3, 0, 7, 8) equals 18.
7	602 ÷ 7 = 86	A number is divisible by 7 if, when you double the last digit and subtract it from the other digits, the result is divisible by 7. For example, using the dividend 602, the last digit 2 is doubled to 4. When 4 is subtracted from the remaining digits (60), we are left with 56 (60 – 4 = 56). Because 56 is divisible by 7, the number 602 must also be divisible by 7.
8	5,224 ÷ 8 = 653	A number is divisible by 8 if its last three digits are evenly divisible by 8, or if the number ends in 000. However, the last 2 digits must also be evenly divisible by 4. The dividend 13,000 is divisible by 8 because it ends in 000 (13,000 ÷ 8 = 1,625). The dividend 5,224 also works because the last three digits (224) are divisible by 8, and because the last two digits (24) are divisible by 4.

9	5,994 ÷ 9 = 666	A number is divisible by 9 if the sum of all of the digits is evenly divisible by 9. With the dividend, 5,994, we add 5 + 9 + 9 + 4 = 27. Because 27 is evenly divisible by 9, the number 5,994 is also divisible by 9.
10	1,111,670 ÷ 10 = 111,167	A number is divisible by 10 if it ends in 0. Thus, the dividend 1,111,670 is perfectly divisible by 10.

Once we have memorized the rules of division for 1 through 10, as shown above, we can begin to tackle most division problems quickly using the same breakdown approach used for addition, subtraction, and multiplication problems.

Consider, for example, the problem, 69 ÷ 4. Quickly, we can break down 69 into two numbers: 60 and 9. We chose 60 because we know that 60 is divisible by 4 (60 ÷ 4 = 15). We then must divide 9 by 4. The answer will be 2 with a remainder of 1. Therefore, we can say that 4 goes into 69 a total of 15 + 2 times, with a remainder of 1. The result is 69 ÷ 4 = 17 with a remainder of 1. (If you find remainders unsettling, you could take the problem further and divide 4 into 1. This will produce a decimal result: 4 ÷ 1 = 0.25. Therefore, 69 ÷ 4 = 17.25. If you were out to dinner with three colleagues and received $69 in change, which had to be divided equally among the four of you, each diner would receive $17.25.)

Let's try a larger problem: 2,865 ÷ 3. We should be able to determine immediately that 2,865 will be evenly divisible by 3 because the sum of its digits (2, 8, 6, 5) equals 21, which is divisible by 3. *How can we quickly determine the quotient?* Let's break it down: Split 2,865 into 2,700 and 165. We choose 2,700 because we can quickly divide 3 into it: 2700 ÷ 3 = 900.

Next, let's attack the 165. Break it down to 150 and 15, and immediately the math becomes evident: 150 ÷ 3 = 50 and 15 ÷ 3 = 5. Therefore, 2,865 ÷ 3 = 900 + 50 + 5 = 955. If a landlord settles an overdue rent claim for $2,865 to be paid in three equal installments, the tenant will be remitting three payments of $955 each.

In tougher division problems, we may need to break down the divisor instead of the dividend. Let's dissect the problem 707 ÷ 87.

707 ÷ 87 First, breakdown 87 into 80 and 7.
Start with the number 80. Ask yourself what number, when multiplied by 80, will come close to the dividend 707 but not exceed it.
8 x 80 = 640 (We choose 8 because 9 would yield too high of a result.)
Next, 8 x 7 = 56. (We must multiply 8 by what remains of 87, which is 7.)
Then, add 640 + 56 = 696.
What remains? Answer: 707 – 696 = 11
707 ÷ 87 = 8, with a remainder of 11
(This can also be expressed as 8 or approximately 8.13.)

Another approach is to *reverse engineer* a division problem by overmultiplying to an easy number. Take, for example, the problem 882 ÷ 89. We can easily multiply 89 × 10 = 890, but that produces a result that is greater than our dividend. In fact, 890 is 8 higher than 882. To reverse engineer this problem, we'll conclude first that the answer must be 9-something instead of 10 since 10 yields too high a number. Since the difference between 890 and 882 is 8, let's subtract 8 from 89, our multiplier. This leaves us with 81. In effect, then, 882 can be divided by 89 a total of 9 times with a remainder of 81. (882 ÷ 89 = 9, with a remainder of 81.)

Doubling and Halving Techniques

Sometimes a division problem can be solved by doubling each number in the equation or by halving each number in the equation. Doubling or halving will not affect the result.

Example: 30,303 ÷ 5
Double it: 60,606 ÷ 10
Answer: 6,060.6

When we first see 30,303 ÷ 5, it stumps us momentarily. We can see that 30,303 is easily divisible by both 3 and 9, in accordance with the division rules we learned above, but that doesn't help us when the divisor is 5. The fastest approach is simply to double both sides of the equation, because 5 will turn to 10, rendering it an easy division problem. Doubling does not change the result: 30,303 ÷ 5 = 60,606 ÷ 10 = 6,060.6.

Let's attack another problem by cutting each of the numbers in half:

Example:	228 ÷ 12
Halve it:	114 ÷ 6
Overmultiply:	6 x 20 = 120 (but 120 is 6 more than 114)
Reverse:	Lower the 20 to 19 (because 20 is obviously too high); then subtract the excess number of 6 from the divisor of 6 (6 – 6 = 0). If the result is 0, then there is no remainder. The answer must be 19. Indeed, 228 ÷ 12 = 114 ÷ 6 = 19.

In the example above, you might have continued to halve the figures a second time to reach the same result:

Example:	228 ÷ 12
Halve it:	114 ÷ 6
Halve it again:	57 ÷ 3
Overmultiply:	3 x 20 = 60 (but that number is 3 too high)
Reverse:	Lower the 20 to 19. Do the math: 3 – 3 = 0. Therefore, 19 is the answer.

4.8. Rapid Squaring

Squaring numbers is an important function in many formulas. Learning how to square quickly can, therefore, be a useful skill.

The 25-and-50 Method

One approach to squaring numbers in your head is to place them between two base numbers, such as 25 and 50. So, for example, what is 38^2? Ask first, what is the difference between 25 and 38. The answer is 13. Then ask, what is the difference between 50 and 38? The answer is 12. Take the second result (12) and square it: 12 x 12 = 144. So, now we must combine the results: 13 and 144. But before we do so, we examine the second figure. If it is three digits, then we add the first digit to the first number. Thus, 13 becomes 14 and 144 sheds the 1 and becomes 44. Your revised answer now consists of 14 and 44. Put it together for the result: 38^2 = 1,444.

Try another in your head:

What is 66^2?
Difference from 25 = 41
Difference from 50 = 16
Square the second number: 16 x 16 = 256
Add the 2 (of 256) to the first difference (41): 41 + 2 = 43
Combine the remaining results: 43 and 56
Result: 66^2 = 4,356

When the second number is not three digits, then the procedure is even quicker. For example, in order to calculate 56^2, we apply the 25-and-50 method in a snap with no adjustments:

What is 56^2?
Difference from 25: (56 – 25 = 31)
Difference from 50: (56 – 50 = 6)
Square the second number: (6 x 6 = 36)
Combine the results: 31 and 36
Result: 56^2 = 3,136

Round and Revise

Another strategy for squaring any two-digit number is to round the number up or down to the nearest multiple of 10. Take 43, for example. To square 43, let's round it down to 40 (the nearest multiple of 10). The difference between 43 and 40 is 3. The shortcut has five quick steps:

1. Round up or down to a new number. Remember the difference between the original number and the rounded number.
2. Add the original number plus the difference (new multiplier).
3. Multiply the rounded number times the new multiplier (result #1).
4. Square the original difference.
5. Add the squared difference to result #1.

Let's apply these five steps to solve 43^2.

Round down: 43 becomes 40; difference = 3
Add difference to original number: 43 + 3 = 46 (new multiplier)

Multiply rounded number times new multiplier: 40 x 46 = 1,840
Square the original difference: $3^2 = 9$
Add the squared difference: 1,840 + 9 = 1,849
Final result: 43^2 = 1,849

Squaring Numbers that End in 5

To square numbers ending in 5, we simply multiply the first digit by itself plus 1. Then place the number 25 at the end. So, for example, if you want to square the number 45 quickly in your head, you multiply the first number (4) times itself plus 1 (4 + 1 = 5). The product of 4 x 5 is 20. Then we place 25 at the end. Thus, 45^2 = 2,025.

Let's try to square 85 quickly using this mental process:

8 x (8 +1) = 8 x 9 = 72
Attach 25 to the answer.
Thus, 85^2 = 7,225.

4.9. Shortcutting and Double-Checking

To further accelerate your ability to perform rapid mathematical functions, you can apply a number of additional shortcuts which are well-known to mathematicians. These include reverse subtraction, cross-multiplication, and the hovering hundreds technique.

Reverse Subtraction

Assume you must find the difference between two large or complex numbers. On paper, this would be a simple subtraction problem, but it might consume time to plug the numbers into a cell phone calculator or to manually calculate the answer by stacking the numbers in a column and subtracting the old-fashioned way. With practice, you can apply a *reverse subtraction* technique with complements to speed up the process.

Consider this question: 1,476.59 – 391.87 = ? If we were to visualize this question in column form, it would look like this:

1,476.59
–391.87
———
= ?

Traditionally, our inclination is to begin subtracting from right to left. But if we're trying to calculate rapidly, either on paper or in our heads, we are momentarily stumped by the numbers on the right side of the decimal point. *What is 59 – 87?* To speed the process, reverse the equation: Instead of asking what is 59 – 87, ask what is 87 – 59? The reverse equation is much easier: We apply high-speed subtraction techniques to calculate 87 – 59 very quickly. The 59 becomes 60 (and we will owe 1). Thus, 87 – 60 = 27. Then add back the 1 to get your answer: 28. Now, we apply the complements of this number:

28
72 (complements)
100

The complement (72) is our answer. Therefore, whatever the result of 1,476.59 – 391.87, we now know that the digits on the right side of the decimal point are 72.

Finishing the problem: Since we've already resolved the calculation on the right side of the decimal point, all we need to do now is subtract the numbers on the left side: 1,476 – 391. However, the second number must be increased by one because we technically borrowed a one when we subtracted the numbers on the right side of the decimal point. Therefore, the remaining equation becomes 1,476 – 392. *How would you solve this equation in your head using high-speed subtraction?* One way to solve this equation quickly is to change 392 to 400 (and hold the difference, 8, in suspension). Now we can easily calculate 1,476 – 400 = 1,076. And then add back the 8. Thus, 1,076 + 8 = 1,084. Finally, connect the complement: 72. Your combined number is 1,084.72. You have now solved the equation: 1,476.59 – 391.87 = 1,084.72.

Cross-Multiplication

Another method of shortcutting is to *cross-multiply* when confronted with a difficult multiplication problem by activating the distributive property of mathematics. So, for example, if you were presented with the problem, 36 x 67 = ?, you could distribute the numbers into their derivative parts: 36 x 67 = (30 + 6) x (60 + 7). Now, by cross-multiplying, you can solve four much easier equations:

36 x 67 = (30 + 6) x (60 + 7)
30 x 60 = 1,800
30 x 7 = 210
6 x 60 = 360
6 x 7 = 42

= 2,412

Therefore, 36 x 67 = 2,412.

Try to cross-multiply again using even larger numbers. Solve this problem: 222 × 196 = ?

222 x 196 = (200 + 20 + 2) x (100 + 90 + 6)
200 x 100 = 20,000
200 x 90 = 18,000
200 x 6 = 1,200
20 x 100 = 2,000
20 x 90 = 1,800
20 x 6 = 120
2 x 100 = 200
2 x 90 = 180
2 x 6 = 12

= 43,512

Answer: 222 x 196 = 43,512

Hovering Hundreds

Another shortcut can be employed quickly when the numbers being multiplied are hovering around 100. Consider, for example, if you were asked to multiply 104 by 106. Both numbers are close to 100. The number 104 is 4 above 100, and 106 is 6 above. We will refer to the 4 and the 6 as the distance numbers since they represent the distance of each number being multiplied from 100. Let's execute the shortcut.

Step One: Add the first number (104) to the second distance number (6): 104 + 6 = 110. Step Two: Multiply the first distance number times the second distance number: 4 x 6 = 24. Now, put the two answers together in sequence (110 → 24) to arrive at your answer: 11024. Thus, 104 x 106 = 11,024.

The same shortcut works for numbers under 100 which hover near 100. Try 98 x 92.

Step One: Add 98 to –8 (the second distance number). Note that the second distance number is a negative figure this time because it is 8 less than 100. Let's complete the equation: 98 – 8 = 90. Therefore, 90 is the first part of your answer. Next, multiply the first distance number (–2) times the second distance number (–8) to obtain +16. Now, put the answers together, 90 and 16 → 9016. And that's the answer: 98 x 92 = 9,016.

Casting Out Nines

Casting out nines is a mathematical technique for double-checking your math. To illustrate how this works, let's start with an addition problem:

3,915 + 4,699 + 5,051 + 837 + 2,604 = 17,106

First, let's simply sum the digits of each of the numbers: For example, for the first number, 3,915, we will add 3 + 9 + 1 + 5. The sum is 18. Let's do it for every number.

Problem:	3,915 +	4,699 +	5,051 +	837 +	2,604 =	17,106
Sums:	18	28	11	18	12 =	15

Next let's simplify each of the sums by adding those digits. So, 18 becomes 1 + 8 = 9.

Problem:	3,915 +	4,699 +	5,051 +	837 +	2,604 =	17,106
Sums:	18	28	11	18	12 =	15
Simplified:	9	10	2	9	3 =	6

Then let's add the resulting *simplified numbers* on the left side of the equals sign:

9 + 10 + 2 + 9 + 3 = 33

Further simplify the new sum by bringing it down to one digit. So, 33 becomes 3 + 3 = 6.

Does the final result for the sum of the figures on the left side of the equal sign equal the final result on the right side of the equal sign? Yes, 6 = 6. Therefore, your math was correct, and you have now verified that 3,915 + 4,699 + 5,051 + 837 + 2,604 = 17,106.

That process seems a bit cumbersome and time consuming. *Can we speed it up?*

To accelerate the process, we need to cast out all 9s while doing the math along with anything that adds up to 9. Let's put this process to a test using the same problem:

3,915 + 4,699 + 5,051 + 837 + 2,604 = 17,106

Notice that the first figure, 3,915, contains a 9. Ignore it—cast it out—when you sum the digits. Thus, you will add 3 + 1 + 5. The second number, 4,699, has two 9s. Ignore them both. The last number, 17,106, does not have a 9, but it has a 7 and two 1s, which equal 9. So cast out the 7 and both 1s. Now let's do the math without the 9s.

Problem:	3,915	+ 4,699	+ 5,051	+ 837	+ 2,604	=	17,106
Cast out:	3 + 1 + 5	4 + 6					0 + 6
Sums:	9	10	11	18	12	=	6
Simplified:	9	1	2	9	3	=	6

In fact, the simplified sums shown above can be further simplified by casting out the 9s again. Simply ignore them, and add 1 + 2 + 3 = 6. If, after casting out the 9s and reducing both sides of the equation to a number less than 9, the two numbers match, then your math is correct.

Simplified: 9 1 2 9 3 = 6
1 + 2 + 3 = 6
And finally . . . 6 = 6

We can also utilize the technique of casting out 9s in simplifying complex multiplication problems. Take, for example, the equation: 621 x 18 = 11,178. Start by reducing each figure to a single digit by summing the digits. Along the way, cast out all 9s. Your answer should be 0 x 0 = 0. Let's break it down:

621 x 18 = 11,178
Sum the digits in 621: 6 + 2 + 1 = 9. Then cast out the 9, leaving zero.
Sum the digits in 18: 1 + 8 = 9. Cast out the 9, leaving zero.
Sum the digits in 11,178: 1 + 1 + 1 + 7 + 8 = 18. Then 1 + 8 = 9. Cast out the 9, leaving zero. You might have accelerated this process when you visualized 11,178. When you saw a 7 and two 1s, you might have cast them out as a 9 from the outset. Then

when you saw that only an 8 and a 1 were remaining, you might have cast them out as another 9, leaving zero.

So, in the end, 0 x 0 on the left side of the equals sign produces a product of 0. Since the reduced number on the right side of the equals sign is also 0, the math checks out: 0 x 0 = 0.

Let's try another: 626 x 343 = 214,718.

Left side of the equals sign:
6 + 2 + 6 = 14, then 1 + 4 = 5
3 + 4 + 3 = 10, then 1 + 0 = 1
5 x 1 = 5

Right side of the equals sign:
214,718
Cast out the 7 and two 1s.
2 + 4 + 8 = 14, then 1 + 4 = 5
Final equation:
5 = 5

Thus, the math checks out, because both sides reduce to 5.

4.10. Percentage Power

How do we calculate percentages at breakneck speed? Let's start with percentages that end in 0 or 5. Try these problems in your head:

100% of 688 = ?
50% of 688 = ?
10% of 688 = ?
5% of 688 = ?

The answers should be quite easy. Obviously 100% of 688 is 688. Knowing this, we can also say that 200% of 688 is 2 x 688, and 500% of 688 is 5 x 688.

Likewise, 50% of 688 is one-half of 100% of 688. Therefore, 50% of 688 equals 344.

We know from our earliest math training that 10% of 688 simply requires us to move the decimal point one position to the left. So, the answer becomes 68.8. And if 10% of 688 = 68.8, then 5% of 688 must equal half of that. Hence, 34.4.

If you know the four simple calculations above, you should be able to handle any percentage calculation that ends in a 0 or 5. Try the following:

95% of 688 = ?
55% of 688 = ?
450% of 688 = ?

To calculate 95%, we simply find 100% and subtract 5%. If 100% of 688 is 688 and 5% of 688 is 34.4, then 95% of 688 must equal 688 – 34.4. In fact, 95% of 688 is precisely that: 653.6.

To calculate 55%, we simply find 50% and add 5%. So, to find 55% of 688, we add 344 + 34.4 = 378.4.

To calculate 450% of 688, we multiply 4 x 100% of 688 = 4 x 688, and then we add 50% of 688 which is 344. Here's the math: 4 x 688 = 4 x 700 – 4 x 12. This becomes 2,800 – 48. Apply complements: The complement of 48 is 52. Thus, 2,800 – 48 = 2,752. Then add back 344. Use high-speed addition for 2,752 + 344. Reduce the 344 to 300 (and hold 44 to the side). Then 2,752 + 300 = 3,052. Then add back the 44. So, 3,052 + 44 = 3,096.

Now, let's suppose you wanted to calculate a percentage in your head that did not end in 0 or 5. Take, for example, these two questions:

34% of 60 = ?
66% of 900 = ?

To determine 34% of 60, we can quickly simplify the question into two equations: 30% of 60 and 4% of 60. First, 30% of 60 = 3 × 10% of 60. Since 10% of 60 is 6, three times that amount is 18. To determine 4% of 60, we must think of 4% as 4 × 1%. We know that 10% of 60 is 6. Therefore, to calculate 1%, we move the decimal point one position to the left. So, 1% of 60 equals 0.6. Accordingly, 4% of 60 must equal 2.4. Putting it all together, 34% of 60 equals 18 + 2.4 or 20.4.

To determine 66% of 900, calculate 60% of 900 + 6% of 900. To solve 60% of 900, we think to ourselves "what is 6 times 10% of 900?" Do the math: 10% of 900 = 90. Then 6 x 90 = 540. Next, we must determine 6%, which would translate into 6 x 1%. If 90 is 10%, then 9 must be 1%. So, 6 x 9 = 54. (Of course, we could have further simplified this process by noting that 60% of 900 = 540. Therefore, 6%

would equal 10% of 540, or simply 54.) Now that we know that 60% of 900 = 540 and 6% = 54, we add the numbers to arrive at our final result: 540 + 54 = 594.

Assume that Attorney Adam plans to take a 33% contingency fee on his personal injury case. He has a $140,000 offer on the table. All of the costs have been prepaid by the client. So Attorney Adam asks himself, what would I stand to earn as my 33% fee if we accepted the $140,000 offer? The equation is 33% x 140,000 (or also 0.33 x 140,000). We can do this quickly: 3 x 14 = 42. Thus, 30% of 140,000 = 42,000. Then, 3% would be one-tenth of that amount, or 4,200. So the answer is $42,000 + $4,200 = $46,200.

4.11. Estimation Techniques

Estimating answers to mathematical problems without precisely solving them can be a helpful technique and a useful litigation tactic, especially when speed is at issue. Imagine, for example, two attorneys delivering oral argument to a judge. Seconds before the first attorney sits down and yields the podium to his adversary, he states that there are 6,977 homes in the community, and each homeowner will receive 1,256 pieces of junk mail during the term of his home ownership, according to a recently released report. The opposing attorney immediately wonders: *Exactly how much mail is that?*

The answer to the question, of course, is a multiplication problem: 6,977 x 1,256. Unfortunately, the judge calls on the opposing attorney to begin his argument seconds later, and there isn't enough time to solve the problem. *Can we quickly estimate the answer without solving it precisely?*

Rounding Numbers

One approach to solving the problem above is to round the numbers. We could round 6,977 up to 7,000. We could then round 1,256 up to 1,300. Then multiply the rounded numbers: 7,000 x 1,300. (Remember your high-speed multiplication techniques: 7,000 x 1,300 is initially 7 x 13. This becomes 7 x 10 + 7 x 3. The answer is 91 plus a total of 5 zeros: 9,100,000.) So, when the opposing attorney begins his argument, he might say, "Your honor, you just heard that there are approximately nine million pieces of mail going to these households."

The precise calculation is: 6,977 x 1,256 = 8,763,112. So, in stating that there are approximately nine million mail pieces, the attorney overestimated by about 300,000. What if he wanted to estimate more accurately? To do this, he would have to round a closer number. For example, instead of rounding 1,256 up to 1,300, he could round it down to 1,250. (1,250 is only 6 less than 1,256, while 1,300 is 44 greater than 1,256.) By rounding down to 1,250, the new equation becomes 7,000 x 1,250. By applying high-speed multiplication techniques, this becomes a quick mental calculation: 7 x 125 = 7 x 120 + 7 x 5 = 840 + 35 = 875. Remember that you can also use the halving and doubling technique for multiplying numbers ending in 5, as discussed in Section 4.6. So, for example, 7 x 125 becomes 6 x 125 (with 1 x 125 kicked to the side for a few seconds). With the equation 6 x 125, we halve the 6 to get 3 and we double the 125 to get 250. Now, the equation is super simple: 3 x 250, which equals 750. But we must add back 1 x 125 (or simply 125). So, 750 + 125 = 875. Of course, 875 is only part of the answer. We must still add a total of four zeros. The final answer is thus 8,750,000.

Now the opposing lawyer, using mental estimation techniques, can say, "Your honor, you just heard that there are approximately 8.7 million pieces of mail going to these households." In quickly estimating through rounding the numbers, the attorney has come remarkably close to the actual, precise answer to the equation (8,763,112).

Rounding can also provide a rapid estimate of numbers being added or subtracted. So, for example, 6,896 – 3,479 can be quickly rounded to 7,000 – 3,500 to produce the answer 3,500. This would not be a bad estimate because the actual answer is 6,896 – 3,479 = 3,417. For a more accurate estimate, one simply must round up or down to closer numbers. Thus, instead of rounding 6,879 up to 7,000, try rounding it up to 6,900. The problem is now 6,900 – 3,500 = 3,400. The answer 3,400 is closer to the actual answer of 3,417 and hence a more accurate estimate.

Benchmarking Fractions

We can estimate the result of an equation that has fractions by identifying the nearest benchmark. This rounding technique assumes that all fractions can be reduced or increased to either 0 or $\frac{1}{2}$ or 1. Consider, for example, this equation: $\frac{15}{16} + \frac{10}{16} = ?$ How would you round up or round down each of these fractions? Given our three choices, what would be the nearest benchmark for each fraction: 0 or $\frac{1}{2}$ or 1? In the case of $\frac{15}{16}$ we can immediately see that this is close to $\frac{16}{16}$, which equals 1. So, 1 is the benchmark for the first fraction. On the other hand, the second fraction, $\frac{10}{16}$ is slightly greater than $\frac{8}{16}$, which equals $\frac{1}{2}$. So we'll round it down to $\frac{1}{2}$. In effect, we can estimate, quite quickly, $\frac{15}{16} + \frac{10}{16} = 1\frac{1}{2}$. In fact, the actual precise answer is that $\frac{15}{16} + \frac{10}{16} = \frac{25}{16} = 1\frac{9}{16} = 1.5625$. This result is barely higher than our estimate of $1\frac{1}{2}$.

Estimating Decimals

If you've mastered high-speed addition and subtraction, then dealing with decimals should not be too troublesome. After all, 23.74 + 74.23 is a simple addition problem (97.97), and the decimal point really poses no problem. When the problem becomes more cumbersome, you may wish to estimate by rounding, and in so doing, remove all numbers to the right of the decimal point.

For example, 2,346.66 + 2,499.99 looks ugly at first. Yet, if we appreciate that anything to the right of the decimal point is less than 1, then we know that removing the numbers to the right of the decimal point will not generally alter our result significantly. We could round up or down to the nearest 1, and that would improve our equation somewhat: 2,347 + 2,500. You can do this now in your head by adding 2,300 and 2,500 and adding back the 47 later. So, 2,300 + 2,500 = 4,800 + 47 = 4,847. This estimate is only slightly different than the actual, precise, solution: 2,346.66 + 2,499.99 = 4,846.65.

Estimating Square Roots

We do not need to estimate square roots for those whole numbers that are perfect squares. A perfect square is the product of two equal integers. In other words, 3 x 3 = 9. The number 9 is a perfect square because it is the product of two equal integers: 3 and 3. We don't need to estimate the square root of perfect squares such as 9 because we already know *exactly* what these square roots are.

We know that 2 x 2 = 4, 3 x 3 = 9, 4 x 4 =16, and so forth. After 10 x 10 is when it gets a bit tricky. Let's look at all the perfect squares up to 15.

$\sqrt{1} = 1$	$\sqrt{36} = 6$	$\sqrt{121} = 11$
$\sqrt{4} = 2$	$\sqrt{49} = 7$	$\sqrt{144} = 12$
$\sqrt{9} = 3$	$\sqrt{64} = 8$	$\sqrt{169} = 13$
$\sqrt{16} = 4$	$\sqrt{81} = 9$	$\sqrt{196} = 14$
$\sqrt{25} = 5$	$\sqrt{100} = 10$	$\sqrt{225} = 15$

How do we determine the square root of a number other than a perfect square? For example, what is the square root of 35? We solve this problem by estimating, and we use the existing perfect squares as our benchmarks.

So, for example, the square root of 35 must be less than the square root of the perfect square 36. It must also be greater than the square root of the perfect square 25 because 35 falls somewhere between 25 and 36. Since we know that it is greater than the square root of 25 but not as great as the square root of 36, we know that the answer must be a number between 5 and 6. In fact, we can estimate that the answer is quite close to 6 because 35 is quite close to 36 which is 6^2. So let's estimate that the answer is 5.9. If we check our math, we discover that 5.9 × 5.9 = 34.81 which is close to 35. *Not a bad estimate.* The actual square root of 35 is a long number that begins with 5.9160 . . . . So, in the end, 5.9 is a solid estimate of the square root of 35.

Try estimating each of these square roots:

$\sqrt{66}$, $\sqrt{10.5}$, and $\sqrt{182}$.

In the first case, $\sqrt{66}$, we know that we are not dealing with a perfect square. But 66 is close to 64 which is a perfect square. Indeed, 64 = 8 × 8, which means that a number greater than 8 (but not too much greater) must be the square root of 66. If you estimate that the answer is 8.1, you would not be far off. The actual answer is a long number that begins with 8.124 . . . . Simply knowing the perfect squares (and knowing $\sqrt{64}$, in particular) allowed us to estimate the answer to this question rapidly and accurately.

In the second case above, $\sqrt{10.5}$ don't be sidetracked by the decimal point. The square, 10.5, is just slightly higher than 9. We know that the square root of 9 is 3. So, we can estimate that the square root of 10.5 is slightly greater. Let's estimate 3.2. (When the squares are lower, our estimates should be slightly higher for each increment above the nearest perfect square.) In fact, the square root of 10.5 is a long number that begins with 3.240 . . . .

In the third example above, $\sqrt{182}$, the answer must be between 13 and 14. We know that $\sqrt{169} = 13$ and $\sqrt{196} = 14$. Because 182 falls in between the perfect squares 169 and 196, the square root of 182 must be some number between the square roots of 169 and 196. *But now the numbers are higher, and 182 is neither close to 169 nor 196.* In fact, 182 is approximately in the mathematical middle of the two numbers (If you wanted to see how close it is to the middle, simply add 169 + 196, and then divide by 2. So, 169 + 196 = 365, and 365 ÷ 2 = 182.5. So, 182 is almost dead center between the perfect squares 169 and 196.) Since 182 is in the middle, our answer should be in the middle of the square roots 13 and 14. We estimate 13.5. Sure enough, when we do the math, $\sqrt{182}$ equals a long number beginning with 13.4907 . . . .

4.12. Memorization Strategies

You're staring at a financial statement, and three large numbers pop out: 64,123; 5,966,512; and 6,038. Each of these numbers represents a different, equally important, financial disclosure. You want to memorize the three numbers in order to recite them later. Unfortunately, these are difficult-to-remember numbers, especially if you must remember all three of them at once. How can we proceed?

The trick is to convert the numbers to words using a mnemonic system. While our brains struggle to remember lots of large numbers, they seem to enjoy memorizing visual images or verbal statements, even unusual or bizarre constructions of language. To make this work, however, we need a uniform code for changing numbers into letters or phonetic sounds. Such a code was invented many years ago, and it is known as the *Major Memory System.* Under this system, the numbers 0 through 9 each have matching phonetic sounds. Let's look at the Major Memory System:

NUMBER	SOUNDS	SAMPLE WORDS	EXPLANATION
0	Z, S, or soft C	zero, soap, ceiling	0 is zero. Think of zero as representing the Z or S sound.
1	T or D	time, duck	D and T have 1 downstroke. The sounds of T and D are quite similar.
2	N	night, near	N has 2 downstrokes. Also, a capital N rotated 90° clockwise looks like a 2.
3	M	moon, mouse	M has 3 downstrokes. Also, a capital M rotated 90° clockwise looks like a 3.
4	R	rock, rope	R is the last letter of four.
5	L	lace, lettuce	L is the Roman numeral for 50.
6	SH, GH, ZH, soft CH, or J	chalk, ship, chef, jam, giraffe	6 facing backward looks somewhat like a J. The phonetic sounds all sound like a sneeze, a wheeze, or a whistle.
7	K, Q, hard C, or hard G	cage, cave, gas, quack, king	An uppercase K looks like two 7s, on their sides, standing back to back.
8	V, F	vase, fish	Think of a V8 motor or a figure 8 maneuver on a skating rink.
9	B, P	book, back, pipe, patch	The lowercase, b and p, can each be spun or flipped to look like a 9.
	W, H, Y	sow, fairy	The WHY letters have no number assigned to them, and they can be used anywhere within a word.
	A, E, I, O, U	sofa, roof, knife	Vowels have no numerical value, and can also be used anywhere within a word.

To master the Major Memory System, you need to memorize the table above. At first, this may seem time consuming, but, after reading the explanations, it becomes easy to memorize the code. Let's try converting a few numbers to words:

33 = mom
76 = cage
95 = belly
99 = pipe

In the first example, 33 consists of two 3s. Since 3 = M, we need a word that has the M sound twice. Thus, 33 can be translated to *mom*. Remember that the O in between the Ms is meaningless because vowels have no numerical effect. The number 76 requires a sound for 7 plus a sound for 6. The 7 translates to a K or hard C sound, and the 6 translates to a J or hard G sound. So, 76 can be converted to *cage.* The number 95 can be *bell* or *ball* or *bail* since the 9 equals a b and the 5 equals an L sound, and since vowels can be used anywhere and are irrelevant to the numerical values. In this instance, we converted 95 to *belly* because the y at the end of the word is also irrelevant. The number 99 consists only of 9s, which translate to Bs or Ps. So, you could convert 99 to *pipe* or *poop* or *babe* or *boob.*

Choosing which words to use is up to you, but it should be words that tie into a story that you can memorize, regardless of how strange the story might be. So, if you had to memorize 33, 76, 95, and 99, and you converted these numbers to mom, cage, belly, and pipe, respectively, you could, for example, construct a scene in your head in which your mom has been put in a cage. When you look at her, you can see her belly, and she's smoking a pipe. The scene is absurd but certainly memorable. When you are called upon to recite the four numbers you've memorized, you'll instantly recall your pipe-smoking caged mom's belly (mom, cage, belly, pipe) and you'll convert these words quickly back to numbers.

Constructing a scene or a story for the words is meant to be as uncomplicated as possible, even when dealing with more complex numbers. How, for example, would you apply the Major Memory System to memorize the number 333,333? There are six 3s, and each 3 equals an M sound. So you could, for example, convert 333,333 to three words, each with two Ms: *mum, mom,* or *mummy.* Tell yourself that you are going to remain *mum* about the fact that your *mom* has become a *mummy.* Or perhaps you can associate this number with the vision of a baby crying *mama, mama, mama.* Three words, six M sounds, converts to 333,333.

How would you convert 491 and 81 if you had to remember them in sequence?

Here are some possibilities: *rabbit food, robot foot,* and *repeat fight.*

Try using the Major Memory System to memorize your client's date of birth and Social Security number. Or use it to memorize a series of important case-related dates, such as:

- The date of your client's accident and her medical treatment dates
- The dates of your client's marriage and the parties' separation, and the dates of her husband's adulterous affairs.
- The dates of publication of an infringing copyright

Try using the system to quickly memorize and recite long numbers on command, which may be relevant in making opening statements, delivering closing arguments, or conducting cross-examination, such as:

- A series of bank account or credit card numbers in a creditor's dispute
- A series of phone numbers dialed by a criminal defendant
- A series of zip codes that are relevant in an administrative hearing involving land use and development issues
- A series of passwords used by an employee accused of pilfering company funds

Let's now return to the opening paragraph of this section and revisit the financial statement that contains three large numbers that you want to memorize: 64,123; 5,966,512; and 6,038. Convert each number under the Major Memory System:

64,123	64 = Ch + R (cherry) and 123 = D + N + M (denim) = *cherry denim*
5,966,512	59 = L and P (loopy); 66 = J and J (judge); 5= L (law); 12= T and N (tone) = A *loopy judge* laid down the *law* in a strange *tone.*
6,038	60 = CH + Z (cheesy); 38 = M + V (move)

If you need to remember these numbers together, or in sequence, you could build a story around the mnemonic conversions you've created under the Major Memory System. Using the examples above, we could, for example, tell ourselves that a woman appeared in court wearing *cherry denim.* She was greeted by a *loopy judge* who laid down the *law* in a strange *tone,* admonishing her that her appearance was a *cheesy move.* An amusing, if not ludicrous story—yes, indeed—but it could help you quickly repeat the numbers 64,123; 5,966,512; and 6,038 on call.

Mnemonic Peg Systems

Another approach to memorizing numbers is to follow a *mnemonic peg system,* in which numbers are pegged to mnemonic images, which are then memorized. For example, in the *Number Rhyme System,* every number is linked to a keyword that defines a memorable image. Common examples of the number rhyme keywords and images are shown below:

0 = hero, arrow
1 = gun, nun, sun
2 = shoe, brew, glue
3 = tree, sea, bee
4 = door, store, core
5 = hive, dive, drive
6 = sticks, hicks, bricks
7 = heaven, tavern, raven
8 = bait, gate, skate
9 = wine, sign, spine
10 = pen, men, hen

Of course, you need not use the particular words listed above. You can associate numbers with your friends and colleagues whose names rhyme with the numbers. Thus, for example, 2 = Stu, 3 = Dee, 7 = Devon or Kevin, 8 = Kate, and 10 = Ben. Likewise, you might choose to associate the numbers with rhyming historical or mythological figures (e.g., 4 = Thor). Or perhaps you prefer commercial references (e.g., 0 = Sterno, 4 = Dior). You could even peg each number to your favorite performers or musical groups, if you prefer (e.g., 6 = Styx).

How you peg the words is important, however, because you will need to construct memorable stories from the combination of keywords and the images they represent. Using the sample keywords provided in the list above, let's try to construct some stories that will generate images that will assist your memory. Assume, for example, that your client's date of birth is February 3, 1987, and you need to compel this date to memory. Let's think of the date as 2-3-87.

2 = shoe
3 = sea
8 = skate
7 = heaven

Can you construct a story from these rhymes? Here's a possibility: "I lost my *shoe* at *sea;* so I wore a *skate* to *heaven*." Preposterous, admittedly, but this strange sentence evokes a series of images: a shoe falling into the sea, and a skate (presumably used in ice skating) being worn on the way through heaven's pearly gates. Thinking of these images, and the rhymes they contain, will force us to recall the numbers 2, 3, 8 and 7, and hence, your client's date of birth.

Try it with the last four numbers of a credit card: 2935.

2 = shoe
9 = sign
3 = tree
5 = hive

"I lost my *shoe.* So, I followed a *sign,* which led me to a *tree*. But all I found there was a *beehive.*" By associating your credit card with the lost shoe story, you should be able to quickly conjure up the words *shoe, sign, tree,* and *beehive*, and convert them back to the rhyming numbers, 2, 9, 3, and 5.

An alternative to the Number Rhyme System is the *Number Shape System,* another mnemonic peg system for memorizing numbers. Under the Number Shape System, we peg each number to an image that looks like the number itself. For example, the number 1 looks like a candle. Therefore, every time we see a 1, we would associate it immediately with the image of a candle. The number 4 is similar to the shape of a sailboat; so every time we see a 4, we'll think of a sailboat.

Common images that look like numbers are listed below:

0 = hole, egg, ball, doughnut
1 = candle, stick, spear
2 = swan
3 = handcuffs, butterfly
4 = sailboat, flag
5 = meat hook, seahorse
6 = golf club, combination lock
7 = boomerang, edge of a cliff
8 = snowman, hourglass
9 = balloon on a string

Let's start with a simple exercise to activate the Number Shape System. How would you remember the number 24? Simply envision a swan (shaped like a 2) and a sailboat (shaped like a 4). Thus, when you see 24, think of a swan on a sailboat. When you see the number 898, think of a snowman handing a balloon on a string to another snowman. Try the number 674. How would you memorize 674 using the Number Shape System?

Experts have developed other mnemonic memory techniques and other memorization shortcuts in general. A full study of the various alternative approaches is beyond the scope of this book. Utilizing the Major Memory System or one of the mnemonic peg systems, however, may prove helpful in recollecting numbers on the fly. Mastering one or more memorization systems will ultimately save time and prevent errors. Moreover, in calculating formulas that involve larger numbers or longer lists of numbers, these memorization skills will prove invaluable.

Chapter 5

The Basic Formulas

5.1. Time Value of Money

The quantum of damages paid by one party to another is inherently inaccurate, unless it is paid at precisely the moment the injury or the loss was suffered. If a defendant breaches a contract causing the plaintiff to suffer damages of $1,000, the plaintiff can only technically be made whole if the $1,000 is paid directly and immediately upon the breach. This is because $1,000 is worth less to the plaintiff as time moves forward. It is worth even less if the parties agree to a $1,000 settlement to be paid a year from the date of the settlement. Indeed, had the plaintiff received $1,000 promptly and invested it at 5% interest, the plaintiff would have $1,050 after one year.

The same principle works in reverse. If a settlement or a judgment provides that a defendant will pay a plaintiff $500,000 in one year, won't the defendant have the benefit of investing the money or earning interest on the funds during the intervening time? If this is the case, isn't there some lesser amount of money that can be paid to the plaintiff today so that over the course of 12 months, the plaintiff can earn interest and build the total up to $500,000? Isn't there some amount that the defendant can pay today (less than $500,000) that will restore to the defendant the financial advantage it would have derived had it held onto the funds for a year?

These examples of future value and present value illustrate the time value of money, one of the fundamental principles of finance and economics. Understanding the time value of money is critical to making accurate calculations of damages. By applying time value principles, attorneys can accomplish a number of important objectives in settling their cases:

- A payment due in the future can be discounted to a certain lower amount to be paid today. This may help a client who needs the funds today and may serve to protect against the risk of the obligor's insolvency in the future.
- A payment due today can be increased to a certain greater amount to be paid in the future. This may help a client who cannot afford to make the payment immediately.
- A choice between a lump sum payment or a structured settlement paid over 20 years can be measured by determining what the 20-year payout will really be worth over time (as compared to the immediate payment of the lump sum).
- The amount of a deposit can be determined in order to open an account that will pay a fixed amount of damages to a party on a monthly or an annual basis. This will assist a business in setting up a reparations fund or a divorce client in establishing an alimony or support account. It can also be used to set up a scholarship fund or a perpetual trust fund.

The calculations for the time value of money revolve around the formulas for future value and present value discussed in sections 2.2 through 2.7. Making these calculations requires some very basic algebra, a chosen interest rate, and a fixed period of time for payments to be made. The interest rate should be agreed on by the parties, or it should be verified by some reliable published standard, of which the court would take judicial notice.

Becoming familiar with the time value calculations provides a relatively quick method for determining missing pieces of information while calculating damages. Five values become critical to the process: (1) Interest Rate; (2) Number of Payment Periods; (3) Payment Amount; (4) Present Value; and (5) Future Value. If given any four of the five values listed above, a judge or an attorney can quickly establish the fifth (missing) value. The calculations are discussed in the formulas that follow.

5.2. Future Value

The future value (FV) starts with the present value (PV). If you have \$1,000 today but you wish to pay it to another party in the future, how much should you pay in the future based on the time value of the money? In this formula, the future payment is the FV, and the \$1,000 is the PV. To build the formula, you will need an interest rate, and a payment period over which the interest rate will be applied. Let's assume that the interest rate will be 4%, and the payment will be due in five years. Let's also assume that the interest rate of 4% will be applied (or compounded) annually.

The question is: What is the future value of \$1,000 in five years based on a 4% interest rate compounded annually?

The formula is:

$$FV = PV\ (1 + i)^n$$

i = interest rate
n = payment period (in years)

The future value equals the present value multiplied by the sum of 1 plus the interest rate, raised to a certain exponential power based on the payment period.

$$\begin{aligned} FV &= PV\ (1 + i)^n \\ FV &= \$1{,}000\ (1 + .04)^5 \\ FV &= \$1{,}000\ (1.04)^5 \\ FV &= \$1{,}000\ (1.2166529024) \\ FV &= \$1{,}216.65 \end{aligned}$$

The interest rate of 4% was converted to a decimal (.04). The five-year payment period provided the basis for the exponent (5).

By applying the future value formula above, we see that \$1,000 owed today will be worth \$1,216.65 if paid in five years at 4% interest compounded annually.

Let's try the formula again, using larger, more cumbersome figures. Assume that the resolution of a contract dispute determines that the defendant owes the plaintiff \$1,155,600.43 in present damages. However, under the terms of the settlement, the plaintiff has agreed to wait two years for payment. The attorneys have stipulated to a 3.5% interest rate. How much should the defendant actually pay in two years when it satisfies the terms of the settlement?

The question is: What is the future value of $1,155,600.43 in two years at 3.5% interest compounded annually?

The formula is:

$$FV = PV\ (1 + i)^n$$
$$FV = \$1{,}155{,}600.43\ (1 + .035)^2$$
$$FV = \$1{,}155{,}600.43\ (1.035)^2$$
$$FV = \$1{,}155{,}600.43\ (1.071225)$$
$$FV = \$1{,}237{,}908.07$$

The future value is $1,237,908.07. Therefore, if the defendant needs two years to pay the actual contract damages of $1,155,600.43, the settlement agreement should require the defendant to pay $1,237.908.07 at two years, based on the stipulated interest rate.

Monthly Compounding

What if the settlement provides that payment can be delayed for two years, but that interest should be compounded on a monthly basis instead of annually? Assuming that the annual interest rate remains fixed at 3.5%, the future value formula will have to be adjusted in two places. First, the annual rate of 3.5% should be divided by 12 to determine the monthly rate (.035 divided by 12 = .0029167). Second, the exponent (2 representing two years) should be multiplied by 12 months. Therefore, the new exponent is 24.

The question now becomes: What is the future value of $1,155,600.43 in two years at 3.5% interest compounded monthly?

The formula is:

$$FV = PV\ (1 + i)^n$$
$$FV = \$1{,}155{,}600.43\ (1 + .0029167)^{24}$$
$$FV = \$1{,}155{,}600.43\ (1.0029167)^{24}$$
$$FV = \$1{,}155{,}600.43\ (1.0723999)$$
$$FV = \$1{,}239{,}265.79$$

Thus, if the settlement figure accrues interest compounded on a monthly basis, the ultimate payoff will be somewhat greater, at $1,239,265.79.

5.3. Future Value of an Uneven Cash Flow

In some cases, it is necessary for a party to pay out a different amount of money each month or each year until a settlement is fully satisfied. For example, a start-up business could agree to settle a claim for an increasing amount each year over a five-year period. A party in a divorce action could agree to pay alimony to the dependent spouse over a five-year period, while paying different amounts each year. These are what are known as uneven cash flows.

Assume, for example, that the payment schedule will span five years, with the following uneven cash flows:

Year 1: Defendant will pay $200,000
Year 2: Defendant will pay $300,000
Year 3: Defendant will pay $400,000
Year 4: Defendant will pay $500,000
Year 5: Defendant will pay $500,000

If the defendant were to make all of the payments immediately, the aggregate payment would total $1.9 million. But we cannot simply determine the future value of $1.9 million because the defendant is not making all of the payments at once. If the defendant pays a portion of the total amount each year, then an interest rate will offset the value of each payment and of the total amount due.

The formula for calculating a future value for an uneven cash flow is:

$$FV = PV\left(1 + \frac{i}{m}\right)^{mn}$$

i = interest rate
m = number of months or other compounding periods within a year
n = number of years remaining

Let's assume the interest rate will be 4%. Let's also assume that interest will be compounded monthly over the course of the five-year payout.

The question is: What is the combined future value of five uneven payments ($200,000, $300,000, $400,000, $500,000 and $500,000), at 4% interest, compounded monthly over five years?

The procedure is to apply the formula above to determine the future value of each payment, and then to add each of the future values together, as follows:

Year 1

$FV = PV\ ((1 + \frac{i}{m})^{mn}$

$FV = \$200{,}000\ (1 + .04/12)^{12 \times 4}$ [12 months times four years]

$FV = \$200{,}000\ (1.0033334)^{48}$

$FV = \$200{,}000\ (1.1732024)$

$FV = \$234{,}640.48$

Year 2

$FV = PV\ ((1 + \frac{i}{m})^{mn}$

$FV = \$300{,}000\ (1 + .04/12)^{12 \times 3}$ [12 months times three years]

$FV = \$300{,}000\ (1.0033334)^{36}$

$FV = \$300{,}000\ (1.1272746)$

$FV = \$338{,}182.38$

Year 3

$FV = PV\ ((1 + \frac{i}{m})^{mn}$

$FV = \$400{,}000\ (1 + .04/12)^{12 \times 2}$ [12 months times two years]

$FV = \$400{,}000\ (1.0033334)^{24}$

$FV = \$400{,}000\ (1.0831447)$

$FV = \$433{,}257.88$

Year 4

$FV = PV\ ((1 + \frac{i}{m})^{mn}$

$FV = \$500{,}000\ (1 + .04/12)^{12 \times 1}$ [12 months times one year]

$FV = \$500{,}000\ (1.0033334)^{12}$

$FV = \$500{,}000\ (1.0407424)$

$FV = \$520{,}371.20$

Year 5

$FV = PV\ ((1 + \frac{i}{m})^{mn}$

$FV = \$500{,}000\ (1 + .04/12)^{12 \times 0}$ [12 months times 0 years]

$FV = \$500{,}000\ (1.0033334)^{0}$

$FV = \$500{,}000\ (1)$ [Anything raised to a power of zero equals 1]

$FV = \$500{,}000$

Total of all future values

Year 1:	$ 234,640.48
Year 2:	$ 338,182.38
Year 3:	$ 433,257.88
Year 4:	$ 520,371.20
Year 5:	$ 500,000.00
Total:	$2,026,451.94

Therefore, at the conclusion of the five-year period, the payments will be worth a total of $2,026,451.94.

Knowing the future value of this uneven cash flow can be helpful as a negotiating tool. If the defendant had agreed to pay $2 million over five years (and assuming that the funds will actually be invested at 4% interest), then the five payments listed above would be a reasonable settlement approach for the plaintiff. Although the five payments total only $1.9 million when added together today, we now know that the future value of the cash flow over the five-year period exceeds $2 million.

5.4. Present Value

Present value is the opposite of future value but can be calculated using the same formula. Instead of asking what value present-day money will have in the future, the calculation for present value asks what value future money will have today (if it were paid today). When calculating the present value of an amount due in the future, it is fair to assume that the amount paid today will be something less than the amount paid in the future. If an obligation will equal a certain amount in three years, it can be discounted to some lesser amount today.

Start again with $1,000, to be paid in three years. How much should one party pay to another today to satisfy a debt that will become due in three years? Assume the interest rate is 4% compounded annually.

The question is: What is the present value of $1,000 to be paid in three years based on a 4% interest rate compounded annually?

The formula is:

$$FV = PV\,(1 + i)^n$$

i = interest rate

n = payment period (in years)

While the present value formula is the same as the future value formula, the FV figure is known to us this time, and the PV figure is missing. As we complete the formula, it will be necessary to apply some simple algebra to determine the PV.

$$FV = PV\ (1 + i)^n$$
$$\$1{,}000 = PV\ (1 + .04)^3$$
$$\$1{,}000 = PV\ (1.124864)$$

[Algebra: We now need to isolate PV on one side of the equation. To do this, divide both sides by 1.124864]

$$\frac{\$1{,}000}{1.124864} = PV$$

$$\$888.99 = PV$$

So, the present value of $1,000 to be paid in three years (at 4% interest) is $888.99. If this were a business transaction or an out-of-court settlement, a payment of $888.99 today would effectively satisfy the obligation to pay $1,000 in three years.

Monthly Compounding

Monthly compounding works to the plaintiff's disadvantage when calculating present value. While plaintiffs who are awaiting a future payment would be inclined to apply monthly compounding, plaintiffs accepting a discounted earlier payoff should apply annual compounding for the greater result. This is because when we apply monthly compounding of interest to a present value formula, the result is somewhat lower.

The question now becomes: What is the present value of $1,000 to be paid in three years based on a 4% interest rate compounded monthly?

Remember that with monthly compounding, the formula will have to be adjusted in two places. First, the annual rate of 4% should be divided by 12 to determine the monthly rate (.04 divided by 12 = .003333). Second, the exponent (3 representing three years) should be multiplied by 12 months. Therefore, the new exponent is 36.

$$FV = PV\ (1 + i)^n$$
$$\$1{,}000 = PV\ (1 + .003333)^{36}$$
$$\$1{,}000 = PV\ (1.003333)^{36}$$
$$\$1{,}000 = PV\ (1.127258)$$

$$\frac{\$1{,}000}{1.127258} = PV$$

$$\$887.11 = PV$$

So, the present value of $1,000 to be paid in three years (compounded monthly at 4% interest) is $887.11.

5.5. Net Present Value

Net present value (NPV) is essentially present value together with a cost-benefit analysis. In other words, by calculating NPV, we can determine whether to accept a certain deal by ascertaining whether we will gain or lose money in the end. We start by determining present value, which means that we will want to discount some future cash payment to a present amount of money. Then, we ask the question: how much will it cost to get there? If the cost (or the investment) to get the future payment exceeds the present value of the payment, then the NPV is negative, and the deal should be rejected. On the other hand, if the cost to obtain the future payment is less than the present value of the future payment, then the NPV is positive, and the deal should be accepted.

For example, assume that we can settle a civil action for $15,000 in one year. Should we take the case? To make this decision, we will want to know the NPV of $15,000 to be paid a year from now. This means we will want to ascertain the present value (which requires a certain interest rate), and we will want to know how much it will cost us to pursue the case (which requires a calculation of internal overhead costs, legal resources, and court costs). So, let's assume that the interest rate is 4%, and that the total cost to the law firm will be $13,500. Is the case worth the investment?

The question is: what is the NPV of $15,000 paid in one year at a cost of $13,500 based on a 4% rate of return?

We start with this formula:

NPV = PV – Cost

Let's first calculate the present value:

$$PV = FV/(1 + i)^n$$

$$PV = \frac{\$15,000}{(1.04)^1}$$

PV = $14,423.08

Then let's determine the NPV:

NPV = PV – Cost
NPV = $14,423.08 – $13,500
NPV = $923.08

In this example, an investment of $13,500 in overhead expenses and court costs would return a positive benefit of $923.08 in today's money, based on a settlement of $15,000 to be paid in one year. In other words, applying the NPV formula, we should accept this case and settle it for $15,000.

Changing the factors, however, may produce a different result. For example, if the overhead expenses and court costs were $14,500, the NPV would be calculated as follows:

NPV = $14,423.08 – $14,500
NPV = –$76.92

Thus, if the investment were $14,500, the NPV would produce a negative result, a loss of almost $77. Therefore, based on an NPV analysis, we would not want to take this case.

Let's assume that the costs and expenses were $13,500, but the settlement amount was changed to $14,500 to be paid in one year. In such a case, we'd have to recalculate the present value of the future settlement, and then determine NPV, as follows:

$$PV = \frac{FV}{(1 + i)^n}$$

$$PV = \frac{\$14,500}{(1.04)^1}$$

PV = $13,942.31

NPV = PV – Cost
NPV = $13,942.31 – $13,500
NPV = $442.31

In this scenario, the NPV is positive, and therefore the settlement is worth pursuing. Notice, however, that the NPV is less positive than in the earlier scenario based on a $15,000 settlement. As the NPV shrinks, the validity of your data becomes more vulnerable. Are the expenses really locked in at $13,500? Is the 4% interest rate (return rate) valid and reliable? If any of these variables changes, the NPV can shift from a positive value to a negative value, uprooting the basis for your decision.

What about a case in which damages will be paid over a series of years? For example, assume that a civil claim is worth $100,000 which, because of the nature of the claim, would pay damages over the course of four years: $20,000 in year 1, $30,000 in year 2, $40,000 in year 3 and $10,000 in year 4. The cost of pursuing the litigation, including legal resources, expert witnesses, and trial preparation, would be $95,000. Assume that interest will be compounded annually at 5%. Is the civil claim worth pursing? Does it make sense to invest $95,000 to obtain $100,000 over four years?

The question is: what is the NPV of cash flows of $20,000, $30,000, $40,000, and $10,000 paid over four years at a cost of $95,000 based on a 5% interest rate compounded annually?

We return to the NPV formula:

NPV = PV – Cost

In this instance, the NPV of pursuing the civil claim is the present value of the four payments (cash flows) minus the cost of $95,000.

The expanded formula is:

NPV = [PV of Year 1 payment + PV of Year 2 payment + PV of Year 3 payment + PV of Year 4 payment] – COST

$$\text{NPV} = \frac{\text{FV}}{(1+\text{i})^{\text{n}}} + \frac{\text{FV}}{(1+\text{i})^{\text{n}}} + \frac{\text{FV}}{(1+\text{i})^{\text{n}}} + \frac{\text{FV}}{(1+\text{i})^{\text{n}}} - \text{COST}$$

Let's do the math:

$$\text{NPV} = \frac{20{,}000}{(1.05)} + \frac{30{,}000}{(1.05)^2} + \frac{40{,}000}{(1.05)^3} + \frac{10{,}000}{(1.05)^4} - \$95{,}000$$

$$NPV = [\$21{,}000 + \$33{,}075 + \$46{,}305 + \$12{,}155.06] - \$95{,}000$$
$$NPV = \$112{,}535.06 - \$95{,}000$$
$$NPV = \$17{,}535.06$$

Therefore, the NPV of the projected cash flows in settlement of the civil claim would be a positive return of $17,535.06. Therefore, we should seriously consider pursuing the civil claim and accepting damages of $100,000. The NPV of the payout is positive, and therefore the $95,000 investment would be a worthwhile investment.

Choosing Between Alternatives

NPV can also be used to determine which of two competing approaches to take. For example, assume that a corporate client can invest $100,000 to settle a case in a year for $200,000 in damages, or it can invest $200,000 to pay for experts, reenactments, demonstrative evidence, and a jury trial, in order to prove damages of $400,000 three years from now. Which alternative makes more sense?

Start by determining the NPV of each alternative. Assume a 4% interest rate.

First Alternative:

$$NPV = PV - Cost$$
$$NPV = \frac{200{,}000}{(1.04)^1} - \$100{,}000$$
$$NPV = \$192{,}307.69 - \$100{,}000$$
$$NPV = \$92{,}307.69$$

Second Alternative:

$$NPV = PV - Cost$$
$$NPV = \frac{400{,}000}{(1.04)^3} - \$200{,}000$$
$$NPV = \frac{400{,}000}{1.124864} - \$200{,}000$$
$$NPV = \$355{,}598.54 - \$200{,}000$$
$$NPV = \$155{,}598.54$$

Assuming the validity of the projected costs and the anticipated amounts of damages, both alternatives are meritorious because they both result in a positive NPV. The second alternative produces the best results—a net present benefit of $155,598.54—and would be the preferred course of action, assuming that the corporate client wishes to litigate over three years.

NPV is one of many decision-making models that can be used to determine whether to accept or reject a deal or to pursue or not pursue a claim. We will see, further along in this book, how to apply NPV to settling or litigating business cases, divorce cases, tort cases, and other kinds of legal claims. NPV is not the only useful formula, however, and decision-makers should consider other formulas and external factors in reaching a final decision.

5.6. Present Value of an Annuity

Let's assume that Baker is seriously injured and has been awarded structured payments of $60,000 for 15 years. His annuity would total $900,000, if Baker were to wait 15 years until the last payment is made. What if Baker wanted to sell the annuity payments in exchange for a lump sum payment today? How much should he sell it for? (Or, if the defendant has offered a lump sum in lieu of the structured settlement, how much should Baker demand as a lump sum settlement to be paid today?) Assume the interest rate is 4%.

The question is: what is the present value of a $60,000 annuity payable for 15 years at 4%?

You will need a financial calculator to perform this calculation. Online financial calculators can be downloaded for free from a number of sites, such as *www.investopedia.com.* To calculate the answer using a financial calculator, input the interest rate (4%), the number of time periods (15 years) and the payment amount ($60,000). You should obtain a present value of $667,103.25.

If you do not have a financial calculator, you can consult an annuity table, which sets forth the precalculated compound interest rates for each period of years at each basic interest rate. Annuity tables are widely published and widely available online (See, for example, the table published at *http://www.annuitylibrary.com/glance_annuities_table.htm*). A typical annuity table depicts the years running down the first column and the rates of interest running across the top row. By finding 15 years on the first column and 4% on the top row, and drawing the points together, you can obtain a precalculated compound interest rate of 11.1184. This rate should then be multiplied by the payment amount. In the example above, we would multiple 11.1184 by $60,000, which yields a present value of $667,104 (nearly exactly the same result as using a financial calculator).

What this means is that Baker should not accept less than $667,104 today in exchange for his annuity payments of $60,000 for the next 15 years. Or, stated otherwise, any lump sum payment offered by the defendants in lieu of the 15-year payout should be at least $667,104.

Try another scenario. An insurance carrier has offered $600,000 to settle a case or, as an alternative, a yearly payment of $45,000 over 20 years. Assume the interest rate is 3%. Which is the best alternative—the lump sum payment of $600,000 or the 20 annual payments of $45,000?

To arrive at the answer, we need to know the present value of 20 annuity payments of $45,000 based on 3% interest. By plugging the interest rate (3%), the number of time periods (20), and the payment amount ($45,000) into a financial calculator, we find that the present value of the annuity is $669,486.37. Or, by using an annuity table, we find that the precalculated compound interest rate for 3% over 20 years is 14.8775. We then multiply 14.8775 by $45,000 to obtain the present value of $669,487.50 (again, quite close to the result obtained by using the financial calculator).

Therefore, we should reject the insurance carrier's offer of $600,000 to settle the case in a lump sum. The annuity payments have a present value of $669,487.50 and therefore present the better deal.

Determining the present value of an annuity can be helpful in negotiating a lump sum settlement in lieu of an annuity payout. In the scenario above, we know that the lump sum settlement must be greater than $669,487.50 in order to exceed the present value of the 20-year annuity. So, for example, one might refuse to negotiate below $670,000. Any lump sum paid above that amount will have a greater present value than the 20-year annuity.

5.7. Present Value of a Perpetuity

A ruptured oil pipeline in the Gulf of Mexico has caused catastrophic environmental problems, destroyed marshlands, ruined breeding bird colonies, and fouled the food chain for hundreds of marine fisheries.

Numerous legal claims have been asserted. As part of the settlement of one of the claims, a corporate defendant has agreed to establish a cleanup fund that will pay $100,000 per year forever.

What is the present value of this so-called perpetuity?

The question is: what will it cost the defendant in today's dollars to generate $100,000 per year in cleanup funds, year after year, in perpetuity?

Assume that interest over the course of time will be 3.5%.

The formula is:

$$\text{PV (Perpetuity)} = \frac{P}{i}$$

P = payment
i = interest rate

In this easy formula, we simply divide the annual payment (P) by the interest rate (i).

Here's the math:

$$PV = \frac{P}{i}$$

$$PV = \frac{\$100{,}000}{.035}$$

$$PV = \$2{,}857{,}142.86$$

Therefore, the defendant will be required to deposit $2,857,142.86 in the bank. Assuming the 3.5% interest rate remains intact, the account will generate $100,000 in interest every year, sufficient to fund the cleanup efforts in accordance with the terms of the settlement.

Growing Perpetuities

In the example above, assume that the annual cleanup funds are expected to increase by 2% per year. Assume that this growth would continue indefinitely; thus, a growing perpetuity. How do we calculate the present value while incorporating this growth rate?

The question now becomes: what will it cost the defendant in today's dollars to generate $100,000 per year in cleanup funds, increasing by 2% each year, in perpetuity?

Assume the same interest rate of 3.5%.

The formula is:

$$PV\ (Perpetuity) = \frac{P}{i} - g$$

P = payment
i = interest
g = growth rate

The growth rate refers to the 2% growth in the annual payment of \$100,000. We will convert the growth rate to a decimal (.02) as we've done with the interest rate (.035).

Here's the math:

$$PV = \frac{P}{i} - g$$

$$PV = \frac{\$100{,}000}{.035 - .02}$$

$$PV = \frac{\$100{,}000}{.015}$$

$$PV = \$6{,}666{,}666.67$$

So, in order for the defendant to generate \$100,000 per year, increasing by 2% each year, in perpetual cleanup funds, the defendant will be required to deposit \$6,666,666.67 in the bank today. Provided that the interest rate of 3.5% remains intact, the account will generate the necessary cleanup funds each year.

5.8. Central Tendency

Central tendency refers to the "number in the middle." This may include the "average" of a set of numbers, the number that falls precisely in the middle of a list of numbers, or simply the number that appears most frequently in a set of numbers. Measures of central tendency are important statistically and financially, as we will see in the examples below.

The Mean

The mean refers to the average of a group of numbers, usually referred to as a population or a sample. To most people, the mean is what we're referring to when we say the average of several numbers. To calculate the mean, simply add up all of the numbers in the group, and divide the sum by the total number of numbers. The formula is sometimes expressed as:

$$\text{Mean} = \frac{\text{Sum of numbers}}{\text{Number of numbers}}$$

Let's try a few examples.

What is the mean of the following eight numbers: 3, 7, 5, 21, 2, 39, 10, and 1?

Simply add up the numbers:

$$3 + 7 + 5 + 21 + 2 + 39 + 10 + 1 = 88$$

Then divide the sum (88) by the number of numbers (8).

$$\frac{88}{8} = 11$$

Therefore, the mean of the set of numbers shown above is 11.

What if one or more of the numbers in the set were negative figures? Simply subtract the negative numbers while you're adding up the other numbers. For example: What is the mean of the following eight numbers: 3, –7, 5, 21, 2, 39, 10, and –1?

Add up the numbers. When you add a negative number, you essentially subtract it.

$$3 + (-7) + 5 + 21 + 2 + 39 + 10 + (-1)$$
$$= 3 - 7 + 5 + 21 + 2 + 39 + 10 - 1 = 72$$

Then divide the sum (72) by the number of numbers (8)

$$\frac{72}{8} = 9$$

Therefore, the mean of this set of numbers is 9.

To consider the mean in a more useful application, assume you wanted to calculate your client's average earnings over a five-year period, in order to respond to an interrogatory pertaining to wage loss. In three of the five years, your client earned reportable income, but in two of those years, your client suffered a loss of income. The five-year earnings summary reflects the following figures:

YEAR	EARNINGS
2007	\$50,000
2008	(\$ 3,000)
2009	\$38,000
2010	(\$12,500)
2011	\$45,000

In 2007, 2009, and 2011, your client reported positive earnings. In 2008 and 2010, he reported negative earnings (or losses). What are his average earnings for the five-year period?

The question is: what is the mean of the five figures \$50,000, –\$3,000, \$38,000, –\$12,500 and \$45,000?

The formula is:

$$\text{Mean} = \frac{\$50{,}000 - \$3{,}000 + \$38{,}000 - \$12{,}500 + \$45{,}000}{5}$$

$$= \frac{\$117{,}500}{5}$$

$$= \$23{,}500$$

Therefore, your client's average earnings for the five-year period 2006 through 2011 were \$23,500 per year (taking into consideration his negative years).

Understanding the mean can also be helpful in determining a missing piece of data. Consider, for example, a litigant who has produced tax returns confirming his annual earnings of \$100,000 for 2006, 2007, and 2008. Other evidence proves that he earned \$150,000 in 2009. He has obtained an extension on the filing of his 2010 taxes and has failed to produce any evidence of his 2010 earnings. Yet he has testified at deposition that between 2006 and 2010 (inclusive), he averaged \$125,000 per year. From this information, we can apply some basic algebra to determine what the litigant earned in 2010.

The formula is:

$$\frac{\$100{,}000 + \$100{,}000 + \$100{,}000 + \$150{,}000 + x}{5} = \$\,125{,}000 \text{ (mean)}$$

$$\frac{\$450{,}000 + x}{5} = \$125{,}000 \text{ (mean)}$$

Multiply each side by 5 to solve for x.

$450,000 + x = $625,000
x = $175,000

Thus, we can conclude that the litigant earned $175,000 in 2010, based on his own testimony.

The Median

The median is another measure of central tendency. In fact, the median is quite literally the central figure. To determine the median, organize the numbers in order by value (from low to high), and then pick the number in the dead center of the list.

For example, assume we have five numbers, 1, 7, 3, 2, and 4.

To find the median, reorganize the numbers in sequence from low to high: 1, 2, 3, 4, and 7. Now pick out the number in the center.

1 2 **3** 4 7
↓
Median

The median is 3. The median and the mean are not always the same. For example, the mean of the five figures above is 3.4. In some cases, it may be necessary to determine a mean in order to determine a median.

Consider, for example, the set of figures below:

5, 10, 15, 20, 25, 35

What is the median? We cannot tell by simply plucking out the middle number because there are an even number of figures this time. To determine the median of this set, we choose the two middle numbers (15 and 20), and we determine the mean of these two numbers.

Thus, 15 + 20 = 35. Then, 35/2 = 17.5.

Therefore, the median of the set of six figures above is 17.5.

Statisticians like the median as a measure of central tendency because exactly one-half of all of the data produced in a set will be lower than the median, and one-half will be higher. The Central Intelligence Agency, for example, maintains a master list of median ages around the world in order to divide the population of every country into two numerically equal age groups—those below the median and those above the median.[1] The U.S. Census Bureau collects data to determine the median household income in every state, and in so doing, can show that exactly one-half of all households will fall below the median, and one-half will fall above the median.[2]

The Mode

The mode is the number that occurs or repeats most frequently in a set of data.

For example, in the set of data, 1, 2, 3, 4, 4, 5, 6, 7, the mode would be 4. The number 4 appears twice, more than any other number. In the set of data, 1, 2, 3, 4, 4, 5, 6, 6, 7, there would be two modes, 4 and 6, because both of these numbers occur more often than the others. In the set of numbers, 1, 2, 3, 4, 4, 4, 5, 6, 6, 7, the mode would be 4 because it occurs three times.

What if every number appears exactly once? For example, consider the set of data, 1, 2, 3, 4, 5, 6, 7. In such a case, there is no mode.

Modes can produce valuable insights when displayed graphically. For example, consider a group of test scores in which 10 of 30 students earned 4 out of a possible 10 points on a test.

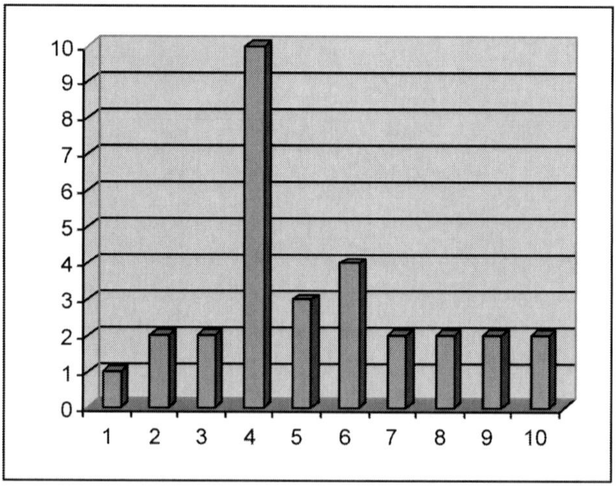

[1]https://www.cia.gov/library/publications/the-world-factbook/fields/2177.html.

[2]http://factfinder.census.gov/servlet/GRTTable?_bm=y&-_box_head_nbr=R1901&-ds_name=ACS_2008_1YR_G00_&-_lang=en&-format=US-30&-CONTEXT=grt.

As the graph above shows, 4 is the mode, occurring more frequently than any other score in the set of scores generated by the 30 students. This so-called unimodal display may provide important guidance to a teacher about the performance trends of her class as a whole.

What if there were two modes? What if seven of the students earned a score of 3, and seven of the students earned a score of 9?

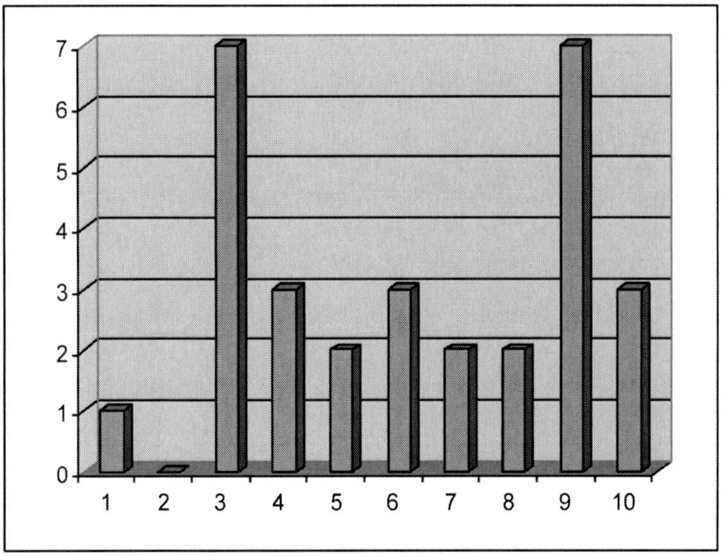

In this bimodal representation, we find that nearly one-quarter of the class is failing the test with a score of 3 while nearly one-quarter of the class is excelling with a score of 9. This kind of information may prompt the teacher to alter his teaching style or to divide the classroom into separate groups. Calculating a mean or a median would not provide the same kind of insight. The data set that produced the results above consists of the following 30 scores:

1	3	3	3	3	3	3	3	4	4
4	5	5	6	6	6	7	7	8	8
9	9	9	9	9	9	9	10	10	10

The mean of these 30 scores is 6.17. The median is 6. Yet only three students (10% of the class) earned a score of 6. The more useful information, in this instance, is the mode, which shows how the majority of the class is performing.

Choosing Between Mean, Median, and Mode

All three measures of central tendency are useful methods for interpreting data. However, they are not all similarly useful in every situation. The mean is best used when the numbers are relatively close to each other (in other words, there are no outliers). For example, if you were calculating the average height of all boys on a Little League team, the mean would make sense, assuming that there are no extremely tall or extremely short players on the team. Generally speaking, the height of boys at a certain age falls within a certain predictable range.

Yet if you were calculating the mean income of salesmen working on commission for a car dealership, one extremely successful salesman with a substantially higher income than all of the others would skew the average.

The median is the better choice when the data is skewed by a number of outliers or extreme numbers. So, if you were calculating the median income of salesmen working at the car dealership, where one of the salesmen has an extraordinarily high income, the median would produce a better measure of central tendency by yielding a number that is generally lower than the mean.

The mode produces a more reliable measure when you seek to make a qualitative judgment about the data rather than a numerical one. As in the case of the scores of 30 students taking a test, discussed above, the mode provides greater insight in cases in which the mean or the median would be distorted by the pattern of data produced.

5.9. Moving Averages

Measures of central tendency are useful provided there are no changing circumstances in progress. In cases in which it is necessary to identify trends or patterns, a moving average may be more appropriate. Stock traders use moving averages to predict trends and price reversals in the market. The logic applied in the stock market can be easily employed in the legal field as well.

A moving average takes an existing average and updates it as new information becomes available. For example, assume that a corporation has filed a lawsuit seeking damages based on an intentional interference with a business relationship. In the first year of the litigation, it claims average annual losses of $332,000 based on a five-year pattern shown below:

YEAR	LOSS
2005	$350,000
2006	$270,000
2007	$390,000
2008	$340,000
2009	$310,000

$$\text{Mean} = \frac{\$350{,}000 + \$270{,}000 + \$390{,}000 + \$340{,}000 + \$310{,}000}{5}$$

$$= \frac{\$1{,}660{,}000}{5}$$

$$= \$332{,}000$$

In the second year of litigation, additional information becomes available, specifically the reported loss for 2010. To calculate the moving average, simply drop 2005 out of the calculation and add 2010 into the calculation, as follows:

YEAR	LOSS
2006	$270,000
2007	$390,000
2008	$340,000
2009	$310,000
2010	$358,000

$$\text{Mean} = \frac{\$270{,}000 + \$390{,}000 + \$340{,}000 + \$310{,}000 + \$358{,}000}{5}$$

$$= \frac{\$1{,}668{,}000}{5}$$

$$= \$333{,}600$$

Moving averages can be calculated year after year, or on a quarterly, monthly, weekly, or daily basis. In each case, however, the number of periods being compared should remain consistent. If you are averaging five years to determine the first mean, then you must average five years to determine each successive mean. In fact, moving averages can be calculated for any number of periods using a variety of popular spreadsheet and financial software programs.

Moving Averages as Predictors

Moving averages can be used as a predictor of gains or losses and thus can be quite useful in settlement negotiations, mediation, arbitration, and litigation. Even though they are classified as lagging indicators because they look at the direction of past data, they can be used to predict future damages or other financial consequences. The example below presents five data periods and five corresponding moving averages. Each data period is five months long. For each successive moving average, we drop the first month and add the newest month.

DATA PERIOD	LOSSES	MOVING AVERAGE
Jan/Feb/Mar/Apr/May	10 + 20 + 30 + 40 + 50 = 150/5 =	30
Feb/Mar/Apr/May/Jun	20 + 30 + 40 + 50 + 60 = 200/5 =	40
Mar/Apr/May/Jun/Jul	30 + 40 + 50 + 60 + 70 = 250/5 =	50
Apr/May/Jun/Jul/Aug	40 + 50 + 60 + 70 + 80 = 300/5 =	60
May/Jun/Jul/Aug/Sep	50 + 60 + 70 + 80 + 90 = 350/5 =	70

What can we learn from this data? First, we can see that during the first nine months (three quarters of the year), losses ranged from 10 to 90. We can also see that the five-month moving average rose from 30 to 70. As a predictive device, the data in this case certainly shows a trend. We can also safely suggest that the losses for October, based on the latest moving average calculated above, would be at least 70 (the average of the last five months).

Moving averages can also be applied to validate or invalidate trends and patterns. For example, assume that an expert witness is asked what losses were sustained between January 1, 2010, and June 30, 2010, and then is asked about the losses between July 1, 2010, and December 31, 2010. He testifies to losses of 21 for the first half of the year and 33 for the second half of the year:

DATA PERIOD	LOSSES	HALF-YEAR AVERAGE
Jan/Feb/Mar/Apr/May/Jun	10 + 50 + 10 + 20 + 35 + 1 =	126/6 = 21
Jul/Aug/Sep/Oct/Nov/Dec	40 + 8 + 10 + 80 + 30 + 30 =	198/6 = 33

Yet this information, standing alone, does not paint a full picture. In fact, it may lead to a hasty conclusion that the losses have grown dramatically during the second half of the year. A moving average, based on rolling six-month periods, provides better insight:

DATA PERIOD	LOSSES	MOVING AVERAGE
Jan/Feb/Mar/Apr/May/Jun	10 + 50 + 10 + 20 + 35 + 1 =	126/6 = 21
Feb/Mar/Apr/May/Jun/Jul	50 + 10 + 20 + 35 + 1 + 40 =	156/6 = 26
Mar/Apr/May/Jun/Jul/Aug	10 + 20 + 35 + 1 + 40 + 8 =	114/6 = 19
Apr/May/Jun/Jul/Aug/Sep	20 + 35 + 1 + 40 + 8 + 10 =	114/6 = 19
May/Jun/Jul/Aug/Sep/Oct	35 + 1 + 40 + 8 + 10 + 80 =	174/6 = 29
Jun/Jul/Aug/Sep/Oct/Nov	1 + 40 + 8 + 10 + 80 + 30 =	169/6 = 28.17
Jul/Aug/Sep/Oct/Nov/Dec	40 + 8 + 10 + 80 + 30 + 30 =	198/6 = 33

Here, we see reduced losses during the spring and summer months, where moving averages equal 19 in two successive periods. We also can more clearly detect the skewing of the pattern by the October 2010 losses of 80—an unusually high-loss month that may be attributable to other economic factors.

Exponential Moving Averages

One way to improve the value of a moving average is to calculate the exponential moving average (EMA). The EMA applies more weight to the most recent data. This is important because moving averages reflect historical information—they lag behind the trend—and thus provide insight into a trend after the trend has unfolded. An EMA is a mathematical device that attempts to speed up the process by weighting new information more heavily and thus signaling us about the new direction of the trend more quickly.

The formula for the EMA is: [Last Data Entry – EMA for Previous Period] x $\frac{2}{n + 1}$ + EMA for Previous Period, where n equals the number of periods measured in the moving average.

For example, let's use the six-month moving averages calculated in the example above.

DATA PERIOD	LOSSES	MOVING AVERAGE
Jan/Feb/Mar/Apr/May/Jun	10 + 50 + 10 + 20 + 35 + 1 = 126/6 = 21	
Feb/Mar/Apr/May/Jun/Jul	50 + 10 + 20 + 35 + 1 + 40 = 156/6 = 26	
Mar/Apr/May/Jun/Jul/Aug	10 + 20 + 35 + 1 + 40 + 8 = 114/6 = 19	
Apr/May/Jun/Jul/Aug/Sep	20 + 35 + 1 + 40 + 8 + 10 = 114/6 = 19	
May/Jun/Jul/Aug/Sep/Oct	35 + 1 + 40 + 8 + 10 + 80 = 174/6 = 29	
Jun/Jul/Aug/Sep/Oct/Nov	1 + 40 + 8 + 10 + 80 + 30 = 169/6 = 28.17	
Jul/Aug/Sep/Oct/Nov/**Dec**	40 + 8 + 10 + 80 + 30 + **30** = 198/6 = 33	

We'll focus on the very last data entry, 30, for December of 2010 [highlighted above]. We'll subtract the previous EMA. For purposes of this example, assume it is 28. (Note: When you do not have an EMA for the previous period, use the previous moving average as the EMA). There are six time periods (six months) being examined at each level. Therefore, our formula looks like this:

$$\text{EMA} = [\text{Last Data Entry} - \text{EMA for Previous Period}] \times \frac{2}{n+1} + \text{EMA for Previous Period}$$

$$\text{EMA} = [30 - 28] \times \frac{2}{6+1} + 28$$

$$\text{EMA} = 2 \times \frac{2}{7} + 28$$

$$\text{EMA} = 28.57$$

Like other data interpretation devices, moving averages and EMAs can be manipulated to provide favorable or unfavorable information. A six-month moving average reflects relatively recent data and may reflect trends very quickly, but longer moving averages contain greater amounts of past data and tend to reflect change less obviously and less rapidly when shown in a graphic format.

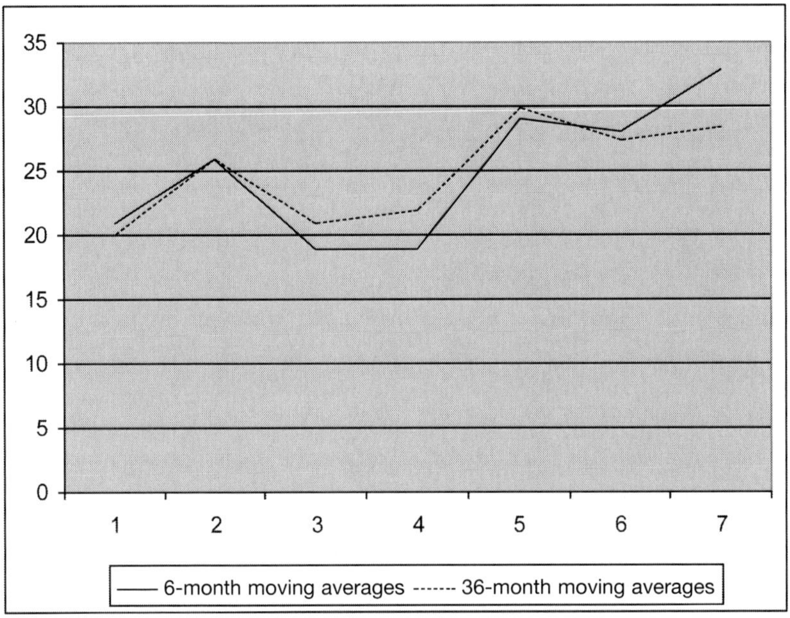

Thus, in the graph above using hypothetical data for the 36-month periods, we see that the 36-month moving averages trudge along more slowly, changing course more patiently over time.

Understanding the value of moving averages is important. But so too is understanding the effect of EMAs and the choice of shorter or longer time periods for calculating averages. In technical analysis of the stock market, where moving averages are applied regularly, experts focus on the crossover between different lines on the graphs. While the subject of crossovers goes beyond the purpose of this book, it is important to note that crossover points can also signal major changes in trends and patterns and may provide yet another tool in predicting a proper financial position.

5.10. Arithmetic Mean versus Geometric Mean

The arithmetic mean is the traditional mean which we have already discussed as the prevailing measure of central tendency. It equals the sum of all of the numbers in a series divided by the number of numbers. The geometric mean is a more complicated formula, but it is necessary in certain circumstances.

First, here are the ugly definitions of geometric mean: (1) It is the n-th root of the product of n numbers, and (2) it is the average of the logarithmic values, converted back to a base 10 number. If you're confused by these definitions, stay on board as we go into more detail.

Suppose you want to calculate the geometric mean of the numbers 4 and 64. To determine a geometric mean, we need to use a log. Let's use a base-2 log in this case.

1. **Convert the first number to a base-2 log.** In other words, convert the number 4 to a number with an exponent where the base of that number is 2. Therefore, with 2 as the base number, the exponent should be 2.

   $4 = 2^2$

   In other words, 4 equals 2 to the second power (2^2).
2. **Convert the second number to a base-2 log.** So, now we must convert 64 to a number in which 2 is the base.

   $64 = 2^6$
3. **Multiply the converted numbers.** Remember that when you multiply numbers with exponents, you simply add the exponents.

   $2^2 \text{ x } 2^6 = 2^8$

   $2^8 = 256$
4. **Calculate the square root of 256.**

   The square root of 256 = 16.

So, the geometric mean of the numbers 4 and 64 is 16.

You might have calculated this result with a shortcut. You could average the two exponents to get the same result. The exponents for 2^2 and 2^6 are 2 and 6. The average of 2 and 6 is 4. Therefore, the result is 2^4 which equals 16.

Let's now reconsider our initial definitions: The geometric mean is the n-th root of the product of n numbers. In this definition, n refers to the number of numbers being examined and it also refers to the number of roots. In our example above, we looked at the square root (16) of the product of two numbers (4 x 64 = 256). In other words, n = 2, referring to the fact that there are two numbers being multiplied, and to the fact that it is the 2nd root (or square root) of the product of those numbers which we seek. Had we examined three numbers (for example, 4, 32, and 64), we would need to calculate the 3rd root (or cube root) of the product of the three numbers.

Applying the shortcut method, the geometric mean is the average of the logarithmic values, converted back to a base 10 number. In other words, it is the average of 2^2 and 2^6 which is 2^4 which is then converted back to 16.

When to Use the Geometric Mean

The geometric mean is necessary when you need to average percentages, such as when calculating the growth in profits or an increase in earnings. An arithmetic mean will work when calculating a change in dollars, but when percentages are used, the geometric mean is the appropriate formula.

Assume that ABC Corporation experienced the following growth over a three-year period:

YEAR	GROWTH ($)
2008	$1 million
2009	$2 million
2010	$4 million

By applying the arithmetic mean, we can easily calculate the average growth of ABC Corporation as $ 2,333,333 per year.

However, XYZ Corporation calculated its growth in percentages over the same three-year period, as follows:

YEAR	GROWTH (%)
2008	3%
2009	4%
2010	5%

We cannot apply an arithmetic mean to these percentages because it would not accurately reflect the real growth. To demonstrate this point, assume that XYZ Corporation started with $10 million. If an arithmetic mean were applied, the average growth over the three-year period shown above would be 4%, yielding the following increase in dollars:

$10,000,000 x 1.04 x 1.04 x 1.04 = $11,248,640.

Note: To reflect the annual average increase of 4% we multiply the running balance by 1.04 each year.

Yet, in reality, XYZ Corporation has actually earned lower profits based on its compounded percentages, calculated as follows:

$10,000,000 x 1.03 x 1.04 x 1.05 = $ 11,247,600.

Note: In this instance, we apply the annual percentage rates of 3%, 4%, and 5% by multiplying the running balance by 1.03, 1.04, and 1.05 respectively.

The geometric mean is based on these growth factors of 1.03, 1.04, and 1.05. In effect, the geometric mean is the cube root of the product of these three numbers.

$[1.03 \text{ x } 1.04 \text{ x } 1.05]^{a}$

Note: To calculate the cube root, we can also use an exponent by inverting the root (3) to a fraction (a).

= 1.0399968

Thus, the cube root of the product of the three growth factors for XYZ Corporation is 1.0399968, which is the geometric mean of XYZ's growth. This translates into an average 3.9% annual growth rate based on the geometric mean, slightly lower than the 4% growth rate based on an arithmetic mean.

The difference between the arithmetic mean and the geometric mean can be significant, especially when larger numbers are being used. In calculating damages to be paid, the geometric mean will generally return a smaller percentage than the arithmetic mean. This point can have strategic implications in the settlement process.

Suppose a fishing enterprise has been put out of business by an oil spill, and the cleanup and restoration of the waterway is expected to take a period of years. In calculating damages, it is important to know how much the fishing enterprise has grown over the last few years. Assume that the accounting records show that the fishing enterprise returned 7%, 5%, and 12% for three years prior to the oil spill. What is the effective rate of return for the three-year period? The answer lies in the geometric mean.

The formula is:

$[1.07 \text{ x } 1.05 \text{ x } 1.12]^a$

$= 1.079602$

Thus, the geometric mean yields an effective rate of return of approximately 7.96%.

By comparison, the arithmetic mean would be 8%, which, if applied, would exaggerate the return enjoyed by the fishing enterprise.

5.11. The Breakeven Formula

One of the most fundamental and most useful devices in finance and business is the breakeven formula. Although it is used chiefly to determine how many units of a product must be sold at a certain price to break even, it has many applications in resolving business, tort, and family law disputes. The central idea of the breakeven formula is that at some point the total revenue from doing something or selling something will equal the total cost. By calculating the breakeven point, you can determine the point at which profit (or excess damages) can be drawn.

Let's assume initially that you're interested only in breaking even. Earning a profit or gaining additional damages is not your objective. All you want is to break even. Assume that your client is fighting for the rights to publish the final manuscript of a recently deceased author. In the estate litigation, the question of who will acquire the publishing rights is on the table. You have determined that the published manuscript, in book form, could be sold to the consumer market for $20 per book. You have also determined that the cost of publishing each book will be $4. In order for your client to undertake the publishing project, it would have to incur annual fixed costs of $20,000 (for editing, binding, printing, and distribution services).

We must carefully classify the available information: The price (P) will be $20. The annual fixed costs (F) will be $20,000. The variable costs per unit (V) will be $4.

The question is: how many published books must we sell for \$20 apiece, at a cost of \$4 per book, with fixed costs of \$20,000, in order to break even?

The formula is:

$$0 = [(P - V) \times X] - F$$

where the 0 represents the profit (when we're seeking to break even, we set the profit at zero), and where X equals the number of books to be sold.

Let's begin by manipulating the formula. We'll apply some basic math in order to isolate X on one side of the equation:

$$0 = [(P - V) \times X] - F$$

$$F = [(P - V) \times X]$$

$$\frac{F}{P - V} = X$$

Therefore, $X = \frac{F}{P - V}$

Now, let's plug in the available information.

$$X = \frac{20{,}000}{20 - 4}$$

$$X = \frac{20{,}000}{16}$$

$$X = 1{,}250$$

Therefore, your client will need to sell 1,250 books annually in order to break even based on the sale price and the related costs.

Breaking Even with a Profit

Perhaps your client wants to earn a profit. If this is the case, we must ask how much profit your client wants. Then we must determine what we need to do in order to not only break even but to draw the specific amount of money the client seeks to earn. In the book publishing example above, the question would become: how many books must we sell at \$20 apiece, at a cost of \$4 per book, with fixed costs of \$20,000, in order to earn a particular profit?

The general breakeven formula is:

$$X = \frac{F}{P - V}$$

In order to convert this formula to a profit formula, we must add the amount of profit to the fixed costs (F), while treating X as being equal to the same amount of profit. So, for example, if your client wishes to earn $10,000 in profit from the sale of the books, the formula would be rewritten as follows:

$$X = \frac{F + \$10{,}000}{P - V}$$

Let's plug in the numbers:

$$X = \frac{20{,}000 - 10{,}000}{20 - 4}$$

$$X = \frac{30{,}000}{16}$$

$$X = 1{,}875$$

So, in order to earn $10,000 in profits from selling the books, your client would have to sell 1,875 copies of the book.

Determining the Price

The breakeven formula can be inverted to tell you what the price should be. There are two variations of the formula that will yield this information.

The first formula for price is:

$$Pr = Q\,(P - V) - F$$

Pr = Profit
Q = Quantity
P = Price
V = Variable Costs
F = Fixed Costs

Let's assume that we wanted to break even; that is, we want to earn zero in profit (Pr), and that we had prospective orders to sell 2,000 copies of the book (Q). We know already that our fixed costs are \$20,000, and our variable costs are \$4. Applying the formula above, we get the following result:

$$Pr = Q\,(P - V) - F$$

$$0 = 2000(P - 4) - 20{,}000$$

$$20{,}000 = 2000\,(P - 4)$$

$$\frac{20{,}000}{2{,}000} = P - 4$$

$$10 = P - 4$$

$$10 + 4 = P$$

$$P = 14$$

Therefore, if we can sell 2,000 copies of the book, with variable costs of \$4 and fixed costs of \$20,000, we should sell each book for \$14 in order to break even.

Let's try it using the second formula for determining price:

$$P = \frac{F}{Q} + V$$

$$P = \frac{20{,}000}{2{,}000} + V$$

$$P = 10 + 4$$

$$P = 14$$

So, here again, we see that at the breakeven point, the price of each book should be \$14.

Chapter 6

Calculating Interest

6.1. Simple Interest

Because money has time value, we apply interest as the basic equalizer. Simple interest calculations account for the time value by raising the principal to a higher number. Calculating interest is a very basic and commonly understood process, but understanding the formula can lead to a number of other helpful determinations.

Let's begin with the basic simple interest formula. Assume that a client has borrowed $10,000 for six months at an annual interest rate of 5%. The question is: what will the client pay in interest on the principal of $10,000, over a six-month period, at an interest rate of 5% per year?

The formula is:

I = P x i x n

I = interest
P = principal
i = interest rate (per month)
n = number of months

To calculate simple interest, we simply multiply principal by interest rate by the number of months (or other time periods) during which the loan remains open.

Here's the math:

$I = P \times i \times n$

$I = \$10{,}000 \times 5\% \times \frac{6}{12}$ (6 months in a 12-month period, since the interest rate is annual)

$I = \$10{,}000 \times 0.05 \times 0.5$

$I = \$250$

Thus, the client will pay $250 in simple interest on a $10,000 loan at 5% over six months. All told, the client will have repaid the loan (principal plus interest) in the total amount of $10,250.

Let's apply the simple interest calculation in another scenario. Assume that $10,000 was the amount of a settlement reached in an auto accident case. After nearly three months following the settlement of the case, the defendant's insurance carrier has failed to tender the $10,000 settlement draft. An enforcement motion is filed by the plaintiff, who complains that the settlement was to have been based on a timely remittance of the settlement funds, a term which the defendant has now ignored. The court, in turn, enters an order compelling the defendant to pay two months' interest on the $10,000 settlement, based on an annual interest rate of 3%.

Here's the formula:

$I = P \times i \times n$

$I = \$10{,}000 \times 3\% \times \frac{2}{12}$

$I = \$10{,}000 \times 0.03 \times 0.1667$

$I = \$50.01$

So, the defendant's insurance carrier will now be required to pay $10,050.01, assuming there are no further delays in issuing the settlement funds.

Understanding the simple interest formula and some basic algebra enables us to determine some other useful figures. For example, assume that a party in a divorce case has indicated on his financial statement that he receives $320 every month from a "Fidelity account" investment. He has not been specific in describing the particular account, and the reference to "Fidelity" could mean many things or refer to any number of investment banks or brokerages. He has been elusive in stating the amount of funds invested (the principal amount), and claims that he doesn't know the amount invested because the investment was established on his behalf many years earlier by his deceased mother. He claims only to be receiving $320 per month from the Fidelity account. Further research reveals that the account earns interest at 7.5%.

So, in this scenario, we have the interest rate (7.5%), the amount of interest being paid ($320), and the period (number of months) over which the interest is paid (one month, because he receives $320 each month). What's missing is the principal (that is, the total amount invested in the Fidelity fund). By rearranging the simple interest formula, we can determine the principal.

$$I = P \times i \times n$$

$$P = \frac{I}{i \times n}$$

$$P = \frac{\$320}{.075 \times 1/12}$$ (one-twelfth, representing 1 month in a 12-month annual period)

$$P = \frac{\$320}{.075 \times 0.08333}$$

$$P = \frac{\$320}{.00625}$$

$$P = \$51{,}200$$

Therefore, $51,200 was invested in the husband's Fidelity account. Having this information may enable the wife's attorney to assess the true financial position of the parties.

6.2. Compound Interest

Suppose a business client were to borrow $100,000 at 7% annual interest. At the end of one year, the client would owe $107,000. Of course, it is easy to make this calculation without a calculator when using such easy numbers as $100,000. What if, however, your client were to borrow $157,000 at 7% interest. To figure out the interest in such a case, we'd need to convert 7% to a decimal form (.07). Thus, a loan of $157,000 at 7% interest would require a payment of $167,990 (the principal of $157,000, plus the interest payment of $10,990). The basic formula is:

$$\$157{,}000 \times 0.07 = \$10{,}990.$$

This is nothing more than a variation of the simple interest formula (I = P x i x n) where the n equals 1 (for 1 payment period). Thus, the principal of $157,000 times the interest rate of .07 times the payment period of 1 equals $10,990 in interest. We will use this formula to determine compound interest.

Start by returning to the easy numbers: $100,000 at 7% interest. This time, assume that your client has invested $100,000 at 7% interest. At the end of one year, your client would be entitled to $7,000 in interest. If she pockets the interest payment, your client would be restored to her principal balance of $100,000, and she would be capable of earning more interest in the subsequent year.

What if your client chose not to withdraw the $7,000 in interest? Instead, she started the next investment year with $107,000 on deposit. Then, she earned another 7% interest on that balance and again chose to redeposit her interest earnings. In year three, your client again earned 7% and again reinvested the interest payment. How much would she have in her investment fund after three years?

The formula is:

Total Balance = P x (1 + i) x (1 + i) x (1+ i)

P = principal
i = interest rate

Here's the math:

$100,000 x 1.07 x 1.07 x 1.07 (based on three years of compounded interest).

If the investment were left in place for five years at 7%, then the formula would be expanded: $100,000 x 1.07 x 1.07 x 1.07 x 1.07 x 1.07

To calculate the total balance, after three years at 7%, we could do the math:

$100,000 x 1.07 x 1.07 x 1.07 = $122,504.30.

Alternatively, we could turn the annual interest rates of 7% for three years into a single multiplier, as follows:

$100,000 x 1.07 x 1.07 x 1.07
= $100,000 x $(1.07)^3$
= $100,000 x 1.225
= $122,500

[The results are essentially the same. The slight difference is a result of rounding off the multiplier in the example above.]

So, if your client invested $100,000 at 7% interest over three years and reinvested her interest earnings with the principal each year, she would have approximately $122,500 after three years. Her compounded interest would be $22,500.

6.3. Principal, Rate, and Time

If you've calculated simple interest using the formula I = P x i x n, then you realize that the amount of interest to be paid in any given fact scenario is a function of three factors: the principal, the interest rate, and the time period in question. These three factors can be manipulated in a variety of useful formulas, depending on what calculation is necessary. If you know the amount of interest and any two of the three factors, you can determine the missing factor. For example, assume that a client wishes to earn $6,000 in interest on a particular investment. A bank will pay a 3.5% annual interest rate on a particular account. The client has $30,000 and is prepared to pay this amount into the account. The question is: how long (in years) must the client keep $30,000 in the bank account at 3.5% interest in order to generate $6,000 in interest? When we apply the formula this time, we will be solving for n.

$$I = P \times i \times n$$

$$\$6{,}000 = \$30{,}000 \times 3.5\% \times n$$

$$\$6{,}000 = 1{,}050 \times n$$

$$\frac{\$6{,}000}{\$1{,}050} = n$$

$$n = 5.714$$

Therefore, it will take the client approximately 5.7 years to earn $6,000 on an initial investment of $30,000 at 3.5% interest.

Now, let's take another fact scenario in which we seek to determine the interest rate. Assume that attorneys are negotiating a settlement of a contract dispute in which one party will pay damages to another party. The principal amount of damages to be paid is $75,000. To enforce payment, the plaintiff has requested a clause in the settlement agreement that imposes a $1,000 per month interest payment on the $75,000 settlement if it is not paid when due. Defendant's attorney indicates that his client will not accept a $1,000 per month interest requirement but would instead consent to a 17% monthly interest rate on the $75,000 payment.

Had defendant's counsel done his homework, he would have accepted the $1,000 per month interest proposal. To illustrate this point, let's apply the simple interest formula, this time solving for i.

$$I = P \text{ x } i \text{ x } n$$

$$\$1{,}000 = \$75{,}000 \text{ x } i \text{ x } \frac{1}{12} \text{ (1 month in a 12-month period)}$$

$$\$1{,}000 = \$75{,}000 \text{ x } \frac{1}{12} \text{ x } i$$

$$\$1{,}000 = \$75{,}000 \text{ x } 0.08333 \text{ x } i$$

$$\$1{,}000 = 6{,}249.75 \text{ x } i$$

$$\frac{\$1{,}000}{6{,}249.75} = i$$

$$i = 0.16 \text{ (meaning 16\%)}$$

Thus, it appears that a payment of $1,000 per month in interest on a $75,000 obligation will be based on a 16% annual interest rate. That's a better deal for the defendant than the defendant's attorney was offering at 17%. At 17%, the defendant would be obligated to pay $1,062.46 in interest.

$$I = P \text{ x } i \text{ x } n$$

$$I = \$75{,}000 \text{ x } 0.17 \text{ x } .08333$$

$$I = \$1{,}062.46.$$

6.4. Real and Nominal Interest Rate

The nominal interest rate is the rate of interest before adjusting for inflation. The real interest rate is the nominal interest rate minus the inflation rate. It can be expressed in the formula:

$$R = N - I$$

where R is the real interest rate, N is the nominal interest rate, and I is the inflation rate.

Consider, for example, a loan made at 5% interest. This nominal interest rate would have little meaning if the inflation rate were also 5%. Applying the formula above, a nominal interest rate of 5% minus an inflation rate of 5% would produce a real interest rate of zero, meaning there would be no positive benefit to the lender.

Suppose that court rules provide for 9% interest per annum on unpaid judgments. This means that a litigant who wins a judgment for $1 million on December 31 would be entitled to collect $1,090,000 on the following December 31. But is the litigant really getting 9% interest? If the rate of inflation is 6% over the same one-year period, and assuming all goods are affected equally, the litigant's net benefit is significantly lower. The real interest rate is 9% minus 6%; thus, only 3%.

The formula above is, in fact, a simplification of a slightly more complicated formula:

$$R = \frac{1 + N}{1 + I} - 1$$

In this formula, the real interest rate is calculated by dividing 1 plus the nominal interest rate by 1 plus the inflation rate, and then subtracting 1 from the result. This formula produces a more technically accurate real interest rate. Let's plug in the numbers from the example above.

$$R = \frac{1 + N}{1 + I} - 1$$

$$R = \frac{1 + .09}{1 + .06} - 1$$

$$R = \frac{1.09}{1.06} - 1$$

$$R = 1.028 - 1$$

$$R = .028$$

The real interest rate is therefore 2.8% (a more accurate calculation than the simplified formula above that produced the 3% rate). The shorter formula is acceptable as an approximation of the real interest rate when dealing with lower nominal rates and inflation rates. However, when using significantly higher numbers, only the more cumbersome formula above should be used.

Here is another variation of the formula for calculating the real interest rate:

$$R = \frac{N - 1}{1 + I}$$

$$R = \frac{.09 - .06}{1 + .06}$$

$$R = \frac{.03}{1.06}$$

$$R = .028$$

Simply recognizing the difference between a nominal interest rate and a real interest rate can be a helpful negotiating tool for attorneys attempting to settle civil actions, commercial disputes, and matrimonial matters. By pointing out the rate of inflation, attorneys can argue for higher interest rates on unpaid debts and judgments.

6.5. Periodic Interest Rate

The periodic interest rate generally refers to the rate of interest that applies for a period shorter than a year. If we know the annual interest rate, then the periodic rate could refer to the monthly rate, the quarterly rate, or perhaps the semiannual rate. For example, let's assume that the annual interest rate is 6%. The periodic interest rate for any given month would be one-twelfth of 6%. The formula is:

$$\frac{\text{Annual Interest Rate}}{12} = \text{Periodic Interest Rate (Monthly Rate)}$$

Thus, using 6% as the annual rate

$$\frac{0.06}{12} = 0.005$$

meaning that the periodic interest rate is 0.5% per month.

Periodic interest rates are important in calculating frequently compounded interest. If you know the periodic interest rate, you can compound interest for each such period, yielding a higher result than simply charging interest on an annual basis. Consider these examples:

Example 1: Using the annual interest rate

Judgment for the plaintiff in the sum of $150,000, with interest set at 5.5% annually.

After three years, the judgment will be worth $176,136.21.

Here is the formula:

Total Balance = 150,000 x (1 + .055) x (1 + .055) + (1 + .055)

Total Balance = 150,000 x $(1.055)^3$

Total Balance = 150,000 x 1.1742

Total Balance = $176,136.21.

Example 2: Using a monthly periodic interest rate

Judgment for the plaintiff in the sum of $150,000, with interest set at 5.5% annually, compounded monthly. After three years, the judgment will be worth $176,839.50.

Total Balance = 150,000 x $(1 + \frac{12}{.055})^{36}$

[The annual interest rate of .055 must be divided by 12 to establish a monthly periodic rate. Then the original exponent (3, reflecting 3 years) must be multiplied by the number of months (12 months) to produce a new exponent of 36.

Total Balance = 150,000 x $(1.004583)^{36}$

Total Balance = 150,000 x 1.17893

Total Balance = $176,839.50.

The total balance (total judgment amount) is slightly higher by compounding monthly using the periodic interest rate instead of compounding annually using the annual interest rate.

6.6. Effective Interest Rate

The effective interest rate is the interest rate that accounts for the effect of compounding. On an annual basis, the effective interest rate is the annual interest rate that measures the additional increment of interest that is paid because of periodic compounding. To illustrate this point, consider a $1,000 judgment subject to 10% annual interest. After one year, the judgment would draw $100 in interest, and the total amount due would then be $1,100. If, however, the interest is compounded monthly, the amount due at the end of the year would be slightly higher at $1,104.70. The formula below shows the math:

$$\text{Total Judgment} = \$1{,}000 \times (1 + \frac{0.1}{12})^{12}$$
$$\text{Total Judgment} = \$1{,}000 \times (1.008333)^{12}$$
$$\text{Total Judgment} = \$1{,}000 \times 1.1047$$
$$\text{Total Judgment} = \$1{,}104.70.$$

The annual interest rate, as stated, is 10%. In fact, it is sometimes referred to as the "stated annual interest rate." Yet, because monthly compounding generated interest of $104.70, the effective interest rate is actually 10.47%. Effectively, the $1,000 judgment earned interest of 10.47% in order to generate an actual interest payment of $104.70 after one year. This effective rate, while based on the stated annual rate of 10%, also takes into account the additional interest earned by compounding interest on a monthly basis.

The effective interest rate can be determined when only a stated annual rate is provided, by applying the following formula:

$$\text{EIR} = (1 + \frac{i}{n})^n - 1$$

EIR = Effective interest rate
i = Stated annual interest rate
n = the number of compounding periods

Let's apply the figures from the example below, in which the stated annual interest rate was 10%, and the compounding periods were 12 (that is, 12 months for a one-year period in which interest in compounded monthly).

$$\text{EIR} = (1 + \frac{i}{n})^n - 1$$
$$\text{EIR} = (1 + \frac{0.10}{12})^n - 1$$
$$\text{EIR} = (1 + 0.0083333333)^{12} - 1$$
$$\text{EIR} = (1.008333333333)^{12} - 1$$
$$\text{EIR} = 1.104713067 - 1$$
$$\text{EIR} = .104713067$$
$$\text{EIR} = 10.47\%$$

Using this handy formula, we can quickly turn an annual rate into a monthly rate or any other periodic rate, simply by imputing the compounding periods. In so doing, we can quickly determine how much money will be gained or lost by changing the compounding period.

Chapter 7

Determining Probability

7.1. Single Event Probability

The probability of a single event happening is the number of desired outcomes divided by the number of possible outcomes. Another way to think of probability is the number of ways in which an event can occur divided by the number of possible events. Probability is initially determined in the form of a fraction. For example, to determine the probability that by tossing a coin, it will land heads up, we would apply the following fraction:

$$\frac{\text{Number of ways in which a coin can land heads up}}{\text{Number of possible ways in which the coin can land}} = \frac{1}{2}$$

The probability of ½ can then be converted to a decimal figure (0.5) or a percentage (50%). Thus, there is a 50% probability that by flipping a coin, it will land heads up.

Consider another example: Assume there is a tray of cupcakes, consisting of four chocolate cupcakes and six vanilla cupcakes. Assume also that it is impossible to tell them apart until one bites into them. What is the probability of choosing a chocolate cupcake? A vanilla cupcake? A chocolate or vanilla cupcake? If you answered 2/5, 3/5, and 1, you would be correct.

$$\text{Probability of choosing chocolate} = \frac{\text{Number of chocolate cupcakes}}{\text{Total number of cupcakes}} = \frac{4}{10} = \frac{2}{5}$$

$$\text{Probability of choosing vanilla} = \frac{\text{Number of vanilla cupcakes}}{\text{Total number of cupcakes}} = \frac{6}{10} = \frac{3}{5}$$

$$\text{Probability of choosing a chocolate or vanilla cupcake} = \frac{\text{No. of chocolate and vanilla cupcakes}}{\text{Total number of cupcakes}} = \frac{10}{10} \text{ or } 1.$$

Another way to express these fractional results is in the form of percentages. In other words, there would be a 40% probability of picking chocolate, a 60% probability of picking vanilla, and a 100% probability of picking one or the other.

Probability calculations are another useful tool that can aid attorneys in making judgments or providing advice. Consider, for example, a jury pool at the courthouse which consists of a variety of local jurors waiting to be selected for duty. Fifty local citizens have reported for jury duty, of which 35 are Caucasian, 10 are African American, and 5 are Hispanic. Of the jurors, 18 are under the age of 30; the remainder are 30 or older. Half are male, and half are female. Assume that the demographic makeup of the jury is relevant in a particular proceeding. Can you quickly calculate the probability of the events listed in the left column below without looking at the answers in the right column below?

What is the probability that:	Answer
1. The first juror selected from the jury pool will be Hispanic?	10%
2. The first juror selected from the jury pool will be a woman?	50%
3. The first juror selected from the jury pool will be under 30 years old?	36%
4. The first juror selected from the jury pool will be either Hispanic or Caucasian?	80%
5. The second juror selected from the jury pool will be an African American (assuming that the first juror selected was not African American)?	20.4%
6. The second juror selected from the jury pool will be an African American (assuming that the first juror selected was African American)?	18.37%

Relative Frequency

Relative frequency is another approach to establishing the probability of an event occurring or a result taking place. We know, for example, that there is a 50% probability of obtaining heads when we toss a single coin. What if, however, we tossed the coin 10 times and found that it landed on heads only three of those times. In such a case, the probability based on relative frequency would be three times out of 10 tries, or 3/10 or 0.3. Statisticians also refer to this figure as empirical probability. It can be a very useful statistic in negotiations, in closing arguments, and in courtroom hearings on enforcement motions.

Assume, for example, that in a commercial real estate foreclosure action, the parties disagree over the number of mortgage payments made, and the dates these payments were tendered and received. The mortgagee's attorney offers evidence detailing the due dates of each payment over a five-year period and the actual payment dates. The number of monthly payments due over five years was 60. The number of late payments, according to the mortgagee's attorney, was 26. The relative frequency was thus 26/60 or 43.33%. In arguing in favor of a final judgment, the attorney can effectively argue that, based on the relative frequency, the probability of late payment has been—and will continue to be—more than 43%, in clear breach of the mortgage loan terms.

A child custody lawyer learns that her client's husband has missed 14 of the 54 scheduled visitations with the children last year. She offers for admission a calendar detailing the court-ordered visitation dates and reflecting each of the 14 cancelled visits. In a hearing in which the father has moved to modify the custody order and increase his parenting time with the children, the mother's lawyer shows that empirically—based on relative frequency—he has missed 14 of the 54 dates that were awarded to him last year. In effect, he showed up only 40 times. The father's probability of visiting his children is therefore 40/54 or about 74%. The mother's custody lawyer would thus argue that no increase in visitation rights is justified based on a 74% probability of compliance.

7.2. Multiple Event Probability

In analyzing the probability of multiple events occurring, we must first ask whether we want them both to occur or either one of them to occur. For example, if a client agrees to purchase a property if the seller repairs a defective plumbing system and repaints an exterior wall, the probability that the plumbing repair and the paint job will both be completed is a combination result that requires one kind of formula. What if, however, the client agreed to purchase the property if the seller either repaired the plumbing system or repainted the wall? This would be an alternative result that requires another kind of formula. Therefore, in considering multiple events, it is important to determine at the outset whether both events must occur or whether either one of them must occur.

Combination Result—Both Events Occurring

Let's apply the facts above. A client agrees to purchase a property if the seller repairs a defective plumbing system and repaints an exterior wall. Both events must occur—a combination result. We would expect that, based on historical facts and circumstances, there is a probability of one event occurring, and a probability of the other event occurring, but that the probability of both events occurring is smaller. It is simply less likely that two events will occur in conjunction with each other. As we will see below, the odds of purchasing the real estate are much greater if the client required only one event to occur.

In this scenario, the question is: what is the probability that the multiple events occur? In other words, what is the probability that the seller will repair the plumbing system AND paint the exterior wall?

The formula is:

$$P(A \text{ and } B) = P(A) \times P(B)$$

P = Probability
A = First Event (Repair of plumbing system)
B = Second Event (Painting of exterior wall)

The probability of A and B both occurring equals the probability of A occurring multiplied by the probability of B occurring. If we knew that the probability of A was 0.5 (50%) and the probability of B was 0.3 (30%), we could then conclude that the probability of A and B occurring is 0.15 (15%).

Here's another example: A married couple wants to have two children. They want to have a boy and a girl. Because they want to have a boy AND they want to have a girl, the probability formula calls for a combination result. Applying the formula above, we must first determine the probabilities of each single event and then multiply them together:

$P(A) = \frac{1}{2}$ [The probability of having a boy is 50% or 1 out of 2 possible outcomes].

$P(B) = \frac{1}{2}$ [The probability of having a girl is also 50% or 1 out of 2 possible outcomes].

$P(A) \times P(B) = \frac{1}{2} \times \frac{1}{2} = \frac{1}{4}$

Therefore, the probability of the married couple having both a boy and a girl is ¼ or 25%. (Notice that the probability of these multiple events—1 boy and 1 girl—is less than the probability of 1 boy or 1 girl).

The same formula applies when there are three or more separate events under consideration. Assume that a hospital has 200 rooms. Asian-born patients can be found in 20 of the rooms. If there are no records of room assignments, and no other method of determining where to find the Asian patients, what is the probability that we will find an Asian patient in each of the first three rooms that we enter? The formula is based on (A) the probability of finding an Asian patient in the first room, multiplied by (B) the probability of finding an Asian patient in the second room, multiplied by (C) the probability of finding an Asian patient in the third room.

$$P(A) = \frac{20}{200} = 0.1$$

$$P(B) = \frac{20}{200} = 0.1$$

$$P(C) = \frac{20}{200} = 0.1$$

$$P(A) \times P(B) \times P(C) = 0.1 \times 0.1 \times 0.1 = 0.001$$

The probability of finding three Asian patients in the first three rooms is 0.1%.

Alternative Result—Either Event Occurring

What if we wanted to know the probability of either of two events occurring? Consider the original set of facts: a client agrees to purchase a property if the seller repairs a defective plumbing system OR if he repaints an exterior wall. This time, the purchase will be made if either event occurs. In this scenario, the question is: what is the probability that either of the multiple events will occur? In other words, what is the probability that the seller will either repair the plumbing system OR that he will paint the exterior wall?

The formula is:

P(A or B) = P(A) + P(B)

P = Probability
A = First Event (Repair of plumbing system)
B = Second Event (Painting of exterior wall)

The probability of either A or B occurring is calculated by simply adding the probability of A to the probability of B. Using the figures provided in the example given above, we said that the probability of A was 0.5 (50%) and the probability of B was 0.3 (30%). Applying the formula, the probability of A or B would be 80% (50% + 30% = 80%).

Notice, again, that the probability of both events occurring is always considerably lower than the probability of either event occurring. The probability of A and B occurring was 0.15 (15 %), compared to the probability of A or B at 80%.

Try another example. The probability of tossing a coin twice and having it land heads up or tails up both times is 50%. Here is the math:

P(A or B) = P(A) + P(B)

A = Heads up both times.
B = Tails up both times.

P(A) = ¼

There is a 1 in 4 chance that two coin tosses will produce two tails-up. The possible results are: (1) Tails, Tails; (2) Heads, Heads; (3) Tails; Heads; (4) Heads; Tails.

P(B) = ¼

Similarly, there is a 1 in 4 chance that two coin tosses will produce two heads-up. The possible results are: (1) Tails, Tails; (2) Heads, Heads; (3) Tails; Heads; (4) Heads; Tails.

P(A) + P(B) = ¼ + ¼ = 2/4 = ½

Thus, the probability of tossing a coin twice and getting two heads-up OR two tails-up is a two-out-of-four probability, reducible to a one-out-of-two chance or a 50% probability.

7.3. Dependent Events

The probability of a particular event occurring may, in some instances, depend on the outcome of another preceding event. Until now, we have been considering only independent events: how one coin lands is independent of how another coin lands. What card a person draws from a deck of cards bears no relationship to what card another person draws from a second deck of cards. But what happens if the outcome of the first event influences or offsets the probable outcome of the second event? What, for example, is the probability of drawing an ace from a deck of cards after already drawing an ace from the same deck? The probability is less than 1%. In fact, it is 0.45%, as will be shown below.

Start by applying the basic probability formula:

$$P = \frac{\text{Number of desired outcomes}}{\text{Number of possible outcomes}}$$

Because there are four aces in a deck of cards, you will succeed at drawing an ace if you pick any one of four cards. There are four desired choices. There are 52 cards in the deck (52 possible outcomes). So, the probability of drawing an ace from the deck of cards the first time is 4/52 or 1/13. Determine the probability of drawing an ace from the same deck on the second draw is not so easy. After removing the first ace (and not returning it to the deck), the number of aces has dropped to three, and the total number of cards has dropped to 51. The second draw is thus dependent on the outcome of the first draw: they are dependent events.

To calculate the probability of drawing a second ace from the same deck, we apply the same formula, using the adjusted figures: P = 3/51. This reduces to 1/17. We still need to determine the probability of drawing two aces from the same deck. In other words, what is the probability of drawing an ace from a deck of 52 cards AND then drawing an ace from a deck of 51 cards missing an ace? Since we know that the formula for the probability of multiple events, considered collectively, is P(A and B) = P(A) x P(B), we simply multiply the probability of picking the first ace (1/13) by the probability of picking the second ace (1/17). The result is 1/221, which translates to 0.00452 or approximately 0.45% (less than half a percent probability that one would draw two aces in a row).

It should be apparent now that there is a clear difference between the probability of drawing an ace from a first deck of cards OR a second deck of cards, the probability of drawing aces from both decks of cards, and the probability of drawing two aces in succession from one deck of cards. Let's compare the math:

Description	Formula	Math	Probability
Two Decks, Either-Or Drawing an ace from EITHER the first deck of cards OR the second deck of cards.	P(A or B) = P(A) + P(B)	4/52 + 4/52 = 8/52 = 2/13	The probability of drawing an ace from either of two decks of cards is 2/13 or roughly 15%
Two Decks, Two Aces Drawing an ace from BOTH the first deck of cards AND the second deck of cards.	P(A and B) = P(A) x P(B)	4/52 x 4/52 = 16/2704	The probability of drawing aces from both of two decks of cards is 16/2704 or roughly 0.6%
One Deck, Two Aces Drawing two aces in a row from one deck of cards.	P(A) [First Draw] P(B) [Second Draw] P(A and B) = P(A) x P(B)	P(A) = 1/13 P(B) = 1/17 1/13 x 1/17 = 1/221	The probability of drawing two consecutive aces from one deck is 1/221 or roughly 0.45%

As the variations above illustrate, strict attention must be paid to formulating the question before determining the probability. A misstatement of the question or a misapprehension of the circumstances may produce an inaccurate probability. Particular attention must be paid to dependent events, as is the case in any calculation in which the first outcome will necessarily affect the factors in the second outcome.

Consider a pool of 100 potential jurors waiting for their juror numbers to be called. Thirty of the potential jurors are under the age of 35. As jury selection is under way, you wonder what is the probability of selecting three jurors younger than 35 from potential jurors in the pool. For this hypothetical, assume that there are no peremptory challenges or for-cause challenges to the jury panel, or any other variables under consideration.

You are in a jurisdiction in which jurors are selected randomly by a courtroom official. A jury of 12 is being selected and 9 jurors have already been empanelled, none of whom is under 35. Assume that no alternate or substitute jurors will be chosen. There are three seats remaining on the jury, and you wish to know the probability of choosing three jurors younger than 35. Because the jury pool consisted initially of 100 potential jurors, and 9 have already been empanelled, the pool now consists of 91 persons. No jurors under 35 have yet been chosen, meaning that all 30 candidates remain available for selection. Here is the math:

A. The probability of selecting a juror under 35 for Jury Seat #10 = 30/91.
B. The probability of selecting a juror under 35 for Jury Seat #11 = 29/90.
C. The probability of selecting a juror under 35 for July Seat #12 = 28/89
D. The probability of all three of the selections above occurring, so that three jurors under 35 have been selected is P(A and B and C) = P(A) x P(B) x P(C) = 30/91 x 29/90 x 28/89 = 24,360/ 728,910 = 0.0334 or approximately 3.3%.

There is essentially a 3.3% chance of selecting three jurors in a row who are each under the age of 35 for the remaining three seats on the jury.

7.4. Mutually Exclusive Events

In order for the probability of multiple events to be accurate, the events must be mutually exclusive. If determining the probability of one also determines the probability of the other or includes the probability of the other, then the two events are not mutually exclusive, and the probability of both of them occurring cannot be accurately determined without some additional math.

Let's consider again the pool of 100 potential jurors discussed above. Thirty of the jurors are under the age of 35. Forty of the jurors are unemployed. What is the probability that a juror selected from the pool will be either under 35 or unemployed? Because this question sets up an either-or equation, we apply the formula P(A or B) = P(A) + P(B). The problem is that some of the jurors under the age of 35 are also unemployed. How do we account for the fact that a certain number of jurors may be counted twice?

The question is: What is the probability that a juror selected from the pool will be either under 35 or unemployed?

The formula is: P(A or B) = P(A) + P(B).

Assume that A equals the probability of a juror under the age of 35, and B equals the probability of an unemployed juror. Assume that no jurors have been chosen so far, and we are starting with a full panel of 100 potential candidates. There are exactly 10 potential jurors who are both under 35 and unemployed.

$$P(A) = \frac{30}{100}$$

$$P(B) = \frac{40}{100}$$

$$\frac{30}{100} + \frac{40}{100} = \frac{70}{100}$$

If we went no further, we'd conclude that there is a probability of 70/100 or 70% that a juror selected from the jury pool will be either under 35 or unemployed. Yet, because 10 of the potential jurors are both under 35 and unemployed, we have counted these 10 persons twice. We have effectively overcounted and we need to reduce the result by the number of jurors who were counted twice. Therefore, the formula is adjusted as follows:

$$\frac{30}{100} + \frac{40}{100} - \frac{10}{100} = \frac{60}{100}$$

The probability that a juror selected from the jury pool will be either under 35 or unemployed is actually only 60%. Because Events A and B are not mutually exclusive, they overlap statistically, and we must make the necessary adjustment to avoid double-counting. To illustrate this adjustment more fundamentally, imagine that you asked all potential jurors under the age of 35 to leave the room and stand in the hallway. Then, you asked all unemployed jurors remaining in the courtroom to leave the courtroom and join the others in the hallway. There would be a total of 60 persons standing the hallway—60% of the total jury pool.

Chapter 8

Rates of Return

8.1. The Basic Calculation

The rate of return (ROR) is a generic reference to the gain or profit derived from a certain decision, investment, or action. There are, in fact, a number of different rates of return, and a variety of formulas for determining the benefit or profitability of a decision, investment, or action. Calculating rates of return is another useful tool for attorneys engaged in a variety of practice areas.

The basic arithmetic calculation for the ROR is expressed as a fraction. The numerator is generally the difference between the money invested or lost and the money earned, gained, or received. The denominator is the money invested or lost. The basic formula is:

$$ROR = \frac{fV - iV}{iV}$$

ROR = Rate of Return
fV = Final Value (Money earned, gained, or received)
iV = Initial Value (Money spent, invested, or lost)

For example, let's assume that you invested $1,000 in a particular business activity. At the end of one year, your initial investment of $1,000 paid off, yielding $1,500. Your iV would be $1,000, and your fV would be $1,500. What is the ROR? Applying the formula, we find that the ROR is 50%.

$$ROR = \frac{fV - iV}{iV}$$

$$\text{ROR} = \frac{1{,}500 - 1{,}000}{1{,}000}$$

$$\text{ROR} = \frac{500}{1{,}000}$$

$$\text{ROR} = \tfrac{1}{2} = 50\%$$

Of course, the ROR must be considered in the context of other external factors, such as the inflation rate and the tax consequences. If inflation was 5% for the year in question, the fV of $1,500 is only worth $1,450, and your real ROR is 45%. Similarly, unless the investment was tax-free or tax-deferred, you'd need to subtract the cost of taxes. If the tax rate was 28%, this percentage would be applied to the gain you enjoyed on your investment. Thus, the $500 in profit would be subject to the 28% tax rate, reducing your fV of $1,500 by $140 to a balance of $1,360. Applying the inflation rate of 5% on this actual balance further reduces the real ROR. Here's the math:

ROR (before adjustment) = 50%

fV (before taxes) = $1,500

Tax-Adjusted fV = fV – Tax = $1,500 – $140 = $1,360

Inflation-Adjusted fV = $1,360 x 95% (since the inflation rate is 5%) = $1,292

$$\text{Adjusted ROR (The real rate of return)} = \frac{\text{Adjusted fV} - \text{iV}}{\text{iV}}$$

$$= \frac{1{,}292 - 1{,}000}{1{,}000}$$

$$= \frac{292}{1{,}000}$$

$$= 29.2\%$$

After adjusting for taxes and inflation, the real ROR equals 29.2%, significantly lower than the nominal ROR of 50%.

8.2. Return on Investment

The return on investment (ROI) is fundamentally the same thing as the basic ROR described in Section 7.1 above. The term ROI, however, is used widely to mean profit or gain (or in some cases, loss), and experts commonly debate which of several formulas is the best measure for ROI. According to some experts, ROI is best measured by calculating earnings per share, net worth, or the return on operating assets. Others say the secret to ROI lies in book value, equity growth rates, dividend yield ratios, or other financial metrics. The many different methods to measure ROI are beyond the scope of this book. However, by looking at several of the basic ROI formulas below, we can develop some shortcuts to evaluating business deals and transactions and assessing case outcomes.

In its simplest form, the formula for ROI is essentially the same as the basic calculation for ROR:

$$\text{ROI} = \frac{\text{Gains} - \text{Costs}}{\text{Costs}}$$

This is essentially a reformulation of the formula $\frac{\text{fV} - \text{iV}}{\text{iV}}$, but is effectively the same formula. If an action produces a gain of \$50,000 (fV) at a cost of \$40,000 (iv), then the ROI (like the ROR) is $\frac{\$50{,}000 - \$40{,}000}{\$40{,}000}$, or ¼ or 0.25. The ROI would be 25%.

The term *return on investment* is frequently generalized to refer to any measure of net gain or net loss. It is often also inaccurate because it fails to account for all of the costs associated with a transaction. As accountants know, it may be better to redefine the formula for ROI as follows:

$$\text{ROI} = \frac{\text{All Inflows} - \text{All Outflows}}{\text{All Outflows}}$$

All cash and losses flowing out are subtracted from all cash and gains flowing in, and then divided by all cash and losses flowing out. If you were selling a home for \$400,000 which you had purchased for \$200,000 some years earlier, it would be insufficient to state that you enjoyed a 100% ROI, calculated as $\frac{\$400{,}000 - \$200{,}000}{\$200{,}000}$. You haven't accounted for the cost of property taxes, homeowner's insurance, plumbing repairs, painting, and other maintenance expenses over the years. To make the formula truly accurate, you must first determine all of the outflows. If you had spent \$100,000 over the years on taxes, insurance, repairs, and maintenance, your ROI would be 50%, calculated as $\frac{\$400{,}000 - (\$200{,}000 - \$100{,}000)}{\$200{,}000}$.

Another way to portray the ROI formula is to think of it as the net benefit divided by the costs, then multiplied by 100:

$$\text{ROI} = \frac{\text{Net Benefit} - \text{Cost}}{\text{Cost}} \text{ x } 100$$

If a transaction costs your client \$100 and yields a benefit of \$150, then the net benefit is \$50. Applying the formula, the transaction would yield a gain of 0.5. To calculate the percentage ROI, we multiply by 100 (0.5 x 100 = 50). Therefore, we say that the transaction produced a 50% ROI.

8.3. Simple Annualized Return on Investment

If you want to know the average annual return on a particular investment, you'll need to extend the formulas above by calculating the simple annualized ROI. To do this, you simply divide your ROI by the number of years in which your funds or payments have been invested in the project, the case, or the decision. So, if it has taken four years for you to generate a \$50 gain on an initial investment of \$100 (a 50% ROI), then you would divide the ROI by 4, yielding a simple annualized ROI of 12.5%.

$$\text{Simple Annualized ROI} = \frac{\text{ROI}}{\text{Y}}$$

where Y equals the number of years during which the investment has been made or held.

8.4. Compound Annual Growth Rate

The problem with a simple annualized ROI is that it is often too simple. Let's say, for example, that you paid \$1,000 on a particular transaction. After one year, it was worth \$2,000. After a second year, it was worth \$1,000 again. Applying the simple annualized ROI, we would show a return of 25%. After one year, you had a gain of 100%. After another year, you had a loss of 50%. Your net gain was therefore 50% (100% – 50% = 50%). Simple annualized ROI equals 50% divided by two years: 25%. But this result could not possibly be accurate because you're back to the same point you were when you made the transaction two years earlier. You have only $1,000, meaning that your real annualized gain must be zero.

In such a case, you would need to calculate the compound annual growth rate (CAGR). As you might expect, the formula for CAGR is not so simple:

$$\textbf{CAGR} = \left[\frac{\text{fV}}{\text{bV}}\right]^{\frac{1}{\text{Y}}} - 1$$

fV = Final value of the investment
bV = Beginning value of the investment
Y = Number of years

Let's calculate the CAGR for the facts above. The bV was $1,000, the amount you initially paid on the transaction. The fV was $1,000, the final amount remaining at the end of the transaction term. The number of years involved is 2.

$$\text{CAGR} = \left[\frac{\text{fV}}{\text{bV}}\right]^{\frac{1}{\text{Y}}} - 1$$

$\text{CAGR} = 1^{1/2} - 1$ (Note: 1 raised to any power equals 1)

$\text{CAGR} = 1 - 1$

$\text{CAGR} = 0$

So now we have confirmation. The CAGR of your $1,000 investment was zero—less than the simple annualized ROI. Knowing the difference between the simple annualized ROI and the CAGR is, indeed, a valuable negotiating tool.

Let's try a somewhat more complicated example. Your client paid $590,000 on June 1, 2011, on a construction project that was promised to generate substantial profits. For the next five years, the initial investment continued to grow, producing the following values:

2011: $590,000 (Initial Investment)
2012: $650,000
2013: $710,000
2014: $980,000
2015: $1,105,000
2016: $1,230,000

What is the CAGR? Let's apply the formula.

$$\text{CAGR} = \left[\frac{\text{fV}}{\text{bV}}\right]^{\frac{1}{\text{Y}}} - 1$$

$$\text{CAGR} = \left[\frac{\$1{,}230{,}000}{\$590{,}000}\right]^{\frac{1}{5}} - 1$$

$$\text{CAGR} = 2.08^{\frac{1}{5}} - 1$$

$$\text{CAGR} = 1.1577 - 1$$

$$\text{CAGR} = 0.1577$$

$$\text{CAGR} = 15.8\%$$

The CAGR on the \$590,000 payment made in 2011 on the construction project is 15.8%. Had we looked only at the simple annualized ROI, we would have found an annual gain of more than 21%, as shown below:

$$\text{ROI} = \frac{\$1{,}230{,}000 - \$590{,}000}{\$590{,}000}$$

$$\text{ROI} = \frac{\$640{,}000}{\$590{,}000} = 1.0847$$

$$\text{ROI} = 108.47\%$$

$$\text{Simple Annualized ROI} = \frac{\text{ROI}}{\text{Y}} = \frac{108.47\%}{5} = 21.69\%$$

Unlike the simple annualized ROI which merely averages the five-year ROI, the CAGR smoothes out the annual returns by producing a percentage rate that reflects what the original \$590,000 would have earned each year had it grown at a steady rate over the five-year period. Technically, the simple annualized ROI is an arithmetic averaging of growth numbers, while the CAGR is a geometric averaging of growth numbers. The geometric average is mathematically the correct growth rate. So, while the simple annualized ROI may be useful as a form of quick shorthand or a negotiating tool, attorneys should recognize the CAGR as the more accurate measure of the ROR on an initial investment over a specific period of time.

8.5. Cash Flow Method

An alternative to the formality of the CAGR formula is a cash flow table or a spreadsheet that takes a more panoramic view of gains and losses. Using the cash flow method, you will be asking, "What is the net cash flow?" as your barometer of gain or loss. For example, if you were to invest $200,000 and draw a gain of $50,000, you might be tempted to say that the ROR is simply 25%, but for how long? Will the initial investment of $200,000 continually produce a $50,000 gain year after year? Or will you start losing money after a few years? The real question you wish to answer is, "What is the net cash flow over time?" In simple cases, this can be calculated manually; in more complicated cases, you will need to use Excel or another spreadsheet platform.

Let's assume, for example, that the initial outlay of $200,000 will actually produce $50,000 for only three of the next five years, and then lower gains for the two years thereafter. Here is what a cash flow table might look like:

	2011	2012	2013	2014	2015	Totals
Initial Investment	–$200,000					–$200,000
Gain	$50,000	$50,000	$50,000	$45,000	$40,000	$235,000
Net Cash Flow	–$150,000	$50,000	$50,000	$45,000	$40,000	$35,000

Here we see that the net cash flow is only $35,000 when considering the cash flows over a five-year period. A 10-year spreadsheet could provide even more valuable information. Displaying the figures in a cash flow table can also provide other insights into the ebb and flow of money, the risks over time, and the length of time necessary to draw a profit.

8.6. Expected Rate of Return

The expected rate of return (ERR) is based on probabilities. It equals the sum of each possible ROR multiplied by the corresponding probability of each return occurring. For example, let's assume that a particular investment of money can produce three possible RORs. We will call them ROR1, ROR2, and ROR3. These RORs are not equally likely to occur. In fact, there is a different probability of occurrence for each one. We will call these probabilities P1, P2, and P3. The probability of ROR1 occurring is P1, the probability of ROR2 occurring is P2, and the probability of ROR3 occurring is P3. Here is the formula for the ERR:

$$ERR = [R0R1(P1) + ROR2(P2) + ROR3(P3)]$$

For example, let's assume that a business venture can produce three possible RORs:

ROR1 = 25%

ROR2 = 10%

ROR3 = –5%

In the first scenario, the business venture enjoys a 25% gain. In the second scenario, it enjoys a 10% gain, and in the third scenario, it suffers a 5% loss. However, the third scenario is the most likely scenario with a 50% probability of occurring. The first scenario and the second scenario (ROR1 and ROR2) each have a 25% probability of occurring. To determine the expected ROR, we apply the formula to the RORs and the probabilities:

ERR = [R0R1(P1) + ROR2(P2) + ROR3(P3)]

ERR = [0.25(0.25) + 0.1(0.25) – 0.5(0.5)

ERR = [0.0625 + 0.025 – 0.25]

ERR = –0.1625

The expected ROR in this instance is negative: a negative return of 16.25%.

By shifting the probabilities, however, we can achieve a much different result. If the probability of a 25% positive return were 50%, and the probability of the other two scenarios was 25% each, the ERR would be a positive return of 2.5%.

ERR = [R0R1(P1) + ROR2(P2) + ROR3(P3)]

ERR = [0.25(0.5) + 0.1(0.25) – 0.5(0.25)

ERR = [0.125 + 0.025 – 0.125]

ERR = 0.025

The expected ROR is a constructive method for attorneys and their advisors to quantify the probable benefits or losses that will result in a case or transaction in which several alternative scenarios may exist. If counsel can clearly articulate the different scenarios, setting forth the RORs in each case, and then ascertain the probabilities of each scenario occurring, an expected ROR can then be calculated.

8.7. Return on Equity

The return on equity (ROE) is another common measure of net income or profitability. It is most frequently used to determine a corporation's financial health by gauging how much profit a business has generated with the money invested by its shareholders. It is essentially the ROR on the ownership interest of the shareholders, known as the shareholders' equity. The ROE is calculated as the net income a corporation earns (after paying taxes and before paying common stock dividends) divided by the shareholders' equity. The basic formula is:

$$\text{ROI} = \frac{\text{Net Income}}{\text{Shareholders' Equity}}$$

ROE is useful to measure profitability, but it also a valuable assessment tool on the performance of management. It reflects how well management is using its money, or more precisely, how well managers are investing the money invested in the company. A high ROE indicates that a company is spending wisely and perhaps efficiently and is likely generating a profit. For publicly traded companies, high ROEs lead to higher stock prices. ROEs calculated for a number of different companies in the same industry can also provide a useful ranking method.

To calculate ROE, you will first need to obtain figures for net income and shareholders' equity. If you were dealing with a private enterprise, you would likely request these figures in pretrial discovery or by subpoenaing records from accountants. Some financial information is also often published on a company's website under menu bar headings for investors. In particular, you would want to see the balance sheet, which provides the shareholders' equity, and the income statement, which provides the net income for a particular year. For publicly listed companies, such information is also generally available on a variety of free and pay services online (for example, Yahoo Finance at finance.yahoo.com), including government websites.

Let's consider some real numbers. Take, for example, MGM Resorts International, which owns a number of casino resorts in the United States. According to its balance sheet and income statement, it suffered some significant reductions in net income during the recession years of 2008 and 2009 as stockholders' equity also declined.

MGM Resorts International (MGM)

All figures are shown in thousands

	2009	2008	2007
Net Income	–$1,291,682	–$855,286	$1,584,419
Stockholders' Equity	$3,870,432	$3,974,361	$6,060,703

Calculating the simple ROEs without any technical adjustments shows that MGM suffered a substantial change in position between its 26% ROE in 2007 and its –33% ROE in 2009. In fact, Yahoo! Finance reported MGM's quarterly ROE in November of 2010 at –50.68%.

ROE is an important calculation because it not only focuses a telescope on management effectiveness but it also reveals the ability of a company to generate cash internally. An attorney who must advise his business client about settling a case with a corporate defendant may wish to know whether the defendant is financially capable of paying, or likely to pay, a settlement over a period of time. Can the defendant truly pay damages over five years as it has promised to do? How well has the defendant managed its stockholders' equity in the last five years? What ROE can be realistically expected? The same analysis may assist a law firm in determining whether to pursue a lawsuit against a particular corporate defendant in the first place.

8.8. Return on Assets

Another ratio that is helpful in determining whether a business is profitable is the return on assets (ROA). Like ROE, ROA is a gauge of management effectiveness. Rather than measuring how well management is using the money invested in the company, ROA measures how efficiently management uses the company's assets to generate earnings. The basic formula for ROA is:

$$\text{ROA} = \frac{\textbf{Net Income}}{\textbf{Total Assets}}$$

The denominator is usually the more difficult figure to establish. The value of total assets should not logically include assets that don't generate income, such as redundant tools and machines or company cars that are never driven. In this respect, the ROA is often stated as the return on *operating assets,* and the denominator is reformulated as *assets that generate revenue*. If ABC Corporation had total assets of $1 million, but $100,000 of them were dormant, redundant, or decommissioned assets serving no profit-generating purpose, then the "Total Assets" denominator would be $900,000. If ABC Corporation generated net income of $200,000 on its total revenue-generating assets of $900,000, the ROA would be $\frac{\$200{,}000}{\$900{,}000}$ or 0.22. The ROA would be 22%.

To calculate ROA, you will need figures for net income and total assets. Net income is a line item on the company's income statement, and total assets is a line item on the balance sheet. While certain adjustments may be required in particular cases, these figures form the basis for building the ROA formula. Let's look at PetSmart, Inc.'s income statement and balance sheet to explore some genuine figures:

PetSmart, Inc.

All figures are shown in thousands

	2009	2008	2007
Net Income	$198,325	$192,670	$258,684
Total Assets	$2,461,986	$2,357,653	$2,167,257

Applying the ROA formula to these figures (without any technical adjustments), we see that PetSmart had an ROA of 11.94% in 2007 which dropped to just barely over 8% in 2008 and 2009. Quarterly reports of management performance by PetSmart as of August 1, 2010, showed an ROA of 10.28%, according to Yahoo! Finance.

Understanding the ROA formula, like other formulas discussed in this book, allows you to apply basic algebra to find missing pieces of information. If you know a company's ROA and the total value of its assets, you should be able to calculate its net income. If you know its ROA and its net income, then you should be able to determine its total assets.

If $\textbf{ROA} = \frac{\textbf{Net Income}}{\textbf{Total Assets}}$ **. . . . Then ROA x Total Assets = Net Income**

If ROA x Total Assets = Net Income . . . . Then $\textbf{Total Assets} = \frac{\textbf{Net Income}}{\textbf{ROA}}$

Attorneys may be able to gather useful pieces of information in published reports, accounting records, pretrial discovery, and expert reports. By recognizing the interplay between net income, total assets, and ROA, attorneys can use their available information sources to draw important conclusions about a party's financial position.

8.9. Net Worth

Net worth is the difference between one's assets and one's liabilities. In a divorce, a spouse's net worth is determined by subtracting all of her loan obligations, credit card debts, and other liabilities from the equity in her home, the value of her personal property, and other assets. In the sale, purchase, or consolidation of a business, net worth is calculated easily from the asset and liability lines on the balance sheets. The formula for net worth is:

NW = Total Assets – Total Liabilities

To make this formula meaningful, however, the value of total assets and of total liabilities must be established accurately. In computing total assets, the fair market value (not the original purchase value, or the tax assessor's value) must be utilized to fix the value of each asset. Intangible assets such as intellectual property rights (if they are going to be included in the calculation of total assets) must also be quantified by an authoritative source. Likewise, total liabilities must be accurately counted. This includes every contractual credit obligation, personal loan, and outstanding bill to be paid.

Net worth provides two useful pieces of information: (a) The financial status of the person or business under consideration, that is, whether they have sufficient assets to cover their debts, and (b) how they compare to another person or business, that is, whether they have a greater or lower net worth. Net worth can also guide attorneys who are attempting to settle cases with individual or corporate defendants. If a person has a low net worth (or a negative net worth), he would be in a presumptively weak position to pay damages (or in the case of a divorce action, to pay cash in distribution of the marital estate). A high-net-worth individual, by contrast, would ostensibly have a surplus, either in funds or in assets that can be liquidated to pay damages.

8.10. Book Value

Book value (BV) is also sometimes stated as the difference between a company's assets and its liabilities. Like net worth, the formula for book value can be simplified as BV = Total Assets – Total Liabilities. To make BV meaningful, however, we must apply several accounting adjustments.

In determining the company's total assets, you should first subtract intangible assets (such as goodwill and other intangibles). When this is done, the BV is considered to be a *tangible book value,* and therefore more useful. (A BV which includes intangibles such as goodwill does not translate into real money that shareholders would receive if the company were to liquidate). The formula for a tangible BV is thus:

BV = Total Assets – Intangible Assets – Total Liabilities

BV can tell us what the owners of the company would receive if the company closed its doors, satisfied its obligations, and liquidated. It is what's left over after all the assets are sold and the debts are paid. By itself, BV is a simple metric that can be calculated and compared to other companies in the same industry. BV for a particular year or quarter can also be compared to prior years or quarters for the same company.

Book Value per Share

Book value per share of stock (BVPS) is another device for quantifying the success of a business. If we know the BV, then the BVPS can be calculated by simply dividing the BV by the number of outstanding shares of common stock.

A more accurate way to think of BVPS is to base it on the *common* shareholders' equity and the shares of common stock outstanding. The basic formula is:

$$\text{BVPS} = \frac{\textbf{Common Shareholders' Equity}}{\textbf{Shares of Common Stock Outstanding}}$$

The formula specifically refers to the ownership interest (the equity) of *common* shareholders. Shareholders with preferred stock are not included. Therefore, if you're starting with a total shareholders' equity figure, you'd need to subtract the value of all preferred stock.

(This can include the cost of the original stock, based on its purchase price, unpaid dividends, and other preferred shareholder increments).

Let's assume that XYZ Corporation has total equity of $10 million, which includes the par value of its common stock, its paid-in capital, and its retained earnings. Let's also assume that the value of liquidating all of the preferred stock is $2 million, leaving a common shareholders' equity of $8 million. If there are 715,000 common shares of stock outstanding, then the BVPS formula would look like this:

$$\text{BVPS} = \frac{\$8{,}000{,}000}{715{,}000} = 11.1888$$

Therefore, the BV would be $11.19 per share. This number, by itself, doesn't tell us much. However, what if we also knew that the common stock for XYZ Corporation was selling for $15 per share? We could then conclude that the company is performing well. If the common stock were selling for $10 per share in the current market—lower than the BVPS—we might conclude that the company is undervalued, and indeed strategic investors might wish to buy the stock now.

It may also be useful to determine the relationship between the market value of common stock and the book value. This is referred to as the price-to-book ratio, to be discussed in the next section of this book. The price-to-book ratio can be determined by dividing the current market price (P) of the stock by the BVPS. In the example for XYZ Corporation above, the calculation would be:

$$\frac{\$15}{\$11.19} = 1.34$$

This means XYZ's common stock is selling for 34% more than its BV. The lower the price-to-book ratio, the more attractive the company's stock will appear to investors looking for a bargain.

8.11. Internal Rate of Return

The internal rate of return (IRR) is a formula that, like the net present value (NPV) discussed in Chapter 2, assists us in determining if a decision, an action, a project, or an investment is financially justified. The IRR is the rate that causes the NPV to be zero. To understand this formula, let's revisit NPV.

NPV equals the present value minus the cost. To obtain the present value, we apply the formula $\text{PV} = \frac{\text{FV}}{(1 + \text{i})^{\text{n}}}$ where PV is present value,

FV is the future value, i is the discount rate (previously, we called it the interest rate), and n is the number of years. So, let's assume that you will be entitled to $1,000 three years from now and that the applicable discount rate is 4%. Let's also assume that you must invest $700 today as your cost of making this investment or pursuing this course of action. Applying the formula, we find that the PV is $888.99. In other words, the present value of $1,000 to be paid in three years discounted at 4% is $888.99. Now that we know the PV, what is the NPV? The NPV equals the PV minus costs; therefore, NPV = $888.99 – $700. NPV = $188.99.

Restating the equation, we now know that the NPV of $1,000 to be paid in three years at 4%, based on an investment of $700, is $188.99. Since we have a positive NPV, the project would be considered a viable or favorable course of action. To get closer to finding the IRR, however, we will need to display this formula graphically and begin tweaking the NPV until we can bring it down to zero.

$$\text{NPV} = \frac{\text{FV}}{(1+\text{i})^{\text{n}}} - \text{Costs}$$

$$\text{NPV} = \frac{\$1{,}000}{(1+.04)^{3}} - \$700$$

$$\text{NPV} = \frac{\$1{,}000}{(1.04)^{3}} - \$700$$

$$\text{NPV} = \$888.99 - \$700$$

$$\text{NPV} = \$188.99$$

The IRR is the *discount rate* that causes the NPV to be zero. Therefore, we will need to manipulate the 4% rate shown above as .04. What new rate would lower the NPV to zero? Let's try 8%.

$$\text{NPV} = \frac{\text{FV}}{(1+\text{i})^{\text{n}}} - \text{Costs}$$

$$\text{NPV} = \frac{\$1{,}000}{(1+.08)^{3}} - \$700$$

$$\text{NPV} = \frac{\$1{,}000}{(1.08)^{3}} - \$700$$

$$\text{NPV} = \$793.83 - \$700$$

$$\text{NPV} = \$93.83$$

We're getting closer to reducing the NPV to zero. If we were to continue experimenting by trial and error, we would eventually find that an interest rate of about 12.62% would reduce the NPV to zero. Accordingly, 12.62% would be the IRR for this set of facts.

You could determine the same interest rate algebraically by manipulating the formula:

$$NPV = \frac{FV}{(1 + i)^n} - Costs$$

$$NPV = \frac{\$1,000}{(1 + i)^3} - \$700$$

Now add \$700 to each side of the equation.

$$\$700 = \frac{\$1,000}{(1 + i)^3}$$

Then multiply both sides of the equation by $(1 + i)^3$

$$\$700 \text{ x } (1 + i)^3 = \$1,000$$

Next, divide both sides of the equation by \$700.

$$(1 + i)^3 = \frac{\$1,000}{\$700}$$

$$(1 + i)^3 = 1.4285714$$

So we can now ask the question: What number cubed (that is, raised to the third power) will equal 1.4285714? Or stated otherwise, what is the cube root of 1.4285714? If your calculator does not calculate cube roots, you can find a free cube root calculator online (for example, visit *http://www.csgnetwork.com/cuberootcubecalc.html*). The cube root of 1.4285714 is 1.1262. Therefore, $(1 + i) = 1 + 0.1262$. Thus the IRR is 12.62%.

Why go to all of this trouble? What value is the IRR?

The value of this exercise is to determine at what rate the project should be accepted or the deal should be made. Under the facts above, the project should be accepted or the deal should be made if the discount rate is less than 12.62%. The deal should be rejected if the rate is above 12.62%.

Stated inversely, the deal should be accepted if the IRR is greater than the discount rate being offered. The deal should be rejected if the IRR is less than the rate being offered.

If several deals or alternatives are under consideration, the one with the highest IRR would the best choice, assuming all other factors are equal. If you simply want to break even, then the discount rate should be exactly the same as the IRR. At an IRR of 12.62%, in the case above, present value of cash inflows equals the present value of cash outflows. That is, the NPV is zero.

8.12. Net Terminal Value

To understand net terminal value (NTV), we begin with terminal value (TV). TV is the value of a certain investment or expenditure of money at the end of a certain period of time, based on a certain rate of interest. It is essentially the value that an investment, a business, a project, or other expenditure will have at the end of a growth period. It is considered a TV because it measures the final value of an investment, using a stable growth rate, when no further change in growth is expected. Attorneys, accountants, and other business advisors may wish to calculate TV in order to assess what a business or a project will be worth at the end of its economic life—that is, when it will be liquidated.

The basic formula is:

$$TV = P(1 + i)^n$$

TV = Terminal value
P = Principal
i = Interest rate
n = number of years

If $1,000 has been invested at 4%, what will it be worth in 20 years?

Applying the TV formula above, we find that it will be worth $2,191.

$$TV = P(1 + i)^n$$

$$TV = \$1{,}000\ (1.04)^{20}$$

$$TV = \$1{,}000\ (2.191)$$

$$TV = \$2{,}191$$

Of course, we cannot expect to generate a positive TV without incurring some cost of capital. The cost of capital must be determined and subtracted from the TV so that we can find out whether the investment was ultimately a gain or a loss. To convert this TV to a NTV, we would subtract the cost of capital from the end of the formula. Let's assume that at the conclusion of the time period under consideration, the sum of $2,000 will have been paid as our cost of capital. The NTV would therefore be equal to the TV of $2,191 minus the outflow (cost) of $2,000, for a net gain of $191. Like NPV, we could conclude that a positive NTV reflects a favorable investment because we ultimately derived a positive gain above the cost of capital.

Another TV formula is known as the perpetuity method. This method is arguably more accurate and meaningful because it assumes some moderate growth rate after the conclusion of the time period under consideration. The formula for the TV based on the perpetuity method is:

$$TV = CF\ [\text{at the end of time}]\frac{1 + g}{r - g}$$

CF (at the end of time) = the cash flow projected to be generated at the end of the time period under consideration.

g = the growth rate (or inflation rate)

r = the discount rate (or interest rate)

Let's assume, for example, that a business is projected to generate positive cash flows for a 10-year period. We believe that in year 11 and thereafter, the business will enjoy no growth except for inflation. The cash flow in the 11th year is projected to be $1 million. Assume that the firm's discount rate is 9%, and inflation is expected to be 2.5%. Applying the TV perpetuity method formula, we will obtain the following results:

$$TV = CF\ [\text{at the end of time}]\frac{1 + g}{r - g}$$

$$TV = \$1{,}000{,}000\frac{1 + .025}{.09 - .025}$$

$$TV = \$1{,}000{,}000\frac{1.025}{.065}$$

$$TV = \$1{,}000{,}000\ (15.77)$$

$$TV = \$15{,}770{,}000$$

To appreciate what this figure means in today's dollars, we'll need to apply the PV formula.

$$PV = \frac{FV}{(1 + i)^n}$$

$$PV = \frac{15{,}770{,}000}{(1.09)^{10}}$$

We use the discount rate of 9% and the time period (n) as 10 years.

$$PV = \frac{15{,}770{,}000}{2.367}$$

$$PV = 6{,}662{,}441.91$$

The PV of the TV of the business at the conclusion of the 10-year period under review will be approximately $6.6 million.

Another variation of the TV formula, based on a stable growth model, assumes that the final cash flows will be reinvested by the business and will grow at a constant rate forever. It produces similar results.

$$TV = \frac{CF}{r - g}$$

$$TV = \frac{\$1{,}000{,}000}{0.065}$$

$$TV = \$15{,}384{,}615.38$$

$$PV = \$6{,}499{,}626.27$$

Chapter 9

Helpful Financial Ratios

9.1. Earnings Per Share

Earnings per share (EPS) is the ratio of a company's earnings to each share of stock. It measures the profitability of the company by producing a number that equals the portion of the overall profit assigned to each outstanding share of common stock. EPS is a critical piece of information for anybody trying to assess the strength of a company. It affects the price of the company's stock and, as discussed in the section below, EPS allows us to determine the important price-to-earnings ratio. Publicly traded corporations are required to report EPS on their income statements. Thus, attorneys can obtain this information easily by conducting an online records search, or by making a pretrial discovery request. Private enterprises are not required to report their EPS, and thus it is useful to know the formula.

The basic formula for EPS is $\dfrac{\text{Net income} - \text{Preferred dividends}}{\text{Average outstanding shares}}$

Let's break down this formula. In order to determine the numerator (the company's earnings), we must first know its gross income, and from that, its net income. Then we must subtract the cost of any dividends it pays to preferred shareholders. Then we have a truly net earnings figure. We could simply divide that figure by the total number of outstanding shares of stock, but the ratio would be inaccurate because all shares are not outstanding for the same period of time. Finance experts, therefore, say that the denominator must be a weighted average of all outstanding shares of common stock.

For example, let's say that XYZ Corporation has 2 million outstanding shares between January 1 and June 30, but the figure increases to 3 million shares for the second half of the year. To calculate the weighted average number of outstanding shares, we multiply 0.5 (representing the first half of the year) by 2 million and 0.5 (representing the second half of the year) by 3 million, and then we add the two figures.

$$[0.5 \times 2{,}000{,}000] + [0.5 \times 3{,}000{,}000]$$
$$= 1{,}000{,}000 + 1{,}500{,}000$$
$$= 2{,}500{,}000$$

Therefore, the weighted average number of outstanding shares is 2.5 million for the period in question.

Let's now test out the EPS formula. Assume that XYZ Corporation has a net income of $16 million, and it pays out $1 million in preferred dividends.

$$\text{EPS} = \frac{\text{Net income} - \text{Preferred dividends}}{\text{Average outstanding shares}}$$

$$\text{EPS} = \frac{\$16{,}000{,}000 - \$1{,}000{,}000}{2{,}500{,}000}$$

$$\text{EPS} = \frac{\$15{,}000{,}000}{2{,}500{,}000}$$

$$\text{EPS} = \$6$$

XYZ Corporation, therefore, earns $6 per share on its stock.

Assuming no changes in the number of stock shares from year to year, EPS can be a helpful metric to compare from year to year. It can provide a quick fix on a company's profit level. Because EPS is based on a ratio, however, we must keep an eye on both the numerator and the denominator. An increase in EPS may not be due exclusively to an increase in net income. It may be the result of a decrease in the number of outstanding shares. A company can manipulate its EPS (and thereby its appearance of profitability) by buying back its shares and reducing the number of outstanding shares divided into its net income to calculate the EPS.

On the other hand, a decrease in EPS may not reflect a decrease in net income. EPS could slide because the company issued additional shares of stock. Was there an increase in stock options awarded during the year? Was there a reconfiguration of the management or organizational structure? These are questions that should be asked and answered before drawing any hasty conclusions about a significant change in EPS. Where EPS is more than a ballpark measure of company profitability, it may be helpful to consult an accountant, a business valuator, or other finance expert. These specialists often use a *fully diluted* EPS which takes into account stock options, warrants, and convertible securities as part of the common stock denominator used in the formula.

Attorneys may find the EPS formula helpful to provide a snapshot of a company's profitability or lack thereof. In a trial, a sliding EPS may support arguments that a company experienced financial trouble and was thus vulnerable to a particular action or course of conduct in dispute. A sliding EPS may also signal a higher risk of failure, insolvency, or default in a firm with whom settlement negotiations are under way. A climbing EPS, however, can be a bargaining tool in demonstrating the financial health and strong management of a company.

9.2. Price-to-Earnings Ratio

One of the most popular formulas, expressed in the form of simple ratio, is the price-to-earnings ratio (P/E). It is used to measure the perception investors hold about a corporation's financial health. A high P/E means the investing public thinks well of the company; a low P/E means the opposite. The change in P/E reflects the shifting values of the public: an increasing P/E indicates increasing public confidence in the growth potential of a company, while a decreasing P/E suggests declining public confidence.

The formula, at its core, is simply a company's stock price divided by its EPS. The P/E ratio is the average market price of a single share of common stock divided by the net income per share, generally characterized as the EPS. The simplified formula is:

$$\text{P/E} = \frac{\text{Price per share}}{\text{Earnings per share (EPS)}}$$

Assume that a share of stock in ABC Corporation sold for \$14, \$18, and \$24 in 2009, 2010, and 2011 respectively. The EPS for those years were \$2, \$3, and \$4, respectively. Applying the simple P/E formula, we might conclude that the company is stagnant as the P/E dropped from 7 to 6.

Year	Stock Price	Earnings Per Share (EPS)	Price to Earnings Ratio (P/E)
2009	$14	$2	7
2010	$18	$3	6
2011	$24	$4	6

Why is this information valuable to attorneys? As an evidentiary device, the P/E ratio is a widely recognized measure of investor confidence, from which a finder of fact could conclude that a company, for example, was experiencing deteriorating financial health. It may reflect, or support, an argument that growth was stagnant, cash flow was drying up, or that the corporation was suffering from significant leadership problems. As a settlement device, the P/E ratio provides a guidepost on how well a company's stock price is performing. The formula can be used to compare two or more companies in the same industry. A P/E ratio that is too low for a corporation relative to the industry average could, in certain cases, indicate an undervalued company, thus representing a fertile opportunity for a corporate takeover, buyout, or other settlement structure. However, a P/E ratio that is too high for its industry may represent an overvaluation and thus a signal to sell.

Understanding P/E provides some shorthand techniques that can be useful in the bargaining process. For example, let's assume that a share of stock sells for $50. Let's also assume that the EPS for the company is $5. The P/E ratio provides some quick math: We can see, in an instant, that P/E equals 10 ($50 divided by $5). We can thus say that investors think the shares of stock are worth 10 times the EPS. To an unsophisticated opponent, such a statement may seem quite powerful (10 times EPS!). In a vibrant market, however, where average stock prices in the same industry are trading at 15 times EPS, a P/E of 10 may fall below market averages.

A P/E ratio should never be used as the only measure of a company's financial health or its perceived financial health. Nor should a single ratio be cited or relied upon for more than it really reveals. A comparison of a company's P/E ratios over time may be useful, as will a comparison of one company's P/E with a competitor's P/E over the same period of time. There is no perfect P/E either, because the number fluctuates with investor trends and interests, reflecting what members of the public are willing to spend, what they believe to be true, and how an overall market is performing. As a negotiating device, a decision-making tool, or a piece of evidence, however, the P/E ratio can be a very helpful, if not tactical, formula.

9.3. Debt-to-Equity Ratio

The debt-to-equity ratio is a measure of a company's leverage, that is, how much of the company's business is funded by debt rather than equity. While the ratio can be expressed as $\frac{\text{Debt}}{\text{Equity}}$, in which the amount of debt is simply divided by the amount of equity, a more complete statement of the D/E ratio is $\frac{\text{Total Liabilities}}{\text{Total Shareholders Equity}}$.

For example, New Age Industries, an American corporation, has recently incurred significant debt expanding into several new Canadian markets. Its equity level is \$100 million with outstanding debt of \$215 million. Its newest market expansion, into British Columbia, will cost another \$45 million. If it follows through with its expansion plans, what will its D/E ratio be?

$$\text{D/E} = \frac{\text{Total Liabilities}}{\text{Total Shareholders Equity}}$$

$$\text{D/E} = \frac{\$215{,}000{,}000 + \$45{,}000{,}000}{100{,}000{,}0000}$$

$$\text{D/E} = 2.6$$

Total liabilities are calculated as consisting of the outstanding existing debt of \$215 million plus the projected debt (cost) of \$45 million for the expansion into British Columbia. This combined debt of \$260 million is then divided by the total shareholders' equity of \$100 million, yielding a debt-to-equity ratio of 2.6.

What does this number tell us? For one thing, it raises concern about the cost of New Age Industries's debt. How much interest does the company pay to carry this debt? How does its debt service compare to its earnings? Its earnings per share? The higher the D/E ratio, the greater the proportion of the company's capital contributed by creditors as opposed to shareholders. The D/E ratio of 2.6 for New Age Industries means that for every dollar of the company owned by shareholders, the company owes \$2.60 to its creditors.

A ratio of 1 to 1 (that is, a D/E of 1) means that there is \$1 of debt for every \$1 of equity or a perfect balance between leverage and actual ownership. In theory, when the owners' interests become greater than the creditors' interests (for example, a ratio of 1 to 2 or a D/E of 0.5), the company is likely to be considered financially strong.

Calculating a company's D/E ratio is easy. Both debt and equity are stated on its balance sheet. For example, the table below shows the actual liabilities and equity for Microsoft Corporation between 2008 and 2010, as taken from its balance sheet:

Microsoft Corporation

YEAR	TOTAL LIABILITIES (In Millions)	TOTAL EQUITY (In Millions)	DEBT TO EQUITY RATIO
2008	36,507	36,286	1.006
2009	38,330	39,558	0.968
2010	39,938	46,175	0.864

Microsoft's debt-equity ratio was, with slight variation, approximately 1 to 1 or better for all three years displayed. In 2008, it was 1.006 to 1. In 2009, debt declined slightly below equity, creating a 0.968 to 1 ratio. In 2010, thanks to the increased equity, the D/E ratio was 0.864 to 1— meaning that for every $1 of Microsoft owned by its shareholders, the company owed only 86 cents to its creditors.

Not all industries can boast such favorable D/E ratios during recessionary times. Barnes & Noble, Inc., the bookseller, for example, had D/E ratios ranging from 2 to 1 in 2008 to 3 to 1 in 2010. This reflected a highly leveraged, debt-dependent financial status.

Barnes & Noble, Inc.

YEAR	TOTAL LIABILITIES (In Millions)	TOTAL EQUITY (In Millions)	DEBT TO EQUITY RATIO
2008	2,175.1	1,074.7	2.020
2009	2,072.3	921.6	2.248
2010	2,803.9	901.8	3.109

So, in 2010, for every dollar of equity owned by Barnes & Noble's shareholders, the company owed $3.11 to its creditors.

Investors routinely expect the D/E ratio in some industries to be higher than in other industries. Industry trends are, in and of themselves, useful ways to measure how a company is faring. Is the company's performance consistent with other companies in that industry? Better or worse? High D/E ratios (or higher-than-average ratios) may raise red flags because they suggest that the company is overburdened with debt and not likely to repay its loans.

A high or low D/E ratio may also influence the method and manner in which a company resolves a legal dispute. Is it capable of paying a settlement? Does it have equity to spare? Is it a bad credit risk? Where a D/E ratio is precariously high, attorneys may wish to formulate contract provisions that would ensure that a particular debt or settlement is paid. One such provision, for example, could compel the corporation to direct any excess cash flow into debt repayment. A provision could also limit the ability of corporate managers to make capital expenditures, except under very controlled circumstances. The owners of the company (shareholders) could also be asked to contribute more equity to the enterprise.

9.4. Quick Balance Sheet Math

If you know the debt and equity for a company for purposes of calculating the D/E ratio, then you can also determine the company's assets. This is because, for accounting purposes, debt plus equity equals total assets. On a balance sheet, the figure for total assets which appears on one side will always match the total for debt and equity which appears on the other side. If you do not have a balance sheet, you can nevertheless do some quick balance sheet math to determine the missing information.

Here are the five formulas you need to know:

1. $A = D + E$
2. $D = A - E$
3. $E = A - D$
4. $\frac{D}{E} = \frac{D}{A - D}$
5. $\frac{D}{E} = \frac{A - E}{E}$

A = Assets
D = Debt (Liabilities)
E = Equity

So, if we wanted to know what Microsoft's total assets were for 2010 without looking at its balance sheet, we could utilize the first formula above (A = D + E) to calculate the answer. In the section above, we saw that Microsoft's reported liabilities and equity for 2010 were $39,938,000,000 and $46,175,000,000. Its total assets must equal the sum of these two numbers, which is $86,113,000,000, which is, in fact, the number that appears on Microsoft's 2010 balance sheet.

If we knew the company's assets and equity, we could determine its debt (its total liabilities) by simply subtracting the equity from the assets (see formula #2 above). Similarly, if we knew the value of total assets and total liabilities, we could ascertain shareholders' equity by subtracting debt from assets (formula #3). We can extend this quick math to help us calculate the D/E ratio when we're missing either the debt or the equity. So, for example, if we want to know the D/E ratio for Larry's Lumber Company but all we know are the value of his assets and his shareholders' equity, we'd apply formula #5 above. Assume Larry's Lumber had assets of $37 million, and equity of 9.1 million. What is Larry's D/E ratio?

$$\frac{D}{E} = \frac{A - E}{E}$$

$$\frac{D}{E} = \frac{\$37M - \$9.1M}{\$9.1M}$$

$$\frac{D}{E} = \frac{\$27.9M}{\$9.1M}$$

$$\frac{D}{E} = 3.07$$

By subtracting the equity from the assets, and then dividing by the equity, we can see that Larry's Lumber is largely leveraged, with a 3 to 1 D/E ratio.

9.5. Dividend Yield

The dividend yield ratio compares what investors are earning from their dividends with the price of the stock. The formula is:

$$\frac{\text{Dividends per share}}{\text{Market price per share}}$$

The formula is useful to determine which of two companies is likely to offer the best payout in dividends. For example, assume that Able Manufacturing, Inc. and Baker Goods, Inc. are both paying annual dividends of $1 per share. Able's stock is selling for $25 per share while Baker's stock is selling for $35 per share. Applying the formula above, we can quickly determine that the dividend yield for Able is $\frac{1}{25}$ or 4% while the dividend yield for Baker is $\frac{1}{35}$ or approximately 2.9%. Able is a better deal.

A high or low dividend yield, by itself, is not automatically a sign of a good or bad investment. Established businesses and mature corporations tend to have higher dividend yields while young startups and growth-oriented firms tend to have lower yields.

Dividend yields are also a way to gauge the progress a single company is making over time. A decline in dividend yields over a period of years may cast a negative image of the company and indeed may be a reflection of diminished growth. Stockholders depending on a certain flow of dividend payments may be prompted to sell if the yield shrinks. Yet such a decline may reflect a change in management philosophy, a corporate reorientation, or some other design to pour more money back into the company instead of paying dividends.

9.6. Earnings Yield

The earnings yield is the reciprocal of the price-to-earnings ratio. It is the EPS divided by the price of a share of stock. Compare the two formulas:

$$\text{P/E} = \frac{\text{Price per share}}{\text{EPS}}$$

$$\text{Earnings Yield} = \frac{\text{EPS}}{\text{Price per share}}$$

You might think of the P/E ratio as how much you'd have to spend on a share of stock to buy a dollar of earnings. The earnings yield presents the inverse relationship: how much earnings you can purchase with $1 of stock. Earnings yield, like dividend yield, is best presented in a percentage form.

Let's return to ABC Corporation, which we discussed in the section on the P/E ratio above. ABC stock sold for $14, $18, and $24 in

2009, 2010, and 2011 respectively. The EPS for those years were $2, $3, and $4, respectively. The P/E ratio, therefore, was 7, 6, and 6 for each of the three years, as shown in the table below. To calculate the earnings yield, we now divide the EPS by the price in each case, producing a yield of 14.29% in 2009 to 16.67% in 2010 and 2011.

Year	Stock Price	Earnings Per Share (EPS)	Price to Earnings Ratio (P/E)	Earnings Yield
2009	$14	$2	7	14.29%
2010	$18	$3	6	16.67%
2011	$24	$4	6	16.67%

The earnings yield ultimately measures the return on a share of stock. For example, in the table above, the earnings yield for 2011 was 16.67% which means that 16.67 cents were earned for every $1 of investment.

The earnings yield is a helpful statistic for comparing with Treasury bonds (which are risk free) and large market indexes (such as the S&P 500). If Treasury bond rates were fixed at 4%, the earnings yield for ABC Corporation would have been a good deal between 2009 and 2011. If the earnings yield on a company fell below the Treasury bond rate, it might have been more prudent to buy bonds, at least in the short run. Still, some investors will buy stocks with a lower earnings yield with the hope that the yield will rise over time (while the Treasury bond rate remains fixed). An investor who plans to hold his stocks in a corporation for 10 years will have made a wise decision if the earnings yield on those stocks passes the Treasury bond rate in seven years.

A divorce lawyer may wish to consider the earnings yield before advising his client whether to bargain for the stocks or the bonds in the marital estate. A business lawyer may want to ascertain the earnings yield among other ratios and formulas in recommending whether a business should be purchased. A low earnings yield may, for example, reveal that a company is overvalued and therefore too expensive to buy.

9.7. Quick Ratio

How fast can a company generate cash? How quickly can it tap its liquid assets such as accounts receivable and marketable securities? The quick ratio (also sometimes called the "acid-test ratio") is a formula for measuring a company's liquidity against its debt. The formula is based on the speed with which assets can be cashed out, and therefore it does not include any calculations for inventory or prepaid expenses. Inventory takes too long to be liquidated. Prepaid expenses are not capable of being converted to cash. So, the quick ratio is essentially limited to cash and things that are equivalent to cash such as securities and accounts receivable. The formula is:

$$\frac{\text{Cash} + \text{Market Securities} + \text{Accounts Receivable}}{\text{Current Liabilities}}$$

Assume there is an Internet company known as Gaggle, Inc. Gaggle has the following assets and liabilities on its financial records:

Cash	\$ 300,000
Marketable securities	\$ 125,000
Inventory	\$1,500,000
Accounts receivable	\$ 500,000
Current liabilities	\$1,000,000

Applying the quick ratio, we can calculate the liquidity to debt relationship as follows:

$$\text{QUICK RATIO} = \frac{\$300{,}000 + \$125{,}000 + \$500{,}000}{\$1{,}000{,}000}$$

$$= \frac{\$925{,}000}{\$1{,}000{,}000} = 0.925$$

Notice that inventory has been excluded from this calculation.

We can conclude that Gaggle has quick ratio of 0.925 to 1. This means that for every \$1 of current debt, Gaggle had only 92 cents in quick assets to cover it. In order to feel secure about Gaggle's ability to generate cash, we would want to see at least a 1 to 1 ratio. The higher the ratio, the more liquid the company.

Quick ratios calculated at various junctures can reveal whether a company is suffering from declining liquidity, a signal that it may experience difficulty meeting its debt obligations. Attorneys may be hesitant to negotiate with a corporate defendant with a low quick ratio insofar as the company would be a poor prospect to pay bills and borrow money. In fact, if the quick ratio is too low, the company may run out of money in the short run. As a bargaining tool, high and low quick ratios can be used to support arguments in favor of, or against, making certain business investments. When presented with a quick ratio, however, an attorney should demand to see the underlying figures. If inventory is included, the results may be falsely inflated.

In the Gaggle example above, the quick ratio would have produced a comfortable liquidity level of 2.43 to 1 had inventory been included. Unloading $1.5 million worth of inventory, however, would have taken a long time and should not realistically have been included in a calculation for quick liquidity.

9.8. Interest Coverage Ratio

The interest coverage ratio is another device for measuring the financial health of a company. It indicates how well interest payments are covered by earnings. If a company is experiencing financial difficulties, the interest coverage ratio provides a reference for how long the firm will be able to service its debt. It is calculated by determining the pretax, preinterest earnings of the company and dividing that figure by the total interest expense. The formula is:

$$\text{Interest Coverage Ratio} = \frac{\text{EBIT}}{\text{Interest}}$$

EBIT = Earnings before interest and taxes

For example, let's assume that Hypothetical Corporation had pretax income as follows:

2009: $1,100,000
2010: $1,200,000
2011: $1,250,000

Let's also assume that Hypothetical's total interest expense rose from $190,000 in 2009 to $210,000 in 2010 to $225,000 in 2011. So, for example, in 2009, we would add the income of $1,100,000 to the interest of $190,000 to arrive at an EBIT of $1,290,000. We would then divide the EBIT by the interest amount of $190,000, yielding an interest coverage ratio of 6.78.

The table below shows the interest coverage ratio for each of the three years:

Year	Pre-Tax Income	Interest	Interest Coverage Ratio
2009	$1,100,000	$190,000	6.78
2010	$1,200,000	$210,000	6.71
2011	$1,250,000	$225,000	6.55

The ratios, considered collectively, provide some insight into the company's financial direction. In 2009, with an interest coverage ratio of 6.78, there was effectively $6.78 in income before taxes and interest for every $1 that Hypothetical Corporation paid in interest. By 2011, however, the company's income fell somewhat behind its increasing interest expense, reducing its interest coverage ratio to 6.55 (effectively, $6.55 in income before taxes and interest for every $1 in interest payments). While Hypothetical Corporation remains in a strong position to cover its interest obligations, the ratios suggest that its margin of safety is starting to slip.

In structuring business deals or evaluating a business defendant's ability to make payments, the interest coverage ratio is an effective negotiating tool and an important decision-making metric. It presages problems on the horizon: the lower the ratio, the more the company is burdened by its interest expense. The longer the ratio continues to decline, the greater the likelihood that the company is on a downward spiral. Ratios under 1.5 are generally considered the danger zone, and under 1.0 means a company is simply not paying its bills.

A high coverage ratio may provide some contrary insight. It may reflect a conservative management style, not prone to borrowing money. It may suggest a nervous leadership, fearful of debt, with higher requirements for a financial buffer. But how safe is too safe? Should Hypothetical Corporation, with its coverage ratios above 6, try to boost its earnings through leverage? Or should it enjoy its current financial position while keeping a watchful eye on the slightly declining ratios it's been experiencing? These are judgment calls based on management philosophy and market trends. A company that incurs debt arbitrarily or unnecessarily may damage its coverage ratio and point itself toward eventual default while a company that neglects growth opportunities by playing it too safe may lose its competitive edge.

9.9. Price-to-Book Ratio

The price-to-book ratio quantifies a corporation's financial health by comparing the price of one share of stock on the stock market to the book value of that share. Investors see this ratio as a method for determining whether a stock is undervalued or overpriced. For attorneys, accountants, managers, and financial advisers, however, the price-to-book ratio is another key indicator of a company heading into a downward spiral or of a company enjoying unusual success.

The formula for the price-to-book ratio (P/B) is:

$$P/B = \frac{\text{Price}}{\text{Book Value Per Share}}$$

For a review of Book Value per Share, see Section 5.10 above.

Let's say that financial records and disclosures produced in pretrial discovery reveal the following information about a particular company:

Assets:	$500,000,000
Liabilities:	$300,000,000
Current Stock Price	$8 per share
Outstanding Shares of Stock:	50,000,000

The P/B ratio begins by calculating the book value of the company. Book value equals assets minus liabilities ($500,000 – $300,000); thus, BV = $200,000. Then, we must determine book value per share (BVPS). $\text{BVPS} = \frac{\text{BV}}{\text{Shares of Common Stock Outstanding}}$ which is another way of saying that it's equal to the common shareholder's equity divided by the number of shares of common stock outstanding. Here there are 50,000 outstanding shares; therefore, BVPS equals $200,000 divided by 50,000, or 4. So the book value per share is $4. To determine the P/B ratio, we simply divide the actual current market price of the stock ($8) by the BVPS ($4), and we discover that the ratio is 2. In effect, the stock is selling for twice its book value.

How do we interpret this ratio? A higher P/B ratio may mean that a company is doing well, and its stock is competitively priced. Yet a higher ratio may also reflect a trend in a particularly popular industry or mirror a larger macroeconomic pattern. If the ratio is too high, it may simply mean the stock is overpriced. In essence, you'd be overpaying for the assets that would remain if the company suddenly went bankrupt. A lower P/B ratio may mean that a company is performing poorly, and its stock is cheap because there are fundamental problems with the company. On the other hand, a lower P/B ratio may be viewed by some investors as an undervalued stock and therefore a great bargain.

The P/B ratio is inherently flawed in cases in which companies fail to show all of their real value on their books. Companies built around unique performers or technical specialists may not be able to assess fully the value of their human capital. The value of patents, copyrights, licenses, and other intangibles is also potentially significant but generally not included in book value. Companies that inflate their book values, legally or otherwise, also produce technically inaccurate P/B figures. So, while the P/B ratio is an effective valuation technique and a useful metric for appraising the progress of a company, it is not fail-safe and should only be used in conjunction with other valid ratios and formulas.

9.10. Inventory Turnover

Another way to evaluate whether a company is failing or succeeding in the marketplace is to inquire how quickly it turns over its inventory. If the age of the inventory is high—meaning that its raw products, works in progress, and completed products remain sitting on warehouse shelves—then the company is tying up too much cash in its inventory. It may be burdened by excess storage costs, and depending on the product, older inventory can expire and become unmarketable.

The inventory turnover ratio is calculated by determining the cost of goods sold (COGS) and dividing that figure by the total value of the inventory. The basic formula is:

$$\text{IT} = \frac{\text{COGS}}{\text{I}}$$

IT = Inventory turnover
COGS = Cost of goods sold
I = Inventory

The cost of goods sold is a common accounting entry that appears on a company's income statement and in its annual report. It can also be calculated by determining the value of all merchandise in inventory at the beginning of an accounting period plus the net purchases of merchandise made by the company minus the value of all merchandise on the end date of the accounting period. If a company started with $250,000 in merchandise and purchased another $350,000 in merchandise, and at the end of the accounting period had $200,000 in merchandise remaining, the cost of goods sold would be calculated as follows:

$$\$250{,}000 + \$350{,}000 - \$200{,}000 = \$400{,}000$$

Inventory turnover could then be easily calculated:

$$IT = \frac{COGS}{I}$$

$$IT = \frac{\$400{,}000}{\$200{,}000}$$

$$IT = 2$$

Note: In this calculation, we used the period-end inventory of $200,000 as the denominator. You may wish to use an average inventory figure for the accounting period if this would be a more representative figure.

In the example above, the inventory turnover ratio is 2, meaning that inventory will turn over twice a year. That is, the company will sell its inventory twice a year. The inventory turnover can also be divided into $\frac{365}{2}$ days to determine the number of days of inventory. In this case, the ratio of tells us that we have an IT ratio equal to 182½ days of inventory in stock.

Let's try the IT ratio on some more complicated figures. ABC Manufacturing Company reports a cost of goods sold at $5,080,172. Its total inventory is reported at $906,000. What is the number of days of inventory on hand at ABC Manufacturing Company?

$$IT = \frac{COGS}{I}$$

$$IT = \frac{\$5{,}080{,}172}{\$906{,}000}$$

$$IT = 5.6$$

Therefore, inventory turns over almost six times a year. Now let's determine the number of days of inventory on hand.

$$\frac{365}{5.6} = 65.18$$

So, we can say that there are approximately 65 days of inventory on hand.

If we were comparing ABC Manufacturing's IT ratio of 5.6 with a competitor's ratio of 3.5, we would conclude that ABC is performing better. A higher inventory turnover indicates that a company's products are selling well. A higher IT ratio will produce a lower number of inventory days on hand. So, if we knew that a competitor turns over its inventory once every 104 days, we would know immediately that ABC is performing better. If all we knew were that the competitor held its inventory for 104 days, we could calculate its IT ratio as approximately 3.5 by tweaking the formula algebraically:

$$\frac{365}{X} = 104 \qquad \text{[X = the competitor's unknown IT ratio]}$$

Multiply both sides by X

$$365 = 104(X)$$

Divide both sides by 104

$$\frac{365}{104} = X$$

$$X = 3.5$$

In addition to comparing one company with another, the IT ratio is a helpful measure of a company's management and risk. If a company's warehouses are filled for lengthy periods of time and its IT ratio is low, it may be a reflection of diminishing sales or sloppy inventory management. Creditors may see such a company as a poor credit risk insofar as inventory is difficult to liquidate. Attorneys, financial experts, and other advisors would be well-guided to question a business with low IT ratios before approving contractual relationships with the firm, or before expecting that it would be capable of generating the cash necessary to pay a damages award or a structured payout arrangement.

9.11. Accounts Receivable Turnover

Another informative ratio is the accounts receivable turnover ratio (ART). How quickly does the company obtain payment on its invoices?

A high turnover of accounts receivable means that more cash is pouring into the company at faster speeds; thus, the company is in a strong position to fund its own activities and pay its current obligations. As a liquidity measurement, the accounts receivable turnover ratio also pinpoints those companies with existing or potential cash-flow problems and identifies potentially bad credit risks.

The formula is:

$$\text{ART} = \frac{\text{Annual credit sales}}{\text{Average accounts receivable}}$$

Let's consider the accounts receivable of a fictitious law firm, Smith and Jones, LLC. The firm reports annual billings (sales) of \$3.9 million. Its average accounts receivable is \$1.9 million. The simple ART ratio for Smith and Jones is 2.05. As with the inventory turnover ratio, we can calculate the number of days in a year that the firm carries its accounts receivable before payment by dividing the ART into 365:

$$\frac{365}{\text{ART}} = \text{Number of days that accounts receivable remain open and unpaid.}$$

$$\frac{365}{2.05} = 178.05$$

Thus, Smith and Jones is carrying its unpaid accounts receivable on its books for about 178 days. Depending on the firm's expectations and the nature of its work and billing practices, it may wish to rethink the level to which it extends credit to its clients before collecting payment.

What if we were examining a corporate party with the turnover rates and collection periods depicted in the table below? What conclusions would you draw?

YEAR	Annual Credit Sales	Average Accounts Receivable	Accounts Receivable Turnover	Collection Period (in days)
2009	\$4,000,000	\$2,135,800	1.87	195
2010	\$4,500,000	\$2,860,050	1.57	232
2011	\$5,000,000	\$3,244,444	1.54	237

It appears that despite an increase in credit sales, the ART ratio is declining each year, from 1.87 to 1.54. As a result of shrinking turnover rates, the collection period is lengthening year-by-year. In 2009, it took the corporation 195 days, on average, to collect its receivables; in 2011, it took 42 days longer. The trend foreshadows an increasing cash-flow problem for the corporation, and it tells us that, without some significant policy changes or protective contractual provisions, this party may not be able to generate cash fast enough in the future.

9.12. Accounts Payable Turnover

The accounts payable turnover ratio (APT) offers another quick snapshot of a company's liquidity. It indicates the number of times per year that a company's purchases are being paid off. To obtain the APT ratio, divide the total purchases made by the company in a given year by the total balance of accounts payable at the end of the year. The formula is:

$$\text{APT} = \frac{\text{Total purchases}}{\text{Total accounts payable}}$$

If Big Business, Inc. ended the year with unpaid bills of \$1.2 million, and made purchases during the year totaling \$7.4 million, we can easily calculate the APT:

$$\text{APT} = \frac{\$7{,}400{,}000}{\$1{,}200{,}000} = 6.17$$

With an APT of 6.17, we can say that Big Business, Inc. pays off its accounts payable approximately six times per year. We can then conclude that its payoff period, on the average, is 59 days:

$$\frac{365}{6.17} = 59.16$$

Another formula for calculating the payoff period is the days-to-payoff (DTP) ratio:

$$\text{DTP} = \frac{\text{Accounts Payable}}{\text{Purchases/365}}$$

First, we divide our annual amount of purchases by 365 to obtain the denominator. Then we divide that number into the total amount of accounts payable.

$$\text{DTP} = \frac{\$1{,}200{,}000}{\$7{,}400{,}000/365}$$

$$\text{DTP} = \frac{\$7{,}400{,}000}{\$1{,}200{,}000}$$

$$\text{DTP} = 59.19$$

Again, we see that the payoff period is approximately 59 days.

The APT and DTP ratios reveal how long it generally takes a company to pay its vendors or suppliers, and in so doing, provides a valuable glimpse of the company's financial position. Like the other turnover ratios we've explored, the accounts payable ratios provide additional metrics for comparing several businesses with each other, or for tracking a single company on a trend line to determine if its liquidity levels are improving or declining.

9.13. Current Asset Turnover

The current asset turnover ratio (CAT) answers this question: How much money is being generated in sales for every dollar's worth of assets? It is calculated simply by dividing the revenue generated from sales by the value of the firm's assets. The formula is:

$$\text{CAT} = \frac{\text{Revenue}}{\text{Assets}}$$

Thus, if The Firm, Inc. generates annual sales of $5 million on total assets of $10 million, its current asset turnover would be 0.5. Each dollar invested in The Firm's assets would produce only 50 cents in sales. If, however, The Firm generated sales revenues of $30 million on the same assets, its CAT would be 3.0. It would then be earning $3 in sales for every dollar invested in its assets. As we can see, the greater the asset turnover, the more efficiently the company is using its assets.

The CAT ratio provides an outlook on a company's productivity and efficiency. A company with a low CAT may have idle or obsolete equipment, generating no return. It may have personnel, systems, or production policies that are ineffective. Such a company perhaps should modify its production protocols, sell its nonproductive assets, or increase its sales. On the other hand, a firm with high turnover rates may be operating at maximum efficiency and optimal levels of asset utilization.

9.14. Current Ratio

The current ratio (not to be confused with the current asset turnover ratio) is a liquidity measurement that targets short-term bill-paying ability. The ratio asks the question: how much are the company's assets worth, in terms of cash, inventory, and receivables, as compared against its liabilities? It is a *current* ratio because it looks at the current state of affairs at the company.

The formula is $\dfrac{\text{Current Assets}}{\text{Current Liabilities}}$.

So, for example, if the company had current assets of \$12 million and current liabilities of \$4 million, its current ratio of assets to liabilities would be 3 to 1. Presumably, with a current ratio of 3 to 1, the company could pay back its current debt on a timely basis. But what if the company's liabilities were actually \$14 million? Then, the current ratio would be 0.8571 to 1. In other words, in such a scenario, the company would have only about 86 cents worth of assets to cover every dollar of liabilities.

The minimum level of acceptable liquidity is 1 to 1, in which the level of current assets essentially equals the level of current liabilities. Higher ratios not only indicate that the company is more liquid and cash-infused, but they suggest that the company is more efficient, better managed, and more cost conscious.

Because the current ratio examines assets and liabilities at any given moment in time, it should not be used to cast a longer-range image about the company. It may be useful to calculate current ratios at various junctures over a timeline to see how well the company has met its current obligations over time. The current ratio is only useful if full discovery is made with respect to the current assets and the current liabilities.

For example, a company may understate its current assets if it has access to a significant line of credit but has not drawn down any cash from that credit line. Such a company could flourish with a 1 to 1 ratio, knowing that it had access to additional cash to pay current liabilities. The current ratio can be skewed by large inventories too. If a company's current assets include a major inventory component, then the asset numerator will be falsely inflated because inventories are difficult to liquidate in the short term. As such, the current ratio should be used together with the inventory turnover ratio to obtain a clearer picture of the company's current assets.

9.15. Capitalization Rate

The capitalization rate, often abbreviated as the "cap rate," is used to measure an investor's potential return on investment. Used primarily in real estate transactions, the cap rate can be adjusted to a number of different decision-making scenarios. The general cap rate formula divides annual income by market value.

$$\text{Cap Rate} = \frac{\text{Annual Income}}{\text{Market Value}}$$

So, if an investor buys a property for \$500,000 that will generate \$50,000 per year in income, the ratio is $\frac{\$50{,}000}{\$500{,}000}$ which equals 10%. The ratio could also be described as follows:

$$\text{Cap Rate} = \frac{\text{Net Operating Income}}{\text{Purchase Price}}$$

In this variation of the ratio, income is more accurately described as being the actual net yearly operating income, and the market value is more accurately described as the purchase price. If the investor were purchasing an apartment complex and calculating income based on rents paid on 10 apartment units, the investor would want to subtract costs and adjustments to arrive at a net operating income before calculating the cap rate.

The cap rate is a handy ratio for calculating the return on investment, but it is not foolproof. If an investor purchased the property described above, and the value of that property doubled a few years later, the cap rate would change based on the increased market value. With an enhanced market value of \$1 million, the cap rate would be $\frac{\$50{,}000}{\$1{,}000{,}000}$ or 5%. The property would have a lower cap rate and therefore be less desirable as an investment. After all, if the property doubled in value to \$1 million, the investor would do better to sell the property.

Knowing the cap rate formula can help one estimate the value of a property or an investment. In the example above, if we knew the cap rate for a property (or a kind of property), and if we knew the net operating income, we could simply divide the income by the cap rate to estimate the value of the property.

$$\text{Estimate value} = \frac{\text{Net operating income}}{\text{Cap Rate}} = \frac{\$50{,}000}{0.05} = \$1{,}000{,}000$$

The 5% cap rate is represented above as 0.05.

By tweaking the cap rate formula, we can say that a property generating $50,000 in net income with a 5% cap rate is worth $1 million.

The cap rate can also be shifted to the stock market. It can be characterized as the income or earnings generated from a share of stock divided by the market price for that share of stock. It is, in essence, the reverse of the price to earnings ratio (P/E), displayed as an earnings to price ratio (E/P):

$\text{Cap rate} = \frac{\text{EPS}}{\text{P}}$ where the EPS is divided by the price per share.

So, if a share of stock has an EPS of $3.50 but is selling on the stock market for $175, its cap rate is $\frac{\$175}{\$3.50}$ which equals 2%. The investor might, in such a circumstance, find the price to be too high and the cap rate to be too low.

The cap rate can be manipulated in a variety of decision-making scenarios whenever one wishes to measure earnings relative to price.

9.16. Benefit-Cost Ratio

The benefit-cost ratio (BCR) is a shortcut to determine if a project or a decision is worthy of pursuit. The question always is whether the benefits of a project or a decision outweigh the costs. In other words, the benefits minus the costs must produce some result greater than zero to justify undertaking the project. We can characterize the decision rule as such:

If $B - C > 0$, then accept the project or vote in favor of the decision.

B = Benefits
C = Cost

In the form of a ratio, the same decision rule looks like this:

If $\frac{B}{C} > 1$, then accept the project or vote in favor of the decision.

Consider, for example, an offer to settle an employee's wrongful termination case for $200,000 in exchange for an agreement that the employee will not seek reinstatement with the employer, nor will he seek employment with a competitor for a two-year period. Let's assume that the cost of not returning to the job and of abiding by the two-year restrictive covenant would be $95,000 per year in earnings and benefits for each of the two years. The employee's total cost for accepting this settlement would be $190,000. His benefit, however, is $200,000. Applying the B/C ratio produces a result of 1.05. Because the result is greater than 1, we can conclude that the employee should accept the settlement.

Of course, a B/C ratio is only as valid as the information used to measure the benefit or the cost. In the example above, we might have quantified the cost to the employee of his long-term losses by not maintaining a continuity of employment. There may have been other benefits the employee enjoyed on the job, which have not been accounted for, and which are now lost. In addition, had we deducted the attorney's legal fee for assisting the employee in securing the settlement, the benefit to the employee would have been lower than $200,000. In fact, to make our analysis even more complete, we would want to express all benefits and costs in present values.

Another version of the B/C ratio attempts to expand on the conventional ratio by considering net benefits and net costs and essentially placing all cash flows in the numerator except for the initial cost. The modified B/C ratio looks like this:

$$\frac{B}{C} = \frac{(B - D) - (C - R)}{I}$$

B = Benefits
C = Costs
D = Disbenefits
C = Operation and maintenance costs
R = Receipts
I = Initial investment

In this expanded version of the ratio, we first try to determine net benefits by subtracting so-called "disbenefits" which refer to negative results or drawbacks that can be quantified. For this, we calculate B-D.

Then we attempt to establish the net costs, not including the initial investment (I). For this, we calculate C-R. Thus, the numerator becomes the difference between the net benefits and the net costs. We then divide that figure by the cost of the initial investment.

Let's assume that a new Internet service will require an initial investment of \$50 million. Annual maintenance and operation costs will total \$25 million. Annual revenue to be generated by the new service is estimated at \$100 million. Activating the new service will cost the company \$5 million in lost revenues from the cancellation of an outdated web-based program. Assume that there are no current receipts. Is the new Internet venture worth pursuing?

$$\frac{B}{C} = \frac{(B - D) - (C - R)}{I}$$

$$\frac{B}{C} = \frac{(\$100{,}000{,}0000 - \$5{,}000{,}000) - (\$25{,}000 - 0)}{\$50{,}000{,}000}$$

$$\frac{B}{C} = \frac{\$95{,}000{,}000 - \$25{,}000{,}000}{\$50{,}000{,}000} = \frac{\$70{,}000{,}000}{\$50{,}000{,}000}$$

$$\frac{B}{C} = 1.4$$

The modified benefit-cost ratio, having produced a result greater than 1, reveals that the Internet service is, indeed, worth pursuing. A word of caution: The example provided above has been simplified in order to explain the modified B/C ratio easily. In a complex venture such as the formation of a new Internet service, many more factors would be taken into consideration to determine the actual benefits, disbenefits, costs, and initial investments. For example, it may be estimated that the Internet service would be sold at a certain future date for an anticipated price. The maintenance and operating expenses would recur annually and would have to be projected over time. Ultimately, too, we would want to consider the present value of the figures in question.

Chapter 10

Handy Numerical Rules

10.1. Rule of 72

The Rule of 72 is a convenient rule of thumb for calculating how long it will take to double money invested in a certain project, decision, or purchase. It does not provide a scientifically perfect answer, but rather an estimate, in years, of the doubling time of an investment. The formula is $\frac{72}{r}$ where r equals a fixed rate of return. So, for example, if you invested \$1,000 at a 4% rate of return, how many years would it take to double the investment? The approximate answer is $\frac{72}{4}$ which equals 18. In other words, you could turn \$1,000 into \$2,000, if invested at 4%, in approximately 18 years. (Had you used a financial calculator, you would have determined that you could have doubled your \$1,000 investment at 4% in exactly 17.673 years). For the best accuracy, the Rule of 72 should be used for interest rates ranging from 6% to 10%.

Knowing the Rule of 72 provides an easy ratio for calculating how long it could take a business client to double a capital investment or how long it might take a spouse in a divorce case to reach a 100% return on a certain fund of money. Although it is not a substitute for a future value calculation or other more technical determinations, the Rule of 72 can provide quick estimates for negotiating purposes in a wide variety of case scenarios.

Tripling and Quadrupling

Applying the same mathematical logic that underlies the Rule of 72, we can establish two additional related rules: the Rule of 114 and the

Rule of 144. The Rule of 114 tells us how long it would take to triple an investment of money at a particular rate of return. The Rule of 144 tells us how long it would take to quadruple the investment. Let's try a few examples:

Your client asks how long it would take to double an investment of $100,000, to triple it, and to quadruple it, if he could obtain an 8% rate of return?

To double it, apply $\frac{72}{r}$. The answer is $\frac{72}{8}$ or effectively nine years to double the money.

To triple it, apply $\frac{114}{r}$. The answer is $\frac{114}{8}$ or 14.25 years to triple the money.

To quadruple it, apply $\frac{144}{r}$. The answer is $\frac{144}{8}$ or 18 years to quadruple the money.

So, you could estimate for your client that his $100,000 fund, invested at 8%, would double in nine years, triple in five years and three months thereafter, and quadruple in less than four more years.

The various rules can also be used to compare rates of return over time. For example, applying the Rule of 144, with an 8% rate of return, we see that it would take 18 years to quadruple one's investment. What interest rate would reduce the timeline to approximately 12 years? Apply some simple algebra: $\frac{144}{r} = 12$. (In this instance, we already know the number of years, 12. What we don't know is the rate of return, r). To solve for r, multiply both sides by r. Therefore, 144 = 12r. Then, divide both sides by 12. So, r = 12. A rate of 12% would thus be necessary to quadruple the $100,000 investment in 12 years.

10.2. Rule of 70

The Rule of 70 is a variation of the Rule of 72 and works the same way. In order to determine how long it will take to double an investment, simply divide the rate of return into 70. Using 70 as a numerator will produce somewhat more accurate results than the Rule of 72 when interest is compounded daily.

Choosing between the Rule of 72 and the Rule of 70 may depend on simple convenience when making rule-of-thumb estimates without the benefit of a financial calculator. The Rule of 72 will produce easy-to-calculate results when the interest rate matches one of the small divisors (numbers that divide easily into 72 as whole numbers). These include 1, 2, 3, 4, 6, 8, 9, and 12. So, for example, if the interest rate is 9%, the Rule of 72 produces the quickest answer—it will take eight years for any given investment to double. The Rule of 70 is the better choice, however, when the interest rate matches one of the divisors for the number 70 (1, 5, 7, 10, and 14). A $1,000 investment with a 7% rate of return would take about 10 years to double, a calculation quickly made with the Rule of 70 (as opposed to the Rule of 72).

One of the virtues of these rules is that the amount of money in question is irrelevant to the ratio. An investment of $957,632.01 at 7% would still take about 10 years to double based on the Rule of 70, regardless of the complexity of the exact amount of funds being invested.

10.3. Rule of 69.3

Probably the best numerator for estimating the time to double an investment is the Rule of 69.3. While it is not easy to identify divisors that easily divide into 69.3, the Rule of 69.3 is mathematically the most accurate figure, especially in cases of daily compounding.

In fact, to achieve the best estimate under the Rule of 69.3, when using high interest rates and daily compounding, the following formula can be used:

$$\frac{69.3147 + r/3}{r}$$

By producing the somewhat larger numerator, this formula adjusts the accuracy level of the Rule of 69.3 when dealing with larger interest rates. For example, if an investment of $1,000 were made at a 21% rate of return, the formula would look like this:

$$\frac{69.3147 + 7}{21}$$

This yields a result of 3.63403, meaning that it would take slightly longer than 3½ years to double the $1,000 investment at 21% using the adjusted Rule of 69.3.

Of course, you could simplify the ratio for the Rule of 69.3 as $\frac{69.3}{21}$ which equals 3.3, but it is unlikely that you would use the Rule of 69.3

unless you were calculating it by hand or with a calculator. If you're going to that effort, then you ought to use the slightly longer enhanced formula of $\frac{69.3147 + r/3}{r}$ which provides the most mathematically accurate estimate among the three rules. In our example above, the enhanced formula yields 3.63403 or approximately 3.6 years to double the $1,000 investment, compared to the slight underestimation of 3.3 years provided by the unenhanced formula.

Double Check Your Math

Because the Rule of 69.3, as well as the Rule of 72 and the Rule of 70, are based on compound interest rates, we can use a compound interest formula to double check our math. The formula is total balance = P x $(1 + i)^n$ where P is the principal, i is the interest, and n is the number of years. In the example above, we learned that an investment of $1,000 made at 21% takes about 3.6 years to double, applying the Rule of 69.3. To double check our calculation under the rule, we can apply the compound interest formula to see if our result equals twice our investment (or $2,000).

$$\text{Total Balance} = P \times (1 + i)^n$$
$$\text{Total Balance} = \$1{,}000 \times (1.21)^{3.6}$$

Our principal investment is $1,000. Our interest rate is 21%. The number of years produced by the Rule of 69.3 is approximately 3.6. In fact, if we want to be even more exact, let's replace the exponent with the extended number of years produced by our calculations in the example above: 3.63403.

$$\text{Total Balance} = \$1{,}000 \times (1.21)^{3.63403}$$
$$\text{Total Balance} = \$1{,}000 \times 1.99915$$
$$\text{Total Balance} = \$1{,}999.15$$

According to the compound interest formula, we can invest $1,000 at 21% interest for 3.63403 years and generate $1,999.15 (just about doubling our money). So, the Rule of 69.3 works as a good rule of thumb for estimating the doubling time for an investment.

10.4. Rule of 78

The Rule of 78—which has nothing to do with doubling or tripling one's money—is a shortcut for determining what portion of a loan repayment will be assigned to principal and what portion will be assigned to interest. The rule can be used to develop amortization schedules, and is particularly popular among bankers and lenders. The Rule of 78 operates on the policy that a borrower of money pays a greater amount of interest at the beginning of his payback period. As time moves forward, the borrower pays a decreasing amount of interest and an increasing amount of principal. The final payment on the loan would be almost entirely principal. In theory, the borrower pays more interest during the early years of his payback term because he enjoys the use of more of the borrowed funds during those years.

The rule is based on the sum of the digits of each month of the year. Let's say that January is Month 1, February is Month 2, and so forth. If we were to add up all of the numbers of each month from January to December, we would be adding 1 + 2 + 3 . . . until 12. The equation would look like this:

$$1 + 2 + 3 + 4 + 5 + 6 + 7 + 8 + 9 + 10 + 11 + 12 = 78$$

As you can see, 78 is the sum of all of the numbers of the months in a 12-month period. To activate the Rule of 78, we then must begin to think of interest for each month as being a fraction based on 78 points. For example, if Frank borrowed $5,000 in January, he would pay $\frac{12}{78}$ of the interest in his first payment. Frank would then pay $\frac{11}{78}$ in his second payment, $\frac{10}{78}$ in his third payment, and so forth. This method effectively reduces the amount of interest paid each month as the balance of the loan decreases correspondingly.

Let's try an example. Assume that Frank borrows $5,000 for 12 months. The annual interest rate is 5%. So, we apply the interest formula: I = P x i x n, where I = interest, P = principal, i = interest rate and n = number of months or years. (For a further discussion of interest calculations, see Section 6.1 above). In this case, the principal of $5,000 multiplied by the annual interest rate of 0.05 and multiplied by a time period of one year yields an annual interest payment of $250. If Frank is going to pay $250 in interest on his $5,000 loan, can we then assume that he would pay approximately $20.83 in interest per month ($250 ÷ 12 = $20.83)? No. Under the Rule of 78, Frank would pay a greater share of interest during the early part of his payback period.

Because Frank has committed to pay $250 in interest on his $5,000 loan, he has agreed to repay a total of $5,250. Let's assume that Frank will make equal monthly payments of principal and interest, which is customary for residential mortgage loans, car loans, and other consumer loans. On a monthly basis, Frank would be paying $437.50 ($5,250 ÷ 12 = $437.50), but how much of it would be principal and how much of it would be interest each month over the 12-month period?

Here is how the Rule of 78 amortizes the loan:

Month	**Fraction** (Rule of 78)	**Percentage** (Based on the fraction)	**Monthly Payment** (Based on annual amount of $5,250)	**Interest** (Percentage times total interest payment of $250)	**Principal**
1	12/78	15.39%	$437.50	$38.48	$399.02
2	11/78	14.10%	$437.50	$35.25	$402.25
3	10/78	12.82%	$437.50	$32.05	$405.45
4	9/78	11.54%	$437.50	$28.85	$408.65
5	8/78	10.26%	$437.50	$25.65	$411.85
6	7/78	8.97%	$437.50	$22.43	$415.07
7	6/78	7.69%	$437.50	$19.23	$418.27
8	5/78	6.41%	$437.50	$16.02	$421.48
9	4/78	5.13%	$437.50	$12.82	$424.68
10	3/78	3.85%	$437.50	$ 9.62	$427.88
11	2/78	2.56%	$437.50	$ 6.40	$431.10
12	1/78	1.28%	$437.50	$ 3.20	$434.30
		TOTALS →	**$ 5,250**	**$ 250**	**$ 5,000**

Let's say that Frank wonders how much interest he might save by prepaying the loan after eight months. Had he laid out a full amortization table as above, Frank could simply total his interest payments for months 9, 10, 11, and 12. The sum of these four interest payments is $32.04; therefore, if Frank paid off the loan after the eighth month, he'd save $32.04 in interest.

However, it might not be easy or quick to amortize the loan in a table format, and in some cases, the loan could last much longer, and the table would be much larger. Applying the Rule of 78, however, we can use a formula that will assist us in answering Frank's question. The formula is: $\frac{n(n+1)}{2}$ where n equals the number of months. It is this very formula that gives us the Rule of 78 in the first place. When we plug 12 months into the formula, we get the following result:

$$\frac{n(n+1)}{2} = \frac{12(12+1)}{2} = \frac{12(13)}{2} = \frac{156}{2} = 78$$

Now, however, Frank wants to know if he'll save enough interest to justify paying off the loan four months early. The question is how much interest will Frank save for four months. The formula provides the answer:

$$\frac{n(n+1)}{2} = \frac{4(4+1)}{2} = \frac{4(5)}{2} = \frac{20}{2} = 10$$

This means that $\frac{10}{78}$ of the interest will be saved. This fraction $\frac{10}{78}$ is approximately 12.82% of $250, which equal about $32.05 in interest payments.

Should Frank pay off his loan early? It depends. After eight months, he would still owe $1,717.96 on the loan. He would save $31.05 in interest, but how would he invest his savings? Would he attempt to borrow funds elsewhere, at a lower interest rate? And if so, at what cost? The Rule of 78, and the formula above, will provide us with specific dollar amounts, but it will not answer all of these business decisions.

The same formula $\frac{n(n+1)}{2}$ can be applied to two-year and four-year loans. A 24-month loan would change the Rule of 78 to the Rule of 300:

$$\frac{n(n+1)}{2} = \frac{24(24+1)}{2} = \frac{24(25)}{2} = \frac{600}{2} = 300$$

A 48-month loan was change it to the Rule of 1176:

$$\frac{n(n+1)}{2} = \frac{48(48+1)}{2} = \frac{48(49)}{2} = \frac{2352}{2} = 1176$$

Were we to amortize a 48-month loan, the interest would be repaid at in month No. 1, in month No. 2, in month No. 3 and so on until the 48th month.

Chapter 11

Personal Injury and Wrongful Death Damages

Lost Earnings

11.1. Putting the Basic Formulas to Work

Before calculating lost earnings, an attorney will need to assess the seriousness of his personal injury or wrongful death case. In the case of a nonfatal injury, physicians, vocational rehabilitation specialists, functional capacity experts, life care planners, or other experts may be required to determine the victim's ability to return to work.

Ultimately, the attorney will want to know his client's earning capacity. He will want to know whether his client can return to the job, and if so, how soon and under what circumstances. Will the client ever be able to perform the same work he did before the accident? Will he ever be able to perform the work as long, as fast, or as productively as before?

A vocational expert may be able to make an *impairment rating* which essentially accounts for the skills, tasks, physical abilities, and mental processes that have been undermined or destroyed as a result of the personal injury sustained by the victim. An impairment rating does not automatically mean that a victim is unemployable, nor does the rating, expressed as a percentage, necessarily translate into a corresponding reduction in working abilities or earning capacity. One victim's injuries may completely prevent him from working at his occupation, while another's injuries may have little effect on the nature of the work performed. So, before putting the basic formulas to work, we will want to know how seriously injured the client is, and what impact, if any, the injuries will have on his ability to perform his work.

The basic formulas discussed in Chapter 4, the interest rate principles discussed in Chapter 5, and the probability formulas discussed in Chapter 6 can then be applied to the analysis of lost earnings. For example, in order to determine the value of future lost earnings for a client who is totally incapacitated and unable to return to work, we will need to establish a present value of the future loss. This process will involve discounting the future paychecks with a real interest rate.

If there is some debate as to whether a particular victim will return to the work force in the future, a probability calculation can then be superimposed on the analysis. One statistic discussed below, which is used to determine work-life expectancy, is based on the combined probability that a particular individual will be living, that he will be participating in the labor force, and that he will be actually employed.

Averaging earnings over a period of time may be necessary in cases in which projected earnings are variable and changing circumstances are unpredictable. Calculating the mean or median salary may be necessary in order to produce the basic information needed to apply other formulas. Measures of central tendency may also be useful in cases involving commission-based employees, as a method for determining their earnings history and their earnings patterns. The basic formulas thus provide a foundation for calculating employment losses credibly and logically without resorting to arbitrary settlement figures.

11.2. Future Earnings Loss

Before we can apply a formula to the loss of future earnings, we must conduct a thorough investigation to ascertain the earnings history of the personal injury victim and to evaluate his work life expectancy. If you represent the personal injury victim, you will want to conduct a comprehensive interview of your client, gathering all relevant earnings documentation such as pay stubs, W-2 forms, tax returns, and Social Security earnings reports. If you are defending the case, you will want to conduct pretrial discovery methodically to ascertain the actual projected earnings and to pin down the realistic work life of the plaintiff.

The general approach for determining how much earnings a personal injury victim will suffer in the future is based on the present value approach. We follow these four steps:

1. Establish the projected amount of future earnings.
2. Determine the work-life expectancy for the plaintiff.
3. Calculate the present value of each year's earnings (in today's dollars).
4. Add up the total of all of the present values of each year's earnings.

To appreciate the importance of these steps, let's first calculate future wage loss the wrong way. Assume that a plaintiff earned $100,000 a year and was injured so badly that he could not return to his job. Assume that he would have worked for another five years before retirement. Can we therefore assume that his future earnings loss equals five years of work expectancy times $100,000 per year for a total loss of $500,000? Not really.

Were we to calculate future wage loss as simply as the sum of all outstanding paychecks to the end of the plaintiff's work life, we would be overpaying the plaintiff. That's because for the plaintiff to actually recover $500,000, had he not been injured, he would have had to wait for five years. Applying the time value of money, however, we know that we must discount each annual paycheck of $100,000 to its present value. We essentially must determine what $100,000 next year will be worth today, if it were paid immediately. What would $100,000 due in three years or four years be worth, if it were paid immediately? In other words, how much should we discount this amount in exchange for being paid off immediately?

We apply the present value formula that we learned in Section 5.5. The formula is:

$$PV = \frac{FV}{(1 + i)^n}$$

The present value equals the future value divided by 1 plus the interest rate (or discount rate), raised to the n power (n equals the number of years in question). So, for example, if the plaintiff expected to earn $100,000 in two years, and if we applied a 4% discount rate to this amount, our formula would look like this:

$$PV = \frac{FV}{(1 + i)^n} = \frac{\$100{,}000}{(1 + .04)^2} = \frac{\$100{,}000}{1.0816} = \$92{,}455.62$$

Therefore, the plaintiff should demand $92,455.62 today as compensation for the $100,000 loss he will suffer in two years, assuming a 4% discount rate.

In our hypothetical case scenario, the plaintiff will lose five years of income. Therefore, we must discount each of those five years to the present value. For purposes of this hypothetical, we will assume that the discount rate remains constant at 4%. The table below shows the present value of each year's earnings and the total discounted wage loss for the five-year period.

YEAR	EARNINGS	PV Formula	Present Value
2011	\$100,000	$PV = \frac{\$100,000}{(1.04)}$	\$ 95,153.85
2012	\$100,000	$PV = \frac{\$100,000}{(1.04)^2}$	\$ 92,455.62
2013	\$100,000	$PV = \frac{\$100,000}{(1.04)^3}$	\$ 88,899.64
2014	\$100,000	$PV = \frac{\$100,000}{(1.04)^4}$	\$ 85,480.42
2015	\$100,000	$PV = \frac{\$100,000}{(1.04)^5}$	\$ 82,192.71
		TOTAL LOSS OF EARNINGS (2011-2015) →	**\$444,182.24**

The total of the present value of each year's earnings during the five-year period is \$444,182.24. Thus, we can see that by discounting the future wage loss to present value, the payout is considerably lower. If the plaintiff were to invest his settlement funds at 4%, however, he would earn back the difference over the five-year period.

The example above is based on a number of assumptions which, if challenged, could significantly alter the final total loss of earnings. For example:

- **Validity of Discount Rate.** The parties may disagree on the discount rate used. In this example, it was 4%, but is that the right number? After all, the rate is an educated guess as to what interest rate the discounted funds could draw if they were invested over the period of loss. Unless set by a court rule, a statute, or case law, the interest rate in a particular jurisdiction is likely to be based on prevailing economic conditions, and may be tied to a safe risk-free investment such as U.S. Treasury bills, notes, and bonds. The longer the period of loss, however, the more likely it is the discount rate will fluctuate. A plaintiff and a defendant might agree to set the discount rate at 4% for a five-year loss of earnings, but their confidence in that rate is likely to be weakened if the case involved a 20-year loss of earnings.

- **Changing Discount Rates.** If the parties were privy to information that suggested that the interest rate was going to climb or drop over the period of loss, they could apply more than one discount rate in the analysis above. For example, let's assume that the parties agreed that the discount rate should remain at 4% for the first three years, but increase to 5% in years 4 and 5. Then, in such a case, the PV formula would be modified to use a denominator of $(1.05)^4$ and $(1.05)^5$ for those two years, producing a somewhat altered final result.
- **Change in Earnings.** We have assumed in this case that the plaintiff will continue earning \$100,000 per year over the five-year period. What if, in fact, he was scheduled for a pay raise or bonus in alternating years? What if the employer was on the frontier of a major growth spurt or an expansion that would have yielded greater compensation to the plaintiff (for example, an upstart pharmaceutical company about to release its first FDA-approved antiobesity drug)? What if, in fact, the plaintiff was likely to have been promoted during the five-year period? Establishing these facts may prompt the plaintiff's attorney to argue that plaintiff's \$100,000 annual earnings should be increased by some percentage each year, or perhaps significantly increased in year 4, for example.
- **Net Discount Rate.** One school of thought is that discount rates are overstated because wages will generally continue to grow over time. The so-called net discount rate (NDR) attempts to adjust for this problem by expressing discount rates in terms of growth rates. The formula for the net discount rate is: $NDR = \frac{1 + i}{1 + g} - 1$, where g equals the growth rate and i equals the interest (or discount) rate. So, if the earnings were expected to grow at 6% and the discount rate was fixed at 4%, we would divide 1.06 by 1.04 and then subtract 1, yielding a net discount rate of 1.9%. *For a further discussion of net discount rates, see Section 11.*
- **Inflation and Other Economic Forces.** The real interest rate can be further adjusted for inflation and other economic events, if these events can be verified and reliably established. The effect of such adjustments is generally to lower the discount rate.

- **Work-Life Expectancy versus Corporate Reality.** It's easy to assume that a plaintiff would have worked for another five years until his retirement age. Such an assumption, however, includes no reference to the life of the employer or the condition of the employer's industry. Was the employer about to go out of business? Was the employer facing extraordinary competition from abroad that would have hastened its move toward plant shutdowns and mass layoffs? Was the employer about to merge with another firm and then reduce its combined labor force? These external factors may have some significant bearing on how the timeline is drawn for calculating a loss of earnings.

Attorneys can apply the PV formula above to estimate the discounted future loss of earnings. The additional considerations addressed above may provide useful leverage in the negotiating process, and may, in fact, provide a basis for challenging assumptions made by opponents and their experts in the courtroom. However, in cases in which large damage awards are sought, or in which lengthy periods of loss are under consideration, counsel should consult a financial expert before drawing specific financial conclusions or offering precise values into evidence.

The same advice holds true in cases in which the plaintiff's employer or the industry in which he works is undergoing rapid change, and in states and communities with growing or shrinking economies. Both microeconomic factors and macroeconomic events may thus be relevant to the final calculations. Experts are likely to be more keenly focused on these dynamics, as well as the appropriate interest rates, growth rates, and other factors that may partially offset the discount value.

11.3. Work Expectancy

The basic calculation for the loss of future earnings is inherently flawed if we assume that all employed injury victims would have worked until the conventional retirement age of 65, or until some other assumed retirement age. Government studies show that men and women historically have different work lives. Moreover, well-educated employees tend to have a longer work life than high school dropouts or those without a college education. Many people have breaks in employment—to pursue education, to have a baby—and some people retire early on disability or for other reasons.

Economists, actuaries, and researchers originally attempted to consider age, sex, race, education, and disability in developing accurate worklife expectancy tables. More recent research has attempted to factor in the effects of marriage, discouragement among job-seekers, and employment discrimination, among other factors.

The U.S. Bureau of Labor Statistics previously maintained work-life expectancy tables, several of which are reproduced below. Since the Bureau stopped publishing these tables, various economists have published updated and modified versions of the tables. These variations have come under critical attack by other economists and researchers and frequently are the subject of academic debate. Reliance on the Bureau's old tables is itself flawed because those tables were drawn from data in the 1970s. Therefore, attorneys would be wise to inquire as to how work-life expectancy is established in any calculation of loss of future earnings.

Another approach, known as the Life-Participation-Employment (LPE) approach, has been introduced to overcome some of the criticisms of the work-life expectancy tables. The LPE approach is based on three major variables: The probability that a particular individual will be living (L), that he will be participating (P) in the labor force, and that he will be actually employed (E). The product of these three probabilities, L x P x E, indicates an arguably more accurate statistic in determining work-life expectancy. To calculate work-life expectancy using the LPE approach, you'll need to determine three probabilities.

STEP ONE: Probability of Living

The best method for determining that a particular plaintiff will be living is to consult the Statistical Abstract of the United States, a national data book published by the U.S. Department of Commerce. The full statistical abstract can be purchased, in book form, from the National Technical Information Service (NTIS), a branch of the U.S. Department of Commerce (*http://www.ntis.gov/products/statabs.aspx* or 1-800-553-NTIS) or for a moderate price from a variety of online booksellers such as Amazon.com. State-specific statistical abstracts can be downloaded for free or for a small fee from state departments of finance, commerce, and/or business regulation.

The statistical abstract, published annually, provides a breakdown of life expectancy by age, race, and sex. Using the actuarial tables provided by the statistical abstract, one can determine how long a particular plaintiff, at a particular age, will remain living.

STEP TWO: Probability of Labor Force Participation

To determine the probability of participation in the labor force, the best source is the data collected by the U.S. Department of Labor's Bureau of Labor Statistics (BLS). The BLS definition of labor force includes the civilian population 16 years old and over. Excluded are persons under 16 years of age, all persons confined to institutions such as nursing homes and prisons, and persons on active duty in the Armed Forces. The labor force includes both the employed and the unemployed, but it does not include those who have no job and are not looking for one. Such persons who are not in the labor force may include those who attend school or are retired.

The BLS website provides scores of tables and statistics which can be very confusing to first-time visitors. (*http://www.bls.gov/ces/home.htm#tables*). To find statistics relating to labor force participation, attorneys should consider the tables relating to both the employed and the unemployed but not those characterized by BLS as "Persons Not in the Labor Force." Up-to-date monthly employment statistics are published at *http://www.bls.gov/opub/ee/home.htm*. State and regional breakdowns are also available. BLS economists are available by e-mail and phone to assist with specific labor force questions. (*http://www.bls.gov/cps/contact.htm* and 202. 691.6378).

STEP THREE: Probability of Employment

The Department of Labor's Bureau of Labor Statistics is also the best source for current data relating to the probability of employment. Monthly, quarterly, and annual employment statistics, displayed on a national level or broken down by state and metro areas, can be downloaded at no charge from the BLS database. (*http://www.bls.gov/data/#employment*).

By multiplying the probabilities of living (L), participating in the labor force (P), and being employed (E), we obtain the joint probability (LPE). Then by multiplying the LPE probability by the present value of each yearly wage loss (based on estimated gross earnings), we can calculate the more accurate earnings loss on an annual basis.

Let's try an example. Assume that a 40-year-old plaintiff has been killed by another's negligence. A complaint for damages has been filed, and settlement negotiations are under way. The plaintiff's attorney is demanding $900,000, based on the sum of the plaintiff's future earnings for 25 more years (until retirement at age 65), minus personal consumption and other adjustments discussed later in this section. The plaintiff's attorney believes the adjusted annual earnings would have been $36,000 for 25 years, which equals $900,000 in total losses. Yet, how do we know that the plaintiff would actually remain living and working for 25 more years? We don't know this, and therefore the defendant's attorney should argue that the more accurate formula for work-life expectancy requires the LPE approach.

Under the LPE approach, a probability percentage would be reached with respect to each of the 25 work years remaining. After multiplying the L probability by the P probability and the E probability, we would arrive at the joint LPE probability for each remaining year of the plaintiff's work life.

Assume, for example, that your math reveals that there would be a joint LPE probability of 0.9010 (or roughly 90% probability) of the plaintiff collecting $36,000 at age 40. This translates into an actual projected earnings loss of $32,436 for that year ($36,000 x 0.9010 = $32,436). In the following year, the LPE probability is 0.8999 (or roughly 89.9%), resulting in projected earnings loss of $32,396 at age 41.

Of course, the probability of living, being in the labor force, and actually working would have continued to decline as the plaintiff aged. Thus, for example, we might have discovered that at age 64, the LPE probability was 0.1504 (or roughly 15%), reducing the plaintiff's projected earnings for that year to merely $5,414.40. By adding up each of the 25 years of projected earnings after applying the LPE probabilities, the defendant's attorney might find that the forecast for lost wages is as much as $200,000 less than the plaintiff is asking for.

The probabilities that underlie the LPE figure take into consideration that some workers are healthy; others are not. Some are smokers; some are overweight; some are employed in dangerous professions with high mortality and injury rates. A plaintiff representing a fit, healthy, nonsmoker employed in a stress-free, danger-free job could argue in favor of higher LPE probabilities, while a defense attorney assessing a plaintiff with numerous health risk factors could argue in favor of lower LPE probabilities.

SAMPLE WORK LIFE EXPECTANCY TABLES

Table A-6. Worklife expectancies for woman by schooling completed, 1979–80

(Average years remaining)

Age x	Life expectancy[1] $^{*}e^{*}_x$	Expectation of active life by schooling completed and current labor force status								
		Less than high school			High school to 14 years			15 years or more of schooling		
		Total $^{*}ea_x$	Currently active $^{a}ea_x$	Currently inactive $^{i}ea_x$	Total $^{*}ea_x$	Currently active $^{a}ea_x$	Currently inactive $^{i}ea_x$	Total $^{*}ea_x$	Currently active $^{a}ea_x$	Currently inactive $^{i}ea_x$
	(1)	(2)	(3)	(4)	(5)	(6)	(7)	(8)	(9)	(10)
16	62.9	22.1	22.8	21.5	—	—	—	—	—	—
17	61.9	21.6	22.3	20.9	—	—	—	—	—	—
18	61.0	21.1	21.9	20.4	28.9	29.6	27.9	—	—	—
19	60.0	20.7	21.5	19.9	28.3	29.0	27.3	—	—	—
20	59.1	20.2	21.1	19.4	27.7	28.4	26.5	31.6	32.2	30.3
21	58.1	19.7	20.6	18.9	27.0	27.8	25.8	30.9	31.4	29.6
22	57.1	19.3	20.2	18.4	26.4	27.2	25.1	30.1	30.7	28.9
23	56.2	18.8	19.8	17.9	25.7	26.5	24.4	29.4	30.0	26.1
24	65.2	18.4	19.4	17.4	25.1	25.9	23.7	28.7	29.3	27.3
25	54.2	17.9	18.9	17.0	24.4	25.3	23.0	27.9	28.6	26.4
26	53.3	17.4	18.5	16.5	23.8	24.7	22.3	27.2	27.9	25.6
27	52.3	17.0	18.1	16.0	23.2	24.1	21.6	26.5	27.2	24.8
28	51.3	16.5	17.7	15.5	22.5	23.5	21.0	25.7	26.5	24.0
29	50.4	16.1	17.2	15.0	21.9	22.8	20.3	25.0	25.9	23.2
30	49.4	15.6	16.8	14.5	21.3	22.3	19.6	24.3	25.2	22.4
31	48.4	15.1	16.4	14.0	20.6	21.7	19.0	23.6	24.5	21.7
32	47.5	14.7	16.0	13.4	20.0	21.1	18.3	22.9	23.8	20.9
33	46.5	14.2	15.6	12.9	19.4	20.4	17.6	22.2	23.1	20.2
34	45.6	13.7	15.2	12.4	18.8	19.8	17.0	21.5	22.4	19.5
35	44.6	13.3	14.6	11.9	18.1	19.2	16.3	20.8	21.7	18.8
36	43.6	12.8	14.4	11.3	17.5	18.6	15.6	20.1	21.0	18.0
37	42.7	12.3	14.0	10.7	16.8	17.9	14.9	19.3	20.2	17.2
38	41.7	11.8	13.5	10.2	16.2	17.3	14.1	18.6	19.5	16.4
39	40.8	11.4	13.1	9.7	15.5	16.7	13.4	17.9	18.7	15.5
40	39.9	10.9	12.7	9.1	14.9	16.0	12.6	17.1	18.0	14.7
41	38.9	10.4	12.3	8.6	14.2	15.4	11.8	16.4	17.3	13.8
42	38.0	9.9	11.8	8.1	13.5	14.8	11.1	15.6	16.5	12.9
43	37.1	9.5	11.4	7.6	12.9	14.2	10.3	14.8	15.8	12.0
44	36.2	9.0	11.0	7.1	12.2	13.6	9.6	14.1	15.1	11.1
45	35.2	8.5	10.5	6.6	11.6	13.0	8.9	13.3	14.4	10.1
46	34.3	8.1	10.0	6.1	10.9	12.4	8.2	12.6	13.7	9.3
47	33.4	7.6	9.6	5.6	10.3	11.9	7.5	11.8	13.0	8.5
48	32.5	7.1	9.1	5.2	9.7	11.4	6.9	11.1	12.3	7.8
49	31.6	6.7	8.7	4.7	9.1	10.8	6.3	10.4	11.6	7.1
50	30.8	6.2	8.3	4.2	8.5	10.3	5.7	9.7	10.9	6.4
51	29.9	5.7	7.9	3.8	7.9	9.8	5.1	8.9	10.2	5.7
52	29.0	5.3	7.5	3.4	7.3	9.3	4.6	8.2	9.6	5.0
53	28.2	4.9	7.1	3.0	6.8	8.8	4.1	7.6	9.0	4.4
54	27.3	4.4	6.7	2.7	6.2	8.3	3.6	6.9	8.3	3.9
55	26.5	4.0	6.3	2.4	5.7	7.7	3.2	6.2	7.8	3.4
56	25.6	3.6	5.9	2.1	5.2	7.2	2.8	5.6	7.2	2.9
57	24.8	3.3	5.5	1.8	4.7	6.7	2.5	5.0	6.7	2.4
58	24.0	2.9	5.2	1.6	4.2	6.3	2.2	4.5	6.3	2.1
59	23.2	2.6	4.9	1.4	3.8	5.8	1.9	3.9	5.8	1.8
60	22.4	2.3	4.6	1.3	3.3	5.4	1.7	3.5	5.4	1.6
61	21.6	2.1	4.3	1.1	2.9	5.0	1.5	3.0	5.1	1.4
62	20.8	1.8	4.1	1.0	2.6	4.7	1.3	2.6	4.8	1.2
63	20.1	1.6	3.9	.9	2.3	4.4	1.1	2.3	4.6	1.0
64	19.3	1.4	3.7	.8	2.0	4.2	1.0	2.0	4.3	.9
65	18.5	1.2	3.5	.6	1.8	4.0	.9	1.8	4.1	.8
66	17.8	1.1	3.3	.6	1.6	3.8	.7	1.6	4.0	.7
67	17.1	1.0	3.1	.5	1.4	3.7	.6	1.4	3.8	.6
66	16.4	.8	3.0	.4	1.2	3.5	.5	1.2	3.7	.5
69	15.6	.7	2.9	.3	1.1	3.4	.4	1.1	3.6	.4
70	14.9	.6	2.7	.2	1.0	3.2	.3	1.0	3.5	.3
71	14.3	.5	2.5	.2	.9	3.0	.3	.9	3.3	.3
72	13.8	.5	2.3	.1	.7	2.8	.2	.8	3.0	.2
73	13.0	.4	2.0	.1	.7	2.5	.1	.7	2.7	.1
74	12.3	.3	1.7	.0	.6	2.1	.1	.6	2.3	.1
75	11.7	.2	1.2	.0	.5	1.5	.0	.5	1.6	.0

[1]Mortality rates used are those of the general female population.

Table A-2. Life and worklife expectancies for men by race, 1979–80
(Average years remaining)

Age	White Men				Black and other men			
		Expectation of active life by Labor force status				Expectation of active life by Labor force status		
Age x	Life expectancy[1] $*e*_x$	Total $*ea_x$	Currently active $^{a}ea_x$	Currently inactive $^{i}ea_x$	Life expectancy[1] $*e*_x$	Total $*ea_x$	Currently active $^{a}ea_x$	Currently inactive $^{i}ea_x$
	(1)	(2)	(3)	(40	(5)	(6)	(7)	(8)
16	56.1	39.9	40.6	39.1	51.4	33.6	34.3	33.2
17	55.2	39.4	40.0	38.4	50.4	33.2	33.9	32.7
18	54.3	38.8	39.4	37.8	49.6	32.8	33.5	32.2
19	53.3	38.2	38.8	37.1	48.6	32.4	33.0	31.7
20	52.4	37.5	38.1	36.4	47.6	31.9	32.4	31.1
21	51.5	36.9	37.4	35.6	46.8	31.3	31.8	30.4
22	50.6	36.1	36.6	34.9	48.9	30.7	31.1	29.7
23	49.7	35.4	35.8	34.1	45.O	30.0	30.4	28.0
24	48.8	34.6	35.0	33.2	44.1	29.3	29.7	28.3
25	47.9	33.8	34.2	32.4	43.3	28.6	28.9	27.5
26	47.0	32.9	33.3	31.5	42.4	27.9	28.2	26.6
27	46.1	32.1	32.4	30.6	41.5	27.1	27.4	25.8
28	45.2	31.2	31.6	29.7	40.7	26.4	26.6	25.0
29	44.2	30.3	30.7	28.7	39.8	25.6	25.8	24.1
30	43.3	29.5	29.6	27.7	39.0	24.6	25.0	23.2
31	42.4	28.6	26.9	26.7	38.1	24.0	24.2	22.3
32	41.4	27.7	28.0	25.7	37.2	23.2	23.4	21.3
33	40.5	26.8	27.1	24.7	36.4	22.3	22.7	20.3
34	39.6	25.9	26.2	23.7	35.5	21.5	21.9	19.3
35	38.6	25.0	25.3	22.7	34.7	20.7	21.1	18.2
36	37.7	24.1	24.4	21.7	33.8	19.9	20.4	17.1
37	36.8	23.2	23.5	20.7	33.0	19.1	19.6	16.0
38	35.9	22.3	22.6	19.6	32.2	18.4	18.9	15.0
39	34.9	21.4	21.7	18.6	31.3	17.6	18.1	14.2
40	34.0	20.5	20.9	17.5	30.5	16.8	17.4	13.4
41	33.1	19.6	20.0	16.4	29.7	18.0	16.7	12.6
42	32.2	18.7	19.1	15.4	28.9	15.3	16.0	11.9
43	31.3	17.8	18.3	14.3	28.1	14.5	15.2	11.1
44	30.4	16.9	17.4	13.2	27.3	13.8	14.5	10.4
45	29.5	16.1	16.6	12.1	26.5	13.1	13.8	9.7
46	28.6	15.2	15.8	11.2	25.8	12.4	13.1	8.9
47	27.8	14.4	14.9	10.3	25.0	11.6	12.4	8.1
48	26.9	13.5	14.1	9.4	24.3	10.9	11.7	7.3
49	26.1	12.7	13.4	8.6	23.5	10.2	11.0	6.5
50	25.2	11.9	12.6	7.8	22.6	9.5	10.4	5.7
51	24.4	11.1	11.8	7.1	22.1	8.8	9.7	4.9
52	23.6	10.3	11.1	6.3	21.5	8.1	9.1	4.3
53	22.8	9.5	10.3	5.6	20.8	7.4	8.4	3.7
54	22.0	8.7	9.6	5.0	20.2	6.8	7.8	3.2
55	21.3	8.0	6.9	4.4	19.5	6.1	7.2	2.8
56	20.5	7.2	8.2	3.8	18.9	5.5	6.6	2.5
57	19.7	6.5	7.5	3.3	18.3	4.9	6.0	2.2
58	19.0	5.8	6.9	2.9	17.7	4.3	5.6	1.9
59	18.3	5.2	6.3	2.5	17.1	3.7	5.1	1.8
60	17.6	4.5	5.8	2.2	16.5	3.3	4.7	1.6
61	16.9	4.0	5.4	2.0	15.9	2.9	4.4	1.5
62	16.2	3.5	5.0	1.8	15.4	2.5	4.1	1.4
63	15.6	3.1	4.7	1.5	14.9	2.2	3.8	1.3
64	14.9	2.7	4.4	1.3	14.3	2.0	3.6	1.2
65	14.3	2.3	4.2	1.2	13.8	1.8	3.5	1.1
66	13.7	2.1	4.0	1.0	13.3	1.6	3.4	1.0
67	13.1	1.8	3.8	.8	12.8	1.4	3.3	.9
68	12.5	1.6	3.6	.7	12.3	1.3	3.2	.7
69	11.9	1.4	3.5	.5	11.8	1.2	3.0	.6
70	11.4	1.2	3.3	.4	11.4	1.0	2.9	.4
71	10.9	1.1	3.1	.3	10.9	.9	2.7	.3
72	10.4	.9	2.9	.2	10.5	.7	2.6	.2
73	9.9	.8	2.6	.1	10.0	.6	2.3	.1
74	9.4	.7	2.3	.1	9.6	.5	1.8	.0
75	8.9	.6	1.6	.0	9.2	.3	1.3	.0

[1]Mortality rates used reflect racial differentials in survival.

11.4. Offset Approaches

Thinking in terms of "offsets" can increase or decrease the value of a personal injury award but can also make the calculating process more complicated and time-consuming. Offsets are based on assumptions that one factor or set of factors will effectively reduce or cancel out another factor or set of factors.

Suppose that a plaintiff would have earned $10,000 in two years, but during those two years the earnings would have grown by 3%. As it turns out, the interest rate used to discount the earnings to present value is also 3%. Thus, the growth rate of the funds is exactly the same as the discount rate applied to calculate present value. We can therefore say that the discount rate was *offset* by the growth rate. In fact, in this example, the offset would be a *total offset*—dollar for dollar—so that the plaintiff would receive exactly $10,000 today as his future loss two years from now.

Among the total offsets that may be applied to a personal injury or wrongful death award are the following approaches:

Alaska Rule: Wage Increase/Discount Rate

Under an old rule known as the Alaska Rule, the amount of growth in one's wages is assumed to be equal to, and thus totally offset by, the interest rate that would be applied for discounting the wages to present value. Under this rule, the growth rate (inflation) and the discount rate (interest) cancel out each other. Calculating wage loss is thus as simple as multiplying the annual earnings on the date of injury by the number of years remaining in the plaintiff's work life.

The Alaska Rule originated in *Beaulieu v. Elliot*, 434 P.2d 665 (Alaska 1967), but was later superseded by a state statute that effectively prevents a total offset. While widely criticized today, the Alaska Rule was recognized as one of the permissible setoff methods in federal cases under the Longshoremen's and Harbor Workers' Compensation Act, under the holding in *Jones & Laughlin Steel Corp v. Pfeifer*, 678 F.2d 453 (3d Cir. 1982). On appeal, however, the U.S. Supreme Court in *Pfeifer* held that while a setoff between wage increases and discount rates may be simple and expedient, and perhaps even accurate, it is not mandatory. 462 U.S. 523 (1983). The court noted, interestingly, that parties may agree to minimize litigation costs by agreeing to the total offset of growth rates and discount rates by stipulation prior to trial.

Medical Cost/Discount Rate Offset

Another total offset theory is based on comparing the increased costs of medical care over time with the discount rate applied to the same time period. Research suggests that the increase in medical care costs may be approximately equal to the interest rate that could be earned by investing funds for the given period. In fact, such an offset may be ultimately more accurate than a total offset between wage increases and discount rates.

So, for example, if a plaintiff was catastrophically injured and was projected to require a certain dollar value in medical care for the rest of his life, the plaintiff's attorney could argue that the increases in the medical care cost over the plaintiff's life would totally offset any suggested discounting to present value requested by the defendant's attorney. The defendant's attorney, of course, could take issue with the suggested increase in the cost of medical care or the estimated discount rates for the applicable time period. If the increases in medical care costs were overstated, or if the interest rates were tied to unreliable interest forecasts, a total offset would be inaccurate.

Tax-for-Tax Offset

The tax-for-tax offset method assumes that income taxes that would have been paid on lost earnings equal the income taxes that should be paid on the interest earned on the settlement funds. This offset is nicely explained in the Hawaii case of *Greene v. Texeira,* 54 Haw. 231 (1973):

> [t]he theoretical measure of the loss of the plaintiff's earning capacity is that sum of money which if invested at a fair rate of return will yield annually the amount by which the plaintiff's earning capacity has been lessened and which will at the end of the plaintiff's life expectancy be reduced to zero. This takes account of the fact that money earns interest each year; and it should be remembered that this interest is taxable. Therefore, if a court is going to use income after taxes as a measure of plaintiff's loss, it must add back the taxes which would be due on the interest earned—else the award would not fully compensate for the loss.

Many states do not acknowledge or require this offset method, principally because lost earnings are not taxable. In federal cases, however, taxes are subtracted from lost earnings, and a number of states follow the same rule.

Tax-for-Benefits Offset

A variation of the tax-for-tax approach is the tax-for-benefits method. With this approach, one assumes that the income taxes that would have been paid on lost earnings equal the fringe benefits that the plaintiff would have received had he continued working at the job. Thus, if the defendant does not attempt to reduce the personal injury award by the value of income taxes that would have been paid from earnings, the plaintiff will not attempt to augment the award by the value of fringe benefits paid in addition to wages.

Building fringe benefits into the equation may, in fact, be a smart tactical move on the part of plaintiffs. Many courts, after all, acknowledge the loss of benefits as a part of the income loss calculation. In *Wood v. SubSea International, Inc.*, 766 So. 2d 563 (La. App. 2000), for example, the court held that the lost income stream of an injured seaman, used to determine his future wage loss, was calculated by adding his gross income at the time of injury to his fringe benefits, and then subtracting the taxes, expenses, and other such required payments.

Partial Offsets

Mathematically, it is more likely that a particular factor will partially offset another factor rather than totally—or perfectly—offset it dollar for dollar. In other words, it is most plausible that, for any given personal injury award, the wage growth rate will be less than (or perhaps more than) the interest rate—more likely, that is, than the two rates being identical. As such, it may be more logical and accurate to speak of *partial offsets* rather than total offsets. In so saying, however, we are immediately confronted with disagreement among experts as to which rates apply and the extent to which one rate will offset another.

Suppose that the interest rate was 7% and the wage growth rate was 4%. We might therefore conclude that wage growth partially offsets interest, reducing the interest rate to 3%.

Partial offset = interest rate (i) – growth rate (r) = 7% – 4% = 3%.

While a defendant could argue that a value placed on wage loss in an injury case should be discounted to present value based on 7% interest, a plaintiff could counter that the discount rate is too high because it doesn't recognize the projected growth in wages over the same period of time. Suppose, for example, that the parties to a civil action agree that a plaintiff will lose $150,000 in wages over a two-year period. The present value of that wage loss at 7% would be $131,015.81, calculated as follows:

$$PV = \frac{FV}{(1+i)^n} = \frac{\$150{,}000}{(1+07)^2} = \frac{\$150{,}000}{1.1449} = \$131{,}015.81$$

A defendant would argue that the proper compensation for the lost wages over two years would thus be $131,015.81, based on the 7% discount rate. The plaintiff, by contrast, would assert that wages were projected to grow by 4% over the same period of time. Therefore, the wage growth rate should partially offset the discount rate, producing an adjusted discount rate of 3%. Applying the plaintiff's partial offset approach, the present value calculation would be:

$$PV = \frac{FV}{(1+i)^n} = \frac{\$150{,}000}{(1+03)^2} = \frac{\$150{,}000}{1.0609} = \$141{,}389.39$$

By arguing for a partial offset, the plaintiff essentially increases his wage loss award by more than $10,000.

Net Discount Rate

The example above provides a simplified method for applying a partial offset to the present value calculation. It is, however, an approximation. To make the calculation more accurate, we need to geometrically adjust the offset. Instead of simply subtracting the growth rate of 4% from the interest rate of 7%, we apply a somewhat different formula: $NDR = \frac{1+g}{1+i} - 1$ where NDR is the net discount rate, g is the growth rate and i is the interest rate. So, using the same hypothetical interest and growth rates, we would calculate the net discount rate as follows:

$$NDR = \frac{1+g}{1+i} - 1$$

$$NDR = \frac{1.04}{1.07} - 1$$

$$NDR = 0.9719 - 1$$

$$NDR = 0.0281$$

The net discount rate is 2.81%. Therefore, for better accuracy, we would use 2.81% in our present value calculation above instead of 3%.

$$PV = \frac{FV}{(1+i)^n} = \frac{\$150{,}000}{(1+0281)^2} = \frac{\$150{,}000}{1.05698961} = \$141{,}912.46$$

By calculating the net discount rate to achieve a more accurate partial offset of the interest rate by the growth rate, the PV formula produces an even more enhanced result for the plaintiff.

11.5. Putting a Quick Value on a Case

Suppose that the plaintiff in a particular case was earning $35,000 per year at the time of his injury. Further suppose that the injuries are so severe that the plaintiff will suffer a loss of earnings for 26 years and 6 months. Assume that the growth rate of the plaintiff's earnings, based on inflation, is projected to be 4.2%, and the interest or discount rate is fixed at 7.5%. A handy formula, published by Professor Gerald D. Martin,[1] provides a reasonably accurate method for estimating the value of a case for loss of future earnings. The formula is:

$$PV = E\left[\frac{\left(\frac{1+g}{1+d}\right)^n - 1}{\left(\frac{1+g}{1+d}\right) - 1}\right]$$

E = Earnings (annual)
g = growth rate
d = discount rate
n = number of years of lost earnings

Let's plug in the figures presented by this hypothetical case:

$$PV = E\left[\frac{\left(\frac{1+g}{1+d}\right)^n - 1}{\left(\frac{1+g}{1+d}\right) - 1}\right]$$

[1] Martin, Gerald H., *Determining Economic Damages,* James Publishing, Inc. (1988).

$1 + g = 1.042 \qquad 1 + d = 1.075$

$\frac{1.042}{1.075} = 0.9693 \qquad (0.9693)^{26.5} = 0.4376$

$E = \$35{,}000$

Therefore . . .

$$PV = \$35{,}000 \left[\frac{0.4376 - 1}{0.9693 - 1}\right]$$

$$PV = \$35{,}000\ [18.32]$$

$$PV = \$641{,}200$$

We can thus conclude that a plaintiff whose injuries will force him to lose \$35,000 per year for 26.5 years should collect \$641,200 today to settle his future wage loss claim, assuming a 4.2% growth rate on his earnings, and a 7.5% discount rate to calculate present value.

Lost Fringe Benefits

11.6. Calculating Lost Benefits

In addition to lost future earnings, a victim of personal injury may have a compensable claim for the loss of fringe benefits. This may include the value of lost health insurance, including hospital, medical, and disability plans, life insurance, pension plans and other retirement programs, stock options, stock purchase plans and other profit-sharing programs, sick leave, personal leave and other paid time off, maternity leave, vacation pay, holiday pay, travel pay, shift premiums, expense accounts, counseling programs, day care facilities, tuition reimbursement, credit union memberships, fitness and recreation programs and gym memberships, unemployment compensation, workers' compensation insurance, housing subsidies, relocation assistance, company cars, company laptops, legal aid, and bonuses. The employer's Social Security contributions for each employee are also a fringe benefit of employment that must be accounted for, unless otherwise replaced in another calculation.

Valuating fringe benefits can be a thorny process: some benefits are easy to quantify; others are not. Some are taxable; others are not. Some are dependent on certain qualifying contingencies, and some are nonrecurrent, awarded arbitrarily, or tied to employer progress or failure. In unionized workplaces, fringe benefits are generally detailed in the union's collective bargaining agreement. In nonunionized workplaces, benefits may be detailed in employee handbooks and publications provided by a human resources department.

Attorneys representing personal injury claimants will want to establish a master list of all fringe benefits that will be lost as a result of their clients' absence from the workplace. Clients can be asked to complete a check-off list of fringe benefits available to them at work. They should provide copies of all insurance cards, summary plan descriptions, handbooks, collective bargaining agreements, bulletins, and notices from the human resources department. Defense attorneys should request such information in pretrial discovery if the plaintiff will be making a claim for lost wages and benefits. While there is a tendency to focus discovery requests on lost earnings, attorneys should not dismiss the value of fringe benefits. Indeed, in some jobs, the fringe benefits will represent one-third or more of the total compensation package.

It is important, too, for attorneys to understand the nature of each of the benefits awarded. For example, a large group health insurance program that provides major medical, hospital, prescription drug, dental, and vision care coverage may cost an employer $250 per employee per month, but may cost a single employee $750 per month to purchase on his own. Simply quantifying the employer's cost for the loss of such a benefit would inadequately compensate the employee.

Retirement programs, likewise, require close scrutiny. In a defined benefit program, an employer promises to pay an employee a specific benefit for life beginning at her retirement. The amount of the benefit is governed by a formula based on age, earnings, and years of service. A specific retirement age is stated, but some defined benefit programs permit early retirement with reduced benefits. In a defined contribution plan, however, employers pay money into a tax-deferred account for each qualifying employee. Employees may also contribute to such accounts, usually through payroll deduction. The most common defined contribution plans are 401(k) plans and individual retirement accounts (IRAs).

What is the value of these lost benefits? The starting point is to ask what the value is to the person or persons who would have received the benefit. What damage did the plaintiff suffer by losing his right to employer-sponsored health insurance? In a wrongful death action, the question becomes: what damage do the plaintiff's survivors now suffer as a result of the plaintiff's death?

There are two approaches to calculating the value of lost fringe benefits: (a) the itemized present value approach, and (b) the percentage-of-earnings approach. Attorneys may choose one approach or the other, or may find it helpful to apply both approaches.

Itemized Present Value Approach

The most technically accurate but more difficult approach to value lost benefits is to itemize each of the benefits, calculate the specific loss of value to the employee in each case, determine the period of time over which the benefit would have been paid or awarded, and then compute the present value of each such loss. So, for example, let's assume that a plaintiff receives the benefit of a family health insurance plan that would cost him $8,000 per year to replace if he were not working. At the time of his injury, the employee has 10 more work years until retirement. Assuming no increase in health insurance costs, and assuming that the employee would remain out of work for the next 10 years, the employee would need $80,000 to cover the value of this lost benefit.

Assume, too, that the employee enjoyed the benefit of a company car, which saved him $2,000 per year in personal car expenses. Prior to the date of the employee's injury, the employer had announced that it would be phasing out its company car program in three years. Therefore, the employee can claim a loss of this benefit for three more years, representing a loss of $6,000. The employee also enjoys defined benefit pension contributions by his employer valued at $4,800 per year, and had every expectation of receiving such contributions for the remaining 10 years of his work life. Assuming no change in the value of the employer's contributions, the employee would thus be entitled to another $48,000 in pension benefits. Let's now plot these fringe benefits on a table and convert them to present value.

Benefit	Value on Annual Basis	Years Remaining on Benefit	Total Value of Benefit	Present Value at 4% discount rate
Health Insurance (Family Plan)	$8,000	10	$ 80,000	$54,046.75
Company Car	$2,000	3	$ 6,000	$ 5,333.98
Pension Fund	$4,800	10	$ 48,000	$32,428.05
		TOTALS →	**$134,000**	**$91,808.78**

In this simplified example, we see that the present value of the three lost fringe benefits of employment is $91,808.78. Making such a calculation can provide tremendous leverage in the negotiating process. Detailed calculations in tabular form, or presented sequentially for one benefit at a time, can significantly enhance answers to interrogatories and other discovery requests. Each and every lost fringe benefit can be summarized in the plaintiff's settlement brochure or settlement demand letter, followed by present values of loss, supporting the ultimate demand for settlement. In fact, effective use of the itemized present value approach can lead to higher settlements and higher verdicts in personal injury cases.

On the other hand, the process can become quite cumbersome if the employee enjoyed 15 or 20 different kinds of benefits. It can become unwieldy if the employer was considering reducing or increasing its employee benefits, in which case it may be necessary to calculate the probability of receiving a particular benefit amount over the employee's work life. The process can become quite time-consuming if certain benefits—for example, the company car—were granted and withdrawn from time to time, without pattern or predictability, a challenge that may require a probability analysis or an averaging process to establish a value for the benefit over the course of several years. In cases in which there are many fringe benefits to be quantified and converted to present value, it may be unreasonable to expect a jury to digest all of the data and return an accurate verdict.

In high value cases, or those cases involving complex benefit programs, attorneys should not hesitate to consult with a financial expert. While the formulas and approaches contained herein will help with negotiating settlements and litigating many kinds of personal injury cases, insurance and retirement programs may involve complex contribution formulas and actuarial assumptions that require further expertise.

Percentage-of-Earnings Approach

The percentage-of-earnings approach seeks to determine what percentage of an employee's fringe benefits are the earnings he receives on the job. The percentage—sometimes called the "fringe rate"—is then converted to a dollar amount and tacked onto the employee's annual earnings, and a loss-of-earnings approach is used to establish the total loss. For example, an employee earns $50,000 per year in wages, but his benefits are valued at 20% of his earnings. We would calculate 20% of \$50,000 (0.2 x \$50,000), which equals \$10,000. We would then say that the earnings-and-benefits loss totals \$60,000. We would then treat this loss as simply an augmented earnings loss. In other words, present value calculations and offsets would be applied to the augmented earnings figure (in this example, \$60,000).

How do we determine the fringe rate? To be precise, we would probably need to itemize each of the benefits and place a value on it, as discussed in the section above. Then we could add up the total value of all benefits, compare it with the value of earnings over the same period of time, and determine the percentage of benefits to earnings. The formula for the fringe rate is a simple ratio:

$$\text{Fringe Rate} = \frac{\text{Total dollar value of all fringe benefits}}{\text{Gross Earnings}}$$

For example, if an employee earns \$45,000 per year, and the value of all of his fringe benefits totals \$14,350, we would calculate the fringe rate as follows:

$$\text{Fringe rate} = \frac{\$14{,}350}{\$45{,}000} = 0.3188$$

Therefore, the employee has a fringe rate of approximately 31.88%. Using the percentage of earnings approach, we would simply add the total value of the fringe benefits to the earnings (\$14,350 + \$45,000), yielding the augmented loss of compensation to the employee (\$59,350).

If we knew the fringe rate and the employee's earnings, we could also determine the dollar amount of the fringe benefits using some simple algebra:

$$\text{Fringe Rate} = \frac{\text{Total dollar value of all fringe benefits}}{\text{Gross Earnings}}$$

$$0.3188 = \frac{X}{\$45{,}000}$$ To solve for X, multiple both sides of the equation by \$45,000.

$$0.3188 \text{ x } \$45{,}000 = X$$

$$\$14{,}346 = X$$

[The slight difference in the results is based on the rounding of figures used in the fringe rate].

This formula could be quite helpful in cases in which you are unable to pin down the exact dollar value of fringe benefits but you have obtained testimony or other evidence disclosing the fringe rate. Many employers, especially large institutional employers, publish their own current and projected fringe rates for various categories of employees and for various types of benefits. For example, Harvard University projects its fiscal year fringe rates for faculty, union members, teaching assistants, and other kinds of workers in more than a dozen benefits categories, including social security, pension, health and dental plans, tuition assistance plans, and short-term disability programs.[2] If you had fringe rate information, but could not easily obtain the dollar value of fringe benefits, you could apply the modified formula, X = Fringe Rate x Gross Earnings, to determine the dollar value of the client's fringe benefits.

Where an employer does not disclose his fringe rate or fails to produce sufficient evidence to permit the calculation to be made from itemized values of fringe benefits, a fringe rate can be presumed and argued based on industry standards. Such rates can be constructed from government studies and statistical reports. For example, the U.S. Department of Labor's Bureau of Labor Statistics publishes regular reports on employee benefits in the United States, divided by occupations, participation rates, and other criteria. The U.S. Chamber of Commerce conducts an annual benefits survey revealing the percentage of the cost of benefits to the overall cost of payroll.

Combining the Approaches

If discovery is conducted thoroughly and efficiently, and if accurate information can be gathered with respect to the dollar value of each fringe benefit, then it may make sense to use both the itemized present value approach and the percentage-of-earnings approach. By first itemizing and calculating the value of all benefits, an attorney can obtain a detailed understanding of what his client actually lost as a result of his injuries. This process can be valuable in and of itself, to the extent that it educates the attorney, provides him with ammunition in the bargaining and negotiating process, and provides mathematical proof of how he ascertained the fringe rate.

[2]http://able.harvard.edu/rates/fy09fringe.pdf.

For settlement purposes, the itemization approach and the calculation of present values provides the attorney with an additional category of damages (the loss of fringe benefits), for which he can argue independent of other categories or combine with other categories as part of an overall settlement package. The percentage of earnings approach then adds an additional layer of support—a more powerful negotiating tool—for arguing that the plaintiff's losses were much greater than simply his straight wages payable over time. Any wage loss claim, the attorney would argue, would have to be augmented by the fringe rate—a percentage that could increase the actual loss suffered by the plaintiff by as much as 20%, 30%, or beyond. The fringe rate is easy to explain to a jury and provides a quick mathematical calculation by which damages can be assessed.

Avoiding Double Counting and Unused Benefits

Employee compensation may include monetary benefits that are listed as—or negotiated by labor organizations as—fringe benefits, but are, in fact, part of the employees' wages. These include, for instance, holiday and vacation pay, sick leave, personal days, and bonuses. These benefits translate into monetary compensation and are usually reflected on W-2 wage and tax statements as part of the employee's gross earnings. Therefore, they should not be double-counted as fringe benefits.

Likewise, it would be inappropriate to calculate a value of a fringe benefit available to an employee, but which he never used. For example, an employer-sponsored day care facility can represent a significant fringe benefit to a working mother who would otherwise have to pay for private child care services, but the value of such a benefit should not be counted by a childless mother or father who is forced to stop working after being injured. Similarly, an employee who opts out of a health insurance plan, because he's covered on his spouse's plan offered through another employer, cannot logically claim a loss of health insurance benefits in calculating his total loss of fringe benefits.

11.7. Stock Options

Stock options are one of the most complex forms of employment benefits to be valued. Because it is an option to buy stock, it is not worth exactly what the stock itself is worth. In fact, it is worth somewhat less than the stock because of a number of variables and uncertainties. The actual fringe benefit is a right granted to the employee, more specifically a right to buy a certain number of shares of the employer's stock at a predetermined price.

Before counting stock options as fringe benefits, an attorney must confirm that the employee qualifies within two applicable time periods: the vesting period and the exercise period. For an employee to obtain a stock option, he must be employed by the employer for a certain period of time known as the vesting period. Once the stock options are granted to the employee, he has a limited period of time within which to exercise the options, after which they will expire. The objective is to activate the option and purchase the stock at the predetermined price when the selling price on the open market is actually much higher.

For example, if an employee has a stock option set at a purchase price of $8 per share, and the stock is trading at $11 per share, the option has an intrinsic value of $3 per share. But what if the employee sits on the option and waits longer before exercising it? The trading price of the stock may fluctuate based on economic events, interest rates, and other factors. Stocks are inherently volatile, and they vary in value over time. Therefore, any formula that would measure the value of a stock option would have to measure not only the difference between the purchase price to the employee and the trading price on the market but also the level of variability—how much the value of the option changes over time. The greater the variability of a share of stock over time, the greater the market value of the stock option.

The formula for calculating the value of a stock option is known universally as the Black-Scholes option-pricing model. It is a complex and daunting formula which we have excluded from this discussion because it relies on a number of intricate statistical concepts. It requires fixing a variance on the continuous return on the stock and on certain probability determinations. The stock's volatility is measured by the annualized standard deviation of the stock price's daily logarithmic returns. *Huh?* The Black-Scholes formula is thus best utilized with the assistance of a financial expert.[3] For those cases in which precise op-

[3]The Black-Scholes formula can be viewed online through any number of Internet searches and is commonly outlined in finance and accounting textbooks.

tion valuation is required, an accounting expert or economics expert should be retained, and the expert should be equipped to run the Black-Scholes formula and to testify about its constituent factors.

As an alternative to Black-Scholes, we can apply some shortcuts to estimate the value of a personal injury victim's stock options. If an option is brand new, it can be said to have the same value as the stock price. There is no intrinsic value per se when the exercise price is identical to the market price. For such cases involving newly issued options, we can say that the option is worth roughly one-third the value of the stock.[4]

For example, suppose that an employee was granted options to purchase 1,000 shares of ABC Corporation at $30 per share. The total value of ABC stock would be $30,000, if the options were exercised and the stock were actually purchased. The options are valued at something less, however. A reasonable estimate is that the options are valued at about one-third of the stock value, or roughly $10,000.

Another shortcut can be applied to stock options that have been held for a period of time and where the price of the stock has increased over time. The following estimating formula[5] can be used:

$$OV = (TP - EP) + EP(0.25)$$

OV = Option value
TP = Current trading price of the stock
EP = Exercise price

Assume that the exercise price of an option is $12 per share. The current trading price of the stock is $15 per share. The multiplier (0.25) above provides an estimate of the five-year time value of the option. So, to obtain the option value using this shortcut, we begin by establishing the intrinsic value (TP – EP), which is $3 ($15 – $12 = $3). We then multiply the exercise price of $12 by 25% (0.25) for a time value calculation of $3. Then, we add the two figures ($3 + $3 = $6). The value of the option at this time is approximately $6 per share.

[4]Author and former tax lawyer Kaye A. Thomas suggests 30% is a reasonable value for a newly issued option that has a life of five or more years, ignoring the value of high volatility.

[5]This formula was built from an explanation given by Kaye A. Thomas in the Fairmark newsletter. http://www.fairmark.com/execcomp/valuation.htm.

11.8. Social Security Benefits

Social Security benefits may include retirement benefits, disability payments, and survivor payments to family members following a plaintiff's death. The first step for attorneys considering Social Security benefits is to identify what they are. What portion of the plaintiff's paycheck was deducted for FICA (Federal Income Contributions Act) contributions? What contribution did the employer make to the employee's Social Security retirement fund? If disability payments are being made, what effect are those payments having on the available retirement balance?

Plaintiff's attorneys will want to argue that the loss of Social Security contributions is another retirement benefit lost as a result of the defendant's negligence. Had the plaintiff not been injured and had he continued working on the job, he would have received increased contributions from the employer over time. Or so goes the argument. Defense attorneys will want to argue that there would have been higher Social Security taxes over time, deducted from the increased earnings.

In some but not all jurisdictions, a plaintiff can claim lost Social Security retirement benefits as a specific item of damages. It is also possible to argue that an injury victim with a reduced earning capacity, who must turn to lower-paying job opportunities because of his injuries, will thus make lower contributions to his Social Security retirement fund. The difference between his prior Social Security contributions and his post-injury contributions (or projected contributions) would thus be a specific item of damages.

Attorneys should not assume, however, that a reduced amount of Social Security contributions in all cases will produce an actual loss to the plaintiff. For one thing, if a plaintiff's earning capacity continues to exceed the income thresholds to which FICA tax applies, there would be no loss to measure. In 2011, for example, the maximum earnings creditable in any one year was $106,800, and with limited exception, this figure increases each year. For an annual table of maximum Social Security earnings, see *http://socialsecurity.gov/OP_Home/handbook/handbook.13/handbook-1301.html.*

There would also be no net loss if the plaintiff's savings in FICA tax payroll deductions attributable to his reduced earnings until retirement exceed the difference in lifetime benefits after retirement. If, for other reasons, the plaintiff did not qualify for benefits under the Social

Security Administration's earnings test, or if there were conditions in which benefits were deemed not payable, then a calculation of damages would be moot. For more information about the reduction or nonpayment of benefits, see Chapter 18 of the Social Security Handbook at *http://socialsecurity.gov/OP_Home/handbook/handbook.18/handbook-toc18.html.*

If the plaintiff qualifies for Social Security Disability (SSD) benefits as a result of the injuries he sustained, the defendant's attorney will likely argue that the value of those benefits should be deducted from any settlement or judgment. Yet this is by no means a universally accepted approach, and plaintiff's attorneys and their experts may wish to analyze more incrementally the effect of SSD payments on long-term retirement payments. Again, the Social Security Handbook may provide additional guidance, in particular Chapter 5, at *http://socialsecurity.gov/OP_Home/handbook/handbook.05/handbook-toc05.html.*

To estimate projected Social Security retirement and disability benefits, the Social Security Administration provides a number of calculators and tables on its website at *http://socialsecurity.gov/OACT/quickcalc/index.html.* A party can gather even more accurate information about future benefits by using the information provided on his Social Security statement. To request a Social Security statement for a client, go to *https://secure.ssa.gov/apps6z/isss/main.html.*

Damage Reducers

11.9. Estimating Personal Consumption

How much did the deceased plaintiff consume from his own income? What amount of his earnings was actually dedicated to his own personal self-consumption? Determining this amount for a wrongful death victim or a personal injury victim can be one of the more stubbornly elusive exercises in calculating damages. After all, few of us can state with any certainty how much we spend on ourselves versus our family members, especially since many of the expenditures are earmarked for the family as a whole (e.g., utility bills, mortgage payments, insurance premiums).

If the quantum of damages is intended to measure the loss to a plaintiff's survivors or beneficiaries, then we must somehow deduct from the plaintiff's earnings the value of his personal consumption. For example, a particular plaintiff may have personally consumed a portion of his earnings for any of the following personal purposes:

- Food
- Clothing and jewelry
- Haircuts and grooming products
- Education
- Cigarettes and alcohol
- Entertainment
- Transportation costs
- Medical/dental expenses
- Reading material
- Personal cell phone charges
- Banking fees
- Gifts purchased for friends and family

Upon the death or permanent disability of such a plaintiff, the survivors or beneficiaries would only fairly be entitled to those damages that remain after accounting for the personal consumption costs of the plaintiff. If we could accurately measure all of the personal consumption costs over time, we could—at least theoretically—deduct that figure from the plaintiff's loss of income in order to ascertain the actual loss suffered by the survivors. If the plaintiff was the main breadwinner for the family, and he alone provided 100% of the family income while personally consuming 20% of the income, the family's net loss would be 80% of the plaintiff's income.

Estimation Methods

Personal consumption can be estimated by comprehensively interviewing family members and friends of the plaintiff to reconstruct the plaintiff's buying and spending habits. This is likely to be a laborious process, inherently unscientific, and susceptible to challenge. Yet it may yield great insight into the plaintiff's economic behavior. Was he frugal? Thrifty? Impulsive? Did he spend lots of money on hobbies or bad habits? Certain assumptions might apply to this process: younger, single wage-earners, for example, tend to have higher personal consumption rates, as they live a single life without family support obligations, and as they focus inordinately on clothing, personal grooming, and entertainment.

One could also attempt to fix a personal consumption figure after deducting all of the other expenditures allocated to family support and general household costs. In effect, personal consumption equals the amount of income remaining after the wage earner spends his paycheck on his family and his home. To approach the personal consumption figure in this manner, attorneys will need to establish the number of plaintiff's dependents, their ages, their support needs, including any special health or disability issues, and the likelihood that the children are college-bound. The costs of supporting the family will include the general household costs, such as electric bills and water service bills, which would not, in most cases, materially change with the absence of the plaintiff.

A self-consumption percentage could also be calculated using the Consumer Expenditure Surveys (CES) published by the U.S. Department of Commerce, Bureau of Economic Analysis (BEA) *http://bea.gov/* or by the U.S. Department of Labor, Bureau of Labor Statistics (BLS) *http://www.bls.gov/cex/#tables*. The BLS tables provide detailed consumer expenditure data displayed according to age, educational background, occupation, race, and other factors.

The Value of Discovery

In jurisdictions where personal consumption costs can or must be deducted from lost earnings calculations, thorough pretrial discovery can assist counsel in arguing for or against a particular cost estimate. Survivors of a deceased plaintiff, for example, may provide deposition testimony or documentary evidence pointing to the plaintiff's pattern of frugality. Or perhaps the evidence will prove the contrary—that the plaintiff was an active sportsman and an impetuous bettor. Evidence of how the plaintiff handled money prior to his injury can not only prompt attorneys to fashion arguments for or against certain personal consumption costs, but it may also assist the trier of fact in assessing the genuine losses to the plaintiff's survivors.

Determining personal consumption costs will also depend on the number of household members or other dependents supported by a particular plaintiff, their individual levels of self-support, the manner and speed in which plaintiff's income was consumed by his dependents, and whether other household members contributed to the support of the dependent family members.

11.10. Estimating Taxes

Taxes due on a plaintiff's earnings should also be deducted from the settlement value of the case and from any jury award. Or so goes the argument in most jurisdictions. Were the plaintiff to have avoided injury and remained working at his occupation, his paychecks would have been reduced by his state and federal income taxes. Thus, one could say that it would be unfair to the defendant to pay the plaintiff a settlement consisting of his *gross* lost wages. Rather, the plaintiff's real loss is his loss of earnings *net of income taxes*. This makes sense particularly if the plaintiff expects to receive a settlement consisting of tax-free damages.

On the other hand, some argue that the tax liability on earned income is offset by the taxes the plaintiff would pay on the interest earned by investing his lump-sum personal injury settlement. In other words, a plaintiff who receives a settlement check for $100,000 is likely to deposit those funds in a risk-free, interest-earning investment. Taxes would thereupon be due and payable on the interest earned. If the plaintiff were to receive a damages award consisting of the present value of his pre-tax earnings, it would be offset by the taxes to be paid on the interest earned on the invested settlement funds.

In practice, such tax setoffs are more hypothetical than scientifically accurate. In fact, a partial setoff is more likely to be appropriate in most cases. If such tax adjustments are required or sought in the jurisdiction in which the plaintiff's case is being handled, then attorneys and their experts will want to consider the plaintiff's tax bracket, the number of available tax exemptions and deductions, and other applicable taxation factors. The extent to which such tax effects are admissible will depend on jurisdiction. The U.S. Supreme Court, ruling in *Norfolk and Western Railway Company v. Liepelt,*[6] a 1980 case brought under the Federal Employers' Liability Act, held that evidence of tax effects on future earnings was admissible, but many states have declined to follow *Liepelt* on state law grounds.[7]

---

[6]444 U.S. 490 (1980).

[7]*See, e.g.* Spencer v. A-1 Crane Service, Inc., 880 S.W. 2d 938 (Tenn. 1994) (finding no error in refusing to instruct a jury on taxability issues because doing so would confuse jurors by making them consider rates of taxation, exemptions, and other speculative factors); McKown-Katy v. Rego Co.,

Other Losses

11.11. Lost Household Services

The death of a loved one leaves his family deprived not only of income from lost future earnings but also of the household and family-type services that the deceased member provided. The loss can be significant as in the case of the death of a young mother who did all of the cooking and cleaning for her children, or the death of a father who did all of the household repairs and handled all of the finances and chauffering responsibilities for the children.

The list of household services commonly provided by parents and spouses can include any of the following:

- Cooking and meal preparation
- Purchasing and mending clothes
- Laundry
- Bathing and grooming children
- Providing spiritual guidance to children
- Providing general social and cultural awareness to children
- Providing financial counsel and building good financial habits in children
- Housekeeping and household maintenance
- Nursing sick children and providing first aid
- Appliance repairs
- Car washing and repairs
- Driving children to and from their activities
- Meeting with the children's teachers, counselors, and coaches
- Lawn care, gardening, mowing, and snow removal
- Grocery shopping and running other errands
- Paying bills and managing a budget
- Assisting children with their homework
- Teaching children to drive and other tasks

---

776 P.2d 1130 (Colo. App. 1989) (holding that the *Liepelt* decision is limited to Federal Employers' Liability Act cases and tax-related jury instructions are misleading and confusing); McElroy v. State, 703 N.W. 2d 385 (Iowa 2005) (refusing to require a tax-related jury instruction where jurors would be left to conjecture over future tax consequences, especially where no evidence was offered at trial concerning the tax consequences of the award).

The list could, in fact, run much longer, depending on the nature of the family and how it lived and functioned together.

There are essentially two methods to estimate the value of lost household services: the opportunity cost method and the replacement cost method. The opportunity cost method focuses on the value of employment opportunities that are *not being pursued* by a person who provides household services. For example, assume that a mother who cooks and cleans for her family all day long could earn \$10 per hour (counting wages and tips) while working in a restaurant or for a catering service. If this is a reasonable estimate, then it can be said that her opportunity cost is \$10 per hour. In effect, one hour of cooking and cleaning at home is equal to one hour of cooking and cleaning in the workplace, and that is equal to \$10. The premature death or permanent injury of such a person would thus implicate a loss of household services valued at \$10 per hour for 40 hours per week.

One could argue, of course, that the decedent in this example never actually worked 40 full hours cooking and cleaning. Instead, she worked only about 20 hours per week performing such functions. If this were true, then the quantum of damages would be \$200. Still, she may have spent another 20 hours per week providing other kinds of compensable household services.

The opportunity cost method is controversial insofar as it presumes that the deceased or injured victim truly might have traded her domestic services for a wage-generating job in the workplace. It presumes a certain earning potential, and may in fact confuse the value of a paycheck with the somewhat different cost of cooking meals at home or vacuuming one's floors.

The replacement cost method takes a different approach to calculating the value of household services. Under this method, the question is: what would it cost to replace the plaintiff in the home with some person or group of persons who could perform the same functions? If the plaintiff cooked three meals a day for three children and cleaned the home daily, what would be the cost of a cook to make each of the meals and a maid to clean the home every day? Could one person perform both functions at a certain cost, or would we need to calculate the independent costs of a cook and a maid? Of course, each of these costs would be fixed to a certain period of time. In other words, the three children would theoretically suffer the loss of their mother as a cook only for the period of their minority, and would at some future point have been expected to start cooking for themselves.

The starting point for calculating a loss of such household services is to determine how much time the deceased or injured plaintiff actually devoted to the specific services. Perhaps such information can be gathered through interviews with the survivors, or records or logs maintained by the plaintiff. Otherwise, the best estimate of such time usage is the BLS American Time Use Surveys which contain breakdowns for average time devoted to housework, cooking, lawn care, financial, and other household management services at *http://www.bls.gov/tus/.*

Let's try a basic example: Suppose that a mother in her mid 20s is tragically killed in an auto accident. Assume that she spent an average of 45 minutes per day preparing meals for her children and related cleanup chores. The replacement cost for this work is hypothetically $9 per hour. Her annual replacement cost for the cooking and related cleanup services would be calculated as follows:

(0.75)(9) x 365 = $2,463.75

The first part of the equation, (0.75) refers to 75% of one hour, or 45 minutes. This figure is multiplied by the hourly rate ($9), to produce the daily replacement cost of $6.75. Assuming that the mother cooked and cleaned for her children every day of the year, the daily replacement cost would then be multiplied by 365 days to yield an annual replacement cost of $2,463.75. This figure would then be multiplied by the number of years during which the services would have been provided in the absence of a wrongful death. The final amount would then be discounted back to present value. This procedure would then be repeated for each category of household services that were lost as a result of the mother's death. A useful source that collects much of this data is *The Dollar Value of a Day,* which repackages federal economic, health, and demographic data for a primary target audience of forensic economists at *http://expectancydata.com/default.aspx.*

Where the loss of household services is at issue, plaintiffs' attorneys should inquire thoroughly of the plaintiff or his survivors. Defense attorneys, in turn, should ask appropriate question in the pretrial discovery process. Among the questions to be asked are the following:

1. What household services did the plaintiff provide to the family or to the home?
2. How often did the plaintiff provide such services (or how many hours per week were devoted to such services)?
3. Were the services the kind that would have been rendered by the plaintiff throughout his life (and therefore we should consider his life expectancy), or were they the kinds of services that were tied to the age of the children (and therefore we should consider the ages of the children benefitting from the services)?
4. Was the plaintiff particularly skillful in any domestic areas (for example, was he a plumber or a skilled carpenter? Was she a particularly accomplished decorator or seamstress)?

Armed with the answers to these questions, attorneys can address the value of lost household services, even before retaining expert witnesses. Rough estimates of the opportunity costs or replacement costs can facilitate meaningful settlement discussions and may add negotiating leverage at mediation sessions.

11.12. Lost Advice, Counsel, and Companionship

What is the value of a parent's advice or guidance? How much is a spouse's insight or consultation worth? In wrongful death cases, the loss of such counsel and companionship is largely recognized but difficult to quantify. In some respects, the loss of advice or guidance can be treated as a loss of household services. A mother who cooks for her children may double as their religious advisor, social mentor, and personal confidante. In a marriage, this loss may translate into a loss of companionship and of conjugal happiness. What is it worth?

While it is difficult to quantify the replacement cost of a beloved advisor or companion, it is not impossible. A survivor may claim a loss of companionship because her husband had accompanied her on dinner dates, picnics, visits to the movie theater, and grocery shopping. Paid companions can be hired, through local nursing agencies, home health care, and employment services, to accompany the survivor and to assist her on grocery shopping trips. Such companions may not be able to function as dinner dates per se, but the value of their services on a shopping trip can be calculated and factored into the damages equation.

Similarly, it may be difficult to find one person who could function as a replacement model for a deceased plaintiff who provided advice, counsel, sensibility, and judgment to a surviving spouse. Yet a replacement cost can be constructed from the cost of counselors, social workers, financial advisers, and other specialists who could provide the kind of recommendations and judgment the survivor expected from the plaintiff.

It must be presumed that in customary relationships, the amount of time dedicated to advice and counsel is considerably less than other more physical forms of household services such as cooking and cleaning. Although little research is available, one might expect that a person would receive something less than one hour's worth of advice from her spouse on a weekly basis, on average, and that a child might receive something between two and four hours of advice and counsel on a weekly basis. Further inquiry into the nature of the relationships and the manner and frequency in which advice was provided will help attorneys to refine the calculation with more reliable information.

11.13. Hedonic Damages

Hedonic damages refer to the intangible loss of life itself or perhaps more accurately the loss of life's pleasures. Like the loss of companionship, hedonic damages are nonpecuniary losses, and as such they are inherently difficult to quantify through any reliable mathematical or scientific method. Perhaps for this reason, hedonic damages are not recognized in wrongful death cases in many states.[8]

---

[8]*See, e.g.,* Delaware: Sterner v. Wesley College, Inc., 747 F.Supp. 263, 274 (D. Del. 1990); Florida: Brown v. Seebach, 763 F.Supp. 574, 583 (S.D. Fla. 1991); Illinois: Bramlette v. Hyundai Motor Co., 1992 WL 213956 at *3 (N.D. Ill. 1992); Wyness v. Armstrong World Indus., Inc., 131 Ill.2d 403, 410, 137 Ill. Dec. 623, 626, 546 N.E.2d 568, 571 (1989); Gonzales v. City Wide Insulation, Inc., 1990 WL 77525 at *4 (N.D. Ill. 1990); Indiana: Southlake Limousine and Coach, Inc. v. Brock, 578 N.E.2d 677, 682 (Ind. Ct. App. 1991); Johnson v. Inland Steel Co., 1992 WL 396296 at *4 (N.D. Ill. 1992); Kansas: Sullivan v. United States Gypsum Co., 862 F.Supp. 317 (D. Kan. 1994); Louisiana: Simmons v. Hartford Insurance Co., 786 F. Supp. 574, 581 (E.D. La. 1992); Chausse v. Southland Corp., 400 So.2d 1199, 1204 (La. Ct. App.), *cert. denied,* 404 So.2d 278 (La. 1981); Mississippi: Buckhalter v. Burlington Northern R.R., 1992 WL 236676 at *1 (N.D. Miss. 1992); Nevada: Pitman v.

Where hedonic losses are permitted, there are a number of theories about how to assess the value of life's pleasures. In one respect, we would want to know about the kind of life the decedent led—his emotional depth, psychological functioning, personal interaction, occupational relationships, his education and intellectual development, his attitude and social adjustment, his sex life, his hobbies, avocations, and recreational activities, his dreams and his goals, his way of life, of living, of learning, of loving. These measures would all seem to tell us something about the decedent's pleasures in life, but placing a value on these intangible aspects of human existence seems utterly impossible.

One formula purports to assess the value of life by the willingness of a person to pay for devices or services to reduce his risk of death. These would include, for example, smoke detectors, security systems, and highly crash-resistant motor vehicles equipped with antilock braking systems, lane departure warning systems, and traction control systems. The decedent's willingness to pay for such safety devices is a measure of his resistance to death and the basis of a hedonic damages formula.

Yet another theory purports to measure the value of bereavement, as suffered by the decedent's survivors. What value then, hypothetically, should a jury place on a survivor's sleeplessness, tearfulness, lack of concentration, malaise, depression, and irritability, all of which are attributable to her grief over the loss of the plaintiff? This approach is intriguing but not clearly associated with the loss of one's life insofar

---

Thorndike, 762 F.Supp. 870, 871-72 (D. Nev. 1991); New Hampshire: Nichols v. Estabrook, 741 F.Supp. 325, 329 (D. N.H. 1989); New Jersey: Clement v. Consolidated Rail Corp., 734 F.Supp. 151, 156 (D. N.J. 1989); New Mexico: Ortega v. Plexco, 793 F.Supp. 298, 300 (D. N.M. 1991); North Carolina: Livingston v. United States, 817 F.Supp. 601, 606 (E.D.N.C. 1993); Ohio: Singleton v. Suhr, 1989 WL 54383 at P*3 (Ohio Ct. App. 1989); Pennsylvania: Willinger v. Mercy Catholic Medical Center, 482 Pa. 441, 447, 393 A.2d 1188, 1191 (1978); *see also* Broome v. Antlers' Hunting Club, 595 F.2d 921, 923 (3d Cir. 1979); Tennessee: Spencer v. A-1 Crane Service, Inc., 880 S.W.2d 938 (Tenn. 1994); Wisconsin: Bell v. City of Milwaukee, 746 F.2d 1205, 1235-36 (7th Cir. 1984); Warsaw Convention: In re Korean Air Lines Disaster of September 1, 1983, 807 F.Supp. 1073, 1083 (S.D.N.Y. 1992); In re Korean Air Lines Disaster of September 1, 1983, 814 F.Supp. 592, 599 (E.D. Mich. 1993) (Same); and Maritime Law: Shield v. Bayliner Marine Corp., 822 F.Supp. 81, 83 (D. Conn. 1993).

as a bereaved party's losses may draw on her individual psychosocial makeup, her coping mechanisms, and her history of loss.

Perhaps because hedonic damages are so speculative and indefinable, no single formula can be offered here. Attorneys handling wrongful death cases or other tort claims in which hedonic damages are recognized (such as mistaken identity leading to the false imprisonment of an innocent inmate for a period of years) should determine initially what law applies in the jurisdiction where the case is pending. If hedonic damages are recognized, attorneys should make further inquiry as to the methods of proof that have been adjudged to be reliable in prior cases. Then, an appropriate economics expert should be retained and asked to assist in the pretrial discovery phase before attempting to state a hedonic damages figure. The request for hedonic damages can be a powerful tool in such cases, if credible evidence can be assembled to support the conclusions of the economics expert.

11.14. Emotional Distress

Damages for emotional distress can be based on a variety of legal proofs. They can be based on the torts of intentional infliction of emotional distress or negligent infliction of emotional distress, although these causes of action are not recognized in every state. They can be tied to a discrete category of damages—such as shock, anxiety, distress, and psychological trauma—sought from the jury on a general negligence cause of action. Yet again, these categories are not universally recognized. In many states, damages for emotional distress are not available without proof of some related physical injury.

Certainly, no formula can measure one's emotional distress per se. In many cases, a judge or a jury is asked to consider a patchwork of evidence, testimony, and documents pointing to the psychological setbacks suffered by a plaintiff. Few emotional distress claims succeed without evidence of some psychological treatment by the plaintiff. In this respect, attorneys often attempt to build a damages portfolio around the psychological treatment undertaken by the plaintiff. Some of the more common techniques include:

- Tracking the client's visits to a psychiatrist, a psychologist, or other therapist or counselor, and tallying up the cost of the office visits, the treatment, and the counseling.

- Asking the mental health professional to issue a narrative report detailing how much additional therapy or treatment will be required of the plaintiff to improve her psychological state, and having the doctor summarize the cost for such treatment. For example, the doctor could state that "this patient will require at least two years of weekly therapy sessions, estimated at a cost of $150 per session, to restore her self-esteem and to address her coping mechanisms following the traumatic accident."
- Asking the mental health professional to make an affirmative diagnosis of the client's condition (e.g., adjustment disorder with mixed anxiety and depressed mood), and then to project the pattern of symptoms, behaviors, and treatment associated with the diagnosis.

For an emotional distress claim to succeed, there must be evidence that the injury suffered by the plaintiff was severe and significantly disruptive of the plaintiff's life. Momentary humiliation or embarrassment or a fleeting emotional reaction do not constitute emotional distress. Unfortunately, many lawyers treat emotional distress claims as secondary to the main physical injury claim, pleading the claim perfunctorily and never thinking twice about proving damages for such losses.

Special Damages

Perhaps the most reliable approach for claiming damages for emotional distress is to present the trier of fact with hard evidence of pecuniary losses. Special damages based on clear, certain, and credible expenditures can be presented, along with specific dollar amounts for future losses attributable to the emotional distress. For example, a table of past and future losses can be constructed as follows:

Description of Loss	Damages Claimed (in dollars)
Past Psychological Treatment and Care	?
Future Psychological Treatment and Care	?
Past Cost of Medications	?
Future Cost of Medications	?
Past Income Loss (missed time from work)	?
Future Income Loss (missed time from work)	?
Past Out-of-Pocket Expenses	?
Future Out-of-Pocket Expenses	?

Pinning down these specific pecuniary losses is one approach to establishing an emotional distress claim. In many cases, however, it will not add up to a substantial amount of money unless a psychological expert can clearly connect the emotional trauma to the plaintiff's loss of past and future earnings. Still, developing a detailed record of special damages is a valuable exercise insofar as it will support the plaintiff's claim for general damages as well.

General Damages

General damages refer to any loss that is nonpecuniary such as pain and suffering, mental anguish, trauma, fear, fright, sleeplessness, loss of appetite, and stress. It embodies medical/psychosocial conditions such as depression and hyperactivity, and it embraces elusive but real setbacks such as the loss of the ability to form intimate relationships and a diminished quality of life. What are these losses worth?

In states that recognize general damages for emotional distress, plaintiffs' attorneys may employ a variety of strategies to persuade a judge or jury to pay a large award. For example, attorneys may elicit testimony about any of the following:

- Changes in the plaintiff's behavior
- Treatment sought from medical/mental health professionals
- Consultations between plaintiff and clergymen or other personal advisors
- The lingering nature of certain symptoms
- Medications taken, their cost, their side effects
- Lifestyle changes
- Missed time from work
- Difficulties performing the job at work
- Plaintiff's reduced interest, dedication, or capacity to pursue social or recreational activities.
- Plaintiff's abandonment of her hobbies (e.g., yoga, ethnic cooking, woodworking).
- Changed relationships with spouses and significant others
- Changed relationships with children
- Changed relationships with parents
- Changed relationships with coworkers
- Changed relationships with classmates

- Changed relationships with neighbors and friends
- Unusual dressing patterns
- Lapses or changes in personal grooming
- Significant changes in spending and buying behavior
- Significant changes in sexual behavior
- Dropping out of school or clubs
- Evidence of cognitive deficiencies (loss of memory, concentration, etc.)
- Recurring bouts of fatigue and malaise

A victim of emotional distress may also be diagnosed as suffering from a *somatoform disorder,* a mental disorder in which the victim suffers physical symptoms that cannot be attributed to any particular physical injury or disease process. Somatoform disorders are real, and the victims truly experience the physical symptoms, but because there is no identifiable physical cause for the symptoms, the treatment involves psychiatric or psychological expertise.

Somatoform disorders include hypochondriasis (excess fear of illness), conversion disorder (numbness, paralysis, tremors, speech problems, and other neurological symptoms), body dysmorphic disorder (extreme preoccupation with body image), somatization disorder (persistent physical symptoms unrelated to any medical condition, usually involving multiple symptoms), and pain disorder (disabling physical pain caused by psychological stress).

One formulaic approach to placing a value on general damages in an emotional distress claim is to choose a multiplier that converts a special damages figure to a general damages figure. For example, let's assume that a plaintiff can show $38,000 in special damages based on the cost of therapy sessions, loss of income specifically attributable to the emotional distress claim, and other out-of-pocket expenses. We could say hypothetically that a multiplier of 7 should be applied. Thus, the value of the emotional distress claim would be 7 times the special damages:

$38,000 x 7 = $266,000

Unfortunately, there is no universally accepted multiplier. An insurance company, acting on behalf of a defendant, may apply a multiplier as low as 1.1, paying only a slight premium over the amount of special damages. ($38,000 x 1.1 = $41,800). Among claims departments that apply such an approach, multipliers of 1.5 or 2 are not uncommon for small cases. More severe emotional distress claims could warrant a multiplier of between 3 and 5, although insurance carriers are much less inclined to settle cases at this level. Plaintiffs' attorneys, by contrast, could argue in favor of even higher multipliers. Ten times special damages would thus not seem unreasonable as a measure to capture *all* of the injured plaintiff's nonpecuniary losses, particularly in a severe case involving permanent injuries.

Because of the lack of uniformity on this issue, plaintiffs' attorneys often find themselves stuck with the dismissive positions of defense attorneys or the low-end multipliers of parsimonious insurance adjusters. Defense attorneys, by contrast, find themselves repeatedly shooting down inexplicably high settlement demands from plaintiffs using arbitrary figures without justification or applying unreasonably high multipliers in weak emotional distress cases. What is needed, at the least, is a table or other reference point that plaintiffs and defendants can rely on in applying multipliers to general damages claims. To address this issue, this author has proposed a set of scales, described at more length in the next section of this book which addresses pain and suffering claims.

11.15. Pain and Suffering

Like emotional distress, *pain and suffering* represents an elusive and indefinable category of personal injury damages. The very term—pain and suffering—has become a popular and controversial legalism in American tort law. However, pain and suffering claims are distinguishable from emotional distress claims in several important ways. Pain and suffering claims are directly derivative of the physical injuries suffered by a plaintiff. If a plaintiff suffered multiple arm fractures in an auto accident, he is entitled to the value of his broken arms (physical injuries) and his special damages (medical bills, lost income, etc.). He is also entitled to his pain and suffering: the unknown monetary value of the difficult-to-measure pain and disability he experienced because of his fractured limbs. Without the physical injury, however, the plaintiff will have sustained no pain; thus, the claim cannot exist in the absence of the physical injury that produces it.

By contrast, an emotional distress claim seeks damages for emotional suffering in its own right. It may be based on the psychological trauma of watching a loved one being killed or suffering a devastating injury; it may be based on nonphysical traumatic events, or it may (as the law requires in some jurisdictions) be associated with a personal physical impact, such as a rape or a physical battery, in which psychological injury exists independent of the physical injury. A victim of a rape resulting from the negligent security of a hotel may overcome her physical injuries much sooner than her emotional distress. The emotional distress, in such an instance, is not intrinsically based on the severity of the physical injury.

To calculate the value of a pain and suffering claim, most attorneys and insurance claims representatives multiply the total amount of special damages by a factor or "multiplier." So, for example, if a plaintiff spent $3,000 in medical treatment for the injuries he sustained, his special damages (pecuniary losses) of $3,000 would be multiplied by some number (generally between 1 and 10), to fix a value for general damages based on pain and suffering. An insurance claims adjuster could offer to pay damages based on a low multiplier such as 1.5, while a plaintiff's lawyer would demand a higher multiplier, such as 5.

Plaintiff's settlement demand: $3,000 x 5 = $15,000
Defense/Insurance counter-offer: $3,000 x 1.5 = $4,500

Which multiplier is correct? No scientific answer to this question exists. As discussed in the previous section on emotional distress damages, the choice of a multiplier is controversial. At one time, plaintiffs' lawyers and defense insurance carriers recognized a "three times specials" rule, in which the multiplier was informally set at 3. Today, it is probably more common to find insurance carriers offering plaintiffs' attorneys anywhere from 1.1 to 2 times special damages on small cases, and perhaps as high as 4 or 5 times specials on larger claims for pain and suffering. In more serious, permanent, and tragic injuries, plaintiffs' attorneys may also seek damages based on much higher multipliers reaching 10 and above.

Because there is no uniformity in choosing multipliers, this author has created several sample scales to assist in the process. The scales which follow are not the product of any scientific analysis or of any consensus between the plaintiff's bar and the defense bar. Rather, they represent an attempt to plot different injuries by severity of pain and suffering, and then to adjust the multipliers assigned to those injuries based on a variety of personal factors. The factors which have been considered here are (1) age, (2) income and employment, (3) credibility and witness quality, (4) hospital/doctor treatment, and (5) previous mental health record.

Age. It is assumed that a younger person who suffers a painful injury should receive a somewhat higher amount of damages, simply because he will live with the pain longer than an older victim. A younger victim would have more years of pain and more likelihood of disability, degeneration, arthritis, and other complications related to the injury.

Income and Employment. A person with a high income level or a high level of employment (and employability) based on work experience, education, and training is treated here as having a somewhat lower amount of continuing pain and suffering. Such persons have greater personal resources and a statistically greater likelihood of overcoming such setbacks.

Credibility and Witness Quality. A plaintiff with a high degree of personal credibility, and for whom there are credible witnesses, deserves a slight upward enhancement of his multiplier. One whose credibility has been called into question, or who has no witnesses, or no reliable witnesses, deserves a slight downward modification of his multiplier.

Hospital/Doctor Treatment. A plaintiff's pain and suffering is likely to be more provable if he has a steady and consistent record of seeking medical treatment following his accident; if he did not ignore therapy sessions for long periods of time; if he was compliant with doctor's orders; if he was confined to a hospital or to home for a period of time. Such a plaintiff deserves an incrementally higher multiplier. Yet, one who has a track record of noncompliance and patternless medical treatment may not qualify for an enhanced multiplier.

Previous Mental Health. A plaintiff with a history of mental or emotional problems should theoretically receive a somewhat lower pain and suffering award because there exist other factors or sources from which the plaintiff experiences pain or suffering. Indeed, there may be no way to separate the personal emotional disruption experienced by a victim of a personal injury who also suffers from multiple preexisting phobias for which she had previously been under psychiatric care.

SAMPLE SCALE BASED ON AGE, INCOME AND CREDIBILITY

Sample Injuries	Basic Multiplier	Age (Under 30)	Age (Over 49)	Income (Under $50,000)	Income (Over $100,000)	Credibility (Low)	Credibility (High)
Severe burns and flesh wounds	5	+1	–1	+ 0.5	–0.5	–1 to –2	+1 to +2
Dislocations, ulna bone fractures, multiple leg fractures	4	+1	–1	+0.5	–0.5	–1 to –2	+1 to +2
Torn ACL, PCL, MCL, meniscus, etc.	3	+1	–1	+0.5	–0.5	–1 to –2	+1 to +2

In this hypothetical scale, it is assumed that severe burns and flesh wounds are the most painful kinds of injuries, thus justifying a basic multiplier of 5—that is, five times special damages. Dislocations and certain kinds of fractures are presumed to be somewhat less painful with a proposed multiplier of 4. Torn ligaments (ACL, PCL, etc.) are rated with a multiplier of 3. Of course, it is impossible to universally grade an injury victim's pain or to state with consistent certainty that a burn victim will experience more pain that a fracture victim. These numbers are ipso facto unscientific. Yet they provide a mechanism for choosing multipliers in pain and suffering cases that holds more promise than random bargaining between zealous plaintiff's lawyers and conservative insurance adjusters.

The basic multiplier can then be upgraded by one point (+1) for young victims or downgraded by one point (–1) for older victims. Victims who earn under $50,000 per year would hypothetically be less equipped to deal with their pain and suffering, and would have fewer resources overall, and would thus be entitled to a slight *bump up* by 0.5. Those earning more than $100,000, by contrast, would suffer a reduction in their multiplier by 0.5. A low-credibility plaintiff, or one with no witnesses or problematic witnesses, might lose a few points, while a highly credible plaintiff, with strong witness support, may gain a point or two in the multiplier.

So, for example, a seriously injured burn victim, who is 20 years old and unemployed, could argue in favor of a higher multiplier of 6.5 times special damages (basic multiplier of 5, plus 1 for being under 30 years old, plus 0.5 for earning under $50,000). A 40-year-old accident victim who suffered a torn meniscus, but who has a long history of dishonesty and has no credible witnesses, could find his basic multiplier of 3 reduced to 1.

SAMPLE SCALE BASED ON MEDICAL TREATMENT AND MENTAL HEALTH HISTORY

Sample Injuries	Basic Multiplier	Well Documented, Consistent Medical Treatment	Poorly Documented, Inconsistent or Questionable Treatment	No Relevant Mental Health History	Significant Relevant Mental Health History
Severe burns and flesh wounds	5	+1	−1	0	−1 to −2
Dislocations, ulna bone fractures, multiple leg fractures	4	+1	−1	0	−1 to −2
Torn ACL, PCL, MCL, meniscus, etc.	3	+1	−1	0	−1 to −2

In this hypothetical scale, the basic multiplier for each category of injuries is augmented by one point for well-documented, consistent medical treatment, but reduced by one point for inconsistent or unnecessary medical treatment. A clean mental health record results in no change in the multiplier while a prior mental history could reduce the multiplier by as much as two points. These ratings and adjustments are, again, sheerly hypothetical, designed simply to offer a prospective scheme for categorizing injuries and personal factors in order to quantify the value of pain and suffering more scientifically.

Under this scheme, a personal injury victim with a dislocated ankle, who waited an extensive period of time before seeking medical treatment and then attended only half of his scheduled therapy sessions, would see his multiplier drop from 4 to 3. A fracture victim with well-documented and timely medical treatment, but with a lengthy history of treatment for clinical depression, could see his multiplier jump from 4 to 5 and then potentially back to 3.

The two sets of sample scales presented above could be conjoined into one expanded scale displaying all five of the factors discussed above. Thus, a 25-year-old burn victim, earning $35,000 per year, with no prior mental history, but with an inadequate and patchy medical treatment record, and no corroborating witnesses, could be assessed for pain and suffering using a multiplier of 4.5.

Augmenting or reducing the multipliers based on such personal factors is a highly subjective practice, but making such adjustments on a scale rather than on a whim could elevate the personal injury settlement process to a more predictable practice.

Chapter 12

Business Damages

12.1. Determining the Best Formula

The economic loss suffered by a business can be measured in a variety of ways, using several different formulas and approaches depending on the nature of the loss and the objective of the calculation. The starting point is to ascertain what *legal events* precipitated the loss. Among the possibilities are the following:

- A **breach of contract** causing significant revenue losses or cost overruns
- An **antitrust** or **unfair trade practice**, such as price-fixing conspiracies that squeeze competitors out of business or otherwise inhibit free competition
- **Wrongful interference** with a business activity or with a contractual relationship
- **Infringement on intellectual property rights** owned by a business enterprise
- The employment of a competitor's **key employee or manager** in violation of a restrictive covenant
- **Embezzlement** or diversion of a significant amount of money by a company employee
- **Breach of fiduciary duties** by a partner, including breach of the duty of loyalty or usurpation of a corporate opportunity, leading to significant business losses

- **Product disparagement, trade libel, slander of title,** and related business defamation torts that impugn the reputation of a company's services or products, including **injurious falsehood** that reflects falsely on the existence, values, or character of a business
- A **fraudulent valuation** in which a business entity or business unit was sold at an inflated value based on fraudulent figures, financial statements, accounts, or representations
- **Fictitious company schemes,** including companies that exchange their worthless stock for the stock of a viable company
- **Malfeasance, misfeasance, and nonfeasance claims** that encompass a wide variety of corporate acts including those undertaken with malicious intent and those committed negligently which represent breakdowns in performance leading to financial losses
- **Unverifiable or falsified trade and bank references** that permit a borrower to obtain bank loans or leases, or to arrange financing, which it could not possibly repay (or which it had no intention to repay)
- **Partnership and corporate director disputes** that place the future of the enterprise in jeopardy
- **Shareholder disputes** such as an action by minority shareholders to dissolve a corporation based on majority shareholders' oppressive conduct
- **Racketeering (Civil RICO) claims** in which a business gains an advantage by conducting an enterprise through a pattern of activity involving interstate commerce that constitutes racketeering (usually mail fraud and wire fraud)
- **Theft of trade secrets** in which a business suffers the loss, publication, release, misappropriation, or revelation of a formula, pattern, compilation, program, device, method, technique, or other process that has economic value
- **Conversion cases** in which a business owner, director, or affiliate engages in unauthorized acts that permanently deprive the business of its property or property rights

Knowing the legal basis for calculating business damages will thus provide a purpose and an objective for choosing one or more formulas to determine the losses. In addition to considering the underlying *legal events,* it is also important to consider the underlying *economic circumstances.* In other words, the damages suffered by a business in a contract or tort dispute, or as a result of an unfair trade practice, can only fairly be measured in the context of the economic circumstances affecting the industry in which the business functions during a particular time frame. In this regard, *economic circumstances* must be construed broadly to include consideration of all of the following factors:

- The general state of the economy
- The particular state of the industry in question (e.g., housing market, metals market, auto industry)
- Political and regulatory environment (e.g., new legislation adopted or forthcoming)
- Social and cultural marketplace trends (e.g., the future of daily newspapers, hybrid cars, traditional grocery stores, coffee cafes)

In some cases, the calculation of damages may boil down to simple math: how much money was stolen by the errant partner? Or, how much money is owed by the customer who failed to pay the remainder due on a building project? In other cases, however, the question of damages is far more elusive: what would that factory have been worth had the sellers not falsified their credit rating and inflated their inventory? What losses could have been avoided had the company we merged with fully disclosed its off-balance sheet liabilities? Is the company going uphill or downhill in the marketplace as a result of (or despite) a particular business deal that went bad, and how exactly do we measure this?

In other cases, it may be necessary to determine the overall valuation of a business. For example, what is the value of a law practice or a chiropractic practice subject to distribution in a divorce case? What is the value of an entertainer's good name or a sports figure's reputation that has been damaged in a business transaction? In many cases, the rates of return discussed in Chapter 7 or the financial ratios outlined in Chapter 8 will provide shortcuts to valuing businesses, or determining losses suffered by those businesses. It may be useful, in fact, to run a variety of formulas and ratios on a set of facts to provide the optimal level of insight about the data gathered in a particular case. Basic calculations, such as net present value and the breakeven formula, will also provide useful guidance as the damage-measurement process unfolds.

12.2. Sources of Information

In order to calculate the value or the changed value of a business or any other measurement of business damages, we will want to consider both internal and external sources of information. Internal sources of information consist chiefly of financial statements, physical assets, facilities, and human resources, the contracts and operations of the company, and its books and records. The external sources of information consist of market indexes and benchmarks that will be used in formula-building, such as the interest rate, inflation rate, currency exchange rate, unemployment rate, and the consumer price index. External information also encompasses a long list of industry-specific data about products and services, such as raw material supplies, salary trends, transportation and warehousing costs, and growth trends.

Internal Sources

The first internal source of information about a business, and the best source, is its financial statements. The balance sheet, the income statement, and the cash flow statement will provide much of the basic information necessary to construct a useful ratio or formula. By examining and dissecting these three kinds of financial statements, lawyers can quickly assess the current condition of a business, and can spot patterns of change in that condition.

Yet the inquiry does not stop with the financial statements. Attorneys conducting discovery should dig deeply in search of source documents, such as invoices, receipts, monthly statements, credit memos, registers, vouchers, and other hard evidence of the underlying financial transactions. A failure to produce such source documents or a reluctance to do so may be a telltale sign of questionable entries on the financial statements. A close examination of such documents may also reveal irregularities, gaps, and inexplicable accounting adjustments that are relevant to a particular cause of action.

The company's journals should also be scrutinized. Whether maintained manually or on a software program, disbursements and receipts are usually recorded in a number of journal entries. A general journal may be available for examination of all noncash items such as earned revenue that hasn't been paid or received yet. A printout of the general ledger should also be inspected for a summarized display of all journal entries.

The company's annual report is also frequently a valuable internal source of information. Although annual reports are frequently conceived as public relations devices designed to promote the company's achievements and good corporate citizenship, they also function as express declarations of the company's financial health, containing both financial and nonfinancial disclosures about the direction of the company. Among the often-useful pages in the annual report are the CEO's letter to shareholders and the signed certification by a company officer attesting to the accuracy of various internal financial reporting controls and procedures. For example, the 2007 Annual Report of Kraft Foods, Inc. features a full-page photograph of company Chairman and CEO Irene B. Rosenfeld which begins with the words "Dear Fellow Shareholder: Welcome to the new Kraft." The introduction, which is signed and dated by the CEO, outlines Kraft's growth strategies but contains the following concession:

> Our bottom-line results, however, were not where we wanted them to be. And so, as we committed last year, our focus in 2008 is to build on our top-line momentum while getting the bottom line growing again.
>
> The biggest challenge we encountered last year was unprecedented high input costs—which impacted everyone in the industry—and the fact that they remained at those levels for an extended time. Because input costs, particularly dairy, stayed so high for so long, our pricing actions did not keep pace with our cost increases. That hurt our gross margins, and as a result, our profits.[1]

---

[1]http://www.kraftfoodscompany.com/assets/pdf/Kraft_07AR_Complete_Book.pdf.

The CEO promised that the company would be "more aggressive with pricing" in 2008, and she outlined plans to reduce overhead costs while investing $100 million in quality upgrades. Like most large corporation annual reports, the 2007 Kraft report contained numerous explanatory footnotes—a fertile repository of additional information about the internal operations of the company, including details of its long-term debt, borrowing arrangements, and interest expense. Reading the narrative sections of annual reports, such as Kraft's, will provide a broader base of knowledge from which proper assumptions can be established and supportable inferences can be drawn.

A company's physical assets, facilities, machinery, equipment, and physical plant also provide an observable source of internal information that may have some bearing on its financial health. Wherever possible and appropriate, attorneys or their expert witnesses should make a physical site visit to the company in question. Under the theory that *one simply doesn't know what he doesn't know,* a physical inspection of the premises may provide leads to other areas of investigation that had not yet been considered. Consider, for example, visible evidence of worker unrest and union demonstrations; evidence of massive fire damage; inactive assembly lines; and barren floors with idle equipment. Such observations may raise further inquiries, prompting one to modify his assumptions or projections about a business entity.

External Sources

Every kind of business has its own peculiar revenue streams, market characteristics and risks, product and service segmentation, and economic forecasts. Data, trends, surveys, and industry ratios for agricultural crop and livestock production will differ from those for forestry and timber operations. The outlook and performance history for the metal ore mining industry will differ from the outlook and performance history for the highway and street construction field. Textile mills will report different cash flow trends, expense details, and profitability levels than industrial chemical manufacturers. In the finance and insurance industries, consumer banks and credit companies will be gauged by merger trends and measured by price-to-earnings multiples that differ significantly from managed health care organizations such as HMO and PPO companies.

Therefore, when building formulas to value businesses or to assess damages and losses, it is important to consult industry-specific sources rather than generalizing about the economy, or about entire industrial segments such as manufacturing, mining, or retail sales. Specific industries can be explored through the North American Industry Classification System (NAICS), which is used by the U.S. Census Bureau and federal statistical agencies to gather data about American business activity. The NAICS classifies North American industries into the following general categories:[2]

- Agriculture, forestry, fishing, and hunting
- Mining, quarrying, and oil and gas extraction
- Utilities
- Construction
- Manufacturing
- Wholesale trade
- Retail trade
- Transportation and warehousing
- Information
- Finance and insurance
- Real estate and rental and leasing
- Professional, scientific, and technical services
- Management of companies and enterprises
- Administrative support, and waste management and remediation services
- Educational services
- Health care and social assistance
- Arts, entertainment, and recreation
- Accommodation and food services
- Other services
- Public administration

There are, in fact, scores of subcategories within each of these categories, enabling one to drill down into a specific industrial classification in search of relevant data. For example, the general NAICS cate-

[2]Based on the 2017 NAICS classification table.

gory for "Manufacturing" above includes several hundred subcategories ranging from starch and vegetable fats and oils manufacturing to dry, condensed, and evaporated dairy product manufacturing; from tobacco stemming and redrying to sheer-hosiery mills; and from burial casket manufacturing to guided missile and space vehicle manufacturing. Choosing the specific industrial classification under the NAICS system will legitimize any external data collected as part of the formula-building process.[3] It will also prevent opposing parties and their experts from misusing data from the wrong industrial classification or from an overgeneralized classification.

Once you've identified a particular industry sector and a particular business subcategory, specific industry data can be obtained through the U.S. Census Bureau's economic census known as "American Factfinder."[4] For example, the American Factfinder data collected for the business subcategory known as "theater companies and dinner theaters" reveals how many U.S. businesses fit this description, the number of establishments, the amount of receipts/revenue, annual payroll, first-quarter payroll, and the number of paid employees. Such information may provide a data portrait that will guide negotiations aimed at valuing a certain business or settling a business loss claim.

In addition to the background information provided by the Census Bureau and other data compilers, it may be necessary to consult external sources to obtain current information about interest rates, discount rates, the prime rate, and other rates. Among the reliable sources are the Federal Reserve's daily publication of selected interest rates,[5] *The Wall Street Journal*'s Market Data Center,[6] Bloomberg,[7] CNN Money,[8] and Yahoo! Finance Forex Central Bank Watch.[9] The Federal Reserve also publishes a wide range of statistics and historical data of principal

---

[3]For a further breakdown of the NAICS classifications, visit the NAICS Association at http://www.naics.com/info.htm.

[4]American Factfinder can be found at www.factfinder.census.gov.

[5]http://www.federalreserve.gov/releases/h15/update/.

[6]http://online.wsj.com/mdc/public/page/2_3020-keyinrates.html.

[7]www.bloomberg.com/markets/.

[8]http://money.cnn.com/data/bonds/.

[9]http://finance.yahoo.com/news/FOREX-CENTRAL-BANK-WATCH-BoC-fxcm-1858437814.html?x=0&.v=1.

economic indicators such as foreign exchange rates and commercial paper rates.[10] The U.S. Department of the Treasury provides daily Treasury yield curve rates, Treasury bill rates, and long-term rates.[11] *The Wall Street Journal* publishes the current *Wall Street Journal Prime Rate*,[12] which is updated every time at least seven of the top ten banks in the United States change their prime rate.

The U.S. Department of Labor home page[13] provides a snapshot of current employment-related data such as the unemployment rate as well as the Consumer Price Index and the Producer Price Index. Foreign exchange rates across the world can be quickly pulled from Yahoo! Finance[14] and a number of other online data compilers.[15]

12.3. Dissecting Financial Statements

To place a value on a company, or to determine what loss it's experienced as a result of a particular legal event, the three key financial statements—the balance sheet, the income statement, and the cash flow statement—should be consulted. In appropriate cases, it may be useful to compare financial statements from one quarter to another, or from one year to another.

The Balance Sheet

Each financial statement provides useful summaries of information. The **balance sheet** reflects total assets, total liabilities, and shareholders' equity. It is based on the essential formula: Total assets = Total Liabilities + Shareholders' Equity. This formula can be algebraically reconfigured into five different formulas.[16] For example, Shareholders' Equity = Total Assets – Total Liabilities.

---

[10]http://www.federalreserve.gov/econresdata/releases/statisticsdata.htm.

[11]http://www.treasury.gov/resource-center/data-chart-center/Pages/index.aspx.

[12]http://www.wsjprimerate.us/.

[13]http://www.dol.gov/.

[14]http://finance.yahoo.com/currency-converter/#from=USD;to=EUR;amt=1.

[15]See, *e.g.*, http://www.exchangerate.com/.

[16]For a look at all five balance sheet formulas, see Section 9.4: Quick Balance Sheet Math.

Dissecting a balance sheet can provide the necessary data to build a formula based on assets, debt, and owner's equity in the company. More specifically, the balance sheet discloses the following **asset** information:

- Current assets
- Investments
- Property, plant, and equipment
- Intangible assets

The balance sheet asset disclosures, in fact, may be considerably more detailed depending on how the company defines assets, what assets it owns, and how it reports these assets. For example, Boeing Corporation's 2009 balance sheet includes the following specific categories of current assets:

- Cash and cash equivalents
- Short-term investments
- Accounts receivable, net
- Current portion of customer financing, net
- Deferred income taxes
- Inventories, net of advances and progress billings

and the following categories of other assets:

- Customer financing, net
- Property, plant, and equipment, net
- Goodwill
- Other acquired intangibles, net
- Deferred income taxes
- Investments
- Pension plan assets, net
- Other assets, net of accumulated amortization

Similarly, a balance sheet can provide valuable data about the company's liabilities. Typically, liabilities are divided into two general categories on the balance sheet:

- Current liabilities
- Long-term liabilities

Like assets, however, liabilities are often divided into subcategories and reported in greater detail, depending on the nature of the company's debt and the manner in which it defines and reports its debt. So, for example, Boeing's 2009 balance sheet divides Total Liabilities into the following categories of current liabilities:

- Accounts payable
- Other accrued liabilities
- Advances and billings in excess of related costs
- Income taxes payable
- Short-term debt and current portion of long-term debt

and the following categories of long-term liabilities:

- Accrued retiree health care
- Accrued pension plan liability, net
- Noncurrent income taxes payable
- Other long-term liabilities
- Long-term debt

Finally, the balance sheet reflects the ownership interest of the shareholders, known as Shareholders' Equity or Owners' Equity. The value of this ownership interest generally consists of the following categories:

- Paid-in capital
- Retained earnings

In a partnership, the owners' equity may be shown as the partners' capital accounts. In a sole proprietorship, it may be shown as the sole owner's capital account. In a corporation, owners' equity will be reflected in terms of paid-in capital and retained earnings. However, corporations may also report owners' equity in a variety of subcategories consistent with their own ownership structure and reporting methods. In Boeing's case, the Shareholders' Equity category on the balance sheet is broken down as follows:

- Common shares issued
- Additional paid-in capital
- Treasury share, at cost
- Retained earnings

- Accumulated other comprehensive loss
- ShareValue Trust shares

Scrutinizing the balance sheet and understanding how data is defined and reported will prevent any mischaracterizations of the data.

Let's now consider how we might use a balance sheet to generate some useful formulas.

For example, let's assume that you wanted to determine a company's return on assets (ROA). The formula for ROA is:

$$ROA = \frac{\text{Net Income}}{\text{Total Assets}}$$

If you have the company's net income (see the next section concerning Income Statements), then you can obtain the total assets from the balance sheet and calculate this formula. Remember, the value of total assets should not logically include assets that don't generate income, such as redundant tools and machines or company cars that are never driven.[17] In this respect, the ROA is often stated as the return on *operating assets,* and the denominator is reformulated as revenue generating assets. This information can also be found (or constructed from the categories) on most balance sheets.

You might also calculate the current asset turnover (CAT) ratio[18] using the amount of total assets reported on the balance sheet. The CAT ratio is:

$$CAT = \frac{\text{Revenue}}{\text{Assets}}$$

Thus, once revenue is ascertained from one of the other financial statements, the CAT can be quickly calculated with the assets figures reported on the balance sheet.

Finding the total amount of assets and liabilities on the balance sheet will also provide the foundation for calculating the price-to-book (P/B) ratio.[19] The P/B ratio begins by calculating the book value of the company. Book value equals assets minus liabilities—a calculation

---

[17]See Section 8.8.

[18]See Section 9.13.

[19]See Section 9.9.

that can be made from the balance sheet alone. If we know our balance sheet formulas, we also know that assets minus liabilities equals shareholder equity. Then, if we can determine the number of outstanding shares of common stock, we can calculate the book value per share (BVPS).

$\text{BVPS} = \frac{\text{BV}}{\text{Shares of Common Stock Outstanding}}$ which is another way of saying that it's equal to the common shareholders' equity divided by the number of shares of common stock outstanding. Once we know the BVPS, we can simply divide the actual current market price of the company's stock by the BVPS to produce the P/B ratio. Thus, if stock was selling at $9 per share, and the BVPS was 3, we would say that the P/B ratio is 3, meaning that stock is selling for three times its book value.

The amount of total liabilities and shareholders' equity shown on the balance sheet also provides the basic information necessary to calculate the debt-to-equity (D/E) ratio.[20] The D/E ratio measures a company's leverage by telling us how much of the company's business is funded by debt rather than equity. The ratio is, essentially, debt divided by equity, but a more complete statement of the D/E ratio is:

$$\frac{\text{Total Liabilities}}{\text{Total Shareholders Equity}}$$

The greater the D/E ratio, the higher the proportion of the company's capital contributed by creditors as opposed to shareholders. A ratio of 2.5 (or 2.5 times as much in total liabilities as in total shareholder equity) means that the company has $2.50 of debt for every $1 of equity. A ratio of 0.5 (or one-half as much in total liabilities as in total equity) means that the company is much stronger financially, with creditors claiming only 50 cents for every $1 of equity claims by the company owners.

Extracting the figures for current assets and current liabilities from the balance sheet can provide additional useful information. A ratio of current assets divided by current liabilities tells us how well a company can pay down its debt in a given fiscal year. The so-called current ratio[21] tells us how much money the company holds in assets in com-

[20]See Section 9.3.

[21]See Section 9.14.

parison to its debt. A current ratio of 2 to 1 means the company has $2 in assets for every $1 in liabilities. A ratio of less than 1 to 1 spells trouble because it means the company has inadequate liquidity; that is, not enough assets to cover its current debt obligations.

Another strategy using the balance sheet is to *common size* each individual type of asset or liability. *Common sizing* refers to a process of determining what portion each asset or liability category represents to the total amount of assets or liabilities. In order to common size the assets, simply divide each category of assets by the company's total assets. To common size liabilities, divide each liability category by the company's total liabilities and shareholders' equity. The same applies to equity: to common size the owner's interest in the company, simply divide each category of shareholders' equity by the company's total liabilities and shareholders' equity.

Why is this important? By breaking down the percentage that each category of assets, liabilities, or equity contributes to the whole, we can quickly ascertain how the company's value or debt is structured. For example, let's assume that ABC Corporation has current liabilities consisting of $350,000 in accounts payable, income taxes payable of $110,000, and short-term debt of $420,000. In addition, it reports long-term liabilities consisting of accrued pension plan liabilities of $185,000 and long-term debt of $589,000. Shareholders' equity is listed at $575,000. Total liabilities and shareholders' equity is reported at $2,229,000. What percentage are each of the specific liability and equity categories of the total amount of reported liabilities and shareholders' equity? By common sizing the figures, we can obtain the following percentages for ABC Corporation:

Category	Percentage of Total Liabilities and Shareholder's Equity
Accounts Payable	15.7%
Income Taxes Payable	4.9%
Short-Term Debt	18.84%
Pension Plan Liabilities	8.3%
Long-Term Debt	26.42%
Shareholders' Equity	25.8%

By analyzing these percentages, we can see that ABC Corporation has a fairly moderate level of pension and tax liabilities. However, its capital structure is somewhat lopsided in favor of debt. The company gets almost 19% of its financing from short-term loans and another 26% from long-term obligations.

The Income Statement

The **income statement** summarizes the company's operations and displays its profits and losses. In fact, the income statement is also known variously as the profit and loss statement, the summary of operations, or the statement of operations. A typical income statement will contain the following income information:

- Revenues
- Cost of goods sold
- Expenses
- Net earnings (income)

These categories can be further divided. Revenues may be stated in terms of sales from one or more corporate units or product lines. Cost of goods sold (COGS) may include inventory, purchases, direct labor costs, and freight charges. Expenses may include sales and marketing expenses as well as general and administrative expenses such as salaries, interest payments, insurance, depreciation, and taxes. Net earnings may be partitioned as earnings before income tax (EBIT) and net earnings after taxes. Depending on what business a corporation conducts and how it reports its income, expenses, and earnings, there may, in fact, be many more specific subcategories on an income statement. For example, Boeing's 2009 "Statement of Operations" includes the following categories:

- Sales of products
- Sales of services
- Total revenues

- Cost of products
- Cost of services
- Interest expense
- Total costs and expenses

- Income from operating investments, net
- General and administrative expense
- Research and development expense, net of credits

- Loss/gain on dispositions, net
- Earnings from operations
- Other expense income, net
- Interest and debt expense
- Earnings before income taxes
- Income tax expense
- Net earnings from continuous operations
- Net loss/gain on disposal of discontinued operations, net of taxes
- Net earnings

One of the most valuable ratios that can be derived from the income statement is earnings per share (EPS).[22] EPS measures the profitability of the company by reducing the amount of earnings to its lowest meaningful denominator; that is, by telling us the portion of the overall profit assigned to each outstanding share of common stock. To build this ratio, we start with the net earnings (net income) generally found at the bottom of an income statement. We subtract the cost of any dividends paid to preferred shareholders. Then we divide the difference by the average number of outstanding shares in a given year.

$$\text{EPS} = \frac{\text{Net income} - \text{Preferred dividends}}{\text{Average outstanding shares}}$$

EPS can be a helpful device for comparing one year's performance to another. Assume, for example, that a party contends that his company's performance has been declining the last three years, pointing to the fact that its net income is slipping by $1 million per year. To test the accuracy of the claim, you have demanded, and obtained, income statements for the last three years. The net income shown on the three statements is as follows:

	2009	*2010*	*2011*
NET INCOME (In Millions)	$16	$15	$14

[22]See Section 9.1.

Assume that the preferred dividends paid for the three years were as follows:

	2009	*2010*	*2011*
DIVIDENDS (In Millions)	$2	$1.5	$1.75

Then, assume that the average number of outstanding shares for the same three-year period was as follows:

	2009	*2010*	*2011*
OUTSTANDING SHARES (In Millions)	$2	$1.8	$1.6

So, let's do the math.

$$\text{EPS} = \frac{\text{Net income} - \text{Preferred dividends}}{\text{Average outstanding shares}}$$

$$\text{EPS (2009)} = \frac{\$16{,}000{,}000 - \$2{,}000{,}000}{\$2{,}000{,}000} = \$7$$

$$\text{EPS (2010)} = \frac{\$15{,}000{,}000 - \$1{,}500{,}000}{\$1{,}800{,}000} = \$7.50$$

$$\text{EPS (2011)} = \frac{\$14{,}000{,}000 - \$1{,}750{,}000}{\$1{,}600{,}000} = \$7.65$$

By using the net income figures provided on the income statement, and applying the formula for EPS, you can challenge the argument that the company's performance has been declining. In fact, the EPS has increased from $7 to $7.50 to $7.65 over the three-year period because dividends have fluctuated and the number of outstanding shares has decreased.

EPS can also be used to compare two or more corporations in the same industry over the same period of time. Assuming other factors remain the same, a comparison of the EPS for multiple companies may reveal which of them is the more profitable enterprise.

The price-to-earnings ratio (P/E)[23] is another useful ratio that can be constructed from the earnings data provided on the income statement. P/E consists of a company's stock price divided by its EPS. The result produces a measure of how the company is viewed—or should be viewed—by the investing public. Where P/E is increasing from period to period, it signals increasing public confidence in the company's growth.

So, for example, assume that a corporation sold its stock at the following price for the years 2009 through 2011:

2009: $15
2010: $20
2011: $26

Borrowing the EPS figures for each of the three years above, the P/E ratios are calculated as follows:

2009: $15/$7 = 2.14
2010: $20/7.50 = 2.66
2011: $21/$7.65 = 2.74

Despite the suggestion that the company is in bad shape due to declining earnings, the P/E in this example is increasing every year, suggesting to the contrary that the company is still growing.

The P/E ratio can be inverted to produce an earnings yield ratio.[24] Earnings yield is calculated by dividing the EPS by the price of a share of stock. By calculating the reciprocal of the P/E ratio, using the figures above, the following earnings yields are produced:

2009: $7/$15 = 0.4666
2010: $7.50/$20 = 0.375
2011: $7.65/$21 = 0.3643

Thus, the earnings yields for the three-year period shrunk from 46.66% to 37.5% to 36.43%. Another way to express these results is to say that in 2009, 46.66 cents were earned for every $1 of investment. In 2010, 37.5 cents were earned, and in 2011, 36.43 cents were earned for every $1 of investment.

---

[23] See Section 9.2.
[24] See Section 9.6.

The income statement is also a road map through the company's costs and expenses. A corporate income statement may, for example, contain line items for cost of goods sold, marketing and selling expenses, administrative expenses, research and development expenses, insurance costs, and federal and state income taxes. We can then common size these costs as a percentage of revenue. Simply divide a particular expense category by the company's total revenue and then multiply by 100. So, for example, if the marketing and selling expenses totaled \$3,333,333, and total revenue equaled \$11,999,999, then the common-sized percentage of marketing and selling expenses would be:

$$\frac{\$3,333,333}{\$11,999,999} = 0.2777 \text{ x } 100 = 27.77\%$$

In other words, for every dollar of revenue, the company spends 27.77 cents for marketing and selling expenses. By common sizing the same expense against total revenue for several years, you can gauge the extent to which expenses are growing or shrinking in particular categories. Spotting trends is part of the basic analysis of a business enterprise and may offer valuable clues as to its ultimate financial health. If net income is growing at a slower pace than revenues, the company may be overburdened by its expenses.

The interest coverage ratio[25] can also be calculated from information found on the income statement. The interest coverage ratio indicates how well interest payments are covered by earnings, and thereby reflects the financial strength of the company. It is calculated by determining EBIT and dividing that figure by the total interest expense. The formula is:

$$\text{Interest Coverage Ratio} = \frac{\text{EBIT}}{\text{Interest}}$$

If, for example, the ratio produced a result of 3.45, it would mean that there was effectively \$3.45 in income before taxes and before interest for every \$1 paid in interest by the company. Calculating the interest coverage ratio for several years by pulling interest and EBIT data from consecutive income statements is therefore a useful device for finding a pattern. If a company has an increasing interest coverage ratio

[25] See Section 9.8.

year after year, it is covering its interest debt with a greater amount of pretax income each year; thus, it's doing well. On the other hand, if the interest coverage ratio is slipping from year to year, the company's ability to cover its interest obligation is becoming weaker over time.

Cash Flow Statement

The statement of cash flows is a critical piece of the financial puzzle in any business case in which the financial value or economic health of a company is in question. The statement reveals how much cash actually is collected by the company and from what sources; how the cash is used or spent; and whether the cash flow is positive or negative at the end of a certain period of time. The cash flow statement begins with the net income (or net profits) for a particular year. It ends with the increase or decrease in the amount of cash and cash equivalents. Typically, the cash flow statement is divided into three major sections: (1) operations; (2) investing; and (3) financing. Among the common categories are the following:

- Net income
- Depreciation expense
- Increased accounts payable
- Increased accounts receivable
- Increased merchandise inventory

which leads to a net cash flow from operating activities. Then, to the net cash flows, we add various investing and financing activities such as:

- Capital expenditures
- Long-term bond proceeds paid
- Dividends paid
- Additions to property, plan, and equipment
- Proceeds from disposal of assets
- Acquisition of businesses
- Sales of investments
- Repurchase of common stock
- Proceeds from short-term debt
- Proceeds from long-term debt

which leads to a net change in the cash for the year.

Cash flow statements may vary somewhat in format based on the manner in which a corporation generates cash, its capital expenditures, and its financial activities.[26] However, they typically follow the three-part pattern of operations, investing, and financing. For example, Boeing's cash flow statement contains these categories:[27]

- **Operating Activities, Cash Flows Provided by or Used In**
  Depreciation
  Adjustments to Net Income
  Changes in Accounts Receivables
  Changes in Liabilities
  Changes in Inventories
  Changes in Other Operating Activities

  Total Cash Flow from Operating Activities
- **Investing Activities, Cash Flows Provided By or Used In**
  Capital Expenditures
  Investments
  Other Cash flows from Investing Activities

  Total Cash Flows from Investing Activities
- **Financing Activities, Cash Flows Provided By or Used In**
  Dividends Paid
  Sales Purchase of Stock
  Net Borrowings
  Other Cash Flows from Financing Activities

  Total Cash Flows from Financing Activities

  Effect of Exchange Rate Changes

  CHANGE IN CASH AND CASH EQUIVALENTS

---

[26]Accountants also distinguish between the *direct method* and the *indirect method* of reporting cash flow. The direct method deducts from operating cash receipts the operating cash disbursements. This results in the presentation of a condensed cash receipts and cash disbursements statement. The indirect method starts with net income and converts it to net cash flow from operating activities. In effect, the indirect method adjusts net income for items that affected reported net income but did not affect cash.

[27]For a three-year comparison of Boeing's Statement of Cash Flows on Yahoo! Finance, click on http://finance.yahoo.com/q/cf?s=BA+Cash+Flow&annual.

Boeing's cash flow statement displays cash flows from three key categories—operating activities, investing activities, and financing activities. A close inspection of the subcategories reveals exactly how Boeing gets its cash and how it spends it, providing deeper insight into how cash flows through the corporation.

In analyzing a cash flow statement, close attention should be paid to the operations section. This section essentially reflects the cash flowing into and out of the company from its core operations. The total cash flow from operating activities should be positive, reflecting a healthy financial condition. Most of the company's cash flow should, in fact, be reflected in the operations section of the statement.

Studying the specific categories within the operations section can provide clues as to the company's real financial condition. For example, a high level of accounts receivable—or an increasing level from year to year—reflects a growing dependency on customer credit, rather than actual cash. Usually displayed in parentheses to represent a negative figure, the accounts receivable category is often an early sign of an impaired cash flow level. Similarly high levels of unused inventory signify reduced levels of cash from operations. If a company is overordering its inventory, and holding it too long, or otherwise failing to move its goods, its inventory value (also portrayed parenthetically as a negative number) will be subtracted from its net income.

The investing section of the cash flow statement compiles the cash expenditures on equipment, assets, and company improvements. The typical subcategories include capital expenditures, acquisitions, and other investments. This portion of the cash flow statement is often the least specific. Thus, a large negative figure for capital expenditures should prompt further inquiry: What is the company buying? How is it investing its money on improvements or enhancements? A large negative figure for acquisitions could reflect the cost of buying a rival company. Such figures may suggest smart investments leading to future growth, or they may imply overburdened company coffers because of costly capital maneuvers.

The financing section of the cash flow statement shows the company's borrowing and debt-repayment activities. It details how cash flows in and out of the company from borrowing money, repaying loans, generating dividends, issuing stock to new investors, or repurchasing common stock. Watching a company's patterns in this section of the cash flow statement can reveal whether the company is borrowing great sums of money or whether it is spending great amounts of money to pay down its debt. Does it have enough cash, year after year, to issue dividends to its shareholders? Is it attempting to raise cash by selling stock? Making these inquiries after scrutinizing the cash flow statement may provide greater insight into the financial health of a particular firm.

Here is some fundamental analysis using the cash flow statement: Start with the operations section. Look at the total cash flow from operations. If the figure is greater than the net income, then the company is likely performing well. A positive level of cash flow from operations, greater than the amount of net income, means the company is generating more cash than it reports to shareholders as earnings. The opposite scenario is likewise true: if cash from operations is less than net income, then the company is cash-strained, generating less money than it reports to shareholders as earnings.

An even stronger indicator of a company's cash flow is the formula for "free cash flow" which measures the amount of cash used by a company, including the cost of improvements and enhancements to its physical plant, machinery, and equipment. The formula for "free cash flow" is:

$$\text{Free cash flow} = \text{Total Cash Flow from Operating Activities} - \text{Capital Expenditures}$$

By subtracting the amount of capital expenditures for a given time period (as listed in the investing section of the cash flow report) from the total cash flow from operations (found at the top or at the bottom of the operations section), you can quickly determine the amount of cash that flows through a company even while it tends to its own maintenance, repairs, and upgrades. Logically, we cannot ignore the fact that a company must spend some amount of money on itself for capital improvements so that it can continue generating cash proceeds at the same rate. Therefore, the free cash flow formula is a truer measure of cash.

Knowing the free cash flow can also help you assess a company's burn rate—that is, how fast it is burning cash, and how soon it will run out of cash. The burn rate formula is:

$$\text{Burn rate} = \frac{\text{Cash and cash equivalents at the end of the year}}{\text{Free cash flow}}$$

The amount of cash and cash equivalents at the end of the year is usually the last line of the cash flow statement.

Let's try an example. XYZ Corporation issues a cash flow statement which reports total cash flows from operating activities as \$51,000. This will be the first figure we will need for the denominator of the burn rate formula: The total cash flow (or net cash) from operating activities = \$51,000. Let's now assume that the capital expenditures for the year total \$34,000, the amount reported in cash outflows to cover equipment upgrades and warehouse expansions for the year. We start by calculating the free cash flow:

Total Cash Flow from Operating Activities – Capital Expenditures
\$51,000 – \$34,000 = \$17,000

Therefore, the free cash flow for the year is \$17,000. In order to calculate the burn rate, we'll also need to know the total amount of cash and cash equivalents at the end of the year. At the very bottom of the cash flow statement, we can find the total amount of cash and cash equivalents on December 31, the end of the fiscal year. Let's assume in this case that the company reports \$9,800 as its total cash and cash equivalents. The burn rate formula can be calculated as follows:

$$\text{Burn rate} = \frac{\text{Cash and cash equivalents at the end of the year}}{\text{Free cash flow}}$$

$$\text{Burn rate} = \frac{\$9{,}800}{\$17{,}000}$$

$$\text{Burn rate} = 0.58$$

Once you have the burn rate, multiply it by the number of months in a year to determine how many months until the company's cash runs out.

0.58 x 12 = 6.96 months

Thus, based on its current financial state, XYZ Corporation has somewhat less than seven months of cash to keep its operations afloat.

Another useful formula to test the financial vitality of a business enterprise is the cash flow coverage ratio (CFC). The CFC is a way of determine how well a company pays back the principal and interest on its loans when they become due. If the cash flow coverage ratio falls below 1.0, it generally signals a company in financial distress. The formula for CFC is:

$$\text{CFC} = \frac{\text{Net income} + \text{Depreciation and Amortization}}{\text{Total Debt Payments}}$$

For example, assume that net income is reported at $229,000, and depreciation and amortization are reported at $99,000. Total debt payments total $66,000. The CFC ratio would equal 4.98, calculated as follows:

$$\text{CFC} = \frac{\$229{,}000 + \$99{,}000}{\$66{,}000}$$

$$\text{CFC} = 4.98$$

The CFC ratio, considered together with the interest coverage ratio,[28] can provide useful insight about a company's actual bill-paying abilities.

Another simple ratio that can gauge a company's liquidity is the operating cash flow (OCF) ratio. The OCF combines information from the balance sheet (current liabilities) with information from the cash flow statement (cash flow from operations) to shed light on how well a company's debt is being managed. The OCF formula is:

$$\text{OCF} = \frac{\text{Cash Flow from Operations}}{\text{Current Liabilities}}$$

The OCF formula is similar to the Quick Ratio[29] insofar as it tells us about a company's ability to pay down (or pay off) its bills. It may, in fact, be a more trustworthy liquidity measure than the quick ratio because it is based strictly on cash flow rather than a hybrid numerator of cash, accounts receivable, and other asset equivalents. So, for example, if a company reported total cash flow from operations of $38.5 million and current liabilities of $50 million, its OCF would be 0.77. In other words, its ratio would be 0.77 to 1, meaning that for every $1 of current debt, the company had only 77 cents in cash flow to cover it.

12.4. What's *Not* in the Financial Statements

As informative as financial statements are, they are not always clear or sufficiently explanatory. By their very nature and design, financial

[28]See Section 9.8.
[29]See Section 9.7.

statements can be inherently ambiguous or falsely suggestive of one financial trend or another. It is thus important to consider all of a company's financial statements together, along with any annual or quarterly reports, and to read all supporting materials, documents, footnotes, and appendixes.

In the most publicized cases involving large-scale financial frauds, regulators have identified a wide range of unlawful management practices, such as illegitimate deferral of expenses, improper revenue recognition, and fictitious or premature sales. If these fraudulent activities have occurred, it may be difficult to detect them by examining the financial statements alone. It is, therefore, necessary to ask questions, demand supporting documentation, and essentially *audit* the company's activities to ferret out any unorthodox accounting procedures.

Attorneys should also be wary of unusually complex transactions, budgets, and organizational structures—any of which may be telltale signs of hidden expenses or other unreported or misreported financial circumstances. Complex business transactions that occur rather suddenly at the end of a fiscal period are suspect, as are a sudden upsweep of end-of-the-year transactions with unknown vendors and newly identified third parties. Strange investment patterns, such as running revenue through offshore tax havens, may also raise red flags, unless otherwise recommended or justified for legal purposes. A management hierarchy that is unnecessarily complex, or in which redundant functions are performed, may also prompt further inquiry.

In cases in which a company's books have been audited, it is useful to see the auditor's report. Was the auditor independent? Did he follow standard accounting practices? Did the auditor ultimately provide a *clean* audit report? Often, an auditor will detect financial events that will call the data in the financial statements into question. These may include, for example, curious or improper transactions between a company and its subsidiaries or affiliates; transactions between a company and other third parties in whom company ownership maintains a personal interest; substantial economic events that changed the course of company's production or earnings potential; or a trend that will inevitably lead to financial disaster if not addressed quickly. Significantly, too, an auditor will generally disclose a change in accounting methods from one year to another, which will almost certainly lead to inconsistencies in comparing annual financial statements.

In terms of fraudulent activity, one need only look at the scandals involving MCI WorldCom, Waste Management, Enron, and other high-profile companies to see how financial statements may fail to tell the whole story. Several of these companies failed to record operating expenses, instead treating them as capital expenditures on their balance sheets. Waste Management also expanded the depreciation time for its property, plant, and equipment, inflating its earnings and making its after-tax profits appear much higher. Issuers of stock options have also run afoul of the law by backdating their options and then misleading stockholders and regulators. When the date that stock options are granted to recipients (the "grant date") differs from the stated date of the options, the company is potentially required to recognize a compensation expense on its income statement. Its failure to do so masks the effect of backdating to investors, tax officials, and other regulators.

Even more flagrant are those companies whose officers forge documents, manipulate inventory records, fictionalize company strategies, sales, or contracts, cover up losses, and report fictitious revenue. While these practices have been widely publicized when they involve large corporations, they are often overlooked, or underpublicized, when they involve smaller, less famous, companies.

Yet another fertile area of corporate fraud is the unreported and undocumented use of corporate assets by other corporations, such as side businesses run by the directors' family members. This may include, for example, using the company jet or its pickup trucks for personal use; requiring the company's janitorial staff to clean personal homes; distributing inventory to family and friends of the company owners; and otherwise using company equipment, machinery, inventory, and personnel for noncorporate purposes.

Of course, fraud and misappropriation are not the only reason that financial statements are potentially misleading. In many cases, it is the nature of the company's business and the design of the financial statements themselves that lead to unclear or deceptive data. For example, on a cash flow statement, the category for capital expenditures which falls under the section on investing activities is often misleading because it lumps together all of the company's capital expenditure activities with no further explanation. However, by performing due diligence, one may find the details in the footnotes in the firm's Form

10-K, the annual report required by the U.S. Securities and Exchange Commission (SEC) and sent to the company's shareholders.[30]

Due inquiry should also be made of a company's off-balance sheet liabilities.[31] A company can artificially inflate its profits or misstate its debt by keeping certain items off the balance sheet. For example, if a firm identifies an asset on its balance sheet but fails to recognize any offsetting liabilities, it may falsely appear to be more financially fortified than it actually is. Even legal off-sheet liabilities should be considered. For example, long-term leases and purchasing agreements could be legitimately excluded from the liability section of the balance sheet under prevailing accounting rules, but that does not mean that such leases or agreements are of no interest. Indeed, the existence and value of such leases or agreements may be highly relevant in establishing the assumptions that underlie a particular formula.

Similarly, contingent liabilities such as pending lawsuits would not ordinarily appear on a balance sheet under the liabilities section since they are not actual current liabilities until a judgment is rendered. Yet a lawsuit that could imperil the financial future of a company is highly relevant. Cursory reliance on a balance sheet with no further inquiry could spell doom in such a case.

12.5. Forms 10-K, 10-Q, and 8-K

It is not a fancy or glossy report, nor does it begin with the colorful displays and promotional statements common to annual reports, but SEC Form 10-K is one of the most valuable sources of detailed information about the financial health of a particular company. Form 10-K is, in fact, a useful blueprint for defining and clarifying the data on a company's financial statements.

Form 10-K must be submitted annually by publicly traded companies, including all domestic issuers of securities, except for small business issuers.[32] It must also be filed by privately traded companies with more than 500 shareholders and $10 million in assets. Quarterly re-

[30] See Section 12.5 below for a discussion of how to dissect the Form 10-K.

[31] See Section 3.6 for a discussion of off-balance sheet liabilities.

[32] 15 U.S.C. §§ 78m, 78o(d), also referred to as Sections 13 and 15(d), respectively, of the Securities Exchange Act of 1934.

ports must then be issued on Form 10-Q, and current reports detailing a number of specified events must be filed on Form 8-K. By examining annual, quarterly, and current reports on these three forms, an attorney can develop significant expertise about a company's actual, recent, and projected financial condition.

Every Form 10-K contains four Parts and 15 Schedules[33] as follows:

PART I

ITEM 1. Description of Business
ITEM 1A. Risk Factor
ITEM 1B. Unresolved Staff Comments
ITEM 2. Description of Properties
ITEM 3. Legal Proceedings
ITEM 4. Submission of Matters to a Vote of Security Holders

PART II

ITEM 5. Market for Registrant's Common Equity, Related Stockholder Matters, and Issuer Purchases of Equity Securities
ITEM 6. Selected Financial Data
ITEM 7. Management's Discussion and Analysis of Financial Condition and Results of Operations
ITEM 7A. Quantitative and Qualitative Disclosures About Market Risk
ITEM 8. Financial Statements and Supplementary Data
ITEM 9. Changes in and Disagreements with Accountants on Accounting and Financial Disclosure
ITEM 9A. Controls and Procedures
ITEM 9B. Other Information

PART III

ITEM 10. Directors, Executive Officers, and Corporate Governance
ITEM 11. Executive Compensation
ITEM 12. Security Ownership of Certain Beneficial Owners and Management and Related Stockholder Matters

---

[33]For explanations and instructions concerning the completion of Form 10-K, see http://www.sec.gov/about/forms/form10-k.pdf.

ITEM 13. Certain Relationships and Related Transactions, and Director Independence

ITEM 14. Principal Accounting Fees and Services

PART IV

ITEM 15. Exhibits, Financial Statement Schedules, Signatures

Scrutinizing these sections can provide valuable insight about a company. For example, Item 3 requires companies to disclose all legal proceedings as required by 17 C.F.R. § 229.103. This regulation, which is also sometimes referred to as Item 103 of Regulations S-K, provides a virtual goldmine of useful information to attorneys. The provision reads:

> Describe briefly any material pending legal proceedings, other than ordinary routine litigation incidental to the business, to which the registrant or any of its subsidiaries is a party or of which any of their property is the subject. Include the name of the court or agency in which the proceedings are pending, the date instituted, the principal parties thereto, a description of the factual basis alleged to underlie the proceeding and the relief sought. Include similar information as to any such proceedings known to be contemplated by governmental authorities.
>
> *Instructions to Item 103:*
>
> 1. If the business ordinarily results in actions for negligence or other claims, no such action or claim need be described unless it departs from the normal kind of such actions.
> 2. No information need be given with respect to any proceeding that involves primarily a claim for damages if the amount involved, exclusive of interest and costs, does not exceed 10 percent of the current assets of the registrant and its subsidiaries on a consolidated basis. However, if any proceeding presents in large degree the same legal and factual issues as other proceedings pending or known to be contemplated, the amount involved in such other proceedings shall be included in computing such percentage.

3. Notwithstanding Instructions 1 and 2, any material bankruptcy, receivership, or similar proceeding with respect to the registrant or any of its significant subsidiaries shall be described.
4. Any material proceedings to which any director, officer or affiliate of the registrant, any owner of record or beneficially of more than five percent of any class of voting securities of the registrant, or any associate of any such director, officer, affiliate of the registrant, or security holder is a party adverse to the registrant or any of its subsidiaries or has a material interest adverse to the registrant or any of its subsidiaries also shall be described.
5. Notwithstanding the foregoing, an administrative or judicial proceeding (including, for purposes of A and B of this Instruction, proceedings which present in large degree the same issues) arising under any Federal, State or local provisions that have been enacted or adopted regulating the discharge of materials into the environment or primary for the purpose of protecting the environment shall not be deemed "ordinary routine litigation incidental to the business" and shall be described if:
   A. Such proceeding is material to the business or financial condition of the registrant;
   B. Such proceeding involves primarily a claim for damages, or involves potential monetary sanctions, capital expenditures, deferred charges or charges to income and the amount involved, exclusive of interest and costs, exceeds 10 percent of the current assets of the registrant and its subsidiaries on a consolidated basis; or
   C. A governmental authority is a party to such proceeding and such proceeding involves potential monetary sanctions, unless the registrant reasonably believes that such proceeding will result in no monetary sanctions, or in monetary sanctions, exclusive of interest and costs, of less than $100,000;

> provided, however, that such proceedings which are similar in nature may be grouped and described generically.

Item 11 of the Form 10-K requires companies to disclose the names and amounts of all executive compensation, in accordance with 17 C.F.R. §§ 229.402 and 229.407(e)(4) and (e)(5). These Item 402 and Item 407 disclosures are likewise rich with details about how the company spends its money, and on whom, and how its structural organization relates to its compensation scheme. These items require clear, concise, and understandable disclosures of all plan and nonplan compensation awarded, earned by, or paid to the top executive officers of the company. The regulation is burdensome in its pursuit of details, including a discussion and analysis section that requires extensive further disclosures by the company:

> **Compensation Discussion and Analysis.**
>
> 1. Discuss the compensation awarded to, earned by, or paid to the named executive officers. The discussion shall explain all material elements of the registrant's compensation of the named executive officers. The discussion shall describe the following:
>   i. The objectives of the registrant's compensation programs;
>   ii. What the compensation program is designed to reward;
>   iii. Each element of compensation;
>   iv. Why the registrant chooses to pay each element;
>   v. How the registrant determines the amount (and, where applicable, the formula) for each element to pay; and
>   vi. How each compensation element and the registrant's decisions regarding that element fit into the registrant's overall compensation objectives and affect decisions regarding other elements.
> 2. While the material information to be disclosed under Compensation Discussion and Analysis will vary depending upon the facts and circumstances, examples of such information may include, in a given case, among other things, the following:

i. The policies for allocating between long-term and currently paid out compensation;

ii. The policies for allocating between cash and non-cash compensation, and among different forms of non-cash compensation;

iii. For long-term compensation, the basis for allocating compensation to each different form of award (such as relationship of the award to the achievement of the registrant's long-term goals, management's exposure to downside equity performance risk, correlation between cost to registrant and expected benefits to the registrant);

iv. How the determination is made as to when awards are granted, including awards of equity-based compensation such as options;

v. What specific items of corporate performance are taken into account in setting compensation policies and making compensation decisions;

vi. How specific forms of compensation are structured and implemented to reflect these items of the registrant's performance, including whether discretion can be or has been exercised (either to award compensation absent attainment of the relevant performance goal(s) or to reduce or increase the size of any award or payout), identifying any particular exercise of discretion, and stating whether it applied to one or more specified named executive officers or to all compensation subject to the relevant performance goal(s);

vii. How specific forms of compensation are structured and implemented to reflect the named executive officer's individual performance and/or individual contribution to these items of the registrant's performance, describing the elements of individual performance and/or contribution that are taken into account;

viii. Registrant policies and decisions regarding the adjustment or recovery of awards or payments if the relevant registrant performance measures upon which they are based are restated or otherwise adjusted in a manner that would reduce the size of an award or payment;

ix. The factors considered in decisions to increase or decrease compensation materially;

x. How compensation or amounts realizable from prior compensation are considered in setting other elements of compensation (e.g., how gains from prior option or stock awards are considered in setting retirement benefits);

xi. With respect to any contract, agreement, plan or arrangement, whether written or unwritten, that provides for payment(s) at, following, or in connection with any termination or change-in-control, the basis for selecting particular events as triggering payment (e.g., the rationale for providing a single trigger for payment in the event of a change-in-control);

xii. The impact of the accounting and tax treatments of the particular form of compensation;

xiii. The registrant's equity or other security ownership requirements or guidelines (specifying applicable amounts and forms of ownership), and any registrant policies regarding hedging the economic risk of such ownership;

xiv. Whether the registrant engaged in any benchmarking of total compensation, or any material element of compensation, identifying the benchmark and, if applicable, its components (including component companies); and

xv. The role of executive officers in determining executive compensation.

SEC Form 10-Q is the quarterly version of the annual Form 10-K. Form 10-Q is filed three times a year, after each of the first three quarters. The 10-K is filed at the end of the fourth quarter. Shorter than the 10-K, every Form 10-Q contains only two parts and 11 items, as follows:

PART I—FINANCIAL INFORMATION

ITEM 1. Financial Statements.

ITEM 2. Management's Discussion and Analysis of Financial Condition and Results of Operations.

ITEM 3. Quantitative and Qualitative Disclosures About Market Risk.

ITEM 4. Controls and Procedures.

PART II—OTHER INFORMATION

ITEM 1. Legal Proceedings.

ITEM 1A. Risk Factors.

ITEM 2. Unregistered Sales of Equity Securities and Use of Proceeds.

ITEM 3. Defaults Upon Senior Securities.

ITEM 4. (Removed and Reserved).

ITEM 5. Other Information.

ITEM 6. Exhibits.

Form 10-Q is a valuable source of information that goes beyond the disclosures in the annual 10-K. The 10-Q, for one thing, provides updated information, which may make an important mathematical difference three months, six months, or nine months after the last 10-K was issued—a difference that can substantially affect a formula.

The updated financial statements provided with the 10-Q may also reveal a developing trend that could not be ferreted out of the last set of financial statements previously provided. So, for example, an updated cash flow statement may show that receivables are climbing much faster than sales, reflecting a growing risk of bad debt or indicating that a company is experiencing collection problems or that management is, for some reason, extending credit more liberally than in the past.

Legal proceedings disclosed in Part II, Item 1 of the Form 10-Q will capture those proceedings that arose after the filing of the last 10-K. The risk factors section in Part II, Item 1A will also contain some insight into the company's response to changing market conditions. In fact, the management discussion and analysis section of Part I, Item 2, may reflect new information and changes in position that occurred since the last annual report was issued. For example, on Morgan Stanley's Third-Quarter 2008 Form 10-Q, in the management discussion section, the firm discussed quarterly net losses of approximately $1.4 billion attributable to the ruined credit market. It pointed to the exacerbating events of Lehman Brothers' bankruptcy filing, the sale of Merrill Lynch to Bank of America, the U.S. government conservatorship of Fannie Mae and Freddie Mac, and the government's loan to AIG. Reading a company's reaction and perception about its financial viability in the face of changing market conditions can assist lawyers to form realistic assumptions about a particular case scenario.

The exhibits attached to the back of the 10-Q may also include any number of relevant disclosures, such as mathematical explanations and data compilations for certain calculations, tables of ratios, contracts, deeds and leases, notes and retirement plan disclosures, and corporate registration documents. For example, the 10-Q filed for Adobe Systems, Inc. in the third quarter of 2000 contained numerous exhibits including the company bylaws, merger documents, indemnity agreements, leases and subleases, details of employee stock purchase plans, confidential executive resignation agreements, promissory notes, details of a stock option plan, and credit agreements.[34] In an appropriate case, such information could prove extremely beneficial in framing the terms of a settlement or grounding the basis for certain decisions used to construct a proper formula.

Finally, SEC Form 8-K, known as a "Current Report," provides the most recent update of a company's financial information. It is required to be filed promptly after the occurrence of any material event, such as the announcement of a layoff or a plant shutdown, the filing of a bankruptcy petition, the resignation of a director, and other events affecting the value and status of assets, bonds, and debentures. Form 8-K contains nine sections, with 28 items, as follows:

Section 1	**Registrant's Business and Operations**
Item 1.01	Entry into a Material Definitive Agreement
Item 1.02	Termination of a Material Definitive Agreement
Item 1.03	Bankruptcy or Receivership
Section 2	**Financial Information**
Item 2.01	Completion of Acquisition or Disposition of Assets
Item 2.02	Results of Operations and Financial Condition
Item 2.03	Creation of a Direct Financial Obligation or an Obligation under an Off-Balance Sheet Arrangement of a Registrant

[34]http://www.adobe.com/aboutadobe/invrelations/pdfs/Q30010Q.pdf.

Item 2.04	Triggering Events That Accelerate or Increase a Direct Financial Obligation or an Obligation under an Off-Balance Sheet Arrangement
Item 2.05	Costs Associated with Exit or Disposal Activities
Item 2.06	Material Impairments
Section 3	**Securities and Trading Markets**
Item 3.01	Notice of Delisting or Failure to Satisfy a Continued Listing Rule or Standard; Transfer of Listing
Item 3.02	Unregistered Sales of Equity Securities
Item 3.03	Material Modification to Rights of Security Holders
Section 4	**Matters Related to Accountants and Financial Statements**
Item 4.01	Changes in Registrant's Certifying Accountant
Item 4.02	Non-Reliance on Previously Issued Financial Statements or a Related Audit Report or Completed Interim Review
Section 5	**Corporate Governance and Management**
Item 5.01	Changes in Control of Registrant
Item 5.02	Departure of Directors or Certain Officers; Election of Directors; Appointment of Certain Officers
Item 5.03	Amendments to Articles of Incorporation or Bylaws; Change in Fiscal Year
Item 5.04	Temporary Suspension of Trading Under Registrant's Employee Benefit Plans
Item 5.05	Amendment to Registrant's Code of Ethics, or Waiver of a Provision of the Code of Ethics
Item 5.06	Change in Shell Company Status
Section 6	**Asset-Backed Securities**
Item 6.01	ABS Informational and Computational Materials
Item 6.02	Change of Servicer or Trustee
Item 6.03	Change in Credit Enhancement or Other External Support
Item 6.04	Failure to Make a Required Distribution
Item 6.05	Securities Act Updating Disclosure

Section 7	**Regulation FD**
Item 7.01	Regulation FD Disclosure
Section 8	**Other Events**
Item 8.01	Other Events (The registrant can use this Item to report events that are not specifically called for by Form 8-K, that the registrant considers to be of importance to security holders)
Section 9	**Financial Statements and Exhibits**
Item 9.01	Financial Statements and Exhibits

When one of the delineated events occurs, a company is required to file a Form 8-K. A catch-all provision in Item 8.01 allows the company to disclose further any "other events" not specifically delineated by the SEC. The 8-K is an indispensible discovery document whenever the actions of management have been called into question insofar as it details changes in the composition of the board of directors. It also reveals changes in the company's accountant, and with that disclosure may come an explanation that prompts further inquiry.

Of course, the 8-K will reveal major company events such as acquisitions, mergers, and bankruptcies within days after they occur (and therefore well in advance of the next quarterly 10-Q or annual 10-K). Whenever P/E ratios or EPS calculations are being made, Form 8-K provides a quick and timely method for determining if any new events have occurred that are likely to affect the future share value of the company's stock. Delinquencies and defaults in the payment of principal and interest of major obligations or arrearages in the payment of dividends will also trigger the filing of an 8-K, and in so doing, provide vital updates to an attorney calculating ratios or formulas based on debt, interest coverage, dividend payments, and other measures of financial condition.

12.6. Applying Net Worth

The net worth of a business is simply its total assets minus its total liabilities. Calculating net worth from one year to the next provides a useful snapshot of the progress the business is making over time. We could say that a positive net worth, in which assets exceed liabilities, is a sign of a financially healthy company and a negative net worth, in which liabilities exceed assets, is a sign of a fiscally troubled company. But these are oversimplifications. A more important question, perhaps, is the minimum net worth a company should have.

The basic formula for net worth[35] is total assets minus total liabilities, but in business cases, it may be useful to apply a more specific formula. In this respect, preferred stock dividends should also be subtracted from total assets. The same is true of any other obligation of the company to make a payment, regardless of whether it is shown on the balance sheet. Only by reducing the total assets by *each and every* liability and obligation can you obtain a genuinely accurate picture of the company's net worth. The more specific net worth formula would thus look like this:

$$\text{Net Worth} = \text{Total Assets} - \text{Total Liabilities} - \text{Preferred Stock Dividends} - \text{All Other Financial Obligations (whether reported or not)}$$

Once net worth is determined, it can be divided by the total shares of stock to produce the company's net worth per share:

$$\text{Net Worth Per Share} = \frac{\text{Net Worth}}{\text{Total Outstanding Common Shares of Stock}}$$

In fact, this formula may be modified to include not only the total number of outstanding shares of stock but also stock options, stock warrants, convertible notes, and convertible debentures. These options, warrants, and bonds can be converted to shares of stock, thus providing an augmented denominator that presents an even more comprehensive picture of the company's current and projected stock ownership. The expanded formula looks like this:

$$\text{Net Worth Per Share (and Projected Share)} = \frac{\text{Net Worth}}{\text{Total Common Stock} + \text{Options} + \text{Warrants} + \text{Convertible Bonds}}$$

[35]See Section 8.9.

Keeping an eye on net worth can be an extremely useful exercise. It can help attorneys make crucial decisions based on the financial path of a business, and to assist clients in satisfying credit and banking requirements. Net worth provides an instant indication of whether a company has sufficient assets to cover its debts. By comparing two or more companies' financial data, we can determine which one has the greater net worth. By tracking one company's financial data over a period of quarters or years, we can see how its net worth changes, draw certain conclusions about the company, and make relevant, documented, decisions.

In business litigation matters, the net worth of a company may reveal its capacity to settle a case; that is, to pay damages. If the net worth is low or negative, the company may be a bad target for protracted litigation and unlikely to satisfy any substantial judgment. Where damages are to be paid, the impact of making a settlement or satisfying a judgment can be gauged by the effect on the company's net worth. Thus, we can factor the cost of a judgment or a series of judgments into the liabilities to be subtracted in the net worth formula:

Net Worth = Total Assets – Total Liabilities – Total Judgments

It is important to remember, however, that any calculation of net worth is time sensitive. As noted in Chapter 2, financial values are technically accurate only at the moment at which they are stated, and there is a continuing forward momentum that imposes an unending risk of change.[36] Every effort should therefore be exerted to ensure that the underlying data used to calculate net worth is up to date and reliable.

12.7. Applying Shareholders' Equity

The term *shareholders' equity* is often used interchangeably with net worth to mean total assets minus total liabilities. In fact, as we know from our quick balance sheet math,[37] the amount of shareholders' equity is equal, for accounting purposes, to assets minus liabilities. Shareholders' equity can also be defined in another way, as we'll discuss below.

Shareholders' equity may come from a number of sources: capital contributions made by the investors who formed the business; addi-

---

[36] See Sections 2.4 (Risk of Change) and 2.5 (Timing Is Everything).

[37] See Section 9.4.

tional infusions of money made thereafter by the owners; and earnings (profit) which the company accumulates over time and is able to retain after paying off its debts and obligations. The last category is referred to as *retained earnings.*

We can think of shareholders' equity as the *share capital* plus retained earnings minus *treasury shares*. Share capital refers to the original funds invested in the company and the cash paid by investors when the company issued stock. Retained earnings refer to the profits accumulated by the company. Treasury shares refer to the stock of the company which is purchased by the company itself. Thus, the formula:

Shareholders Equity = Share Capital + Retained Earnings – Treasury Shares

If we consulted a balance sheet and discovered that Hypothetical Corporation had total assets of $100,000 and total liabilities of $60,000, then we could conclude easily that the shareholders' equity in Hypothetical Corporation would be $40,000. We might also learn that Hypothetical's share capital was $55,000 when it first issued shares to its investors. After several years in business, the company reported retained earnings of $45,000. But the company bought back $60,000 worth of stock as treasury shares. Applying the formula above, we reach the same result:

Shareholders Equity = Share Capital + Retained Earnings – Treasury Shares

Shareholders Equity = $55,000 + $45,000 – $60,000

Shareholders Equity = $40,000

Because shareholders' equity is effectively net worth, one might also say that net worth can be determined by adding share capital to retained earnings and subtracting treasury shares. Because this is true, the formula for shareholders' equity can replace net worth in the various formulas discussed in Section 11.5 above.

Another helpful device is to determine a company's *average shareholders' equity.* Average shareholders' equity (ASE) provides an arguably more legitimate picture of the true ownership value than the reported shareholders' equity at the beginning of an accounting period or at the end of the period. The formula is:

$$\text{ASE} = \frac{\text{Beginning Shareholders Equity} - \text{Ending Shareholders Equity}}{2}$$

First, find the shareholders' equity at the end of the previous year. That figure will be the *beginning shareholders' equity* for the current year. Then, add the shareholders' equity for the last reported period for the current year. Divide the sum by two to find the average shareholders' equity.

Knowing the shareholders' equity for a particular corporation also permits us to calculate the rate of return on such equity. The return on shareholders' equity, also known as return on equity (ROE),[38] is simply the net income divided by the shareholders' equity:

$$\text{ROE} = \frac{\text{Net Income}}{\text{Shareholder's Equity}}$$

By calculating the ROE, we can evaluate the financial position of a corporation in terms of its profitability. How much profit is generated by the money invested by the shareholders—that's the question. If the ROE is low, it may reflect low profitability or poor management. A high ROE, by contrast, reflects greater profit and wiser money management. ROE is thus a useful device for comparing a corporation's progress from year to year, and for comparing one corporation with another.

12.8. Applying EPS

Earnings per share (EPS)[39] tells us how profitable a business is, in terms of each share of stock. EPS data is generally reported on income statements and is mandatorily reported by public corporations. EPS is calculated by dividing the net income of the corporation (determined after paying out dividends to preferred shareholders) by the average number of outstanding shares:

$$\text{EPS} = \frac{\text{Net income} - \text{Preferred dividends}}{\text{Average outstanding shares}}$$

So, for example, if a corporation reported net income of $20 million and paid out $2 million in dividends, with an average of 3,000,000 in outstanding shares, its earnings per share would equal $6, calculated as follows:

---

[38]See Section 8.7.

[39]See Section 9.1.

$$\text{EPS} = \frac{\text{Net income} - \text{Preferred dividends}}{\text{Average outstanding shares}}$$

$$\text{EPS} = \frac{\$20{,}000{,}000 - \$2{,}000{,}000}{3{,}000{,}000}$$

$$\text{EPS} = \frac{\$18{,}000{,}000}{3{,}000{,}000}$$

$$\text{EPS} = \$6$$

Knowing the EPS for a corporation can lead to a number of other useful calculations. For example, assume that an issue in a business dispute is whether a particular enterprise was experiencing steady growth or sporadic growth during a particular period of time. Merely showing an increase or a decrease in earnings provides a somewhat superficial forecast of the company's financial position. However, the EPS can be used to determine a growth rate that will indicate whether the company's growth trend is accelerating or declining. This growth rate is known as the EPS Growth Rate (EPSGR) and is calculated as follows:

$$\text{EPSGR} = \frac{\text{Ending EPS} - \text{Beginning EPS}}{\text{Beginning EPS}}$$

For example, if the EPS at the beginning of an accounting period is \$6, and it grows to \$8 by the end of the period, the EPSGR would be 33%, as shown below:

$$\text{EPSGR} = \frac{\$8 - \$6}{\$6}$$

$$\text{EPSGR} = 0.33$$

The EPSGR provides a multiplier that can be used in calculating the company's market value. Determining the EPSGR for a series of accounting periods (year after year) will provide a much more meaningful indication of whether—from an investment standpoint—the company is, was, or has been growing steadily or sporadically.

Another method of applying EPS data is to calculate the *annual growth factors* for the EPS and then calculate the geometric mean for a period of time. Start by determining the EPS for a period of years. In the example below, we provide a 10-year portrait of EPS figures for the hypothetical ABC Corporation.

ABC CORPORATION

EPS BY YEAR

2002: $3.50	2007: $6.35
2003: $4.10	2008: $7.44
2004: $6.05	2009: $7.56
2005: $6.15	2010: $7.90
2006: $5.80	2011: $8.25

Next, starting with 2003, establish a series of year-to-year EPS ratios, dividing the current year by the prior year EPS:

$4.10 / $3.50
$6.05 / $4.10
$6.15 / $6.05
$5.80 / $6.15
$6.35 / $5.80
$7.44 / $6.35
$7.56 / $7.44
$7.90 / $7.56
$8.25 / $7.90

Now calculate the annual growth factors for each of the ratios above:

2003 $4.10 / $3.50 = 1.1714
2004 $6.05 / $4.10 = 1.4756
2005 $6.15 / $6.05 = 1.0165
2006 $5.80 / $6.15 = 0.9430
2007 $6.35 / $5.80 = 1.0948
2008 $7.44 / $6.35 = 1.1716
2009 $7.56 / $7.44 = 1.0161
2010 $7.90 / $7.56 = 1.0449
2011 $8.25 / $7.90 = 1.0443

Once you've calculated the growth factors, you need only subtract 1 to determine the EPSGR. In 2003, the EPSGR was 1.1714 – 1, or 0.1714. Thus, in 2003, ABC Corporation enjoyed a positive EPS growth of 17.14%. In 2006, however, ABC experienced a negative EPS growth of –5.7% (calculated as 0.9430 – 1 = –0.057).

Next, by calculating the geometric mean[40] of the nine growth factors above, we can draw some meaningful conclusions about ABC Corporation's growth. *Why do we calculate a geometric mean rather than an ordinary arithmetic mean?* Remember that the geometric mean is necessary when you wish to average percentages. The growth rates above are essentially percentages, and the most accurate averaging process is derived from the geometric mean.

To calculate the geometric mean, first calculate the product of all nine growth factors by multiplying them by each other.

1.1714 x 1.4756 x 1.0165 x 0.9430 x 1.0948 x 1.1716 x 1.0161 x 1.0449 x 1.0443 = 2.356. Therefore, the product is 2.356.

Next, determine the 9th root of the product. Remember that in order to calculate a root, we can raise the product to an exponent of the reciprocal: in other words, the 9th root of 2.356 is the same as 2.356 raised to a power of one-ninth. Thus:

Geometric mean = $(2.356)^{1/9} = 1.099899$
Mean Growth Rate in Earnings Per Share = 1.099899 – 1 = 0.099899

So, we can say that ABC Corporation had a mean EPSGR of more than 9.9% over the period 2002 through 2011.

The geometric mean of the EPS growth factors can also be calculated using a shortcut. Divide the final year (2011) EPS of \$8.25 by the first year (2002) EPS of \$3.50, and then determine the 9th root of the result.

$$\frac{\$8.25}{\$3.50} = 2.357$$

$$(2.357)^{1/9} = 1.099958$$

Rounding off the result, we can see again that ABC Corporation had a mean EPSGR of 9.9% over the same 10-year period.

Understanding EPS and EPSGRs is not only important for investors. These financial formulas can assist attorneys in proving or dis-

[40]See Section 5.10.

proving the financial trajectory of a corporation in a business dispute. They can assist legal advisors in making recommendations to clients about the fiscal strength of a corporation. They can provide key indicators to guide deal-makers in contract negotiations and merger and acquisition analyses, and they can help determine whether a company has sufficient earnings capacity to pay damages. In a punitive damages claim, where a company's financial status may be relevant and admissible, the mean EPSGR provides a strong indicator of the company's growth over time.

12.9. Applying the P/E Ratio

The Price to Earnings Ratio (P/E)[41] measures investor confidence in a company. The higher the P/E, the greater the level of investor confidence about the company's performance and financial health. The P/E also provides a *multiple* of a stock, meaning that it tells us—at least, in theory—how much investors are willing to pay *per dollar of earnings.* A P/E of 10 suggests that investors are willing to pay \$10 for every \$1 earned by the company.

The formula is simply the average market price of a single share of common stock divided by the net income per share of stock (expressed as the earnings per share).

$$P/E = \frac{\text{Price per share}}{\text{Earnings per share (EPS)}}$$

In litigation, arbitration, mediation, and negotiations, the P/E ratio is a handy gauge of a company's performance, and of the public perception of its performance. It can be used to portray the financial health of a company, or lack thereof, or to prove or disprove the existence of certain financial conditions necessary to establish an opportunity, a motive, or a pattern that is critical to a party's theory of the case. However, a simple P/E calculation may have minimal value by itself. It is necessary to apply, compare, and project the P/E scenarios properly to obtain the greatest benefit from this useful ratio.

---

[41]See Section 9.2.

Comparables

A P/E ratio of one company can be compared to the P/E of other companies, but the comparison would be folly unless both companies were engaged in the same business or industry. Industries known for low growth rates such as the oil and gas industry or the utilities field in general should not be compared to companies in the technology sector. Lower P/E ratios are common in mature industries in which earnings and sales grow at a slower, more stable pace.

Overpricing and Underpricing

Beware of the tendency to assume that high or low P/Es reflect overpriced or underpriced stock. For example, assume that a company's stock is priced at $50 per share with an EPS of $5. Its P/E would be 10, meaning that investors are willing to pay $10 for every $1 the company generates in earnings. If the stock were priced at twice as much, $100 per share, with an EPS of $5, the P/E ratio would jump to 20, meaning that investors would dole out $20 for every $1 of earnings. This doesn't sound like such a good deal. Surely the company's stock must be overpriced at $100 per share, right?

Not necessarily. A closer look is necessary. If the company is a robust, fast-moving business, in an emerging growth pattern, it may be reliably projected to generate significantly higher earnings in the future. Perhaps the company is capable of commanding a higher stock price today because its prospects for the future are very promising. Moreover, the company may have a very trustworthy earnings history, suggesting that its reported earnings will *actually* be received. It thus presents a low investment risk as compared with a lower P/E company with uncertain earnings patterns and greater investment risk.

Forward P/E Ratio

Some experts argue that P/E data is flawed because it relies on outdated information that can change at any moment. Indeed, the risk of change[42] is inherent in a P/E calculation because the denominator of

[42]See Section 2.4 (discussing Rule 4 for dealing with formula, "Risk of Change").

the formula contains past earnings, rather than current or future earnings. Of course, the EPS, as reported on financial statements, is generally an audited number which the company has shared with government regulators and is likely to be considered trustworthy and admissible in legal proceedings. Still, the reported EPS is a *trailing* figure because it tells us only about the earnings over the 12 months that have already gone by. If the P/E ratio is relevant to a business dispute or to litigation involving past events, then a reliable published trailing figure would be quite useful. On the other hand, if the P/E ratio is sought to determine the investment worthiness of a company, going forward, then the trailing figure would arguably be outdated and risky.

Under such circumstances, it would seem more accurate to know what the EPS will be in the future. In order to project the future, it will be necessary to obtain reliable earnings forecasts from dependable financial monitors and/or expert witnesses. Informally, it may be possible to make some generalized projections about a company's earnings by analyzing the status of its projects, its products and inventory, its loans and debts, the future value of certain funds and receipts, and other factors found on its financial statements. Generally, however, it is best to leave the business of forecasting future earnings to the Wall Street specialists and economic advisors who publish such results on a regular basis. Once a projected or expected EPS can be established, moving forward, then we can calculate the Forward P/E, as follows:

$$\text{Forward P/E} = \frac{\text{Price per share}}{\text{Projected Earnings per share}}$$

Instead of dividing stock price by the EPS to obtain the P/E, we divide the stock price by an estimated EPS, a projection of what we believe earnings will be in a future year. This forward-looking P/E ratio may prove to be a more credible evaluation tool if the projected earnings are based on trustworthy data and conservative conclusions.

The PEG Ratio

Another way to overcome the drawback of using trailing data is to calculate the P/E ratio while measuring the growth in earnings during a fixed period of time. The so-called price-earnings-growth ratio (PEG) measures the price of a stock against the earnings per share and against the company's expected growth.[43] PEG thus produces a growth factor derived from dividing the P/E ratio by the annual EPSGR. The formula is:

$$\text{PEG} = \frac{\text{P/E}}{\text{Annual EPS Growth}}$$

For example, assume that "Defendant Corporation" experienced 10% annual growth in earnings and a P/E ratio of 40. Its PEG ratio would be 40 divided by 10, which equals 4. The result would shrink if the P/E ratio declines. Thus, a P/E ratio of 20 would reduce Defendant Corporation's PEG to 2. Likewise, the result would shrink if the annual EPS growth increases. So, if Defendant Corporation had a P/E of 40 but enjoyed a 20% annual growth rate, its PEG would also be 2. Simple math, but what does it mean?

A lower PEG may signal an undervalued stock. For investors, a lower PEG is often treated as good news, that is, a "good buy" or a cheaper investment. A PEG of 1 or lower is thought to be a solid investment risk, assuming no other countervailing factors. If a company is growing at 25% per year and has a P/E of 25, its PEG would be 1, meaning that there is a balanced trade-off between stock price and company growth. In fact, we might say that a fairly priced company stock will equal its growth rate. In other words, P/E = Annual EPS Growth. PEG ratios greater than 1 suggest that a company is overvalued, but some advisors say that ratios of 2 to 3 are acceptable. PEG ratios less than 1 indicate an undervalued company. With a PEG of less than 1, the company may outpace the market, returning higher profits, signaling investors that it is a good bargain.

The PEGY Ratio

While the PEG ratio could help us gauge the value of a company, it may also be an incomplete measure of the company because it does not take into consideration the dividend yield.[44] Companies that pay divi-

---

[43] A company's growth can be estimated informally, by applying various rates of return, estimates, and projections. Alternatively, estimated growth rates for various companies may be found through a wide variety of online reporting services and analyst reports, including, for example, Yahoo! Finance.

[44] See Section 9.5.

dends to their shareholders typically have higher earnings growth than companies that don't pay dividends. In a legal setting, it is important to know what you're dealing with—a company that pays no dividends, a company that pays dividends steadily and predictably, or a company that pays dividends erratically, or perhaps in unsustainably high amounts. Because dividend paying is a measure of a company's financial strength and its management practices, many financial experts recommend that the PEG formula be modified to include a measure of the dividend-paying practices of the company, the so-called dividend yield.

The price-to-earnings-to-growth-and-yield ratio (PEGY) is the answer. It is calculated as follows:

$$\text{PEGY} = \frac{\text{P/E}}{\text{Annual EPS Growth} + \text{Dividend Yield}}$$

For example, assume that Defendant Corporation has a P/E of 30 and projected annual EPS growth of 10%. Its PEG would be 3. However, if we also determine its dividend yield, we might obtain a clearer picture of the interrelationships between stock price, earnings, growth, and dividend payouts.

Dividend yield by itself compares what investors are earning from their dividends with the price of the stock. The formula is:

$$\frac{\text{Dividends per share}}{\text{Market price per share}}$$

It is expressed in percentage form. If Defendant Corporation's stock sells for $25 per share, and it pays dividends of $1 per share, its dividend yield is 1/25 or 4%.

Let's put it all together now. If Defendant Corporation has a P/E of 30, earnings growth of 10%, and a dividend yield of 4%, then its PEGY ratio would be 2.14, calculated as follows:

$$\text{PEGY} = \frac{\text{P/E}}{\text{Annual EPS Growth} + \text{Dividend Yield}}$$

$$\text{PEGY} = \frac{30}{10\% + 4\%}$$

$$\text{PEGY} = 2.14$$

Had we looked only at the PEG ratio of 3, we might have evaluated Defendant Corporation too high and regarded its stock price as too expensive. By using the PEGY ratio, however, we can obtain a better, more accurate, picture of the company that takes into consideration the value of it dividend yield. In business litigation, as well as in corporate deal making, the more textured picture that can be drawn from inquiring about dividend payments and calculating the PEGY may prove to be a critical deal closer or a deal breaker.

12.10. Applying Rates of Return

Because we already know a number of basic formulas from Chapter 4, and various rates of return from Chapter 7, we can now apply some algebraic techniques to make constructive calculations in business cases.

Let's start with a variation of present value. As you may recall, present value (PV) can be determined by manipulating the formula for future value (FV). $FV = PV\ (1 + i)^n$ where i is the interest rate and n is the number of years. Thus, we can use some basic algebra to state the formula for present value as follows:

$$PV = \frac{FV}{(1 + i)^n}$$

In most cases, we know the future value, and we're trying to determine the present value. Or we know the present value, and we're trying to determine the future value. But what if we knew the present value *and* the future value, and we want to determine the rate of return—that is, the interest rate or the discount rate in a particular case? For example, Company A has its eye on two potential acquisition targets: Company B and Company C. It can acquire either company for $5 million. A financial projection of the Company B acquisition indicates that a $5 million investment made today in Company B would be worth $17 million in three years. A financial projection of the Company C acquisition indicates that a $5 million investment made today in Company C would be worth $28 million in five years. Which is the better deal?

	Company B	**Company C**
PV	$5,000,000	$5,000,000
FV	$17,000,000	$28,000,000
n	3 years	5 years
i	?	?

To determine whether Company B or Company C would be the better investment, we must rewrite the present value formula to solve for i (the interest rate).

$$PV = \frac{FV}{(1+i)^n}$$

$$i = \left[\frac{FV}{PV}\right]^{\frac{1}{n}} - 1$$

Let's plug in the math for each of the target acquisitions.

Company B

$$i = \left[\frac{FV}{PV}\right]^{\frac{1}{n}} - 1$$

$$i = \left[\frac{17}{5}\right]^{\frac{1}{3}} - 1$$

$$i = 1.5037 - 1$$

$$i = .5037$$

Therefore, the Company B deal pays 50.37% interest on the original $5 million investment.

Company C

$$i = \left[\frac{FV}{PV}\right]^{\frac{1}{n}} - 1$$

$$i = \left[\frac{28}{5}\right]^{\frac{1}{5}} - 1$$

$$i = 1.4114 - 1$$

$$i = .4114$$

Therefore, the Company C deal pays 41.14% interest on the original $5 million investment.

The better deal, then, is for Company A to invest the $5 million in acquiring Company B. By calculating the interest rates for each deal, we are able to determine that the greater rate of return can be found in the Company B deal.

ROE[45] is another important ratio that can be applied and modified in business cases. ROE measures a company's profitability by showing how much profit is generated with the money invested by the company's shareholders. The basic formula is:

$$\text{ROE} = \frac{\text{Net Income}}{\text{Shareholder's Equity}}$$

So, for example, assume that a company reported net income of \$1.5 million on its income statement, and stockholders' equity of \$6.6 million on its balance sheet. Without making any technical adjustments, the simple ROE would be:

$$\text{ROE} = \frac{\$1{,}500{,}000}{\$6{,}600{,}000}$$

$$\text{ROE} = 0.26666$$

$$\text{ROE} = 26.67\%$$

This basic calculation can be modified, however, to reveal the return on equity for common shareholders. The general ROE formula considers *all* forms of shareholders' equity, including equity attributable to preferred shareholders. The so-called return on common equity (ROCE), however, removes the preferred stockholders' stake from the formula. To calculate ROCE, we must reduce net income by the value of preferred dividends and then reduce shareholders' equity by the value of preferred equity. The formula is:

$$\text{ROCE} = \frac{\text{Net Income} - \text{Preferred Dividends}}{\text{Shareholder's Equity} - \text{Preferred Equity}}$$

Yet another way to examine ROE is to average the shareholders' equity for a given year. A basic ROE calculation is arguably an inadequate measure because the shareholders' equity that is used is the amount of equity reported on a balance sheet at the end of a fiscal year. Perhaps it would be more appropriate to determine what the average shareholders' equity was during the course of the fiscal year. To deter-

[45]See Section 8.7.

mine the average shareholders' equity, simply add the beginning shareholders' equity (derived from the prior year's balance sheet) to the ending shareholders' equity (which is the amount reported on the current balance sheet), and then divide by two. Thus, the formula for return on average equity (ROAE) is:

$$\text{ROAE} = \frac{\text{Net Income}}{\text{Beginning Shareholder's Equity} + \text{Ending Shareholder's Equity} \div 2}$$

$$\text{ROAE} = \frac{\text{Net Income}}{\text{Average Shareholders Equity}}$$

The ROA ratio[46] is another device for gauging management performance. Unlike ROE which compares net income to equity, ROA compares net income to assets. It answers the question: how efficiently is management using the company's assets to generate profit? The basic ROA formula is:

$$\text{ROA} = \frac{\text{Net Income}}{\text{Total Assets}}$$

The numerator of this ratio (net income) can be found on the company's income statement, and the denominator (total assets) can be found on the balance sheet. So, for example, if a company reported net income of $350,000 and total assets of $1.8 million, the ROA would be:

$$\text{ROA} = \frac{\text{Net Income}}{\text{Total Assets}}$$

$$\text{ROA} = \frac{\$350{,}000}{\$1{,}800{,}000}$$

$$\text{ROA} = 0.1944$$

$$\text{ROA} = 19.44\%$$

Assume, however, that in structuring a deal involving a company, the sellers of the company argue that their ROA is really quite a bit higher than the 19.44% shown above because not all of their assets are truly being utilized by the company. Assume, for example, that the company can show that it has redundant machinery, outdated equip-

[46]See Section 8.8.

ment, and other idle assets totaling $150,000 in value. It could argue that the basic ROA calculation is not an accurate measure of the extent to which company assets generate revenue because the denominator is inflated by the value of assets that are not actively employed by the company. Rather, a return on operating assets (ROOA) should be calculated, as follows:

$$\text{ROOA} = \frac{\text{Net Income}}{\text{Total Assets} - \text{Unused, Idle or Unproductive Assets}}$$

So, in the instant case, if there were unused, idle, or unproductive assets totaling $150,000, our ROAA would be calculated as follows:

$$\text{ROOA} = \frac{\$350{,}000}{\$1{,}800{,}000 - \$150{,}000}$$

$$\text{ROOA} = 0.2121$$

$$\text{ROOA} = 21.21\%$$

By applying the ROOA instead of the ROA, the company's counsel can now argue that there is, in fact, a greater return on assets than previously suggested.

Perhaps the value of assets is challenged as being too high or too low in a particular accounting period. After all, a company that generates $1 million in net income on $5 million of assets will have a greater ROA than a company that generates $1 million on $10 million of assets. If net income is fixed and agreed upon, the value of the assets may be disputed, especially where fluctuations from one quarter to another are questioned. To resolve this issue, the ROA formula can be modified to take into consideration the average value of assets during a given year. The return on average assets (ROAA) works like the ROAE: an average value of assets is determined by adding a beginning value to an ending value and dividing by two. Such an average can cover a quarter or a fiscal year. Once the average value of the assets is determined, the ROAA can be calculated:

$$\text{ROAA} = \frac{\text{Net Income}}{\text{Average Total Assets}}$$

In cases where averaging the value of total assets will provide better, more current, or more reliable information, the ROAA is the preferable measuring device.

Applying ROA, ROE, and the variations on these ratios strategically can assist attorneys in assessing the value, performance, and profitability of business entities in a variety of transactional and litigation scenarios.

12.11. Liquidity versus Indebtedness

How easily and how quickly a company can convert assets into cash is a key measure of the company's financial health, its performance and profitability, and the quality of its management team. So, too, is the question of how deeply the company depends on borrowed funds. While some degree of leverage is desirable to facilitate capital growth and augment cash flow, too much dependency on creditors' funding can place a company in a weak and vulnerable financial position. In sizing up a company, therefore, most ratios and formulas are designed to provide a yardstick of liquidity or indebtedness.

Measuring the liquidity and leverage of a company also provides important statistical information to attorneys and accountants in a variety of applications. In a transactional scenario, discovering illiquid business enterprises and overleveraged companies may serve to terminate a negotiation or to alter the course of negotiations before credit is extended or a dangerous deal is struck. Discovering liquidity issues or debt-coverage difficulties before making a deal serves the attorney's objective of performing due diligence while allowing him to cover his own tracks with hard mathematical evidence.

In a litigation environment, knowing how to ascertain the level of a company's liquidity or indebtedness can support proof of the opportunity or motive for a company to have acted in a particular way when confronted with certain economic events. Mathematical proof of a significant change in liquidity may cast a light on a corporate atmosphere in which the company was fraught with the risk of theft or fraud. Establishing certain ratios can also lay the predicate for an expert's opinion or for an entire trial theme.

From a settlement perspective, the liquidity of a company or its ability to pay its debts may influence decisions about its capacity to pay a judgment or the structure under which any such judgment should be paid. Working the ratios to make an argument can solidify the settlement demands or counteroffers contained in demand letters, settlement brochures, and offers of judgment. The ratios and formulas for liquidity and leverage may also provide attorneys with tactical bargaining tools in mediation sessions and settlement conferences.

Liquidity Measures

To measure liquidity using the balance sheet, we can run three simultaneous calculations: (1) the quick ratio, (2) the current ratio, and (3) the working capital calculation. The quick ratio[47] is a quick snapshot of cashable assets as measured against company debt. The quick ratio is calculated as:

$$\frac{\text{Cash} + \text{Market Securities} + \text{Accounts Receivable}}{\text{Current Liabilities}}$$

The formula, by design, excludes calculations for inventory which cannot be quickly converted to cash.

The current ratio[48] expands on the quick ratio by adding back inventory and other current assets. It pulls from the balance sheet the total amount of current assets and current liabilities and strikes a simple ratio:

$$\frac{\text{Current Assets}}{\text{Current Liabilities}}$$

Although it is simple to state and easy to calculate, the current ratio provides a meaningful measure of liquidity by computing the company's short-term bill-paying ratio. For example, if current assets were worth $20 million and current liabilities were worth $10 million, the current ratio would be 20-to-10 or 2-to-1, meaning that the company would have $2 worth of assets to cover every $1 of debt—an acceptable level of liquidity.

The working capital (WC) calculation is simply the difference between current assets and current liabilities:

$$\text{WC} = \text{Total Current Assets} - \text{Total Current Liabilities}$$

So, for example, if current assets were $20 million and current liabilities were $10 million, the working capital would be $10 million. The math is quick, but the information is substantial: The company has a current cash flow of $10 million in working capital.

---

[47]See Section 9.7.

[48]See Section 9.14.

Leverage Measures

A useful leverage measure, the debt-to-worth ratio (DTW), can also be built from data readily available on the balance sheet. The ratio is:

$$\text{DTW} = \frac{\text{Total Liabilities}}{\text{Net Worth}}$$

Net worth[49] should be calculated first. Net worth equals total assets minus total liabilities. Once this calculation is made, the figure for net worth is divided into total liabilities to produce the DTW ratio. The ratio reveals how leveraged the company is. In other words, it tells us how heavily dependent on debt the company is, and therefore whether the company appears to be more or less liquid. The greater the DTW ratio, the more undesirable the company will appear to creditors, investors, and acquisition suitors.

Turnover ratios can also illuminate the balance between liquidity and indebtedness. These include, for example, the inventory turnover, accounts receivable turnover, accounts payable turnover, and current asset turnover ratios.[50] For example, the accounts receivable turnover ratio (ART) can tell us how many days customer accounts receivable remain open and unpaid. If this time period is increasing over time, then the company may be experiencing an evolving cash flow problem and hence diminished liquidity.

12.12. Profit Margins

Measuring gross profit and net profit is another approach for appraising the financial status of a business enterprise. Profit margins can be examined on a quarter-to-quarter or year-to-year basis, indicating a particular company's trend or pattern over time. Profit margins for several similar companies can also be compared with each other to ascertain which of them is most or least profitable.

To calculate profit margins, we turn to the income statement where we can obtain figures for the amount of sales, the cost of goods sold, and other expenses.

---

[49]See Section 8.9.

[50]See Sections 9.10, 9.11, 9.12, and 9.13 respectively.

Gross Profit Margin

The gross profit margin (GPM) ratio calculates a percentage of "profits" remaining after manufacturing the goods sold in order to meet the expenses of the company. The GPM formula is:

$$\text{GPM} = \frac{\text{Net Sales} - \text{Cost of Goods Sold}}{\text{Net Sales}}$$

In effect, the GPM ratio starts with the amount of gross profit in the numerator. Gross profit, which is usually calculated and stated on the income statement, is the difference between the dollar value of sales revenue and the reported COGS. The amount of COGS equals the total cost of materials used to create the goods along with the direct labor costs associated with the production.[51] Thus, if we subtract the COGS from the sales revenue figure, we'll have a "gross profit" figure as our numerator.

The denominator of the GPM ratio is simply the amount of net sales. By dividing net sales into the gross profit figure, we can obtain a percentage, known as the GPM, that gauges the company's ability to satisfy its overhead expenses.

Example: Life Enterprises, Inc. reports net sales of $1 million and a cost of goods sold of $770,000. Its gross profit is, therefore, $1 million minus $770,000, or $230,000.

Its GPM is 23%, calculated as follows:

$$\text{GPM} = \frac{\$230{,}000}{\$1{,}000{,}000}$$

$$\text{GPM} = 0.23$$

Once you know the GPM, you can assess whether the company is an industry leader or laggard. Before making comparisons, however, be sure to determine whether all other companies being compared share the same accounting procedures for calculating cost of goods sold.

Net Profit Margin

A further analysis—and perhaps a more meaningful one—is to determine the net profit margin after taking into consideration the other ex-

[51] For another application of COGS, see Section 9.10.

penses of the corporation (other than the COFS). This will include all kinds of operating expenses as well as income taxes. The net profit margin (NPM) ratio accounts for these additional liabilities.

$$NPM = \frac{\text{Net Income After Taxes}}{\text{Net Sales}}$$

Net income can be plucked from the bottom of the income statement, and net sales (or revenues) can generally be found at the top of the statement. Where an income statement is not available, then the numerator of the NPM must be calculated manually as follow:

Net income after taxes = Net Sales – COGS – operating expenses – income taxes

After the net income after taxes is determined, the net sales are divided into the figure to produce a NPM.

Example: World Enterprises, Inc. sells five million doohickeys for $25 each, but it costs the company $15 to manufacture each doohickey. World Enterprises also has operating expenses of $15.5 million, and a tax liability of $13.3 million. To calculate the NPM, we begin by determining the net income after taxes.

Net Sales = 5,000,000 doohickeys @ $25 each = $125,000,000

Cost of Goods Sold = 5,000,000 doohickeys @ $15 each = $75,000,000

Operating Expenses = $15,500,000

Income Taxes = $13,300,000

Net income after taxes = $125,000,000 – $75,000,000 – $15,500,000 – $13,300,000 = $21,200,000. We can now build the NPM formula:

$$NPM = \frac{\$21{,}200{,}000}{\$125{,}000{,}000}$$

$$NPM = 0.1696$$

Thus, we can conclude that the NPM for World Enterprises, Inc. is 16.96%.

The NPM ratio is particularly useful in gauging the trajectory of a particular company over time. However, when it is used to compare one company with another, the comparison will be flawed if the companies enjoy different tax rates or benefit from different tax breaks or setoffs. In such cases, it is safer to modify the NPM ratio so that taxes are not deducted from the numerator. Where the information is being pulled from an income statement, the numerator should be the net income before taxes.

12.13. Devising Your Own Specific Business Ratios

It may be useful in business negotiations and in litigation matters to perform certain calculations with respect to a specific question about a business operation that cannot be directly addressed by any of the formulas discussed above. In this regard, you can devise your own specific business ratio, setting two questions in opposition (or in relation) to each other. The relationship of the number of X to the number of Y converts mathematically to $\frac{X}{Y}$. If we can obtain the figures for X and Y through negotiations, investigations, or pretrial discovery, then we may be able to design our own ratio setting the figures in relation to each other and generating a percentage. The range of possibilities is endless.

If a company sells 300 widgets per month and 500 whatchamacallits per month, we might want to know the relationship between these two sales figures. How we pitch the question determines how we set up the ratio. What is the ratio of widgets to watchamacallits is $\frac{\text{Widgets}}{\text{Watchamacallits}}$ which equals $\frac{300}{500}$ which equals 0.6 or 60%. We can then conclude that the company sells 6 widgets for every 10 watchamacallits it sells. If we ask, instead, what is the ratio of watchamacallits to widgets, the ratio is stated as $\frac{\text{Watchamacallits}}{\text{Widgets}}$ which equals $\frac{500}{300}$ which equals 1.66 or 166%. By subtracting 1 from the result (1.66 – 1), we can say that the sales of watchamacallits are 0.66 or 66% greater than the sales of widgets.

Useful business ratios can be designed to address any number of valuable questions that arise in the course of client discussions or courtroom battles. For example, in contract negotiations with organized labor, or in a wrongful discharge case brought by an aggrieved employee, we may want to calculate the rate at which factory workers are leaving the company. How would we calculate an *employee turnover ratio* for factory workers alone?

In a dispute between companies over which one originated a series of sales over a period of time, we may be interested to know how many sales were generated through a company's website in relation to the number of prospective buyers who viewed the company's home page. How would we calculate a *sales-to-home page hits ratio* as a measure of a particular sales department's activity?

Or, consider a shipping department with a troublesome track record of untimely deliveries, which has now led to a breach-of-contract lawsuit. In discovery, attorneys disagree over the percentage of orders that are shipped on a timely basis. How would we calculate a *timely order shipping ratio* to ascertain exactly what level of untimeliness the shipping department experienced in fulfilling orders during a certain period of time?

Each of these examples can be addressed through a ratio that fixes a relationship between a specific factor and a more general factor.[52] For example, in the case of factory worker turnover, in order to devise a useful formula, we would want to know two basic figures: first, the total number of factory workers employed at the company at a specific point in time, and second, the number of factory workers who resigned, retired, or were fired. Essentially, we are asking the question: what is the relationship between the total number of employees (general factor) and the specific number of employees who left the company (specific factor)? Or, stated otherwise, what percentage of the total number of factory workers resigns, retires, or gets fired at any given time? The formula is simply:

$$\text{Factory Worker Turnover Ratio} = \frac{\text{Number of Factory Workers Who Resigned, Retired or Were Fired}}{\text{Total Number of Factory Workers}}$$

By constructing a department-specific ratio (factory workers), we are able to formulate a basic mathematical relationship between the specific figure in the numerator and the larger, more general figure in the denominator. So, for example, if a corporation employed 1,400 workers, of which 850 worked in the factory, we would use the figure 850

[52]The use of the term *factor* is meant here to refer to both the figure expressed in the numerator of the fraction, which is properly known as a *dividend,* and the figure expressed in the denominator, properly known as the *divisor.* The result of dividing the divisor into the dividend produces the *quotient,* which, for purposes of simplicity and clarity, is referred to herein as simply the *result* or the *ratio.*

as our denominator. Of the 175 employees who left the company, 100 of them were factory workers; so, we would then use the figure 100 as our numerator. Applying the ratio shown above, we can calculate a factory worker turnover ratio of 11.76%, as follows:

$$\frac{100}{850}$$

$$= 0.1176$$

In effect, the company is losing about 12 factory workers for every 100 factory workers employed.

There are many ways to fine-tune this formula, based on the various mathematical devices applied earlier in this chapter. For example, if we want to establish an accurate number of factory employees for a particular calendar year, and assuming that the number fluctuated throughout the year, we would calculate an average number of total factory workers employed during the year. To do this, we would add the total number of factory workers employed at the beginning of the year to the total number at the end of the year, and divide by 2. We could also modify the formula by changing the numerator to reflect only the number of resigning factory workers OR the number of retiring factory workers OR the number of terminated factory workers, or some combination of these figures, rather than a hybrid number of all factory workers who resigned, retired, or were fired during the applicable period.

The logic of comparing a specific factor against a more general factor, or a specific figure against a more global or broader figure, is the fundamental technique of ratio-building. By appreciating how a ratio generates a useful percentage, one can devise any number of different ratios to address specific concerns within specific corporate departments and divisions.

Let's try another example, this time applying the s*ales-to-home page hits ratio* mentioned above. At issue is the question of what percentage of the people visiting a company's Web page actually purchase the company's products. The answer to this question could illuminate negotiations in a business dispute between two sales representatives selling the same product. Or perhaps it could settle specific questions that arise in the course of litigation over the success of a Web-based advertising campaign. To fix the ratio, we need to gather two pieces of information: First, the general factor for the denominator—in this case, the total number of home page views by prospective customers. Then, the specific factor for the numerator—in this case, the number of home page views that turned into sales closed through the website. The formula is:

$$\frac{\text{Total Number of Web-Based Sales}}{\text{Total Number of Home Page Views}}$$

Let's plug in some sample numbers. Assume Company A and Company B are both selling a holiday trinket set. For the month of December 2011, the two companies are reporting the following Web-based sales and home page views:

	Number of Sales	Home Page Views
Company A	690	71,084
Company B	548	56,111

Which company has the greater sales-to-page-hits ratio for the holiday trinket set? Let's do the math:

$$\textit{Company A: } \frac{690}{71{,}084}$$
$$= 0.009706$$
$$= 0.9\%$$

$$\textit{Company B: } \frac{548}{56{,}111}$$
$$= 0.009766$$
$$= 0.9\%$$

It's a virtual tie. Both companies have a sales-to-hits ratio of approximately 0.9% (Company B has a technically higher ratio, but by a de minimus degree). For what it's worth in the case at hand, neither company can claim better results from Web-based sales of the trinket set.

The third example offered above deals with a shipping department with a troublesome track record of untimely deliveries. But exactly how untimely is the shipping department? Can we somehow construct a *timely order shipping ratio?* To do this, we would need to think first about the general factor: the total number of orders shipped. Then, we would state a smaller number to be measured against the total number of orders shipped. The smaller number would be the total number of timely shipments. So, for example, if a company shipped 50,000 units, but only 19,000 of them were shipped on time, we would construct the ratio as follows:

Timely order shipping ratio =

$$\frac{\text{Number of Timely Shipments}}{\text{Total Number of Shipments}}$$

$$= \frac{19{,}000}{50{,}000}$$

$$= 0.38$$

$$= 38\%$$

Therefore, only 38% of the shipments leaving the shipping department are on time.

We could tweak this formula by changing the specific factor to be measured against the total number of shipments. Instead of asking what the timely shipping ratio is, we could inquire about the untimely or overdue shipping ratio. We could thus construct an *untimely order shipping ratio,* as follows:

Untimely order shipping ratio =

$$\frac{\text{Number of Timely Shipments}}{\text{Total Number of Shipments}}$$

The number of untimely shipments would equal the total number of shipments (50,000) minus the number of untimely shipments (19,000), or 31,000.

$$= \frac{31{,}000}{50{,}000}$$

$$= 0.62$$

$$= 62\%$$

Therefore, the company is suffering a late shipment rate of 62%.

As you might have detected, you can also determine the untimely shipment rate by subtracting the timely shipment rate from 1. Thus, if the *timely order shipping ratio* produces a timely shipping rate of 0.38, then the untimely shipping rate must be 0.62 (1 – 0.38). This shortcut can be applied whenever there are only two alternatives, such as timely or untimely, open or closed, male or female, Caucasian or non-Caucasian.

Almost any question that arises in a business or corporate setting can be examined more quickly by way of a ratio. The value of the ratio depends on how the questions to be examined are framed. For example:

- A business executive wonders whether she's employing too many secretaries, clerks, and other support staff. The question she's actually asking is "What is the number of support staff in relation to the total number of employees?" The ratio is:

$$\frac{\text{Number of Support Staff}}{\text{Total Number of Employees}}$$

- A company's outstanding receivables are mounting, and a question arises as to how long it has been carrying such a high amount of accounts receivable. Perhaps we want to know what the relationship is between the amount of money owed for more than 60 days and the total amount of receivables outstanding. The ratio is:

$$\frac{\text{Total Amount of Accounts Receivable over 60 days old}}{\text{Total Amount of Accounts Receivable}}$$

- At issue in a dispute between a company and commission-based employees is the question of whether direct-mail-order campaigns and telemarketing campaigns were successful or profitable during a period of time. An arbitrator wonders what level of success was enjoyed from direct mail sales and from cold calls to sales prospects. Two ratios can be envisioned: First, we can gauge the success of the direct-mail-order campaign by fixing the relationship between the total number of direct mail pieces actually placed in the mail and the number of sales generated by the mail pieces. The ratio is:

$$\frac{\text{Total Number of Direct Mail Sales}}{\text{Total Number of Direct Mail Pieces Actually Mailed}}$$

Then, we can gauge the success of the telemarketing campaign by asking what the total number of cold call sales is in relation to the total number of cold calls made to prospective buyers. The ratio is:

$$\frac{\text{Total Number of Cold Call Sales}}{\text{Total Number of Cold Calls Actually Made}}$$

As these examples show, the kinds of issues and questions that can be measured by a ratio are quite varied and specific. By thinking of ratios as tools for establishing rates and percentages that can be used as comparing devices, we can enhance the process of making business decisions, providing legal advice, and arguing for or against certain legal positions.

12.14. Dealing with Professional Practices and Small Businesses

What is a law practice or a dental practice worth? How do we measure the value or the change in value of a business that sells professional services only and maintains no inventory of goods or products? Is a one-man chiropractic office or a one-woman architectural firm worth anything, as a business, if the chiropractor or the architect stops working?

Placing a value on such professional service corporations is often difficult, and data gathering can be elusive. Because these businesses rely so heavily on personal reputation, word-of-mouth referrals, and a history of service dedicated to a particular community or physical location, it is necessary to measure the *goodwill* of the business, not just its physical assets, accounts receivable, and cash on hand.

The need to place a value on a professional practice or small personal service business is important in a variety of legal scenarios:

- A retiring pediatrician wishes to sell his medical practice to a corporate medical practice group that is establishing a chain of pediatric centers. Attorneys have been retained to handle the sale.
- A two-man law partnership is dissolving as one of the lawyers has been named to a judgeship. Outside attorneys have been

retained to oversee the buyout of the firm and transfer of the firm's assets to the surviving partner.

- A successful veterinary practice is listed as an asset in a divorce case. The wife, who is the veterinarian and the sole owner of the business, minimizes the value of the business. The husband insists that it has been a lucrative professional practice, which has largely supported their family for many years. The value of the veterinary practice is in question.
- A tragic flood in a waterfront community has destroyed the offices of a real estate firm. A dispute arises between the displaced firm and its insurance carrier over the claim for coverage attributable to the flood. Because of environmental and safety issues, the real estate firm will not be permitted to rebuild its offices in the same location and will thus lose its advantageous location. At issue is the value of the real estate firm.
- An individual debtor has filed a petition for bankruptcy under Chapter 13. Before incurring insurmountable debt, the debtor operated a financial advisory service in which he provided investment advice. Chartered as a limited liability company, the financial advisory service continues to do business, although it is having difficulty meeting its recurring debt obligations. In reviewing his Chapter 13 confirmation plan, the bankruptcy trustee has expressed concern about the value of the ongoing business.

While each of these scenarios calls for legal intervention, lawyers alone may not be able to provide all of the necessary valuation answers. Indeed, in most such scenarios, it is necessary to retain an accredited business valuator or other qualified financial expert to place a value on the business.[53] However, it may be useful to perform certain rough valuation calculations in the early stages of negotiation, litigation, or client counseling. It is also quite useful to appreciate the methods of valuation that will be considered or applied by financial experts. Two of the most common methods used to valuate businesses are discussed below.

---

[53]For a discussion on choosing the right expert, see Section 20.1.

Capitalization of Earnings Method

One of the most common and historical methods of small business valuation is known as the *capitalization of earnings method.* This method determines the value of a professional practice of a personal service corporation by dividing future earnings by a capitalization rate. The capitalization rate ("cap rate") is essentially a discount rate minus a growth rate, but selecting these discount and growth rates is often highly subjective and controversial. The basic formula for the capitalization of earnings method is:

$$\text{Business Value} = \frac{\text{Future Earnings}}{\text{d} - \text{g}}$$

in which d refers to the discount rate and g refers to the growth rate, and together (d – g) they refer to the cap rate.

For example, assume that a business earned $750,000 last year. A discount rate of 28% is chosen (discussed below), and the growth rate is expected to be 3%. The simplified calculation for the capitalization of earnings method would be:

$$\begin{aligned} \text{Business Value} &= \frac{\text{Future Earnings}}{\text{d} - \text{g}} \\ &= \frac{\$750{,}000}{0.28 - 0.03} \\ &= \frac{\$750{,}000}{0.25} \\ &= \$3{,}000{,}000 \end{aligned}$$

Therefore, the value of the business is $3 million.

The formula, though simply stated, relies on a number of complicated and potentially controverted determinations, for which expert assistance is generally required. Let's examine each part of the formula:

Future Earnings. The only reasonable method for determining future earnings is to look at the historical earnings of the business. Maximum integrity is required in this process, for the future earnings figure selected can be based on inflated past earnings if those past earnings include one-time nonrecurring payments or other unusual windfalls that increased the bottom line. Generally, the "earnings" amount refers to EBIT, but in some cases it could refer to earnings before interest, taxes, and depreciation (EBITD)—a point that needs to be clarified. Earnings may also include the owner's salary and benefits, but if these amounts are added back into the total annual earnings, then a higher capitalization rate must be used.

The future earnings figure is perhaps inherently flawed because the capitalization of earnings method assumes that earnings will be constant in the future. However, the capitalization of earnings method eliminates the need to place specific values on customer files, works in progress, and goodwill.

Discount Rate. The greatest amount of controversy surrounds the selection of a discount rate and the method used by accountants, valuators, and other experts to determine this rate. In the most general sense, the discount rate is the annual rate of return that a buyer of the business would require in order to purchase the business and all of the risk associated with it. If there were one reliable source that published discount rates for similar businesses, the discount rate could be selected from that source. Comparison could also logically be made to other similar professional practices whose discount rates have been published or otherwise disclosed. Logically, too, a discount rate is a number that embraces a number of different kinds of risks, and so it may make sense to *build* the discount rate from the various constituent risks.

The *build-up method* (BUM) has four components:

(1) **The Safe Rate (SR)**, which is also sometimes known as the risk-free rate of return. It is essentially the cost of money represented by a rate on investments that have no risk of default. This source for this rate is the rate for the current 20-year U.S. Treasury bond.
(2) **The Equity Risk Premium (ERP)**, which is a premium that measures the additional risk that investors take by investing in an equity market rather than in long-term government securities. The source for this rate is Ibbotson Associates which publishes annual market risk data.[54]

---

[54]Ibbotson Associates is widely recognized in the business valuation community as the source for such data. It is owned by Morningstar, Inc, a leading provider of independent investment research. Ibbotson's annual publication, *SBBI (Stocks, Bonds, Bills and Inflation Valuation Yearbook* and *Cost of Capital Yearbook)* are generally accepted among all business valuators.

(3) **The Small-Size Risk Premium (SRP)**, which measures the increased risk experienced by smaller companies. This premium takes into consideration the difficulty that smaller companies have in raising financing, their higher sensitivity to business risks, their lack of economies of scale, the lack of internal controls and infrastructure, and other risks. The prevailing source for SRPs is Ibbotson Associates.

(4) **The Specific Company Risk Premium (SCRP)**, which is a highly subjective premium that considers the risks associated with the specific company under consideration and/or the risks associated with the specific industry in which the company operates. This premium considers the quality of management, the amount of leverage, cash flow, and other considerations, many of which can be analyzed using the liquidity and leverage ratios discussed earlier in this chapter. Although the CRP is generally drawn from an expert's own judgment and appraisal of the company, Ibbotson has developed studies associated with specific industries to provide a foundation for this premium too.

Thus, applying the BUM method, we can establish a discount rate (d) based on the four components above, effectively applying this formula:

$$d = SR + ERP + SRP + CRP$$

For example, assume that the SR for a particular time period is 7%, the ERP was 8%, the SRP was 4% and the CRP was 6%. We could then conclude that the proper discount rate should be 25% using the BUM method:

$$d = SR + ERP + SRP + CRP$$
$$d = 7\% + 8\% + 4\% + 6\%$$
$$d = 25\%$$

Growth Rate. The growth rate (g) assumes a steady rate of growth. It starts with a beginning value and a final value (or a past figure and a present figure). If we were concerned only with a one-year growth rate, we could say that the rate of growth from one year to the next would equal the difference between the two years' values divided by last year's value. The basic formula would be:

$$\frac{\text{This Year's Value} - \text{Last Year's Value}}{\text{Last Year's Value}}$$

So if the company was worth \$5,000 last year and \$6,800 this year, we would calculate its growth at 36%, as follows:

$$\frac{\$6{,}800 - \$5{,}000}{\$5{,}000}$$

$$= 0.36$$

Let's say we knew the growth rate, and we wanted to determine the present value of the company and we also knew the value of the company three years ago. We could apply a variation of the formula as follows:

$$\text{This Year's Value} = \text{Beginning Value (three years ago)} \times (1 + g)^n$$

where n equals the number of years. This time, let's assume that the company was valued at \$5,000 three years ago. We know the growth rate at 36%. What should this year's value be?

$$\text{This year's value} = \$5{,}000 \times (1.36)^3$$

$$= \$5{,}000 \times 2.515456$$

$$= \$12{,}577.28$$

Therefore, this year's value of the company should be \$12,577.28.

You might have noticed that the formula above is the same formula for calculating future value: $FV = PV(1 + i)^n$ That is, future value equals present value multiplied by 1 plus the interest rate raised to a power that equals the number of years in question.[55] If we think of the growth rate as the interest rate, we can apply the future value formula. Consider the question, somewhat modified: what would the future value of the business be in three years at a 36% interest rate if the business has a present value of \$5,000?

$$FV = PV(1 + i)^n$$

$$FV = \$5{,}000(1.36)^3$$

$$FV = \$5{,}000(2.515456)$$

$$FV = \$12{,}577.28$$

[55] For a review of future value, see Section 4.2.

Looking at the revised question, we can say that in three years at 36%, the business which is presently valued at $5,000 will be worth $12,577.28.

In trying to establish a growth rate for purposes of a business valuation, and in basing that rate on a period of years, we'll need a formula that isolates the growth rate to one side of the equation. Algebraically, we must modify the formula above. Start with the formula, as initially stated: This Year's Value = Beginning Value x $(1 + g)^n$. Next divide both sides by the Beginning Value. Then, transfer the exponent and convert it to 1/n. Subtract 1 from both sides of the equation, and you will have a new formula for growth rate, as follows:

$$g = \left[\frac{\text{This Year's Value}}{\text{Beginning Value}}\right]^{\frac{1}{n}} - 1$$

This formula restates the formula for compound annual growth rate (CAGR)[56] using slightly different terms.

Let's try an example. Assume that a medical practice is worth $555,000 this year. Ten years ago, it was valued at $243,000. With the assumption that there was a steady rate of growth, the formula produces the following result:

$$g = \left[\frac{\text{This Year's Value}}{\text{Beginning Value}}\right]^{\frac{1}{n}} - 1$$

$$g = \left[\frac{\$555{,}000}{\$243{,}000}\right]^{\frac{1}{10}} - 1$$

$$g = [2.28]^{\frac{1}{10}} - 1$$

$$g = 1.0859 - 1$$

$$g = 0.0859$$

$$g = 8.59\%$$

Therefore, the annual growth rate for the medical practice over the 10-year period was approximately 8.6%. In projecting the future growth of the medical practice—and again, assuming a steady rate of growth—the 8.6% estimate would be reliable.

---

[56]For a discussion and illustration of CAGR, see Section 7.4.

It may also be appropriate to add in the inflation rate. In other words, the cap rate would consist not merely of the discount rate minus the growth rate, but of the discount rate minus the sum of the growth rate plus the inflation rate. Thus, if inflation were at 2%, then the growth rate of 8.6% would be bumped up to 10.6%.

Putting It All Together. In order to apply the capitalization of earnings method, assume that we have hypothetically established or gathered the following information with respect to an optometry practice that is up for sale:

Future earnings of the optometry practice based on prior years' figures =	$300,000
Current book value of the business =	$666,000
Book Value of business five years ago =	$491,000
Safe Rate =	7%
Equity Risk Premium =	8%
Small-Company Risk Premium =	4%
Specific Company Risk Premium =	6%
Inflation Rate =	1%

For purposes of this exercise, we will accept the future earnings figure of $300,000 as the numerator of our formula, without any challenge.

To determine the discount rate (d), we'll apply the BUM, using the formula: d = SR + ERP + SRP + CRP. Therefore, d = 25%.

To determine the growth rate (g), we'll apply the growth rate formula

$$g = \left[\frac{\text{This Year's Value}}{\text{Beginning Value}}\right]^{\frac{1}{n}} - 1$$

$$g = \left[\frac{\$666{,}000}{\$491{,}000}\right]^{\frac{1}{5}} - 1$$

$$g = 1.061 - 1$$

$$g = 0.061$$

Therefore, the growth rate equals 6.1%. We'll increase the growth rate by the rate of inflation (1%), to give us an enhanced growth rate of 7.1%.

Now, we are ready to apply the formula for the capitalization of earnings method:

$$\begin{aligned}\text{Business Value} &= \frac{\text{Future Earnings}}{d-g}\\ &= \frac{\$300{,}000}{0.25-0.071}\\ &= \frac{\$300{,}000}{0.179}\\ &= \$1{,}675{,}977.65\end{aligned}$$

Thus, by capitalizing the earnings of $300,000, the business is valued at more than $1.6 million.

The process outlined above requires a more extensive examination of the various factors shown above and, therefore, attorneys are cautioned that they should consult with financial experts in attempting to place values on professional practices and other small business enterprises. Understanding the capitalization of earnings method, however, can inform the direction of pretrial discovery, stimulate the course of negotiations, and add greater relevance to the data obtained in financial statements, annual reports, and other materials.

The Excess Earnings Method

A simpler business valuation method, but one which has been challenged as technically flawed, is the *excess earnings method.* This method, also sometimes known as the *formula approach*, divides a company's assets into two categories: tangible assets and intangible assets, such as goodwill (good name and reputation).

The first step in the excess earnings method is to determine the average net earnings of the business, not including owner's compensation, generally referred to as *normalized earnings*. If the company averages $500,000 per year in net earnings, but the owner pays himself $300,000, then the proper amount of normalized earnings is $200,000.

The next step is to determine the value of all tangible assets. This includes all physical assets as well as the value of all accounts receivable in excess of all accounts payable. In calculating the value of tangible assets, use the "net" value representing the actual value of the assets minus any loans, liens, or other setoffs against the value. If the value of the tangible assets has changed during the course of a year, then an average annual value should be established.

The third step is to estimate an appropriate rate of return applicable to the tangible assets. This rate can be found in published reports for various industries, or it can be estimated using various formulas.[57]

Then, apply the rate of return to the value of all net tangible assets. You now have a dollar figure that represents the appropriate return on the tangible assets. By subtracting this amount from the total normalized earnings, we can determine the dollar amount that represents the return on *intangible* assets.

Let's try an example. Assume that normalized earnings for a business are $200,000 as explained above. Net tangible assets total $425,000. The rate of return selected for the tangible assets is 9%. Applying this rate to the tangible assets of $425,000, our return on the tangible assets is calculated as $38,250 ($425,000 x 0.09 = $38,250). By subtracting the dollar amount for the return on tangible assets from the total amount of normalized earnings, we can determine the dollar amount representing the return on intangible assets:

Normalized earnings = $200,000

Net tangible assets = $425,000

Rate of return = 9%

Return on tangible assets = $38,250

Return on intangible assets = Normalized earnings – Return on tangible assets = $200,000 – $38,250 = $161,750.

Therefore, the earnings attributable to intangible assets such as goodwill or copyrights, patents, and leases are $161,750. This is essentially the "excess earnings" generated by the business. But we're not done yet. In order to place a value on the business, we must now capitalize the excess earnings. This is a fertile area of disagreement among experts, although the IRS has said that the range of capitalization rates generally runs from 15% for low-risk businesses with stable earnings to 20% for high-risk businesses with irregular earning pat-

[57]For example, see the formula for return on assets at Section 7.8.

terns.[58] Let's assume, in this instance, that the capitalization rate will be 18%. Applying this rate to the return on intangible assets of \$161,750, we can make the following calculation:

$$\frac{\$161{,}750}{0.18}$$
$$= \$898{,}611.11$$

We now know that the capitalized earnings attributable to intangible assets (goodwill, etc.) are \$898,611.11. Now we must add this figure to the value of the net tangible assets of \$425,000, in order to arrive at the total value of the business:

$$\$898{,}611.11 + \$425{,}000 = \$1{,}323{,}611.11$$

By adding the net value of tangible assets and the capitalized value of the excess earnings attributable to intangible assets, we can conclude that the business is worth approximately \$1.3 million.

Other Methods and Models of Business Valuation

While the capitalization of earnings and excess earnings methods are widely cited and relied upon, they are not the only approaches to business valuation. Other methods may be found to be more reliable or applicable to a particular set of circumstances.

The **Discounted Future Earnings Method**, for example, is a variation of the capitalization of earnings method. Instead of assuming that earnings will remain constant in the future, however, the discounted future earnings method calculates the sum of the present values of the earnings projected to be generated over a period of time, plus the pres-

[58] *See* IRS Revenue Ruling 68-609, which addresses both the rates of return on tangible assets as well as the capitalization rates on intangible assets: "The 8 percent rate of return and the 15 percent rate of capitalization are applied to tangibles and intangibles, respectively, of businesses with a small risk factor and stable and regular earnings; the 10 percent rate of return and 20 percent rate of capitalization are applied to businesses in which the hazards of business are relatively high." *See also,* Revenue Ruling 65-192 stating that the excess earnings method should only be used as a last resort "if there is no better basis" available.

ent value of the terminal value[59] or liquidation value of the business. This approach may prove more reliable in cases in which the business is projected to exist for a finite number of years, with declining earnings over time.

An **Asset-Based Valuation Model** calculates the values of fixed assets, equipment, leasehold improvements, inventory, and discretionary cash. This method is sometimes used by retail businesses and manufacturing operations which are heavy in assets and inventory.

The **Multiples Method** fixes a number by which income or earnings is multiplied to place a value on the business. If a business is in an industry in which a multiple of five times net income is accepted, and if the business generates net income of $100,000, then the selling price for the business should be $500,000. Certain multiples are commonly tied to businesses in particular professions and occupational fields. Revenue multiples are most frequently used in an attempt to measure the value of a company relative to the revenue it generates. Yet earnings multiples, sales multiples, and profit multiples may be more appropriate than revenue multiples in valuing certain kinds of businesses. A price earnings multiple, for example, multiplies the P/E ratio by net income to fix a value for the business.

A quick, but unscientific, multiples approach is the **Owner Benefit Valuation**, best used in businesses whose value is derived from their ability to generate high cash flow and profits. In this method, the owner's discretionary cash flow for one year is multiplied by 2.2727 to estimate the market value of the business.

In still other cases, business valuations may be based on book values or adjusted book values, dividend capitalization, liquidation value, or asset replacement value. Comparisons to other businesses that have been valued, liquidated, or recently sold may provide other meaningful benchmarks in the valuation process.

---

[59]For a discussion of how to calculate the net present value of a series of future cash flows, see Section 4.5. For a discussion of net terminal value, see Section 7.12.

Chapter 13

Employment Law Damages

13.1. Statutory Damages Framework

The practice of employment law is driven by a long list of federal and state statutes governing workplace discrimination, wages and fringe benefits, insurance and retirement programs, occupational health and safety, labor union organization, and dispute resolution. Fortunately, this takes the guesswork out of the process of identifying those categories of damages that may be available in employer-employee disputes. Statutes and regulations often specifically identify the awards and forms of compensation available to claimants who succeed in proving their claims. These may include, for example, any of the following:

- Compensation for lost wages, including past wages and future wages
- Compensation for lost overtime or unpaid past overtime wages
- Compensation for unpaid benefits or entitlements
- Liquidated damages
- Punitive damages
- Attorneys' fees and costs

Unlike some other areas of law, however, employment law statutes often provide other penalties and remedies for aggrieved employees. In addition to a right to damages in a civil action, there may be administrative fines and penalties or criminal liability. For example, the child labor provisions of the Fair Labor Standards Act (FLSA) impose civil penalties of up to $11,000 per employee for violations of the Act.[1] The Age Discrimination in Employment Act (ADEA) provides that any employer who intimidates or interferes with the Equal Employment Opportunity Commission (EEOC) in its investigation of an age discrimination claim may be fined up to $500 or imprisoned for up to one year, or both.[2]

Employment law statutes also commonly contain provisions for reinstatement, restoration of benefits, promotion, or special injunctive relief, all of which may be substituted for monetary compensation and/or be blended with a damages award or settlement agreement. Federal government contractors who violate employment laws may also face termination of their contracts and/or debarment from future contracts.

The variety of damages and other remedies available to litigants in the employment sector is, for the most part, neither automatic nor mandatory. Some statutes are drafted in general language; others are more specific. Some statutes recognize multiple tiers of monetary and nonmonetary relief; others recognize only an election of remedies. Under the federal framework, moreover, litigants are usually required to exhaust administrative remedies with the EEOC or another federal or state agency[3] before seeking damages in a court of law. Exhaustion requirements vary depending on the nature of the claim, and the statutes under which the claim is raised.

The Top 40 Federal Employment Statutes

Although there are many highly specific federal enactments governing the rights of public and private employees, the top 40 federal statutes containing provisions for damages, penalties, or other sanctions in employment-related matters are:

---

[1] 29 U.S.C. § 216(e)(1)(A)(i).

[2] 29 U.S.C. § 629.

[3] Other federal agencies that investigate, process, and/or adjudicate employment disputes include, for example, the U.S. Office of Personnel Management, the Merit Systems Protection Board, and the Office of Federal Contract Compliance Programs. The states also maintain human relations commissions and/or civil rights divisions which consider complaints of job discrimination under state statutory law.

1. Age Discrimination in Employment Act (ADEA)
2. Americans with Disabilities Act (ADA)
3. Black Lung Benefits Act (BLBA)
4. Civil Service Reform Act (CSRA)
5. Consolidated Omnibus Budget Reconciliation Act (COBRA)
6. Consumer Credit Protection Act (CCPA)
7. Contract Work Hours and Safety Standards Act (CWHSSA)
8. Copeland Act (CA)
9. Davis-Bacon and Related Acts (DBRA)
10. Defense Base Act (DBA)
11. Employee Polygraph Protection Act (EPPA)
12. Employee Retirement Income Security Act (ERISA)
13. Equal Pay Act (EPA)
14. Executive Order 11246 (EO 11246)
15. Fair Credit Reporting Act (FCRA)
16. Fair Labor Standards Act (FLSA)
17. Family and Medical Leave Act (FMLA)
18. Genetic Information Nondiscrimination Act (GINA)
19. Immigration and Nationality Act (INA)
20. Immigration Reform and Control Act (IRCA)
21. Labor Management Relations Act (LMRA)
22. Labor Management Reporting and Disclosure Act (LMRDA)
23. Longshore and Harbor Workers' Compensation Act (LHWCA)
24. McNamara-O'Hara Service Contract Act (SCA)
25. Migrant and Seasonal Agricultural Worker Protection Act (MSPA)
26. Mine Safety and Health Act (MSHA)
27. National Labor Relations Act (NLRA)
28. Occupational Safety and Health Act (OSH Act)
29. Older Workers Benefit Protection Act (OWBPA)
30. Personal Responsibility and Work Opportunity Reconciliation Act (PRWORA)
31. Pregnancy Discrimination Act (PDA)
32. Railway Labor Act (RLA)
33. Rehabilitation Act (RA)
34. Sarbanes-Oxley Act (SOX)
35. Surface Transportation Assistance Act (STAA)
36. Civil Rights Acts (CRA), including Title VII and Section 1981

37. Uniformed Services Employment and Reemployment Rights Act (USERRA)
38. Vietnam Era Veterans' Readjustment Assistance Act (VEVRAA)
39. Walsh-Healy Public Contracts Act (PCA)
40. Worker Adjustment and Retraining Notification Act (WARN)

In addition to these federal statutes, a varied and somewhat overlapping list of state and local statutes governs job discrimination, wages and hours of employment, workplace health and safety, and related issues. For example, California's Fair Employment and Housing Act (FEHA)[4] provides for the hiring, reinstatement, and upgrading of employees found to be victims of job discrimination, along with restoration of missed pay, and damages for emotional injuries including pain and suffering, inconvenience, mental anguish, loss of enjoyment of life, and other nonpecuniary losses up to $150,000, other actual damages, administrative fines, and civil penalties up to $25,000.

Navigating the statutory damages framework is thus the first step for all practitioners dealing with employment law cases. Although a particular case may include common law causes of action, and a particular state may permit open-ended damages claims, actions arising under particular statutes may be circumscribed by limited remedies, specific procedures, and monetary caps on the amounts recoverable.

13.2. Front Pay

Front pay is compensation for future wage loss that results from present employment-related circumstances. In most scenarios, it serves as a form of future wage-based restitution for victims of job discrimination. However, front pay is only available where reinstatement is not possible or appropriate. Thus, if a job has been filled or no longer exists, or if the employer-employee relationship has been so severely damaged that the relationship is unsalvageable, then front pay may be awarded as an item of damages.

In a Title VII employment discrimination case, one federal court has articulated nine factors to be considered in determining whether to award front pay to a successful plaintiff: (1) whether the employer is

[4]Cal. Gov. Code § 12970.

still in business, (2) whether there is a comparable position available for the employee to assume, (3) whether an innocent employee would be displaced by reinstatement, (4) whether the parties agree that reinstatement is a viable remedy, (5) whether the degree of hostility or animosity between the parties—caused not only by the underlying offense but also by the litigation process—would undermine reinstatement, (6) whether reinstatement would arouse hostility in the workplace, (7) whether the employee has since acquired similar work, (8) whether the employee's career goals have changed since the unlawful termination, and (9) whether the employee has the ability to return to work for the defendant employer—including consideration of the effect of the adverse employment action on the employee's self-worth.[5]

Therefore, before thinking about front pay, employment lawyers must think about the prospects of reinstatement for the aggrieved employee, and whether they are likely to recover front pay in a contested case.

In calculating front pay owed to a victim of employment discrimination, the following basic rules must be followed:

- There must be a start date (usually the date specified in a settlement or the date of a judgment).
- There must be an end date (based on work-life expectancy or other factors).
- There must be an adjustment for wages the employee could earn in the future using reasonable efforts.

Other adjustments may be warranted because of the particular character of the parties or the peculiar circumstances of a dispute. For example, a front pay award may be reduced by a factor that represents an employee's uncertain future in a position (such as may be determined based on the employee's declining health or a history of short-term employment and frequent job-hopping). The calculation of front pay may be adjusted to account for the availability of comparable employment opportunities and the time reasonably required for the employee to secure substitute employment. For older employees, it may also be adjusted to take into consideration the employee's projected retirement age.

---

[5]Ogden v. Wax Works, Inc., 29 F. Supp. 2d 1003 (N.D. Iowa 1998).

Front pay can also include projected promotions, bonuses, pay raises, and cost-of-living increases that the employee would have enjoyed had she not been terminated or forced to leave the job. However, proof of such enhancements will need to be gathered and produced in the form of admissible evidence before a court will infer that an employee would have earned greater amounts of compensation in the future.

A court considering an employment discrimination case may also apply other factors to substantiate the likelihood that an employee seeking front pay would likely have earned future wages with the same employer over a particular period of time. These may include, for example, the employee's intention to remain with the employer until retirement, the length of time other employees typically hold such positions, the length of time persons in similar positions at other companies generally hold such positions, and the status of the current job market and industry.

Calculating Front Pay

The basic, unadjusted, formula for front pay is essentially the same as the basic formula for loss of future earnings used by personal injury lawyers.[6] Since we know what the employee would have earned in future years (or at least we are proceeding on that assumption), our objective is to determine the PV of the future wage loss. We thus begin with the formula for present value: $PV = \frac{FV}{(1+i)^n}$.

Assume that an employee would have earned exactly $100,000 for five more years, at which time he would have resigned or retired from employment. The question, unaffected by any adjustments or special considerations discussed above, is simply: what is the PV of $100,000 paid in each of five consecutive years? To answer this question, we must add the PV of $100,000 in year 1 to the PV of $100,000 in year 2, and then to the PV of $100,000 in year 3, and so forth until year 5. The formula is:

$$PV = \frac{FV}{(1+i)^1} + \frac{FV}{(1+i)^2} + \frac{FV}{(1+i)^3} + \frac{FV}{(1+i)^4} + \frac{FV}{(1+i)^5}$$

Let's assume that the applicable discount rate (i) will be 4% (or .04) throughout the five-year period. Here's the math:

[6] See Section 11.2.

$$PV = \frac{\$100,000}{(1.04)} + \frac{\$100,000}{(1.04)^2} + \frac{\$100,000}{(1.04)^3} + \frac{\$100,000}{(1.04)^4} + \frac{\$100,000}{(1.04)^5}$$

PV = \$95,153.85 + \$92,455.62 + \$88,899.64 + \$85,480.42 + \$82,192.71

PV = \$444,182.24

So, assuming no other considerations, we can say that the discounted amount of future wage loss (that is, the front pay for the five-year period) would be $444,182.24.

We may wish to modify the numerator in each the fractions above if we could establish, for example, that the employee seeking front pay would have enjoyed certain increased wages after two years. The same would hold true if we had reason to believe that the employee's income would decline at some point over the five years.

We may also wish to modify the denominator in the fractions above if we have reason to believe that interest rates (discount rates) would increase or decrease at some point during the five-year period. Growth rates and inflation rates may also offset our discount rate, as discussed in Section 10.2.

While this hypothetical assumes a five-year future wage loss, other cases may suggest that the aggrieved employee would have continued working for the employer for the rest of his life, or, more appropriately, the rest of his working life. The cutoff date for front pay, however, cannot be arbitrarily pinned to a projected retirement age (such as 65 or 70). The more reliable approach is the LPE method,[7] which considers the probability that a particular individual will be living (L), that he will be participating (P) in the labor force, and that he will be actually employed (E). The product of these three probabilities, L x P x E, indicates an arguably more accurate statistic in determining work-life expectancy. Notwithstanding this approach, many courts have expressed a reluctance to award front pay beyond 10 years.[8]

---

[7]For a further discussion of the LPE approach and a look at sample work-life expectancy tables, see Section 11.2.

[8]*See, e.g.,* Hukkanen v. International Union of Operating Engineers, Hoisting & Portable Local No. 101, 3 F.3d 281, 286 (8th Cir. 1993); United Paperworkers International Union, AFL-CIO, Local 274 v. Champion International Corp., 81 F. 3d 798, 805 (8th Cir. 1996); Sellers v. Mineta, 358 F. 3d 1058 (8th Cir. 2004).

In order for a front-pay formula to be accepted, it must therefore rationally adjust for the realities of the workplace, the logical progression of the employee's work life, and other applicable factors. Consider, for example, an employee who has lost a job paying $100,000 per year, but has been able to find a new job paying $55,000 per year. Her front pay is thus reduced by her replacement pay, leaving her with a net annual loss in future earnings of $45,000 per year. Let's also assume that the employee's employment history, pretrial testimony, and personal characteristics lead to the conclusion that she would have worked for the first employer for only four more years. Let's also assume that earnings were expected to grow at 2% during the four-year span, and the interest rate was set at 4%. Here is how to proceed:

Step 1: Determine the net discount rate (NDR).[9] The NDR is technically more accurate than a simple discount rate because it considers both the market interest rate and a growth rate. We might therefore say that the *net* discount rate is nothing more than the discount rate (or market interest rate) minus the growth rate. Thus, NDR = i – g, where "i" is the interest rate and "g" is the growth rate.[10] In our hypothetical, the interest rate is 4% and the growth rate is 2%; therefore, NDR = 4 – 2, or 2%. The more accurate adjustment for NDR, however, comes from a slightly more complicated formula, which will produce a result close to 2%, but even more precise:

$$\text{NDR} = \frac{1 + i}{1 + g} - 1$$

$$\text{NDR} = \frac{1.04}{1.02} - 1$$

$$\text{NDR} = 1.01960 - 1$$

$$\text{NDR} = 0.01960$$

$$\text{NDR} = 1.96\%$$

Step 2: Determine the net wage loss per year. As noted above, if the employee was earning $100,000 at the first job, and now earns $55,000 at the second job, her net wage loss per year is $45,000.

---

[9]See Section 11.4.

[10]Other publications may refer to the interest rate "i" as "r" and may cite the formula for NDR as being r – g.

Step 3. Plot the formula by adding the PVs for each year. Restate the PV value formula for each year in question. The numerators should state the amount of future net wage loss, and the denominators should state the NDR (1 + NDR). The NDR for each year is raised to the nth power, where "n" equals the year in question. The sum of each year's PV calculation provides the PV for the entire four-year stream.

$$PV = \frac{\$45{,}000}{(1.0196)} + \frac{\$45{,}000}{(1.0196)^2} + \frac{\$45{,}000}{(1.0196)^3} + \frac{\$45{,}000}{(1.0196)^4}$$

$$PV = \$44{,}134.95 + \$43{,}286.53 + \$42{,}454.43 + \$41{,}638.32$$

$$PV = \$171{,}514.23$$

Therefore, the employee in this hypothetical case scenario would be entitled to front pay of $171,514.23.

13.3. Back Pay

Back pay is the amount of compensation that would have been paid to the employee had she not been wrongfully terminated from employment—up to the point that front pay is calculated. In effect, back pay runs from the last paycheck the employee received after being discharged until the point at which future wage loss is calculated. Or, stated otherwise, back pay consists of all wage loss from the moment of termination to the entry of judgment.

Back pay also necessarily includes salary increases, bonuses, and other pay enhancements that the employee would have received had she not been terminated. It includes fringe benefits such as profits from employer stock options that the employee could have exercised during the period between termination and judgment. Like front pay, however, the amount of back pay must be reduced by the actual amount of earnings received by the employee through other employment opportunities, including any amounts that could be imputed to her as payments she could have claimed to mitigate her losses.

Determining Base Salary

The time between a discharge from employment and a trial on a wrongful termination claim can be lengthy. In a state in which there is a two-year statute of limitations to bring such claims, and in which the backlog for a trial runs three years, a judgment for back pay could come five years from the last day of employment. Thus, the first step is to determine the amount of earnings at the time of termination *and* the amount of time that has elapsed until the time of trial.

It may be easiest, in fact, to state the amount of monthly or weekly earnings rather than yearly earnings in order to simplify the math. For example, if a discharged manager was earning $85,000 per year, and if the time between discharge and trial was 2 years, 11 months, and 1 week, it may be easiest to reduce his annual earnings to a time period that matches the most specific measure of the time between discharge and trial—that is, to a weekly basis. At $85,000 per year, the manager was earning $1,634.61 per week. His pretrial period of termination from employment spans 153 weeks altogether. Therefore, his gross wage loss—assuming no replacement employment or other offsets—is $250,095.93, calculated by multiplying $1,634.61 by 153.

Adjusting Base Salary

The better advocate will seek to augment the base salary before doing the math. There may be a number of reasons for using a base salary figure greater than the amount that appears on pay stubs or W-2 wage statements. These include:

- The likelihood that the employee would have been promoted to a higher paying job during the back-pay period.
- The likelihood that the employee would have received a pay raise during the time span.
- The likelihood that the employee would have enjoyed a bonus or other salary enhancement during the same period.
- The likelihood that the employee would have enjoyed a certain additional volume of overtime pay or received shift differentials or other forms of additional compensation.
- The likelihood, in certain occupations, that the employee would have received an increased amount of commissions or gratuities.
- Evidence that the employee suffered an unlawful reduction in his pay rate or in his hours, such that his last recorded payroll amount understates what he should have been earning.

- Evidence that the employee was otherwise a victim of discrimination, such as a victim of the Equal Pay Act or the Fair Labor Standards Act, resulting in an unfairly depressed amount of earnings prior to discharge.

If competent, reliable, and admissible evidence can be gathered to support any of these conditions, an aggrieved employee can argue that his pretrial losses are greater than his prior paycheck suggests, justifying a higher award of back pay. In a fast-moving industry, for example, where wages are known to be growing by a certain percentage each year, it may be useful to produce documentary evidence of the wage growth or to call an expert witness on the subject. Published inflation rates, cost-of-living adjustments, and growth rates can provide other evidence to support an inference that an employee's back pay would have been greater than his last paycheck indicates during a multiyear pretrial period. In fact, the Department of Labor's Employment Cost Index[11] provides a seasonally adjusted statistic that measures the change in employers' payroll costs, yielding another factor by which wage growth can be gauged.

The calculation of an accurate base pay can be particularly controversial in cases in which an employee claims she was forced to leave a job based on sexual harassment or other forms of job discrimination. For example, consider a regional sales manager who claims that her sales territory was systematically eroded and redrawn by her boss in retaliation for her cooperating in another sales manager's sex discrimination claim during the course of a protracted EEOC investigation.

The cooperating employee (sales manager) arguably has a claim for Title VII damages based on retaliation by the employer. She asserts that as a result of the remapping of her sales territory, her annual earnings dropped from $110,000 in 2010 to $70,000 in 2011. She was terminated from employment on what she claims were false pretenses in 2011. In her wrongful discharge lawsuit, she may wish to establish that her base earnings, for purposes of calculating back pay, were $110,000 rather than the $70,000 per annum which she claimed at the end of her

---

[11]Published by the U.S. Department of Labor, Bureau of Labor Statistics on a quarterly basis. See http://www.bls.gov/news.release/eci.toc.htm.

employment. If she can establish that her sales territory—and thus her earnings—were diminished as a result of employer retaliation, then her base wage figure would be the greater amount.

The amount of base salary must also be adjusted upward to reflect any bonuses or additional compensation that was routinely paid by the employer. If an employee always received a fixed bonus at the end of each calendar year, then the calculation is quite easy and predictable. If the amount of bonus was tied to employer earnings or to employee performance, then additional evidence will need to be gathered so that a trier of fact will infer that the base salary—as augmented—reflects a rational aggregate amount of earnings for the displaced employee.

Adjusting the Back-Pay Period

Back pay runs from the date the employee was terminated (or from the date that she suffered another adverse employment action) to the date of judgment at the conclusion of a trial—unless there is some reason to shorten the time period. For example, if an employee waited five years from the date of termination to the date of judgment, back pay of five years' wages would *not* be reasonable if the company went out of business and terminated everybody three years after the employee was discharged. In this respect, plant closings, mass layoffs, periodic reductions in force, mergers and acquisitions, consolidation of divisions and departments, and discontinuation of product lines can all indicate that an employee's actual work expectancy with a particular employer would have been limited following his termination.

A back-pay period may also be compressed by a superseding event, such as the discovery that the employee had planned to quit and take another job, or perhaps return to school for an advanced degree, at a particular time in the future. Consider, for example, an employee who seeks back pay for a five-year period, but pretrial discovery reveals that she had accepted an offer of admission to medical school commencing in August of her second year following termination. It would seem unfair or illogical to assert that the employee would have remained at the job beyond the two-year mark had she not been terminated.

Most states also recognize a duty by the employee to mitigate her losses by actively seeking replacement employment. Thus, a terminated employee who remains employable, but forgoes available employment opportunities, may not be able to claim lost wages for a lengthy back-pay period. A court may equitably constrict the back-pay period to end on a date by which, in the court's view, the employee should have obtained replacement employment.

Evidence that the employee would have been fired from the job at some subsequent point, for reasons unrelated to her discharge, could also warrant a compression of the back-pay period. So, for example, if an employee charging discrimination and seeking back pay for a five-year period was determined one year after his discharge to have embezzled $500,000 several years earlier, the back-pay period would extend only for one year, to the point when the employer actually discovered the embezzlement.

Fringe Benefits

A party claiming lost wages may also be claiming lost benefits. While fringe benefits are not always delivered in the form of monetary compensation, they may include quantifiable values for lost health insurance, including hospital, medical, and disability plans, life insurance, pension plans and other retirement programs, stock options, stock purchase plans and other profit-sharing programs, sick leave, personal leave and other paid time off, maternity leave, vacation pay, holiday pay, travel pay, shift premiums, expense accounts, counseling programs, day care facilities, tuition reimbursement, credit union memberships, fitness and recreation programs and gym memberships, unemployment compensation, workers' compensation insurance, housing subsidies, relocation assistance, company cars, company laptops, legal aid, and bonuses.[12]

The calculation of back pay can thus be augmented by an additional amount that reflects the loss of fringe benefits between the date of termination and the date of judgment. For example, let's assume that an employee would be required to expend $12,000 per year to replace his company-sponsored family health insurance plan, either through the payment of COBRA continuation benefits or by purchasing a private health plan for his family. Let's also assume that the employee would lose $6,500 per year in employer contributions to his pension plan. The employee could argue that, in addition to his loss of salary, he lost a total of $18,500 per year in fringe benefits. If his annual salary loss were $85,000, then he would argue that his annual wage-and-benefit loss amounts to $103,500.

---

[12]For a further discussion of valuing fringe benefits, see Section 11.6.

Another approach is to determine the *fringe rate*,[13] which is a percentage of earnings attributable to fringe benefits.

$$\text{Fringe Rate} = \frac{\text{Total dollar value of all fringe benefits}}{\text{Gross Earnings}}$$

If the total dollar value of all fringe benefits was \$17,000, then we could easily find the fringe rate:

$$\text{Fringe rate} = \frac{\$17{,}000}{\$85{,}000} = 0.2$$

In this example, the fringe rate is 0.2, or 20%. Thus, 20% becomes the factor by which base wages are enhanced to account for the loss of fringe benefits. A wage loss of \$85,000 is enhanced by 20% to reflect an annual wage-and-benefit loss of \$102,000. If the wage loss in the next year was found to be \$90,000, and assuming a constant fringe rate, the next year's wage-and-benefit loss would be \$108,000.

While these calculations are quite simple, it may be necessary to consider other, more mathematically complex, calculations for lost benefits, such as stock options and Social Security benefits,[14] and setoffs (if applicable and recognized) for severance pay, unemployment compensation, public welfare and health care assistance programs, and third-party charitable donations of replacement benefits.

Other Adjustments

Back pay need not be discounted like front pay because it's being paid after the fact. Because it's being paid later than it would have been earned, had there not been a termination from employment or other adverse employment action, back pay should enjoy the opposite time-value effect: that is, it should bear interest. The right to pre-judgment interest, in fact, is recognized in many federal and state statutes and in most state civil codes. The amount of interest can be tied to federal Treasury bill rates, adjusted prime rates, or other commonly recognized interest rates, or it may be set by state law or court rule in a particular case.

---

[13] Section 11.6.

[14] For stock options, see Section 11.7. For Social Security benefits, see Section 11.8.

Of course, back pay is also taxable, like any form of earned wages. If an employment law dispute leads to a settlement, and the assumption is that the employee will be responsible for his own tax liability, then the settlement should be based on gross pretax wages and benefits. If an employee will recover a significant lump sum in settlement of a claim, or if he wins a substantial judgment, the payment of a large sum in one calendar year may have significant tax consequences for the employee, which ought to be considered and addressed in the litigation or the settlement. Victims of job discrimination who receive lump-sum back-pay awards covering a multiyear period are likely to incur higher federal and state income taxes than they would have had they received their wages in due course, a fact that the IRS has sought to address.[15]

13.4. Nonpecuniary Losses

The Civil Rights Act of 1991 added remedial provisions to Title VII which authorize compensatory damages for a plaintiff's "future pecuniary losses, emotional pain, suffering, inconvenience, mental anguish, loss of enjoyment of life, and other nonpecuniary losses."[16] Not only did these amendments spring open the door to a wide variety of pain-and-suffering claims, but they also triggered a new generation of unspecified claims for nonpecuniary damages in employment litigation.

For example, the Seventh Circuit has recognized the right of a plaintiff to *lost future earnings*, separate and distinct from her right to front pay. In *Williams v. Pharmacia, Inc.*,[17] the court characterized such lost future earnings as "an intangible nonpecuniary loss" and analogized it to an "injury to professional standing" and an "injury to character and reputation." Citing the civil rights provisions for nonpecuniary losses, the court distinguished front pay from lost future earnings. It found that front pay compensates the employee for the actual lost earnings from the job, had she been able to return to the job, and measured by the period of time she would have remained working

---

[15]See Memorandum GC 11-08 issued March 11, 2011, by the Office of the General Counsel. http://lawprofessors.typepad.com/files/gc11-08.pdf.

[16]42 U.S.C. § 1981a(b)(3).

[17]137 F. 3d 944 (7th Cir. 1998).

at that job. Lost future earnings, by contrast, compensate the employee for a lifetime of diminished earnings resulting from the reputational harms she suffered as a result of the discrimination she experienced.

To calculate lost future earnings, pain and suffering, and other nonpecuniary losses, a judge or a jury may require additional relevant evidence, not to mention the possible guidance of an economics expert. Formulas used in personal injury and wrongful death litigation may also provide guidance.[18] Yet, because there is no precise mathematical formula for calculating the intangible losses suffered by a victim of employment discrimination, juries are often asked to agree upon *reasonable compensation* for a victim's pain and suffering or other nonpecuniary losses.

The jury's domain is perhaps sacrosanct, and some may say that no attempt should be made to render the process of assessing such damages more scientific or formulaic. On the other hand, attorneys, arbitrators, judges, and jurors who are trying to settle an employment case, or who wish to take the guesswork out of the process of fixing a nonpecuniary loss, may wish to apply a more precise and justifiable approach.

One such approach is to construct a table of multipliers that would tie a victim's pain-and-suffering, inconvenience, mental anguish, social isolation, and loss of enjoyment of life to the actual amount of back pay paid or payable in a compensable case.[19] The underlying question asks: what amount, when added to a victim's back pay, will compensate the victim for his nonpecuniary losses? The formula asks: what number, when multiplied by the total amount of back pay, will produce a dollar amount that fairly and reasonably compensates the victim for his nonpecuniary losses? In attempting to find such multipliers, it would seem that the longer the victim remains unemployed or otherwise adversely affected by the challenged employment action, and the greater the amount of his back pay, the larger the multiplier should be to properly

---

[18]For how to calculate lost earnings, see Sections 11.1 through 11.5. For emotional distress and pain and suffering damages, see Sections 11.14 and 11.15.

[19]Tying the calculation of nonpecuniary damages to back pay essentially associates the actual loss of past wages due with the actual pain and suffering already experienced. It would seem less appropriate to apply multipliers to front pay, which covers future wage loss, insofar as one would have to speculate about the residual pain-and-suffering or mental anguish a victim might suffer *after* judgment is entered in his favor.

compensate him for the nonpecuniary aspect of the case. For example, a sample table of multipliers might look like this:

Back Pay	Multiplier	Nonpecuniary Damages
$0 to $25,000	0.33	$0 to $8,250
$25,001 to $100,000	0.5	$12,500 to $50,000
$100,001 to $500,000	0.75	$75,000 to $375,000
$500,001 to $1,000,000	0.875	$437,500 to 875,000
$1,000,001 and above	1.0	$1,000,001 and above

Using this sample table, we would apply a multiplier of 0.33 to a back pay award of $25,000 to produce an additional award of $8,250 to compensate the victim for pain and suffering, reputational injury, mental anguish, and related nonpecuniary damages. A victim who remained out of work for a much longer time period, or who experienced a much greater financial loss attributable to job discrimination, and who would thereby be entitled to a back pay award of $400,000, would be entitled to an additional (nonpecuniary) award of $300,000, using the hypothetical 0.75 multiplier shown above.

A table of multipliers could also be applied to psychological costs where pain-and-suffering from loss of employment is a significant part of the claim. Thus, for example, an employee who files suit for sexual harassment and is forced to leave the workplace to avoid a clearly hostile work environment would be entitled to her Title VII damages for back pay and front pay, as well as some unspecified quantum of compensation for her emotional grief, anxiety, shock, and the disruption in her life.

Assuming that the emotional and nonpecuniary damages were significant enough to require the victim to enlist the help of a psychologist, the evidence will likely include the cost of psychological therapy as a specific item of damages. That cost could then be augmented, by a multiplier, to cover the value of the victim's pain-and-suffering and related nonpecuniary claims. Consider, for example, a variation of the table of multipliers, this time based on therapy costs:

Therapy Costs	Multiplier	Nonpecuniary Damages
$0 to $5,000	1.0	$0 to $5,000
$5,001 to $10,000	1.5	$7,500 to $15,000
$10,001 to $50,000	2.0	$20,000 to $100,000
$50,001 and above	2.5	$125,000 and above

In this scenario, a victim who incurs $10,000 in psychotherapy costs as a result of her isolation, displacement, and mixed emotional problems following her sexual harassment in the workplace would be entitled to reimbursement of her therapy costs *plus* an additional $15,000 as nonpecuniary damages to cover her pain and suffering.[20]

13.5. Liquidated Damages

Liquidated damages consist of a stipulated amount of damages that the parties agree to, or that they are subject to, in the event of a proven claim for relief. In the employment law sector, liquidated damages may refer to a specific dollar amount, set forth in an employment contract, to be paid upon the employer's breach. They may also refer to a method or formula for calculating a specific dollar amount in the event of a breach of contract or a statutory violation. The federal FLSA, for example, provides that a victim is entitled to liquidated damages calculated by doubling the amount of back pay the victim is owed.[21]

Because liquidated damages, by their very nature, are stated as a specific dollar amount, or are based on an ascertainable specific dollar amount (such as by doubling back pay), it is not usually necessary to apply any fanciful formulas or mathematical calculations.

A liquidated damages clause in an employment contract may, however, state a novel or creative method or formula for calculating damages. For example, in *GFI Brokers, LLC v. Santana,*[22] a federal court was confronted with a liquidated damages provision governing a currency options broker who facilitated trades between and among large

[20]The choice of multipliers is sheerly hypothetical in these examples. A victim's actual pain and suffering may be significantly greater than would be allowed by the suggested multipliers above. On the other hand, it may be appropriate, in fixing the value of the multipliers, to progressively lower the increase in multipliers from level to level and/or to ultimately cap the maximum multiplier, to avoid excessive awards of nonpecuniary damages at the highest levels.

[21]29 U.S.C. § 216(b). The provision entitles victims to a doubling of their unpaid wages or their unpaid overtime wages, as the case may be. Liquidated damages provisions also appear in the Equal Pay Act, Age Discrimination in Employment Act, and Family and Medical Leave Act.

[22]2009 WL 2482130 (S.D.N.Y.), decided August 13, 2009.

financial institutions. The broker's contract stipulated that he would work for GFI until a specific date, and that he could neither work for a competitor nor solicit GFI's clients for four months after leaving GFI. The contract further provided that if the broker violated the noncompetition or nonsolicitation clauses, he would pay GFI liquidated damages calculated as the greater of:

> "the product of (x) the monthly average of [Santana's] Net Revenues for the twelve (12)-month period immediately preceding the termination of [Santana's] employment with GFI . . . , and (y) the number of months remaining unfulfilled under this Agreement and the term of any prohibition contained in [the Non-Solicitation Clause and the Non-Competition Clause]
>
> or
>
> the Net Revenues earned by [Santana] or by [Santana's] new employer as a result of [Santana's] efforts during the same time period described above."

Before the GFI agreement expired, the broker resigned and started working for a competitor. The employer sued, and the liquidated damages formula was challenged. The U.S. District Court for the Southern District of New York upheld the liquidated damages clause as being reasonably and logically connected to the broker's revenue stream for a specified period of time.

Controlling the Amount of Liquidated Damages

If a statute provides that a victim of job discrimination who proves her case is entitled to liquidated damages equal to twice her back pay, then the formula for calculating liquidated damages is inextricably tied to the calculation of back pay. If back pay is augmented to include lost commissions, lost bonuses, and lost insurance benefits, then the value of the liquidated damages will be substantially greater. This is not a fleeting consideration insofar as the federal courts have repeatedly recognized the right of claimants to calculate their augmented back pay before determining their liquidated damages. Thus, for example, in claims brought under the ADEA, where doubling back pay is recognized as the method for calculating liquidated damages,[23] the compu-

[23] 29 U.S.C. § 626(c).

tation has included the value of lost sales commissions,[24] fringe benefits,[25] and even the lost use of a company car.[26]

Attorneys representing employees would thus be well-advised to consider all of the available forms of compensation and employment benefits in order to fix a maximum value of back pay *before* doubling the value to determine liquidated damages.

On the other hand, attorneys representing employers will want to consider all possible setoffs and evidence of mitigation by the employee that will reduce the employer's exposure. Federal circuit courts have widely acknowledged that before doubling back pay, any amounts of money earned by the employee from other sources must be subtracted from the total amount of wages and benefits.[27] In addition, some jurisdictions recognize the right to set off state unemployment and disability compensation, severance pay, and pension payouts. Whether prejudgment and postjudgment interest will be awarded in addition to liquidated damages and back pay may also vary from state to state.

In a hypothetical case that pulls together all of the considerations noted above, the simple doubling-of-back-pay formula for calculating liquidated damages under various federal statutes would be rendered more cumbersome:

> *Liquidated damages* = 2 x [(back pay + commissions + bonuses + health insurance + life insurance + other fringe benefits) – (wages earned from replacement employment + unemployment benefits received + severance pay + pension payouts)].

Attacking the Award of Liquidated Damages

While statutory provisions for liquidated damages cannot be easily challenged, contractual provisions are often tested in the judicial sys-

---

[24]Buchholz v. Symons Mfg. Co., 445 F. Supp. 706 (E.D. Wis. 1978).

[25]Aledo-Garcia v. Puerto Rico National Guard Fund, Inc., 887 F. 2d 354 (1st Cir. 1989).

[26]Berndt v. Kaiser Aluminum & Chemical Sales, Inc., 604 F. Supp. 962 (E.D. Pa. 1985).

[27]*See, e.g.,* Padilla v. Metro-North Commuter Railroad, 92 F. 3d 117 (2d Cir. 1996); EEOC v. O'Grady, 857 F. 2d 383 (7th Cir. 1988); Acrey v. American Sheep Industry Association, 981 F. 2d 1569 (10th Cir. 1992).

tem. Those subject to liquidated damages clauses in employment contracts frequently attack them as being unconstitutional, unduly oppressive, punitive, or clearly unrelated to any actual damages. The history of litigation and debate over liquidated damages clauses has produced the following general policies:

1. **The Amount Cannot Be Punitive.** The courts have said that the amount of liquidated damages must not be so high or so disproportionate to the actual damages as to unduly penalize the offending party. The objective is to compensation the aggrieved party.
2. **The Amount or Method Cannot Be Arbitrary.** There must be some logical or reliable method for calculating the amount of liquidated damages. If a fixed amount of damages is stated, it must bear some reasonable relationship to the anticipated loss. If a method of calculation is used, it must likewise be reasonable under the circumstances.
3. **Actual Damages Must Be Somewhat Elusive or Unquantifiable.** In order for the courts to enforce a liquidated damages clause, the amount of actual damages must not be easy to compute, or the method for doing so must be difficult or impossible to accomplish under the circumstances.

Understanding these policies can be quite useful to an attorney who also recognizes the value of employing strategic formulas to calculate damages. For example, where an employment agreement provides that an employee will pay liquidated damages to an employer in the event that a particular breach occurs, the provision may be attacked as unreasonable or unenforceable where a specific formula can show exactly what loss the employer suffered as a result of the purported breach. Indeed, knowing how to calculate damages precisely, using the formulas discussed in these pages, may serve to illustrate the extent to which a particular liquidated damages clause is punitive or unreasonable, and may thereby result in the clause being rendered unenforceable in favor of a lower (more accurate) calculation of actual damages.

Consider, for example, a contract provision that requires an employee found to be liable for leaking trade secrets to pay liquidated damages of $100,000 to the employer. Is this clause punitive? Is

$100,000 an arbitrary amount? Is there no way to calculate the employer's actual losses attributable to the employee's misconduct? Perhaps the evidence will show that the leaked trade secrets diluted the net sales of the company for a fixed period of time. Using data from the change in net sales and cost of goods sold, the gross profit margin[28] for a period of time can be calculated, yielding a specific measure of loss.

Other measures, such as inventory turnover, accounts receivable turnover, and future earnings loss may provide other indicia of actual loss. Where the evidence demonstrates that the amount of liquidated damages is arbitrary, punitive, unreasonable, or clearly inconsistent with the victim's actual losses—as shown by the strategic application of formulas—a court is likely to reject the liquidated damages clause in favor of a fairer calculation.

13.6. Punitive Damages

Punitive damages are extremely limited and difficult to recover in employment law cases, but in the field of employment discrimination, the right to punitive damages continues to expand. The principal federal antidiscrimination law applicable to the workplace is Title VII of the Civil Rights Act of 1964 which outlaws discrimination based on sex, race, color, national origin, and religion. Title VII did not originally recognize a right to punitive damages. However, the Civil Rights Act of 1991 modified the law, introducing a statutory right to punitive damages in cases involving intentional discrimination.[29]

The amount of punitive damages that can be awarded in a Title VII discrimination claims runs from $50,000 to $300,000, depending on the size of the company.[30] The Act specifically provides:

> The sum of the amount of compensatory damages awarded under this section for future pecuniary losses, emotional pain, suffering, inconvenience, mental anguish, loss of enjoyment of life, and other nonpecuniary losses, and the amount of punitive

[28]See Section 11.12.

[29]42 U.S.C. § 1981a(a)(1); (b)(1). The provisions do not apply to inadvertent discrimination (disparate impact cases).

[30]42 U.S.C. § 1981a(b)(3).

damages awarded under this section, shall not exceed, for each complaining party—

(A) in the case of a respondent who has more than 14 and fewer than 101 employees in each of 20 or more calendar weeks in the current or preceding calendar year, $50,000;
(B) in the case of a respondent who has more than 100 and fewer than 201 employees in each of 20 or more calendar weeks in the current or preceding calendar year, $100,000; and
(C) in the case of a respondent who has more than 200 and fewer than 501 employees in each of 20 or more calendar weeks in the current or preceding calendar year, $200,000; and
(D) in the case of a respondent who has more than 500 employees in each of 20 or more calendar weeks in the current or preceding calendar year, $300,000.

Punitive damages are also available through other workplace discrimination claims, including, for example, disability claims charging intentional discrimination under the ADA and the RA, and retaliation claims demonstrating willful conduct by employers in violation of the ADEA. Punitive damages are not available, however, under the EPA or the FLSA.

State law may provide other variations on the availability of punitive damages in the employment arena and the caps on the awards available to claimants who prosecute claims under state statutes.

How to Calculate Punitive Damages

The amount of punitive damages is generally left to the jury in civil cases, and as such it is often attacked as being irrational or excessive. No single uniform formula or mathematical principle controls the value of such an award because, by its very nature, punitive damages are designed to advance a number of elusive legal and social objectives. Often referred to as *exemplary damages,* a punitive award is said to serve as an example, or to send a message, to other prospective tortfeasors and offending parties that intentional or outrageous conduct of the sort being punished will not be tolerated in the future. Punitive damages are thus characterized as a deterrent against the repetition of unlawful conduct.

Yet even more difficult to pin down is the objective of punishing the individuals or the business entities who committed the offending conduct. Punishment, in financial terms, must necessarily vary depending on the levels of culpability, the size or wealth of the offending parties, and the risk that the award of damages may inflict punishment upon innocent third parties (such as innocent shareholders of a corporation).

Still, there should be some theoretical, if not practical, guidance on how much a jury should award in punitive damages. In *State Farm Mutual Automobile Insurance Co. v. Campbell,*[31] the U.S. Supreme Court pointed to a long-standing historical practice of setting punitive damages at two, three, or four times the size of compensatory damages, noting that "single-digit multipliers are more likely to comport with due process." Doubling, tripling or quadrupling compensatory awards may, in fact, work out to be more mathematically logical if the risk of deterrence could be statistically measured. Yet this approach has not always reached the trier of fact, which has sometimes given enormous punitive damages awards to punish defendants who have fallen out of social favor.[32]

It therefore becomes necessary to attach some economic or financial methodology to the determination of punitive damages—something better perhaps than simply doubling or tripling the compensatory damages award and better than permitting the arbitrary and limitless freedom of having a jury pick an inflated number that will punish the defendant and somehow deter future misconduct.

Professors A. Mitchell Polinsky and Steven Shavell[33] have developed a tangible approach to calculating punitive damages when a defendant is found liable. Their approach considers the optimal amount

---

[31]538 U.S. 408, 425 (2003).

[32]*See, e.g.,* Philip Morris USA v. Williams, 549 U.S. 346 (2007), in which the Supreme Court vacated a punitive damages award for a heavy cigarette smoker's widow, which had been previously reduced from a jury award of $79.5 million to $32 million.

[33]See Polinsky and Shavell, *Punitive Damages: An Economic Analysis,* 111 Harv. L. Rev. 869 (Feb. 1998). The analysis above is abbreviated in the context of this chapter. The Polinsky and Shavell article, which readers are recommended to consult, makes certain assumptions and discusses certain variations and other considerations that invite deeper analysis.

of damages when the defendant is found to be liable *with certainty* versus the case in which the defendant could possibly escape liability. Where certainty exists, then the proper measure of damages is equal to the harm the defendant has caused.

Of course, if the amount of damages equals the amount of harm, then those who cause injuries or damages to be suffered will be incentivized to spend money on economically justified precautions. Suppose, for example, that by spending $50,000 on a precaution, a firm can prevent a harm of $100,000. Suppose, further, that the precaution is socially desirable. In this scenario, a firm would surely spend $50,000 to prevent certain liability of $100,000. But what if the level of harm (that is, the liability to the company) is only $30,000? It would not spend $50,000 for a precaution—even a socially desirable one—to prevent a $30,000 harm.

The converse analysis also makes sense. If, for example, the precaution would cost $250,000 instead of $50,000, it would be regarded as excessive and undesirable. A firm would have no incentive to spend $250,000 to avoid a liability of $100,000. *But what if punitive damages increased the liability?* If punitive damages could be applied in order to raise the amount of total damages beyond the amount of harm, then the company would theoretically take the necessary precautions to avoid the harm, even at a cost of $250,000. Assume then, applying the Polinsky/Shavell model, that $200,000 is added to the compensatory damages of $100,000, so that the total damages equal $300,000. In such a scenario, the firm would be impelled to take the $250,000 precaution because the damages are now greater.

Therefore, in a strict liability sense, if we knew with certainty that a company could have avoided an adverse event, from which a claim for damages has arisen, by expending $250,000 on a precaution, then the formula for calculating punitive damages would be based on equalizing the total damages (compensatory plus punitive) to match the total cost of the precaution:

$$TD = CD + PD$$

where TD is total damages, CD is compensatory damages, and PD is punitive damages.

$$TD = TC$$

where TC is the total cost of the precaution.

Therefore,

CD + PD = TC

To solve for punitive damages:

PD = TC – CD

Let's plug in the numbers above. Assume that the total costs of the precaution are $250,000, and the known harm for which compensatory damages would be paid is $100,000.

PD = TC – CD

PD = $250,000 – $100,000

PD = $150,000

Thus, in order for a company to justify a precaution costing $250,000, where the known harm will create a liability of $100,000 (compensatory damages), it must be facing punitive damages of more than $150,000. At exactly $150,000 in punitive damages, the company would break even; that is, the precaution would cost exactly the same as the prospective total damages. At less than $150,000 in punitive damages, there would be no incentive to take the precaution, because the precaution would cost more than the total amount of damages.

What would be the optimal amount of damages when the defendant could potentially escape liability? In other words, how much should be awarded in punitive damages where the liability of the defendant is uncertain? Under the Polinsky/Shavell approach, the method for determining such a value requires some factor that accounts for the probability of escaping liability. Assume, for example, that there is only a one-in-four chance that a company will be found liable for an injury or other form of loss valued at $100,000. In effect, on average, the company would be required to pay $25,000 in damages every time it causes the harm. If a $50,000 precaution would have prevented the harm from occurring, the company would not likely take the precaution. Indeed, its cost of prevention would be twice the toll of its average loss in damages.

To address this concern, punitive damages must be fixed in an amount that will increase the total amount of damages so that the average damages will equal the harm caused by the company. Assume, for example, that instead of paying $25,000 in damages for an injury or loss valued at $100,000, the company is required to pay $400,000 in damages. If there is still only a one-in-four chance of liability, then, at $400,000, the company would be effectively paying $100,000 every time it causes the harm. This would create an incentive for the company to incur the costs of precaution to avoid risky behavior. A total damage award of $400,000 would include both compensatory and punitive damages. If the plaintiff is entitled to $100,000 in compensatory damages for his actual losses, then punitive damages would be $300,000.

The formula to calculate punitive damages, based on the uncertain possibility of escaping liability, is the harm (or loss) multiplied by the reciprocal of the probability that the company will be found liable. If the probability that a company would be found liable is one-in-four, then we convert this probability to a decimal (0.25), and we set up the reciprocal as follows: $\frac{1}{.25}$. This reciprocal equals 4. Therefore, the multiplier is 4, meaning that this is the number that will be multiplied by compensatory damages to determine the total damages.

CD = $100,000

TD = $100,000 x 4 = $400,000

PD = TD – CD

PD = $400,000 – $100,000

PD = $300,000

Thus, the optimal level of punitive damages is $300,000. For practical purposes, punitive damages should be greater than $300,000, so that when combined with the compensatory damages of $100,000, the risk to the company is too great even considering the company's three-in-four chance of escaping liability.

13.7. Prejudgment Interest

Prejudgment interest is generally authorized in employment law cases, and is specifically recognized in Title VII litigation. By applying interest to the back pay award, a court effectively adjusts the back pay to present value. Three pieces of information are necessary: the principal amount of the back pay award, the interest rate to be applied, and the period of time over which prejudgment interest will be awarded. The formula for simple interest is I = P x i x n, where I = interest, P = principal, i = the interest rate and n = the number of months, years, or other applicable time period.[34]

If a back pay award of $150,000 is subject to 3% prejudgment interest for three years, our simple interest formula would be $150,000 x 0.03 x 3 = $13,500. This would bring the total back pay award to $163,500.

If the interest award is compounded annually for three years at 3% interest, we would apply the following formula:

$$\$150{,}000 \text{ x } (1.03)^3$$
$$= \$150{,}000 \text{ x } 1.092727$$
$$= \$163{,}909.05$$

Thus, with annual compounding, the final result is somewhat higher.

An even higher result flows from monthly compounding.[35] For example, if prejudgment interest is to be compounded on a monthly basis for the same $150,000 award, applying the same 3% interest rate, the formula would become:

$$\$150{,}000 \text{ x } \left[1 + \frac{.03}{12}\right]^{36}$$

With monthly compounding, it is necessary to convert the 3% annual interest rate (.03) to a monthly interest rate; thus it is divided by 12. The original exponent (3, reflecting 3 years), must then be multiplied by the number of months per year (12) to produce a new time period of 36 months. Let's do the math:

$$\$150{,}000 \text{ x } \left[1 + \frac{.03}{12}\right]^{36}$$
$$= \$150{,}000 \text{ x } [1.0025]^{36}$$
$$= \$150{,}000 \text{ x } 1.094$$
$$= \$164{,}100$$

---

[34] See Section 6.1.
[35] See Section 6.5.

Choosing the proper interest rate and the frequency of compounding interest are likely to be the most controversial aspects of assessing prejudgment interest in an employment law case. Approaches to choosing the interest rate abound. Some say it should be tied to the prime rate or to a market index, such as the return a plaintiff would have earned had he received his back pay earlier and invested it in a diversified portfolio of stocks. Others argue in favor of a risk-free interest rate based on the U.S. Treasury bill rate. Still others promote variable rates and floating rates. Local precedent and court rules may provide guidance on the choice of an applicable rate.

Another area of concern is the start date for assessing prejudgment interest. While interest would seem to run from the date on which the adverse employment action occurred, some jurisdictions may fix the filing date of the complaint, petition, or grievance as the start date for assessing interest. But what if a plaintiff unreasonably delays the filing of an action, thus protracting the litigation, in a state in which interest accrues at the moment the injury or adverse employment action occurred? What if a plaintiff unreasonably prolongs the litigation through improper, redundant, or cumulative discovery tactics or multiple requests for adjournments? These are unsettled questions that may require an equitable adjustment of the prejudgment interest period.

Chapter 14

Real Estate Damages

14.1. Origin of Property Damage Claims

Before calculating the amount of damages in a real estate case, it is important to consider how property damage claims originate. Appreciating the source and origin of the damages suffered in a particular case will provide a foundation for selecting the best formula. Among the many kinds of natural, legal, social, and economic events that may affect the value of real estate are the following:

- Contract and financing issues, such as when a buyer backs out of a deal.
- Architectural and engineering issues, which make a property unsafe or uninhabitable.
- Construction delays or noncompliance issues, such as when a builder cannot finish a job within code specifications on a timely basis.
- Natural disasters, such as wild fires, floods, and hurricanes.
- Zoning and eminent domain, such as when a government-sponsored building project encroaches on private property.
- Health and environmental conditions, including mold, radioactive elements, lead paint, asbestos, and contaminated water supplies.
- Socioeconomic and cultural issues, such as high crime, neighborhood deterioration, racial tensions, and gang presence.

- Insolvency issues, including bankruptcies, foreclosures, and short sales.
- Public and private nuisance conditions, such as, for example, unreasonable noise from a nearby airport, or unbearable smoke from a nearby industrial chimney stack.
- Infestation problems from pests and rodents.
- Access issues, which may relate to blocked rights of way or the need for easements, design changes, or special licenses.
- Tainted image problems, such as where a property was the scene of a gruesome crime, or where it is believed to be haunted or jinxed.

This list, of course, is only a glimpse of the wide variety of political, regulatory, cultural, contractual, transactional, environmental, climatological, and structural issues that may adversely affect the value of real estate. In addition, ordinary and extraordinary market forces may have an impact on the value of real estate and the calculation of damages in a particular case. Market conditions include the impact of inflation on buyers' purchasing power, job growth and unemployment rates, new housing construction patterns, 30-year fixed mortgage rates and Treasury bond yields, rental vacancy trends, and other economic drivers.

Identifying, classifying, and distinguishing the cause and origin of a particular loss in a real estate case permits a sensible assessment of the kinds of factors that ought to be considered in applying a valuation method or a damages formula. It may also assist attorneys in finding statutory and regulatory support for a particular damages assessment. For example, mudslides and erosion cases may be eligible for certain disaster relief funds from a government agency, the payment of which is subject to strict proofs and specific caps. Such funds may not be available or such caps may not be applicable if the damage is shown to be attributable to seismic shifts, tornados, or violent storms.

14.2. Sales Comparison Approach

Real estate appraisers commonly apply three general approaches to valuing real estate: (1) the sales comparison approach; (2) the cost approach; and (3) the income capitalization approach. Each of these approaches can be modified to explore the amount of damages suffered in a real estate case.

The sales comparison approach essentially compares a particular property with comparable properties that have recently been sold to establish a property value. Applying the principle of *substitution,* this approach assumes that a buyer would not purchase a property for any price greater than what he would pay for a comparable property, consisting of similar features and characteristics, and presumably sold in the same locale under similar market conditions.

When a legal dispute arises and the value of a certain property has been thereby diminished, the sales comparison approach can be utilized to determine the monetary damage affecting the subject property. The specific method is known as *matched pair analysis* or *paired sales analysis.*

Let's assume, for example, that a homeowner claims that his home has been devalued by a manufacturing plant that has recently expanded its operations onto a bordering tract of land, causing loud machinery noises and malodorous air pollution. His home is described as a two-story Colonial, with four bedrooms, two-and-a-half baths, a two-car garage, and a large backyard sitting on one-half acre in a suburban residential tract.

Using the matched pair analysis, the subject home would be compared to one or more similar homes located elsewhere in the community that are not affected by the deafening machines or the foul-smelling air quality. The comparable homes should be two-story Colonials with four bedrooms, two-and-a-half baths, and other similar characteristics. If the match between the subject home and the comparable home is accurate, then the difference in the sales prices should reflect the value of the damages attributable to the nuisance caused by the abutting manufacturing plant.

Assume then the subject property has sold (or can be sold) for \$300,000. Three similar properties not affected by the noise or the pollution (Comp 1, Comp 2, and Comp 3) have sold for higher amounts. The damage suffered by the subject property owner would be an averaged difference between the sales price for the subject home and the sales price of each of the comparable homes, as shown below.

Comparable Properties	Sales Price	Difference ($$) from Subject	Difference (%) from Subject
SUBJECT	$300,000		
COMP 1	$412,000	$112,000	27.18%
COMP 2	$368,000	$ 68,000	18.48%
COMP 3	$379,000	$ 79,000	20.84%
Average of Comps	$386,333	$ 86,333	22.35%

As the table depicts, the three comparable homes, unaffected by the adverse conditions, drew higher sales prices than the subject property. The average price of a comparable home was $386,333, which was $86,333 more than the sale price of the subject property. This represented a difference (a loss in sales value) of more than 22%.

Attorneys who use a matched pair analysis must be prepared to defend against two common attacks on this approach. The first attack is that the homes chosen for the comparison are not comparable. Challengers will frequently argue that the homes selected as being comparable homes are, in fact, differentiated by some feature or amenity. While the "comps" may all be two-story Colonials, with four bedrooms, two-and-a-half baths, and two-car garages, other distinctions may render the match invalid.

For example, one of the comps may have stand-alone, window-based air-conditioning units instead of central air-conditioning. Another comp may have a swimming pool or a fully built basement. If this is the case, it may be necessary to adjust the figures to account for the differences. Therefore, if a comparable home with a swimming pool sold for a greater amount partly because of the swimming pool, then the value which the swimming pool added to the sales price would have to be subtracted from the sales price used to make the comparison.

An abbreviated way to depict the matched pair approach, with such an adjustment, is:

Damages =
Sales Price of Comp Home
– Adjustment (Swimming Pool Value)
– Sales Price of Subject Home

If a comparable property with a value-adding swimming pool sold for $400,000, of which $10,000 could be attributed to the swimming pool, and if the subject property could draw only a $300,000 purchase price, then the dollar value of the damages suffered by the subject homeowner would be:

$400,000 – $10,000 – $300,000 = $90,000

A loss of $90,000 off the price tag would represent a 22.5% reduction.

The second common attack on the matched pair analysis is the proximate cause argument. Challengers are likely to assert that the differences in price between a subject property and comparable property are not attributable exclusively to the event or the circumstances on which the legal action is based. If the case is based on a civil tort claim for damages based on nuisance theories attributable to noise and air pollution, the defendants may argue that other factors—market conditions, age of the properties, or specific transactional conditions—account for the difference in the sales prices. The defense would contend that the industrial operations at the nearby plant are not the proximate cause (or the exclusive cause) of the difference in the market values of the subject property and comparable homes elsewhere in the community.

Expert testimony may provide the necessary evidence to prove causation and damages. Yet perhaps the parties can settle the claim before trial by agreeing that the defendant is responsible for a certain percentage of the diminution in value of the subject property. If the defendant concedes 60% responsibility, then the formula shown above can be modified as follow:

Damages =
Sales Price of Comp Home
– Adjustment (Swimming Pool Value)
– Sales Price of Subject Home
multiplied by percent of responsibiliity

Using the figures above, we'll apply 60% as the percent of responsibility:

$400,000 – $10,000 – $300,000 = $90,000
$90,000 x 0.60 = $54,000

The defendant would then be obligated to pay $54,000 in damages, assuming that the cause of action was otherwise proven and the matter was amicably settled.

Appraisers and other technical experts may apply the sales comparison approach using a variety of other, more sophisticated, comparison techniques. These include trend analysis, proximity analysis, and multiple regression analysis which use larger data sets and/or survey research. However, the simplified matched pair analysis discussed above, as modified by the appropriate adjustments, offers a reasonable approach for calculating damages in a real estate case.

14.3. Cost Approach

The basic tenet of the cost approach is that the value of a property, once damaged or impaired by a compensable event, is equal to the cost of rebuilding, repairing, and restoring the property to its undamaged and preimpaired condition. To calculate a property value using this approach, one must estimate the value of land, the replacement cost of building on the land, and the applicable level of depreciation. In essence, the formula for calculating damages for a ruined property must yield a value that would restore the claimant to an unruined property of equal condition and utility.

Like the sales comparison approach, the cost approach relies on the principle of substitution, holding that the replacement value of a property should be no greater than the cost of comparable land and improvements.[1] The cost approach, however, focuses on cost, not sales, and it targets the cost of the constituent parts of the property, not the property as a whole.

Suppose that a nuclear mishap at a local power plant has contaminated a farmer's land and rendered his home uninhabitable and his grain silo unusable. Applying the cost approach, we would estimate each cost associated with replacing the property, as follows:

Step One. Estimate the value of the land (without improvements).
Step Two. Estimate the construction cost of the buildings.

[1]The cost approach, however, provides a useful alternative to the sales comparison approach, especially in cases in which there are no comparable properties from which to make a comparison, or in which the subject property has unique, impossible-to-compare features.

Step Three. Determine the depreciation in value of the buildings.[2]
Step Four. Estimate any other replacement costs.
Step Five. Estimate any incidental and consequential costs.
Step Six. Add all of the estimated costs, and then subtract the depreciation amount.

Damages =
Land + Buildings + Other replacement costs, incidental and consequential costs – Loss due to depreciation

In the case of a nuclear mishap, the cost approach may, in fact, require much more data, rendering the six steps above an oversimplification. For example, it may be impossible to rebuild on the site of the farmer's land or anywhere nearby. Even if the farmer could safely return to this property, there may be cleanup costs, engineering studies, laboratory analysis, site inspections, and regulatory compliance costs, all before the property can be restored or reoccupied. The value of the farmer's crops, livestock, grain storage, and other assets would also necessarily need to be assessed.

What if an office building were rendered unusable by the nuclear mishap? A proper expansion of the cost approach might take into consideration any number of incidental and consequential costs, such as:

- Tenant relocation costs
- Customer and client notification costs
- Special insurance endorsements
- Moving costs
- Special advertising costs
- Additional property management or security costs
- Lease modification and other legal costs
- Additional operating expenses
- Lost tenant and extended vacancy costs
- Furniture, fixtures, and equipment (sometimes listed as FF&E).

[2]Depreciation represents a loss in value of the buildings on the property due to any number of different reasons. It includes physical deterioration due to age and weather; functional deterioration in which the use of the property has become impaired due to the obsolescence of the structure, and depreciation attributable to external economic factors.

Not only is it important to account for all of the replacement costs, but it is also necessary to recognize all preexisting circumstances that may have reduced the value of the damaged property before the damage was done. For example, a homeowner claiming damages for total loss of his home should not enjoy 100% replacement costs if the home was in disrepair, or had a nonfunctional heating system or a defective roof.

Let's consider a factually detailed property claim arising from a flood. Assume that Helen Homeowner has a two-story, four-bedroom Colonial-style home in the Oak Village section of town. The home and the adjacent storage shed on the property were destroyed in a flash flood when a cement infrastructure collapsed, breaching a dam on the local riverfront and flooding all of Helen's land. Helen's home is 10 years old, and it spans 2,300 square feet. The roof, which has a 20-year guarantee, was severely damaged before the flood. According to contractors, the roof will cost $7,500 to replace. Sheds can be rebuilt for $2,200. The typical life of a home in Oak Village is 40 years. Local builders could rebuild Helen's home at a cost of $75 per square foot. Vacant lots in Oak Village sell for $25,000. The cost of moving Helen and her salvageable belongings is $3,500.

To apply the cost approach to this factual scenario, let's return to the original six-step process, this time accounting for the additional information known to us.

The first step is to estimate the value of Helen's land (without improvements). Vacant lots sell for $25,000; so this will be our first cost.

The second step is to estimate the construction cost of Helen's home. If we were to build Helen's home from scratch—a brand new home—the cost would be equal to the square footage multiplied by the builder's estimate of $75 per square foot.

2,300 square feet x $75 = $172,500

So the reconstruction costs for Helen's home will be $172,500.

The third step is to determine the depreciation in value of the property. First we must consider the physical deterioration of the home, specifically the roof. Helen's property was already 10 years old when the flood occurred, and the roof carries a 20-year guarantee. Therefore, she is entitled to only 50% of the replacement cost of the roof. The roof will cost $7,500 to replace; therefore, we will deduct $3,750.

As for the depreciated value of the home, we will look at the age of the home and its projected life. The home is 10 years old, and it has a projected life of 40 years. Therefore, even before the flood, the home had lost one-fourth (10/40) of its full value. We will thus subtract 25% of the construction cost of $172,500.

$172,500 x 25% = $43,125

As our fourth step, we must look at any other replacement costs. The shed on Helen's property will cost $2,200 to replace.

Our fifth step is to account for any incidental and consequential costs. In this case, Helen will incur $3,500 in moving expenses.

Our final step is to add all of the costs and to subtract the depreciation costs.

$25,000 (land) + $172,500 (home) + $2,200 (shed) +
$3,500 (moving expenses)
– $43,125 (depreciation of home) – $3,750 (roof)
= $156,325

The value of the property claim—that is, the adjusted damages to be paid to Helen Homeowner—is $156,325.

14.4. Direct Income Capitalization Approach

The income capitalization approach is the best valuation technique for income-producing properties that have been damaged, or whose value has been impaired by a legally compensable event. Its most common application involves commercial properties that are leased to business tenants and which thereby generate income through rental payments.

There are two income capitalization approaches: the direct capitalization technique, discussed here, and the DCF model, discussed in the next section below.

The direct capitalization technique is based on a simple formula in which the net operating income (NOI) of a property in its first year is divided by the market capitalization rate (cap rate). The formula is expressed as:

$$\text{Value} = \frac{\text{NOI}}{\text{Cap Rate}}$$

The difficulty lies in determining an accurate NOI and a valid cap rate.

Net Operating Income

The NOI of a property is equal to the annual income produced by that property after deducting operating expenses. It requires three levels of data:

1. **Potential Gross Income (PGI)**[3] which consists of all of the gross rents possible, and any other income the property potentially generates, such as parking fees, laundry fees, and vending receipts.
2. **Effective Gross Income (EGI)**, which consists of vacancy losses and collection losses.
3. **Operating Expenses**, which consist of all operational, administrative, and maintenance costs, including utilities, insurance, repairs, and property taxes. However, operating expenses do not include debt service, depreciation, income taxes, and capital expenditures.

   To calculate NOI, first calculate PGI; then apply these two equations:

   PGI – Vacancy and Collection Losses = EGI
   EGI – Operating Expenses = NOI

   The simplified statement of these equations produces this formula:

   NOI = PGI – Vacancy and Collection Losses – Operating Expenses

Let's plug in some numbers using data from a hypothetical office building known as Trinity Tower:

[3]Potential Gross Income (PGI) is also sometimes referred to as Gross Potential Income (GPI).

Trinity Tower
Net Operating Income

Gross Rents Possible	$175,000
Parking Fees	$ 5,200
Tenant Signage Fees	$ 2,450
PGI	**$182,650**
Vacancy Costs	$ 5,400
Collection Costs	$ 950
EGI	**$176,300**
Utilities	$ 21,000
Insurance	$ 18,500
Maintenance and Repairs	$ 6,750
Property Taxes	$ 24,100
NOI	**$105,950**

Applying the data shown above, we now have the numerator for the direct capitalization formula, that is, the NOI for Trinity Tower. To determine the property value, we must next determine the market capitalization rate.

Market Capitalization Rate

The market capitalization rate, or cap rate, is often well-known to investors and lenders in a particular market at any particular moment in time. It is generally based on market characteristics and trends (location, crime, property type, and other risk factors). The cap rate is used to estimate the value of income producing properties by reflecting the recent pattern of buyers and sellers in the same marketplace. If we knew the value (or asking price) of a property, and if we knew its NOI, then we could modify the value formula, $\text{Value} = \frac{\text{NOI}}{\text{Cap Rate}}$, to determine the cap rate. In other words, if $\text{Value} = \frac{\text{NOI}}{\text{Cap Rate}}$, then $\text{Cap Rate} = \frac{\text{NOI}}{\text{Value}}$. Thus, using Trinity Tower's NOI of $105,950, and a hypothetical asking price of $1,100,000, we can calculate the cap rate:

$$\text{Cap Rate} = \frac{\text{NOI}}{\text{Value}}$$

$$\text{Cap Rate} = \frac{\$105{,}950}{\$1{,}100{,}000}$$

$$\text{Cap Rate} = 0.096$$

Therefore, the cap rate for Trinity Tower would be 9.6%.

This example assumes that we knew the value of the property. But what if the *value* of the property is what we were trying to determine? What if the entire purpose of knowing the cap rate was to activate the first formula, Value $= \frac{\text{NOI}}{\text{Cap Rate}}$? In such a case, there are only two choices: either (1) apply a cap rate provided by a reliable investment source based on the most current information, or (2) establish your own cap rate based on bank lending terms and your desired return on equity (ROE).[4] Let's look at the second alternative.

To derive our own cap rate based on bank lending terms and ROE, we need to gather some data about the financing terms available to purchase the property in question. Let's assume that a bank is willing to lend \$800,000 at 6% interest to be repaid over 20 years. The annual debt service can be easily calculated using an online loan calculator.[5] In this example, the monthly payments on a 20-year loan of \$800,000 at 6% would come to \$5,731.45. This converts to an annual debt service on the loan of \$68,777.40.

Next, calculate the *loan constant* by dividing the annual debt service amount by the principal amount of the loan:

$$\text{Loan Constant} = \frac{\text{Annual Debt Service}}{\text{Loan Principal}}$$

$$\text{Loan Constant} = \frac{\$68{,}777.40}{\$800{,}000}$$

$$\text{Loan Constant} = 0.08597175$$

This produces a loan constant of approximately 8.6%, which is effectively the bank's own cap rate for this transaction.

The next step is to determine the ROE. The general formula for ROE is:

$$\text{ROE} = \frac{\text{Net Income}}{\text{Shareholder's Equity}}$$

Let's assume that a buyer in the marketplace would invest \$50,000 toward the purchase of the subject property, from which he would ex-

---

[4]For a further discussion of ROE, see Section 8.7.

[5]See, for example, the free mortgage loan and amortization calculator at bankrate.com. http://www.bankrate.com/calculators/mortgages/loan-calculator.aspx.

pect to generate $7,500 per year in income. Applying the ROE formula, we can quickly determine that this buyer seeks a 15% pre-tax ROE:

$$\text{ROE} = \frac{\$7{,}500}{\$50{,}000}$$

$$\text{ROE} = 0.15$$

In effect, 15% is the investor's equity cap rate.

We now have two cap rates, the bank's loan constant of 8.6% and the investor's ROE of 15%. In order to construct a *market cap rate*, we need to blend these two rates into one rate. To do this, we will need to determine the loan-to-value ratio (LTV).

The LTV ratio is simply a statement of how much a bank will lend a borrower against the appraised value of a property, expressed in the form of a percentage. It is stated in terms of the amount of money a borrower must borrow (his mortgage principal) divided by the appraised value of the property:

$$\text{LTV} = \frac{\text{Amount of Mortgage Loan}}{\text{Appraised Property Value}}$$

In this case, the mortgage loan is $800,000, and the property value is stated at $1.1 million. Therefore, LTV = 73%. In effect, the bank will provide 73% of the financing for the property at its cap rate, and the equity market will provide the remainder at the ROE rate. To blend the rates, we effectively weight the rates according to the LTV percentages. The bank's loan constant of 8.6% accounts for 73% of the market cap rate; therefore, we multiply 0.086 x 0.73, which equals 0.06278. If the bank's rate accounts for 73%, then the LTV for the equity cap rate is 27%. Therefore, we multiply the ROE of 15% by 27%, or 0.15 x 0.27, which equals 0.0405. By adding the two results (0.06278 and 0.0405), we arrive at a market cap rate of 0.10328, or 10.33%. Here's a visual display of the calculations:

<table>
<tr><td>Bank's cap rate (loan constant) = 8.6%
Bank's LTV debt ratio = 73%
Bank's weighted cap rate = (0.086 x 0.73)</td><td>Investor's cap rate (ROE) = 15%
Investor's LTV equity ratio = 27%
Investor's weighted cap rate = (0.15 x 0.27)</td></tr>
<tr><td colspan="2">Formula:
Market Cap Rate = (0.086 x 0.73) + (0.15 x 0.27) = 0.10328 (10.33%)</td></tr>
</table>

Tying It All Together

Let's now return to the formula for the direct income capitalization approach: Value $= \frac{\text{NOI}}{\text{Cap Rate}}$. Since we know that the NOI is \$105,950 and the market cap rate is 10.33%, we can now calculate the value of the Trinity Tower property:

$$\text{Value} = \frac{\text{NOI}}{\text{Cap Rate}}$$

$$\text{Value} = \frac{\$105{,}950}{0.1033}$$

$$\text{Value} = \$1{,}025{,}653.44$$

Therefore, we can now say that a property with NOI of \$105,950 in a market with a cap rate of 10.33% is worth \$1,025,653.44.

The same formula can be recast to apply to investment decisions and to set the parameters in legal claims. For example, if Value $= \frac{\text{NOI}}{\text{Cap Rate}}$ then $\frac{\text{NOI}}{\text{Cap Rate}}$ also equals the maximum purchase price a buyer should pay under current market conditions. Likewise, $\frac{\text{NOI}}{\text{Cap Rate}}$ also equals the optimal amount of a settlement or a judgment to be awarded for property damage or impaired property value, assuming that 100% liability has been established and that 100% of the property has been damaged or impaired. If a settlement or a judgment is based on a defendant who is 80% responsible for the impaired value of the property, based on a comparative negligence standard, then the final property value would be multiplied by 80% as follows:

$$\text{Value (Based on defendant's 80\% liability)} = \frac{\text{NOI}}{\text{Cap Rate}} \text{ x } 0.8$$

Another variation on the property value formula is to convert the cap rate to a cap factor and then multiply it by the NOI. To convert a cap rate to a cap factor (that is, a multiple), simply divide 1 by the cap rate. In this case, 1 divided by the cap rate of 10.33% is $\frac{1}{0.1033}$ which equals approximately 9.68. With a cap factor of 9.68, the formula is simply stated:

$$\text{Value} = \text{NOI x cap factor}$$

$$\text{Value} = \$105{,}950 \text{ x } 9.68$$

$$\text{Value} = \$1{,}025{,}596$$

The property value of $1,025,596 is quite close to the result obtained using the original cap rate formula above, the slight difference being attributable to the rounding of the cap factor.

14.5. Discounted Cash Flow Approach

The discounted cash flow (DCF) approach can be used to estimate the lost value of income-producing property that has been destroyed, damaged, or otherwise impaired. While the DCF method has many applications in the making of investment decisions,[6] it is used here to compare the projected cash flows of an undamaged property over a period of time to the actual cash flows of the property in its damaged state.

The starting point is to project the cash flows for a particular income-producing property over a period of years and then to calculate the present value (PV) of each of those cash flows. The sum of the present values of the cash flows, minus the cost of the original investment in the property, provides us with the net present value (NPV) of the property. The formula for NPV, as you may recall, is:

$$NPV = \frac{FV}{(1+i)^n} + \frac{FV}{(1+i)^n} + \frac{FV}{(1+i)^n} + \frac{FV}{(1+i)^n} + \frac{FV}{(1+i)^n} - COST$$

where FV stands for future value, i stands for interest rate (or discount rate) and n stands for the number of years. Let's substitute CF (cash flows) for FV, as a reference to our future cash flow of income from the subject property. Let's also populate each fraction with the number of the year for a five-year period. The revised NPV formula for our subject property looks like this:

$$NPV = \frac{CF}{(1+i)^1} + \frac{CF}{(1+i)^2} + \frac{CF}{(1+i)^3} + \frac{CF}{(1+i)^4} + \frac{CF}{(1+i)^5} - COST$$

In effect, this formula represents a calculation of the PV of the net cash flow in year 1, plus a calculation of the PV of the net cash flow in year 2, plus a calculation of the PV of the net cash flow in year 3, and so

[6]For other applications of the DCF model, see the discussions of Future Value of an Uneven Cash Flow in Section 5.3 and of Net Present Value in Section 5.5.

forth until the fifth year. The sum of the PVs is then calculated, from which the cost of the investment is deducted, yielding the *net* present value of the cash flows for the five-year period.

Let's apply some hypothetical figures. Assume that a commercial property was purchased for $1 million. It is expected to produce potential gross income (PGI) of $300,000 in year 1, $400,000 in year 2, $450,000 in year 3, and $500,000 in years 4 and 5. Assume consistent vacancy rates of 10%, and consistent operating expenses of $100,000 each year. Let's calculate NOI, which is effectively our cash flow for each year:

YEAR	1	2	3	4	5
Potential Gross Income (PGI)	300,000	400,000	450,000	500,000	500,000
Vacancy Rate (10%)	30,000	40,000	45,000	50,000	50,000
Effective Gross Income (EGI)	270,000	360,000	405,000	450,000	450,000
Operating Expenses	100,000	100,000	100,000	100,000	100,000
Net Operating Income (NOI)	170,000	260,000	305,000	350,000	350,000
CASH FLOW	170,000	260,000	305,000	350,000	350,000

Assuming a discount rate of 7%, we can calculate the PV of each year's cash flow using the formula $\frac{CF}{(1+.07)^n}$ where n will be 1, 2, 3, 4, or 5 depending on the year in question. Let's do the math:

YEAR	CASH FLOW	FORMULA	PRESENT VALUE
1	170,000	$\frac{CF}{(1+.07)^1}$	158,878
2	260,000	$\frac{CF}{(1+.07)^2}$	227,094
3	305,000	$\frac{CF}{(1+.07)^3}$	248,970
4	350,000	$\frac{CF}{(1+.07)^4}$	267,013
5	350,000	$\frac{CF}{(1+.07)^5}$	249,545
TOTALS	$1,435,000		$1,151,500

To calculate the NPV, we must add together the present values for each year, and then subtract the cost (the initial investment of $1 million).

$$NPV = \frac{CF}{(1+i)^1} + \frac{CF}{(1+i)^2} + \frac{CF}{(1+i)^3} + \frac{CF}{(1+i)^4} + \frac{CF}{(1+i)^5} - COST$$

As show in the table above, the NPV is calculated as follows:

NPV = \$158,878 + \$227,094 + \$248,970 + \$267,013 + \$249,545 – \$1,000,000

NPV = \$151,500

Therefore, the NPV of the projected five-year cash flow for the commercial property is \$151,500.

Calculating Damages Using the DCF Model

By projecting the cash flows for the five-year period shown above, we are able to determine the NPV of owning the property, but this NPV is based on the assumption that the property is habitable and income-producing. What if a negligent electrical installation caused a fire that rendered much of the property uninhabitable and out of service, forcing most of the commercial tenants to move? To calculate damages using the DCF model, we would essentially have to reduce each year's cash flow by the cost of repairing the building, and by the increased vacancy rates, along with any additional costs attributable to the fire. Let's assume that the fire occurs at the beginning of year 2. A total of 75% of the tenants are forced from their commercial space in year 2, and 50% are displaced in years 3 and 4. In year 5, the vacancy rate drops to 20%. To account for these displacements, the vacancy rate will need to be adjusted on the cash flow table:

YEAR	1	2	3	4	5
Potential Gross Income (PGI)	300,000	400,000	450,000	500,000	500,000
Vacancy Rate	30,000	300,000	225,000	225,000	100,000
Effective Gross Income (EGI)	270,000	100,000	225,000	225,000	400,000
Operating Expenses	100,000	100,000	100,000	100,000	100,000
Net Operating Income (NOI)	170,000	0	125,000	125,000	300,000
CASH FLOW	170,000	0	125,000	125,000	300,000

Let's further assume that, as a result of the fire, there will be structural repairs of \$110,000 in year 2, \$65,000 in year 3, and \$42,000 in year 4; restoration and smoke damage remediation of \$15,000 in year

2; furniture, computer, and equipment replacement costs of $32,000 in years 2, 3, and 4; chemical, corrosion, and acid decomposition abatement costs of $10,000 in years 2 and 3; and soot-and-tar cleanup in the HVAC system totaling $21,000 in year 3. Add another $25,000 in year 2, $15,000 in year 3, and $9,500 in year 4 for tenant relocation and interruption costs. Let's revise the cash flow table to account for these additional costs:

YEAR	1	2	3	4	5
Potential Gross Income (PGI)	300,000	400,000	450,000	500,000	500,000
Vacancy Rate	30,000	300,000	225,000	225,000	100,000
Effective Gross Income (EGI)	270,000	100,000	225,000	225,000	400,000
Operating Expenses	100,000	100,000	100,000	100,000	100,000
Structural Repairs		100,000	65,000	42,000	
Restoration and Smoke Damage		15,000			
Furniture, Computer, and Equipment		32,000	32,000	32,000	
Chemical, Corrosion, and Acid		10,000	10,000		
Soot and Tar Cleanup			21,000		
Tenant Relocation		25,000	15,000	9,500	
Net Operating Income (NOI)	170,000	(182,000)	(18,000)	41,500	300,000
CASH FLOW	**170,000**	**(182,000)**	**(18,000)**	**41,500**	**300,000**

As a result of the repair, restoration, and relocation costs, and the increased vacancy rates beginning in year 2, the cash flow dropped significantly, reflecting negative cash flow in years 2 and 3.

The next step is to recalculate NVP, using the revised cash flow figures:

YEAR	CASH FLOW	FORMULA	PRESENT VALUE
1	170,000	$\frac{CF}{(1 + .07)^1}$	158,878
2	(182,000)	$\frac{CF}{(1 + .07)^2}$	–158,965
3	(18,000)	$\frac{CF}{(1 + .07)^3}$	–14,693
4	41,500	$\frac{CF}{(1 + .07)^4}$	31,660
5	300,000	$\frac{CF}{(1 + .07)^5}$	213,895
TOTALS	$311,500		$230,775

NPV equals the sum of the present values minus the cost (the initial investment of $1 million). Therefore, $230,775 – $1,000,000 = –$769,225. Thus we can conclude that the NPV of the property *after the fire* is negative-$769,225.

What are the damages?

Before the fire, the property had a positive NPV of $151,500. After the fire, it has a negative NPV of –$769,225. The difference between these two figures equals the PV of the damage caused by the fire:

–$769,225 – $151,500 = $920,725.

Therefore, the optimal amount of damages to be claimed by the property owners in their suit against the contractor responsible for the negligent electrical installation would be $920,725. Based on the DCF model, this figure represents the best assessment of the financial loss, as measured by the five-year reduction in cash flow, discounted to today's dollars.

14.6. Rental Loss Formulas

In some cases, the primary damage suffered by a property owner is the loss of rental income. This can result from high vacancy rates, market forces, rent collectability problems, and physical property damage. The formulas below—while not perfectly scientific—provide expedient shortcuts for estimating damages attributable to lost rental income.

Quick Rental Loss Formula

The quick rental loss formula (QRL) is a handy device for estimating damages caused by nonpayment of rents and vacant office suites or apartment units. Determining the quick rental loss requires the NOI, the anticipated rent increase (RI), the estimated vacancy rate (EVR), and the estimated rental default rate (ERD). The formula is:

QRL = NOI x RI x (EVR + ERD)

Suppose an environmental catastrophe causes 20% of the tenants in an apartment building to cancel their leases or to opt out of renewing their leases. Another 10% of the available units are unrentable because of the stigma created by the nearby environmental calamity. The apartment therefore has an EVR of 30%. Let's also assume that another 10% of the tenants simply stop paying their rents: thus, an estimated ERD of 10%. Let's also say that, in this case, the NOI for the apartment building was $65,000. The anticipated RI for the upcoming year is 4%. Let's apply the formula:

QRL = NOI x RI x (EVR + ERD)

QRL = $65,000 x 1.04 x (.30 + .10)

QRL = $65,000 x 1.04 x .40

QRL = $27,040

So, based on the figures provided, the anticipated rental loss for the upcoming year will be $27,040. While the QRL formula is not scientifically precise, and in fact is only as valid as the estimates used in the formula (RI, EVR, ERD), it provides a convenient shorthand for calculating damages in a case in which the loss of rental income is the primary setback.

Property Damage Loss Formula

The property damage loss (PDL) formula tells you how much money will be lost as a result of the physical destruction of rental premises by an undesirable tenant or by an external source. The formula essentially calculates the net costs of repairing the premises plus the net market loss. It requires the following pieces of information: the amount of any unpaid rent (UR); the departing tenant's security deposit being held on account (SD); the total cost of repairs (TR); the budgeted (anticipated) rent charge for the next rental period (BR); and the actual reduced amount of rent which the market will bear (RR). The difference between the BR and the RR represents the market loss (ML). The formula for calculating the property damage loss is:

PDL = UR + TR + ML – SD

Let's plug in some hypothetical numbers. Assume that an uncooperative tenant defaults on the lease and destroys his rental unit prior to his abandoning the property. He has left unpaid rent due of $5,000. The costs for repairing the premises are as follows:

Painting	$2,200
Cleaning	$ 900
Junk Removal	$ 450
Key Replacement	$ 10
New Carpets	$1,850
Window Repairs	$ 260
Plumbing Repairs	$ 380
Refurbishing Woodwork and Other Repairs	$ 545
TOTAL	$6,595

Assume that the tenant left a security deposit of $7,500 on account. Based on market trends, and assuming that there was no diminution in the value of the rental unit, the unit would be budgeted in the next rental period for (or would have an anticipated rental charge of) $3,000 per month, or $36,000 per year (BR). However, because of the diminished quality of the premises, despite the many repairs, the market will only bear a reduced rental price of $2,300 per month, or $27,600 per year (RR). The market loss (ML) is the difference between the BR and the RR.

ML = BR – RR

ML = $36,000 – $27,600

ML = $8,400

Let's put the entire PDL formula together now.

PDL = UR + TR + ML – SD

PDL = $5,000 + $6,595 + $8,400 – $7,500

PDL = $12,495

Therefore, the damages arising out of the tenant's property damage total $12,495, after applying the tenant's security deposit to his unpaid rent and to the total repair costs. The outcome of the PDL formula will vary, of course, when all of the components of the formula are not present. For example, there may be no unpaid rent, and so the UR would be 0. Likewise, there may be a ML of 0 in a good rental market.

Eviction Loss Formula

When a tenant is evicted, the landlord suffers the value of his lost rent. This loss, however, must be augmented by any costs associated with the eviction process, and then reduced by any rental payments received from a replacement tenant. The easy formula for an eviction loss is:

EL = ALR – PR + LF – RTR

where EL is the eviction loss, ALR is the annual rent charge according to the lease (annual lease rent), PR is the rent actually paid by the tenant (paid rent), LF is the legal fees and court costs associated with the eviction process, and RTR is the replacement tenant rental payments received.

For example, assume that Christopher signs a lease with Condor Commons, an apartment lessor, to pay $1,500 per month in rent for a one-year lease running from January 1 through December 31. Christopher dutifully pays rent for January through April; then he stops paying. It takes three months to give Christopher notice of the eviction, to file a landlord-tenant complaint against him, to complete the eviction process, and to install a replacement tenant at the same monthly rental amount. The new tenant takes up occupancy of the premises on August 1. Condor's lawyer charged $450 for handling the eviction case and advancing the court filing and service fees. Let's do the math:

ALR = $18,000, based on $1,500 per month for 12 months.

PR = $6,000, equaling four monthly payments of $1,500 (January through April)

LF = $450, as the legal fee and court costs

RTR = $7,500, the total of five monthly payments of $1,500 paid by the replacement tenant (August through December).

The EL is calculated as follows:

EL = ALR – PR + LF – RTR

EL = $18,000 – $6,000 + $450 – $7,500

EL = $4,950

So, the losses attributed to the nonpayment of rent by, and subsequent eviction of, the first tenant total $4,950.

The EL formula can be modified in cases of property damage by adding to the formula the cost of repairs (TR). Thus, for example, if Christopher ruined the carpets because of an untrained dog, and if carpet replacement was estimated at $1,600, the revised formula would look like this:

$$EL = ALR - PR + LF - RTR + TR$$

$$EL = \$18{,}000 - \$6{,}000 + \$450 - \$7{,}500 + \$1{,}600$$

$$EL = \$6{,}550$$

If a security deposit (SD) could be claimed by the landlord, then the amount claimed would be subtracted, extending the formula further. Assume the court permitted the landlord to claim an SD equal to one month's rent of $1,500.

$$EL = ALR - PR + LF - RTR + TR - SD$$

$$EL = \$18{,}000 - \$6{,}000 + \$450 - \$7{,}500 + \$1{,}600 - \$1{,}500$$

$$EL = \$5{,}050$$

Special provisions contained in a lease may also permit the landlord to claim other losses in the event of an eviction. Any such additional losses should be added to the formula.

14.7. Income Loss Formulas

Another way to calculate the amount of damages suffered in a real estate case is to assess the loss of income generated by an income-producing property. Several formulas accomplish this task.

Debt Service Coverage Ratio

The debt service coverage ratio (DSCR) answers the question: how much income is available to pay down debt after operating expenses have been paid. The formula explores the relationship between NOI and debt obligations.[7] It actually produces a net income percentage, and the difference in that percentage from one point in time to another reflects a potential item of damages. The formula is $\frac{\text{NOI}}{\text{Debt}}$ where the

[7]For a variation on the DSCR, see the Interest Coverage Ratio discussed in Section 8.8. Compare also to the Current Ratio discussed in Section 8.14.

debt consists of principal plus the interest, such as in the case of a mortgage payment.

For example, let's say that Oscar has a rental property with an NOI of \$50,000. He has mortgage payments (principal plus interest) totaling \$39,800. Oscar's debt service coverage ratio is 25.6%

$$\text{DSCR} = \frac{\text{NOI}}{\text{Debt}}$$

$$\text{DSCR} = \frac{\$50{,}000}{\$39{,}800}$$

$$\text{DSCR} = 1.256$$

$$[1.256 - 1 = 0.256]$$

If Oscar's mortgage debt were as high as his NOI (\$50,000), his income-to-debt ratio would by 1 (or effectively, 1 to 1), meaning that his rental property would generate only enough money in income to cover its debt. In the example above, however, Oscar's DSCR is 1.256, meaning that he is generating 25.6% more in income than he needs to cover his debt (to pay his mortgage).

Let's now assume that the contamination of a water system by an industrial polluter prompts civil litigation over the adverse effects suffered by Oscar's rental properties. One way to explore the damages Oscar suffered is to examine the difference in debt service coverage both before and after the adverse events occurred.

After the water system contamination, Oscar's NOI may have dropped to \$40,000. His DSCR now looks like this:

$$\text{DSCR} = \frac{\text{NOI}}{\text{Debt}}$$

$$\text{DSCR} = \frac{\$40{,}000}{\$39{,}800}$$

$$\text{DSCR} = 1.005$$

$$[1.005 - 1 = 0.005]$$

His revised DSCR is now just 0.5%—a significant drop from the 25.6% he enjoyed before the contamination occurred.

Or, let's assume that Oscar's NOI remains the same at \$50,000, but that his special plumbing, piping, and water supply replacement costs rise significantly, raising his total recurring debt to \$51,500. The DSCR ratio now produces a problematic result:

$$DSCR = \frac{NOI}{Debt}$$

$$DSCR = \frac{\$50{,}000}{\$51{,}500}$$

$$DSCR = 0.970$$

$$[0.970 - 1 = -0.03]$$

Now, Oscar is not generating enough income to meet his debt. In fact, he is negative 3%, that is, 3% short. His damages, based on the pre-contamination DSCR of 25.6%, are nearly 29% (representing the difference between a positive 25.6% and a negative –3%).

Another approach to the DSCR formula is to account for the tax rate in calculating debt. In this variation, NOI is treated as earnings *before interest and taxes*. Debt is treated as principal plus interest, but the principal is divided by the inverse of the tax rate (that is, 1 minus tax rate). The revised formula is:

$$DSCR = \frac{\text{Operating Income (Earnings before interest and taxes)}}{\frac{\text{Principal}}{1 - \text{Tax Rate}} + \text{Interest}}$$

We'll assume that the operating income is \$100,000, and that the interest due is \$20,000. The principal of \$50,000 is divided by 1 minus the tax rate, which we'll say is 33% in this case.

$$DSCR = \frac{\$100{,}000}{\frac{\$50{,}000}{1 - 0.33} + \$20{,}000}$$

$$DSCR = \frac{\$100{,}000}{\frac{\$50{,}000}{0.67} + \$20{,}000}$$

$$DSCR = \frac{\$100{,}000}{\$74{,}626.87 + \$20{,}000}$$

$$DSCR = \frac{\$100{,}000}{\$94{,}626.87}$$

$$DSCR = 1.056$$

$$[1.056 - 1 = 0.056]$$

The DSCR is therefore 5.6% at a 33% tax rate.

Return on Investment

The basic formula for return on investment (ROI)[8] can also be explored to gauge damages in a real estate action. ROI, in its simplest form, is stated as the gains minus the costs, divided by the costs:

$$\text{ROI} = \frac{\text{Gains} - \text{Costs}}{\text{Costs}}$$

This could also be stated as income minus costs divided by costs:

$$\text{ROI} = \frac{\text{Income} - \text{Costs}}{\text{Costs}}$$

It is essentially the difference between the before-and-after ROIs that provides a snapshot of our damages in a given case.

Example: A mudslide occurs on a residential tract causing significant structural damage, attributable to negligent engineering, design, and construction work. Before the mudslide, the subject property generated $2.4 million in income at a cost of $800,000. After the mudslide, it generates $1.9 million in income at a cost of $950,000. Using the simplified formula for ROI, we can compare before-and-after scenarios:

BEFORE	***AFTER***
$\text{ROI} = \frac{\text{Income} - \text{Costs}}{\text{Costs}}$	$\text{ROI} = \frac{\text{Income} - \text{Costs}}{\text{Costs}}$
$\text{ROI} = \frac{\$2{,}400{,}000 - \$800{,}000}{\$800{,}000}$	$\text{ROI} = \frac{\$1{,}900{,}000 - \$950{,}000}{\$950{,}000}$
ROI = 2	ROI = 1
2 x 100% = 200%	1 x 100% = 100%
Before the mudslide, there was a 200% return on investment.	After the mudslide, there was a 100% return on investment.

Another variation of the simplified ROI is to divide net profit by assets. In this approach, costs are deducted from the numerator to produce a single *net* profit amount. If, for example, net profit was stated at $85,000, and assets were valued at $225,000, the formula would look like this:

---

[8]See Section 8.2.

$$ROI = \frac{\$85{,}000}{\$225{,}000} = 0.3777$$

ROI is therefore approximately 38%. Again, a before-and-after analysis can provide a useful snapshot of the damages suffered in a given case.

Another way to characterize the ROI formula using the terms we've discussed in this chapter is to treat the numerator as the NOI, which is roughly the equivalent of income minus costs or net profit. In this variation, we divide the NOI by the total investment:

$$ROI = \frac{\text{NOI}}{\text{Total Investment}}$$

Assume that an investor wishes to purchase a large income-producing property and, under current market conditions, can make the purchase for a down payment of $100,000. The sellers, however, did not relinquish the premises on a timely basis, and because of the delay, the investor lost the advantage of a lower interest rate, costing him an additional $10,000. Moreover, the sellers fraudulently concealed a construction defect which the investor was forced to repair at a cost of $33,000. Altogether, the investor's total investment equals $143,000.

If the investor's NOI was $17,500, then his ROI would be roughly 12%, calculated as follows:

$$ROI = \frac{\text{NOI}}{\text{Total Investment}}$$

$$ROI = \frac{\$17{,}500}{\$143{,}000}$$

$$ROI = 0.122$$

But what if the sellers had conveyed the property on a timely basis, so that the investor could obtain the lower interest rate? And what if the sellers had delivered a structurally sound property without a costly construction defect? The investor's total investment would then be only $100,000, and the ROI formula would be 17.5% as follows:

$$ROI = \frac{\$17{,}500}{\$100{,}000}$$

$$ROI = 0.175$$

The difference between the originally projected ROI of 17.5% and the actual resulting ROI of 12.2% is 5.3%. In other words, the investor's damages amount to a 5.3% reduction in his ROI.

Gross Rent Multiplier

The gross rent multiplier (GRM) is a price-to-income ratio, or more specifically a ratio that compares the sale or purchase price of certain real estate to its potential or projected gross income.

The formula is $\frac{\text{Price}}{\text{Gross Income}}$, but it might be recast in a number of different ways. The numerator "Price" could be sales price, purchase price, or fair market value. The denominator "Gross Income" could be stated as potential gross income; annual gross income, or projected, anticipated, expected, or scheduled gross income. In determining the income, however, it is important to consider the total amount of rent payable, not only from occupied units, but from vacant units as well.

Let's try an example, using the formula $\frac{\text{Purchase Price}}{\text{Gross Scheduled Income}}$. We will refer to purchase price as P and gross scheduled income as GSI. Assume that a buyer has paid $450,000 for an office building that contains five offices that generate rents of $750 each per month. On an annual basis, the office building generates $45,000 in rent. ($750 x 5 units x 12 months = $45,000). The GRM would be 10.

$$\text{GRM} = \frac{\text{P}}{\text{GSI}}$$

$$\text{GRM} = \frac{\$450{,}000}{\$45{,}000}$$

$$\text{GRM} = 10$$

If we know the GRM, we can invert the formula to calculate the purchase price:

$$\text{P} = \text{GRM x GSI}$$

$$\text{P} = 10 \text{ x } \$45{,}000$$

$$\text{P} = \$450{,}000$$

What does GRM tell us? The number alone tells us nothing. However, it can be a useful benchmark in comparing before-and-after scenarios, or in comparing one property with another. For example, let's say that you wanted to sell a property in a community in which property owners have sued an industrial polluter. The typical GRM for the community was 10, but it has now dropped to 9. If the GSI is still $45,000, then the price of the property must be $405,000. (GSM of 9 multiplied by GSI of $45,000). At $405,000, the property has lost $45,000 in value. Assuming all other market forces have remained stable, this diminution in value would be one indicator of the seller's damages.

Suppose that a litigant has filed suit claiming that a certain defendant's actions caused the value of his property to decline. An appraisal of the property indicates that it is worth $750,000, and in fact the highest offer on the property has been $738,000. The property has an established GSI of $88,000. The GRM of comparable properties, recently sold in the same market but unaffected by the legal claim, is 10.5. By simple math, we can determine that the property should have a market value of $924,000 in a market with a GRM of 10.5.

P = GRM x GSI

P = 10.5 x $88,000

P = $924,000

If the litigant could establish proximate cause and demonstrate that the diminution in the value of his property is not attributable to any other intervening factors, then he could assert that the expected market value of $924,000 in the GRM 10.5 market was reduced to an actual market value of $738,000 (as if the property were situated in a market with a GRM of 8.4). This represents damages in amount of $186,000.

GRM is a handy benchmark that can be used as a negotiating tool, but it is not a precise or perfectly accurate measure of value or of losses. GRMs are inherently flawed because they do not account for operating expenses such as utilities, taxes, and insurance, and they are derived from property pricing and valuation techniques that may be inconsistent or unreliable. To establish meaningful proofs, a cap rate comparison and DCF analysis would be recommended. A GRM comparison, however, can provide quick information that may assist an attorney in estimating the value of a loss or in prompting a settlement negotiation.

Chapter 15

Environmental Damages

15.1. Methods of Valuation

In cases involving environmental damage, destruction of natural resources, or contamination of air or water supplies, the general methods for calculating damages are largely spelled out in federal statutes, such as the Comprehensive Environmental Response, Compensation, and Liability Act (CERCLA)[1] and the Oil Pollution Act (OPA),[2] and their corresponding regulations. There are, in fact, dozens of highly specialized and targeted federal environmental laws administered by the U.S. Departments of Interior, Energy, Agriculture, Commerce, Defense, and Health and Human Services, the U.S. Environmental Protection Agency (EPA) and the U.S. Fish and Wildlife Service (FWS).[3]

Moreover, every state has at least one environmental protection agency, and many states have specialized agencies, departments, and

---

[1]42 U.S.C. § 9601, *et.seq.* Commonly known as the Superfund law, CERCLA was enacted by Congress in December 1980, and thereafter amended by the Superfund Amendments and Reauthorization Act (SARA) in October of 1986.

[2]33 U.S.C. § 2701, *et.seq.* (signed into law in August 1990).

[3]These include, for example, the Clean Air Act (CAA), 42 U.S. § 7401, *et seq.,* the Clean Water Act (CWA), 33 U.S.C. § 1251, *et.seq.,* the Emergency Planning and Community Right-to-Know Act (EPCRA), 42 U.S.C. § 11001, *et.seq.,* the Hazardous Materials Transportation Act (HMTA), 49 U.S.C. 5101, *et.seq.,* and the Chemical Safety Information, Site Security and Fuels Regulatory Relief Act (CSISSFRRA), 42 U.S.C. 7412(r).

boards for conservation and protection of natural resources, pollution control, air and water quality measurement, nuclear safety, coastal management, mining, oil and gas drilling, and solid waste disposal.[4] Thus, in addition to federal statutes and regulations, state laws provide a complex, often overlapping, matrix of fines and penalties and damage assessment schemes for polluters, waste dumpers, and other environmental offenders.[5]

The statutes and regulations provide the federal and state governments with methods for assessing damages against those who destroy or impair natural resources. They also provide guidance for determining damages in a civil action brought by private parties who are adversely affected by an environmental mishap or a negligent or reckless event.

Conceptually, there are many ways to think of damage to the environment: The fair market value of the land or the water supply that was destroyed; the cost of cleanup; the cost of replacing or rebuilding contaminated property; the loss of enjoyment of an aesthetically pleasing waterway, meadow, field, garden, or orchard. Statutes and commentators refer to the following terms in calculating damages:

- Lost value
- Restoration
- Removal and remediation
- Rehabilitation
- Replacement
- Acquisition of equivalent resources and services
- Use value
- Committed use value
- Passive use value
- Option value
- Existence value

---

[4]California, for example, has an Air Resources Board, a Department of Conservation, an Environmental Protection Agency, a Department of Toxic Substances Control, a Department of Water Resources, and an Integrated Waste Management Board.

[5]See, e.g., Florida's Settlement Guidelines for Civil and Administrative Penalties, at http://www.dep.state.fl.us/legal/penalty/files/dep_923_civil_penalty_directive.pdf.

While the precise definitions of these terms may vary, or may be subject to varying opinions, they serve to illustrate the different approaches to valuation that have evolved in the statutory and regulatory framework.

Natural Resource Damage Assessments

The U.S. Department of the Interior (DOI), responding to the mandate under CERCLA, developed two procedures for assessing natural resource damages. Type A Natural Resource Damage Assessments (NRDAs) are procedures for addressing smaller environmental mishaps covering smaller areas or involving smaller or shorter term releases (e.g., smaller oil spills). Type B NRDAs cover more significant environmental events, requiring determination of the injury, quantification, and ultimately assessment of the damages. The most significant work in measuring damages in a Type B case is determining the costs of restoration, rehabilitation, replacement, and/or acquisition of equivalent resources.

Determining Costs

The cost of restoration, rehabilitation, replacement, and/or acquisition of equivalent natural resources is the primary valuation determinant in an environmental case. Federal regulations under CERCLA recognize these costs both in terms of direct costs and indirect costs.[6] Direct costs, for example, include the compensation of employees for their time and effort devoted to replacing the damaged property, the cost of materials acquired, consumed, or expended, equipment and other capital expenditures, and other necessary expenses. Indirect costs include somewhat elusive categories of costs relating to activities or items that support the cleanup or replacement work being done but are not directly related to the actual cleanup or replacement activities. For example, a portion of the lease costs for a building that contains the offices of employees working on an environmental rehabilitation project could be measured as an indirect cost. Regulations recognize the use of an "indirect cost rate" for such overhead costs under appropriate circumstances.[7]

---

[6]43 C.F.R. § 11.83(b).

[7]43 C.F.R. § 11.83(b)(1)(iii).

In dealing with an environmental disaster under federal law, six cost estimating methodologies are recognized by statute. An authorized official responsible for estimating damages is free to choose among the different methodologies or can choose any other methodology that satisfies the government's acceptance criteria. A glimpse at the six recognized cost estimating methodologies provides yet another perspective on the inherent complexity of determining damages in an environmental case:[8]

- **(i) Comparison methodology.** This methodology may be used for unique or difficult design and estimating conditions. This methodology requires the construction of a simple design for which an estimate can be found and applied to the unique or difficult design.
- **(ii) Unit methodology.** This methodology derives an estimate based on the cost per unit of a particular item. Many other names exist for describing the same basic approach, such as order of magnitude, lump sum, module estimating, and flat rates, and involve various refinements. Data used by this methodology may be collected from technical literature or previous cost expenditures.
- **(iii) Probability methodologies**. Under these methodologies, the cost estimate represents an "average" value. These methodologies require information which is called certain, or deterministic, to derive the expected value of the cost estimate. Expected value estimates and range estimates represent two types of probability methodologies that may be used.
- **(iv) Factor methodology**. This methodology derives a cost estimate by summing the product of several items or activities. Other terms such as ratio and percentage methodologies describe the same basic approach.
- **(v) Standard time data methodology.** This methodology provides for a cost estimate for labor. Standard time data is a catalogue of standard tasks typically undertaken in performing a given type of work.

[8] 43 C.F.R. § 11.83(b)(2).

(vi) Cost- and time-estimating relationships (CERs and TERs). CERs and TERs are statistical regression models that mathematically describe the cost of an item or activity as a function of one or more independent variables. The regression models provide statistical relationships between cost or time and physical or performance characteristics of past designs.

These cost-estimation methodologies require much greater attention and analysis than this volume can provide. Attorneys involved in litigation over governmental claims for damages to environmental and natural resources will almost certainly require economic experts to apply one or more of these methodological approaches in accordance with the applicable regulatory procedures.[9]

Understanding the statutory and regulatory framework, however, can provide useful insight to practitioners dealing with smaller private environmental claims, toxic tort litigation, industrial health and safety actions, and the like. The categories of damages and methods of valuation discussed in federal and state laws provide meaningful guidance on how to measure the damage to a property, a person, or a natural resource in civil litigation involving environmental accidents.

15.2. Change in Value

In a case involving property damage caused by environmental pollution, the easiest formula for calculating damages is the lost value formula based on the difference in value prior to and subsequent to the damage. In other words, the change in value (CV) equals the value before damage (VBD) minus the value after damage (VAD).

$$CV = VBD - VAD$$

[9]The need for experts is certainly clear in mass disaster litigation such as the Exxon Valdez oil spill in March 1989. The ensuing litigation involved 60 experts for the plaintiffs and 120 experts for the defendants. For an interesting account, see N. Robert Stoll, *Litigating and Managing a Mass Disaster Case: An Oregon Plaintiff Lawyer's Experience in the Exxon Valdez Oil Litigation*, 56 Or. St. B. Bull. 14, 15 (1995).

This formula applies in cases in which the amount of damages, or the method for calculating damages, is not expressed in a contract between the parties. In other words, a lost value or change-in-value formula is most appropriate when the plaintiff is the landowner, and the defendant is an unrelated third-party polluter whose conduct or misconduct somehow devalues the landowner's property.

Consider, for example, a case in which a landowner owns a large tract of land, consisting mostly of swamps, adjacent to an industrial waste disposal site. The corporation that owns the waste disposal site has been sued by the landowner because waste materials dumped into a disposal pit on the corporation's property leaked onto the landowner's tract. The leakage has been attributable to faulty construction of the pit, which allowed chlorinated hydrocarbons and other toxic substances to overflow onto the landowner's property and into the swamps.

Before it was polluted, the landowner's property was used for grazing cattle, for hunting and fishing, and, commercially, for growing timber. An appraisal prior to the waste disposal mishap valued the landowner's property at \$795 per acre or \$703,575 for the 885 acres affected. After it was polluted, however, the acreage was rendered useless to cattle, off-limits to hunters and fishermen, and commercially inactive. Experts have testified that the swamps are now devoid of animal and vegetable life. Dead or dying trees are everywhere visible, and are said to be the result of the corporation's pollution. At best, the land has a current fair market value of \$100 per acre, or a total value of \$88,500. What are the landowner's damages, using the simple lost value formula?

$$CV = VBD - VAD$$

$$CV = \$703{,}575 - \$88{,}500$$

$$CV = \$615{,}075$$

The change in value in this case is \$615,075. The difference between the before-and-after values is essentially the lost market value of the property as a result of the pollution.

15.3. Restoration Costs

A second approach to assessing property damage in an environmental case is to determine the cost of restoration if the property can be adequately renewed, repaired, and refurbished. Restoration costs can be extensive, taking into account geophysical and topographical renovations, soil, rock, and surface alterations, heavy machinery, specialized equipment, testing facilities, and a significant investment in human resources.

The analysis is no less complicated for governmental damage claims against polluters. For example, on January 14, 1999, the engine room of the *M/S Star Evviva,* a Norwegian cargo ship, was unmanned as the ship sailed approximately 30 to 50 miles off the coast of South Carolina. Due to the malfunction of a fuel oil transfer system in the engine room during these hours while oil was being transferred from one tank to another, the *Star Evviva* pumped fuel oil onto the deck and overboard, spilling approximately 24,000 gallons into the Atlantic Ocean. Two days later, oiled birds—mostly common loons and red-throated loons—began washing ashore along the coastline from Folly Beach, South Carolina, to Topsail Beach, North Carolina.

In wrestling with the costs of restoration of the loon habitat, the U.S. Fish and Wildlife Service and the South Carolina Department of Natural Resources were required to compare the purchase of 3,234 hectares of a loon nesting habitat in Ontario, Canada, at a cost of $1,018,710 ($315 per hectare) to the cost of purchasing two islands consisting of thousands of acres of salt marsh that would provide a winter habitat for the loons. Also considered were the costs of building an Oiled Bird Rehabilitation Center together with a Combined Use Avian Medical Center.

Charting Restoration Costs

Before determining if a restoration project is economically justified, it is necessary to identify every incremental cost that will be incurred in the restoration process over time. This can be a technical objective, requiring the expertise of specialists in a number of different fields. Let's assume, for example, that the contamination of a tract of land with hazardous and toxic chemicals will require the following restoration costs:

1. Soil acquisition
2. Chemical removal and remediation
3. Excavation

4. Site design and redevelopment
5. Permits, licenses, and approvals
6. Site monitoring
7. Maintenance and oversight

How long will it take to fully restore the property? And how will the costs of restoration be spread over the timeline for completing the project? These are other questions that may require expert guidance. Let's assume the entire project will take six years.

By charting the various restoration costs over the timeline of the project, we can begin to assess our total restoration costs. The chart below depicts each of the seven stated restoration cost categories listed above, for each of the six years beginning in 2012. Hypothetical cost figures have been provided.

YEAR	1. Soil Acquisition	2. Chemical R&R	3. Excavation	4. Site Design and Re-Devlmt.	5. Permits, Licenses, Approvals	6. Site Monitoring	7. Maint. and Oversight
2012			$10,000	$20,000			
2013	$25,000	$65,000		$10,000	$8,500	$5,000	$7,000
2014		$15,000				$5,000	$7,000
2015						$5,000	$7,000
2016						$5,000	$6,500
2017						$5,000	$6,000

Once we have plotted the costs on a table, we are ready to calculate the total annual costs for each year of the restoration project. Let's now add another column to the table:

YEAR	1.	2.	3.	4.	5.	6.	7.	Total Annual Costs
2012			$10,000	$20,000				$ 30,000
2013	$25,000	$65,000		$10,000	$8,500	$5,000	$7,000	$120,500
2014		$15,000				$5,000	$7,000	$ 27,000
2015						$5,000	$7,000	$ 12,000
2016						$5,000	$6,500	$ 11,500
2017						$5,000	$6,000	$ 11,000

We can further expand the table to provide us with the total of all annual costs, essentially the total project cost:

YEAR	1.	2.	3.	4.	5.	6.	7.	Total Annual Costs
2012			$10,000	$20,000				$ 30,000
2013	$25,000	$65,000		$10,000	$8,500	$5,000	$7,000	$120,500
2014		$15,000				$5,000	$7,000	$ 27,000
2015						$5,000	$7,000	$ 12,000
2016						$5,000	$6,500	$ 11,500
2017						$5,000	$6,000	$ 11,000
TOTAL								$212,000

So we can now see that the restoration project will cost $212,000 over the six-year period. This figure, however, must be discounted to present day value, as discussed below.

Determining Present Value

Present value (PV),[10] as you may recall, discounts tomorrow's dollars to today's value by applying an interest rate or discount rate. PV poses the question: what amount of money today, if invested at a particular interest rate, would produce the amount of money we will need in the future? Using the table of figures above, we can restate the question more specifically as follows: how much must we invest in today's dollars to cover the restoration costs of $212,000 over the six years of the restoration project?

Because the total restoration costs are divided over six years, we must calculate the PV of each year's annual costs. The formula for present value is: $PV = \frac{FV}{(1 + i)^n}$ where FV equals the future value, i equals the interest rate or discount rate, and n equals the number of years. To calculate the combined PV of the project, we must add the PV of the 2012 costs to the PV of the 2013 costs to the PV of the 2014 costs, and so forth. Let's assume a 3% discount rate. The table below coverts each of the annual costs shown above to their PV.

[10]For a review of present value, see Section 5.4.

YEAR	Total Annual Costs*	Formula	Discounted Annual Restoration Costs (Present Value by Year)
2012	$ 30,000	$\frac{\$30{,}000}{(1.03)^1}$	$ 29,126.21
2013	$120,500	$\frac{\$120{,}500}{(1.03)^2}$	$113,582.81
2014	$ 27,000	$\frac{\$27{,}000}{(1.03)^3}$	$ 24,708.82
2015	$ 12,000	$\frac{\$12{,}000}{(1.03)^4}$	$ 10,661.84
2016	$ 11,500	$\frac{\$11{,}500}{(1.03)^5}$	$ 9,920.00
2017	$ 11,000	$\frac{\$11{,}000}{(1.03)^6}$	$ 9,212.33
TOTALS	$212,000		**$197,212.01**

*Total costs could also be increased before discounting to take into consideration projected inflation rates

In today's dollars, based on a 3% discount rate, the restoration price tag of $212,000 would cost $197,212.01.

Applying Net Present Value

Once the restoration costs are estimated, it is necessary to calculate the net present value (NPV) of a restoration project to determine if the cost justifies the effort.[11] If the NPV is positive, then the restoration approach may be the preferred choice for assessing environmental damages. If the NPV is negative, the lost value formula or another approach may be better.

Let's start by calculating PV in another hypothetical scenario. Assume that an oil spill has destroyed the habitat of yellowfin tuna off the coastline of Hawaii. Restoration of the yellowfin tuna habitat will cost $8 million (PV), but is projected to generate an expanded catch among artisanal fisheries valued at $12.5 million in 10 years. What is the PV of $12.5 million in 10 years in today's dollars? Assume a 4% discount rate.

[11]For a review of net present value, see Section 5.5.

$$PV = \frac{FV}{(1 + i)^{10}}$$

$$PV = \frac{\$12{,}500{,}000}{(1 + .04)^{10}}$$

$$PV = \frac{\$12{,}500{,}000}{1.48}$$

$$PV = \$8{,}445{,}945$$

The PV of the future gain from restoring the tuna habitat is \$8,445,945. To gauge whether the restoration project is economical under the circumstances, we need to calculate the *net* present value. The formula for NPV is PV – Cost. Remember that the cost of the restoration project is \$8 million. We now know that the PV is \$8,445,945. Therefore, we can quickly determine that there is a positive NPV and the project is therefore economically justified:

$$NPV = PV - Cost$$

$$NPV = \$8{,}445{,}945 - \$8{,}000{,}000$$

$$NPV = \$\ 445{,}945$$

Because there is a positive NPV of \$445,945, the investment in restoration costs is justified. Whether it is the best assessment of environmental damages, however, is a judgment to be rendered after considering alternative methods of assessing damages.

Applying Benefit-Cost Analysis

Another approach to determining if a restoration project is justified is to construct a benefits-cost equation or a benefits-cost ratio.[12] The benefits-cost equation is simply benefits (B) minus costs (C). The rule is if $B - C > 0$, then the project is economically justified. In the form of a ratio, the same decision rule looks like this: If $\frac{B}{C} > 1$, then the project is economically justified.

Let's apply the figures which we used in the hypothetical yellowfin tuna habitat restoration project above. The benefit of the project is \$8,445,945, which represents the PV of the projected gain. The cost is \$8 million.

[12]For a review of benefit-cost ratios, see Section 9.16.

The benefits-cost equation is:

$8,445,945 – $8,000,000 = $445,945

If B – C > 0, then the project is economically justified. Since $445,945 is greater than zero, the restoration project is justified.

The benefits-cost ratio provides the same conclusion:

$$\frac{\$8,445,945}{\$8,000,000} = 1.0557$$

If $\frac{B}{C} > 1$, then the project is economically justified. Here, the ratio produces a result of 1.0557 which is greater than 1. Therefore, the project is justified.

Assuming that a benefit-cost analysis shows that a restoration project is economically justified, then the cost of restoration would be a meaningful quantum of damages.

15.4. Replacement Costs

A third approach to calculating damages in an environmental case is to determine the costs of replacement, minus reasonable depreciation. This approach generally makes sense when the cost of restoration is excessive and unjustified by the projected value (as shown by a negative NPV or a benefit-cost ratio less than 1).

Damages based on replacement costs are essentially equal to the cost of finding a substitute that yields the equivalent flow of goods and services. This is easier said than done. In some cases, there are no comparable substitutes that would replicate an ecosystem destroyed by toxic pollutants, a unique natural resource created over millennia, or distinctive and irreplaceable forms of fish, animal, or vegetable life endemic to a particular place or region. In other cases, the cost and time of finding suitable replacements invalidates the process from both an environmental and an economic standpoint. Even the process of pricing replacement goods and services is potentially complex and time-consuming.

In *Commonwealth of Puerto Rico, et al. v. the SS Zoe Colocotroni, et al.,*[13] a federal circuit court confronted precisely this kind of difficulty in applying replacement costs. The oil tanker, SS Zoe Colocotroni, had run aground on a reef off the south coast of Puerto Rico.

[13]628 F.2d 652 (1st Cir. 1980).

To refloat the vessel, the captain ordered the dumping of more than 5,000 tons of crude oil into the surrounding waters. An oil slick four miles long, and a tenth of a mile wide, floated towards the coast and came ashore at an isolated peninsula on the southwestern tip of the island, killing thousands of invertebrate organisms. The Commonwealth of Puerto Rico sued to recover damages for harm done to the coastal environment by the spilled oil.

At issue was which method of calculating damages was most likely, and most appropriate environmentally and economically, to compensate for the lost organisms. Economist Philip E. Sorenson estimated $5,526,583 as the replacement value of the invertebrate organisms. How he reached this estimate illustrates the complexity of the process.

Using the reports of other experts, Dr. Sorenson extrapolated the differences in number of organisms found in 10-centimeter core samples over a square meter area to determine the net difference in creatures per square meter. Since six samples were taken at each of four "stations" in the coastal area and in a control area, he determined this involved multiplying the results of each set of six samples by 21.22. Results from one of the four stations, where more animals were found at the coastal area than at the control area, were not included. The net difference was calculated to be 1,138 creatures per square meter. This figure in turn yielded the sum of 4,605,486 creatures per acre, and a total of 92,109,720 creatures of the 20 acres of mangroves allegedly impacted by oil.

Then, to arrive at an estimate of damages, Dr. Sorenson consulted catalogs from biological supply houses. From these catalogs he determined that many of these species sold at prices ranging from $1 to $4.50, and that no animal on the list sold for less than 10 cents. Dr. Sorenson assigned an average replacement value to each creature, regardless of species, of six cents. Multiplying 92,109,720 by .06 resulted in an estimate of $5,526,583 as the replacement value of the organisms missing from the sediments in the affected area.[14]

---

[14]In fact, a replacement value approach alone was not sufficient to Dr. Sorenson's analysis. He also estimated the cost of a 10-year scientific monitoring program at $1,393,200. His total estimate of the damages was thus $14,733,755.60, consisting of $7,176,363.71 for mangrove and sediment removal, $559,500 for mangrove replanting, $5,526.583 for the replacement value of organisms, $1,393,200 for monitoring, and $78,108.89 for cleanup costs.

In the end, the Commonwealth of Puerto Rico had no intention of purchasing 92 million *replacement* organisms but rather commissioned Dr. Sorenson's research as a yardstick of damages. The First Circuit rejected what it called an "abstract recovery" based on a "theoretical loss." It recognized, in fact, that actually purchasing the creatures would kill them again if they were returned to the oil-soaked sands, and in fact they would probably replenish themselves naturally once a restoration took place. It rejected the replacement value approach in favor of a more nuanced restoration value approach.

The lesson learned from the *SS Zoe Colocotroni* case is that a replacement value approach to calculating damages is unlikely to be adopted by a court if the process is too theoretical, the cost is too high, and the likelihood of actually replacing the damaged goods or services is too remote.

Net Replacement Value

If a reasonable replacement value could be determined in the case of a damaged or destroyed asset, the actual quantum of damages payable by an environmental offender would have to be adjusted to account for any salvage value and then further adjusted to account for depreciation. The general formula is:

$$\text{NRV} = \frac{\text{RC} - \text{SV}}{\text{UL}} \text{ x RL}$$

where NRV equals net replacement value, RC equals replacement cost, SV equals salvage value, UL equals useful life of the damaged or destroyed asset, and RL refers to the remaining life of the asset prior to the adverse environmental event. Before applying the formula, let's first consider salvage value.

Let's assume that a leaking underground storage tank causes widespread contamination of soil and groundwater with toxic petroleum hydrocarbons.

The cost of replacing the soil and the groundwater system would provide one simple measure of the value of the damages caused by the incident. But what if the hydrocarbon-contaminated soil could be sold to a buyer who sought to clean the soil through a bioremediation process using spent mushroom compost? The salvage value of the soil should then be deducted from any claim for damages.

Assume that 220 acres of soil have been adversely affected by the hydrocarbon leak. To recover salvage value for the 220 acres of soil, we'll need to translate the amount of contaminated soil into cubic yards. First, we start by calculating square feet. To convert acres to square feet, we multiply by 43,560.

220 x 43,560 = 9,583,200 square feet

Assume that the contaminated soil was laid at an average depth of three feet. To convert square feet to cubic feet, we apply this formula:

Square feet x average depth in feet = cubic feet

9,583,200 x 3 = 28,749,600 cubic feet

Then, to determine cubic yards, we divide by 27.

$$\frac{28{,}749{,}600}{27} = 1{,}064{,}800 \text{ cubic yards}$$

Assume that a buyer will pay $5 per cubic yard for the contaminated soil. The salvage value would thus be:

1,064,800 x 5 = $5,324,000

If we knew that the replacement cost of the soil was $18 per cubic yard, we could then say that our damages based on net replacement value would be calculated as follows:

Replacement Cost (RC): 1,064,800 x 18 = $19,166,400

Salvage Value (SV): 1,064,800 x 5 = $5,324,000

Net Replacement Value (NRV) = $19,166,400 – $5,324,000 = $13,842,400

We could also subtract the cost per cubic yard offered by the salvage buyer from the replacement cost per cubic yard (18 – 5 = 13) and then multiply by the number of cubic yards:

NRV = 13 x 1,064,800 = $13,842,400

But note: The NRV in these equations does not (yet) account for depreciation.

While these equations account for the salvage value, they do not fully adjust the replacement costs in every case. Let's assume that the property or asset destroyed in a particular case has a useful life, after which it will cease to be a productive asset. The value of the damaged or destroyed asset should be depreciated to account for the expenditure of its useful life before the adverse environmental event occurred.

Suppose that the soil in the example above had a useful life of 35 years, and that when the groundwater contamination occurred, the soil had *expended* 20 years of that useful life. It would therefore have a remaining life of 15 years. Let's return to our original formula:

$$NRV = \frac{RC - SV}{UL} \text{ x } RL$$

To determine the net replacement value, we'll start by subtracting the salvage value of the soil (SV) from the replacement costs (RC), using the figures from the example above:

$$\$19{,}166{,}400 - \$5{,}324{,}000 = \$13{,}842{,}400$$

The useful life (UL) of the soil is 35 years, of which the remaining life (RL) is 15 years.

$$NRV = \frac{RC - SV}{UL} \text{ x } RL$$

$$NRV = \frac{\$13{,}842{,}400}{35} \text{ x } 15$$

$$NRV = \$395{,}497.14 \text{ x } 15$$

$$NRV = \$5{,}932{,}457.10$$

As we analyze this formula, we can generate several different calculations of damages based on replacement value. For one thing, the gross replacement value is simply the RC of $19,166,400 to purchase 1,064,800 cubic yards of soil at $18 per cubic yard. We can produce a NRV of $13,842,400 based on SV of $5,324,000. We can further refine the NRV depreciating the value of the property over its useful life. Thus, if the property had a useful life of 35 years, it would have expended $395,497.14 of its value in each year of its existence. If, in fact, 20 years had elapsed before the environmental mishap occurred, then the property would have only 15 years remaining on its useful life. The

NRV would then consist of $395,497.14 per year for 15 more years, for a total of $5,932,457.10 in damages.[15]

15.5. Hedonic Pricing Method

The value of a particular property is based in part on the economic benefit attributable to certain environmental factors, such as air quality, water quality, aesthetic views, and the size and proximity of flourishing trees and vegetation, wildlife, and woodland. That same value is reduced by the economic detriment attributable to adverse environmental conditions such as air pollution, water pollution, excessive noise, and proximity to roads, highways, densely populated tracts, and commercial or industrial activities. The hedonic pricing method is based on the theory that value is derived from the sum of the value of *all* of a property's characteristics.

The value of some characteristics, of course, is elusive and impossible to quantify scientifically. *What is clean air worth?* However, we can isolate a particular environmental factor and place a market value on it by changing it from a positive to a negative condition. For example, assume that a lakefront estate surrounded by a thriving wooded area is worth $1 million. Now, redefine the property as a lakefront estate with a contaminated water supply, surrounded by a thriving wooded area. If the market value of the property drops to $750,000—and assuming all other conditions remain constant—we might say that the value of the contaminated water is $250,000. This, of course, is a simple change-in-value approach (the value before damage minus the value after damage). Yet we can also isolate the value of an adverse environmental condition by comparing two identical properties, only one of which suffers from the adverse condition. In the same vein, a property located beside a hazardous waste site may be priced $150,000 less

[15]This method is based on a straight-line depreciation approach. It assumes that replacement value damages in an environmental case would be measured by the remaining life of a particular asset. Not every case can utilize this method, nor will it be possible in every case to estimate an asset's useful life.

than an identical property located far from the waste site, suggesting that proximity to the waste site is the single factor accounting for the differential.

The hedonic pricing method is best used as a model for estimating the value of an adverse environmental condition when a large number of properties with similar characteristics can be observed and where environmental conditions can be carefully defined and separated from other conditions (noise pollution may be intertwined with motor vehicle traffic caused by the opening of a new roadway). Data must be taken from only one market and must be measured under comparable conditions during the same period of time. A lakefront property worth $1 million *five years before* the water supply became contaminated cannot be fairly compared to the fair market value of a contaminated property today.

Hedonic pricing theory applied across a spectrum of properties can also be used to determine incremental value based on proximity to an environmental problem. For example, assume that six identical properties are located at varying distances from a hazardous Superfund site:

Property Number	Distance from Superfund Site	Market Value
1	7 miles	$550,000
2	5 miles	$510,000
3	4 miles	$490,000
4	2 miles	$451,000
5	1 mile	$430,000
6	1,000 feet	$405,000

The greater the distance from the hazardous waste site, the more valuable the property value. Significantly, each mile from the site increases the value of the property by about $20,000.

The hedonic pricing method is sometimes classified as a *surrogate market approach* or an *indirect approach* because it attempts to monetize environmental resources without any actual defined market for clean air or clean water. By constructing a surrogate market based on what consumers are willing to pay (or not pay) based on air quality, water quality, and other environmental features, the hedonic pricing method provides another gauge for quantifying loss in an environmental law case.

15.6. Travel Cost Method

Another indirect approach to calculating loss in the event of an environmental mishap is the travel cost method. The travel cost method attempts to place a value on a recreational site or cultural amenity by determining the cost for visitors to visit the site and to enjoy its benefits. Thus, for example, if a beach is closed because of a coastal pollution event, we would ask the following questions:

1. How often do individuals visit the beach?
2. How much do visitors incur in travel costs (time and out-of-pocket expenses) to visit the beach?
3. How many people are affected?
4. What is the average demand for visits to the beach by consumers in various geographical zones?

The travel cost method first attempts to sum up all travel-related expenses, which could, for example, include fuel costs for travel to and from the beach, bridge and highway tolls, parking fees, beach admission fees, and other costs and incidentals. One might assume that visitors living closer to the beach would spend less money to get there and would likely visit the beach more often. Thus, the per capita travel costs for local visitors would be correspondingly lower but the total travel costs for such locals, in the aggregate, could be much greater.

Let's try an example. Suppose that the beach in question draws visitors from Atlantic County, Burlington County, and Cumberland County. Atlantic County residents are nearest to the beach; Cumberland County residents are farthest away. The table below displays the number of visits by residents of each county, the total population of each county, and the travel costs (including transportation fuel costs, travel time, and beach admission fees).

COUNTY	POPULATION	NUMBER OF BEACH VISITS	TRAVEL COSTS
Atlantic	140,000	45,000	$ 40
Burlington	50,000	6,000	$ 90
Cumberland	100,000	4,000	$135

Next, let's calculate the number of trips each county resident takes to the beach, that is, the *per capita trip rate*.

$$\text{Atlantic County: } \frac{45{,}000}{140{,}000} = .32$$

$$\text{Burlington County: } \frac{6{,}000}{50{,}000} = .12$$

$$\text{Cumberland County: } \frac{4{,}000}{100{,}000} = .04$$

Let's now consider how beach visitors from each county would be affected if an environmental event closed their beach and they were required to spend an additional $55 to travel to the nearest environmentally safe beach in Cape May.

County	Population	Number of Beach Visits	Per Capita Trip Rate	Travel Costs	Additional Travel Costs	Total Travel Costs
Atlantic	140,000	45,000	.32	$ 40	$55	$ 95
Burlington	50,000	6,000	.12	$ 90	$55	$145
Cumberland	100,000	4,000	.04	$135	$55	$190

We can quickly apply this data to make a rough estimate of damages using the travel cost method. For example, if every beach visit in each of the three counties will now cost $55 more per visit, then the combined amount of additional costs attributable to the environmental mishap will be:

Atlantic County: 45,000 visits x $55 = $2,475,000

Burlington County: 6,000 visits x $55 = $330,000

Cumberland County: 4,000 visits x $55 = $220,000

Total Additional Costs for the 3 Counties = $3,025,000

We can reach the same approximate results by multiplying the per capita trip rate by the $55 expense, and then multiplying the product by the total population. Thus, in the case of Atlantic County:

.32 x $55 = $17.60

$17.60 x 140,000 = $2.4 million

The travel cost approach is imperfect, at least to the extent it is addressed here. In order to be more accurate and reliable, we would want to know the mileage each visitor's car gets and the depreciation of the car caused by the trip. We want to measure the investment of time each visitor expends, and the value of that time, measured by an after-tax wage rate (assuming that each visitor would have chosen to work if he was not visiting the beach). Statistically, a certain number of beachgoers would forego their beach visits altogether if the cost increased by $55, choosing perhaps to enjoy other, less expensive, recreational alternatives. In the end, too, the travel cost method measures the monetary loss to members of the public but ignores or perhaps understates the cost of remediating the polluted waters.

Still, the travel cost approach provides another useful device for measuring and estimating damages in an environmental case, especially in government claims against polluters where the public's interest is what's been most severely affected.

15.7. Contingent Valuation Method

The contingent valuation method (CVM) is a hypothetical and controversial valuation method for assessing what members of the public are willing to pay to correct an environmental problem. The CVM approach uses questionnaires to infer the amount of damages in an environmental case from consumer responses about what they would pay to fix the problem. By determining what consumers of an environmental asset (e.g., a beach) would spend—that is, their maximum willingness-to-pay (WTP)—to correct an environmental mishap, attorneys and experts can place a value on the damage that was done. The CVM approach is not based on any real market for public goods; rather, it solicits WTP data that is *contingent* on a hypothetical scenario described in the consumer questionnaires.

One approach is to survey a well-defined community of consumers about a clearly specified and carefully articulated environmental cleanup program. Consumers are then asked to specify their maximum WTP for the described environmental action. The survey also generally collects demographic data about the respondents, in order to categorize and test the WTP results.

The CVM approach provides a relatively quick snapshot of consumer preferences. It also provides a glimpse of how consumers value an environmental asset for its *nonuse* characteristics, such as the aesthetic enjoyment of a body of water, as distinguished from its *use* characteristics (drinking water, fishing area, etc.). By canvassing the public about their willingness to pay for an environmental cleanup program, we can assess what passive value the public places on a natural resource.

Critics have attacked the CVM approach as being extremely hypothetical and unscientific, based on strategic and behavioral biases and inappropriate and skewed survey methods. The National Oceanic and Atmospheric Administration (NOAA), however, has found that CVM may produce a reliable starting point for a judicial assessment of damages.[16]

A simple application of the CVM approach can be illustrated as such: Assume that a CVM survey indicated that Atlantic County households were willing to pay an average maximum of $18 per month (or $216 per year) to purify a contaminated waterway. Therefore, WTP = 216. If Atlantic County has 99,500 households, then the CVM value would be calculated as follows:

CVM Value = WTP x Number of Households

CVM = 216 x 99,500

CVM = $21,492,000

At approximately $21.5 million, the CVM approach may well exceed the actual costs of restoration and remediation. Yet the calculation provides a useful marker of the passive value the public consumer places on an unpolluted waterway. Having this information may have a significant impact on the course of negotiations and the value of a final settlement, judgment, or verdict.

15.8. Total Economic Value

Environmental economists use the term *total economic value (TEV)* to capture both the *use value* and the *nonuse* value of an environmental

---

[16]Report of the NOAA Panel on Contingent Valuation, January 11, 1993. http://www.darrp.noaa.gov/library/pdf/cvblue.pdf.

asset. TEV is essentially the whole value of an environmental asset. It embraces the use value attributable to end users, such as those who would swim in a lake, or fish on a waterway. It also includes the nonuse value, defined as the passive value of simply having a unique asset remain in place, unchanged by pollution, erosion, or other adverse consequences.

TEV is ultimately a more accurate yardstick of the value of an environmental asset, and therefore a better gauge for calculating damages. By incorporating both use value (UV) and nonuse value (NUV), TEV considers both the loss to consumers who utilize environmental assets and those who do not use such assets but nevertheless place a value on the intrinsic benefit and aesthetic, cultural, or social advantages of keeping such an asset unchanged (that is, the value of preserving the waterway, keeping the park open, or saving the loons that nest or the salmon that spawn in the area).

To economists, TEV equals UV plus NUV. Thus, if TEV = UV + NUV, we can also say that:

TEV – UV = NUV
and
TEV – NUV = UV

Economic scholars have further dissected the value of TEV by breaking down the constituent values of the use and nonuse of an environmental asset. In the use value category, for example, there are both direct values and indirect values. Direct value is generally the value placed on removing and using a specific natural resource, such as fish, foul, water, or timber. Indirect value relates to the irremovable products of nature such as a spectacular canyon, an unobstructed vista, or a cascading waterfall. Indirect value has also been categorized as a "functional" value, referring to ecological functions of forests such as biodiversity and watershed management.

The UV category also recognizes an *option value*, consisting of the right or option to use the natural environment in the future. This value recognizes the worth attributable to preserving the environment in anticipation of enjoying it at some other time. In this vein, preserving diverse plant life is believed to facilitate our future access to the raw materials necessary to develop pharmaceuticals. Even if we claim no present use of plants at this time, the option value accounts for the inherent value of preserving them for the future.

Therefore, we can say that the use value of the environment consists of the direct value plus the indirect value plus the option value:

UV = DV + IV + OV

The nonuse value of the environment has likewise been divided into its constituent parts. NUV has been defined as the *existence value (EV)* plus the *bequest value (BV).* EV is the value placed by the public on the mere existence of a natural asset, the passive nonuse value attributable to the asset's unique physical, aesthetic, or cultural features. EV is most commonly assessed by use of the CVM and is calculated by determining the public's WTP for an environmental asset or cleanup project, as discussed in Section 15.7 above.

Bequest value is the willingness to pay to preserve a desirable natural asset for a future generation. BV assumes that today's consumers would thus place a value on maintaining clean air, clean water, and fertile soil for their descendants.

We can then say that the nonuse value of an environmental asset includes both the existence value and the bequest value:

NUV = EV + BV

In so breaking down UV and NUV, we can now expand the formula for TEV.

TEV = DV + IV + OV + EV + BV

By applying basic math, we can use this expanded formula to isolate and calculate particular damage categories. For example, assume that $1 million were offered as a global settlement of a particular environmental claim, and that four of the five constituent categories were valued as follows:

DV = $250,000
IV = $205,000
EV = $235,000
BV = $280,000

We could solve for the missing category, OV, by applying the formula.

TEV = DV + IV + OV + EV + BV

\$1,000,000 = \$250,000 + \$205,000 + OV + \$235,000 + \$280,000

\$1,000,000 = \$970,000 + OV

OV = \$1,000,000 – \$970,000

OV = \$30,000

With an option value of only \$30,000, the calculation may, in fact, tell us that the \$1 million offer is inadequate, and that the global figure must be upgraded to account for a much greater option value.

To calculate an environmental loss from scratch applying the TEV approach, it would be necessary to investigate fully the incremental aspects of the loss and to engage the necessary experts to assist in this process. Suppose, for example, that we wanted to calculate damages for the destruction of a section of a forest known as Washington Woods. We would want to discover and determine what *exactly* has been lost in the destruction of Washington Woods—what natural resources, what recreational uses, what aesthetic or physical attributes. What is the DV of the loss? The IV? The OV? And so forth.

Let's assume that we've done the legwork, gathered the information, and summed up the value of the various specific losses suffered by the destruction of Washington Woods. Let's now use some hypothetical figures to calculate the TEV of the loss:

TEV CATEGORY	SPECIFIC LOSS	LOSS AMOUNT
DV	Timber	\$48,000,000
DV	Hunting	\$16,500,000
DV	Other Recreational Uses	\$15,000,000
DV	Mushrooms	\$11,900,000
IV	Soil Preservation	\$27,610,000
IV	Carbon Storage	\$35,800,300
OV	Pharmaceutical (Medicinal Plants)	\$7,000,700
EV	WTP for Preservation of Wilderness	\$3,400,000
EV	WTP for Protection of Endangered Species	\$3,050,000
BV	Lost Future Value of Fresh-Water Stream	\$1,500,000

Next, let's apply the TEV formula using the loss amounts shown on the table above. Since there are multiple DV, IV, and EV values, we will add them all in calculating the TEV.

$$\text{TEV} = \text{DV} + \text{IV} + \text{OV} + \text{EV} + \text{BV}$$

$$\text{TEV} = \$48{,}000{,}000 + \$16{,}500{,}000 + \$15{,}000{,}000 + \$11{,}900{,}000 + \$27{,}610{,}000 + 35{,}800{,}300 + 7{,}000{,}700 + \$3{,}400{,}000 + \$3{,}050{,}000 + \$1{,}500{,}000$$

$$\text{TEV} = \$169{,}761{,}000$$

Therefore, we can say that the total economic value of the destruction of Washington Woods, taking into consideration both the use values and nonuse values of the asset, is more than \$169 million. This result could be further augmented by considering other value categories (e.g, camping as a direct value), or it could be adjusted to account for externalities that might limit the real value of the assets presently or in the future.

Chapter 16

Bankruptcy Risk

16.1. Bankruptcy Ratios

As we saw in Chapter 8, there are a number of helpful financial ratios that tell us about a company's liquidity, indebtedness, and cash flow. What if we could combine a number of those ratios to predict a company's failure? In fact, research conducted by finance professor Edward I. Altman, a renowned expert on corporate bankruptcy, and other scholars,[1] explains that it is possible to predict default and bankruptcy by testing a series of ratios and then weighting the results as part of a longer formula. Six key ratios will be discussed in the sections below, followed by a discussion of the Z-score formula.

It is worth noting that any ratio that measures liquidity or debt, or any combination of such ratios, may shed light on the financial trajectory of a company. These include, for example, the following ratios:

- Current Ratio (See Section 9.14)
- Quick Ratio (See Section 9.7)
- Inventory Turnover (See Section 9.10)
- Accounts Receivable Turnover (See Section 9.11)
- Accounts Payable Turnover (See Section 9.12)

[1]Among the scholars who have contributed to the literature on predicting corporate failure are Professors William H. Beaver, Cindy Yoshiko Shirata, and James A. Ohlson.

In addition to the ratios discussed in this volume, other ratios can be constructed from data maintained by companies and readily available in their accounting statements. For example, a company that is overstocked in inventory, or that moves its inventory slowly, could be reporting a skewed figure for working capital and thus overestimating its short-term cash flow. Working capital is generally defined as accounts receivable plus inventory minus accounts payable. (WC = AR + I – AP). When the inventory figure is unusually large, due to low turnover, the working capital calculation could be dangerously inflated. To test this hypothesis, we would construct an inventory-to-working capital ratio, as follows:

$$\frac{I}{WC}$$

So, for example, let's assume that a company's inventory is growing faster than its working capital. A three-year analysis of the trend could reveal the problem, as shown by the hypothetical figures depicted below:

Year	2010	2011	2012
Inventory	$2,110,000	$2,965,005	$3,688,000
Working Capital	$5,400,400	$6,000,110	$6,377,000
Inventory-to-Working Capital Ratio	$\frac{I}{WC}$ = 39%	$\frac{I}{WC}$ = 49%	$\frac{I}{WC}$ = 58%

Here, we see that the company's inventory is growing at a rate greater than the working capital, forcing the inventory-to-working capital ratio to jump nearly 20% over three years. This information, combined with a low inventory turnover rate, could signal cash-flow problems for the corporation. Without some kind of management intervention, the company could fail in its attempt to satisfy its short-term accounts, pointing it toward a possible Chapter 11 bankruptcy petition.

Let's try another ratio that will measure a company's solvency. Suppose we want to know whether a company's cash flow can cover the interest payments on its debt obligations and, if so, by how many times. Is the company generating enough money to pay its interest expense? Twice as much? Three times as much? The more excess funding the company generates after covering its interest payments, the greater its solvency. If this excess level begins declining, however, the business may lose its comfort zone and may be heading in the wrong direction.

To test this inquiry, let's construct a cash flow-to-interest expense ratio (sometimes known as a "times interest earned ratio"). The ratio requires us to simply divide the average cash flow (which consists of net income plus depreciation plus amortization) by the average interest expense. We can think of the ratio as either

$$\frac{\text{CF}}{\text{Int}}$$

where CF is the average cash flow, and Int is the average interest expense, or as

$$\frac{\text{NI} + \text{D} + \text{A}}{\text{Int}}$$

where NI is net income, D is depreciation, and A is amortization.

Assume now that we've done the math, and the resulting ratios show a continuous decline in cash flow-to-interest expense over a five-year period. The following ratios are produced for each year:

2007: 2.8
2008: 2.5
2009: 2.1
2010: 1.6
2011: 1.2

In fact, we can appreciate the downward trend of the cash flow by plotting these results on a graph.

The downward curve portends financial distress for the company. Unless the cash flow trend is reversed, the company will soon experience difficulty meeting its debt obligations.

These ratios demonstrate several relatively simple methods for forecasting the fate of a company. By applying these ratios and other such financial comparisons, separately and in combination with one another, rational predictions can be made about the financial course of a business entity. The consistency of the information, the severity of the debt, the shortfall in liquidity, and the speed and pattern of the trend, considered collectively, can foretell whether the company can be saved, or whether, ultimately, the enterprise is headed toward bankruptcy.

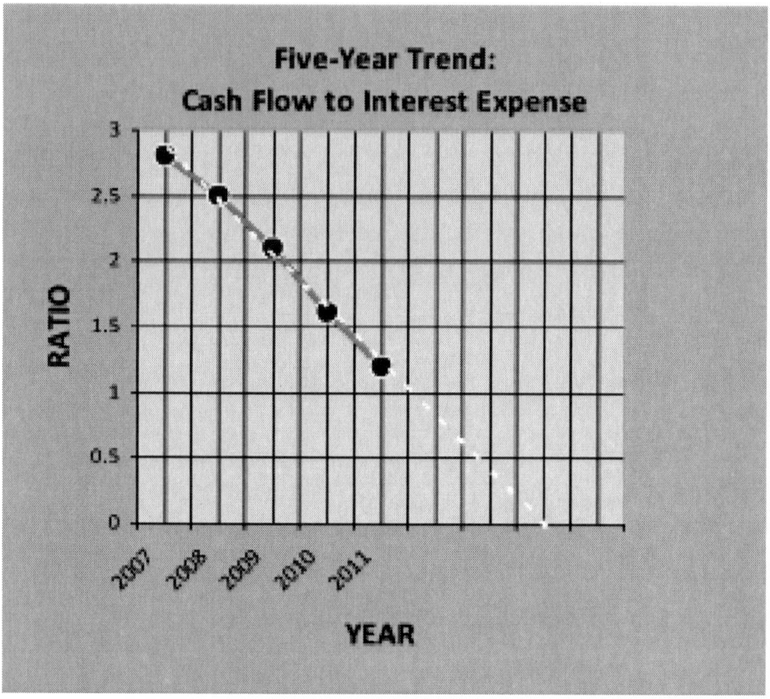

16.2. Working Capital to Total Assets

One of the most useful liquidity ratios is the working capital-to-total assets ratio. It asks the question: what percentage of the capitalization of the business is the net working capital? The greater the percentage, the greater the liquidity of the company. A company with a high working capital-to-total assets ratio can pay its bills on time and thus presents itself to lenders as an attractive borrower and to suppliers as a reliable buyer. By contrast, a company with a low ratio may have cash flow problems, casting it as untrustworthy to its creditors and suppliers. The lower the ratio—and the longer the low ratio persists—the greater the risk of bankruptcy.

The ratio can be displayed as $\frac{\text{WC}}{\text{TA}}$ where WC is the net working capital and TA is the total assets of the company. If ABC Corporation reports net working capital of \$950,000 and total assets of \$4.7 million, its working capital-to-total assets ratio is:

$$\frac{\text{WC}}{\text{TA}} = \frac{950{,}000}{4{,}700{,}000} = 0.2021 = 20.2\%$$

A ratio of 20.2% does not necessarily bespeak financial distress, but it may signify a need for managerial intervention. If the ratio dropped to 10% or 5%, financial disaster could be imminent.

Let's try another example, using figures pulled from ABC Corporation's balance sheet:

Cash	$ 150,000
Accounts Receivable	$ 780,000
Inventory	$1,900,000
Real Estate	$3,500,000
Accounts Payable	$ 650,000
Notes Payable	$ 170,000
Long-Term Debt	$1,400,000

To calculate working capital, start by adding cash, accounts receivable, and inventory, and then subtract accounts payable, notes payable, and long-term debt.[2]

$$\$150{,}000 + \$780{,}000 + \$1{,}900{,}000$$
$$-\$650{,}000 - \$170{,}000 - \$1{,}400{,}000$$
$$= \$2{,}830{,}000$$
$$-\$2{,}220{,}000$$
$$= \$\ 610{,}000$$

Therefore, ABC's working capital is $610,000.

To calculate the total assets, we will want to sum up cash, accounts receivable, inventory, and real estate.

$$TA = \$150{,}000 + \$780{,}000 + \$1{,}900{,}000 + \$3{,}500{,}000$$

$$TA = \$6{,}330{,}000$$

The working capital-to-total assets ratio for ABC Corporation is:

$$\frac{WC}{TA} = \frac{610{,}000}{6{,}330{,}000} = 0.0963 = 9.6\%$$

[2]This hypothetical has been abbreviated for purposes of brevity. In analyzing an actual balance sheet, all current assets and all current liabilities should be counted in calculating the net working capital.

A low ratio such as the 9.6% shown in this example may indicate that the company is unable to pay its creditors and suppliers on a timely basis, even though it may hold significant assets and report a profit. Further inquiry is warranted: if the company is experiencing recurrent operating losses, or if sales are drying up, bankruptcy may lie ahead. This is not always the case, however. The company may have made a significant investment. It may have adopted a fiscal policy that deliberately reduces the level of working capital because such funds draw little interest. If the percentage of working capital is slipping, however, due to diminishing sales and other setbacks, the company's future may be imperiled.

16.3. Retained Earnings to Total Assets

The retained earnings (RE)-to-total assets (TA) ratio is a profitability and leverage measure. It tells us the extent to which assets have been paid for by company profits or debts. Retained earnings are reported in the shareholder's equity section of a company's balance sheet. They can be thought of as the net total of reinvested earnings and losses a business reports over time. They are also referred to as the "earned surplus."

In effect, retained earnings are the portion of the net income that the company retains (as distinguished from the portion that it distributes to shareholders as dividends). Thus, retained earnings are often referred to as an indicator of *cumulative profitability*. By building a ratio of retained earnings to total assets, we can obtain a snapshot of whether a company finances its assets through profit or whether it borrows those funds. Over time, the RE-to-TA ratio casts a picture of either cumulative profitability or increasing debt dependency.

Let's consider a few examples. ABC Corporation, a young firm in existence for only two years, reports retained earnings of \$66,465, and total assets of \$191,082. Its RE-to-TA ratio is calculated as follows:

$$\frac{\text{RE}}{\text{TA}} = \frac{\$66{,}465}{\$191{,}082} = 0.3478 = 34.8\%$$

XYZ Corporation, an older, more well-established firm, reports retained earnings of \$195,333 and total assets of \$199,600. Its RE-to-TA ratio is considerably greater:

$$\frac{\text{RE}}{\text{TA}} = \frac{\$195{,}333}{\$199{,}600} = 0.9786 = 97.8\%$$

ABC's ratio of 34.8% is not problematic and may, in fact, be satisfactory for a new upstart company. If its ratio began slipping, however, it could signal an increasing risk of failure. A low RE-to-TA ratio means that the firm's growth may not be sustainable because of an increasing reliance on debt.

On the other hand, XYZ's ratio of 97.8% provides a desirable level of cumulative profitability. At nearly 100%, XYZ's ratio tells us that retained earnings and total assets have an almost one-to-one relationship. At this level, XYZ's growth is clearly being financed through its profits rather than through increasing debt.

The RE-to-TA ratio is also utilized to measure a company's internal growth rate (IG). The IG rate is effectively the highest level of growth that a business can achieve without borrowing money from external sources.

$$\text{IG} = \frac{\text{RE}}{\text{TA}}$$

In the example above, ABC Corporation would be said to have an IG rate of 34.8%, meaning that 34.8% is the highest level of investment that ABC can make in itself, whether by buying new equipment and machinery, pursuing research and development opportunities, or otherwise—without external financing. Of course, thinking of the RE-to-TA ratio as the IG rate invites a restrictive assumption that the firm will borrow no more money or issue no new shares of stock to facilitate its growth. Calculating the ratio for a series of years may nevertheless provide a meaningful gauge of where the company is headed. For example, assume IG rates for ABC Corporation over a five-year period declined as follows:

2008: 34.8%
2009: 28.4%
2010: 26.1%
2011: 17.8%
2012: 14.5%

The constant downward movement of the growth rate, and the decline in growth by 20% over five years, should be cause for concern.

Another method for calculating the IG rate involves the return on assets (ROA)[3] and reciprocal concepts known as the dividend payout ratio (DPR) and the retention ratio (RR). The DPR is the percentage of the company's earnings that are paid to shareholders as dividends. It is calculated as follows:

$$DPR = \frac{\text{Annual Dividends Per Share}}{\text{Earnings Per Share (EPS)}}$$

This ratio is often simplified as simply dividends divided by net income:

$$DPR = \frac{D}{NI}$$

The RR is the opposite of the DPR. It reflects the percent of earnings credited to retained earnings. What's not paid out in dividends is retained as surplus by the company; what's not part of the DPR is part of the RR. Therefore, the formula for the RR is simply:

$$RR = 1 - DPR$$

To calculate the internal growth rate using this alternative method, the formula is:

$$IG = \frac{ROA \text{ x } RR}{1 - (ROA \text{ x } RR)}$$

Assume that ABC Corporation reported a ROA of 25% and paid out 30% of its earnings to shareholders as dividends. Its RR would thus be 70%. Its IG rate would be calculated as follows:

$$IG = \frac{ROA \text{ x } RR}{1 - (ROA \text{ x } RR)}$$

$$IG = \frac{.25 \text{ x } .70}{1 - (.25 \text{ x } .70)}$$

$$IG = \frac{.175}{1 - .175}$$

[3]See Section 8.8.

$$IG = \frac{.175}{.825}$$

$$IG = .2121$$

$$IG = 21.21\%$$

Applying this formula to the facts provided above, we can now say that ABC Corporation has an IG rate of 21.21%, which is the maximum rate that it can grow without external financing. How this formula changes over time may indicate the direction of the company. A decline in growth over time may indicate that the company needs to rethink its level of leverage or adjust its target DPR. Depending on its access to external funds, its capital structure, and other considerations, a declining IG rate may spell trouble for the company.

16.4. EBIT to Total Assets

EBIT is the earnings before interest and taxes which the company reports on its income statement.[4] The ratio of EBIT to total assets indicates the productivity level of the company's assets. The higher the ratio, the higher the company's earning power.

The EBIT-to-TA relationship asks the question "what are the company's assets worth?" where the answer is expressed in terms of how much earning power the assets have. The ratio is thus often referred to as the *basic earning power ratio.* If a company's liabilities exceed the true value of its assets, then it is insolvent. The earnings generated by the assets, however, reflect the company's level of solvency. How much the assets generate in earnings is a measure of the earning power of the assets and of the solvency of the company.

EBIT can be calculated in a number of ways. On an income statement, earnings are generally displayed as net income. In some statements, a line item appears for net income *before interest and taxes.* In other statements, a line item appears for net income *before taxes*, requiring interest expense to be added. EBIT can also be determined by using the final net income figure which appears at the bottom of the income statement and adding interest and taxes to it.

$$EBIT = NI + Interest + Taxes$$

---

[4]For a closer look at income statements, see Section 12.3.

Once EBIT has been determined, the EBIT-to-TA ratio is easy. Suppose, for example, that Miscellaneous Company reports EBIT of \$750,000 with total assets of \$5,996,000. Its EBIT-to-TA (basic earning power) ratio would be 12.5% as shown below:

$$\frac{\text{EBIT}}{\text{TA}} = \frac{\$750{,}000}{\$5{,}996{,}000} = 0.125 = 12.5\%$$

In other words, the assets of Miscellaneous Company have a basic earning power of 12.5% return on the assets before considering the impact of taxes and debt. This information can be useful if we wanted to compare Miscellaneous Company's performance with other companies with different debt and tax structures. If we knew, for example, that other firms in the same industry as Miscellaneous Company had an average EBIT-to-TA ratio of 22%, we would know that the earning power of Miscellaneous's assets was well below average.

Perhaps more important, a low EBIT-to-TA ratio, or a declining ratio over time, could signal a gradual unraveling of the company. Certainly, if the ratio became negative, the prospect of bankruptcy would loom inasmuch as there would be no earnings to cover assets (effectively, assets with zero earning power).

16.5. Equity to Debt

The equity-to-debt ratio, not to be confused with the debt-to-equity ratio,[5] measures the value of a company's assets in terms of its debt. While the debt-to-equity ratio measures a company's financial leverage, the equity-to-debt ratio measures its strength in assets. As a company's asset value declines toward 0% of its debt, it moves closer to bankruptcy.

To obtain the numerator of the equity-to-debt ratio, determine the market value of the company's common and preferred stock. To obtain the denominator, add the company's current and long-term liabilities, readily available from a balance sheet. The formula is presented as follows:

---

[5]See Section 9.3.

$$\text{Equity-to-Debt Ratio} = \frac{E}{D} = \frac{\text{Market Value of Common Stock + Preferred Stock}}{\text{Sum of Current Liabilities and Long-Term Liabilities}}$$

Suppose that Barely Solvent, Inc. shows the following stock and debt values:

Market Value of Common Stock:	\$ 7,590
Market Value of Preferred Stock:	\$ 1,612
Total Current Liabilities:	\$13,502
Total Long-Term Liabilities:	\$ 9,800

The equity-to-debt ratio would be completed as follows:

$$\frac{E}{D} = \frac{\$7{,}590 + \$1{,}612}{\$13{,}502 + \$9{,}800}$$

$$\frac{E}{D} = \frac{\$9{,}202}{\$23{,}302}$$

$$\frac{E}{D} = 0.3949 = 39.5\%$$

With an equity-to-debt ratio of 39.5%, Barely Solvent, Inc. is not in a safe position. Its assets need only decline by 39.5% in value before the business becomes insolvent. To illustrate this risk, assume that the value of the common and preferred stock for Barely Solvent, Inc. declined significantly, reducing the market value of all stock to \$4,050. Let's see how this changes the equity-to-debt ratio:

$$\frac{E}{D} = \frac{\$4{,}050}{\$23{,}302}$$

$$\frac{E}{D} = 0.1738 = 17.4\%$$

Now, the company has barely any cushion against insolvency. With an equity-to-debt ratio of just 17.4%, it survives in a precarious and vulnerable financial position. Another drop in value, or a major new debt, could paralyze the firm.

If Barely Solvent, Inc. had an equity-to-debt ratio of 100%, it would effectively have \$1 in asset value for every \$1 in debt it owed.

At 200%, it would have $2 in assets for every $1 in liabilities. And as the percentage grows, the risk of bankruptcy would correspondingly shrink.

16.6. Sales to Total Assets

The sales-to-total assets ratio indicates the extent to which a company's assets are generating revenue. The ratio is also known as the *asset turnover* or *asset utilization* ratio because it measures how efficiently companies utilize their assets to make sales. A low ratio is generally bad news. Consistently low ratios, or continuously declining ratios, may mean that the company is on a downward spiral.

To construct this ratio, obtain a figure for the amount of sales or net sales from the company's income statement. Determine the total assets from the company's balance sheet. So, for example, if Seller Inc. reports net sales of $2,650,000 and total assets of $1,140,000, its sales-to-total assets ratio would be 2.32 to 1, as calculated below:

$$\frac{S}{TA} = \frac{\$2,650,000}{\$1,140,000} = 2.32$$

In effect, Seller Inc. generates 232% revenue off its assets. It draws $2.32 in sales for every $1 in assets. This would generally be considered a healthy position.

Consider another hypothetical company, Slacker, Inc. Slacker generates sales of $980,150 with assets of $8,976,000. Its sales-to-total assets ratio paints a different picture:

$$\frac{S}{TA} = \frac{\$980,150}{\$8,976,000} = 0.1091$$

For Slacker, the ratio is roughly 0.11 to 1. Each dollar invested in assets produces only 11 cents in sales—a far less secure condition than Seller, Inc.

A low sales-to-total assets ratio may not, by itself, mean that a company is in dire condition. It is important to consider the industry in which the company conducts business and the industry trend. *Are other companies doing much better? Are low sales-to-total asset ratios typi-*

cal of the industry? It is also important to consider the ratio together with the other ratios discussed in this chapter. *Do all ratios paint a gloomy picture, or is this ratio uniquely low?* The company's sales-to-total assets ratio should also be compared to historical data for the firm. In some cases, a sales-to-total assets ratio will produce a high or low result because of a pricing strategy. Companies with low profit margins tend to have high asset turnover rates while those with high profit margins have lower asset turnover rates. In other cases, a ratio can plummet temporarily because of a corporate strategy, such as, for example, an initiative that quickly increases that amount of cash, and thus inflates the amount of total assets.

If a company's sales have recently become sluggish, it may be useful to break down the denominator of the ratio into its constituent parts. In other words, total assets should be divided into various asset categories, such as cash and accounts receivable, and then compared to net sales. This will produce a number of more specific ratios, including:

$$\frac{\text{Sales}}{\text{Cash}} \qquad \frac{\text{Sales}}{\text{Accounts Receivable}} \qquad \frac{\text{Sales}}{\text{Inventory}}$$

$$\frac{\text{Sales}}{\text{Property, Plant and Equioment}} \qquad \frac{\text{Sales}}{\text{Intangible Assets}}$$

By plugging in specific asset data from the balance sheet, it is possible to identify where a company's asset utilization is the weakest, and to make management decisions accordingly. For example, if the sales-to-accounts receivable ratio is dangerously low, the firm may need to act to improve its collections and to minimize the time period during which credit accounts remain open. If the sales-to-inventory ratio is too low, the firm should act to move its inventory faster, develop policies to avoid overstocking, and eliminate outdated goods from its shelves.

Ultimately, a company should not hold assets unless they generate sales or otherwise contribute to the firm's profitability. A continuously low sales-to-total assets ratio that cannot be improved through better asset management and/or increased sales, and that cannot be explained through pricing policies or other deliberate actions, may be a telltale sign of trouble on the horizon.

16.7. Z-score Bankruptcy Prediction Formula

The Z-score prediction formula, developed by finance professor Edward I. Altman, is a model that combines the five ratios discussed above:

- Working Capital to Total Assets
- Retained Earnings to Total Assets
- EBIT to Total Assets
- Equity to Debt
- Sales to Total Assets

By statistically weighting these ratios in combination with each other, Dr. Altman was able to predict, with considerable accuracy, the likelihood that a company would go bankrupt in the future. The Z-score formula requires each ratio to be calculated and then weighted by being multiplied by a certain weighting factor. Then each of the weighted ratios is added together to produce the Z score.

To run the formula, we begin by assigning a letter X to each of the five ratios. Thus,

X_1 = working capital to total assets
X_2 = retained earnings to total assets
X_3 = EBIT to total assets
X_4 = equity to debt
X_5 = sales to total assets

By weighting X_1 through X_5 and summing up the figures, Altman was able to predict the likelihood of bankruptcy. Here is the Z-score formula:

$$\mathbf{Z = 1.2X_1 + 1.4X_2 + 3.3X_3 + 0.6X_4 + 0.999X_5}$$

In other words, Z equals 1.2 multiplied by the working capital-to-total assets ratio, plus 1.4 times the retained earnings-to-total assets ratio, plus 3.3 times the EBIT-to-total assets ratio, plus 0.6 times the equity-to-debt ratio, plus 0.999 times the sales-to-total assets ratio.

Let's plug in some hypothetical figures. Assume that one company, Rebound Inc., has the following ratios (all of which we originally explored in Sections 15.2 to 15.6 above with a variety of hypothetical companies):

RATIOS FOR REBOUND, INC.

Working Capital to Total Assets **(X_1)**

$$\frac{WC}{TA} = \frac{950{,}000}{4{,}700{,}000} = 0.2021 = 20.2\%$$

Retained Earnings to Total Assets **(X_2)**

$$\frac{RE}{TA} = \frac{\$66{,}465}{\$191{,}082} = 0.3478 = 34.8\%$$

EBIT to Total Assets **(X_3)**

$$\frac{EBIT}{TA} = \frac{\$750{,}000}{\$5{,}996{,}000} = 0.125 = 12.5\%$$

Equity to Debt **(X_4)**

$$\frac{E}{D} = \frac{\$9{,}202}{\$23{,}302} = 0.3949 = 39.5\%$$

Sales to Total Assets **(X_5)**

$$\frac{S}{TA} = \frac{\$980{,}150}{\$8{,}976{,}000} = 0.1091 = 11\%$$

To apply the Z-score prediction formula, we need to weight each of the ratios. The table below captures the numerical result for each of the ratios above and applies the applicable weighting factor:

X VARIABLES	CALCULATED RATIO	WEIGHTING FACTOR	WEIGHTED RESULT
X_1	.2021	1.2	.24252
X_2	.3478	1.4	.48692
X_3	.125	3.3	.4125
X_4	.3949	0.6	.23694
X_5	.1091	0.999	.1089909

To calculate the Z-score, we now must total the weighted results.

The formula is: $Z = 1.2X_1 + 1.4X_2 + 3.3X_3 + 0.6X_4 + 0.999X_5$

Therefore, $Z = .24252 + .48692 + .4125 + .23694 + .1089909$

$Z = 1.4878709$

The rounded Z-score is thus about 1.5. *What does this mean?* Unfortunately, a score of 1.5 means there is a high bankruptcy risk for Rebound, Inc. According to Altman, any Z-score of 1.8 or lower presents a high probability of financial catastrophe. A score above 3.0 means that a company is unlikely to go bankrupt. Scores between 1.8 and 3.0 represent a grey zone, with the risk of insolvency growing as the score slips closer to 1.8.

The Z Chart

Score	Interpretation
≤ 1.8	High Probability of Bankruptcy
> 1.8 and < 3.0	Grey Zone (Uncertain Future)*
≥ 3.0	Low Probability of Bankruptcy

*A more detailed interpretation of the mid-range scores holds that scores between 2.7 and 1.8 predict that a company will go bankrupt within two years. Companies scoring between 2.7 and 3.0 are not quite in the safe zone, and while their financial condition is acceptable, their condition is considered guarded.

The Z-score provides a valuable quantitative predictor of business failure. Corporate attorneys, bankruptcy practitioners, and other business specialists can employ this device to advise clients on prospective mergers, acquisitions, and consolidations, on potential investment and buyout deals, and on the timing and settlement of costly litigation. The Z-score can also support recommendations for dissolving businesses, reforming management policies, discharging unproductive leaders, closing unprofitable divisions, and discontinuing failed product lines. Considered together with other financial analyses and market-based judgments, the Z-score can provide the impetus for the capital and financial restructuring of a going concern, and may intercept a disastrous business model before it's too late.

16.8. Cash Flow Ratios

Cash is king. So goes the classic expression about the fiscal strength of a company. Where there is a strong cash flow, there is, arguably, a high level of creditworthiness, a steady level of debt reduction, and a significant commitment to capital development and investment opportunities. A cash-strapped company not only risks default on its obligations but may fail to achieve growth in a competitive marketplace.

Thus, the patterns by which a company receives and consumes cash, as measured against the value of its assets and liabilities, provide a further measure of its risk of failure. A variety of cash flow ratios can be constructed to examine this risk more closely.

Cash Flow to Debt

The cash flow-to-debt ratio reveals how much cash is available to pay down a company's debt obligations. A company with less than \$1 in cash flow for every \$1 in debt is potentially in a financially unhealthy position. On the other hand, a company with \$2 in cash flow for every \$1 in debt can not only meet its current debt commitments, but it can likely borrow more money safely.

Suppose, for example, that InHock Corporation reports cash flow of \$850,000 and total debt of \$2,140,000. Its cash flow-to-debt ratio would look like this:

$$\frac{CF}{D} = \frac{\$850{,}000}{\$2{,}140{,}000} = 0.3971 = 39.7\%$$

With a 39.7% ratio, InHock Corporation is likely experiencing a liquidity problem. It effectively has less than 40 cents in cash to service every \$1 of debt. If InHock's cash flow-to-debt ratios have been declining over time, the firm is probably facing increased difficulty in paying its bills, expanding the prospect of bankruptcy. A ratio less than 100% is not always a sign of impending doom, and in fact many large successful corporations have had ratios below 100% for many years. Whether a low ratio foretells problems depends on the capital structure and payment obligations of the company and its cash generation patterns. Still, a persistently low or quickly declining cash flow-to-debt ratio, taken together with other low ratios, can signal a company on the brink of collapse.

The cash flow-to-debt ratio can be constructed in several formats and can be further dissected into more specific ratios. Start by determining cash flow by obtaining net income from the company's income statement. Net income can also be pulled from the first line of a cash flow statement prepared using the indirect method.[6] Net income should

[6]See Section 12.3.

not include sales made on credit. In fact, the best measure of cash flow is the firm's *operating cash flow* (OCF), which is calculated by adding EBIT to depreciation and then subtracting taxes:

$$\text{OCF} = \text{EBIT} + \text{Depreciation} - \text{Taxes}$$

An even more conservative approach is to limit cash flow only to the cash a company can generate after earmarking the funds necessary for capital expenditures. This so-called *free cash flow* (FCF) effectively allows the firm to set aside money for its own expansion and development before measuring what funds remain to pay down its debt. FCF is calculated as follows:

$$\text{FCF} = \text{EBIT} + \text{Depreciation} - \text{Taxes} - \text{Capital Expenditures}$$

Or simply:

$$\text{FCF} = \text{OCF} - \text{Capital Expenditures}.$$

The cash flow-to-debt ratio can thus be refined as the OCF-to-debt ratio or the FCF-to-debt ratio to provide an even more specific measure of the extent to which actual cash flow covers the company's debt commitments.

Yet another variation modifies the denominator of the ratio. Total debt could, in fact, be misleading in a company in which short-term obligations vary significantly throughout the year. It may therefore be more useful in some cases to replace total debt with long-term debt. Long-term debt, which refers to debts lasting more than one year, can be found on the company's balance sheet.[7] This includes, for example, notes payable, bonds payable, and outstanding leases. By constructing a ratio of cash flow to *long-term* debt, one can measure how well today's cash is paying off the firm's long-term liabilities.

In effect, the cash flow-to-debt ratio can be refined as an OCF or FCF to long-term debt ratio:

$$\frac{\text{OCF}}{\text{Long-Term Debt}} = \frac{\text{EBIT} + \text{Depreciation} - \text{Taxes}}{\text{Notes, Bonds and Lease Repayments}}$$

$$\frac{\text{FCF}}{\text{Long-Term Debt}} = \frac{\text{EBIT} + \text{Depreciation} - \text{Taxes} - \text{Capital Expenditures}}{\text{Notes, Bonds and Lease Repayments}}$$

---

[7]Long-term debt is also sometimes referred to as noncurrent liabilities or long-term liabilities.

How to interpret the results of these ratios depends on the industry in which the company operates and the industry's historical trends; the performance, cash flow, and debt coverage history of the company and the extent to which the ratios produce noteworthy departures from historical results; the pattern of cash flow-to-debt ratios over time; and any patterns revealed by comparing the cash flow-to-debt ratios to a variety of liquidity and leverage formulas.

A cash flow-to-debt ratio of 80% means that a company's debt load is 20% greater than its operating cash flows. Still, the ratio could be considered high enough for a particular company in a particular industry. Even a ratio of 70% could be acceptable in some sectors. Ratios below 100% should nevertheless prompt further inquiry. *If the company is not generating enough new cash to cover its debts, is it defaulting on those debts or otherwise failing to meet its obligations? Is the company's ratio slipping year after year? Are the percentages dropping drastically?*

The lower the cash flow-to-debt ratio, the more serious and urgent the inquiry must be. A 50% ratio means that the company is generating operating cash flows of only 50 cents for every dollar of debt. Not only the percentage but the trend, and the length of the trend, may prompt a deeper concern. Consider, for example, a company that reports the following cash-flow-to-debt percentages for a five-year span:

2007: 105%
2008: 101%
2009: 95%
2010: 89%
2011: 82%

In 2007, with a ratio of 105%, the company was generating more than enough cash to cover its debt load. But the figures have slipped each year for five years in a row, and the annual amount of decline is increasing. By 2011, the company's cash-flow-to-debt coverage had slipped significantly by 23% over five years. The trend is ominous, and unless it can be reversed, the company will eventually decline into default on its debt obligations.

Operating Cash Flow to Capital Expenditures

The ratio of operating cash flow to capital expenditures compares how much a company spends to maintain its property, plant, and equipment to its operating cash flow. Operating cash flow (OCF), as discussed above, does not include taxes or dividends. It also does not include any cash generated by new loans or by the issuance of new stock. Property, plant, and equipment (PP&E) is listed as one of the itemized accounts under assets on the balance sheet. PP&E represents the total value of the company's manufacturing plant, equipment, and machinery, and other property items minus any amortization. PP&E is thus a *current* value of the property, plant, and equipment based on the depreciated economic value of the items throughout their useful life.

To construct this ratio, we'll need to divide the operating cash flow by the capital expenditures made for PP&E. Suppose, for example, that a company reports $1,903,000 in capital expenditures for PP&E, with cash flow of $3,908,000. Its ratio would look like this:

$$\frac{\text{OCF}}{\text{Capital Expenditures}} = \frac{\$3{,}908{,}000}{\$1{,}903{,}000} = 2.05$$

At 2.05, the company carries a solid margin to maintain its PP&E and fund the purchase of additional capital assets. In fact, the greater the ratio of OCF to capital expenditures, the greater the cash flow for capital expansion—a sign of a flourishing business. *But what if the numerator and the denominator were reversed?* If the company had capital expenditures of $3,908,000 and operating cash flow of $1,903,000, its situation would be much different:

$$\frac{\text{OCF}}{\text{Capital Expenditures}} = \frac{\$1{,}903{,}000}{\$3{,}908{,}000} = 0.49$$

With an OCF-to-capital expenditures ratio of less than 0.5, the company has inadequate cash flow to maintain or upgrade its PP&E. Besides indicating that the company may not be able to compete in the marketplace, a low ratio may bespeak a sinking ship, drifting toward inevitable bankruptcy.

Operating Cash Flow to Dividends

Another useful measure of a company's financial position is how well its cash flow covers the cash dividends it pays to its owners. The operating cash flow-to-dividends ratio puts this question to the test by asking whether the operating cash flow covers the cost of dividends; if not, then by what percentage does it fall short, and if so, then what percentage of free cash flow exceeds the cost of the dividend payments.

Assume that a company reports operating cash flow of $3,908,000, and pays dividends of exactly $3 million. It ratio of 1.30 should leave investors with a sense of security since the company can safely continue paying cash dividends with cash flow remaining to cover its other obligations.

$$\frac{\text{OCF}}{\text{Dividends}} = \frac{\$3{,}908{,}000}{\$3{,}000{,}000} = 1.30$$

In fact, a ratio of 1.30 indicates that the company generates 30% more cash flow than it needs to cover its dividend payments. This fact, alone, may not prove that the company is thriving, any more than a low ratio would prove that the company is sinking. Considered together with other ratios and measures, however, the OCF-to-dividends comparison provides another indicator of the company's financial position.

Where the ratio produces a result under 1, it means that the company is unable to cover its cash dividends with its current level of cash flow. A ratio of 0.85, for example, means that the firm is generating only 85% of the cash flow necessary to pay its dividends. This should prompt action. Perhaps the company should stop paying dividends, or should begin paying smaller amounts to its investors. Or perhaps its management should reconsider the larger issues impeding its cash flow. While a decrease in dividend payments does not suggest that bankruptcy is on the horizon, a continuous decline in this coverage ratio, combined with other adverse measures, can present a negative projection for the company's future.

Cash Flow Adequacy Ratio

The cash flow adequacy ratio (CFAR) attempts to combine the logic of several of the ratios discussed above by measuring cash flow against debt payments, capital purchases, and dividends—all at the same time. The formula is:

$$\text{CFAR} = \frac{\text{OCF}}{\text{Long-Term Debt} + \text{Capital Purchases} + \text{Dividends}}$$

To construct this ratio, we need to sum up the line items that constitute the denominator:

Long-term Debt Paid
+ Fixed Assets Purchased
+ Cash Dividends Distributed
= *Total Amount of Obligations Sought to be Covered by Cash*

In effect, this ratio tells us if the cash flow generated through the company's operations is adequate to cover everything it needs to cover: the company's leases and other long-term debts; the capital expenditures of PP&E and additions to inventory, and the cash dividends paid out to investors. *Is there enough money to go around?* If the company generates exactly enough cash flow to cover these obligations, then its ratio will be 1. Anything less than 1 reflects a lagging cash flow and suggests that a watchful eye should be focused on the company.

Consider this scenario: XYZ Corporation has total long-term debt of \$3.7 million, asset purchases of \$775,000, and dividend distributions of \$980,000. Its operating cash flow is exactly \$5 million. *Is XYZ's cash flow adequate?* The cash flow adequacy ratio answers this question:

$$\text{CFAR} = \frac{\text{OCF}}{\text{Long-Term Debt} + \text{Capital Purchases} + \text{Dividends}}$$

$$\text{CFAR} = \frac{\$5{,}000{,}000}{\$5{,}455{,}000}$$

$$\text{CFAR} = 0.9165$$

The answer is that XYZ's cash flow is *not quite* adequate. With a ratio of just under 0.92, XYZ is generating only 92% of the cash it needs to cover its debt, its purchases, and its dividends. It is operating at 8% shy of the necessary level of cash coverage. Depending on the ebb and flow of business, the due dates on debt commitments, and the timing of dividend distributions, XYZ may not immediately sense any financial distress. However, a ratio of 0.92 also means that XYZ may have difficulty attaining its desired level of growth or maintaining a competitive advantage in the marketplace. Its attention may be focused on *keeping up*, rather than *getting ahead.* If the ratio continues to slide downward, XYZ may need to consider external sources of financing to stay afloat.

The scenario would be far worse for XYZ if its ratio dropped to, say, 70% or 50% or 30%. In fact, if XYZ chose to discontinue paying dividends to its investors, and the cash flow adequacy ratio were still quite low, then XYZ would not have enough cash to cover its debts and its capital expenditures. With dividends removed from the equation, XYZ's ability to improve the ratio becomes much more limited. In such a case, if the company had persistently low ratios, or continuously declining ratios, the risk of financial collapse would be an issue, with the possibility of bankruptcy looming nearby.

Chapter 17

Intellectual Property Damages

[Patents]

Lost Profits

17.1. Conceptual Framework

Lost profits on sales are widely recognized as a fundamental measure of damages in a copyright, trademark, or patent infringement action. When one infringes on the intellectual property rights of another, he must account for the profits so derived, and the value thereof represents the loss to the rightful property owner. Lost profits, however, do not include sales lost to lawful competitors or as a result of unfortunate social, political, or economic circumstances. In fact, calculating lost profits would seem all too simple if one needed only to demand an accounting from the infringer and to tally up the value of his profits. In practice, determining lost profits actually may entail a number of other considerations, such as:

- Changes in the price of raw materials
- Variations in manufacturing and production costs
- The contracting or expanding market during the period of infringement
- The delivery and marketing efficiencies (or lack thereof) of the infringer

- The introduction of new competitors, and the infringer's success against them
- The disappearance of old competitors, and the infringer's timeliness in claiming their market
- The presence or absence of general macroeconomic trends: depression, recession, inflation, etc.
- The presence or absence of industry-specific trends (e.g., the declining consumer interest in compact disks and videotapes).

Moreover, an infringer may be capable of raising defenses that, if established, would reduce the calculation of damages to the lawful property owner. These could include, for example, quantitative determinations of the following:

- The market share of the owner versus the infringer, both before and after the infringed product entered the market
- The size of the market both before and after the infringing product entered the market
- Whether the infringing product has certain advantages over the patented product that increased its marketability
- Whether the infringer adopted smarter marketing strategies and/or more strategic pricing policies

To illustrate the potential complexity of determining lost profits, consider the case of two companies, Owner, Inc. and Stealer, Inc. Owner, Inc. holds the registered patent on Freedom Widgets, a consumer product. Stealer, Inc. recently entered the market with a substantially similar product marketed as Liberty Widgets, which Owner claims to be an infringement on its product design. Owner captured 20% of the widget market before Stealer came along, selling 500,000 units of the Freedom Widget at a price of $10 each. This represented a profit of $5 million to Owner.

Assume, initially, that Stealer usurps one-fifth of Owner's market, slicing Owner's sales to 400,000 units by aggressively peddling Liberty Widgets in the same market. If Owner could prove its infringement case, it would claim lost profits for all of the sales appropriated by Stealer, representing damages of $1 million (100,000 lost sales multiplied by $10 per widget in lost profits). Yet, what if Stealer successfully captured a 30% market share with its Liberty Widgets—more than Owner ever had—by reducing the price of the product to $8, and by giving away a free Liberty Gadget with every Widget purchase? What if Stealer also entered a foreign market that Owner would never have been able to enter because of licensing restrictions that Stealer alone had overcome years ago? Could all of Stealer's profits then be attributed to its infringement of Owner's Freedom Widget product? Would it be equitable to require Stealer to disgorge 100% of its profits under the circumstances?

A fair calculation of lost profits would logically have to include the value of the patent, trademark, or copyright holder's lost sales, plus the lost profits on the actual sales, minus whatever adjustments are necessary for the infringer's own internal manufacturing and design initiatives and external marketing and distribution advantages. Additionally, the calculation would include such other adjustments as will account for changes in the entire market structure due to the infringer's entry into the market and for larger macroeconomic events and circumstances. Conceptually, at least, we might say that lost profits are measured as follows:

$$\mathbf{LPr = LS + LPr_{AS} - Inf.C \;\forall\; \Delta Mkt \;\forall\; \Delta Econ}$$

where:

$\forall$ = The upside down A means "for all", as in, for all changes in the marketplace or in the economy.

LPr = Lost Profits

LS = Lost Sales, which represents the value of the sales the owner would have made had the infringer not made the sales

LPr_{AS} = Lost Profits from actual sales, such as, for example, the cost to the owner of lowering the price on the actual sales of its product during the infringement period (See Price Erosion section below).

Inf.C = Credit for the infringer's own distinguishable market initiatives and advantages

ΔMkt = Changes in the marketplace attributable to the infringer's entry

ΔEcon = Changes in the economy, including such macroeconomic forces as inflation, recession, taxation, and consumption trends and patterns.

Conceptualizing lost profits, of course, is easier than actually calculating them. Indeed, the formula could theoretically take into consideration many other economic variables, such as price elasticity and shifts in the demand curve based on, for example, an increase in the price of substitute products in the marketplace. Economists interested in intellectual property damages have, in fact, explored and debated a variety of other economic influences that could potentially improve the final calculation of lost profits in an infringement case—an inquiry that goes well beyond the scope of this book. Suffice it to say that, for purposes of our calculations here, it is important to remember that a simple short cut—lost sales, for example—may provide an imperfect, or potentially inaccurate, measure of damages without considering other factors and circumstances.

17.2. Lost Sales

The starting point for calculating damages in an infringement case is to determine the value of lost sales. Before the owner of an intellectual property right (the patentee) can raise a claim, it must satisfy the so-called "but for" test; that is, it must prove that it would have made a greater amount of sales *but for* the infringement. A company that manufactures only 10,000 units of a patented product cannot claim damages greater than 10,000 units if it had no intention or capacity to produce a greater quantity. *But for* the infringement, it would have perhaps sold 10,000 units, but it would not have sold 15,000 units simply because the infringer managed to sell a much greater quantity.

In fact, in order to recover lost profits, the lawful owner of a patent is required to demonstrate that it would have made additional profits, under all of the attending circumstances, *but for* the misconduct of the infringer. A four-pronged test for satisfying the "but-for" rule, laid out in *Panduit Corp. v. Stahlin Brothers Fibre Works, Inc.*,[1] requires the patentee to establish (1) there is demand for the patented product; (2) there are no noninfringing substitutes; (3) the patentee had the manufacturing and marketing capability to exploit the demand; and (4) the amount of profit the patentee would have made absent the infringing conduct. Assuming that the patentee can satisfy the first three prongs of the *Panduit* test, a great deal of discretion often surrounds the fourth

[1]575 F. 2d 1152 (6th Cir. 1978).

prong in the method and manner in which the proof of the amount of lost profit is actually established.

Incremental Income Approach

A common method of calculating lost profits is to apply the incremental income approach. This approach eliminates *fixed costs*, such as management, salaries, property taxes, and insurance, from the calculation of damages. Such fixed costs do not change with an increased volume of sales. On the other hand, *variable costs*, such as labor and materials, do change with an increased volume of sales. Therefore, lost profits from lost sales can be calculated as the difference between the incremental revenue that the patentee would have obtained if it had sold its product instead of the infringer's sales, and the variable costs attributable to that incremental sales volume.

Let's examine the process more closely by determining variable costs for a hypothetical company. Assume that ABC Corporation sells DigiWidgets for $10 apiece and has the following variable costs associated with an annual production of 1 million DigiWidgets:

Raw Materials:	$1,100,000
Direct Labor:	$4,500,000
Manufacturing Supplies:	$ 97,000
Sales Commissions	$ 380,000
Packing and Shipping:	$ 55,000
Temporary Factory Staff:	$ 106,000
Clerical/Billing Activities:	$ 120,000
Total Variable Costs:	$6,358,000

If ABC is producing 1 million DigiWidgets at $10 apiece, its projected revenue is $10 million. With variable costs of $6,358,000, we can then determine XYZ's incremental cost ratio at approximately 63.6%, as follows:

$$\frac{\text{Variable Costs}}{\text{Revenue}} = \frac{\$6{,}358{,}000}{\$10{,}000{,}000} = 0.6358 = 63.58\%$$

So, for example, if ABC received an order for 3,600 DigiWidgets, it could calculate its projected profit using the same information:

3,600 x $10 = $36,000

$36,000 x 0.6358 = $22,888.80 (variable costs)

$36,000 – $22,888.80 = $13,111.20 (profit)

If, in fact, ABC's DigiWidgets were copied by an infringer, who sold 3,600 units of the product before ABC successfully enjoined the infringer's sales, ABC could claim a loss of profits in the amount of $13,111.20.

Capturing Other Losses

The incremental approach to lost profits is incomplete in cases in which the patentee would have sold other nonpatented products along with its patented product. Under the so-called *entire market rule,* a patentee may be entitled to additional damages if there is a functional relationship between the patented product and some other product or if the infringement of a patented product necessarily infringes on the sales of another related product.

In *Rite-Hite Corp. v. Kelley,*[2] for example, the court awarded damages for infringement of two different kinds of vehicle restraining devices used to lock vehicles to loading docks during the loading process. Only one of the vehicle restraint products was covered by the patent on which the infringement suit was based. The other device, an earlier model not covered by the patent in question, was still for sale by Rite-Hite. In fact, the court found that "but for" the actions of the infringer, Rite-Hite would have made 80 more sales of the patented product and 3,243 more sales of the other restraining device not covered by the patent. The court recognized lost profits of both of these products, which were often sold as packages to wholesalers.

A patentee may also be entitled to damages for lost sales of *convoyed products.* Convoyed products include accessories, replacement parts, supplies, and other collateral sales made in connection with the patented product. So, for example, a manufacturer of laser printers could rely heavily on convoyed sales of toner and ink cartridges. A manufacturer of cameras could include in its anticipated profits the convoyed sales of specialty lenses and other camera equipment. In such cases, the lost sales of the patented product represent only the primary loss, but the convoyed sales of accessories and replacement parts constitute a significant secondary loss.

Convoyed sales may also include *bundled sales*, such as when a handheld dictation machine is packaged and sold with a charging unit, or a set of specialty wine glasses is bundled and sold with a decanter.

[2]56 F. 3d 1538 (Fed. Cir. 1995).

They may also include bundled service contracts. Thus, a wheelchair manufacturer claiming infringement on a specially motorized scooter design may also allege lost sales of its convoyed maintenance contracts, typically sold to all new scooter buyers.

Shortcut Formulas

In simple markets with only two competitors (patentee and purported infringer), a series of simple equations can be applied to evaluate a case based on approximate figures.

For example, lost sales can be measured, at least in the most general sense, by multiplying the number of units infringed (N) times the profit per unit (P) and then subtracting the change in the patentee's variable costs, calculated as the increase in its production costs (ΔVC). Thus, if an infringer unlawfully sold 50,000 items, depriving the patentee of \$1.15 in profit for each item, and if the patentee would have spent an additional \$32,456 in materials and labor to produce and sell the 50,000 items, we could quickly calculate the damages from lost sales (LS).

$$LS = N \times P - \Delta VC$$

$$LS = 50{,}000 \times \$1.15 - \$32{,}456$$

$$LS = \$25{,}044$$

Another shortcut formula targets the infringer's income from the unlawful sales. In this formula, the change in variable costs is simply subtracted from the infringer's income (Inf.Inc.). So, if the infringer's income was \$141,060 and the change in variable costs was \$96,555, lost profits based on lost sales would be calculated as follows:

$$LS = \text{Inf.Inc.} - \Delta VC$$

$$LS = \$141{,}060 - \$96{,}555$$

$$LS = \$44{,}505$$

Where collateral or convoyed sales are lost as a consequence of the infringement, these formulas would be extended to account for those losses as well. For example, $LS = N \times P - \Delta VC$ would be restated as:

$$LS = (N_1 \times P_1 - \Delta VC_1) + (N_2 \times P_2 - \Delta VC_2)$$

where the subscript numbers refer to Product 1 (the main product) and Product 2 (the convoyed product). Depending on the circumstances, these formulas could be further extended to cover even more related, connected, collateral, and bundled products.

While these shortcut formulas are helpful in making rough estimates of the value of a potential case, they are not necessarily scientific calculations. Particularly in complex markets with multiple variables and numerous competitors, the need for an expert valuator cannot be understated.

17.3. Price Erosion

Under a price erosion theory, a patentee claims that the infringer sold its competing product at a reduced price, forcing the patentee to lower its prices in order to compete in the market. Price erosion can also occur when the infringing product disrupts the market in such a manner as to force the patentee to discount prices, or when the patentee planned on increasing prices but cannot do so now because of the entry into the market of the lower-priced infringing product.

The burden of proof lies with the patentee to prove that it would have been capable of selling its product at the same price, or a greater price, *but for* the conduct of the infringer. Moreover, if a patentee lowers its price in response to a lower-priced infringing product, then the patentee carries the burden of proving that its reduced price is not lower than necessary to compete in the same market.

One simplified method of measuring price erosion is to think of it as the difference between the patented product's actual price (AP) and its potential price (PP), multiplied by the number of product units affected (N).

Damages from Price Erosion = (PP – AP) x N

So, if the potential price of a DigiWidget is $10, but the patentee was required to discount the product to $8.85 to compete in the market where the infringed product was introduced, its loss per unit of $1.15 is then multiplied by the number of infringed units (assume 120,000). Thus,

(PP – AP) x N

($10.00 – $8.85) x 120,000

$1.15 x 120,000

= $138,000

In this scenario, the patentee lost $138,000 as a result of price erosion caused by the infringer. Caution must be exercised, however, not to assume the scientific certainty of such information based on this simplified formula. An expert, for example, would certainly analyze whether consumers would have purchased the same volume of DigiWidgets in the marketplace at the higher price. According to the law of demand in the study of economics, consumers will always purchase fewer units of a product at a higher price.[3]

17.4. Combined Losses

When considering a patentee's damages from lost sales and price erosion, it is important not to double-count or to misclassify the losses. A patentee may, ultimately, claim damages for lost profits based on lost sales *and* lost profits based on price erosion. Considered collectively, these two aspects of the lost profits calculus will yield a total amount of damages based on lost profits.

Consider this example involving Patco, Inc., the patent owner of a new brand of long-life electric car batteries, and Infro, Inc., an infringer who has recently introduced a competing product. Patco manufactures the Ultimatic Battery with its proprietary "steel-cell technology." The company touts its product as maintaining the longest battery life with 10 times the vibration resistance of competing products. Patco's battery also claims to be steel-encased to prevent acid leakage and all-season resistance to the elements. Patco can demonstrate that Infro's competing Super-Traction EVB-100 battery copies its patented cell technology and infringes on its proprietary design. In the emerging electric car market, Patco claims that Infro has significantly disrupted its market leadership by diverting thousands of customers who are concerned about battery life and energy efficiency—aspects that Patco monopolized before Infro came along.

---

[3]Every student of economics is familiar with the term *price elasticity of demand*, a calculation that measures the percentage change in demand for a product based on the percentage change in price. An economics expert, confronted with a price erosion case, would be interested in the elasticity of the demand, the availability of substitute goods, and other market factors in quantifying actual loss to a patentee.

Before Infro introduced its Super-Traction EVB-100 into the market, Patco could sell 21,000 batteries at $275 each, at a marginal cost to Patco of $175 per unit. Patco reported total profits of $2.1 million.

After Infro introduced its battery, the best Patco could do was to sell 15,000 batteries at $249 each. Its total profits slipped to $1,110,000.

Infro was also able to sell 15,000 units of its Super-Traction EVB-100 product at $249. Interestingly, with Infro's infringement, the market output for electric batteries containing the patented long-life and leak-resistant cell technology jumped from Patco's original volume of 21,000 units to a combined 30,000 units (15,000 units of Patco's Ultimatic and 15,000 units of Infro's Super-Traction EVB-100).

Under infringement, Patco's lost profit is $990,000 ($2,100,000 preinfringement profit minus $1,110,000 postinfringement profit). How do we know what portion of the $990,000 in lost profits is attributable to lost sales, and what portion is tied to price erosion?

Lost profits from lost sales equals the difference in preinfringement and postinfringement sales to Patco multiplied by the marginal cost per unit, calculated as the difference between the sale price and the cost of manufacturing. In this set of facts, we know that Patco sold 21,000 batteries before Infro's infringement and 15,000 batteries after the infringement.

21,000 – 15,000 = 6,000

We also know that the price (P) of Patco's Ultimatic was $275 per unit, manufactured at a cost of $175 per unit.

$275 – $175 = $100

Therefore, lost sales account for $600,000 of Patco's lost profits:

6,000 x $100 = $600,000.

If Patco's total lost profits were $990,000, and lost sales accounted for $600,000, we could then conclude that price erosion accounted for the balance of $390,000 in lost profits. Price erosion could also be independently calculated by multiplying the number of units sold at the reduced price (N) times the difference in potential price (PP) and actual price (AP):

(PP – AP) x N

($275 – $249) x 15,000

$26 x $15,000

= $390,000

Thus, putting it all together, we can say that Infro's infringement on Patco's patented batteries caused Patco to suffer damages of $990,000—the difference between Patco's preinfringment profit of $2,100,000 and postinfringement profit of $1,110,000. The damages of $990,000 suffered by Patco are attributed to lost sales of $600,000 and price erosion of $390,000.

17.5. Future Lost Profits

Assume that, using the hypothetical in Section 17.4, Infro continued to draw profits from sales of its Super-Traction EVB-100 battery product *after* the Patco vs. Infro case was settled. In other words, what if the infringer enjoyed profits from its infringement *after* the lost profits calculation was completed and the case was concluded? How would Patco recover these additional *future* lost profits?

If the plaintiff in such a case can rationally estimate the likelihood of future postsettlement sales, then it should apply a discounted cash flow calculation to the timeline of projected lost revenues to determine the net present value of the future lost profits.[4] Suppose, for example, that a market study commissioned by Patco projected that Infro would draw profits totaling $69,400 from additional battery sales through retailers and resellers, even after the infringement case was concluded, a permanent injunction was entered, and manufacturing was halted. According to the projection, Infro would earn $36,000 in the first year following the settlement, $22,000 in the second year, $10,000 in the third year, and $1,400 in the fourth year.

To include these future lost profits in the settlement negotiations, Patco would want to discount them to present value. A discount rate should be chosen carefully because there may be great uncertainty about future market conditions and variables.

---

[4]See Sections 5.4, 5.5.

Let's assume that the discount rate is projected to be 3% for the first two years following the settlement and 4% for the next two years. Let's also assume that Patco's costs tied to the increased production and manufacturing of batteries during the four-year postsettlement period would be \$27,600. The net present value (NPV) formula would be applied, using the NPV formula for a cash flow:

$$\text{NPV} = \frac{\text{FV}}{(1+\text{i})^{\text{n}}} + \frac{\text{FV}}{(1+\text{i})^{\text{n}}} + \frac{\text{FV}}{(1+\text{i})^{\text{n}}} + \frac{\text{FV}}{(1+\text{i})^{\text{n}}} - \text{COST}$$

where FV is future value, i is the interest or discount rate, and n is the number of years.

Plugging in the numbers from Patco's projected future losses, we arrive at the following calculation:

$$\text{NPV} = \frac{\$36{,}000}{(1+.03)^1} + \frac{\$22{,}000}{(1+.03)^2} + \frac{\$10{,}000}{(1+.04)^3} + \frac{\$1{,}400}{(1+.04)^4} - \$27{,}600$$

$$\text{NPV} = \$34{,}951.46 + \$20{,}737.11 + \$8{,}889.96 + \$1{,}196.73 - \$27{,}600$$

$$\text{NPV} = \$38{,}175.26$$

Therefore, in negotiating a settlement that includes projected future lost profits, Patco should demand an additional \$38,175.26 as the NPV of those future lost profits.

The same logic can be applied to recover loss of goodwill. Thus, if Patco has lost future profits but it cannot quantify them based on any rational projection of future sales, it might consider reaching an agreement with Infro on the loss of goodwill. If the parties negotiated a goodwill loss figure, the figure could similarly be discounted to present value and added into the final settlement package.

17.6. Accelerated Entry Damages

In a perfect market, where no infringement exists, a company could wait patiently for a competitor's patent to expire and then proceed efficiently to fight for the available market share. Yet, what if the company were not so patient? What if it infringed the patent—or began to do so—at some point before the patent expired? In such a case, one might argue that the infringing company enjoyed an early advantage in relation to the eventual expiration of the patent. In fact, once the patent expires, the infringer, having previously geared up to infringe on the patent, would claim a larger market share sooner, or reduce the patentee's market share faster, than it would have under ordinary circumstances had no infringement occurred.

Such accelerated entry into the open marketplace by the infringer gives the infringer an unfair advantage, allowing it to establish a customer base quickly, to the detriment of the patent holder who, despite the expiration of the patent, expected to enjoy residual competitive advantages for a period of time.

One remedy in such a situation is for the court to enjoin the infringer from selling its product for a period of time. A more common approach, however, would be to assess accelerated entry damages against the infringer as a portion of the former patentee's lost future profits.[5] To quantify such damages, one would want to know (a) what share of the market was wrongfully taken by the infringer; (b) how long did the wrongful intrusion upon the market persist; and (c) how much profit was generated by the infringer, or lost to the patentee, because of the infringer's accelerated entry into the market.

Suppose, for example, that the infringer enjoyed a six-month advantage once the patentee's patent expired. Because the infringer had developed the mechanisms, procedures, and prototypes for the infringing product, and had already infringed on the patent, it was ready to enter the market aggressively on the first day after the patent expired. Expert estimates now indicate that the infringer had a six-month lead that it would not have enjoyed in the absence of its earlier infringement. Let's also assume that the patentee would have enjoyed an average postpatent profit of roughly $120,000 per month based on its prepatent experience (as gradually reduced to recognize the rising competition of new entrants in the marketplace). In other words, after scrutinizing the entire market and considering what portion of it the patentee would have retained after its patent expired, we can approximate the patent's projected profits at roughly $120,000 per month.

---

[5]*See BIC* Leisure Products, Inc. v. Windsurfing International, Inc., 687 F. Supp. 134 (S.D.N.Y. 1988) (noting that damages for future losses based on the infringer's accelerated reentry in the market are essentially attempts to make the patentee whole for past infringements, rather than an attempt to extend the life of a patent beyond its expiration date).

Under ordinary circumstances, no competitor would have made a significant dent into the patentee's profit margin during the first six months following the expiration of the patent. But the accelerated entry into the market by the infringer resulted in the patentee's profits being cut in half to $60,000 immediately after the patent expired.

Accelerated entry damages under this simplified scenario would thus amount to six months times $60,000, or $360,000. In effect, the patentee lost $360,000 in profits it would have enjoyed as a residual benefit of its expired patent in a market in which it expected that competitors were still learning how to produce and sell a competing product. Because a single infringing competitor enjoyed a head start attributable to its unlawful infringement, the former patentee is entitled to damages caused by its accelerated entry into the market.

Royalties

17.7. Reasonable Royalty

When lost profits cannot be determined from lost sales, the patentee is entitled to damages based on a *reasonable royalty*.[6] A reasonable royalty is essentially the amount for which the patentee would license the patent to another company. In effect, if the patentee and another company sought to negotiate a licensing agreement, what reasonable royalty would they agree on as the cost of sharing in the patent rights?

The analysis necessarily draws on a variety of qualitative and quantitative factors. The most reliable—but admittedly incomplete—list of factors appears in *Georgia-Pacific Corp. v. U.S. Plywood Corp.*,[7] in which a federal court delineated 15 relevant factors:

1. The royalties received by the patentee for the licensing of the patent in suit, proving or tending to prove an established royalty.
2. The rates paid by the licensee for the use of other patents comparable to the patent in suit.
3. The nature and scope of the license, as exclusive or non-exclusive; or as restricted or non-restricted in terms of territory or with respect to whom the manufactured product may be sold.

---

[6] 35 U.S.C. § 284.

[7] 318 F. Supp. 1116 (S.D.N.Y. 1970).

4. The licensor's established policy and marketing program to maintain his patent monopoly by not licensing others to use the invention or by granting licenses under special conditions designed to preserve that monopoly.
5. The commercial relationship between the licensor and licensee, such as, whether they are competitors in the same territory in the same line of business; or whether they are inventor and promoter.
6. The effect of selling the patented specialty in promoting sales of other products of the licensee; that existing value of the invention to the licensor as a generator of sales of his non-patented items; and the extent of such derivative or convoyed sales.
7. The duration of the patent and the term of the license.
8. The established profitability of the product made under the patent; its commercial success; and its current popularity.
9. The utility and advantages of the patent property over the old modes or devices, if any, that had been used for working out similar results.
10. The nature of the patented invention; the character of the commercial embodiment of it as owned and produced by the licensor; and the benefits to those who have used the invention.
11. The extent to which the infringer has made use of the invention; and any evidence probative of the value of that use.
12. The portion of the profit or of the selling price that may be customary in the particular business or in comparable businesses to allow for the use of the invention or analogous inventions.
13. The portion of the realizable profit that should be credited to the invention as distinguished from non-patented elements, the manufacturing process, business risks, or significant features or improvements added by the infringer.
14. The opinion testimony of qualified experts.
15. The amount that a licensor (such as the patentee) and a licensee (such as the infringer) would have agreed upon (at the time the infringement began) if both had been reasonably and voluntarily trying to reach an agreement; that is, the amount which a prudent licensee—who desired, as a business proposition, to obtain a license to manufacture and sell a particular article embodying the patented invention—would have been

willing to pay as a royalty and yet be able to make a reasonable profit and which amount would have been acceptable by a prudent patentee who was willing to grant a license.

These 15 factors can be intricately examined and then applied in any number of different approaches. They can *all* be considered, or they can be selectively considered. Other unlisted, case-specific factors, can also be considered. One or more of the factors may require special consideration, perhaps through weighting. While some of the *Georgia-Pacific* factors can be measured economically and financially, others elude easy quantification. Conducting a factor analysis is ultimately the most time-consuming approach but perhaps the most thorough, balanced, and defensible method for determining a reasonable royalty.

Experts have also attempted to fix a baseline royalty rate to approximate what a patentee would be willing to pay to a licensee in a hypothetical negotiation. Under the now-defunct "25% Rule," a reasonable royalty is said to be 25% of the marginal profits realized by using the patented product—or at least that's the starting point in a hypothetical negotiation. To apply the 25% Rule, we would estimate the infringer's projected profits derived from the infringed product (PPr). We would then divide the projected profits by the projected net sales (PNS) and multiply the result by 25% to arrive at the royalty rate (RR). The formula for the 25% rule is:

$$RR = \frac{PPr}{PNS} \text{ x } 25\%$$

If the infringer's projected profits were $410,000, and its projected net sales were $2 million, then the royalty rate would be slightly more than 5%, as shown below:

$$RR = \frac{\$410{,}000}{\$2{,}000{,}000} \text{ x } 25\%$$

$$RR = 20.5\% \text{ x } 25\%$$

$$RR = 5.125\%$$

This royalty rate would then be applied to the infringer's net sales to determine the royalty payment. Of course, the 25% baseline could be increased or reduced based on the *Georgia-Pacific* factors.

Despite its longevity and popularity in the patent law field, the 25% Rule was essentially abandoned in early 2011 after the U.S. Court of Appeals for the Federal Circuit held that it was a "fundamentally flawed tool for determining a baseline royalty rate in a hypothetical negotiation."[8] The court said that there must be some factual basis to establish a reasonable royalty rate, and that casual reliance on a 25% baseline, even as a starting point for discussions, lacked the necessary connection to the parties, products, or patents at issue.

The Federal Circuit's rejection of the 25% Rule probably spells doom for any baseline approach, although such an approach is not objectionable in all cases and may, in fact, serve as a starting point for negotiations in an appropriate case. If nothing else, the Federal Circuit's decision underscores the importance of the *Georgia-Pacific* factors and emphasizes the need for a fact-specific analysis of the parties, products, patents, and markets under consideration in each case.

17.8. Analytical Approach

The so-called *analytical approach* provides an estimate of a reasonable royalty by determining the profit differential between the patented product and a comparable unpatented product. The formula is simply the difference between the profit margin derived from the infringing product and the profit margin that was or would have been derived from a same or similar noninfringing product:

Inf.Pr. – Ninf.Pr. = Diff.Pr.

where Inf.Pr. is the infringing product profit margin, NInf.Pr. is the noninfringing product profit margin, and Diff.Pr. is the profit differential.

For example, assume that an infringer enjoys a 72% profit margin on a product that infringes another firm's patent. Were it to market a noninfringing version of the product, it would enjoy a profit margin of 45%. Applying the analytical approach, we can quickly find the differential:

Inf.Pr. – Ninf.Pr. = Diff.Pr.

72% – 45% = 27%

Therefore, the reasonable royalty to be paid by the infringer would be 27% or, depending on circumstances, an amount somewhat more or less than 27%. Scientific certainty may not always apply to volatile

[8] Uniloc USA, Inc. v. Microsoft Corp., 632 F. 3d 1292 (Fed. Cir. 2011).

markets with changing profit margins. The analytical approach seeks to restore the profit margin enjoyed by the patentee, but many variables, such as the fixed costs, industry trends, and alternative licensing options, may offset the profit differential.

If, for example, the patentee had more lucrative licensing options in the marketplace, it should not be limited to a reasonable royalty equal to only the infringer's profit differential. On the other hand, if the infringer's profit margin on the infringed product is significantly enhanced by technological innovations, cost containment initiatives, or other internal controls unique to the infringer's business, the profit differential produced through the analytical approach may be unfairly high as a reasonable royalty.

17.9. Weighted Average Cost of Capital

Another approach to fixing a reasonable royalty is to conduct a return-on-assets evaluation based on the weighted average cost of capital (WACC).[9] In this approach, the patentee seeks to determine what investment return is needed to service the capital required by the infringer. Any excess return attributable to the use of the intellectual property would be a reasonable royalty amount.

The WACC method, recognized widely in the business community as a project valuation device, is founded on the principle that a project (in this case, the hypothetical licensing of a patent right to an infringer) is financed with both debt and equity. The cost of capital is a weighted average of the cost of debt and the cost of equity.

The formula for WACC is:

$$\text{WACC} = \frac{E}{E + D} R_E + \frac{D}{E + D} R_D(1 - T_C)$$

E = Equity
D = Debt
R_E = Cost of Equity
R_D = Cost of Debt
T_C = Corporate Tax Rate

[9]For a basic review of the formula for return on assets, see Section 8.8.

Before plugging in numbers, it is important to conceptualize what the WACC formula seeks to determine. WACC has essentially two pieces—the equity side and the debt side. The equity side consists of the infringer's equity divided by the total value of its equity and debt combined, depicted as $\frac{E}{E+D}$. This amount is then multiplied by the cost of equity (R_E). The debt side consists of the infringer's debt divided by the total value of its equity and debt combined, depicted as $\frac{D}{E+D}$. This amount is then multiplied by the cost of debt (R_D). The cost of equity is often elusive because it involves the determination of a risk premium.[10] The cost of debt, however, is relatively simple because it consists of the interest rate paid to bankers or bondholders for borrowed funds. The cost of debt must be adjusted so that it applies only to that portion of debt not paid in corporate taxes; thus, we include the calculation $(1 - T_C)$ where T_C is the tax rate.

Let's try a hypothetical. Assume that the infringer has a market value of equity at $500 million and debt at $375 million. The cost of equity is 19.5%, and the cost of debt is 7% with a tax rate of 34%. Here is the WACC calculation.

$$\text{WACC} = \frac{E}{E+D} R_E + \frac{D}{E+D} R_D(1 - T_C)$$

$$\text{WACC} = \frac{500}{875}(0.195) + \frac{375}{875}(0.07)\ (1 - 0.34)$$

$$\text{WACC} = \frac{500}{875}(0.195) + \frac{375}{875}(0.07)\ (1 - 0.34)$$

$$\text{WACC} = (0.57)\ (0.195) + (0.43)\ (0.07)\ (0.66)$$

$$\text{WACC} = 0.11 \text{ (rounded)} + 0.02 \text{ (rounded)}$$

$$\text{WACC} = 0.13$$

$$\text{WACC} = 13\%$$

The WACC figure of 13% tells us the required return for the infringer's business as a whole. Now we must consult the infringer's balance sheet (and/or other financial statements) to obtain a list of the infringer's various assets. Our first objective will be to determine what

---

[10]For a further discussion of how to calculate a return on equity, see Section 8.7.

portion of the $875 million in total equity and debt is attributable to intellectual property other than the infringed product under patent.

Let's assume that the infringer reports the following assets:[11]

	Value	Percentage of Total
All Assets	$875,000,000	100%
Cash and Cash Equivalents	$ 65,400,000	7.5%
Inventory	$190,000,000	21.7%
Property, Plant, & Equipment	$265,700,000	30.4%
Other Intangibles	$ 38,555,000	4.4%
Other Assets	$126,000,000	14.4%
Intellectual Property (not including infringed patent)	$189,345,000	21.6%

Subtracting the value of cash and cash equivalents, inventory, property, plant, and equipment, other intangibles, and other assets from the total value of all assets of $875 million leaves a value of $189,345,000 which the marketplace, by default, ascribes to the right to use intellectual property. Essentially, this is the value of intellectual property other than the infringed patent. By default, we can conclude that the intellectual property represents a value of 21.6% of the infringer's assets with a monetary value of $189,345,000.

Next, we need to determine the appropriate rate of return for the intellectual property. Again, we can establish this figure by default after estimating rates of return for each of the other assets and subtracting them from the weighted average rate of return of 13%. For purposes of illustrating this process, rates of return have been estimated in the table below. However, rates of return should be given great consideration and should be based on reliable indicators or expert advice. Typically, for example, cash and other liquid assets are considered low-risk investments and would be assigned a safe rate of return. Here, below, arbitrary rates of return have been assigned to each of the asset categories to demonstrate the process for establishing the default rate of return attributable to intellectual property.

[11]For the method of charting assets to establish a default value for intellectual property, see Siebrasse, Norman V. and Alexander J. Stack, *Damages Calculations in Intellectual Property Cases in Canada,* first published in the Canadian Intellectual Property Review, as A.J. Stack, A.S. Davidson, and S.R. Cole, *Damages Calculations in Intellectual Property Cases in Canada,* 18(1) C.I.P.R. 1 (2001).

	Value	Percentage of Total	Rate of Return	Weighted Rate of Return
All Assets	$875,000,000	100%		13%
Cash and Cash Equivalents	$ 65,400,000	7.5%	7%	0.53%
Inventory	$190,000,000	21.7%	10%	2.17%
Property, Plant, & Equipment	$265,700,000	30.4%	9%	2.74%
Other Intangibles	$ 38,555,000	4.4%	12%	0.53%
Other Assets	$126,000,000	14.4%	10%	1.44%
Intellectual Property (not including infringed patent)	$189,345,000	21.6%	25.88%	5.59%

Doing the math, we can see that each category of assets has a certain weighted rate of return derived from its percentage of the total assets and its rate of return. For example, property, plant, and equipment represent 30.4% of the infringer's total assets. With a rate of return of 9%, the weighted rate attributable to property, plant, and equipment is 2.74%:

0.304 x 0.09 = 0.02736 (rounded to 2.74%)

Once we've calculated all of the weighted rates of return and subtracted them from the WACC of 13%, we see that noninfringing intellectual property has a weighted rate of 5.59%. Then, we can divide the weighted rate of 5.59% by the percentage of total for intellectual property (21.6%) to arrive at the rate of return for intellectual property of 25.88%. Assuming the accuracy of these percentages, the infringer will need a 25.88% rate of return on intellectual property to achieve the WACC of 13%.

Let's now return to the WACC of 13%. *What does this percentage mean?* A WACC of 13% means that the infringer must spend 13% of the total value of its assets to cover its WACC and satisfy its debt service.

Total Assets ($875,000,000) x WACC (0.13) = $113,750,000.

In other words, with a WACC of 13%, the infringer must spend a total of $113,750,000.

Assume that the infringer was earning $300 million after taxes. Because the WACC included fair returns on all of the assets, the excess earnings—that is, the amount beyond the WACC—can be attributable to the infringed patent. Thus, in this case, if the infringer has net pre-debt income of $300 million and WACC costs of $113,750,000, it has excess earnings of $186,250,000.

Next, we retrofit the tax rate. If the infringer's income had been taxed at a rate of 34%, its excess earnings of $186,250,000 would have derived from pretax earnings of $547,794,117.65 (calculated as $186,250,000 divided by 0.34). In other words, $547,794.117.65 is the total amount of annual income available to the infringer to pay a royalty to the patentee.

The Final Drill-Down

Now that we know that the infringer earned additional, infringement-based, pretax income of $547,794,117.65, we can apply this figure to the specific number of units of the infringed product sold by the infringer. If the infringer sold 650,000 units, then royalties per unit (RPU) would be calculated as follows:

$$\text{RPU} = \frac{\text{Excess Pre-Tax Income}}{\text{Unit Sales}} = \frac{\$547{,}794{,}117.65}{\$650{,}000} = \$842.76$$

Thus, the royalty per unit would be $842.76. If the infringer sold each unit for $2,400, then the royalty percentage would have been approximately 35%.

$$\frac{\text{RPU}}{\text{Sale Price}} = \frac{\$842.76}{\$2{,}400} = 0.35115 = 35\% \text{ (rounded)}$$

Using the WACC approach and drilling down deeper into the per-unit sales, we can now conclude that the infringer enjoyed a pretax income of more than $547 million attributable to the infringed patent, that this income translates into $842.76 per unit sold, and that ultimately the patentee is entitled to 35% of the net sales generated by the infringing product.

[Trademarks]

Valuation Methods

17.10. Overview

Like the valuation of an infringed patent, the valuation of an infringed trademark entails a measure of the asset's lost profits, a consideration of the condition of the marketplace in which the infringement takes place, and an account of available substitute products and additional competitors. Lost profits attributable to a trademark infringement can also be based on lost sales and price erosion.

Courts have, in fact, broadly considered a variety of damage categories in entering judgments for patent infringement, including:

- Actual lost sales
- Reduction in net profits
- Unjust enrichment
- Damage for business reputation
- Increased costs attributable to infringement
- Punitive damages (under state law)
- Attorneys' fees

Under the federal Lanham Act,[12] a trademark holder can also claim statutory damages equal to the infringer's profits, the trademark holder's actual losses, and the costs of the action. This could include, for example, the cost of corrective advertising. In cases involving the unlawful use of counterfeit marks, courts may award damages ranging from $1,000 to $200,000 per violation, and for willful violations, up to $2 million per counterfeiting incident.[13] The Act also recognizes a right to treble damages[14] and to nonmonetary remedies such as injunctive relief to prevent dilution by blurring or by tarnishment of a trademark by an infringer.[15] In fact, the Act even gives courts discretionary power to increase or decrease damages if they find that the recovery of profit by the trademark holder is either inadequate or excessive.

While the term "reasonable royalty" is generally recognized primarily in patent law as a foundation for calculating damages where lost profits are not readily quantifiable, trademark damages can also apply a reasonable royalty in appropriate cases. Such a royalty, for example, may take into consideration any royalty rates previously received by the trademark licensor or paid by licensees, the scope of the licensee's use, the value and profitability of the infringement, and other evidence of what amount the parties would have agreed upon voluntarily.

---

[12] 15 U.S.C. §§ 1051, *et. seq.*
[13] 15 U.S.C. § 1117(c).
[14] 15 U.S.C. § 1117(b).
[15] 15 U.S.C. § 1125(c).

17.11. DCF Approach

Because one measure of damages in a trademark case is the lost sales, and therefore the lost income, to the trademark holder, we can calculate damages from infringement by determining the present value of future lost sales.[16] Of course, the best estimate of future lost sales is the most accurate record of past and present sales. The need for accuracy cannot be underestimated: any projection of future lost sales must consider, at a minimum, the sales record for the trademarked products in question, the evolution and trajectory of the current market for such products, the reasonable life of the products, and the presence or absence of other external economic influences.

By applying the discounted cash flow (DCF) approach, as we saw in our earlier discussions of future value and present value,[17] we can determine what a projected future income stream would equal in today's dollars, for purposes of settling a trademark infringement case. Assume, for example, that an analysis of sales over time, measured against all verifiable trends in the marketplace, reveals that a particular trademark would have generated additional income of $575 million had no infringement occurred. According to the projection, the following cash flow would have been generated over a 10-year forecast period:

YEAR 1:	$100,000,000	YEAR 6:	$ 50,000,000
YEAR 2:	$ 90,000,000	YEAR 7:	$ 50,000,000
YEAR 3:	$ 80,000,000	YEAR 8:	$ 50,000,000
YEAR 4:	$ 70,000,000	YEAR 9:	$ 20,000,000
YEAR 5:	$ 60,000,000	YEAR 10:	$ 5,000,000

Once these future returns on the trademark can be established, we would need to discount them to present value using an appropriate discount rate. Again, this is easier said than done. Great care must be exercised to fix a discount rate, or rates, that truly and rationally meas-

[16]This is often referred to as the "income method" of calculating damages, to be distinguished from the cost and market-based approaches described below.

[17]For a discussion of future value of an uneven cash flow, see Section 5.3. For an application of the DCF approach in calculating net present value, see Section 5.5.

ure market conditions, growth, risk, and other factors. For purposes of this example, let's assume a discount rate of 5% throughout the forecast period.

Applying the DCF approach, the question becomes: what is the present value of the 10 annual cash flows shown above based on a 5% interest rate compounded annually? In fact, if we knew that there would be a cost associated with generating the income of $575 million over the 10-year forecast period, we would want to measure the net present value (NPV) after accounting for the cost. NPV equals present value (PV) minus cost. If, for example, the trademark holder's costs would be $460 million, we would want to know what the PV of $575 million over 10 years would be, after deducting $460 million in costs.

The formula requires us first to determine the PV of each year's cash flow. It is, essentially, the PV of the Year 1 cash flow, plus the PV of the Year 2 cash flow, plus the PV of the Year 3 cash flow, and so forth . . . and then, minus the cost of $460 million. To do the math, we'll need to plot each year's cash flow as a future value (FV) to which the trademark holder would be entitled.

$$\mathrm{NPV} = \frac{\mathrm{FV}}{(1+i)^n} + \frac{\mathrm{FV}}{(1+i)^n} + \frac{\mathrm{FV}}{(1+i)^n} + \frac{\mathrm{FV}}{(1+i)^n} + \frac{\mathrm{FV}}{(1+i)^n} + \frac{\mathrm{FV}}{(1+i)^n}$$

$$+ \frac{\mathrm{FV}}{(1+i)^n} + \frac{\mathrm{FV}}{(1+i)^n} + \frac{\mathrm{FV}}{(1+i)^n} + \frac{\mathrm{FV}}{(1+i)^n} - \mathrm{COST}$$

where i equals the interest or discount rate (in this case 5%) and n refers to the year in question (running from 1 through 10).

Let's now do the math:

YEAR 1:	$100,000,000
YEAR 2:	$ 90,000,000
YEAR 3:	$ 80,000,000
YEAR 4:	$ 70,000,000
YEAR 5:	$ 60,000,000
YEAR 6:	$ 50,000,000
YEAR 7:	$ 50,000,000
YEAR 8:	$ 50,000,000
YEAR 9:	$ 20,000,000
YEAR 10:	$ 5,000,000

$$NPV = \frac{100{,}000{,}000}{(1.05)^1} + \frac{90{,}000{,}000}{(1.05)^2} + \frac{80{,}000{,}000}{(1.05)^3} + \frac{70{,}000{,}000}{(1.05)^4} + \frac{60{,}000{,}000}{(1.05)^5}$$

$$+ \frac{50{,}000{,}000}{(1.05)^6} + \frac{50{,}000{,}000}{(1.05)^7} + \frac{50{,}000{,}000}{(1.05)^8} + \frac{20{,}000{,}000}{(1.05)^9} + \frac{5{,}000{,}000}{(1.05)^{10}}$$

$$- \$460{,}000{,}000$$

$$\begin{aligned} NPV = {} & \$\ 95{,}238{,}095.24 \\ & + \$\ 81{,}632{,}653.06 \\ & + \$\ 69{,}107{,}007.88 \\ & + \$\ 57{,}589{,}173.24 \\ & + \$\ 47{,}011{,}569.99 \\ & + \$\ 37{,}310{,}769.83 \\ & + \$\ 35{,}534{,}066.51 \\ & + \$\ 33{,}841{,}968.10 \\ & + \$\ 12{,}892{,}178.32 \\ & + \$\ 3{,}069{,}566.27 \\ & - \$460{,}000{,}000 \end{aligned}$$

$$NPV = \$\ 13{,}227{,}048.44$$

Therefore, the NPV of the projected cash flows would be \$13,227,048.44. The trademark holder would argue that it has been deprived of these cash flows, and thus its actual damages from lost sales equal \$13,227,048.44 in today's dollars.

A DCF approach is a helpful analytical tool in estimating damages, but it is not unassailable if the projected cash flows, the forecast period, or the discount rate are unreliable.

17.12. NTV Approach

The net terminal value (NTV) approach[18] is another income method for quantifying losses in a trademark case. It produces a value for the trademark at the end of a certain span of time, based on a certain interest rate. The starting point is to calculate terminal value (TV). The formula for TV in this context is:

$$TV = CF(1 + i)^n$$

TV = Terminal value
CF = Cash Flow

[18]See Section 8.12.

i = interest rate
n = number of years

If, for example, a trademark generated a cash flow of $1 million, we might want to know what it would be worth in 20 years, invested at 4%. Applying the TV formula above, we find that it would be worth more than $2.1 million at the end of 20 years:

$$TV = CF(1 + i)^n$$

$$TV = \$1,000,000\ (1.04)^{20}$$

$$TV = \$1,000,000\ (2.191123143)$$

$$TV = \$2,191,123.14$$

Of course, we would also need to consider the costs incurred over the relevant time period. Like an NPV calculation, NTV should be calculated by subtracting costs. Thus, if the same trademark would incur costs of $1.5 million, its NTV would be $691,123.14.

$$NTV = TV - Costs$$

$$NTV = \$2,191,123.14 - \$1,500,000$$

$$NTV = \$691,123.14$$

In practice, TV calculations are more complicated because of the recognition of some level of growth after the forecasting period expires. So, for example, if we had a TV of $1 million in year 20, how would we adjust that value where the discount remains at 5% but the inflation rate is 2.5%? We call this the perpetuity calculation, and it looks like this:

$$TV = CF\ (Final)\ \frac{1 + g}{r - g}$$

where the cash flow represents the value in the final year, at the end of the forecasting period, and where r stands for the discount rate and g stands for the growth or inflation rate.

$$TV = \$1,000,000\ \frac{1 + .025}{.05 - .025}$$

$$TV = \$1,000,000\ \frac{1.025}{.025}$$

$$TV = \$1,000,000\ (41)$$

$$TV = \$41,000,000$$

If $41 million were the TV of a trademark asset, calculated with the perpetuity method, we would then calculate its PV using the 5% discount rate and the 20-year time frame:

$$PV = \frac{FV}{(1 + i)^n}$$

$$PV = \frac{\$41{,}000{,}000}{(1 + .05)^{20}}$$

$$PV = \$15{,}452{,}468.79$$

So, now we know that a TV of $1 million in 20 years, adjusted for perpetual growth, and reduced to present value, is approximately $15.4 million.

Another variation of the TV formula, based on a stable growth model, predicts that the final cash flows will be reinvested by the business and will grow at a constant rate forever. It produces similar results.

$$TV = \frac{CF}{r - g}$$

$$TV = \frac{\$1{,}000{,}000}{0.025}$$

$$TV = \$40{,}000{,}000$$

$$\text{PV of } \$40{,}000{,}000 = \frac{\$40{,}000{,}000}{(1 + .05)^{20}}$$

$$PV = \$15{,}075{,}579.31$$

In an appropriate case, the DCF formulation over a particular forecasting period would be considered together with the NTV in valuing the full range of lost income to the trademark holder. As noted above, however, such calculations are not incontrovertible where the inputs are unreliable. Moreover, the complexity of forecasting values and adjusting the incremental returns for trademarks, especially under changing economic circumstances, is often best left to financial and economic experts.

17.13. Replacement Cost Method

What did it cost to create, develop, and commercialize the trademark in question? Stated otherwise, if the trademark were infringed or diluted, what would it cost to replace it—by designing an equivalent substitute trademark (or brand name), promoting and advertising the new trademark, and investing fully in its commercial distribution and market penetration? By examining the actual costs as well as the opportunity costs, and adding them to lost sales and profits during the period of substitution and redevelopment, a trademark holder can estimate the value of the loss from an infringement.

The theory underlying the replacement cost method is that a company would not invest in designing, marketing, and advertising a trademark unless the return on the investment would exceed the cost. Calculating the total cost (TC), therefore, provides a foundation for determining damages suffered as a result of an infringement. Of course, accounting for *all of the costs* can be a significant task, encompassing design, graphical and artistic costs, market research expenses, professional fees and office labor costs, application and development costs, production and registration costs, advertising, marketing, and promotional charges, contract, licensing, and miscellaneous obligations.

Added to the actual costs of replacing a trademark are both prejudgment damages and postjudgment damages determined by measuring lost sales and profits. Essentially, in order to restore the trademark holder to the position it would have occupied in the absence of an infringement, we need to add replacement costs to lost profits. In most cases, however, the determination of lost profits will be calculated to the moment of a trial and the ensuing judgment.[19] As such, lost profits would be divided into pretrial or prejudgment lost profits (essentially, past lost profits) *and* posttrial or postjudgment lost profits (essentially, future lost profits).[20]

Each of these categories would then be adjusted to present value (PV). The TC would necessarily require up-to-date cost figures, accurate as of the date of trial. The pretrial lost profits would need to be adjusted to future value (FV), and the posttrial future lost profits would need to be discounted to PV.

[19]However, lost profits may be determined up until the moment that a financial expert renders a report; until pretrial discovery is provided; or until a mediation, an arbitration, or a settlement conference occurs.

[20]The process applies to whatever dividing point is used. Thus, if lost profits are fixed at the moment that interrogatories are answered, then lost profits would be divided into preinterrogatory lost profits (as past lost profits) and postinterrogatory lost profits (as future lost profits).

In effect, the formula for valuing a misappropriated trademark under the replacement cost method can be stated as follows:

Damages = TC + FV of pretrial lost profits + PV of posttrial lost profits.

Let's address the TC aspect first. Suppose, for example, that ABC Corporation made the following financial investments in the creation of its trademark:

DESCRIPTION	COST
Design and development	$3,400,000
Application, registration and legal	$ 150,000
Production and replication	$1,800,000
Advertising and marketing	$2,100,000
Labor and management	$1,526,230
Miscellaneous overhead	$ 450,000
Total Costs (Unadjusted)	$9,426,230

ABC's total unadjusted costs for its trademark were $9,426,230. These are, of course, yesterday's costs. ABC will want to calculate the difference between yesterday's design, production, labor, and advertising costs and today's costs.[21] Let's assume, for purposes of this example, that it is 22% more costly today to create, produce, and promote a new trademark. Therefore we need to adjust the TC by 22%; that is, to multiply by 122% or 1.22.

TC = $ 9,426,230

$9,426,230 x 1.22 = $11,500,000.60

Therefore, ABC Corporation will be required to invest $11.5 million in today's dollars to create a new trademark and brand identity.

[21]The upward or downward modification of total costs depends on many factors, including the length of time since the original trademark was designed; the specific line items for which costs were previously incurred and for which they will be incurred today; and the change in consumer prices over time. The historic costs would have to be adjusted to present value by applying the applicable inflation rate. The rate of price inflation over a particular period of time can be measured by the change in the Consumer Price Index.

ABC has also determined, through one or more other formulas, that its lost profits throughout the period of infringement until the date of trial amount to \$35.2 million. ABC can further demonstrate that its future lost profits will total \$14.1 million over time, as a measure of its projected posttrial losses running until the point that a replacement trademark would restore its market position. To calculate ABC's losses, we would adjust each figure and add them together, as follows:

TC = \$11,500,000 (adjusted to present value)

FV of pretrial lost profits of \$35,200,000. For the purposes of this hypothetical, we'll assume a 4% interest rate and a three-year pretrial period of infringement. Thus, $FV = \$35{,}200{,}000 \times (1.04)^3 = \$39{,}595{,}212.80$.

PV of posttrial lost profits of \$14,100,000. For the purposes of this hypothetical, we'll assume a 4% discount rate and a five-year posttrial period of recovery. Thus, $PV = \frac{\$14{,}100{,}000}{(1.04)^5} = \$11{,}589{,}172.21$.

ABC's damages in this case:

= TC + FV of pretrial lost profits + PV of posttrial lost profits

= \$11,500,000 + \$39,595,212.80 + \$11,589,172.21

= \$62,684,385.01

To be made whole, ABC would claim \$62,684,385.01 in damages—a figure that not only represents a PV of its past and future lost profits but also incorporates the current cost of designing, developing, and marketing a new trademark. While this method provides a straightforward technique for analyzing damages under a cost-based approach, it is, like the other approaches discussed here, neither fail-safe nor absolutely complete. Cost accounting can be a technical science unto itself, and the calculation of lost profits is, again, only as accurate as the factors and inputs on which the calculations are based. Attorneys should therefore not hesitate to consult appropriate experts for anything beyond preliminary case evaluations, discussions, and negotiations.

17.14. Market Comparables Method

The market comparables method, sometimes referred to simply as the "market approach," measures the value of a trademark by looking at the sale of substantially similar intangible assets. By comparing the trademark with a set of comparable benchmarks, the value of a trademark can be appraised in much the way residential real estate is appraised.

The use of "comps," however, is only reliable if the other assets being compared are truly comparable. Trademarks cannot be arbitrarily compared with any other intangible asset or even any other form of intellectual property. They should not be compared with assets that were sold or licensed a long time before the infringement took place because the information will be outdated. They should not be tied to incompatible benchmarks, such as situations in which an asset belonging to a failing company or a merging enterprise was auctioned at steep discounts, or where a sale price was inflated by an unusual or unique market event.

The market comparables approach, however, benefits from its own self-correcting, automatic-updating character. Actual sales, licensing, and transfers of trademark rights provide a veritable measure of the fair market value of the trademark in a current market. Still, it may be necessary to make downward or upward adjustments to the average value of comparable assets to account for the passage of time, fluctuations in the marketplace, and other factors.

The formula for activating the market comparables approach is:

$$MV = \frac{C1 + C2 + C3}{3} (X\%)$$

where MV is the market value, C1, C2, and C3 are three comparable sales figures, and X% refers to the upward or downward adjustment for the lapse of time and the changes in the marketplace. In this formula, we are seeking an average of three comparable sales figures; thus, we add the three figures (C1 + C2 + C3) and divide by 3. Were we to consider five comparable sales (C1 . . . C5), we would add them and divide by 5.

Let's assume that we have collected sales figures for three comparable assets, as follows:

C1: $1,600,000

C2: $2,050,000

C3: $1,850,000

Let's also assume that the asset in question is at least 50% greater than any of the comparable assets in terms of its market saturation, global reach, and unique position in the marketplace. Therefore, we are going to adjust the average of the comps by a multiplier of 150%. Here's the math:

$$MV = \frac{C1 + C2 + C3}{3}(X\%)$$

$$MV = \frac{\$1{,}600{,}000 + \$2{,}050{,}000 + \$1{,}850{,}000}{3}(150\%)$$

$$MV = \$1{,}833{,}333.33\ (1.5)$$

$$MV = \$2{,}750{,}000$$

Using the market comparables method, as adjusted, we can now value the asset in question at $2.75 million.

Estimation Models and Rules of Thumb

17.15. Profit Split Methods

Profit split methods are designed to determine what portion of a company's profit is attributable to the brand or the trademark in question. To apply a profit split, we would need to clearly isolate the branded products from other intangible and tangible assets and to allocate revenue to those products. Two basic profit split methods are the excess earnings rate method and the residual earnings rate method.

The Excess Earnings Rate Method

The excess earnings method compares the price and cost of branded or trademarked products with nonbranded and nontrademarked products. There are three simple formulas:

(1) We start with the rule that price (P) minus cost (C) equals earnings (E). In the case of the branded product, this would yield branded earnings (BE), and in the case of the unbranded product, unbranded earnings (UBE).
(2) BE minus UBE equals excess earnings (EE).
(3) EE divided by the branded price (BP) equals the earnings rate (ER).

Assume, for example, that a branded radial tire and an unbranded generic radial tire are sold for the following prices, incurring the following costs:

	BRANDED	UNBRANDED
Price	\$99	\$69
Cost	\$75	\$54
Earnings Per Tire	\$24	\$15

Let's apply the three formulas to determine the excess earnings rate.

(1) P – C = E
Branded Tire: \$99 – \$75 = \$24 BE
Unbranded Tire: \$69 – \$54 = \$15 UBE

(2) BE – UBE = EE
\$24 – \$15 = \$9

(3) $\frac{EE}{BP} = ER$

$\frac{\$9}{\$99} = .10 = 10\%$

Therefore, we can say that the branded radial tires have a 10% earnings rate—a figure that can be used in estimating a reasonable royalty or building a damage loss formula.

Residual Earnings Rate Method

The residual earnings approach calculates the value of a brand or a trademark by first determining the company's total profits and then subtracting its profits attributable to all other nonbrand/nontrademark assets. Residual earnings (RE) are then divided by total revenues (TR) to establish an earnings rate attributable to the brand or the trademark.

The first step is to determine the company's total net earnings or profit (Pr). We then subtract the profit attributable to every kind of asset except for the subject brand or trademark. This could include, for example, profit attributable to fixed assets, working capital, and other intangible assets. Assume that a company had total profit of \$100 million, of which \$40 million was attributable to fixed assets, \$3 million was attributable to working capital, and \$37 million was attributable to other intangible assets. We could easily calculate the value of the trademark by determining the RE.

RE = Pr – profit attributable to fixed assets, working capital, and other intangibles.

RE = \$100 – \$40 – \$3 – \$37

RE = \$20

The residual earnings attributable to the brand or trademark amount to \$20 million. To fix the residual earnings rate, divide the ER by the total amount of revenue for the company. So, for example, if the company generated revenue of \$997 million, the ER would be approximately 2% as shown below.

$$\frac{\text{RE}}{\text{Revenue}} = \text{ER}$$

$$\frac{\$20{,}000{,}000}{\$997{,}000{,}000} = .02006 = 2\%$$

We can thus conclude that the branded or trademarked product carries an earnings rate of 2%, again producing a measure that can be used to estimate a reasonable royalty or serve as a foundation for calculating damages.

17.16. Premium Pricing Method

The premium pricing method compares the price of a trademarked product (P_T) to the price of a nontrademarked product (P_{NT}). The difference between these two prices is the Premium (Prem), from which a value for the trademark can be calculated. Here are the formulas:

(1) First, subtract the price of the P_{NT} from the price of the P_T to determine the Prem.
(2) Multiply the Prem by the number of units sold of the trademarked product (Sales) to determine lost sales revenue (Rev).
(3) Project sales over a period of years to determine Rev for each year.
(4) Add each year's Rev together.

For example, assume that the price of trademarked tires is \$100 and of nontrademarked tires is \$78. Assume that Tire Empire, Inc. sells

17,000 tires bearing the Empire trademark in a given year. Growth is projected at a steady 10% over the next three years. Follow the formulas to approximate the value of the trademark:

$P_T - P_{NT} = \text{Prem}$

$100 – $78 = $22

Prem x Sales = Rev

$22 x 17,000 = $374,000 (Year 1 revenue loss)

We can now plot this revenue loss for the next three years, based on the 10% projected annual growth in sales.

	Year 1	**Year 2**	**Year 3**	**Year 4**
Price of Empire Branded Tire	$100	$100	$100	$100
Price of Generic Tire without trademark	$78	$78	$78	$78
Premium	$22	$22	$22	$22
Annual Sales of Empire Tires	17,000	18,700	20,570	22,627
Revenue Tied to Lost Sales	$374,000	$411,400	$452,540	$497,794

Finally, we add each year's revenue loss to determine the loss over four years attributable to the lost premium price:

Year 1: $374,000
Year 2: + $411,400
Year 3: + $452,540
Year 4: + $497,794
Total: = $1,735,734

Thus based on the projection above,[22] Tire Empire, Inc. will suffer a $1.7 million loss in sales revenue attributable to the infringement of the trademarked premium-priced Empire brand tire.

---

[22]The project assumes, for purposes of this hypothetical, that the price of the tires will remain constant over the four-year period depicted. It also assumes steady 10% growth in sales over the forecast period. Both of these assumptions may be flawed in an actual analysis of a fluctuating market.

17.17. Scale Comparison Method

The infringement of a trademark can also interfere with a company's ability to save money by reducing its economies of scale. After all, a company holding a valuable trademark right may command a dominant position in the marketplace, buying raw materials at volume discounts, maximizing the efficiency of machinery and equipment, and utilizing resources at optimal levels with minimal waste. The scale comparison method thus seeks to capture the losses attributable to the lost economies of scale suffered by the company as a result of the infringement on its trademarked product.

Here are the formulas:

(1) Calculate the total profit (Pr) and the total sales revenue (Rev) of the company that lawfully holds the trademark. Generally, profit is the difference between Rev and the costs of good sold.
(2) Calculate the Pr and Rev of the infringer.
(3) Determine the profit-to-sales revenue ratio (Pr/Rev) for the lawful trademark holder.
(4) Determine the Pr/Rev for the infringer.
(5) Multiply the Pr/Rev for the infringer by the trademark holder's Rev to arrive at the relative income (RI).
(6) Subtract RI from the trademark holder's actual Pr.

Let's plug in some hypothetical numbers. Suppose that the trademark holder reported total profit of $750,000 on sales of $2,250,000, and that the infinger reported total profit of $1,900,000 on sales of $7,999,999. Let's calculate each company's gross margin by using the Pr/Rev ratio:

$$\text{Trademark Holder: } \frac{\text{Pr}}{\text{Rev}} = \frac{\$750{,}000}{\$2{,}250{,}000} = .3333\ (33.33\%)$$

$$\text{Infringer: } \frac{\text{Pr}}{\text{Rev}} = \frac{\$1{,}900{,}000}{\$7{,}999{,}999} = .2375\ (23.75\%)$$

Next, let's multiply the infringer's Pr/Rev ratio by the trademark holder's revenue.

$$\frac{\text{Pr}}{\text{Rev}} \text{ x Rev} = \text{RI}$$

$$.2375 \text{ x } \$2{,}250{,}000 = \$534{,}375$$

Then, subtract the result from the trademark holder's actual profit:

$750,000 – $534,375 = $215,625

Thus, we can say that the trademark holder has suffered damages of $215,625. Because of the lost economies of scale, the trademark holder is earning $215,625 less than it would have earned in the absence of an infringement.

17.18. Return on Assets Employed

The ratio for return on assets employed (ROAE) is generally a measure of a company's operating efficiency.[23] It reveals the extent to which a company generates a positive return with the minimum investment of assets. In its simplest form, the ratio is $\frac{\text{Profit}}{\text{Assets}}$. However, it is often expressed or refined more specifically in one or more of the following ratios:

$$\frac{\text{Net Profit}}{\text{Total Assets}} \qquad \frac{\text{Net Income}}{\text{Total Assets}} \qquad \frac{\text{Net Profit}}{\text{Average Total Assets}}$$

$$\frac{\text{Net Operating Profit After Taxes (NOPAT)}}{\text{Total Assets}}$$

$$\frac{\text{Earnings Before Interest and Taxes (EBIT)}}{\text{Average Total Assets}}$$

$$\frac{\text{Earnings Before Interest, Taxes Depreciation and Amortization (EBITDA)}}{\text{Average Total Assets}}$$

Other variations are also in popular use.

Depending on the purpose of the calculation, the denominator of the ROAE ratio can be limited to one or more categories of assets. For example, a more targeted ROAE ratio could be expressed as $\frac{\text{Net Profit + Interest}}{\text{Fixed Assets}}$. These ratios can assist a company in determining how profitably it is operating, relative to its total assets, its fixed assets, or any other particular subcategory of assets. Indeed, because the denominator can be modified, we can use the ROAE ratio to isolate the profitability of a trademark asset.

---

[23]For a basic discussion of the return on assets (ROA) ratio, see Section 8.8.

Before calculating the ROAE, it is important to account for those assets that are actually *employed*. Dormant, inactive, and nonperforming assets that do not contribute to the generation of income to the company should not counted in the denominator.

Assume, for example, that Free Trade, Inc. reports net profits of $385,000 on total employed assets of $4.5 million. Its ROAE would be:

$$\frac{\$385{,}000}{\$4{,}500{,}000} = 0.08555 \text{ (approximately 8.6\%)}$$

Free Trade can improve its ROAE by either raising its profits or reducing its employment of assets. If Free Trade nets $100,000 more in assets, its ratio will improve:

$$\frac{\$485{,}000}{\$4{,}500{,}000} = 0.1077 \text{ (approximately 10.8\%)}$$

Similarly, if Free Trade can improve its warehouse management and reduce its inventory by $100,000 (thus lowering its calculation of total assets), it can improve its ROAE ratio:

$$\frac{\$385{,}000}{\$4{,}400{,}000} = 0.0875 \text{ (exactly 8.75\%)}$$

In the context of a trademark infringement case, multiple ROAE calculations must be made, each one aimed at determining the return on a particular category of assets.[24] We would then continue to calculate the ROAE for each category of assets, except for intangible assets (the trademark asset). When we are finished, we should be left with the ROAE for the trademark asset.

For example, we might begin by *backing out* the return on property, plant, and equipment (PP&E). Let's assume that the company applies the ratio $\frac{\text{Net Profit}}{\text{PP \& E Employed}}$ and finds that its return on property, plant, and equipment is 18%. We would then multiply 18% by the net profit to determine the portion of the profit attributable to PP&E. Then, that amount would be subtracted from the net profit. The process

[24]A sophisticated variation of the ROAE procedure discussed above is followed in a proprietary program known as the ValCALC methodology, developed by CONSOR at http://www.consor.com/.

is then repeated for each category of assets, subtracting from net profit the amount in each case attributable to that category of assets. The balance remaining in net profit, after subtracting the amounts attributable to every category of assets except the trademark asset, will yield the return on the trademark asset.

For the sake of simplicity, let's assume that Free Trade, Inc. has five asset categories: PP&E, Working Capital, Accounts Receivable, Inventory, and Intangible Assets (consisting only of its single trademark asset). Let's further assume that after doing the math, we've calculated the following specific ROAEs and applied them to Free Trade's net profit of $385,000:

	RATIO	ROAE	CORRESPONDING PROFIT
PP&E	Net Profit / PP & E Employed	18%	$69,300
Working Capital	Net Profit / Working Capital Employed	14%	$53,900
Accounts Receivable	Net Profit / Accounts Receivable Employed	7.5%	$28,875
Inventory	Net Profit / Inventory Employed	21%	$80,850
Intangible Assets	Net Profit / Intangible Assets Employed	**39.5%**	**$152,075**

In this example, the ratios have all been expressed with specific denominators in order to target specific asset categories. The ROAE calculations are provided (without showing any underlying dollar figures). The ROAE calculations are then each multiplied by Free Trade's net profit of $385,000. So, for example, in the case of PP&E, 18% of $385,000 corresponds to profit of $69,300. After determining what portion of the profit corresponds to each of the four nontrademark asset categories (PP&E, Working Capital, Accounts Receivable, and Inventory), the value of the fifth category (Intangible Assets)—that is, the value of the trademark—can be determined by subtracting the other values from Free Trade's net profit of $385,000.

Thus, $385,000 – $69,300 – $53,900 – $28,875 – $80,850 = $152,075.

We can then conclude that the return on Free Trade's trademark asset is $152,075. We can also conclude, through simple math, that the percentage of profits attributable to the trademark is 39.5%. These figures may need to be corrected to account for particular circumstances, and the return of $152,075 may need to be adjusted to PV, depending on which figures were used to calculate the ratios.

17.19. Shortcuts and Rules of Thumb

Shortcuts and rules of thumb for estimating trademark damages are inherently flawed and should be approached with great caution. They are generally not reliable for constructing a true scientific measure of damages, nor will they withstand attack when used arbitrarily in a courtroom. However, several shortcuts and rules of thumb may assist attorneys in making rough initial evaluations about the value of a case and may, in fact, provide useful preliminary yardsticks for evaluation.

The Subtraction Method

The subtraction method is a useful form of quick math when two similar companies can be compared, one of which possesses the trademark asset, and the other of which does not. If Company A_T possesses the trademark and Company B_{NT} has no trademark, then we can compare the difference in value or in cash flows between the two companies:

$A_T - B_{NT}$ = Infringement Damages

Assume that Company A_T is manufacturing tires using a stolen brand or trademark, and it shows cash flows of $100,000. Company B_{NT} manufactures tires but uses no such brand or trademark, and it has cash flows of $67,000. Using the subtraction method, we can quickly estimate that the value of the trademark is $33,000, the difference in cash flows between the two companies:

$A_T - B_{NT}$ = Infringement Damages

$100,000 – $67,000 = $33,000

The Proportionate Value Method

The proportionate value method essentially inquires into what infringement has occurred and what portion of the value of the company's brand or trademark is burdened by that infringement. For example, assume that Sammy Food Service Corp. has manufactured a popular brand of popcorn branded as *Sammy's Sweet and Salty Pop-*

corn. The packaging features a happy boy ("Sammy") swirling in a flurry of popcorn. The depiction of the happy boy has become an instantly recognizable logo image used by Sammy Foods in its billboard advertising and supermarket merchandising. The Sammy's Sweet and Salty brand is now valued at $25 million.

Assume that a Mexican peanut seller has penetrated the U.S. market aggressively, using an image that features a very similar happy boy, swirling in what appears to be a whirlwind of peanuts. If Sammy Foods pursues an infringement action against the peanut maker for encroaching upon its happy boy design, it may wish to know what portion of the market value of Sammy's brand should be apportioned to the image of the happy boy. In other words, what share of the market value of $25 million represents the proportionate value of the happy boy design? If the happy boy design were estimated at being 20% of the Sammy's brand, then the proportionate value of the infringed logo would be 20% of $25 million ($25 million x .2 = $5 million).

The 25% Rule

The 25% rule holds that a fair royalty rate equals about one-quarter of a licensee's (infringer's) anticipated pretax profits. Once popular in patent infringement cases, the rule has now been rejected by the Federal Circuit Court of Appeals and is no longer a reliable gauge for calculating damages in an intellectual property context. However, it still provides a starting point for discussions and negotiations in trademark cases where the parties are attempting to establish a reasonable royalty, and where data is available to support the market values being used.

In a royalty calculation, an infringer would be obligated to pay damages equal to a hypothetical royalty owed to the intellectual property owner, as if the infringer had licensed the property rather than infringed upon it. The 25% rule treats the infringer as the hypothetical licensee who must pay a hypothetical royalty rate based on 25% (or more) of the marginal profits realized by using the asset in question. The 25% rule is flawed for many reasons, and it may ultimately overestimate the value of a reasonable royalty. Still, if data from product sales and other market measures can be used to substantiate a 25% rate, then the rule is arguably still a viable shortcut for establishing a baseline royalty rate.

The 5% Rule

The 5% rule is another crude rule of thumb for determining a royalty rate. Under this rule, the starting point for negotiations is 5% of gross sales. For speedy off-the-cuff discussions, this rule requires only a gross sales figure. If an infringer has made gross sales of $2.2 million, the 5% rule would hold that a reasonable baseline royalty for stealing the trademark would be $110,000. Negotiations could then ensue with the purpose of fine-tuning the figure, perhaps by incorporating other factors such as the cost of overhead tied to the reported sales.

As with all rules of thumb, the 5% rule fails to consider industry-specific factors and the wide variety of costs and other factors that may invalidate such mathematical shortcuts. Indeed, it may be more appropriate in some cases to fashion a rule-of-thumb based on a percentage of *net sales*. Still, as a benchmark, the 5% rule or variations thereof permit attorneys to roughly impute royalty values to an infringer, initiating the process of assessing damages.

17.20. Other Techniques and Considerations

As noted in various disclaimers, the use of formulas, ratios, and shortcuts for calculating damages in the context of a trademark infringement is potentially fraught with error if based on inadequate data, computed without appropriate adjustments for particular circumstances, or considered without necessary verification. Each case raises a peculiar set of circumstances arising in a specific market, in a specific industry, affecting specific products, and unfolding during a specific period of time.

Because of the many variables, and the need to apply specific approaches to specific cases, it is important to consider the full range of statutory rights in a trademark infringement case, as well as the ever-growing variety of damage calculation techniques. Here, below, are brief summaries of some of the other considerations, theories, approaches, and techniques available in calculating patent infringement damages.

Disgorgement. A trademark infringement plaintiff, unlike a patent infringement plaintiff, is authorized to seek a disgorgement of the defendant's profits. This alternative to establishing lost profits allows the trademark plaintiff simply to prove the revenue generated by the infringer through the sales of infringing products. The burden then shifts to the infringer (defendant) to prove its costs and expenses tied to the sales. Revenue minus costs equals profit, and that is what the infringer must disgorge.

Orderly Disposal Value. Under the orderly disposal method, a trademark is valued at its liquidation value, as if the company were dissolving and selling off its assets in an orderly fashion. This approach necessarily reduces the value of the trademark by eliminating the context of a profitable going concern. On the other hand, the value is intended to be based on an orderly, unrushed disposal, not a forced liquidation or "fire sale" situation, and should therefore reflect a full liquidation value in the marketplace. Such an approach could apply to a trademark that is infringed while its owner is in bankruptcy.

Expected Profit Margin. This theory assumes that an infringer is collecting excess profit by virtue of the infringement. Therefore, the lawful owner of the trademark should receive the excess profits, measured as that quantum of profit that exceeds the infringer's normal profit. Calculating the infringer's normal profit margin (that is, what it would earn in a particular industry and marketplace without the infringed trademark) is perhaps an elusive, if not impossible, estimate to project. Yet, if reliable evidence of a normal profit margin can be established, then this margin should be subtracted from the *expected* profit margin with the infringed trademark in order to establish a reasonable royalty rate to use in a damages calculation.

Monte Carlo Simulation. Monte Carlo simulation refers to a series of computerized data generated randomly through a process of simulating different scenarios in which the trademark is being used. A Monte Carlo simulation will generate a random set of data, from which values can be drawn. The value of the trademark is determined from this distribution of values based on the inputs used in the process. Monte Carlo methods are widely recognized in finance, in the sciences, and in other fields where statistical methods are applied to account for risk and uncertainty.

Specific Statutory Damage Ranges. Statutory damages are specifically recognized, within a range of amounts, in a number of areas, such as for the use of counterfeit marks and the infringement of domain names. Damages may also be available for "cyber-squatting," that is, for unlawfully using another's domain name or a name that infringes a trademark or another domain name.

Blurring, Tarnishment, and Dilution. Blurring refers to chipping away at a trademark by distorting its purpose and intention and thereby eroding its distinctive character. Tarnishment occurs when an unauthorized party ties a trademark to lower-quality goods or takes other action to tarnish the image of the lawful trademark owner's product. Dilution refers more generally to the process of undermining the ability of the trademark owner to identify and distinguish its goods, effectively watering down the value of the trademark by some unlawful usage or improper competitive practice. These concepts are covered variously by the Federal Trademark Dilution Act and the Trademark Dilution Revision Act, as well as a wide variety of state laws, and various federal and state regulations.

Cost Savings. A trademark owner may realize cost savings and operating profit advantages because of the positive economic impact that the trademark has on advertising, branding, promotion, and sales expenses. By quantifying the advantage enjoyed by these reduced costs, the trademark holder can establish another element of damages caused by an infringement.

Product Sales Volume. A trademark owner may also realize heightened sales of particular products that carry the trademark in question. An infringement may correspondingly destroy the advantage enjoyed by the trademark owner by reducing the product sales volume. Determining the value of this incremental reduction in sales volume adds another measure of damages.

Unjust Enrichment. Damages based on unjust enrichment are recognized in trademark law and may be calculated as equaling the amount of the defendant's profits, regardless of whether the defendant exhibited any willful or deliberate conduct.

Loss of Goodwill. Damages for trademark infringement can also include a loss to a company's goodwill, particularly when the company's image has been devalued by the infringer's sale of counterfeit goods of lower quality. While the measure of goodwill in such a case can be elusive, a projection reduced to PV would represent a valid claim for damages in an appropriate case.

Treble Damages. The Lanham Act permits an award of three times actual damages in an appropriate case. Ordinarily, willful infringement must be shown in such cases. Courts are given full discretion as to whether to award treble damages.

Attorneys' Fees. The Lanham Act also permits an award of attorneys' fees to the prevailing party in "exceptional cases."

[Copyrights]

Statutory Damage Schemes

17.21. Actual Damages Plus Profits

Under the U.S. Copyright Act,[25] an infringer of a copyright is liable for either (1) the copyright owner's actual damages *and* any additional profits earned by the infringer, *or* (2) statutory damages as provided by the Act. The first approach—actual damages plus profits—requires the copyright owner to present proof of the infringer's gross revenue.[26] The infringer must then prove his deductible expenses and the elements of profit attributable to factors other than the copyrighted work.[27] Then, the copyright owner may add any additional profits enjoyed by the infringer which were not taken into account in computing the actual damages. The formula is:

Infringer's Gross Revenues
– Infringer's Deductible Expenses
– Infinger's Profits Unrelated to the Copyrighted Work
+ Infringer's Additional Profits Not Already Counted in Gross Revenues
= Copyright Owner's Recoverable Damages

An infringer has the burden of showing its deductible expenses that should be deducted from the amount of its gross revenues. It cannot arbitrarily or simplistically report its expenses. It must demonstrate the nexus between its actual overhead and its production of the infringing material. The infringer's overhead expenses could include, for example, rent, personnel costs, entertainment, and public relations ex-

[25] 17 U.S.C. § 501, *et. seq.*
[26] 17 U.S.C. § 504(b).
[27] *Id.*

penses. The court will likely not scrutinize these expenses, line item by line item, but may inquire into the proofs as to how they are connected to the production of the goods or products in question.

In addition to identifying its deductible expenses and their nexus to the infringing material, the infringer must demonstrate a fair, accurate, and practical method of allocating the overhead expenses to the infringement.[28] In this regard, there is no single allocation formula. The burden falls on the infringer to offer a fair and acceptable formula for determining what portion of its overhead is attributable to the infringing items at issue. Three of the recognized approaches are the cost-of-production method, the number-of-products method, and the sales revenue method.

Cost of Production Method

Under the cost-of-production method, the infringer calculates a percentage of its total production costs attributable to the infringing items. So, for example, assume that a particular infringement produced the following data:

Gross Revenues From Infringing Products	$14,500,000
Total Production Costs	$ 8,300,000
Percentage of Production Costs Assignable to Infringing Items	25%
Profits Unrelated to the Copyrighted Work	$ 1,570,000
Additional Profits	—0—
Actual Damages	$10,855,000

In this simplified scenario, the infringer can credibly and verifiably allocate only 25% of its $8.3 million in production costs to the $14.5 million in revenue. In other words, its production costs attributable to the infringement are $2,075,000, which are then subtracted from revenues, to produce an adjusted revenue figure of $12,425,000. From that figure, we would further credit the infringer with its profits unrelated to the infringement, thus subtracting another $1,570,000.

[28] *See, e.g.,* Hamil America, Inc. v. GFI, 193 F. 3d 92 (2d Cir. 1999).

Since there are no additional profits to which the copyright owner is entitled, the total amount of actual damages (recoverable damages) is $10,855,000.

Number-of-Products Method

Another approach to allocating overhead expenses is the number-of-products method. Particularly well-suited for cases involving copyrighted music in which publishing costs per song are indistinguishable,[29] this approach simply allocates overhead equally among all of the products produced by the infringer, including both the copyrighted items and unrelated items. Suppose, for example, that a music publisher infringed the copyright of a particular song entitled "I Love the Law," and that this particular song was just one of its 30 published songs. Let's assume, too, that the fixed indirect overhead costs for the publisher were $950,000—an expense that was not demonstrably attributable to any one song more than another. Applying the number-of-products method, we would calculate the portion of the overhead attributable to the infringing title, "I Love the Law," as representing $\frac{1}{30}$ of the total overhead expense.

Gross Revenues from Infringing Products	$2,100,000
Total Publishing Overhead	$ 950,000
Number of Infringing Songs	1
Total Number of Songs	30
Percentage of Songs	3.3%
Profits Unrelated to the Copyrighted Work	$ 175,000
Additional Profits	$ 64,900
Actual Damages	$1,958,550

In this approach, the infringing song represents only $\frac{1}{30}$ or 0.33 or 3.3% of the total publishing overhead of $950,000. This means that, all things being otherwise equal, the title, "I Love the Law," accounts for $31,350 in proportional publishing-related overhead expenses. This amount deducted from the revenue of $2.1 million yields an adjusted revenue figure of $2,068,650. The infringer's profits unrelated to the

[29] *See, e.g.*, Wilkie v. Santly Brothers, 139 F. 2d 264 (2d Cir. 1943).

copyrighted song are then subtracted ($175,000), and the infringer's additional profits which are derived from the infringing activity but have not already been accounted for ($64,900), are added back, resulting in actual damages of $1,958,550.

The Sales Revenue Method

The revenue generated by selling the infringing product represents a percentage of the infringer's overall revenue. That percentage of sales can thus be presumed to be the percentage of overhead attributable to the publication of the infringing product. Assume a book publisher has published seven titles, of which one is claimed to be an infringement of a copyrighted manuscript published years earlier. If the overhead attributable to the publication of the infringing book is not easily distinguishable or incrementally assignable to that book, then the revenue generated by the sales of the book would provide a gauge of the estimated overhead attributed to the infringing publication.

Suppose that the infringing publication grossed $500,000 in sales, while all seven books together grossed $2.5 million in sales. The dollar sales from the infringing product could then be set as $\frac{\$500,000}{\$2,500,000}$ or $\frac{1}{5}$ or 20%. Overhead expenses attributable to the infringing title would then be set at 20% of the publisher's overhead.

The three methods for calculating the infringer's deductible expenses discussed above are not the exclusive methods and, in fact, each case presents specific peculiar circumstances that may require the application of other reasonable and reliable approaches. As discussed herein, these methods have been simplified in order to present a comprehensible illustration. In particular cases, however, the circumstances may be significantly more complicated, requiring the introduction of other weighting factors, adjustments, or corrections to the final amount of actual damages.

Under the Copyright Act, too, the copyright owner elects to waive its right to actual damages, choosing instead to invoke the second prong of the Act's damages provision and demand statutory damages, as discussed in the section below.

17.22. Statutory Damages

Under the Copyright Act, the copyright owner may choose at any time before final judgment is rendered to recover, instead of actual damages and profits, an award of statutory damages.[30] A court may award statutory damages, in its discretion, ranging from $750 to $30,000, and where a willful infringement has been proven, up to $150,000. On the other hand, an innocent infringer who is demonstrably not aware of the infringement could be forced to pay a reduced statutory damage award of as little as $200.

The statute does not imply or presume that proof of willful infringement will automatically entitle the copyright owner to the maximum award of $150,000. Indeed, a judge has full discretion, and could order a willful infringer to pay an amount just barely over the nonwillful infringement limit of $30,000, depending on the circumstances of the case.[31] Statutory damages are not intended to provide a plaintiff with a windfall recovery, and some courts have observed that the statutory award should bear some relationship to the actual damages suffered by the copyright owner.[32] Smaller statutory copyright infringement judgments have also been approved in cases in which the infringer's profits were shown to be quite meager, and where the infringer was sufficiently punished by having to incur its own attorneys' fees.[33]

Under the Act, the award of damages is based on the number of copyrighted works infringed, and the number of infringers, but not on the number of incidents of infringement. A single infringer of a single work is liable for a single amount of damages under the statute, no matter how many acts of infringement are claimed, and regardless of whether the acts were separate, isolated, related, or unrelated.

While stated simply, the determination of how many separate registered works are infringed is often highly controverted, taking into account whether the works were registered jointly on a single application

---

[30]17 U.S.C. § 504(c).

[31]*See, e.g.,* Clever Covers, Inc. v. Southwest Florida Storm Defense, LLC, 554 F. Supp. 2d 1303 (M.D. Fla. 2008) (awarding $31,000 for each of two infringed copyrights, for a total statutory damage award of $62,000).

[32]*See, e.g.*, Peer International Corporation v. Luna Records, 887 F. Supp. 560, 568-69 (S.D.N.Y. 1995).

[33]*See* Bryant v. Media Right Productions, Inc., 603 F. 3d 135 (2d Cir. 2010), in which the court awarded statutory damages of only $2,400, finding that a music wholesaler's infringement generated meager profits and deterrence was effectuated by defendants having to pay their own attorneys' fees.

as a single self-contained work or whether they each have some independent economic value.[34] The court may also consider how the copyright owner organizes, publishes, markets, and sells its copyrighted material, as evidence of whether one or more items represent a single compilation of works or separately copyrighted works, each individually infringed.[35]

In addition to statutory damages, the Copyright Act also provides for injunctive relief,[36] the impoundment and destruction of infringing articles,[37] costs and attorneys' fees,[38] and criminal penalties,[39] including forfeiture and destruction of infringing works and restitution to the copyright owner.[40] These legal remedies are beyond the scope of this book, but they may have an impact on the court's determination of damages and ought to be considered concurrently with any claim for statutory damages.

17.23. Punitive Damages

While the Copyright Act makes no mention of punitive damages, it does not necessarily prohibit them. There are, in fact, competing schools of thought about the availability of punitive damages, and different courts have offered divergent responses to the idea. The weight of authority today is clearly against the availability of punitive damages, but proponents of punitive damages are tenacious in their efforts.

The strict interpretation of the Copyright Act holds that punitive damages are precluded by law because the statute specifically delineates those categories of damages that are available, recognizing, in fact, that under the statute, a willful infringer can already be saddled

---

[34]37 C.F.R. § 202.3(b)(4)(i); Gamma Audio & Video, Inc. v. Ean-Chea, 11 F. 3d 1106, 1117 (1st Cir. 1993).

[35]*See, e.g.*, Tattoo Art, Inc. v. TAT Intern., LLC,—F. Supp. 2d—, 2011 WL 2585376 (E.D.Va. 2011) (in which the court recognized one statutory damage award of $20,000 per book of tattoos infringed, for each of 24 books, totaling $480,000, rather than awarding damages for each tattoo image infringed).

[36]17 U.S.C. § 502.

[37]17 U.S.C. § 503.

[38]17 U.S,C. § 505.

[39]17 U.S.C. § 506.

[40]17 U.S.C. § 506((b).

with a judgment as high as $150,000. The U.S. Supreme Court and various federal district courts have thus stated that the remedies for infringement consist only of those expressly prescribed by the Act.[41]

On the other hand, punitive damages have been awarded in cases in which malice, wrongful motive, or reckless indifference have been established. In such cases, punitive damages have often been pleaded under a state law and/or common law theory.[42] In one case, a federal jury in Tennessee awarded $3.5 million in punitive damages for a copyright infringement, but the verdict was later reversed as excessive.[43] Most of the pro-punitive cases seem to be based primarily in New York, and they have largely been discounted or rejected by more recent rulings.

Infringer's Accounting Methods

17.24. Full Absorption Costing

In presenting its expenses attributable to the infringing products, the infringer can apply a full absorption costing approach or a variable costing approach. The full absorption costing approach, sometimes known as simply "full costing," treats all costs as part of the cost of goods sold (COGS), without distinguishing them as fixed costs or variable costs. It effectively expenses *all* costs incurred in the manufacture of a product, including direct costs, such as materials and labor, and overhead costs, such as physical plant and utility costs.

With full absorption costing, the costs of manufacture are said to be fully absorbed by the units being produced. To depict the full absorption method on an income statement, we would simply subtract the COGS from the lost sales to show the gross profit. Selling costs, general, and administrative (known as SG&A) would then be deducted to

---

[41]Sony Corp. of America v. Universal City Studios, Inc., 464 U.S. 417,431, 104 S. Ct. 774 (1984); Curcio Webb LLC v. National Benefit Programs Agency, Inc., 367 F. Supp. 2d 1191 (S.D. Ohio 2005).

[42]*See, e.g.*, Roy Export Co. Establishment of Vaduz, Liechtenstein, Black Inc. v. Columbia Broadcasting System, Inc., 503 F. Supp. 1137 (S.D.N.Y. 1980); TVT Records v. Island Def Jam Music Group, 288 F. Supp. 2d 506 (S.D.N.Y. 2003); Blanch v. Koons, 329 F. Supp. 2d 568 (S.D.N.Y. 2004).

[43]Bridgeport Music Inc. v. Justin Combs Pub., 507 F.3d 470 (6th Cir. 2007).

produce net income. Consider this abridged income statement for Hypo Company showing the full absorption costing approach:

HYPO COMPANY

Income Statement

Full Absorption Costing Approach

LOST SALES	$990,000
COGS	$750,000
GROSS PROFIT	$240,000
TOTAL SG&A	$157,000
NET INCOME **(Lost Profit)**	$ 83,000

As we see above, the COGS is stated as one hybrid figure ($750,000) and is not separated into fixed and variable costs. As such, costs are fully attributed to the products in question and are therefore totally deducted from the sales revenue of $990,000. The resulting profit of $240,000 is then reduced by total selling expenses of $157,000, which are, again, not separated into fixed and variable costs. This leaves a net income (or in the case of an infringement, a lost profit) of $83,000.

17.25. Variable Costing

Variable costing assigns only variable production costs to the COGS. In other words, those costs that vary with the volume of production—such as raw materials, labor, and manufacturing overhead—are deducted from sales to produce the contribution margin, which is effectively the lost profits. Fixed costs are shifted out of this first equation. After the contribution margin is calculated, then fixed costs are deducted.

Using the figures for Hypo Company shown on the income statement in the preceding section above, assume that the COGS ($750,000) actually consisted of variable product costs of $500,000 and fixed costs (physical plant and factory operations) of $250,000. Assume, also, that the total SG&A ($157,000) consisted of variable SG&A of $80,000 and fixed SG&A of $77,000. Here is what Hypo

Company's income statement might look like, in abridged format, applying the variable costing approach:

HYPO COMPANY

Income Statement

Variable Costing Approach

LOST SALES	$990,000
VARIABLE COGS	$500,000
VARIABLE SG&A	$ 80,000
CONTRIBUTION MARGIN **(Lost Profit)**	$410,000
FIXED COSTS (Plant/Factory)	$250,000
FIXED SG&A	$ 77,000
NET INCOME	$ 83,000

Under the variable costing approach, lost profit is stated as the contribution margin and is calculated after deducting only the variable manufacturing costs (COGS) and variable selling expenses (SG&A).

The significance of the two accounting methods—full absorption versus variable costing—boils down to the definition of variable and fixed costs. In a copyright infringement case, the parties may disagree as to what constitutes a variable cost. Applying a variable costing approach, an infringer will want to argue that a greater share of the company costs are actually variable costs and are therefore deductible from sales in determining the lost contribution margin (lost profits). Some costs are, in fact, partly fixed and partly variable, such as electricity. Electricity is generally a fixed operational cost of running the factory, the warehouse, and other facilities necessary in the production of goods. Yet electrical usage may vary with increased output and is, therefore, a variable cost too.

Exactly which expense is defined as variable and which is defined as fixed depends ultimately on whether the expense changes with an increase in production. If, for example, ordinary fixed expenses, such as heating, increase as a consequence of increased output, they must be considered above-the-line, as variable expenses deducted from sales in calculating the contribution margin. More precisely, it is the portion of the heating bill, electric bill, or any other overhead expense that is actually increasing with production which thereby becomes deductible from the ultimate revenue generated from sales. In this regard, both plaintiff and defendant in a copyright case will want to analyze closely what costs are defined as variable and fixed.

In the end, full absorption costing will provide a snapshot of what the infringer's liability would be if all costs were tied to the units of production, were grouped together, and were deducted collectively as COGS. A full absorption income statement may also provide a useful comparison in cases where the infringer insists that a greater amount of its overall expenses should be treated as variable and therefore deductible. But it is the variable costing method that will yield the most direct procedure for isolating the lost contribution margin and calculating lost profits. For the infringer to assign any portion of its overhead (fixed costs) to the variable cost category, it will need to show exactly how that overhead varies with production of the infringing products.

Chapter 18

Family Law Formulas

Time Value Calculations

18.1. Division of Assets

Perhaps no area of law entails more creative and tenacious negotiating tactics than family law. Dividing the assets in a divorce case can be a difficult exercise, both financially and emotionally. Suddenly confronted with the prospect of living separately, divorce clients grapple with paying separate mortgage and utility bills, dividing their assets, and supporting their children, while losing their economies of scale.

There is no single method for settling a divorce case, dividing marital property, or resolving an alimony, palimony, or child support action. *What's the value of the house? The boat? The pension? The family business?* These are often challenging questions. Even after the value of the property is established, there may no easy way to divide it, or for one party to afford to buy out the opposing party's interest.

Of course, a party could agree to pay less than he actually owes, but that would require an estimate of what he actually owes. Similarly, a party could agree to pay a lump sum sometime in the future—say, for example, three years from now—but that would require a determination of the future value of the payment. In other cases, a party could agree to an installment payment plan, but even then, it would be necessary to determine how many installments, over what period of time, and how the recipient would be compensated for the delay in receiving full payment.

In fact, most divorce cases involve a series of trade-offs in which the parties separately relinquish their interest in various jointly held assets. For example, a wife may agree to waive her interest in her husband's pension, in exchange for the husband's agreement to waive his claim to his share of the equity in the marital home. The parties may also trade property rights for support rights, such as when a party waives an interest in a home or a business or a motor vehicle, in exchange for some term of alimony or spousal support.

Is any of this scientific?

Is it sufficient to say that one party will waive her right to $100,000 in future retirement funds in exchange for the other party waiving his $100,000 share of the value of a family home? What if the retirement funds would not possibly be paid for another 10 years? What if the house would not logically be sold until after the youngest child graduates from high school, five years from now? Each of these scenarios implicates the time value of money. Thus, it is necessary to calculate the present value or the future value of the deal, as discussed in Chapter 4.[1]

Present Value

Calculating present value allows us to accept a *discounted* amount of money today instead of the actual amount we're entitled to receive at some point in the future. So, for example, if a wife is entitled to receive $100,000 in three years from her husband, there must be some lesser amount that he can pay her today to buy out her $100,000 future interest. We would thus want to calculate the present value of $100,000.

Similarly, if a husband plans to waive his claim for $300,000 that he would be entitled to receive five years from now, the amount he is presently waiving is something less than $300,000. We would want to know the present value of $300,000. Unless all assets in a negotiation consist of assets that are immediately available and distributable, then it may be necessary to apply the present value test to discount those assets to today's dollars.

Let's apply a specific example. Mr. and Mrs. Jones hold a secure investment that is slowly and safely growing and will be worth $800,000 in two years. They agree that they are each entitled to one-half of the funds. The investment earns 8% interest but will not be

[1]See Sections 5.1 through 5.5.

available for distribution for two years. Mr. Jones wants to claim the entire investment when it matures in two years. How much should he pay to Mrs. Jones to buy out her $400,000 share today? The question asks: what is the present value of a specific amount to be paid in the future? Assume 8% interest.

Let's revisit the steps for calculating present value.

Step 1: Add the interest rate to the number 1. This gives us 1.08.

Step 2: Raise 1.08 to the second power because the money will not be available for two years. Thus, $1.08^2 = 1.1664$.

Step 3: Now, divide $400,000 by 1.1664 to determine the present value. Thus, $400,000 divided by 1.1664 equals $342,935.53. That is the amount which Mrs. Jones must demand today (assuming 8% interest) in order to waive her right to $400,000 in two years.

Here is the formula:

$$PV = \frac{FV}{(1 + i)^n}$$

where PV equals present value, FV equals future value, i is the interest rate (or discount rate) and n is the number of years.

$$\text{Thus, } PV = \frac{\$400{,}000}{(1 + .08)^2} = \frac{\$400{,}000}{1.1664} = \$342{,}935.53.$$

Let's try another scenario. Mr. and Mrs. Smith, through their attorneys, enter into a stipulation that provides the following:

(a) Mr. Smith will transfer his right, title, and interest in the marital home to Mrs. Smith.

(b) Mrs. Smith will occupy the home until the youngest child graduates from high school in seven years. At that point, Mrs. Smith will sell the home or refinance it in her name alone.

(c) Mr. Smith will receive his 50% share of the current equity in the home equal to $150,000, without any assessment of interest, at the time the home is sold or refinanced.

(d) Mrs. Smith will pay all mortgage payments and household bills from the alimony Mr. Smith is paying her, until such time as the house is sold or refinanced.

Before the Smith divorce is finalized, however, Mr. Smith expresses an interest in obtaining payment of his $150,000 share right away. He recognizes that he will have to accept a lesser amount if payment is going to be made immediately. Mrs. Smith has told her lawyer that she would renegotiate the stipulation and buy out her husband's $150,000 claim against the property if she could get a better deal. *What would be a better deal?* Let's start by calculating the present value of $150,000. Assume that a 4% interest rate applies under current market conditions.

$$PV = \frac{FV}{(1 + i)^n}$$

$$PV = \frac{\$150{,}000}{(1.04)^7}$$

$$PV = \frac{\$150{,}000}{1.32}$$

$$PV = \$113{,}636.36$$

The present value of $150,000 due seven years from now, based on a 4% interest rate (discount rate), is $113,636.36. In other words, in order to get a better deal, Mrs. Smith should be willing to pay her husband any amount today that is less than $113,636.36. The less Mr. Smith will accept (below $113,636.36), the better the deal. Under no circumstances should Mrs. Smith pay her husband more than $113,636.36, given the current interest rate.

Net Present Value

Net present value,[2] as you may recall, is the present value minus the investment. In other words, it is the present value of an asset, reduced by the cost of obtaining it. In the context of a divorce case, net present value can be viewed as the present value of a particular asset minus the cost to the spouse who wants that asset. If Mr. Smith wants his share of the house today, instead of seven years from now when the house is sold, he will need to know the present value of his share *and* what he will have to trade, or waive, or spend, to obtain the share.

Assume that Mrs. Smith will not pay anything to Mr. Smith to settle the issue over the equity in the house unless Mr. Smith gives her the coin collection, the stamp collection, and a Victorian doll collection. The appraised values of the three collections are:

[2]See Section 5.5.

Coin Collection:	\$ 9,650
Stamp Collection:	\$ 8,210
Doll Collection:	\$20,060
Total	\$37,920

Mr. Smith's 50% share of the three collections: $\frac{\$37,920}{2} = \$18,960$

In effect, Mr. Smith will have to give away his 50% share of the three collections (or \$18,960 in assets) to get a payment of \$150,000 in seven years for his share of the house. Assume that Mrs. Smith was willing to pay the \$150,000, discounted to present value, provided that Mr. Smith transfers the coin collection, the stamp collection, and the Victorian doll collection. We learned above that the present value of \$150,000 payable in seven years, calculated at 4% interest, is \$113,636.36 today. The net present value, however, requires us to lower this figure by Mr. Smith's cost; that is, by the \$18,960 he will spend to close the deal. The formula for net present value is:

$$NPV = \frac{FV}{(1 + i)^n} - \text{Cost}$$

$$NPV = \frac{\$150,000}{(1.04)^7} - \text{Cost}$$

$$NPV = \$113,636.36 - \$18,960$$

$$NPV = \$94,676.36$$

In the end, Mr. Smith should only make this deal if he is willing to part with the coins, the stamps, and the Victorian dolls, and if he is willing to accept what amounts to a net payment of \$94,676.36 for waiving his rights in the marital home.

Net-Net-Net Present Value

In the tug of war of a matrimonial dissolution case, the calculation of net present value may, in fact, be only the first stage of negotiations. Imagine this chain of events:

March 5. Mr. Smith demands \$150,000 as his share of the marital home, payable in seven years.

March 6. Mrs. Smith tentatively agrees.

March 10. Mr. Smith determines that he needs cash much sooner, and indicates that he will accept a lesser payment if Mrs. Smith will pay it today.

March 15. Mrs. Smith demands that Mr. Smith give her the coin collection, the stamp collection, and the doll collection before she'll pay him anything today.

March 24. Mr. Smith tentatively agrees, but indicates that he wants to keep the stocks in BIG Corporation, valued at $18,300.

March 28. Mrs. Smith tentatively agrees, provided that Mr. Smith gives her a painting worth $1,900.

When a pattern of trade-offs unfolds, as is common in divorce cases, it has the effect of requiring the net present value calculation to be extended and netted over and over again. Indeed, if Mr. Smith's share of the house is the driving issue in the negotiations, the calculation of net present value effectively becomes a determination of net-net-net present value.

$113,636.36 – $18,960 + $18,300 – $1,900
= $111,076.35

At the end of the negotiation,[3] Mr. Smith would be netting only $111,076.35 and keeping the BIG Corporation stocks.

Future Value

Assume that Mr. and Mrs. Lawful are part-owners of a family business that is subject to equitable distribution in their divorce. The Lawfuls own 50% of the business, and another couple owns the other 50%. Mr. Lawful intends to remain in the business after the divorce while Mrs. Lawful is happy to relinquish her share for a reasonable sum of money. Under an agreement between the two couples, however, no portion of the business may be divided, distributed, or sold for four years. The couples have further agreed that the buyout amount for any party would be fixed at $125,000, payable at the four-year mark. Under the

[3]Of course, this example simplifies the negotiation by excluding other asset tradeoffs, tax considerations, and the impact of alimony or child support, some or all of which could also potentially change the bottom line for Mr. and Mrs. Smith.

agreement, if Mr. Lawless sought to acquire his wife's share in the business, he would be obligated to pay her $125,000.

As part of their negotiations, Mr. Lawful agrees to give Mrs. Lawful $90,000 today instead of paying her $125,000 and dividing a business interest that won't be available for distribution for another four years. *Is $90,000 a good number?* The answer is to determine the future value of $90,000—in other words, what $90,000 would be worth in four years. Assume, in this instance, that Mrs. Lawful would invest the money and earn 8% interest. So the question is: What will $90,000 paid today be worth in four years at 8% interest? Follow the procedure for calculating future value:

Step 1: Add the interest rate, in decimal form, to the number 1. Thus, $1 + 08 = 1.08$

Step 2: Raise 1.08 to the fourth power, to account for the four years. $(1.08)^4 = 1.36$

Step 3: Multiply $90,000 by 1.36. [90,000 x 1.36 = $122,400]

The formula is:

$$FV = PV\ (1 + i)^n$$

$$FV = \$90{,}000(1.08)^4$$

$$FV = \$90{,}000(1.36)$$

$$FV = \$122{,}400$$

Mr. Lawful now knows that $90,000 paid to his wife today is the equivalent of $122,400 paid in four years. For Mr. Lawful, this would be an acceptable deal because he is spending less than the $125,000 he would be obligated to pay in four years.

On the other hand, if Mrs. Lawful demanded $95,000 today for her share of the business, Mr. Lawful would be overpaying (assuming the 8% interest rate remains in effect).

$$FV = PV\ (1 + i)^n$$

$$FV = \$90{,}000(1.08)^4$$

$$FV = \$129{,}200$$

A payment of $95,000 today is the equivalent of paying approximately $129,200 in four years, which is greater than Mr. Lawful's contractual obligation of $125,000.

By examining the relationship between present value and future value, we can quickly calculate the actual value of assets under negotiation, while taking into consideration the timing of the transfer or payment of those assets. In this case, we know that $90,000 is an acceptable number for Mr. Lawful, and that $95,000 is too great a number. So what number should Mr. Lawful pay to his wife today if he wants to give her exactly the value of the $125,000 she would be entitled to in four years—no more and no less. Let's revisit present value. The question is, what is the present value of $125,000, that would be payable in four years, using an 8% discount rate?

$$PV = \frac{FV}{(1+i)^n}$$

$$PV = \frac{\$125{,}000}{(1.08)^4}$$

$$PV = \$91{,}911.76$$

Therefore, Mr. Lawful should pay no more than $91,911.76 today to satisfy his wife's entitlement to $125,000 in four years.

Calculating these figures can provide useful bargaining leverage for both of the parties. It can also assist lawyers in advising their clients as negotiations are unfolding. For example, assume that Mrs. Lawful had been willing to accept $90,000 today to buy out her interest in the business. However, Mrs. Lawful demanded that Mr. Lawful pay her attorney's outstanding bill of $1,500 as a final deal closer.

Mr. Lawful is offended at this request and refuses to make the deal. Mr. Lawful's attorney, however, has calculated the present values and future values of the deal. He encourages Mr. Lawful to counter-offer $750 toward the attorney's fees, in order to lay the issue to rest. After all, by paying Mrs. Lawful $90,000 for her interest in the business plus $750 toward her attorney's fees, Mr. Lawful has still spent less than the present value of $125,000 ($91,911.76), a point that leaves Mr. Lawful with a sense of momentary victory.

18.2. Alimony and Spousal Support

In many family law cases, the more financially endowed spouse (often known as the obligor or payor spouse) does not wish to pay alimony, spousal support, or maintenance to the dependent spouse. Although alimony is no longer tax-deductible to the payor, there may be a number of reasons why he might resist or object to making periodic support payments to his spouse. The scenarios below demonstrate how some of the basic formulas discussed in this book can be put to good use in Family Court.

Discounted Cash Flows

Husband doesn't want to pay alimony. But he will make a deal by which a certain amount of his own money can be invested at 5% to generate a cash flow to his wife over the next five years. The parties negotiate long and hard. Wife proposes that she receive a cash flow of $100,000 in year 1, $300,000 in years 2, 3, and 4, and $100,000 in year 5. She demands that Husband invest $1 million to fund the cash flows which she seeks. Husband tells his lawyer that he has no objection to Wife's yearly cash flows, but seeks the lawyer's advice as to whether a $1 million investment is appropriate. How far will $1 million stretch, at 5% interest, over five years, given the precise payout schedule Wife wants?

The inquiry is answered by the discounted cash flow procedure.[4]

Step 1: Add the interest rate to 1. Thus, 1 + 05 = 1.05.

Step 2: Use 1.05 for year 1. For year 2, use 1.05 to the second power. For year 3, it's 1.05 to the third power . . . and so forth.

Step 3: Divide the amount to be paid in each year by the finalized interest rate. Thus, in year 1, we divide $100,000 by 1.05. In year 2, we divide $300,000 by 1.1025 (which is 1.05 the second power). In year 3, we divide $300,000 by 1.1576 (which is 1.05 to the third power) . . . and so forth.

Step 4: Add each year's totals together.

Follow the complete formula below:

YEAR 1: $\$100{,}000/1.05$
YEAR 2: $+\ \$300{,}000/(1.05)^2$
YEAR 3: $+\ \$300{,}000/(1.05)^3$
YEAR 4: $+\ \$300{,}000/(1.05)^4$
YEAR 5: $+\ \$100{,}000/(1.05)^5$
Total: = $951,666.

[4]See Section 5.5.

So, the net present value of the cash flows to the Wife would be $951,666.

In other words, Husband will need to invest only $951,666 to meet Wife's five-year cash flow proposal, not $1 million. Demonstrating how the discounted cash flow procedure works could thus save Husband over $48,000.

Permanent Alimony (Perpetuities)

Husband doesn't want to write alimony checks, but the parties agree that Wife qualifies for permanent alimony. The parties agree that Wife should receive $100,000 per year for life. If Husband has a significant estate and is able to invest a lump sum at 10%, how much should he invest to generate cash flows of $100,000 per year for Wife? Answer: $1 million. The formula is simple: Divide the Wife's annual amount by the interest rate: $100,000 divided by .10 = $1 million.

This formula is known as the present value of a perpetuity because it continues in perpetuity. Thus, in structuring a deal, the parties must address the eventual pay-out of the corpus ($1 million) upon the payee's death (or upon her remarriage, as the case may be). Unlike alimony, the payment of a perpetuity to generate annual lifelong cash flows to the Wife will not automatically terminate upon the death of the Husband.

What if Husband agreed to pay Wife $50,000 per year for life? Assume that a 6% interest rate applies. How much should Husband invest now to guarantee annual payments of $50,000?

$50,000/0.06 = 833,333.33

In this scenario, Husband should invest $833,333.33, assuming a stable 6% interest rate.

Limited Term Alimony (Present Value of an Annuity)

Assume that Wife is seeking $2,000 per month in alimony, and Husband is not conceptually opposed to the amount. Husband doesn't want to write the monthly checks. Husband consults his attorney about converting one of his assets to an account or an investment to fund the monthly alimony payments. The parties negotiate, and they agree that Wife would get $2,000 per month in limited duration alimony for a period of 10 years. How much must Husband deposit now to fund the payments for the 10-year term?

There are eight steps:

Step 1: Annualize the alimony. In other words, $2,000 per month equals $24,000 per year.

Step 2: Determine the available interest rate. Let's assume 5%. Add the interest rate to 1, creating the multiplier of 1.05.

Step 3: Raise 1.05 to the tenth power, because 10 is the number of years that the limited duration alimony will be paid. Thus, $(1.05)^{10} = 1.63$.

Step 4: Multiply the interest rate (.05) by 1.63, which equals .08.

Step 5: Divide 1 by .08, which equals 12.5.

Step 6: Divide 1 by the interest rate (.05). Thus, $1 \div .05 = 20$.

Step 7: Subtract 12.5 (Step 5) from 20 (Step 6). Thus, $20 - 12.5 = 7.5$.

Step 8: Multiply the annual alimony payment ($24,000) by 7.5. Hence, $24,000 x 7.5 = $180,000.

Conclusion: In order to fund a limited term of alimony of $2,000 per month for 10 years, Husband must set aside $180,000 today at 5% interest. This calculation is often known by financial experts as the present value of an annuity. Here is the official formula:

$$\text{PV of an Annuity (PV:A)} = C\left[\frac{1}{r} - \frac{1}{r(1+r)^t}\right]$$

where C equals the cash or alimony which the Wife will be receiving annually, r equals the interest rate, and t equals the number of years in the term. Let's do the math:

$$\text{PV:A} = \$24{,}000 \times \frac{1}{.05} - \frac{1}{.05(1+.05)^{10}}$$

$$\text{PV:A} = \$24{,}000 \times 20 - \frac{1}{.05(1.63)}$$

$$\text{PV:A} = \$24{,}000 \times 20 - \frac{1}{.08}$$

$$\text{PV:A} = \$24{,}000 \times (20 - 12.5)$$

$$\text{PV:A} = \$24{,}000 \times 7.5$$

$$\text{PV:A} = \$180{,}000$$

18.3. Assessing Interest

Because of the many settlement scenarios in family law in which a payment will be delayed or deferred to a future point in time, it is useful to assess interest, wherever applicable. As you may recall from Chapter 5, the formula for compounding interest is $X(1+r)^t$ where X refers to the principal amount, r refers to the interest rate (sometimes denominated as i), and t refers to time, as in the number of years. Thus, for example, if you wanted to know what \$50,000 at 6% interest will be worth in five years, you'd multiply \$50,000 by 1.06 to the fifth power.

$$X(1+r)^t$$

$$\$50{,}000(1.06)^5$$

$$= \$50{,}000(1.338)$$

$$= \$66{,}900$$

If a husband agreed to pay \$50,000 to a wife in five years at 6% interest, he would owe her \$16,900 in interest, for a total payment of \$66,900. As shown, this basic interest formula is essentially the same as the formula for future value.

However, the actual payment arrangements in a typical divorce may not be expressed as easily as the example above. For example, what if interest was compounded semiannually? If the annual interest rate remained at 6%, then the semiannual rate would be 3%. This would change the formula as follows:

$$\$50{,}000 \text{ x } (1.03)^{5 \text{ x } 2}$$

Notice that we've used 1.03 instead of 1.06 because only half of the annual interest rate has been earned in a semiannual calculation. Notice also that the time exponent (based on five years) is now 5 times the number of annual compounding periods (2). In other words, interest will be compounded twice per year for five years. The exponent 5 x 2 becomes 10. The revised formula is, therefore, $\$50{,}000 \text{ x } 1.03^{10} = \$50{,}000 \text{ x } 1.3439 = \$67{,}195$. By compounding semiannually, the recipient spouse draws a somewhat higher interest payment.

Taking the process one step further, assume that the \$50,000 will earn 6% interest per annum, but it will be compounded monthly. The formula becomes $\$50{,}000 \text{ x } (1.005)^{5 \text{ x } 12}$. Notice that the annual interest rate of .06 must now be calculated on a monthly basis. Thus, .06 divided by 12 equals .005. So, the figure in the parentheses becomes 1.005. Notice also that the exponent becomes 5 x 12, representing 5 years times 12 compounding periods per year. So, the revised formula is \$50,000 x 1.005^{60} = \$50,000 x 1.34885 = \$67,442.50. Again, notice that by compounding interest more often, we have again boosted the total interest payment.

Such interest calculations produce what is often referred to as the *nominal interest rate*. In a changing economic environment, however, inflation may also affect the value of property over time. Suppose for example, that the interest rate was 6% while the inflation rate was 2%. In effect, the recipient spouse would be enjoying a 6% boost in the payment she will receive while at the same time experiencing a 2% setback due to the rate of inflation. We can approximate the net result by simply subtracting the inflation rate from the interest rate to obtain the *real interest rate.*

Real Interest Rate = Nominal Interest Rate – Inflation Rate

Real Interest Rate = 6% – 2%

Real Interest Rate = 4%

For quick estimates, you could thus say that the interest rate, after considering the inflation rate, is about 4%. But this is only an approximation. The actual formula for calculating the real interest rate is:

$$\text{Real Interest Rate} = \frac{1 + \text{Nominal Interest Rate}}{1 + \text{Inflation Rate}} - 1$$

$$\text{Real Interest Rate} = \frac{1 + .06}{1 + .02} - 1$$

$$\text{Real Interest Rate} = \frac{1.06}{1.02} - 1$$

Real Interest Rate = 1.039 – 1

Real Interest Rate = .039

Hence, we can see that the real interest rate is actually 3.9%.

Ratio Analysis

18.4. Debt-to-Asset Ratio

In considering a spouse's entitlement to support or an award of interim counsel fees, courts generally examine a number of factors, such as the obligor spouse's ability to pay, the dependent spouse's financial need, the parties' access to other financial resources and liquid assets, and their exercise of good faith or bad faith in the proceedings. A helpful way to interpret several of these factors is to examine the debt-to-asset ratio.

The debt-to-asset ratio determines how much of each party's assets are financed or encumbered by debt. As such, it provides a measure of the dependent spouse's need for support compared to her access to valuable assets.

The data necessary to construct this ratio is readily available in the financial disclosures that parties are required to make as part of the pretrial discovery process in a divorce action. So, for example, a spouse's total debt, or her total assets, can be gleaned from the Statement of Net Worth used in New York proceedings, the Affidavit of Financial Information used in Arizona, the Case Information Statement required in New Jersey divorces, or the Financial Affidavit required in Florida and many other states. There are three simple steps: First, calculate a spouse's total debt. Then, calculate total assets. Then, divide total debt by total assets.

For example, assume that Wife's total liabilities are $300,000, and her total assets are $500,000. The debt-to-asset ratio is 0.60 ($300,000 divided by $500,000). This means that for every 60 cents in total debt, the Wife has total assets of $1. If Husband has a ratio lower than 0.60, then his financial position is better. The objective is to have a lower number because it is better not to owe too much money. Thus, in arguing alimony and support motions, it is useful to note which party has the lower (better) debt-to-asset ratio. If Wife has a ratio of .60 and Husband has a ratio of .20, one might argue that the Husband has a stronger (more asset-rich) financial foundation and has a clear ability to pay more support. In a jurisdiction in which the court will attempt to equalize the financial positions of the parties, one might argue that Husband should pay enough money to the Wife to equalize both of their ratios at .40—effectively giving them a comparable debt-to-assets balance.

Consider another scenario. On his financial disclosures, an unemployed Husband reports total debt at $219,650. Having been dispossessed of his only real estate in a foreclosure action, the Husband counts $132,000 in personal assets. His debt-to-asset ratio is disquieting:

$$\frac{\text{Debt}}{\text{Asset}} = \frac{\$219{,}650}{\$132{,}000} = 1.66$$

The ratio indicates that for every $1.66 in debt, the Husband has only $1 in assets. His *top-heavy* or *upside-down* condition may very well help him to argue for alimony, spousal support, maintenance, or an award of interim counsel fees from a more financially secure Wife.

The ratio may also assist the Husband in arguing for a reassignment of assets as part of the marital dissolution proceedings. In the scenario above, the Husband has only $1 worth of assets to cover every $1.66 of debt. If Husband were to liquidate his assets—essentially selling everything to pay off his debt—he would be able to cover only about 60% of his obligations.

$$\frac{\$1}{\$1.66} = 0.6024$$

In this regard, Husband could argue that he should receive an award of additional assets. In a mathematically perfect world, for example, Husband could assert that an additional $87,650 in assets would bring his debt-to-asset ratio to 1:1, that is, exactly $1 of debt for every $1 of assets.

$$\frac{\text{Debt}}{\text{Asset}} = \frac{\$219{,}650}{\$132{,}000 + \$87{,}650} = \frac{\$219{,}650}{\$219{,}650} = 1$$

In a more likely scenario, however, there could be insufficient assets to bring each party down to a ratio of 1, or there may be enough assets to lower each party's ratio to a comparable number below 1.

Suppose that at the time of their separation, Husband had debt of $219,650 and Wife had debt of $111,000. Husband had assets of $132,000 and Wife had assets of $121,000. In the divorce which ensues, the Husband contends that he is the dependent spouse and demands a financial and/or property distribution from his Wife. Wife, in defense, points out that Husband walked away with $11,000 more in assets than she has. Let's compare each party's debt-to-asset ratio:

$$\text{Husband: } \frac{\text{Debt}}{\text{Asset}} = \frac{\$219{,}650}{\$132{,}000} = 1.66$$

$$\text{Wife: } \frac{\text{Debt}}{\text{Asset}} = \frac{\$111{,}000}{\$121{,}000} = 0.91$$

Here, it is evident that Wife is not nearly as financially burdened as Husband. In the event of a full liquidation, Wife could cover her indebtedness because she has only 91 cents in debt for every dollar in assets. The disparity in the two ratios offers a negotiating opportunity to Husband's counsel. While it may not be appropriate to settle a divorce exclusively on the basis of the disparity in these ratios, the information produced by these ratios provides a useful bargaining tool. Consider two approaches:

Approach #1: Reassigning Debt

Husband's attorney could seek a payment of alimony or spousal support from Wife that would assist Husband in reducing his debt more quickly. Or, Husband's attorney could argue that a particular debt should be reassigned from Husband to Wife in order to equalize (or nearly equalize) their debt-to-asset ratios. For example, let's say that Husband had been assuming responsibility for a $44,650 bank loan, among his other debts. Husband's attorney argues that this particular loan (which was marital in nature) should be shifted to Wife in order to apportion the parties' debt commitments more equitably. If Wife agreed to assume responsibility for the $44,650 bank loan, the respective debt-to-asset ratios would be adjusted as follows:

$$\text{Husband:}\quad \frac{\text{Debt}}{\text{Asset}} = \frac{\$219{,}650 - \$44{,}650}{\$132{,}000} = \frac{\$175{,}000}{\$132{,}000} = 1.32$$

$$\text{Wife:}\quad \frac{\text{Debt}}{\text{Asset}} = \frac{\$111{,}000 + \$44{,}650}{\$121{,}000} = \frac{\$155{,}650}{\$121{,}000} = 1.28$$

By reassigning the bank loan to Wife, Husband has lowered his debt-to-asset ratio to 1.32 while Wife has raised her ratio to 1.28. The ratios are now quite close, and with other minor adjustments between the parties, an equitable resolution of the divorce can be achieved.

Approach #2: Reassigning Assets

The second approach to equalizing or approximately balancing the ratios is to reassign assets from one spouse to the other. Using the original ratios for Husband and Wife provided above, let's assume that there are no reassignable debts. However, Wife's assets of $121,000 consist of a number of investments, two of which can be safely transferred without any penalties, fees, or tax consequences. The two investments are valued at \$16,000 each, for a total of \$32,000. By transferring these investment assets to Husband, the parties will achieve somewhat more comparable debt-to-asset ratios:

$$\text{Husband: } \frac{\text{Debt}}{\text{Asset}} = \frac{\$219{,}650}{\$132{,}000 + \$32{,}000} = \frac{\$219{,}650}{\$164{,}000} = 1.33$$

$$\text{Wife: } \frac{\text{Debt}}{\text{Asset}} = \frac{\$111{,}000}{\$121{,}000 - \$32{,}000} = \frac{\$111{,}000}{\$89{,}000} = 1.24$$

While the ratios are not identical, the disparity between the parties has been significantly reduced. With other financial or equitable adjustments between the parties, the prospect of a fair settlement now seems much more achievable.

The debt-to-asset ratio, like the debt-to-equity ratio,[5] is a common calculation on the corporate frontier. It is not, however, limited to business analysts and corporate lawyers. The debt-to-asset ratio provides a practical snapshot of a separated spouse's financial condition. A ratio under 1 means that a majority of that spouse's assets are financed through equity; a ratio greater than 1 means they are financed more by debt. The higher the ratio above 1, the more debt-leveraged the spouse. Knowing this information can help a dependent spouse qualify for support or for a redistribution of assets. It may also assist an obligor spouse in arguing that he is already too leveraged by debt to pay support or to relinquish any unencumbered property.

Like all ratios, however, the debt-to-asset comparison should not be considered in isolation. Rather, it should be used as one of several tools aimed at structuring a reasonable settlement, or as one of several devices to persuade a judge to enter a well-reasoned judgment.

18.5. Liquid Assets to Take-Home Pay Ratio

The ratio of liquid assets to take-home pay indicates whether a divorce litigant's current earnings are enough to pay her current bills. A rule-of-thumb is that liquid assets should be equal to six months of take-home pay. A range of three to six months is acceptable but not preferable. Under three months is inadvisable.

---

[5]See Section 9.3.

The first step in building this ratio is to determine which assets are *liquid assets.* Generally, any asset that can be sold or transferred quickly is liquid, provided that it can be exchanged for cash and will draw a sale value equal to the market value of the asset. Liquid assets include cash on hand, funds in checking and savings accounts, money market accounts, certificates of deposit, mutual funds, U.S. Treasury bills, stocks, and bonds. The cash value of a life insurance policy can also be considered a liquid asset, along with readily accessible trust funds, tax refunds, and personal injury settlements. Real estate, by contrast, is *not* a liquid asset because selling a home requires time and negotiation and—in most cases—the property is not quickly convertible to cash.

A total value of liquid assets should thus be calculated by examining the spouse's financial affidavit or other pretrial disclosures. Then, the amount of take-home pay should be noted (while also noting the pay period: i.e., weekly, biweekly, monthly). For example, assume that Molly has liquid assets of $50,000, and her monthly take-home pay is $10,000. The liquid assets to take-home pay formula is $50,000 divided by $10,000, which equals 5. Therefore, Molly can cover the loss of her take-home pay for five months. Molly's lawyer could argue that Molly needs a higher liquid balance in her assets, perhaps by claiming sole ownership of a particular investment in stocks or mutual funds.

This ratio provides another tactical device for negotiating the redistribution of assets. Suppose, for example, that at the time of their separation, Molly and her husband, Henry, have the following liquid assets:

ASSET	VALUE
Cash	$ 3,500
Checking Account (Bank of America)	$ 2,600
Savings Account (Bank of America)	$ 9,100
Savings Account (Wells Fargo Bank)	$ 2,400
Certificate of Deposit (36-month)	$ 5,800
Series EE Bonds	$ 2,100
Toy-Tech Stocks	$ 6,700
Life Insurance Cash Value	$ 8,900
Total Liquid Assets	$41,100

As part of their settlement negotiations, Molly and Henry have agreed to divide their liquid assets as follows:

MOLLY'S SHARE

ASSET	VALUE
Cash	$ 3,500
Savings Account (Wells Fargo Bank)	$ 2,400
Certificate of Deposit (36-month)	$ 5,800
Life Insurance Cash Value	$ 8,900
Total Liquid Assets	$20,600

HENRY'S SHARE

ASSET	VALUE
Checking Account (Bank of America)	$ 2,600
Savings Account (Bank of America)	$ 9,100
Series EE Bonds	$ 2,100
Toy-Tech Stocks	$ 6,700
Total Liquid Assets	$20,500

While Molly will receive a slightly higher distribution of the assets, Henry is willing to accept this arrangement as part of the global settlement of all issues in the divorce case.

Unfortunately, this division of assets doesn't truly measure either party's liquidity. The liquid assets to take-home pay ratio provides more insight. Assume, for example, that Molly earns $1,333 per week in take-home pay. Henry earns $1,590.25 per week. Let's apply the ratio to each party:

$$\text{Henry: } \frac{\text{Liquid Assets}}{\text{Take-Home Pay}} = \frac{\$20{,}500}{\$1{,}590.25} = 12.89 \text{ Weeks}$$

$$\text{Molly: } \frac{\text{Liquid Assets}}{\text{Take-Home Pay}} = \frac{\$20{,}600}{\$1{,}333} = 15.45 \text{ Weeks}$$

Here, we see that Molly will receive sufficient assets to cover her take-home pay for nearly 15½ weeks. If she lost her weekly pay, Molly would be able to liquidate her liquid assets quickly enough to keep herself afloat for approximately four months. Henry, on the other hand, should not be so gracious as to divide the liquid assets without further analysis. Henry's ratio shows that he could cover his take-home pay for less than 13 weeks. In effect, if Henry lost his job, he'd be able to stay afloat by liquidating assets for only about three months. In this respect, Molly is enjoying an advantage that is greater than the mere $100 difference in the division of the liquid assets.

Using the liquid assets to take-home pay ratio to Henry's advantage, Henry's attorney can now negotiate an improvement to Henry's distribution of assets to roughly equalize the parties' liquidity. Henry's attorney suggests that the parties divide the cash account down the middle, each taking $1,750. This will reduce Molly's total liquid assets by $1,750, while increasing Henry's total liquid assets by that amount. The attorney recalculates the ratios to show why this will produce a more equitable deal:

$$\text{Henry: } \frac{\text{Liquid Assets}}{\text{Take-Home Pay}} = \frac{\$20{,}500 + \$1{,}750}{\$1{,}590.25} = \frac{\$22{,}250}{\$1{,}590.25} = 13.99 \text{ Weeks}$$

$$\text{Molly: } \frac{\text{Liquid Assets}}{\text{Take-Home Pay}} = \frac{\$20{,}600 - \$1{,}750}{\$1{,}333} = \frac{\$18{,}850}{\$1{,}333} = 14.14 \text{ Weeks}$$

Now, the parties have almost identical ratios, with each of them holding a sufficient amount of liquid assets to cover approximately 14 weeks of take-home pay.

The liquid assets to take-home pay ratio is beneficial in cases in which liquidity is an issue. It is also a useful strategic device for redirecting attention away from a disparity in assets, such as in the calculations above, where Henry is receiving $22,250 in liquid assets, $3,400 more than Molly. Like all ratios, this ratio does not operate in a vacuum: it may be necessary to adjust the distribution of real property and other illiquid assets, or to renegotiate support and maintenance payments to achieve an equitable conclusion to a divorce case.

18.6. Take-Home Pay to Debt-Service Ratio

Another way to measure the financial strength of a spouse in a divorce case is to look at the ratio of take-home pay to debt-service charges. This ratio determines how well one's net wages cover her monthly payments of principal and interest on credit cards and loan accounts.

Debt service can be calculated by determining the sum of all payments due on loans, credit accounts, and other debts for a fixed period of time. New Jersey's Case Information Statement, for example, provides a line item for debt service under the listing of the party's personal expenses. In other jurisdictions, it may be necessary to ascertain the debt service from several line items on the financial affidavit or other disclosure document.

Assume that Molly has a monthly debt service of $2,099, calculated as follows:

Creditor	**Amount**
American Express	$ 185
Citibank Visa	$ 95
Key Bank MasterCard	$ 26
SteelBank Credit Line	$ 260
Ally Financial Account	$ 450
Stafford Student Loan	$ 188
Apartment Rent	$ 895
TOTAL DEBT SERVICE	$2,099

If Molly nets $6,500 in monthly wages, with a total debt service of $2,099, then her take-home pay-to-debt service ratio would look like this:

$$\frac{\text{Take-Home Pay}}{\text{Debt Service}} = \frac{\$6{,}500}{\$2{,}099} = 3.09$$

In other words, Molly would have a ratio of 3.09. This means that she has $3.09 in take-home pay for every $1 dedicated to paying credit card bills and loan accounts. *Not bad.* In fact, a ratio above 3 is considered favorable; under 2 is considered risky. For Molly and her attorney, the goal is to obtain a higher ratio.

Of course, the ratio can be utilized and compared in a number of different ways. If, for example, Molly has obtained a wage garnishment order that withdraws alimony and child support from Henry's paycheck each week, then Henry's take-home pay will be correspondingly lower. If the amount of the support payments is too high, and if Henry's ratio drops considerably lower than Molly's, Henry may choose to challenge the support orders or other aspects of the divorce case.

So, for example, assume that Molly has a take-home pay-to-debt service ratio of 3.09 and Henry has a ratio of 6.4. As a measure of liquidity, this comparison would suggest that Henry is in a much stronger position. This could be attributable to Henry's higher paycheck alone. Or perhaps Henry has fewer credit card bills. In matrimonial negotiations, such a disparity in ratios presents an opportunity for Molly's attorney. As in the case of the debt-to-asset ratio, a significant disparity between take-home pay-to-debt service ratios can be addressed from several approaches, one of which considers the numerator (take-home pay), and one of which considers the denominator (debt service).

Approach #1: Modifying Support

By requiring Henry to pay more spousal support or child support, Molly can essentially reduce Henry's take-home pay, and in so doing reduce his take-home pay-to-debt service ratio. If Molly were to receive an additional infusion of net cash (after payment of any taxes on alimony), her ratio would correspondingly increase. For example, an additional monthly payment of $1,000, effectively increasing Molly's take-home pay to $7,500, would boost her ratio to 3.57.

Suppose Henry had a significantly lower take-home pay-to-debt service ratio of 1.2. This means that his paycheck would provide only $1.20 to cover every dollar of debt repayment he was obligated to make—a very small cushion. Henry's attorney would thus argue that Henry's support obligations should be reduced because he is in a far less liquid condition than Molly. By lowering Henry's support obligations, Henry's take-home pay would increase, and his ratio would correspondingly grow.

Approach #2: Reducing Debt Service

If take-home pay cannot be adjusted, then the ratio can be modified by reassigning debt between the spouses. If Molly then reduces her debt service, even without altering her take-home pay, she will enjoy a higher ratio. So, for example, if Molly's attorney can persuade Henry's attorney that Henry should assume responsibility for the Citibank Visa and SteelBank Credit Lines, he will have shifted $355 in debt service to Henry. By reducing Molly's debt service by this amount, Molly's new take-home pay-to-debt service ratio would be 3.72.

$$\frac{\text{Take-Home Pay}}{\text{Debt Service}} = \frac{\$6{,}500}{\$2{,}099 - 355} = \frac{\$6{,}500}{\$6{,}500} = 3.72$$

Now, Molly has $3.72 to cover every $1 of debt.

The opposite scenario is also true. If Henry had a lower ratio of 1.2, as suggested under Approach #1 above, and if he was unable to persuade his wife or a judge to lower his support obligations, he might wish to turn his attention toward reassigning his debt service. By transferring one or more of his credit obligations or monthly bills to Molly, Henry would reduce his debt service, while increasing his ratio, and Molly would increase her debt service, while reducing her ratio.

18.7. Liquid Assets to Current Liabilities

How quickly can a spouse tap her liquid assets to cover her current liabilities? That is the question that underlies the liquid assets-to-current liabilities ratio. How fast can cash be generated, and what is the relationship between that quick cash and current debt commitments? In the business world, this ratio is often referred to as the acid test ratio or simply the quick ratio.[6]

The significance of the liquid assets-to-current liabilities ratio is quite basic: If the ratio falls below 1, it means that a party does not have sufficient liquid assets to cover her current debt. If the ratio is exactly 1, then there is exactly enough value in the liquid assets to cover current debt. As the ratio rises, the financial condition improves. So, for example, a ratio of 3 would indicate that a spouse has three times as much value in her liquid assets as she needs to cover to her current liabilities.

For this example, assume that Molly has total liquid assets of $1,811, and total current liabilities of $950. Her liquid assets-to-current liabilities ratio would look like this:

$$\frac{\$1,811}{\$950} = 1.9$$

With a ratio of 1.9, Molly is easily covering her debt. She effectively has $1.90 in money which she can quickly generate from her liquid assets in order to cover every $1 in current debt that she must repay.

Is a ratio of 1.9 enough? One cannot say with absolute certainty that 1.9 is good enough for Molly, without knowing more about her financial situation and family concerns. For example, will Molly and her husband, Henry, be sending a child to college in the next year? Will there be an infusion of cash in the coming months, when an estate of a deceased relative disburses a sizeable beneficial share to Molly? Are

---

[6]See Section 9.7.

there deferred obligations that will be coming due shortly which will increase the total current liabilities? Is the value of any of the liquid assets declining or at risk (because of a volatile stock market, for example)? Each of these considerations could cast a different light on a ratio of 1.9, and in some cases, could cause the ratio to change.

An effective strategy is to compare a spouse's liquid assets-to-current liabilities ratio over time. Let's assume, for example, that Molly and Henry have been separated for three years, and during that time period, Molly's ratios were calculated as follows:

2009: 1.9
2010: 1.2
2011: 0.95

Clearly, Molly is experiencing declining liquidity. After three years, Molly files for divorce. She argues that the continuous and significant deterioration in her liquidity now imperils her ability to meet creditors' demands and that she requires an immediate, *pendente lite* order of spousal support. The downward pattern in her ratios will help to prove that her 2011 ratio of 0.95 was not simply an anomaly but rather a reflection of a declining state of affairs.

Valuation Formulas

18.8. Actual Cash Value

What's the value of a big-screen television that is five years old? Imagine that a husband and wife are fighting over this particular item in the course of a mediation session, at which they're trying to resolve the equitable distribution of their marital assets. A similar new 82-inch, 120-hertz, 3D television could be purchased for $3,000, and has an expected life of 10 years. Before the Wife will consider giving the big-screen TV to the Husband, she wants to know what it's worth.

The solution to this problem lies in the actual cash value (ACV) formula:

$$\text{ACV} = \text{P} - \left[\text{A}\left(\frac{\text{P}}{\text{t}}\right)\right]$$

where P is the purchase price of the replacement item (new television), A is the age of the old item (old television), and t is the expected life or time (in years) of the replacement item.

Let's apply this formula to the television negotiations in this case. First, divide \$3,000 by the expected life of 10 years. Then, multiply the result by the age of the old television (300 x 5 = 1,500). Finally, subtract \$1,500 from the purchase price of the replacement television (3,000 – 1,500 = 1,500).

$$ACV = P - \left[A\left(\frac{P}{t}\right)\right]$$

$$ACV = \$3{,}000 - \left[5\left(\frac{\$3{,}000}{10}\right)\right]$$

$$ACV = \$3{,}000 - 5(\$300)$$

$$ACV = \$3{,}000 - \$1{,}500$$

$$ACV = \$1{,}500$$

Therefore, the actual cash value of the five-year-old big-screen TV, based on the facts above, is \$1,500 (only half of the replacement value). The actual cash value is often used by insurance claims adjusters as a basis for reimbursement of lost, stolen, and destroyed items. As we see here, it is also an effective method for valuing a personal property item subject to distribution in a divorce case.

18.9. Home Affordability Tests

Divorce litigants are often required to sell the family home. Or, in many cases, one of the parties agrees—or is forced—to move out of the property. Inevitably, at least one of the parties will be shopping for a new place to live. Yet, in many cases, the cost of new housing is ignored or downplayed. Not uncommonly, a relocating spouse finds herself unable to cover the mortgage payment, insurance, and utilities costs on her new home, even with an award of alimony or other support.

Attorneys are therefore duty-bound to explore the question of affordability with their family law clients. *Should they rent or buy a new place? If they buy a new home, how much should they spend?* The answers to these questions will have an impact on the other applications for relief sought in the divorce case. To get started, we turn to several rules of thumb developed by financial planners and mortgage lenders.

The Gross Income Multiple Test

The first rule of thumb is that the price of a new home should not exceed X times the party's gross annual income. *What is X?* A conservative lender would perhaps say that a buyer (or borrower) should not spend more than 1.5 times his gross annual income. So, if you earned $50,000, you should not spend more than $75,000. An aggressive lender might say that a buyer should not spend more than 3 or 4 times his gross annual income. With a multiple of 4, for example, one who earns $50,000 should be able to buy a home for $200,000.

Exactly which multiple is best could depend on a variety of factors, such as: (a) the current lending market; (b) the current housing market; (c) the buyer's credit history; (d) the deductibility of mortgage interest and other tax issues; (e) the amount of the buyer's downpayment, and (f) the vast geographical differences in utility and insurance costs. Measuring each of these factors would require a more scientific algorithm.

Most market analysts apply a middle-of-the-road approach, using 2.5 as the multiple of gross annual income. Assume that a Husband has moved out of the marital home with the children and is searching for a comparable three-bedroom home in a nearby community. He earns $98,750 per year in gross income. With a multiple of 2.5, the Husband can afford a home priced up to $246,875.

$98,750 x 2.5 = $246,875.

Of course, as a rule of thumb, this approach is not fail-safe. For one thing, the rule, as stated, does not account for the down payment to be made by the buyer. What if the Husband walked away from the marriage with $150,000 in cash, as his equitable share from the transfer of the former marital home to his Wife? Were he to deposit that $150,000 as a down payment on a new home, he would likely qualify for a much pricier property than one priced at $246,875. In such cases, it may be better to amortize the amount of any mortgage loan over the term of the loan, and to examine the borrower's ability to pay the monthly mortgage payment based on his annual income.

While the 2.5 multiple-of-gross-income rule of thumb may assist in negotiations or in post-divorce planning, it does not take into consideration other significant home-related expenses. Property taxes, for example, may have a significant impact on affordability, especially in states such as New Jersey and New York which impose the highest levels of taxation. The affordability of a new home should also account for electrical and/or gas service, water utilities, homeowner's insurance, and, in communities managed by homeowner associations, the monthly maintenance fee or other membership fee. Where these other costs are comparatively high, then a multiple of 2.5 is arguably too aggressive and should be somewhat lowered.

The Gross Income Percentage Test

A variation on the gross income multiple test is to use a percentage of gross income. More specifically, a buyer should not spend more than X percent of his gross income to cover his mortgage payment, real estate taxes, and homeowner's insurance premium. Historically, financial advisors recommended that X = 25%. Thus, a buyer who grosses $6,000 per month should not spend more than $1,500 per month to cover her mortgage loan, taxes, and insurance bill. While a gross income percentage approach is still a useful strategy for testing affordability, the 25% rule may not be appropriate in all locations or under all conditions and circumstances.

The list of potential circumstances that may offset the 25% rule is endless. For example, an old home purchased in "as is" condition as a so-called "handyman's special" could incur significant maintenance and repair costs on a monthly basis. A large estate on an expansive tract of land could require a substantial monthly investment for lawn, yard, and garden care. In such cases, the 25% rule would have to be restated as requiring that a buyer should not spend more than 25% of her gross income to cover her mortgage, taxes, insurance, *and repair or maintenance costs.*

Of course, if a buyer makes a larger down payment on the purchase of her home, she can thereby reduce her monthly mortgage payments. Attorneys negotiating the distribution of proceeds from the sale of a marital home, or the equitable distribution of other marital assets, may wish to consider how much cash their clients would need to tender a down payment on a new home sufficient to reduce the new mortgage payments within the parameters of the 25% rule (or any other percentage that is applied). Similarly, a buyer may find that she can satisfy the 25% rule only if she had a greater amount of monthly gross income. In this respect, attorneys may wish to argue for more alimony, or for front-loaded alimony increases, to augment the gross income received by the buyer.

The Take-Home Pay Test

Instead of using gross income, the take-home pay test measures affordability using net income. Under this approach, a borrower should not commit to pay more than 35% of his monthly take-home pay for mortgage, taxes, and insurance. As a rule of thumb, the 35% test is widely acknowledged, but likewise widely criticized.

Assume that a spouse netted $3,210 per month in take-home wages. Under the take-home pay test, she could afford to pay $1,123.50 per month for her home. As a mathematical shortcut, this test may prove helpful in negotiations and mediation sessions. It may fall under attack, however, if offered as a scientific measure of affordability.

The inherent flaw in the take-home pay test is the location variant. A spouse who nets $3,210 per month in Omaha or Fort Wayne could potentially afford a suitable home with monthly housing costs of $1,123.50, but that same spouse would be unlikely to find an affordable and comparable deal in other housing markets, such as New York, Los Angeles, and Honolulu. Indeed, cost of living, as a variable, is not accurately measured by a blanket 35% rule. Food, transportation, and other living expenses are more costly in America's big cities and in resort towns. Interest rates, home appreciation, and increases in the cost of utilities provide additional variables. The 35% rule also does not account for individual household or personal factors that may limit one's ability to pay, such as a court order that requires a payment of child support or installments on an outstanding civil judgment.

This does not mean that the take-home pay test is useless. It may require tweaking, however, to account for higher interest rates, pricier housing markets, and special personal circumstances. Depending on the circumstances, a buyer may feel secure, for example, in applying a 45% rule. As a general rule, however, the higher the percentage, the riskier the investment and the less affordable the purchase.

The PITI Tests

The conventional method for mortgage lenders was to apply their own gross income percentage test based on the sum of the principal (P), interest (I), taxes (T), and insurance (I). The first so-called PITI test is essentially a ratio of P+I+T+I to gross monthly income (GI):

PITI Test #1:

$$\frac{\text{PITI}}{\text{GI}}$$

The calculation of the PITI numerator could also be increased in cases in which a homeowner is also required to pay mortgage insurance or homeowners' association fees on a monthly basis.

The conventional rule was that if the ratio of PITI-to-GI produced a percentage that was not greater than between 25% and 28%, a lender should extend credit to the home buyer. Like other rules of thumb, however, the first PITI test is location-dependent, and the percentage that a lender would accept—and that a family lawyer might use for negotiating purposes—is contingent on both personal financial and macroeconomic factors.

For example, suppose that a spouse had the following monthly housing costs:

Mortgage Principal	\$ 210.00
Mortgage Interest	\$1,160.00
Taxes	\$ 504.00
Insurance	\$ 118.00
TOTAL PITI	\$1,992.00

If her annual earnings were \$36,700, she'd be in a weak position to qualify for a mortgage loan. Let's do the math, first by converting the gross annual earnings of \$36,700 to a monthly figure (\$36,700 ÷ 12 = \$3,058.33).

$$\frac{\text{PITI}}{\text{GI}} = \frac{1{,}992}{\$3{,}058.33} = 0.65$$

In this scenario the spouse would need to dedicate 65%—almost two-thirds—of her gross monthly income to afford a mortgage and pay her property taxes and homeowner's insurance premium. For a family lawyer, this ratio is a valuable bargaining tool. It shows the buyer-spouse's inadequate financial position and may thereby justify a petition for alimony or an enhanced distribution of marital assets.

What if the buyer-spouse could obtain alimony payments of \$250 per week, putting another \$1,082.50 per month in her bank account. We could treat this additional cash as gross income, and rebuild the PITI-to-GI ratio as follows:

$$\frac{\text{PITI}}{\text{GI}} = \frac{1{,}992}{\$3{,}058.33 + \$1{,}082.50} = \frac{1{,}992}{\$4{,}140.83} = 0.48$$

Now, the buyer-spouse would be dedicating 48% of her monthly gross income to her housing costs. While the percentage is still higher than most lenders would approve in most locales, it demonstrates how the PITI-to-GI formula can be a basis for negotiating a matrimonial settlement.

In a case in which a spouse's ability to afford a new home is a critical issue, the continuous manipulation of this ratio can serve as a tool for settlement. Here, the buyer-spouse's attorney may choose to fight for more financial assets that would boost the GI denominator and thus lower the ratio further. If all else fails, and if a particular case provides no greater hope of producing additional sources of income for the buyer-spouse, then counsel may wish to use this formula to advise the buyer-spouse that she simply cannot afford the house in question and ought to shop for a property with a lower mortgage payment or lower tax and insurance costs.

A second PITI test expands the numerator of the ratio to include long-term debts (LTD) such as car loans, student loans, and credit card balances that will take more than a year to pay off. Under this second PITI approach, lenders historically required that the sum of principal, interest, taxes, insurance, *and long-term debts* did not exceed between 33% and 36% of monthly income. For all of the reasons mentioned above, the 33% to 36% rule is not scientific and is subject to challenge based on location, interest rates, personal factors, and other external economic considerations.

Let's reconsider the buyer-spouse's condition by adding her long-term debt to her total PITI:

Mortgage Principal	$ 210.00
Mortgage Interest	$1,160.00
Taxes	$ 504.00
Insurance	$ 118.00
Ally Car Loan	$ 399.00
Visa/MasterCard	$ 95.00
PLUS Student Loan	$ 160.44
TOTAL PITI + LTD	$2,646.44

In this example, we've increased the spouse's PITI by her long-term debt, consisting of her monthly car loan, her Visa and MasterCard payments, and her federal PLUS student loan payment. Let's do the math:

PITI Test #2:

$$\frac{\text{PITI} + \text{LTD}}{\text{GI}} = \frac{\$2{,}646.44}{\$4{,}140.83} = 0.63$$

Here, again, we find that the buyer-spouse must dedicate too much of her monthly gross income to satisfy her housing costs as well as her long-term debt. At a ratio of 63%, she would not satisfy lenders who follow the conventional 33% to 36% rule. Still, the ratio provides a meaningful gauge of where the buyer-spouse stands in a matrimonial proceeding in which her ability to relocate to another home is at issue. Confronted with a 63% ratio of PITI+LTD-to-GI, a family lawyer might choose, for example, to reapportion the marital debt. Perhaps the nonbuyer-spouse should be paying the Ally car loan or some other combination of expenses to improve (lower) the buyer-spouse's ratio.

The Residual Income Test

The residual income model, developed by Professor Michael E. Stone,[7] a community planning expert, eschews the income ratio tests of affordability in favor of an analysis that targets the amount of money that's left over *after a party pays all of her housing costs.* It essentially recognizes that when a person cashes her paycheck, the largest and least flexible claim on her after-tax income is the mortgage bill and related mandatory housing costs (property taxes, insurance). The more a person spends on these housing costs, the less she has to spend on nonhousing needs. Therefore, the residual income test is simply a basic subtraction equation:

Net Income – Housing Costs = Residual Income

By examining whether the residual income is sufficient to cover a homeowner's nonhousing needs, this test forces the homeowner to re-

---

[7]For further discussion of this approach, see, Stone, Michael, et. al., *The residual income approach to housing affordability: the theory and the practice,* http://bsllibrary.org.au/housing/the-residual-income-approach-to-housing-affordability-the-theory-and-the-practice-ahuri-6349/.

think whether the cost of housing is too high. Technical application of the residual income test is beyond the scope of this book. However, the model can be used, in its simplest form, as another method for approaching home affordability questions. For example, if a spouse must cover child care costs, special health care costs, and extensive transportation costs, is there enough residual income to cover these important obligations? If not, perhaps the cost of housing is too high. An attorney for a home buyer who cannot afford to pay her child care, health care, and transportation costs would thus be forced to inquire as to whether the home buyer can afford the house, or whether some further petition or negotiating tactic is necessary to close the gap.

Where residual income is inadequate to cover nonhousing costs, the burdened spouse has limited options. She can either fight for more financial support, reassign some of her nonhousing costs to the other spouse, make lifestyle changes that will reduce or eliminate certain nonhousing costs, or search for a cheaper house. Because housing costs come off the top—that is, they are generally drawn first from a party's paycheck—a cheaper house means more residual income to pay for everything else.

The Affordability Index

The Housing Affordability Index (HAI) is a monthly benchmark published by the National Association of Realtors (NAR). It is, effectively, a ratio between median family income and the qualifying income needed to own a median single-family home. Stated otherwise, the HAI is the median household income (MHI) divided by the amount of qualifying income (QI):

$$\text{HAI} = \frac{\text{MHI}}{\text{QI}} \text{ x } 100$$

To calculate this ratio, we need to know the median price of single family homes, the mortgage rate, the monthly payment, and the homeowner's monthly income. First, we'll need to establish the median price of existing single-family homes. This information can be quickly found online by consulting the Median Sales Price of Existing Single-Family Homes for Metropolitan Areas, published by the NAR.

Next, we'll need to determine the effective annual mortgage rate. The effective annual mortgage rate is the effective interest rate (EIR)[8] that applies to mortgage loans. The formula for EIR is:

$$EIR = (1 + \frac{i}{n})^n - 1$$

where i is the stated annual interest rate and n is the number of compounding periods. In calculating the HAI, however, the effective mortgage rates published by the Federal Housing Finance Agency are generally the best source. For state-specific information, current rate tables can also be obtained from HSH Associates.[9]

The third step is to calculate the monthly payment on a median-price home at the effective mortgage rate. To make this calculation, we will assume that a home buyer would commit a down payment of 20% to the purchase, and would therefore borrow 80% of the sale price. Here's the formula:

$$MP = MedP \text{ x } 0.8 \text{ x } (ER/12) \ / \ 1 - [1/1 + (ER/12)]^{360}$$

where MP equals monthly payment, MedP is the median price, and ER is the effective mortgage rate.

Let's assume, hypothetically, that after plugging in the median home price for a particular city, and the effective mortgage rate, you arrived at a monthly payment of $1,080. The NAR's formula assumes that a homeowner uses no more than 25% of his household income for mortgage payments. Therefore, to calculate monthly income, we would multiply the mortgage payment amount by 4.

Monthly Income = MP x 4
Monthly Income = $1,080 x 4 = $4,320

Then, to determine the necessary annual income, we would multiply the monthly income by 12.

---

[8]See Section 6.6.

[9]http://www.hsh.com/mortgage-quotes/ratetable.php.

Therefore, annual income = MP x 4 x 12, or annual income equals monthly income x 12. So, with a monthly mortgage payment of $1,080, the necessary amount of annual income a homeowner would need to earn is $1,080 x 4 x 12 = $51,840. Therefore, the qualifying income (QI) to be used in the HAI formula will be $51,840.

The final step is to determine the median household income (MHI) for the city in question. MHI data can be found in the Census Bureau Decennial Survey. It may be necessary to tweak this data if the decennial survey has become outdated and economic circumstances have changed. Let's assume, for purposes of this hypothetical, that the MHI is $89,500.

We are now in a position to calculate the HAI using our original formula:

$$\text{HAI} = \frac{\text{MHI}}{\text{QI}} \times 100$$

$$\text{HAI} = \frac{\$89{,}500}{\$51{,}840} \times 100$$

$$\text{HAI} = 1.73 \times 100 = 173$$

Because the HAI is based on a scale of 100, a score of 173 means that a party earning the median family income has 173% of the income necessary to qualify for a mortgage loan on a median-priced home, assuming a 20% down payment. An index below 100 would mean that a home buyer earning a median family income would not be entitled to a mortgage on a median-priced home.

A divorce lawyer engaged in settlement negotiations on behalf of a client who is relocating to another home can apply the HAI index to make a preliminary determination as to his client's eligibility for a mortgage under the current terms of the divorce settlement. Where a client, for example, scores an HAI of 95%, the client falls below the mortgage-qualification mark, assuming that she would earn a median level of income, that she would purchase a median priced home, and that she would make a downpayment of 20%. In such circumstances, the attorney would be well-advised to consider renegotiating the divorce settlement, or perhaps counseling the client to consider other housing and mortgage options. The HAI should also be used cautiously during changing economic times, as its technical validity may be questionable during changing market conditions.[10]

The Price-to-Rent Ratio

Is it more affordable to rent or to buy a new home? The price-to-rent ratio offers another measure of home affordability focused on the cost of leasing versus owning a property. To build this ratio, you will need to know a typical monthly rent for a particular location. Fair market rents for every county in America are reported by the U.S. Department of Housing and Urban Development (HUD) for each calendar year.[11]

The next step is to multiply the monthly rent by 12. So, for example, HUD reports that a two-bedroom apartment in Chico, California, had a fair market rent (FMR) of $874 for fiscal year 2011. Therefore, the annual FMR for Chico would be $874 x 12 = $10,488.

Then, you'll need to find the median home price for the city in question. This information is available from the National Association of Realtors website[12] and from other information sources such as zillow.com.[13] The media sale price for a Chico home during the same period was $254,900. The price-to-rent ratio can now be stated:

$$\frac{\text{Price}}{\text{Rent}} = \frac{\$254{,}900}{\$10{,}488} = 24.3$$

To interpret the price-to-rent ratio, the following rules generally apply:

(1) If the ratio is less than 16, then owning a home is less expensive than renting.

(2) If the ratio is greater than 16, then renting is generally less expensive.

---

[10]Critics claim that NAR's housing affordability index is founded on an improper baseline that almost never shows that housing is unaffordable; that it unreasonably assumes that most home buyers can actually tender a 20% down payment today, and that it underestimates the indebtedness of the average American household, meaning that most homebuyers cannot devote 25% of their monthly gross income to pay their mortgage principal and interest.

[11]http://www.huduser.org/portal/datasets/fmr.html.

[12]http://www.realtor.org/research/research/metroprice.

[13]zillow.com/local-info/.

In the case of Chico, California, as shown above, with a ratio of 24.3, the rental market is clearly more affordable, under typical circumstances.

18.10. Adequacy of Life Insurance

Complex algorithms are often used to determine the proper amount of life insurance coverage, but one useful shortcut is available to family lawyers in fashioning settlements and in approximating the possibilities. This formula operates on the assumption that life insurance should be set at somewhere between 5 to 10 times one's annual gross income. The greater the need for support for dependents, the higher the multiplier should be.

Thus, for example, if there are children and a stay-at-home mother, the Husband's life insurance coverage should be closer to 10 times his annual gross income. Unlike the declining term coverage approach that is often used to insure support payments, or the more generalized amounts of coverage that are imposed by some courts, this method is based sheerly on a multiple-of-income approach.

For example, let's assume that Husband earns $75,000 in gross income per year, and he has three children and a dependent Wife. If the Wife wants him to provide the maximum amount of coverage within the recommended range, then Husband should obtain coverage equal to $75,000 times 10, or $750,000.

Of course, the multiple-of-income approach is not scientific, and in certain cases, it may underestimate or overestimate the amount of necessary coverage. A more accurate method is to estimate the actual cost (or the actual loss) to one's dependents caused by the death of the insured party. These costs could include, for example, any or all of the following:

- Funeral and burial expenses.
- Unsatisfied mortgage loans, car loans, student loans, lines of credit, and other credit card debt.
- Alimony and child support payments, and contributions toward the college expenses of any children.
- Health insurance coverage for dependents.
- Pension benefits that will lapse upon the death of the pension participant.

In most divorce and domestic relations cases, life insurance is ordered by the family court in order to secure the future payment of court-ordered alimony or child support. For example, if the obligor spouse is required to pay \$1,000 per month in combined alimony and child support, for a period of 15 years, we could say that his obligation will total \$180,000. But that would potentially understate his real obligation. Were the obligor to die during the third year of his 15-year obligation, he would not experience the cost-of-living increases and other changes in circumstance that would possibly increase his obligations over time. Because child support is based, partly, on the time that the obligor spends with the children in exercising his shared custody and parenting rights, the obligor's death also places a new, costly burden on the recipient spouse.

Another approach to setting a life insurance value is the return-on-investment approach. Under this method, the dependent spouse would calculate all of the payments that she is scheduled to receive from the obligor spouse over the course of a year. Let's assume, hypothetically, that she would receive the following payments in one year's time:

Alimony	\$16,000
Child Support	\$ 4,426
Equitable Distribution Payout	\$ 6,120

Therefore, the dependent spouse would want to insure that she purchased enough coverage to replace total annual receipts of \$26,546 from the obligor spouse. How much insurance will ensure that the dependent spouse can cover this amount of money year after year? The answer lies in the formula for the present value of a perpetuity.[14]

$$\text{PV (Perpetuity)} = \frac{P}{i} \text{ where P = payment, and i = interest rate}$$

Let's assume, for this hypothetical, that the dependent spouse could invest a certain amount of money over time at an interest rate of 4% in order to generate a return of \$26,546 per year. The formula would be:

$$\frac{P}{i} = \frac{\$26{,}546}{.04} = \$663{,}650$$

[14]See Section 5.7.

Therefore, the dependent spouse in this scenario should insist on insurance coverage of at least $663,650.

Other Useful Devices

18.11. Break-Even Analysis

Often, in the course of negotiations in a divorce case, it becomes necessary to determine when a party who is making a particular investment will reach his *break-even* point. The investment can come in the form of a lump sum payment to the other spouse, in exchange for a future benefit, a right in property, or some other favorable trade-off. Or, the investment can represent an actual investment in property, in a business, a project, a job, or in the purchase of securities. Predicting the breakeven point can be a useful planning tool, not to mention a tactical negotiating device.

Let's consider a hypothetical scenario. A wife is in the process of moving out of the marital home. She has fixed costs of $10,000 to make the move. Her husband refuses to contribute toward her moving expenses. The husband's lawyer, in fact, dismisses the request for moving expenses, arguing that the Wife can work part-time and pay for her relocation herself. In fact, the wife can work part-time earning $250 per week, but it will cost her $65 per week in travel expenses, lunches, and related expenses. Exactly how long would it take the Wife to break even, were she to cover her moving expenses through part-time employment?

In a business setting, the breakeven formula would be stated as follows:[15]

$$X = \frac{F}{P - V}$$

where X is the breakeven point, F is fixed costs, P is price, and V is variable costs. This same formula can be redefined to fit the facts of this hypothetical. In this case, the fixed expenses are the $10,000 in moving expenses. This figure is *fixed* because it doesn't change based on how much or how little the Wife works at a part-time job. However, her cost of working at the job, $65 per week, is *variable* because it varies depending on how many weeks she works. The value of her work—essentially the figure that replaces the P for price—is her

[15]See Section 5.11.

weekly wages of \$250. So, the breakeven formula can be calculated by dividing the wife's fixed expenses (\$10,000) by the difference between the value of her work and the cost of working (\$250 – \$65 = \$185). Here's the math:

$$X = \frac{F}{P - V}$$

$$X = \frac{\$10{,}000}{\$250 - \$65}$$

$$X = 54.05$$

Therefore, the wife will have to work slightly more than 54 weeks to break even—that is, in order to generate enough money to cover her moving expenses.

Let's apply the breakeven formula in another scenario: Suppose that the Husband is challenging alimony based on the Wife's employability. The Husband contends that his Wife can earn a good living selling handmade dolls for children, a specialty she developed as a hobby and turned into a fledgling business. How long would it take for Wife to realistically generate a meaningful income for herself from the sale of dolls?

The Wife's attorney has collected the necessary information: Fixed expenses of \$5,000 are necessary to buy a sewing machine, various supplies, and handicraft tools. Each doll sells for \$35, but it costs the Wife \$7 in fabric, plastic moldings, and other materials to assemble each doll. Apply the breakeven formula:

$$X = \frac{F}{P - V}$$

$$X = \frac{\$5{,}000}{\$35 - \$7}$$

$$X = 178.57$$

In this instance, the fixed costs of \$5,000 are divided by the difference between the price of a doll (\$35), and the variable cost of a single doll (\$7), producing a breakeven figure of 178.57. In other words, the Wife will have to sell 179 dolls before she breaks even. Her lawyer will surely argue that she won't even generate a dime of support for herself until she sells the 180th doll—an unreasonable expectation in defense of a claim for alimony.

The breakeven formula, in fact, is also useful in projecting how long it will take a spouse to break even *and* to generate a profit (or any particular additional sum of money). For example, what if we wanted to know, as part of our divorce negotiations, how long it would take the very same Wife to generate an income of $10,000 from selling her dolls? In effect, we'd be asking, how many dolls the wife would have to sell in order to break even *and* to generate a $10,000 profit. To answer this question, we simply apply the breakeven formula, but we add the desired profit ($10,000) to the numerator:

$$X = \frac{F + \$10{,}000}{P - V}$$

$$X = \frac{\$5{,}000 + \$10{,}000}{\$35 - \$7}$$

$$X = 535.71$$

So, Wife would have to sell 536 dolls to generate an income of $10,000. If this is an unreasonable expectation, then selling dolls would not be a rational argument for generating $10,000 for the Wife.

18.12. Gross and Net Analysis

A simple, yet often overlooked, device in matrimonial negotiations and in family court litigation is to distinguish income, savings, and worth by gross versus net figures. Sloppy litigants often toss around numbers that are inherently inaccurate because they have not been properly adjusted to account for recognized tax deductions and other necessary corrections. Yet a diligent dedication to the *adjustments* can have a major impact on the final results of any negotiation or litigation.

Adjusted Gross Income

Adjusted gross income (AGI) is important because it represents a party's gross income, *after* deduction of retirement deductions, moving expenses, and a variety of other statutory adjustments.[16] The formula for AGI is simply gross income minus up to 20 different recognized deductions:

---

[16]26 U.S.C. § 62. Many of the specific deductions are limited by the terms and conditions set forth in other statutory provisions.

$$\textbf{AGI} = GI - TBD - PL - PE - PD - PPA - RS - EWP - RE - SUCR - JP - CFV - ME - AMSA - ELI - HEE - HSA - DSC - WSC$$

where GI is gross income; TBD is trade and business deductions; PL is property loss, including losses from the sale or exchange of property; PE is property expenses for rent-producing properties; PD is property depreciation allowed in cases involving life tenants on property or income beneficiaries of property; PPA is pension, profit-sharing, and annuity plan deductions for self-employed individuals; RS is the recognized retirement savings deduction; EWP is penalties of early withdrawals from savings accounts; RE is reforestation expenses; SUCR is repayment of supplement unemployment compensation benefits; JP is jury duty pay remitted to employers; CFV is the clean-fuel vehicle deduction; ME is moving expenses; AMSA is Archer Medical Savings Accounts; ELI is interest on education loans; HEE is higher education expenses; HAS is health savings accounts; DSC is costs involving discrimination suits, such as allowable deductions for attorneys' fees and court costs; WSC is costs involving whistleblower suits.

Casually referring to a party's *income,* without a qualifier, is thus a dangerous practice. Where *gross income* is at issue, it should be explored fully to include all of its constituent sources: wages and salaries, unemployment benefits, tips and gratuities, dividends, rents, royalties, annuities, and a percentage of Social Security benefits. Many state statutes and rule books further define gross income, especially for purposes of calculating alimony and child support. The Internal Revenue Code itself has an expansive definition, including everything from prize money won in a contest to the fair market value of property sold at a cheaper price to a political organization.[17] Where *adjusted gross income* is at issue—or ought to be—then the income figure is likely to be considerably lower based on the deductions shown in the formula above.

Adjusted gross income is generally found on the bottom of the first page of a party's IRS Form 1040, and it is then copied again to the top of the second page.

---

[17]26 U.S.C. §§ 71 through 90.

Taxable Income

Taxable income refers to the adjusted gross income minus any deductions, exemptions, or other adjustments recognized by law. It is the taxable income that is *taxed*. In other words, it is the taxable income, found on Line 43 of a federal tax return, that is subject to the tax rate. Therefore, it is important—and indeed, it may be quite strategic—to specify exactly whether a particular negotiation involves gross income, adjusted gross income, or taxable income. Especially in the case of self-employed spouses, it is not simply the tax bracket that counts, but also the taxable income to which it applies.

If taxable income for a particular year has not yet been reported on a tax return, then it can be determined from gross income. First, gross income must be adjusted to determine adjusted gross income. Then, adjusted gross income must be further adjusted by subtracting personal exemptions and deductions to arrive at taxable income.

On a federal tax return (Form 1040), a taxpayer can claim a standard deduction depending on his or her filing status, which is a preset amount set by the IRS.[18] In the alternative, a taxpayer can file itemized deductions for allowable expenses, such as charitable contributions, mortgage interest, and certain medical expenses. The Internal Revenue Code recognizes additional deductions for taxpayers who are 65 or older and their spouses, for blind taxpayers and their spouses, and for real property taxes, disaster losses, and motor vehicle sales tax.

Where taxable income is at issue in a divorce case, attorneys should demand discovery of Schedule A of Form 1040, in which itemized deductions are listed. Schedule A provides spaces for medical and dental expenses, state and local taxes and sales tax paid, interest payments and mortgage insurance premiums, charitable gifts, job-related expenses, and other miscellaneous deductions—any of which may be a fertile source of information or a trigger for deeper inquiry. The total amount of itemized deductions is then reported on line 40 at the top of the second page of Form 1040. Line 43 of the tax return then subtracts the itemized deductions and allowable exemptions to produce the amount of taxable income.

In some cases, it is also valuable to identify what income is *nontaxable income*. Nontaxable income includes child support, 401K funds rolled over into another 401K account or IRA account when switching jobs, disability income on benefits purchased with after-tax

[18] 26 U.S.C. § 63.

dollars, and funds paid in to a variety of retirement plans. Family practitioners should consult the federal Tax Cuts and Jobs Act (TCJA), adopted during the Trump Administration. Under the TCJA, there is no deduction for alimony for the payer. Furthermore, alimony is no longer treated as gross income to the recipient. For divorces and legal separations that are executed after 2018, the alimony-paying spouse will not be able to deduct the payments, and the alimony-receiving spouse will not be required to include them in gross income or pay federal income tax on them.

Net Savings

Savings is an important aspect of a family's financial structure. In many cases, attorneys find themselves arguing to preserve the savings component of a couple's standard of living. As such, it is not always enough to negotiate how much cash will change hands for immediate bill-paying and family support purposes; it is also sometimes necessary to address how much money will be deposited or invested as part of an established saving pattern. Especially where college trust funds have been established for the children, a couple's savings history represents a measurable aspect of their financial lifestyle.

Net savings refers to a calculation of all income remaining—and available for saving—after all expenses have been paid. If a spouse earns $120,000 and has expenses of $90,000, then his net savings is $30,000. Notwithstanding any other adjustments, claims, or tax issues that might be asserted, the net savings is simply the amount unassigned to any cost, expense, or obligation and therefore is the net amount available for saving.

Actual spending patterns, however, are relevant because one's net savings may vary once the parties separate. The amount of net savings is thus reduced by replacement costs, discretionary expenditures, and day-to-day variables. Replacement costs refer to those expenditures that become necessary for the first time once a spouse occupies new living quarters (such as the cost for lawn service or a parking permit). Discretionary expenditures refer to nonmandatory spending that recurs in a particular pattern, such as daily purchases of a newspaper, or coffee and a donut on the way to work. Day-to-day variables expand the discretionary category to account for those occasional and patternless purchases, such as the cost of an occasional night at the movies or visit to the ballpark, or the charge for a periodic shoeshine or a massage. By tallying all of these expenditures, the true *net* savings can be determined.

Unless a spouse conducts a study of her own day-to-day activities and scientifically calculates all of her discretionary and variable spending habits over a period of time, it may be difficult to scientifically report every conceivable expenditure. This analysis is nonetheless useful, and it may be fruitful to estimate spending patterns to calculate a reasonable figure for net savings. The following formula can be utilized to estimate net savings:

$$NS = NI - BillsP - RDExp - AVE$$

where NS is net savings, NI is net income, BillsP is bills paid, RDExp is regular discretionary expenditures, and AVE is averaged variable expenses. Net income in this equation refers to take-home pay; that is, income net of taxes, but not (yet) net of personal expenses. Bills paid refers to all regular bills, such as mortgage or rental payments, car payments, credit card payments, loan payments, and other ordinary periodic obligations. Regular discretionary expenses refers to the spending patterns that define a party's lifestyle, such as a standing monthly manicure, a regular weekend dinner at the pub, or biweekly trips to the dry cleaner. Averaged variable expenses represents an estimate of the total of occasional and/or nonrecurring expenses (car washes, weekend getaways to the mountains or the beach, purchase of cell phone accessories or upgrades).

Only after counting all of one's expenditures, or carefully and thoroughly estimating them, should this formula be applied. The more thorough the calculation of expenses, the more likely the net savings will not be overstated.

Net Worth

The fundamental formula for net worth[19] is nothing more than assets minus liabilities. The calculation may be found on financial affidavits and financial disclosure forms used in some states. The calculation is, however, frequently inaccurate because its constituent parts are inconsistent, inflated, incomplete, or unadjusted.

To fine-tune the calculation, the formula must be based on *total assets* and *total liabilities.* We could say that net worth is the difference

[19]See Section 8.9.

between total assets and total liabilities: NW = TA – TL. However, if assets are under- or overreported or liabilities are incorrect, then the calculation is inaccurate or incomplete. So, for example, if liabilities (as garnered from a financial affidavit) do not account for tax consequences, then the net worth formula would have to be modified as such: NW = TA – TL – Tax. A spouse with assets equal to $800,000, liabilities of $200,000, and tax consequences of $75,000 would have a net worth of $525,000.

In the absence of a financial affidavit or other form of financial disclosure, a rough estimate of net worth must be made with a genuine commitment to thoroughness. Asset calculations must take into consideration the market value of homes and other real property, the market value of motor vehicles, the amount of cash on hand, funds on deposit in checking and savings accounts, investments and securities, the value of life insurance contracts, retirement account balances, certificates of deposit, money market and other bank accounts, all forms of personal property, all forms of intangible property (copyrights, for example), collectibles, jewelry, valuable legal rights (easements, licenses, contract options), guaranteed employment benefits, personal loans owed to the individual, and all other kinds of personal belongings. Likewise, liability calculations must be comprehensive, including all mortgage balances, car loans, credit card balances, personal loans and lines of credit, student loans, unpaid medical bills, legal bills, and other professional expenses, unpaid taxes, and unsatisfied liens and judgments.

Net worth can be used to compare one spouse with another, particularly when an attorney seeks to equalize each party's standard of living. Net worth can also be used as a measure for equitably distributing marital assets: where one party's net worth dwarfs the other party's net worth, then it is necessary to shift assets between them to balance their positions more equitably. In addition, net worth can be plotted on a graph in a time series analysis to forecast a trend that is, or soon will, affect a spouse either favorably or unfavorably. Thus, for example, where a timeline of net worth values shows that a separated wife's net worth has continuously declined by 10% each year over five years, an attorney may be able to argue persuasively in favor of a disproportionately greater allocation of assets to her and/or a more aggressive allocation of debts to her spouse.

Net worth is also a fundamental aspect of measuring the value of a family business that is subject to division in a divorce case. As in the case of an individual's net worth, the net worth of a business must be comprehensive. Assets must include all money invested into the company since its creation, including its retained earnings and the value of its intangible assets (such as patents, franchise rights, and goodwill). Liabilities must include all categories of short-term and long-term debt, including, for example, unpaid taxes and unsatisfied liens or judgments.

18.13. Wilcox's Prediction Formula

A frequent point of contention in a divorce is the value of a spouse's small business, particularly when the business is run like a hobby, on an informal or part-time basis. Consider, for example, a wedding photography business or a landscaping operation that a spouse runs as a side business. Not infrequently, the spouse who runs the business will claim that the business is valueless, dormant, or unprofitable, making it inappropriate to include in any settlement talks. The other spouse, meanwhile, may believe that the business is more active, more profitable, or more valuable than claimed.

If the business is flourishing and lucrative, then it may be appropriate to retain an expert business valuator to determine the value of the enterprise. If it is clear, however, that the business is not active or profitable, then it may be appropriate to consider the liquidation value of the company's assets. For this scenario, we would apply *Wilcox's Gambler's Ruin Prediction Formula*.

This formula estimates the liquidation value of a failing (or failed) business in a manner that will quickly produce a figure that can be used in negotiations or in argument at trial.

The formula for Wilcox's Prediction Formula is:

$$C + MS + 0.7(I + A/R + PE) + 0.5(FA + OA) - CL - LTL$$

where C is cash, MS is marketable securities, I is inventory, A/R is accounts receivable, PE is prepaid expenses, FA is fixed assets, OA is other assets, CL is current liabilities and LTL is long-term liabilities. In the liquidation of company assets, an owner would not likely get 100% of the book value of his assets. Thus, the Wilcox formula considers only 70% (0.7) of inventory, accounts receivable, and prepaid expenses. It assumes that other assets, including fixed assets, would draw only 50% (0.5).

Let's try an example. Suppose that Margaret works full-time in the accounting department of a major corporation. She runs a private bookkeeping service from her home, through which she has assisted friends with their tax returns and personal budgets at a reasonable price. During her divorce, Margaret's husband contends that Margaret earned at least $1,000 per week during tax season, and that, over the course of a year, she made a significant supplemental income running her bookkeeping service. Margaret counters that her bookkeeping service is not a formal business but rather a casual sideline; that her friends pay her insignificant amounts of money to help them with their taxes; and that the service is barely operational at this point.

Margaret's husband's attorney conducts pretrial discovery to explore these issues. He asks Margaret to produce a balance sheet and other financial statements showing the assets and liabilities for the bookkeeping service. The following asset and liability values are gleaned from the documents:

Margaret's Bookkeeping Service	
Cash	$6,000
Inventory	$ 500
Accounts Receivable	$5,100
Prepaid Online Access to Accounting Program	$1,239
Prepaid Errors & Omissions Insurance	$ 490
Computer/Printer, Calculators, Fax Machines, Scanner, Register and Binders	$4,600
Office Furniture	$1,050
Accounts Payable	$2,530
Interest Payments	$ 259
Commissions Owed to Referral Sources	$ 601
Telephone Expenses	$ 590
Long-term Liabilities	$4,300

Let's do the math by applying the Wilcox Prediction Formula:

C + MS + 0.7(I + A/R + PE) + 0.5(FA + OA) – CL – LTL

$6,000 + 0 + 0.7($500 + $5,100 + $1,239 + $490) + 0.5($4,600 + $1,050) – $2.530 – $259 – $601 – $590 – $4,300

= $6,000 + $5,130.30 + $2,825 – $2,530 – $259 – $601 – $590 – $4,300

= $5,675.30

According to the formula, Margaret's bookkeeping service has a liquidation value of $5,675.30. Applying this formula will permit her husband's attorney to argue, rationally and credibly, that the assets and liabilities of the bookkeeping business should be appropriately considered in the divorce settlement discussions. Even if the business is defunct or unproductive, Margaret's husband will declare his fair share of the *fire sale* value of the assets—that is, the liquidation value determined by the Wilcox formula.

Margaret, in fact, can utilize the formula herself to challenge any attempt by her husband to distribute the full book value of her bookkeeping business assets, or to ignore her accounts payable and accrued expenses. Were Husband's lawyer to add up the assets and liabilities shown on the table above without considering the Wilcox formula, he might argue that the net book value of Margaret's business is $10,699. As we see, however, the book value is significantly greater than the liquidation value of $5,675.30.

The Wilcox formula is used in business settings as a predictor of business failure. The lower the liquidation value, and the closer that value slips toward zero, the greater the risk of insolvency. In family court settings, however, where the value of a lapsed family business or inactive side business is at stake, the formula provides a realistic model for quantifying the value of the enterprise.

18.14. Pressing vs. Patient Liabilities

In every household, there are those debts that are pressing because they need to be paid when due, without fail. These include, for example, bank loans and taxes. There are also patient liabilities which consist of accounts payable that can be delayed, manipulated, temporarily ignored, or controlled by variations in discretionary spending habits. The ratio of pressing current liabilities to patient current liabilities is a marker of how well a party will be able to sustain a marital lifestyle. A lower ratio yields greater liquidity and presumably a better standard of living.

Consider a Wife's pressing and patient liabilities over a three-year period:

Liability	**2009**	**2010**	**2011**	**Nature of Debt**
Bank Loans Payable	\$29,000	\$31,200	\$30,666	Pressing
Taxes Due	\$ 6,000	\$ 7,005	\$ 8,710	Pressing
Accounts Payable	\$45,000	\$40,000	\$40,000	Patient

The Wife's ratios of pressing debt to patient debt would be:

$$2009: \frac{\$35,000}{\$45,000} = 0.78$$

$$2010: \frac{\$38,205}{\$40,000} = 0.95$$

$$2011: \frac{\$39,376}{\$40,000} = 0.98$$

Wife's growing ratio over the course of the three years indicates that her pressing debt load is increasing in proportion to her patient debt load. It means that she is beginning to experience liquidity problems. As such, the ratios, as depicted, would help Wife demonstrate her need for increased support to meet her cash flow needs and to cover her pressing debt.

Ratios of pressing versus patent liabilities can be compared between spouses too. So, for example, if a Wife has a ratio of 0.95 in the same year as the Husband has a ratio of 0.75, then Wife's attorney could argue that Husband's lower liquidity risk puts him in a stronger position to reallocate support dollars to his Wife, or to assume responsibility for some of her pressing debt.

Chapter 19

Admiralty and Aviation Law Damages

19.1. Scope

The fields of admiralty and aviation law share many features that distinguish them from other legal specialties. They are both largely governed by federal law. They both include multiple, often inconsistent statutes of limitations. They both frequently entail pre-suit notice requirements, and both often involve choice-of-law questions. They are also both hybrid practices, incorporating contract law as well as tort law, including personal injury and product liability law, along with environmental law, criminal law, commercial law, labor and employment, worker's compensation, and international law.

Admiralty, also known as *maritime law,* covers virtually all legal questions and controversies occurring on navigable waters. This may include contract violations, shipping accidents in which commercial cargo is lost or damaged, accidents involving damage to commercial vessels, and accidents involving injury or death to passengers. It also embraces maritime workers' rights and remedies; hazardous travel and working conditions; health, safety and labor violations on the open seas; employee injuries; and wrongful death. In addition, admiralty includes a wide array of criminal laws, such as piracy; robbery; unlawful smuggling of exotic plants and animals; unauthorized transport of weapons; cargo-related tax fraud; unauthorized fishing; unauthorized entry into a nation's marine boundary; oil and gas drilling violations; injuring protected marine wildlife; discharging sewage, oil, sludge, garbage, and other pollution offenses; hazardous dredging activities; homeland security offenses; and illegal trafficking in drugs or persons, including sex trafficking and immigration violations. While these criminal offenses are generally outside the scope of this book, the calculation of damages is relevant to the assessment of restitution, such as where an unlawful oil discharge by a shipowner disrupts a coastal zone ecosystem and interferes with beaches, swimming, and recreational boating.

Aviation law is a similarly broad field that covers not only airplane crashes, but also the various legal issues pertaining to aircraft design; airworthiness; navigation and maintenance; air traffic control; safety; pilot, mechanic, and crew licensing and training; and airport operations. It comprises the contract law of charter, interline, codeshare, catering, maintenance, and jet fuel purchasing agreements. Even more broadly, aviation law encompasses joint ventures among airline competitors, air cargo damage, delay and destruction, cargo screening, acceptance and security procedures, terrorism prevention initiatives, dangerous goods regulations, route network competition, price-fixing and antitrust law, aircraft financing law, data protection, public and private international law including multilateral agreements, unlawful tarmac delays, passenger baggage loss, noise pollution and air pollution by aircraft, third-party surface damage claims, infrastructure defects, and inaccessible airports and connected facilities under the Americans with Disabilities Act. Aviation law today also embodies the fast-growing fields of private commercial spacecraft, the issues relating to protection of public and private property during launch or reentry of commercial spacecraft, and the regulation of unmanned aircraft systems including drones.

Admiralty and aviation law overlap when helicopters are used in oil rig operations, when amphibious aircraft (i.e., sea planes) are used for maritime patrolling, firefighting, transport, and rescue operations, or when a commercial jet makes an emergency landing or crashes into a body of water. In most cases, admiralty law has governed these blended situations,[1] and federal courts have applied a choice-of-law analysis in addressing the issue of compensatory damages.

Understanding the nuances of these legal specialties is the critical first step in any damages claim arising within the fields of admiralty or aviation law. *Where does jurisdiction lie? What choice of law will apply? What international treaties, federal statutes or regulations, state law or common law principles are applicable?* The next step is to determine which fields of law will drive the analysis: *Is it a contract law case? A personal injury or wrongful death case? A lost cargo or delayed freight case? A commercial damages case?* Answering these essential questions will frame and narrow the damages analysis and will ultimately define the scope and magnitude of the claim.

Admiralty Law

19.2. Legal Framework for Admiralty Cases

Before applying any damages calculation to an admiralty case, an attorney must determine which statutes or regulations may apply to the issues in dispute. A glimpse at some of the various federal statutes governing admiralty practice provides insight into how important it is to understand the law in general and the specific differences between the laws:

> **Death on the High Seas Act (DOHSA).**[2] This statute authorizes damages for the death of a person by wrongful act, neglect, or default occurring on the high seas. The amount of recovery "shall be a fair compensation for the pecuniary loss sustained by the individuals for whose benefit the suit is brought."[3] The Court must also apportion the recovery among those individuals in proportion to the loss each has sustained.[4] A wrongful death action under DOHSA

---

[1]28 U.S.C. § 1333. *See, e.g.,* Executive Jet Aviation, Inc. v. City of Cleveland, 409 U.S. 249 (1972); Hammill v. Olympic Airways S.A., 398 F. Supp. 829 (D.D.C. 1975); Smith v. Pan Isla Corp., 684 F.2d 1102 (5th Cir. 1982); Isla Nena Air Services, Inc. v. Cessna Aircraft Co., 380 F. Supp. 2d 74 (D. Puerto Rico 2005).

[2]46 U.S.C. §§ 30301 through 30308.

[3]46 U.S.C. § 30303.

[4]*Id.*

may be filed within three years, but the states may have shorter statutes of limitations. The Act does not affect the law of the state regulating the right to recover for death.[5] Damages may include calculations of life expectancy, work expectancy, past and future earning capacity, living expenses, a surviving child's benefits during minority, means of support available to adult beneficiaries, actual contributions which the decedent made to the beneficiaries, the probability of future contributions, and prejudgment interest.

Longshore Harbor and Workers Compensation Act (LHWCA).[6] The LHWCA provides compensation for "employees" who are defined as persons "engaged in maritime employment, including any longshoreman or other person engaged in longshoring operations, and any harbor-worker including a ship repairman, shipbuilder, and ship-breaker."[7] To recover under the Act, an employee must be injured "upon the navigable waters of the United States (including any adjoining pier, wharf, dry dock, terminal, building way, marine railway, or other adjoining area customarily used by an employer in loading, unloading, repairing, dismantling, or building a vessel).[8] The Act prescribes a variety of compensation timelines and caps on recovery. For example, compensation for disability or death not paid in a lump sum may not be greater than twice the applicable national average weekly wage,[9] and for total disability, may not be less than 50% of the applicable national average weekly wage.[10] The LHWCA has a 30-day pre-action notice requirement,[11] and a strict one-year statute of limitations.[12]

Jones Act.[13] A maritime tort statute, the Jones Act is limited to claims by seamen injured or killed in the course of employment.

[5] 46 U.S.C. § 30308.
[6] 33 U.S.C. § 901, *et. seq.*
[7] 33 U.S.C. § 902(3).
[8] 33 U.S.C. § 903(a).
[9] 33 U.S.C. § 906(b)(1).
[10] 33 U.S.C. § 906(b)(2).
[11] 33 U.S.C. § 912.
[12] 33 U.S.C. § 913.
[13] 46 U.S.C. §§ 30104-30105.

Only a seaman's employer may be sued; the Act does not permit claims against third parties.[14] The Jones Act is based on the Federal Employees Liability Act (FELA)[15] and extends to seamen the same remedies and liability standards recognized under FELA.[16] Case law now also extends a seaman's damages claim to include hedonic damages[17] as well as punitive damages.[18] A Jones Act claim is governed by a three-year statute of limitations.[19]

Outer Continental Shelf Lands Act (OCSLA).[20] The OCSLA extends the Constitution and laws and civil and political jurisdiction of the United States to the subsoil and seabed of the outer Continental Shelf and to all artificial islands, and to all installations and other devices attached to the seabed, such as oil rigs.[21] It provides for civil and criminal penalties for harming fish and other aquatic life and for damaging property or mineral deposits or the marine, coastal or human environment. Citizens may file OCSLA suits after a 60-day notice period, but the notice period does not apply when there is an imminent threat to public health or safety or an immediate effect on the legal interests of a plaintiff.[22] If the Attorney General commences an OCSLA action, citizens cannot file their own suits but must, in such cases, intervene in the government's suit.[23] The Act sets civil penalties of not more than $20,000 per day.[24]

---

[14]*See, e.g.,* Daughtry v. Jenny G., LLC, 703 Fed. Appx. 883, 886 (11th Cir. 2017).

[15]45 U.S.C. § 51, *et seq.*

[16]Ferguson v. Moore-McCormack Lines, Inc., 352 U.S. 521, 77 S. Ct. 457, 1 L. Ed. 2d 511 (1957); Wilson v. Zapata Off-Shore Co., 939 F.2d 260 (5th Cir. 1991).

[17]Perkins v. American Electric Power Fuel Supply, Inc., 91 Fed. Appx. 370 (6th Cir. 2004).

[18]Atlantic Sounding Co., Inc. v. Townsend, 557 U.S. 404, 129 S. Ct. 2561, 174 L. Ed. 2d 382 (2009).

[19]46 U.S.C. § 30106.

[20]43 U.S.C. § 1301, *et. seq.*

[21]43 U.S.C. § 1333(a)(1).

[22]43 U.S.C. § 1349(a)(3).

[23]43 U.S.C. § 1349(a)(2)(B).

[24]43 U.S.C. § 1350(b).

Abandoned Shipwreck Act (ASA).[25] ASA divests the federal courts of admiralty jurisdiction over claims to embedded shipwrecks. Under the Act, the United States asserts title to any abandoned shipwreck embedded in submerged lands of a state or in coralline formations protected under state law, or which is determined to be eligible for inclusion in the National Register.[26] At issue in ASA cases is whether a shipwreck is actually abandoned or whether maritime laws governing salvage are applicable. While abandonment may be inferred from the surrounding circumstances,[27] there is a presumption against finding abandonment,[28] especially when an owner appears and seeks to recover its long lost property.[29]

Maritime Transportation Security Act.[30] This 2002 statute requires all cargo shippers to provide cargo documents prior to the unloading of such cargo in a U.S. port. The Customs and Border Patrol must receive the vessel's cargo declaration 24 hours before the cargo arrives at port.[31] Disclosures include information concerning the quantity and classification of cargo, the port where it was loaded, the identity of the shipper, and consignee.[32] Finally, all carriers are required to maintain an International Carrier Bond. The production of these records may be critical in gathering verifiable information to be used in a subsequent cargo delivery damages claim.[33]

Ocean Shipping Reform Act (OSRA).[34] OSRA, which amended the Shipping Act of 1984, includes financial responsibil-

---

[25]43 U.S.C. §§ 2101 through 2106.

[26]43 U.S.C. § 2105(a).

[27]Northeast Research LLC v. One Shipwrecked Vessel, her Tackle, Equipment, Appurtenances, Cargo, 790 F. Supp. 2d 56 (W.D.N.Y. 2011).

[28]Hener v. United States, 525 F. Supp. 350, 356–357 (S.D.N.Y.1981).

[29]Sea Hunt, Inc. v. Unidentified Shipwrecked Vessel or Vessels, 221 F. 3d 634 (4th Cir. 2000).

[30]19 U.S.C. § 70101, *et. seq.*

[31]19 C.F.R. 4.7(b)(5).

[32]19 C.F.R. 4.7(a)(c).

[33]*See, e.g.*, NIC Holding Corp. v. Lukoil Pan America, LLC, No. 05-CIV-9372, 2008 WL 4212462 (S.D.N.Y. 2008).

[34]46 U.S.C. § 40901, *et. seq.*

ity provisions for ocean transportation intermediaries and provides for the right of a common carrier to compensate an ocean freight forwarder for authorized shipments.[35] The Act prohibits common carriers from paying compensation more than once on the same shipment. It also prohibits an ocean freight forwarder from receiving compensation from a common carrier or a shipment in which the ocean freight forwarder has a direct or indirect beneficial interest.[36]

Wreck Act.[37] Under this law, the federal government can obtain damages against anyone who anchors, sinks, or wrecks vessels or watercraft in navigable channels so as to obstruct the passage of other vessels and craft. Masters, pilots, and engineers can be made personally liable. Although the Wreck Act is a criminal statute, it is also recognized as establishing the standard of care defining civil liability.[38] The costs of removal or destruction and disposal is recoverable under the law.[39]

Oil Pollution Act (OPA).[40] Under the OPA, enacted in 1990, all responsible parties who allow a vessel to discharge oil into navigable waters or adjoining shorelines are liable for all removal costs and damages arising therefrom. This includes removal costs incurred by any governmental agency or Indian tribe, damages to natural resources and to private real estate or personal property, loss of subsistence use of natural resources, loss of profits or impairment of earning capacity of damaged property, and damages for the net costs of providing increased public services during or after removal activities.[41]

Carriage of Goods by Sea Act (COGSA).[42] This law places primary responsibility for the safety of cargo upon the vessel and

---

[35]46 U.S.C. §§ 40902, 40904.

[36]46 U.S.C. § 40904.

[37]33 U.S.C. § 409, *et. seq.*

[38]Morania Barge No. 140, Inc. v. M. & J. Tracy, Inc., 312 F. 2d 78 (2d Cir.1962).

[39]33 U.S.C. §§ 414(b), 415(c).

[40]33 U.S.C. § 2701, *et. seq.*

[41]33 U.S.C. § 2701(b).

[42]46 U.S.C. § 30701, *et. seq.*

its operators and owner. It eliminates various contractual schemes in which a carrier might attempt to shield itself from liability. In an action for damaged cargo brought under COGSA, a carrier may enjoy limited liability pursuant to a bill of lading, but the carrier's negligent agent, who is neither a party to nor an express beneficiary of the bill of lading, would not be protected by the limited liability provision.[43]

Thus, even though the general marital liability law provides for the right of passengers to sue vessels and their owners for personal injury and damage to their baggage,[44] and to make claims against ship mates, engineers, and pilots,[45] it is important to analyze every potentially applicable admiralty law which could impose jurisdictional exclusions, financial limitations or caps on prospective damage claims. It is equally important to scrutinize contracts of passage, stowage, affreightment, and cabotage, and to analyze carrier certificates, invoices, and bills of lading for details that may affect the rights and liabilities of passengers, shipowners, and workers. Cruise line passengers, for example, generally have no rights under admiralty law because the cruise line owner customarily includes contractual language prescribing notice provisions and a one-year statute of limitations.

19.3. Damages Available

Before calculating the amount of damages, it is important to identify all categories of damages that are available under admiralty law. The potential damages that are available will vary depending on whether the claimant is a seaman, another kind of maritime worker, a passenger, or otherwise.

Damages for Injured Seamen

In a typical worker's compensation case, an injured worker would present a claim for lost wages, reimbursement of medical bills, and disabil-

---

[43]Robert C. Herd & Co. v. Krawill Machinery Corp., 359 U.S. 297, 79 S. Ct. 766, 3 L. Ed. 2d 820 (1959).

[44]46 U.S.C. § 30102.

[45]46 U.S.C. § 30103.

ity benefits, generally classified as temporary total disability (TTD), temporary partial disability (TPD), permanent total disability (PTD), or permanent partial disability (PPD) benefits. Liability can be established *without* proving the fault or negligence of the employer. Under the law of admiralty, however, the injured worker (seaman) can seek damages, as in other personal injury cases, by proving negligence or *unseaworthiness* to sustain a claim under the Jones Act. Unseaworthiness includes any number of possible mishaps resulting from unsafe conditions on a vessel, such as when a seaman slips and falls on an oil slick on the ship's deck or when he is injured by improperly maintained equipment. Under general maritime law, a seaman is also entitled to several unique categories of damages, which, like worker's compensation law, do not require any proof of fault. These damages include (1) maintenance, (2) cure, (3) unearned wages, and (4) found.

Maintenance refers to a payment that will compensate the seaman for lodging beginning on the date that he leaves the vessel. It may include food and travel expenses associated with medical treatment. A maritime employer must pay maintenance as long as the employment relationship has been established, regardless of any negligence or unseaworthiness of the vessel, and despite any proof of any contributory negligence by the seaman. Maintenance payments must be continued until the seaman reaches a status known as *maximum medical cure,* which occurs when the seaman's condition will no longer improve with additional medical treatment.

Cure refers to medical treatment, including the costs of hospitalization, doctor's bills, therapy, and medications. The right to cure continues until the seaman is fit for duty or reaches a level of maximum medical cure. The right to cure is also based purely on the employment relationship, and no proof of negligence or unseaworthiness is necessary.

Unearned wages refers to the regular pay that the seaman would have earned had he not been injured and had he fulfilled the terms of his contract or completed his voyage. Unearned wages include all amounts that would have been paid, such as overtime, compensatory time, accumulated shore leave, gratuities, bonuses, and other employment benefits. The amount of unearned wages payable may be defined or limited by an employment contract or a collective bargaining agreement.

Found refers to a claim for damages, as part of a lost wages claim, that represents the value of the meals and lodging a seaman would have received had he remained in active service.

An award for found can be made only when actual food and lodging expenses are incurred.

Damages for Other Maritime Workers

Non-seaman and non-crew members who nevertheless work in maritime trades and occupations are generally covered by the LHWCA. This include longshore workers, ship-repairers, shipbuilders or shipbreakers, and harbor construction workers. Covered injuries must occur on the navigable waters of the United States or in the adjoining areas, including piers, docks, shipyards, terminals, wharves, and those areas used in loading and unloading vessels. Non-seaman may also be covered if they perform their work on navigable water and their injuries occur there.

The LHWCA provides for the payment of compensation, medical care, and vocational rehabilitation services to employees disabled from on-the-job injuries that occur on the navigable waters of the United States, or in adjoining areas used for loading, unloading, building or repairing a vessel. The Act also provides for payment of survivor benefits to dependents if the work injury causes, or contributes to, the employee's death. These benefits are typically paid by the self-insured employer or by a private insurance company on the employer's behalf.

Employees working on offshore oil drilling rigs or in other occupations in the development or exploration of natural resources on the Outer Continental Shelf of the United States are covered by the OCSLA. The Act, however, specifically provides that compensation for the disability or death of an Outer Continental Shelf employee shall be payable under the provisions of the LHWCA.

As in other nonmaritime cases, special damages are also reduced to present value and discounted for the effect of income tax.

General Maritime Damages

Under general maritime law, wrongful death claims may include only pecuniary damages, such as loss of services, loss of support, loss of nurture, loss of inheritance, loss of fringe benefits, and funeral expenses. A survival action may bring further damages in the form of medical expenses, lost wages, and pain and suffering prior to death. Pain and suffering by beneficiaries is not recognized, and in most federal circuits, loss of consortium claims are also not recognized. However, punitive damages may be available in an appropriate case.

Injured passengers and nonmaritime workers are entitled to the broadest variety of damages, including past and future medical expenses; past, present, and future wage loss; future loss of earning capacity; pain and suffering, including loss of the enjoyment of life; emotional distress damages; physical injury and disfigurement; loss of family services; loss of consortium; and in some cases, punitive damages. Prejudgment interest is also available, running from the date of injury until the date judgment is entered.

19.4. Calculating Damages

Each claim for damages arising under admiralty law will fall into one or more preordained categories depending on whether it's a personal injury claim, property claim, cargo claim, or other contract claim, and whether it involves a seaman or other maritime worker. Which category applies—and which statutes or other laws may apply—will dictate what specific facts will be necessary to calculate a final damage award. Let's consider some examples:

Property Damage Claim

Let's assume that an oil tanker known as the *Duchess* crashes into a pier owned by the Florida Port Authority (FPA). The FPA sues the *Duchess* and its owner, American Duchess Fleets, for the property damage to the pier. Partial summary judgment is granted to FPA as to liability and causation insofar as the *Duchess* could not rebut the presumption that it was at fault for causing the allision. The *Duchess* sustained an indentation to its bow as a result of the allision, which did not affect its seaworthiness. The damage to the tanker, which was repairable, is not at issue. However, the vessel was fully loaded with nearly 40,000 tons of cargo at the time of the accident, which occurred when the *Duchess* was steering from one berth to another berth at approximately three knots. The heavy vessel struck the southwest corner of the FPA pier.

When the allision occurred, the pier had already been damaged and had deteriorated due to the passage of time. Originally built as a wooden structure, the pier had been fortified with concrete pilings and a concrete deck, but the original wooden pilings had never been removed. A renovation project was thus underway on the pier before the accident with the *Duchess*. As part of the renovation project, a contractor had been hired to repair some of the existing outer piles, to construct a large concrete pile cap, and to construct a U-shaped element to bolster the end of the structure supporting the fenders and to provide lateral-load capacity.

At issue in the case brought by FPA is what dock damage was caused by the *Duchess* and what damage preexisted the allision. Under FPA's tariff and regulations, all vessels, their owners, charterers, and agents are liable for the costs to repair damage or destruction caused by them, and the associated losses, together with litigation costs and attorneys' fees. An additional 15% of the replacement or repair costs is also assessed. Accordingly, the outline of possible damages would look like this:

1. Repair Costs plus 15%
2. Interest
3. Prejudgment Interest
4. Litigation Costs
5. Attorneys' Fees

Awarding 100% of repair costs to FPA would seem unfair, however, if the pier, once repaired, would enjoy an extended life. In fact, as a general rule, if a repair or replacement to a damaged structure adds new value to or extends the useful life of a property, the court should reduce the full repair or replacement costs.

Betterment Based on Useful Life Extension

To calculate the *betterment* amount based on a useful life extension, we need to know (1) what the useful life was prior to the casualty, (2) what is or will be the expected useful life of the repaired or replaced property, and (3) what amount should be deducted to account for prior depreciation or any anticipated betterment. The recoverable repair costs (RRC) will thus equal the total replacement and repair costs (TRC) minus the extended useful life (EUL) divided by the sum of the pre-allision remaining useful life (RUL) plus the EUL, then multiplied times the TRC, depicted as follows:

$$RRC = TRC - \left(\frac{EUL}{RUL + EUL} \times TRC\right)$$

Let's plug in some numbers. Assume, for example, that the total repair costs proved by FPA totals \$295,000. The pre-allision useful life of the pier was 20 years, but as a result of the repairs, the useful life will be extended by another 10 years. Using these figures, we can calculate the recoverable repair costs:

$$RRC = TRC - \left(\frac{EUL}{RUL + EUL} \times TRC\right)$$
$$RRC = \$295{,}000 - \left(\frac{10}{20 + 10} \times \$295{,}000\right)$$
$$RRC = \$295{,}000 - (0.33 \times \$295{,}000)$$
$$RRC = \$295{,}000 - \$97{,}350$$
$$RRC = \$197{,}650$$

Thus, the recoverable repair costs would be \$197,650. Depending on the applicable law, this figure may have to be further adjusted by the effects of depreciation, present value, and any other improvements or betterment to the pier that was anticipated. If depreciation is applicable, it may be applied to various expenses that constitute the TRC before applying the formula above. This may include, for example, engineering fees and surveying costs.

In admiralty law, unjust enrichment of a party who suffers damage to its property is not permitted. Therefore, the provision in the FPA's tariff and regulation that would award an additional 15% of repair costs will generally not be allowed. Such a penalty or surplusage would run counter to federal law. Likewise, attorneys' fees, even when recognized by state-based offers of judgment, may contravene federal maritime law. However, prejudgment interest is recognized and would be payable from the date the damages were incurred until the date judgment is entered against the responsible party.

Damages for Physical Injury to Seaman

Suppose that a seaman is injured by an explosion on his ship. He brings an action against the shipowners, alleging negligence under the Jones Act and unseaworthiness. The seaman spends the first four weeks following his injuries at the Walter Reed National Military Medical Center, where he undergoes surgery and a course of rehabilitation.

When he is thereafter discharged by the hospital, the seaman immediately joins the crew on another ship on a voyage for 22 days. The experience on that voyage is terribly painful, however, and the seaman, still suffering from his injuries, withdraws from active maritime service thereafter. After another 60 days, the seaman finds work as a chef at a hotel restaurant.

As we know from general maritime law, when a seaman is injured in the service of his vessel, the shipowner has an obligation to pay *maintenance,* such as room and board; *cure,* such as medical expenses, and *unearned wages.* The seaman's right to maintenance and cure continues until the seaman reaches maximum medical improvement (MMI). The employer's obligation to pay maintenance and cure exists even where the employer is not at fault.[46]

What will a court need to know in order to resolve a dispute involving maintenance and cure? In order to address any dispute involving maintenance and cure, the Court will need to determine:

A. The time when maintenance and cure should begin;
B. The time when maintenance and cure should terminate;
C. The per diem allowance for maintenance and the expenses of cure;
D. The total amount of money that the seaman has earned at the time of trial through any shore employment (within the bracket of time defined in (A) and (B) above);
E. The total amount of expected future earnings from shore employment between the time of trial and the termination of maintenance and cure.

In this case, we must first construct a formula to fix the seaman's daily maintenance rate (DMR).

The daily rate will be determined by dividing the monthly maintenance rate by 30.42 (the number of days in an average month). The monthly cost of maintenance will be a total of all room and board expenses, including, for example, rent or mortgage payments; electric-

[46]Under the Jones Act, the injured seaman may nevertheless present his negligence claim to a jury and seek a separate award of damages based on the circumstances that caused the explosion. To calculate personal injury damages arising from a negligent act, see Chapter 11, *Personal Injury and Wrongful Death Damages.*

ity, water, gas, and garbage removal bills; car loan payments; car maintenance and fuel expenses; and the cost of food. Let's simplify these expenses as follows:

Rent	$ 850.00
Utilities:	$ 150.00
Car Expenses:	$ 350.00
Food:	$ 750.00
Total:	$2,100.00

To convert the monthly maintenance cost to DMR, we next divide by 30.42.

$$\frac{2{,}100.00}{30.42} = 69.03$$

Therefore, DMR = 69.03. Let's now add the following hypothetical information to the maintenance calculation:

Date of Injury: December 1, 2018
Days in Hospital: 28
Days on 2nd Voyage: 22
Start Date for Subsequent Employment: March 22, 2019
Amount Earned at Time of Trial on November 1, 2019: $26,061.75
Future Earnings Until Termination of Maintenance: ? ? ?

In this hypothetical scenario, the seaman was injured by the explosion on December 1, 2018. We are told that he spent four weeks (28 days) at the hospital. Therefore, these first 28 days following the injury, during which the seaman was living at the hospital at government expense, will not be counted in the total maintenance award. His excludable hospital time (EHT) equals 28. We are also told that the seaman boarded another ship and joined its crew immediately after being released from the hospital, and he remained in the second ship's employment for the next 22 days, during which his room and board were provided.[47] Therefore, the seaman's excludable employment time (EET) equals 22. We know, therefore, at the outset, that the final main-

[47]The obligation to pay maintenance does not terminate automatically upon service on another ship, according to the law of some circuits. Employment aboard another vessel, however, generally provides strong evidence of the fact that the seaman has fully recovered.

tenance award (FMA) must be reduced by any excludable hospital time or excludable subsequent employment time that the seaman spent under the care of others. We can begin our formula as follows:

FMA = DMR x (N – EHT – EET)

where the FMA will equal the DMR multiplied by the number of days (N) between the start date of the injury and the MMI, minus the EHT and minus the EET. If the seaman had hypothetically reached MMI on May 5, 2019, we could then determine that the number of days between his injury date (December 1, 2018) and his MMI date (May 5, 2019) is 155 days. We could then determine FMA as follows:

FMA = DMR x (N – EHT – EET)
FMA = 69.03 x (155 – 28 – 22)
FMA = 69.03 x 105
FMA = $7,248.15

In our hypothetical case, however, the seaman finds work 60 days after returning from his second voyage, on March 22, 2019. This is 111 days after the date of injury. The right to maintenance does not end simply because a seaman has found subsequent shore employment.

In fact, if a seaman can establish that he has not fully recovered, then his return to work does not terminate his right to maintenance and cure from the vessel in whose service he was injured.

In the end, the determination of the cutoff date for maintenance—the MMI date—is a medical one, not a legal one. It is achieved when it appears probable that further treatment will result in no betterment of the seaman's condition, such as when the seaman's condition is incurable or when future treatment will merely relieve pain and suffering but not otherwise improve the seaman's condition.

What if the determination of MMI was contested? A seaman may claim that he is still disabled and still requires treatment months after being injured, but what if he takes a new full-time job that involves an equivalent amount of physical labor? The nature of the new work, whether it is full time or part time, and the state of the seaman's health are all factors that may affect the determination of when MMI should be established.

Under admiralty law policies, a seaman receiving maintenance has a duty to mitigate his damages. Let's assume that the seaman's new job as a chef pays a gross salary of $42,900 per year, or $3,575 per month. Between the date he acquired the job (March 22, 2019) and the time of trial (November 1, 2019), the seaman worked 7.29 months, grossing $26,061.75. He will continue to earn $3,575 per month as future earnings thereafter. An employer may wish to argue that the MMI date should coincide with the seaman's date of subsequent employment as a chef. If the employer can support this position with a medical opinion, then the seaman's period of eligibility for a maintenance award would run from the date of his injury, less the EHT and the EET, *until* March 22, 2019, the MMI date, being also the date of the subsequent employment. The number of days between the injury and MMI is 111. Therefore, the employer would argue that maintenance should be determined as follows:

FMA = DMR x (N – EHT – EET)
FMA = 69.03 x (111 – 28 – 22)
FMA = 69.03 x 61
FMA = $4,210.83

The calculations shown above are designed to illustrate an approach to establishing an FMA, but, of course, they can be manipulated by altering the DMR or any of the constituent parts of the multiplier. Thus, if a seaman did not actually incur living expenses for a period of time because he stayed with another person who fully paid for and supported him during this period, an employer could seek a lower number of eligible days (N). Similarly, if a seaman's food budget or his transportation expenses were unreasonably inflated, the employer might argue for a lower DMR. The terminal date for payment of a maintenance award would also necessarily be impacted by the payment for cure. A seaman's right to cure continues until he is fit for duty or reaches MMI. An employer may contend, however, that the amount of medical expenses for treatment, testing, or medications is excessive or unnecessary.

Damages Payable on Maritime Salvage Claim

A maritime salvage award is potentially payable to all who render beneficial aid at sea. It is given as a matter of public policy to ensure the safety of life and property at sea; to restore property to its owners; to induce and encourage others to risk life and limb, if need be, in the interest of saving distressed property; and to eliminate any temptation on the part of the rescuers to despoil the saved property. No mathematical formula exists for the calculation of salvage awards, but many of the factors constituting such awards rely on damage and loss calculations addressed elsewhere in this book. In guiding the courts to determine a fair salvage award, several tests have been developed to consider the highly circumstantial nature of salvage claims.

The Six-Factor Blackwall Test

The U.S. Supreme Court, in *The Blackwall,*[48] laid out the six-factor test for calculating salvage claims under general maritime law. Under this test, a court considering a salvage claim should consider:

1. The labor expended by the salvors in rendering the salvage service
2. The promptitude, skill, and energy displayed in rendering the service and saving the property
3. The value of the property employed by the salvors in rendering the service, and the danger to which such property was exposed
4. The risk incurred by the salvors in securing the property from the impending peril
5. The value of the property saved
6. The degree of danger from which the property was rescued

The *Blackwall* factors do not readily translate into a formula. The Fifth Circuit, however, has advised courts to use the first, second, third, fourth, and sixth factors to construct a percentage to apply to the fifth factor.[49]

The 10-Factor Treaty Test

The *International Convention on Salvage 1989,*[50] a maritime treaty ratified by the United States and at least 10 other countries, requires a salvage award "to be fixed with a view to encouraging salvage operations." It prescribes ten factors to be taken into account:

---

[48]77 U.S. 1, 19 L. Ed. 870 (1869).

[49]Margate Shipping Co. v. M/V JA Orgeron, 143 F. 3d 976 (5th Cir. 1998).

[50]1953 UNTS 165; S. Treaty Doc. No. 102-12; adopted on April 28, 1989, ratified by the U.S. Senate on October 31, 1991, and entered into force on July 14, 1996.

1. The salved value of the vessel and other property
2. The skill and efforts of the salvors in preventing or minimizing damage to the environment
3. The measure of success obtained by the salvor
4. The nature and degree of the danger
5. The skill and efforts of the salvors in salving the vessel, other property, and life
6. The time used and expenses and losses incurred by the salvors
7. The risk of liability and other risks run by the salvors or their equipment
8. The promptness of the services rendered
9. The availability and use of vessels or other equipment intended for salvage operations
10. The state of readiness and efficiency of the salvor's equipment and the value thereof

Article 13 of the Salvage Treaty further provides that a salvage award "shall be made by all of the vessel and other property interests in proportion to their salved values." Under the treaty, a participating country may impose the salvage liability on just one party, subject to a right of recourse against the other interests for their respective shares.

Applying the Factors

Assume that a helicopter operated by HeliCo makes an emergency landing on a ship owned by Mayflower Maritime while the helicopter is ferrying passengers to an offshore oil platform in the Gulf of Mexico. The ship, a bulk freighter engaged in international trade, then carries the helicopter and its crew and passengers safely back to the port. Mayflower Maritime sues HeliCo in a salvage claim, seeking the costs of its additional fuel, lost time and demurrage charges, survey and related expenses, and a claim for value of the helicopter and the lives saved by the vessel's rescue efforts.

For purposes of this analysis we will apply the 10 factors under the Salvage Treaty.[51] It may be helpful to visualize the factors, as we populate a table with some hypothetical facts.

---

[51]Which set of factors actually applies is a legal decision that would first need to be made, based on the parties and circumstances involved and the prevailing law of the circuit court where the venue lies.

FACTORS	ANALYSIS	VALUE	AWARD
Salved Value	What is the value of the helicopter? The court is not likely to make a separate "life salvage" award for saving lives.	Assume the helicopter is worth $1.9 million.	Yes
Skill/Effort in Preserving Environment	What environmental damage was at risk from the helicopter?	Assume no evidence that the helicopter would have crash-landed in the water or dumped its fuel.	N/A
Success Obtained	Mayflower Maritime effectively took care of the helicopter crew and passengers and safely transported them to shore.	Assume Mayflower Maritime incurred costs for , food accommodations, and transportation.	Yes
Nature/Degree of Danger	Assume the helicopter was clearly in danger while flying but that danger was averted once it landed on the ship.	Assume that the danger level was moderate.	Yes
Skill/Effort in Salving Property and Life	The ship's crew assisted the helicopter crew and passengers mostly after they landed on the vessel.	Assume that the ship was extremely forthright in providing lodging, food, and fire prevention services.	Yes
Time/Expenses/ Losses of Salvors	Assume that Maritime Mayflower incurred expenses for loss of use, additional fuel consumed, additional agency fees, local survey, classification survey attendance, and hatch cover manufacturer's attendance.	Assume that the total cost of the salvor's time and expenses (in the various categories noted) is $25,000.00.	Yes $25,000.00
Risks to Salvors	Assume that the helicopter was well controlled by its pilot when it landed on the ship. There was a low risk that the helicopter could have hit the mast, piping, and equipment or raised hatch covers when it landed, but it did not do so.	Assume that the risk level was moderate.	Yes

FACTORS	ANALYSIS	VALUE	AWARD
Promptness	The Mayflower Maritime crew quickly greeted the helicopter when it landed, had fire hoses ready, and efficiently diverted off course to deliver the helicopter back to port.	Assume that the salvors provided services promptly and effectively.	Yes
Availability and Use of Vessel/ Equipment	The necessary equipment was available, but was not designated or maintained for emergency use.	Assume the equipment was properly maintained, even though the vessel's crew were not professional salvors and no special efforts were undertaken in anticipation of a possible casualty.	N/A
Readiness of Equipment	The vessel's equipment was maintained and efficiently employed to assist the helicopter, although no special efforts were applied to maintain a state of readiness.	Assume the equipment was held in a general state of readiness, even though the vessel's crew were not professional salvors and no special efforts were undertaken in anticipation of a possible casualty.	N/A

To construct a formula from the hypothetical facts displayed in the table above, we must first ascertain which factors justify a salvage award. The last column in the table denominates the factors justifying an award with a "Yes," with all others being not applicable under the circumstances of this case. *But what is a "Yes" worth?* Only the sixth factor, which quantifies the time and expenses incurred by the salvors, provides us with a specific dollar amount (i.e., $25,000, which represents the cost of the vessel's additional fuel, the agency fees, surveys, etc.).

To construct a formula based on the "Yes" categories, we can say at this point that the value of the salvage award is the sum of the separate values that we assign to Factors 1, 3, 4, 5, 6, 7, and 8. (Only Factors 2, 9, and 10 are inapplicable in this hypothetical.) Therefore, the salvage award equals:

	Factor 1 Value
	Factor 3 Value
	Factor 4 Value
	Factor 5 Value
	$25,000.00
	Factor 7 Value
+	Factor 8 Value
=	Salvage Value

Assigning values to each factor can be difficult, but they should be fixed based on real market conditions and costs. Indeed, one court has noted that "the purpose of salvage awards is to encourage rescues in settings of high transaction costs by simulating the conditions and outcomes of a competitive market. In an ideal world, every meeting of salvor and salvee would result in a freely negotiated contract for salvage services priced at a competitive level. In the real world, however, most meetings of salvor and salvee cannot be resolved in this fashion."[52]

To complicate the analysis even further, consider the fact that only the owner of the ship, Mayflower Maritime, filed the lawsuit against HeliCo. Under general maritime law, a court would apportion any salvage award between the owner, the master, and the crew. Owners are generally awarded the largest share of any salvage award, because the vessel (rather than the crew) plays the largest role in facilitating the success of the salvage operation. Moreover, the failure of the master and the crew to join in the litigation inures to the benefit of the owner of the salved property, not to the plaintiff who actually brought the suit. Thus, if a court found that the total salvage award was equal to $100,000, and the vessel owner is entitled to 75% of that award, then the vessel owner could recover only $75,000 from the salved property owner.[53] Additionally, in an apportionment case, the actual costs

[52]Margate Shipping Co. v. M/V JA Orgeron, supra, 143 F, 3d. at 986.

[53]In an international law case, in which the Salvage Convention applies, a U.S. court would potentially be required to apply a different apportionment rule if the vessel is governed by another country's national law and that law conflicts with U.S. law.

and expenses incurred, as represented by the sixth factor, would not always be bundled with the values assigned to each of the other factors. These expenses are incurred entirely by the vessel owner, and it would not be appropriate to burden the salving crew with any portion of them. Thus, the expenses would be added back to the proportional award made to the vessel owner after apportioning the award between all actual and potential plaintiffs. Finally, prejudgment interest, which is available in admiralty cases, would be added to the proportionate salvage award.

Considering all of these aspects collectively, we can now expand the equation for calculating a salvage award to the vessel owner, as follows:

	Factor 1 Value
	Factor 3 Value
	Factor 4 Value
	Factor 5 Value
	Factor 7 Value
±	<u>Factor 8 Value</u>
=	Interim Salvage Value x 75% + $25,000.00 + I

In this example, the sum of the various values applied to each salving factor (interim salvage value) is multiplied times the percentage of the award apportioned to the actual plaintiff (the vessel owner, Mayflower Maritime) + the actual costs and expenses incurred by the owner for additional fuel, surveys, and related costs ($25,000) + prejudgment interest (I).

Remember that the formula for interest (I) is P x i x n, where P represents the principal, i represents the interest rate, and n represents the number (of years, months, or days). To calculate prejudgment interest, we would simply multiply the principal times the annual interest rate, divided by 365 to arrive at a daily interest rate, and then multiply by the number of days from when the principal became due.

Let's put it all together. Assume that the interim salvage value was $100,000, that the date when the salvage judgment became due was 656 days ago, and the annual interest rate on any award was 2.75%.

Salvage Award = Interim Salvage Value x 75% + $25,000 + I
= $100,000 x 0.75 + $25,000 + I
= $100,000 + I

I = Principal x Annual Interest Rate ÷ Days in Year x Days Since Salvage
Judgment Became Due
= $100,000 x 0.0275 ÷ 365 x 656
= $4,942.46

Salvage Award = $100,000 + $4,942.46 = $104,942.46

Therefore, in the hypothetical helicopter rescue, the final salvage award recoverable by Mayflower Maritime from HeliCo, is $104,942.46.

Aviation Law

19.5. Legal Framework for Aviation Cases

Like admiralty, the field of aviation law is driven by a variety of federal laws, state laws, international treaties, and common law principals drawn from contract and tort law. It also relies on a number of administrative pronouncements by the Federal Aviation Administration, including Airworthiness Directives (ADs), Advisory Circulars (ACs), as well as Notices to Airmen (NOTAMS) and Temporary Flight Restrictions (TFRs) issued by the Flight Data Center (FDC), and other general and specific orders, notices, and policy statements. Aviation law is particularly defined by federal regulations published in the Code of Federal Regulations, governing everything from crew member fatigue to aircraft engine horsepower to airport zoning. The following summary of relevant laws provides a general, albeit incomplete, overview of the treaty, statutory, and regulatory environment in which aviation practice is conducted:

Title 14, Code of Federal Regulations, Subchapter G (Air Carrier Certification and Operations)

Part 117 Flight and Duty Limitations and Rest Requirements: Flightcrew Members

Part 119 Certification: Air Carriers and Commercial Operators

Part 120 Drug and Alcohol Testing Program

Part 121	Operating Requirements: Domestic, Flag, and Supplemental Operations
Part 125	Certification and Operations: Airplanes Having a Seating Capacity of 20 or More Passengers or a Maximum Payload Capacity of 6,000 Pounds or More; and Rules Governing Persons on Board Such Aircraft
Part 129	Operations: Foreign Air Carriers and Foreign Operators of U.S.-Registered Aircraft Engaged in Common Carriage
Part 133	Rotorcraft External-Load Operations
Part 135	Operating Requirements: Commuter and On Demand Operations and Rules Governing Persons on Board Such Aircraft
Part 136	Air Tours and National Parks Air Tour Management
Part 137	Agricultural Aircraft Operations
Part 139	Certification of Airports

(Airmen, Pilots, and Instructors Certification—Selected Provisions)

14 C.F.R. § 61.3.	Requirement for certificates, ratings and authorizations
14 C.F.R. § 61.4.	Qualification and approval of flight simulators and flight training devices
14 C.F.R. § 61.11.	Expired pilot certificates and re-issuance
14 C.F.R. § 61.13.	Issuance of airman certificates, ratings, and authorizations
14 C.F.R. § 61.15.	Offenses involving alcohol or drugs
14 C.F.R. § 61.16.	Refusal to submit to an alcohol test or to furnish test results
14 C.F.R. § 61.18.	Security disqualification
14 C.F.R. § 61.19.	Duration of pilot and instructor certificates and privileges
14 C.F.R. § 61.23.	Medical certificates: Requirement and duration
14 C.F.R. § 61.35.	Knowledge test: Prerequisites and passing grades
14 C.F.R. § 61.37.	Knowledge tests: Cheating or other unauthorized conduct
14 C.F.R. § 61.41.	Flight training received from flight instructors

	not certificated by the FAA
14 C.F.R. § 61.51.	Pilot logbooks
14 C.F.R. § 61.53.	Prohibition on operations during medical deficiency
14 C.F.R. § 61.55.	Second-in-command qualifications
14 C.F.R. § 61.59.	Falsification, reproduction, or alteration of applications, certificates, logbooks, reports, or records
14 C.F.R. § 61.65.	Instrument rating requirements
14 C.F.R. § 61.66.	Enhanced Flight Vision System Pilot Requirements
14 C.F.R. § 61.73.	Military pilots or former military pilots: Special rules
14 C.F.R. § 61.75.	Private pilot certificate issued on the basis of foreign pilot license
14 C.F.R. § 67.103.	Eye
14 C.F.R. § 67.105.	Ear, nose, throat, and equilibrium
14 C.F.R. § 67.107.	Mental
14 C.F.R. § 67.109.	Neurologic
14 C.F.R. § 67.111.	Cardiovascular
14 C.F.R. § 67.113.	General medical condition
14 C.F.R. § 67.405.	Medical examinations: Who may perform?
14 C.F.R. § 67.409.	Denial of medical certificate

Title 14, Code of Federal Regulations, Subchapter F (Small Unmanned Aircraft Systems and Drones – Selected Provisions)

14 C.F.R. § 107.5.	Falsification, reproduction or alteration
14 C.F.R. § 107.7.	Inspection, testing, and demonstration of compliance
14 C.F.R. § 107.9.	Accident reporting
14 C.F.R. § 107.12.	Requirement for a remote pilot certificate with a small UAS rating
14 C.F.R. § 107.15.	Condition for safe operation
14 C.F.R. § 107.17.	Medical condition
14 C.F.R. § 107.19.	Remote pilot in command
14 C.F.R. § 107.21.	In-flight emergency
14 C.F.R. § 107.23,	Hazardous operation

14 C.F.R. § 107.25.	Operation from a moving vehicle or aircraft
14 C.F.R. § 107.27.	Alcohol or drugs
14 C.F.R. § 107.29.	Daylight operation
14 C.F.R. § 107.31.	Visual line of sight aircraft operation
14 C.F.R. § 107.36.	Carriage of hazardous material
14 C.F.R. § 107.37.	Operation near aircraft; right-of-way rules
14 C.F.R. § 107.38.	Operation over human beings
14 C.F.R. § 107.43.	Operation in the vicinity of airports
14 C.F.R. § 107.49.	Preflight familiarization, inspection, and actions for aircraft operation
14 C.F.R. § 107.65.	Aeronautical knowledge recency

Title 49, United States Code, Subtitle VII, Part A, Subpart III, Chapter 448.
(Unmanned Aircraft Systems – Selected Provisions)

49 U.S.C. § 44805.	Small unmanned aircraft safety standards
49 U.S.C. § 44806.	Public unmanned aircraft systems
49 U.S.C. § 44808.	Carriage of property by small unmanned aircraft systems for compensation or hire
49 U.S.C. § 44810.	Airport safety and airspace hazard mitigation and enforcement

Title 49, United States Code, Subtitle VII, Part A, Subpart I, Chapter 401.
(General Provisions – Selected Provisions)

49 U.S.C. § 40103.	Sovereignty and use of airspace
49 U.S.C. § 40106.	Emergency powers
49 U.S.C. § 40108.	Training schools
49 U.S.C. § 40117.	Passenger facility charges
49 U.S.C. § 40125.	Qualifications for public aircraft status
49 U.S.C. § 40127.	Prohibitions on discrimination
49 U.S.C. § 40128.	Overflights of national parks

Title 49, United States Code, Subtitle VII, Part B, Chapter 471, Subchapter I.
(Airport Improvements – Selected Provisions)

49 U.S.C. § 47107.	Project grant application approval conditioned on assurances about airport operations

49 U.S.C. § 47112.	Carrying out airport development projects
49 U.S.C. § 47123.	Nondiscrimination
49 U.S.C. § 47130.	Airport safety data collection

Title 49, United States Code, Subtitle VII, Part A, Subpart III, Chapter 449.
(Security – Selected Provisions)

49 U.S.C. § 44901.	Screening passengers and property
49 U.S.C. § 44901.	Refusal to transport passengers and property
49 U.S.C. § 44904.	Domestic air transportation system security
49 U.S.C. § 44906.	Foreign air carrier security programs
49 U.S.C. § 44909.	Passenger manifests
49 U.S.C. § 44910.	Agreements on aircraft sabotage, aircraft hijacking, and airport security
49 U.S.C. § 44913.	Explosive detection
49 U.S.C. § 44917.	Deployment of federal air marshals
49 U.S.C. § 44918.	Crew training
49 U.S.C. § 44919.	PreCheck Program
49 U.S.C. § 44925.	Deployment and use of detection equipment at airport screening checkpoints
49 U.S.C. § 44926.	Appeal and redress process for passengers wrongly delayed or prohibited from boarding a flight
49 U.S.C. § 44945.	Disposition of unclaimed money and clothing
49 U.S.C. § 44947.	Air cargo security division

Sample Airworthiness Directives, Advisory Circulars, Temporary Flight Restrictions, and
Notices to Airmen Issued by the Federal Aviation Administration

AD 2019-03-02	Pacific Aerospace Limited Airplanes
AD 2018-21-14	Zodiac Aerotechnics Oxygen Mask Regulators
AC 21-29D	Detecting and Reporting Suspected Unapproved Parts
AC 21-49	Gaining Approval of Seats with Integrated Electronic Components
FDC 9/1599	Restricting airspace over El Centro, California on March 9, 2019, during aerobatic demonstration by the Navy Blue Angels

FDC 9/0826	Imposing a 7-day TFR from March 3, 2019, through March 10, 2019, at Anderson Air Force Base in Guam, for special security reasons
!PHL 03/068	NOTAM: PHL SVC SMR Out of Service 1903041400-1903041700
!FLL 03/015	NOTAM: (KFLL A0275/19) FLL TWY G AT SHELTAIR RAMP CLSD 1903041044-1903041700.

The Montreal Convention – Chapter III
(Liability of the Carrier and Extent of Compensation for Damage – Selected Provisions)

Article 17	Death and Injury of Passengers – Damage to Baggage
Article 18	Damage to Cargo
Article 19	Delay
Article 20	Exoneration
Article 21	Compensation in Case of Death or Injury of Passengers
Article 22	Limits of Liability in Relation to Delay, Baggage and Cargo
Article 23	Conversion of monetary units
Article 24	Review of Limits
Article 25	Stipulation on Limits
Article 26	Invalidity of Contractual Provisions
Article 27	Freedom to Contract
Article 28	Advance Payments
Article 29	Basis of Claims
Article 30	Servants, Agents – Aggregation of Claims
Article 31	Timely Notice of Complaints
Article 32	Death of Person Liable
Article 33	Jurisdiction
Article 34	Arbitration
Article 35	Limitation of Actions
Article 36	Successive Carriage
Article 37	Right of Recourse against Third Parties

Understanding the broad scope of treaty law, the statutory and regulatory provisions, and other laws that govern aviation practice is a mandatory prerequisite to performing damage calculations in civil disputes. Without a complete analysis of the applicable laws, attorneys may run afoul of jurisdictional exclusions, preemption issues, limits on liability, conditions precedent to establishing a claim, and other legal principles that would invalidate their assessment of the claim from the outset. Moreover, it is crucial that attorneys fully investigate the underlying facts of any claim, considering all potentially relevant details that may alter the status, character, or classification of the parties involved, the cargo or baggage at issue, and the claims in dispute. In some jurisdictions, for example, a carrier's liability may be altered by the circumstances leading to the loss of property (e.g., in New York, where the courts have interpreted the Warsaw Convention, which preceded the Montreal Convention, to exclude an employee theft of passenger property and thus removing the limitation on the carrier's liability).

19.6. Damages Available

The determination of damages in an aviation case depends on many factors. The two key questions to be asked at the outset of any case are: (1) Who or what has been damaged or delayed, and (b) Where specifically, or in connection with what kind of flight, were the damages or injuries sustained? As to the question of who or what has been damaged, cargo loss, misplaced or delayed passenger baggage, and other kinds of property claims are subject to one set of laws, while bodily injury or death claims are subject to another set of laws. As to the question of where the loss was sustained, domestic cases may trigger state and federal laws, while international cases will also almost always be governed by the Montreal Convention and its damage caps.

International Regime

In cases involving international flights, damages are measured by a kind of artificial currency known as *special drawing rights* or simply SDRs. The SDR is an international reserve asset created by the International Monetary Fund (IMF) in 1969 to supplement its member countries' official reserves. Every day, the IMF recalculates the currency value of the SDR by summing the values in U.S. dollars, based on market exchange rates, of a group of major currencies (the U.S. dollar, Euro, Japanese yen, pound sterling, and the Chinese renminbi). The collective valuation is then reviewed and adjusted every five years.

The last time the IMF updated the SDR values (prior to release of this book), the limitations placed on damage awards in international airline mishaps were as follows:

- For destruction, loss, damage, or delay of baggage: 1,131 SDRs
- For destruction, loss, damage, or delay of cargo: 19 SDRs per kilogram
- For damage caused by delay: 4,694 SDRs
- For bodily injury or death (where strict liability applies): 113,100 SDRs

As noted above, the path for claiming damages varies, depending on the facts and circumstances of the case and the subject of the claim (i.e., baggage, cargo, personal injury). In an injury case, for example, an international carrier is strictly liable under the Montreal Convention for provable damages. The strict liability rule, however, applies only to death or bodily injury claims worth up to 113,100 SDRs. For all damage claims exceeding 113,100 SDRs, the carrier is not liable unless it was negligent. The burden of proof is on the carrier, in the higher damage cases, to prove that it was not negligent or otherwise at fault.

In the case of a baggage claim, however, the Convention reads:[54]

> The carrier is liable for damage sustained in case of destruction or loss of, or of damage to, checked baggage upon condition only that the event which caused the destruction, loss or damage took place on board the aircraft or during any period within which the checked baggage was in the charge of the carrier. However, the carrier is not liable if and to the extent that the damage resulted from the inherent defect, quality or vice of the baggage. In the case of unchecked baggage, including personal items, the carrier is liable if the damage resulted from its fault or that of its servants or agents.

In order to determine the amount of loss from an international injury claim or a baggage loss claim, a plaintiff would ultimately need to establish its entitlement to a certain number of SDRs, and then convert those SDRs to the appropriate currency. At the time of this book's publication, 1 SDR equaled approximately 1.39 USD (U.S. dollar).

[54] Art. 17, & 2.

Stated inversely, the exchange rate was roughly 1 USD = 0.72 SDR. Once determining the payable SDRs and knowing the applicable exchange rate, the determination of a specific amount of damages, expressed in USD, is a matter of simple math. *For an example of how a court would make a baggage loss award based on SDRs, see Section 19.7 below.*

Domestic Regime

In cases involving U.S. domestic claims, the amount payable in damages is partly statutory, partly regulatory, and partly a fact question to be determined by the trier of fact. The first consideration is whether the issue at bar is covered by any regulation that limits a carrier's liability or otherwise affects the amounts potentially payable on a claim. Thus, for example, there are regulations governing damages awardable to passengers who are denied seats or whose baggage is lost *en route* to a destination:

14 C.F.R. § 250.5	Sets the amount of compensation payable to passengers on an interstate flight who are bumped from the flight because the flight is oversold by the carrier.
14 C.F.R. § 254.4	Prohibits a carrier from limiting its liability for damages resulting from the disappearance of, damage to, or delay in delivery of passenger's baggage, to an amount less than $3,500.

In domestic aviation personal injury cases, the damages recoverable by, or on behalf of, an injured person, can potentially run the full gamut of provable losses, including:

1. Reasonable and necessary medical expenses
2. Costs of ongoing medical care, treatment, medication, therapy, and/or rehabilitation
3. Lost wages, past and future
4. Vocational impairment, including a reduction in earning capacity
5. Lost profits or reduced net income by a person engaged in business

6. Cost of hiring aids, assistants, and other attendants, including the cost of chauffeurs or taxi services, cooks, housekeepers, gardeners, and home health care workers
7. Pain and suffering, past and future
8. Mental distress, depression, anxiety and psychological damages, such as posttraumatic stress disorder
9. Hedonic damages (impairment of the quality of life, or the ability to enjoy life)
10. Punitive damages (where applicable)
11. Prejudgment interest
12. Court costs and other litigation expenses

In a death case, surviving dependents would potentially be able to recover wrongful death damages as well as survival claim damages and other out-of-pocket expenses. This may include the value of financial support from the decedent's earnings; the loss of a parent's advice, counsel, and guidance; the loss of companionship; and the loss of a prospective inheritance from the death of the victim. It may also include the value of a survivor's own grief and mental anguish, her loss of consortium, comfort, care, instruction, support, and contribution toward household services. In some jurisdictions, loss by a parent of a minor's services may also be recoverable. Where a survival claim is recognized, the damage portfolio may also include pain and suffering experienced by the decedent prior to his death. Funeral and burial expenses are also generally recognized and recoverable.

Courts may also recognize discrete claims for *preimpact* pain and suffering as well as *postimpact* pain and suffering. Damages for the mental anguish associated with preimpact fear of death or injury may also be recoverable. In some locales, however, psychological injuries are not cognizable in the absence of physical injuries.

As discussed in the earlier chapters of this book, a damages calculation for a personal injury or wrongful death victim can be made from the discounted present value of the victim's pretax earnings and the present and future values of the goods and services he would have produced. Stated more specifically, full economic loss is the sum of the discounted value of the victim's present and future market and non-market economic losses. Market loss is the value of the victim's lost future earnings, and nonmarket loss represents the present and future values of his total output. Where the lost value of a decedent's life is the measure of damages, the calculation is based on the discounted present value of the decedent's pretax market earnings, plus the discounted present value of the decedent's nonmarket services (where no deduction is made for the decedents personal consumption).

In addition, any calculation based on lost wages must take into consideration wage growth that might have occurred during the decedent's life. In this regard, discount rates used to determine present value would be overstated. The net discount rate (NDR) formula, discussed in Section 11.4 above, attempts to adjust for this problem by expressing discount rates in terms of growth rates.

19.7. Calculating Damages

The actual calculation of damages in an aviation case begins after a significant assessment of the applicable law, and a comprehensive evaluation of the relevant facts, has concluded. Let's consider some hypothetical cases.

Destruction of Cargo

Assume that La Vie France (LVF) is a manufacturer of highly specialized digital radiography equipment used in veterinary medicine. Organic Farms, Inc., a U.S. food wholesaler, orders five identical portable X-ray systems for its farming operations in Kentucky, at a cost of $62,500. The five LVF units are shipped DDP[55] by air on March 1, 2019, from France to Cincinnati/Northern Kentucky International Airport. Because of a loading mishap on Gallic Air, in which heavy goods were dropped during transit, two of the five 85-pound X-ray units were damaged beyond repair.

Organic Farms files suit against LVF, Gallic Air, and the insurer, Mutuelle Assurance (MA) for damages. If Organic Farms spent $1,890 for an expert to survey the damaged goods, and $2,400 in other recov-

[55]The incoterm DDP stands for delivered duty paid. In this case, the seller has assumed all risks and costs of transport up until the final destination, including export fees, carriage, insurance, and destination port charges.

erable incidental costs, what is the value of Organic's total claim for damages?

Let's first approach this question as an insurance claim. Assuming that LVF maintained full insurance coverage for the loss, then the amount of Organic's claim, for purposes of this hypothetical, is:

The value of two X-ray units + $1,890 in survey fees + $2,400 incidental costs[56]

Because LVF charged $62,500 for five units, and only two of them were damaged in transit, we must first determine the value of the two lost X-ray units:

$$\frac{62{,}500}{5} = 12{,}500 \times 2 = 25{,}000$$

If each unit cost $12,500, then two completely damaged units equals $25,000. Therefore, our insurance claim is:

$$\$25{,}000 + \$1{,}890 + \$2{,}400 = \$29{,}290$$

Let's further assume that MA pays the claim in full. Now MA, as the subrogated insurer, makes a claim against Gallic Air for recovery of the amount paid. Gallic has admitted its liability, and the only question is how much Gallic should pay. According to the facts of this case, a loading mishap occurred on Gallic Air, in which heavy goods were *dropped during transit.* Article 18 of the Montreal Convention provides that a carrier is liable for destruction or loss of cargo if "the event which caused the damage so sustained took place during the carriage by air." Assuming, therefore, that the Montreal Convention applies, what damages should be paid by Gallic Air for the destruction of the two X-ray units?

The answer is a relatively simple three-step formula. First, we must ascertain the weight of the lost shipment and convert it to kilograms (kg). Secondly, we must multiply the total kilograms by 19 because the Montreal Convention sets the value for destruction, loss, damage, or delay of cargo at 19 SDRs per kilogram. Thirdly, we must convert SDRs to USD. Let's plug in the numbers here:

---

[56]The hypothetical assumes that Organic Farms has no cognizable claim, or insurable loss, for loss of use, or for other incidental and consequential damages.

Weight of each X-ray unit = 85 pounds
Two X-ray units = 170 pounds
1 pound = 0.453592 kg. Therefore, 170 x 0.453592 = 77.11 kg.
77.11 kg x 19 SDR = 1,465.09 SDR
Exchange Rate on March 1, 2019: 1 SDR = 1.39448 USD
Therefore, 1,465.09 x 1.39448 = 2,043.04 USD

Under the Montreal Convention, and under the hypothetical facts provided, Gallic Air is liable for $2,043.04. By destroying 170 pounds (or 77.11 kilograms) of cargo, Gallic became liable for 19 SDRs for each kilogram of lost cargo. Its total liability of 1,465.09 SDRs must then be converted from the artificial currency of SDRs into an actual national currency in which damages can be paid. Since this is a U.S. case, the damages value of 1,465.09 converts back to USD at the applicable exchange rate, in this case approximately 1.39 USD per 1 SDR. Thus, at 1,465.09 SDRs, Gallic's total liability equals 2,043.04 USD.

Baggage Loss

Natalie Noluck is a hypothetical traveler on SiberAir, which provides regular passenger flights and cargo charters across Eastern and Western Siberia. Natalie alleges that SiberAir lost her checked luggage during a flight from New York's John F. Kennedy International Airport (JFK) to Russia's Tolmachevo Airport (OVB). Under Article 17(2) of the Montreal Convention, SiberAir is liable to Natalie if "the event which caused the destruction, loss or damage took place on board the aircraft or during any period within which the checked baggage was in the charge of the carrier." Natalie files suit against SiberAir, alleging that, in addition to her clothing and personal effects, she lost valuable scientific letters, materials, and reports packed in her checked baggage, which she had intended to present at a conference in Novosibirsk, a city near the airport renowned for its scientific work.

Natalie's complaint, filed in U.S. District Court for the Southern District of New York, contains counts for property loss, emotional distress, and punitive damages. The actual, provable value of Natalie's lost baggage is $4,550. She seeks a trial to recover her $4,550 in property loss and to assess the value of her emotional distress and punitive damages claims.

What should Natalie recover?

Under Article 22(2) of the treaty, as updated, the liability of the carrier for destroyed, lost, damaged, or delayed baggage is limited to 1,131 SDRs. If Natalie qualifies for the maximum number of SDRs, she would be able to claim whatever the USD equivalent is for 1,131 SDRs. To calculate this amount, we will apply an exchange rate of 1 SDR = 1.39448 USD, as applied in the cargo loss example given above. This exchange rate can also be expressed as $1 = 0.7171 SDRs. The formula is quite simple:

1,131 SDRs x 1.39448 = 1,577.15688

Therefore, if she proves all of her damages, Natalie will receive a maximum of $1,577.16 in damages for her loss of baggage under the Montreal Convention. If she had not purchased flight or baggage insurance, Natalie will have no further claim under international aviation law. In fact, Natalie's claims for emotional distress and punitive damages would likely be dismissed on summary judgment. The Convention does not recognize emotional damages unless they are specifically and demonstrably connected to physical injury,[57] and punitive damages are expressly prohibited under Article 29.

Aviation Death Claim

A domestic aviation casualty, resulting in a wrongful death claim, is subject to the same economic considerations and financial formulas as discussed in Chapter 11. However, certain additional considerations, such as preimpact fear and terror, may also be quantified by a jury as part of an ultimate damage award. Without comprehensively delineating all of the financial criteria that an expert witness might consider, we cannot—in this limited volume—provide a complete amount of damages. Let us, however, consider some of the formulas and factors that would contribute to the analysis.

Let's assume that a father and his infant child board a helicopter for transportation to a medical facility for an emergency surgical proce-

---

[57]*See, e.g.,* Booker v. BWIA West Indies Airways, Ltd., 307 Fed. Appx. 291 (2009).

dure. The helicopter crashes when an engine equipped with newly installed compressor turbine blades fails en route, killing everybody on board. The surviving wife (and mother of the child) files strict product liability wrongful death claims on behalf of her husband and son against the manufacturer of the replacement compressor turbine blades in the helicopter engine.

Analyzing the infant child's case first, we will begin with some assumptions. First, we presume that the education level that would have been achieved by the child would be equivalent to his parents' education levels.[58] So, we will assume that the child, like each of his parents, would have graduated from high school. The median usual weekly earnings for a high school graduate is $712.[59] To convert this into an annual figure, simply multiply by 52.

$$\$712 \text{ x } 52 = \$37{,}024.$$

Therefore, the medium *annual* earnings for a high school graduate is set at $37,024.

Next, we need to determine the value of the child's future fringe benefits. As discussed in Section 11.6, the value of fringe benefits can be determined either by an itemized present value approach or a percentage-of-earnings approach, which generates a fringe rate. Since the child has no work history, however, and thus no measurable benefits, we must predict his future fringe rate. The U.S. Bureau of Labor Statistics (BLS) maintains tables of employer costs per hour for various fringe benefits including the employer's contributions for Social Security retirement and Medicare benefits; paid vacation, holiday, and sick leave; life, health, and disability insurance, and contributions to the employer's pension plan. For purposes of this hypothetical, we will use a combined fringe rate of 28.6%, as published by the

[58]There is a strong correlation between the educational attainment of parents and their children. *See, e.g.*, Lawrence M. Spizman & John Kane, *Loss of Future Income in the Case of Personal Injury to a Child: Parental Influence on a Child's Future Earnings*, 5 J. Forensic Econ. 159 (1992).

[59]This figure is provided by the U.S. Bureau of Labor Statistics as the median weekly earnings for a worker with a high school diploma but no college education for the year 2017. An expert would possibly make adjustments for wage growth or other considerations.

BLS as its rate for all benefits for service employees as of September 2018.[60]

Next, we must determine how many years the child would have worked, had he not perished in the helicopter accident. This calculation relies on his *work-life expectancy,* the calculations for which we discussed in Section 11.3. Let's assume that the work-life expectancy, in this case, of a male high school graduate, is 38.6 years at the age of 20.

Finally, we will need to determine a cost of maintenance, which is how much the child would have spent to sustain his life. This includes the child's predictable consumption costs necessary for his personal and physical subsistence.[61] The deduction of personal consumption serves to ensure that the estate and/or survivors are not overcompensated. To determine an annual consumption or maintenance expense (AME), we will apply the following formula:

$$\text{Consumption Rate} \times \text{Annual Earnings} + \text{Poverty Threshold} = \text{AME}.$$

Let's set the consumption rate at 14.7 cents per dollar.[62] In effect, for every one dollar earned in pretax income, the decedent would have spent 14.7 cents in maintenance expenses. We must also recognize the poverty threshold, which in 2018 was $13,064 for a single person under the age of 65.[63] Let's plug in the data:

$$\text{Consumption Rate x Annual Earnings} + \text{Poverty Threshold} = \text{AME}$$
$$0.147 \text{ x } 37{,}024 + 13{,}064 = \$18{,}506.53$$

Therefore, we can now state that the deceased child's AME is estimated to have been $18,506.53 per year, had he not died in the helicopter accident.

---

[60]See *Employer Costs for Employee Compensation – September 2018,* U.S. Department of Labor, Bureau of Labor Statistics, USDL-18-1941, at https://www.bls.gov/news.release/pdf/ecec.pdf.

[61]See Section 11.9.

[62]For an analysis of how this rate was obtained, see James D. Rodgers & Robert J. Thornton, *Making Operational the Concept of Maintenance Consumption,* 8 J. Legal Econ. (Spring 1998).

[63]See *Poverty Thresholds for 2018 by Size of Family and Number of Related Children Under Age 18,* U.S. Census Bureau, at https://www.census.gov/data/tables/time-series/demo/income-poverty/historical-poverty-thresholds.html.

How do we put it all together? The simplified formula for estimating the child's total economic losses is as follows:

$$\text{Loss} = (\text{E} + \text{Fr} - \text{AME}) \times \text{WLE}$$

where E represents the earnings the child would have collected, Fr represents the annual fringe benefits in dollars, AME represents the annual maintenance expense, and WLE represents the child's work-life expectancy. To convert the 28.6% fringe rate to a dollar amount, simply multiply it by the earnings:

$$\$37{,}024 \times 0.286 = \$10{,}588.86$$

Let's apply the formula for total economic losses:

$$\text{Loss} = (\text{E} + \text{Fr} - \text{AME}) \times \text{WLE}$$
$$\text{Loss} = (\$37{,}024 + \$10{,}588.86 - \$18{,}506.53) \times 38.6$$
$$\text{Loss} = \$29{,}106.33 \times 38.6$$
$$\text{Loss} = \$1{,}123{,}504.34$$

After adding the child's projected earnings to his projected fringe benefits and then deducting his maintenance (consumption) costs and multiplying by the projected work-life expectancy of 38.6 years, we can declare that the child's total economic loss would be $1,123,504.34.

As for the deceased father, the analysis essentially follows the various wage loss and fringe benefit loss calculations described in Chapter 11, taking into consideration personal consumption and other damage reducers, and factoring in other available damage categories such as pain and suffering and hedonic damages. In an aviation case, one could also seek compensation for *predeath* pain and suffering (including preimpact fear and terror), where such categories are recognized under state law. Of course, a victim can also seek damages for *postimpact* pain and suffering, where the victim is conscious after the injury-causing event. In such cases, the burden falls on the plaintiff to identify and prove that the victim was conscious after the accident.

For an adult wage earner, the calculations could conceivably require many incremental calculations: future earnings and earnings growth; the value of fringe benefits; the value of services and goods the decedent would have provided; the value of the decedent's care, support, maintenance, and other services provided to family members;

his medical and funeral expenses; his expected work life; income tax considerations; present value discounts for future earnings, including investment earnings; lost household contributions; the value of a potential inheritance; and future consumption. Noneconomic damages, beyond the general categories of physical pain and mental anguish, include the loss of love, comfort, companionship, guidance, advice, nurturing, and training. In some cases, and in particular jurisdictions, prejudgment interest, punitive damages, attorneys' fees and litigation costs may also be recoverable.

Chapter 20

Forensic Experts

20.1. When to Retain an Expert

Even an attorney who has mastered all of the formulas and shortcuts in this book may find it necessary to consult or retain a forensic expert in one of the various accounting or financial specialties. Indeed, it would be shortsighted to assume that every case can be settled, or submitted to a trier of fact, based on the mathematical calculations of an able lawyer, acting alone.

Some cases may simply present economic considerations or financial calculations that are difficult to pin down, or that are too elusive to apply to a unique set of circumstances, without the aid and counsel of an expert. Other cases may require extensive testimony about assumptions that underlie the calculations, and only an expert witness could present and defend those assumptions within the parameters of the rules of evidence. In still other cases, a financial or accounting expert may be necessary simply to advise as to which of several formulas is best suited to the factual questions at issue.

Of course, this volume should prove useful even when expert witnesses are necessary. It will help attorneys determine the financial merits of a claim and estimate the costs of litigation. It will enable attorneys to approximate quickly the amount of damages under a given case scenario. It will focus attorneys on the kinds of calculations, and the kinds of experts, that may be necessary. It will also prepare attorneys to question their own experts, and opposing experts, and to appreciate the science and mathematics that drive the experts' opinions.

What is important is to know whether a particular case requires expert testimony or would benefit from such evidence; whether the value of the claim justifies the retention of a forensic expert; and whether the rules of procedure and evidence require (or suggest) that the necessary financial data and underlying testimony about the data could only realistically be admitted through an expert witness.

In some situations, an attorney may be able to avoid hiring an expert witness throughout much of the pretrial stage, provided that he is not time-barred from retaining one as part of the discovery process. Settlement negotiations, mediations, arbitration proceedings, and pretrial hearings could all possibly be conducted with financial evidence gathered, interpreted, and calculated by attorneys alone. In an appropriate case, where the math is readily comprehensible, an attorney may wish to "go the distance" without an expert witness. Should he succeed in settling the case in mediation without the aid of an expert witness, he may have saved his client a considerable amount of money. In other cases, where the stakes are high, or the economic and financial issues are substantial, it may be more prudent to utilize an expert witness as early as possible in the case, including in the negotiation, mediation, and arbitration process.

In fact, if a case presents sufficient damages to warrant the cost of an expert, then an expert can prove extremely helpful in the pretrial discovery process. By retaining or at least consulting an expert early in the process, an attorney can develop unanticipated theories of damages and thereby propound interrogatories or subpoena documents in support of those theories. With the assistance of an expert, an attorney can develop efficiently the list of exhibits he will need to prove the calculations of damages. He can identify the kinds of depositions that will be necessary and the particular questions that should be asked. An expert can also strategically assist an attorney in preparing to depose other parties, and other experts, and to target the weak spots of a witness during cross-examination. A good forensic expert can also recommend other specialists who may be helpful to the lawyers, such as a vocational rehabilitation expert or an enrolled actuary specializing in pensions.

In professional liability claims, expert witnesses are generally required by statute or court rule. Most states require plaintiffs to produce an affidavit or certificate of merit signed by an expert and attesting to the technical merits of the case. Thus, for example, if a plaintiff brings a malpractice action against an accounting firm for negligent preparation of his tax returns, the plaintiff will almost certainly be required to retain an accounting expert to testify about the proper accounting procedures, the negligent missteps taken by the defendant, and the calculations of damages suffered by the plaintiff.

An expert witness may also be necessary when questions of scientific reliability arise, discussed further below. Therefore, if one's calculations rely on a procedure, a calculation, or an assumption that is questionable or not widely accepted within the financial or accounting fields, it may be necessary to further develop and elucidate the approach through expert testimony.

20.2. Educational Credentials

Damages experts come in many varieties, and it is important to select a specialist who possesses the best combination of educational credentials, professional experience, certifications, and personal attributes. The best fit for a particular case is not always the most educated, the most experienced, or the most court-savvy expert, but rather the expert who has the best combination of such qualifications.

Professional training among damages experts varies widely: some are accountants, others are actuaries; some are economists, others are vocational evaluators; some are finance specialists, others are statisticians. Some experts identify themselves as *forensic* experts, but the usage has been expanded widely to cover many different areas of expertise with no uniform or common qualifying credential. Among the titles and specialties claimed by damages experts are the following:

- Accountant
- Forensic Accountant
- Public Accountant
- Certified Public Accountant
- Management Accountant
- Cost Accountant
- Tax Accountant
- Financial Accountant
- Auditor

- Forensic Auditor
- Internal Auditor
- External Auditor
- Economist
- Forensic Economist
- Labor Economist
- Econometrician
- Financial Economist
- Monetary Economist
- Industrial Economist
- Organizational Economist
- Public Finance Economist
- Agricultural Economist
- Certified Real Property Appraiser
- Registered Real Property Appraiser
- Personal Property Appraiser
- Accredited Jewelry Appraiser
- Statistician
- Biostatistician
- Mathematical Statistician
- Industrial Statistician
- Statistical Analyst
- Life Actuary
- Health Actuary
- Pension Actuary
- Property Actuary
- Casualty Actuary
- Enrolled Actuary
- Financial Planner
- Certified Financial Planner
- Chartered Financial Analyst

In fact, the list is considerably longer because there are so many different certifications and designations now available to financial experts beyond (or as an alternative to) their formal academic education. See Section 18.3 below. Therefore, at the outset, it is important to consider what general category of expert can guide a particular case. An accountant? An economist? Then, it may be useful to inquire into subspecialties: Is it perhaps a tax accountant that would be most useful in a particular case? Or, an economist knowledgeable about pricing methods? The inquiry inevitably leads to the question of academic credentials and board certifications.

No specific level of education is necessary to qualify one as an expert witness. In fact, a highly experienced expert or skilled practitioner may hold only a bachelor's degree. Still, it is common for financial and economic experts to hold master's degrees and doctorate degrees in their specialties. Here, for example, are some of the most common advanced degrees held by such experts.

Ph.D. The Doctor of Philosophy degree is widely recognized as the terminal degree in the natural and social sciences and in a number of financial specialties. It is important to know the specialty in which the Ph.D. was earned—for example, economics, finance, accounting, management, statistics, or business administration. Even within a doctoral-level business program, some schools designate more specific research and training areas such as decision sciences, marketing, operations management, and strategy.

Ph.D. programs in various economic or finance specialties may, in fact, be offered by different schools and programs within one university. A Ph.D. in economics may be classified as a social science degree offered by a university's college of arts and sciences, while a Ph.D. in business administration could be offered by a college of business studies, or similar such unit of a university system.

It is also important to inquire about special areas of concentration within the expert's Ph.D. studies. An expert who holds a Ph.D. in economics, but who concentrated on international macroeconomics, may not be the best choice for litigation that involves an inquiry into a corporation's internal product pricing patterns. Virtually all Ph.D. graduates are also required to complete a dissertation at the conclusion of their degree programs. The choice of dissertation topic frequently forms the foundation for a doctoral student's future research, writing, and teaching specialties. Knowing about an expert's dissertation topic, therefore, may provide useful guidance in the expert selection process.

DBA. A Doctor of Business Administration degree, while of more recent vintage, is a widely respected doctorate degree throughout the world. Although many DBA programs are academically equivalent to Ph.D. programs in terms of rigor and research, the degree is often regarded as less theoretical and more practical. DBA programs are generally housed in schools and colleges of business and often expose their students to extensive clinical opportunities and practice laboratories. Many DBA programs offer specialty tracks, such as management information systems, technology and operations management, accounting, entrepreneurship, and strategic leadership. The DBA degree has been aggressively embraced by the online education and distance learning community, and course requirements for the degree vary widely. Some DBA programs conclude with dissertations; others require extensive case studies or capstone projects. Learning more about an expert's DBA program can thus provide valuable insight into the expert's core training.

Specialty Doctorates. A damages expert may also possess a doctorate in a business or economic specialty that is neither a Ph.D. degree nor a DBA degree. These include, for example, a doctor of management, a doctor of economic sciences, and a doctor of finance degree—just a few of the variations of specialty doctorates offered at institutions around the world.

MBA. The Master of Business Administration degree is the most widely recognized graduate business degree offered by U.S. and foreign universities and colleges. The degree is commonly held by industry leaders worldwide as well as financial experts used in litigation. All MBA students take courses in finance, statistics, accounting, microeconomics, and macroeconomics. Many specialize, thereafter, in more focused elective courses, such as "advanced corporate finance," "fixed income securities," or "small business management." Although the MBA degree is a generalist degree, many colleges have been offering specialty MBAs in recent years, including, for example, MBA degrees in computational finance, health care, and information technology.

Like DBA programs, MBA programs are readily available through online and distance education providers. The quality of such programs varies significantly, and not all of them are accredited by the recognized accrediting agencies, the Association to Advance Collegiate Schools of Business (AACSB), the Accreditation Council for Business Schools and Programs (ACBSP), and the International Assembly for Collegiate Business Education (IACBE). Where an expert holds an MBA degree, it is thus best to inquire more deeply about the nature and accreditation of the program from which he was graduated.

MS and MAc (Accounting). Master's degrees in accounting are generally offered as a Master of Science (MS) in accounting or as a Master of Accountancy (MAc or MAcc) degree. Many schools offer specialized concentrations in taxation, forensic accounting, auditing, public accounting, governmental accounting, and accounting information systems. An expert with such specialized training, at the graduate level, may be particularly well-suited for a case requiring such expertise.

Other Specialty Master's Degrees. Master's degrees are offered in a number of other business and financial specialties with an ever-growing variety of degree titles. Among the varied graduate degrees currently available are the following:

- MS in management
- MS in information management
- MS in project management
- MS in personal financial planning
- MS in taxation
- MTax master of taxation
- MS in banking and financial services management
- MS in predictive analytics
- MS in marketing
- MS in integrated marketing
- MS in international marketing management
- MA in international economics and finance
- MS in financial mathematics
- MS in applied mathematics
- MA in pure mathematics
- MS in financial markets with information systems
- MS in financial services
- MS in accounting and taxation
- MS in risk management and insurance
- MS in real estate and urban land economics
- MS in operations and supply chain management
- MS in statistics
- MS in applied statistics
- MS in applied mathematics and statistics
- MA in economics
- MS in economics

- MS in economics and applied econometrics
- MPA in public financial administration
- Master of probability and statistics
- Master of actuarial science
- Master of commerce

While the curriculum featured in these graduate degrees is often sampled by many of the more generic graduate degrees, such as the MBA, an expert with a specialized master's degree may prove particularly valuable in a case requiring unique training or proficiency in a subspecialty.

20.3. Certifications and Designations

Financial and accounting experts may also hold one or more specialty certifications, licenses, designations, or other distinctions. Understanding the letters that appear after an expert's name is an important part of the selection process. In fact, many acronyms are similar or identical, and further inquiry may be necessary to determine an expert's actual training and certification status.

Both in retaining an expert, and in cross-examining an opposing expert, it is useful to understand the range of requirements for various financial certifications and designations. Some certifications and designations are granted on the basis of prior experience, or on the completion of an application and payment of an application fee. Other such distinctions require substantial educational or experience requirements and passage of a board certification examination. Still others require significant continuing education commitments, character references, and compliance with ethical codes.

While many of the certifications are based in finance, accounting, or economics, other specialists, such as vocational experts and life-care planners, may be used as part of damage calculation process, particularly in personal injury and wrongful death cases.

Following is a list of the most common certifications and designations which appear on the curricula vitae of expert witnesses:

AAMS. An Accredited Asset Management Specialist is an investment specialist who completes a 12-module professional education program and passes a qualifying examination administered by the College for Financial Planning.

ABA. An Accredited Business Accountant is a specialist in financial accounting, financial reporting, financial statement preparation, taxation, and business consulting services who is accredited by the Accreditation Council for Accountancy and Taxation.

ABV. An Accredited Business Valuator is a specialty designation awarded to CPAs by the American Institute of Certified Public Accountants (AICPA). ABVs typically provide sophisticated business valuation services to attorneys and business executives.

ABVE/P. The abbreviation stands for American Board of Vocational Experts/Professional, but it actually refers to the ABVE's Professional Forensic Certification. The Professional Forensic Certification, introduced in June 2011, is granted to vocational experts who can testify about labor market surveys, provide vocational assessments and evaluation services, and contribute to vocational case management evidence.

ADPA. An Accredited Domestic Partnership Advisor is specially trained in wealth transfers for domestic partners, federal taxation issues, retirement planning, financial, medical, and end-of-life needs for domestic partners. The ADPA designation is granted by the College for Financial Planning upon completion of an online or self-study program and passage of a final examination.

AEP. An Accredited Estate Planner is a designation conferred by the National Association of Estate Planners & Councils to attorneys, CPAs, trust officers, CLUs, CFPs, or ChFCs who complete two graduate courses administered by the American College.

AFA. Accredited Financial Analyst is a designation of the International Management Consultants Certification Board that requires three to five years of professional experience, an applicable college degree, commitment to continuing education requirements, and compliance with ethical standards.

AFC. An Accredited Financial Counselor is an individual who passes a series of courses given by the Association for Financial Counseling and Planning Education (AFCPE) and who satisfies the Association's experience, ethics, and peer reference requirements.

AFE. Accredited Financial Examiners are generally insurance industry professionals, with an accounting background, who pass a test in life, health, property, and liability insurance administered by the Society of Financial Examiners. *See also CFE.*

AMLP. The Anti-Money Laundering Professional Certification is awarded by the Bank Administration Institute (BAI) to those professionals who demonstrate expertise with the Bank Secrecy Act, the USA PATRIOT Act, and related regulations.

APMA. An Accredited Portfolio Management Advisor is a professional designation given by the College for Financial Planning to those who complete a course of study, pass a final examination, complete an interactive case study, and comply with a Code of Ethics. APMA coursework covers investment risk and return, portfolio performance evaluation, fixed income securities, derivatives, foreign investments, mutual funds, taxation, and other issues.

ARA. Estate and trust planning and retirement plan expertise are the specialties that fall within the status of an Accredited Retirement Advisor, a designation of the Accreditation Council for Accountancy and Taxation.

ASA. Accredited Senior Appraisers are designated as such by the American Society of Appraisers based on education, appraisal experience, and the quality of appraisal reports. ASAs are required to pass a comprehensive examination in the field.

ATA. An Accredited Tax Advisor handles sophisticated tax-planning issues involving closely held businesses, qualified retirement plans, and estate tax planning, and is so qualified by the Accreditation Council for Accountancy and Taxation.

ATP. The Accredited Tax Preparer credential, also offered by the Accreditation Council for Accountancy and Taxation, is awarded to those specialists who demonstrate thorough knowledge of the Tax Code and of Form 1040 issues in particular.

AVA. An Accredited Valuation Analyst is trained to perform business valuations and is so accredited by the National Association of Certified Valuators and Analysts (NACVA).

AWMA. The Accredited Wealth Management Advisor title is granted by the College for Financial Planning to professionals who complete an online educational or self-study program, pass a final examination, and comply with a Code of Ethics. Coursework covers the asset management process, risk, return and investment performance, investment strategies, taxation of investment products, deferred compensation, insurance products, and estate planning.

CA. A Chartered Accountant is roughly the foreign equivalent of the American CPA. Like certified public accountants trained in the

United States, CAs are the Canadian and English standard for professional accountants, employed most frequently to render advisory services and expert opinions in accounting matters.

CAM. Chartered Asset Manager is a designation of the American Academy of Financial Management (AAFM) granted upon proof of qualifying work experience and satisfaction of necessary educational milestones completed through the Thomas Jefferson School of Law. Coursework covers wealth management, private banking, international estate planning, estate and gift tax, investment management, offshore financial services, and financial instruments. The AAFM also requires proof of academic degrees from accredited or government-sanctioned programs and appropriate professional licenses.

CAMC. Certified Anti-Money Laundering Consultant is a designation of the International Board of Standards and the American Academy of Financial Management (AAFM) granted upon proof of qualifying work experience and satisfaction of necessary educational milestones completed through the Thomas Jefferson School of Law. Coursework covers anti-money laundering and compliance procedures, financial crimes and security, cyber-crimes, and offshore financial services. The AAFM also requires proof of academic degrees from accredited or government-sanctioned programs and appropriate professional licenses.

CAP. A Chartered Advisor in Philanthropy must complete three courses administered by the American College in the fields of family wealth, charitable strategies, and gift planning.

CAPA. Certified Asset Protection Analyst is a designation of the International Board of Standards and the American Academy of Financial Management (AAFM) granted upon proof of qualifying work experience and satisfaction of necessary educational milestones completed through the Thomas Jefferson School of Law. Coursework includes either international estate planning and asset protection or immigration and international tax planning. The AAFM also requires proof of academic degrees from accredited or government-sanctioned programs and appropriate professional licenses.

CASL. A Chartered Advisor for Senior Living is a financial specialist who completes five courses offered by the American College in such areas as estate planning and long-term care financing.

CB. A Certified Bookkeeper, so qualified by the American Institute of Professional Bookkeepers, has successfully passed a series of tests in bookkeeping entries and adjustments, bank reconciliations, payroll, depreciation, inventory, internal controls, and fraud prevention.

CBA. A Certified Bank Auditor is qualified by the Bank Administration Institute (BAI) in four areas: accounting, auditing principles and bank laws and regulations, auditing practices, and general business.

CCA. Chartered Compliance Analyst is a designation of the International Board of Standards and the American Academy of Financial Management (AAFM) granted upon proof of qualifying work experience and satisfaction of necessary educational milestones completed through the Thomas Jefferson School of Law. Coursework covers anti-money laundering and compliance, financial crimes and security, online contracting, privacy law, invest and risk management, and consumer financial services. The AAFM also requires proof of academic degrees from accredited or government-sanctioned programs and appropriate professional licenses.

CCAA. A Certified Career Assessment Associate is a designation of the Commission on Rehabilitation Counselor Certification awarded to certified rehabilitation counselors who pursue additional training in vocational interviewing, standardized testing, job analysis and training analysis, functional skill assessment, and professional development.

CCSA. The Certification in Control Self-Assessment is a specialty status conferred by the Institute of Internal Auditors to those persons who specialize in risk identification and assessment, as well as control theories and applications.

CDE. Certified Disability Evaluators are divided into CDE 1s (physicians), CDE 2s (those who assist physicians, such as physical therapists and speech pathologists), and CDE 3s (others who assist in disability litigation, such as vocational evaluators and rehabilitation counselors). CDEs are designated by the International Commission on Health Care Certification based on their professional training and their satisfactory completion of an examination.

CDFA. The Institute for Divorce Financial Analysts offers the credential of Certified Divorce Financial Analyst to those who have been trained and successfully tested in all financial aspects of divorce, including collecting and evaluating financial data, dividing family businesses, identifying hidden assets, and pension and tax issues.

CEA. A Certified E-Business Analyst is a distinction granted by the International Management Consultants Certification Board to those management consultants who have satisfied the necessary education and experience requirements and who commit to eight hours of continuing education per year.

CEBS. The Certified Employee Benefit Specialist title is conferred after an eight-course college-level curriculum cosponsored by the International Foundation of Employee Benefit Plans (IFEBP) and the Wharton School of the University of Pennsylvania. Coursework covers group health plans, retirement plans, human resources and compensation management, asset management, personal wealth management, health care financing and economics, executive compensation, and other areas.

CEC. Certified E-Commerce Consultant is a designation of the International Project Management Commission and the American Academy of Project Management (AAPM). Coursework includes e-commerce law, global e-commerce taxation, and online contracting. The AAPM also requires proof of academic degrees from accredited or government-sanctioned programs and appropriate professional licenses.

CEPA. Chartered Economic Policy Analyst is a professional management consulting designation granted by the International Management Consultants Certification Board. CEPAs must demonstrate requisite experience, educational achievement, ethical compliance, and continuing education.

CFA. A Chartered Financial Analyst is a specialist qualified by the CFA Institute in a wide variety of quantitative methods, economic principles, financial reporting, and corporate finance skills. CFAs are also trained in equity investments, fixed income, derivatives, and portfolio management.

Cr.FA. A Certified Forensic Accountant designation is offered to CPAs by the American College of Forensic Examiners International after completion of an examination testing forensic accounting, auditing, and investigative skills. Certified forensic accountants are used to calculate and estimate economic damages and to probe illegal financial activities.

CFC. A Certified Forensic Consultant is a designation of the American College of Forensic Examiners International. CFCs are trained and tested in their familiarity with the American judicial system.

CFE. Certified Financial Examiners must first be AFEs, and must complete additional management education and be tested in the areas of analysis and evaluation procedures, reinsurance, and financial analysis in an examination administered by the Society of Financial Examiners.

CFE. CFE is also the acronym for Certified Fraud Examiner, a credential conferred by the world's largest antifraud organization, the Association of Certified Fraud Examiners. Certified Fraud Examiners are trained and tested in fraud prevention and deterrence, fraudulent financial transactions, fraud investigation, and the legal elements of fraud.

CFF. The Certified in Financial Forensics designation is awarded to CPAs by the American Institute of CPAs after successful proof of their specialized knowledge of forensic accounting in such fields as bankruptcy, family law, business valuations, damage calculations, and fraud prevention.

CFFA. The Certified Forensic Financial Analyst credential is awarded by the National Association of Certified Valuators and Analysts (NACVA) to those persons who satisfy specific education and experience requirements in forensic financial support, and who pass the organization's testing requirements.

CFP. A Certified Financial Planner must satisfy educational, experience, and ethical requirements, and then must pass an examination administered by the Certified Financial Planner Board of Standards. CFPs are tested in a variety of financial planning areas, such as insurance and risk management, investments, taxation, employee benefits, retirement, and estate planning. They are also required to know cash flow managements, mortgage financing, and financial planning in special cases such as divorce and disability.

CFS. Certified Fraud Specialist is a distinction conferred by the Association of Certified Fraud Specialists to auditors, accountants, loss prevention specialists, and other investigative professionals who demonstrate knowledge and experience in such fields as white collar crime, auditing, accounting, and law.

CFS. A Certified Fund Specialist, which also uses the abbreviation CFS, is a designation for financial services professionals who successfully complete a 60-hour course and pass a qualifying examination given by the Institute of Business and Finance.

CFSA. Certified Financial Services Auditors are qualified by the Institute of Internal Auditors to perform internal audits and are tested in banking, insurance, or securities.

CGAP. Certified Government Auditing Professionals are qualified by the Institute of Internal Auditors for public-sector internal auditing activities, including fund accounting.

CGFM. Certified Government Financial Managers are qualified by the Association of Government Accountants and are tested in the fields of governmental accounting, financial reporting and budgeting, and governmental financial management and control.

ChE. Chartered Economist is a distinction granted by the American Academy of Financial Management to economists who complete coursework in securities law, asset management, international taxation, investment management and compliance, wealth management, and private banking.

ChEA. Chartered Economic Analyst is a designation conferred by the National Institute for Continuing Education on qualified individuals who maintain an insurance license, pass the Series 6 or 7 and Series 63 exam, attend a three-day educational program, and pass a rigorous exam.

ChFC. The Chartered Financial Consultant credential is awarded by the American College to financial professionals who complete a nine-course curriculum dealing with income taxation, insurance planning, investments, estate planning, executive compensation, and related areas.

CHFP. A Certified Healthcare Financial Professional designation is generally held by mid-level healthcare professionals who have successfully passed an examination in revenue cycles, disbursement functions, budgeting and forecasting, internal control, financial reporting, and contract management, administered by the Healthcare Financial Management Association.

ChHC. The designation of Chartered Healthcare Consultant is conferred by the American College upon completion of six courses covering such subjects as individual health insurance, group benefits, executive compensation, managed care, and long-term care financing for seniors.

ChMA. A Chartered Marketing Analyst is a professional certification granted by the International Management Consultants Certification Board based on education, experience, ethical compliance, and continuing education.

CIA. A Certified Internal Auditor is a designation awarded by the Institute of Internal Auditors to those who satisfy certain training requirements and pass a four-part examination.

CIC. A Chartered Investment Counselor is a designation awarded by the Investment Advisor Association to CFAs who devote more than 50% of their time to investment counseling and portfolio management activities and who otherwise satisfy the Association's experience, education, and membership requirements.

CIMA. A Certified Investment Management Analyst is a specialty certification in investment consulting awarded by the Investment Management Consultants Association. CIMAs are required to pass prequalifying and certification exams, and fulfill educational and experience requirements.

CIPM. The Certificate in Investment Performance Measurement is awarded by the CFA Institute to those professionals who meet certain training requirements and pass two examinations in investment performance measurement, attribution, and appraisal.

CIPM. This acronym also stands for Certified International Project Manager, a distinction conferred by the International Project Management Commission and the American Academy of Project Management.

CISA. A Certified Information Systems Auditor is a credential awarded to audit, control, and security professionals by ISACA, formerly known as the Information Systems Audit and Control Association. ISACA also awards the Certified Information Security Manager (CISM) and Certified in Governance of Enterprise IT (CGEIT) designations.

CITA. Certified International Tax Analyst is a designation of the International Board of Standards and the American Academy of Financial Management (AAFM) granted upon proof of qualifying work experience and satisfaction of necessary educational milestones completed through the Thomas Jefferson School of Law. Coursework covers international tax planning, tax treaties, offshore financial services, and international antiavoidance legislation. The AAFM also requires proof of academic degrees from accredited or government-sanctioned programs and appropriate professional licenses.

CITP. The Certified Information Technology Professional designation, conferred by the American Institute of CPAs, is given to CPAs who master risk assessment, fraud techniques, internal controls, auditing procedures, data analysis, and reporting techniques, among other performance criteria.

CLCP. A Certified Life Care Planner may provide the foundation for calculating the funding needed to care for a personal injury victim. The certification is granted by the International Commission on Health Care Certification to qualified health care providers who meet training and experience thresholds.

CLF. Financial professionals can obtain the designation of Chartered Leadership Fellow by completing a business curriculum with the American College and producing evidence of experience in a managerial or supervisory role for a requisite period of time.

CLU. A Chartered Life Underwriter is generally an insurance or financial services professional who has met the American College's three-year business experience requirement, passed its eight-course program, and agreed to abide by its code of ethics.

CM. The Institute of Certified Professional Managers offers the Certified Manager title to those management professionals who successfully complete three management skills programs and pass the applicable examinations.

CMA. Certified Management Accountant is an advanced professional certification for practicing accountants and financial managers offered by the Institute for Management Accountants (IMA). An earlier designation, Certified Financial Manager (CFM), has been discontinued but is still supported by the IMA.

CMA. This is also the abbreviation for Chartered Market Analyst, a designation of the American Academy of Financial Management (AAFM) granted upon proof of at least seven years of professional experience and completion of two courses in investment management and compliance and wealth management.

CM&AA. A Certified Merger and Acquisition Advisor is a designation awarded by the Alliance of Merger & Acquisition Advisors to financial service professionals who demonstrate competence in their knowledge of the private capital marketplace, corporate finance, business valuation, M&A tax issues, acquisition and growth financing, and legal considerations.

CMFC. A Chartered Mutual Fund Counselor has been so qualified by the College for Financial Planning after successfully completing nine courses, passing an examination, and subscribing to a code of ethics.

CMS. The Compensation Management Specialist designation is given to those who complete three courses in human resources and compensation management, compensation concepts and principles, and executive compensation, delivered by the International Foundation of Employee Benefit Plans.

CNLCP. Certified Nurse Life Care Planners are registered nurses with at least five years' experience in nursing and at least two years' experience in life care planning or case management services. CNLCPs are required to demonstrate their education and experience and pass a certification examination given by the Certified Nurse Life Care Planner Certification Board.

CPA. The commonly recognized acronym for Certified Public Accountant, CPA is the certification awarded by each of the state boards of accountancy to those accounting professionals who satisfy the education and experience requirements and pass the certifying examination.

CPC. A Certified Project Consultant is a professional designation granted by the International Management Consultants Certification Board based on education achievement, plus three to five years' professional experiences, ethical compliance, and continuing education.

CPCU. The Chartered Property Casualty Underwriter title is conferred by the American Institute for Chartered Property Casualty Underwriters after completion of nine courses, a national essay examination, and proof of professional experience.

CPEA. A Certified Professional Environmental Auditor must meet certain professional experience, auditor training, and character reference standards before passing a six-hour examination administered by the Board of Environmental, Health & Safety Auditor Certifications. In addition to environmental, health, and safety experience, CPEAs are experienced with compliance audits of business activities, procedures, processes, and techniques.

CPFO. A Certified Public Finance Officer has passed five examinations covering the major disciplines of public finance. The tests, administered by the Government Finance Officers Association of the United States and Canada, cover governmental accounting, auditing, financial reporting, cash management investments, debt management, operating and capital budgeting, pensions and benefits, risk management, and procurement.

CPM. Chartered Portfolio Manager is a designation of the American Academy of Financial Management (AAFM) granted upon proof of qualifying work experience and satisfaction of necessary educational milestones completed through the Thomas Jefferson School of Law.

Coursework covers financial instruments, including debt and equity instruments, and derivatives and alternative investments. The AAFM also requires proof of academic degrees from accredited or government-sanctioned programs and appropriate professional licenses.

CPP. The American Payroll Association tests and qualifies persons experienced in payroll production, reporting, accounting, taxation, and administration as Certified Payroll Professionals.

CPRM. A Certified Project Risk Manager is an analyst who has experience in managing risk teams and leading project managers. The certification is conferred by the American Academy of Project Management.

CQA. Certified Quality Auditor is a designation conferred by the American Society for Quality on professionals who meet certain auditing standards and who pass an examination on internal auditing, process auditing, systematic problem-solving, and related areas.

CRA. Certified Risk Analyst is a designation granted by the American Academy of Financial Management upon completion of several courses, delivered by the Thomas Jefferson School of Law, covering financial crimes, institutional risk, cyber-crimes and techno-torts, money laundering, investment management, international tax planning, and risk management.

CRC. A Certified Rehabilitation Counselor is a rehabilitation counselor who has met certain education and experience requirements set by the Commission on Rehabilitation Counselor Certification, and who has passed the Commission's examination. Testing covers insurance and health care benefits, Social Security programs, financial support, and funding sources for disabled persons.

CRISC. The "see-risk" acronym stands for the Certification in Risk and Information Systems Control awarded by ISACA for those professionals who have developed expertise in risk identification, assessment, and evaluation, risk monitoring and response, and information system control, design, and implementation.

CRP. A Certified Risk Professional specializes in risk management in financial services and must successfully satisfy the testing, education, experience, and ethical requirements of the Bank Administration Institute (BAI).

CRPC. A Chartered Retirement Planning Counselor designation is awarded by the College for Financial Planning to those professionals who complete a course of study and pass a final examination covering personal savings, employer-sponsored plans, deferred compensation, incapacity, disability and long-term care, retirement plan distributions, income taxes, and retirement cash flow considerations.

CRPS. A Chartered Retirement Plans Specialist is a variation of the CRPC designation, also offered by the College for Financial Planning. CRPS designees must also complete a course of study and pass a final examination. Coursework focuses on the types and characteristics of retirement plans, including all forms of 401(k) plans, IRAs, and SEP plans.

CSEP. A Certified Specialist in Estate Planning is a designation awarded after completion of eight courses (and eight related tests) dealing with estate and gift tax returns, fiduciary income tax returns, trusts, valuation issues for closely held businesses, and estate and business succession planning using life insurance. The designation is given to CPAs and other financial professionals by the National Institute for Excellence in Professional Education, LLC.

CSRP. A Certified Specialist in Retirement Planning is a designation given to CPAs and financial planners who complete seven courses (and seven related tests) dealing with retirement plans, tax implications and tax planning strategies, life insurance products, elder care planning, rollovers and distributions of IRAs, Roth IRAs, SEPs and SIMPLEs, and Social Security, Medicare, and prescription drug retirement benefits. The CSRP designation is conferred by the National Institute for Excellence in Professional Education, LLC.

CTEP. Chartered Trust and Estate Planner is a designation of the American Academy of Financial Management (AAFM) granted upon proof of qualifying work experience and satisfaction of necessary educational milestones completed through the Thomas Jefferson School of Law. Coursework covers trusts and company law, administration and compliance, international estate planning and asset protection, estate and gift taxation, wealth management, and private banking. The AAFM also requires proof of academic degrees from accredited or government-sanctioned programs and appropriate professional licenses.

CTFA. The Certified Trust and Financial Adviser distinction, granted by the Institute of Certified Bankers, requires designees to demonstrate their personal trust experience and education and to pass an examination on tax law, investment management, personal finance, insurance and estate planning, and fiduciary and trust activities.

CTP. Certified Treasury Professional is a title conferred by the Association for Financial Professionals upon treasury management specialists and others who are familiar with corporate liquidity, investing and borrowing activities, and management strategies for current assets and liabilities. Testing involves competency in financial accounting, cash management, risk management, payment systems, collections and disbursements, financial decisions, capital structure and dividend policy, and other related areas.

CTS. A Certified Transfer Pricing Specialist has completed special training in the law of intellectual property, tax treaties, international transfer pricing, and office financial services, delivered by the Thomas Jefferson School of Law. The designation is awarded by the American Academy of Financial Management.

CVA. A Certified Valuation Analyst is a credential offered to CPAs who have special training in business valuation and have been so qualified by the National Association of Certified Valuators and Analysts.

CVE. Certified Vocational Evaluation Specialist is a designation of the Commission on Rehabilitation Counselor Certification awarded to certified rehabilitation counselors who pursue additional training in vocational evaluation, standardized assessment techniques, and occupational information.

CVE. The acronym also previously referred to Certified Vocational Evaluators, a designation of the now-defunct Commission on Certification of Work Adjustment and Vocational Evaluation Specialists. Certified Vocational Evaluators are now recognized by PVE status (see below), and a more recent designation of Certified Vocational Evaluation Specialist, also known as CVE (see above) is offered by the Commission on Rehabilitation Counsel Certification.

CVE. The acronym is also sometimes used to refer to a Certified Vocational Expert, a designation of the American Board of Vocational Experts (ABVE). ABVE-certified experts must hold at least a master's degree, meet certain technical training and experience requirements, and pass a Board examination.

CWA. Certified Work Adjustment Specialist is a designation of the Commission on Rehabilitation Counselor Certification awarded to certified rehabilitation counselors who pursue additional training in the functional aspects of disability, situational assessments, behavior management, task analysis, functional living skills, and restructuring of work environments.

CWM. Chartered Wealth Manager is a designation of the American Academy of Financial Management (AAFM) granted upon proof of qualifying work experience and satisfaction of necessary educational milestones completed through the Thomas Jefferson School of Law. Coursework covers wealth management, private banking, investment management and compliance, international estate planning, asset protection, and estate and gift planning.

EA. An Enrolled Agent is a tax practitioner licensed by the U.S. Department of the Treasury to represent taxpayers before all administrative levels of the IRS on issues involving collection, audits, and appeals. EAs, who are represented by the National Association of Enrolled Agents, also provide tax planning and other financial services to individuals and industry.

ECS. An Elder Care Specialist is a specialist in retirement planning, estate and trust planning, and other financial areas affecting the elderly. The designation is conferred by the Accreditation Council for Accountancy and Taxation.

FAD. The Financial Analyst Designation is a variation of the Chartered Market Analyst (CMA) designation granted by the American Academy of Financial Management. See CMA for further details.

FCPA. The Forensic Certified Public Accountant designation is awarded by the Forensic CPA Society to certified public accountants (or equivalent qualified accountants from foreign countries) who pass a five-part certification examination covering such areas as forensic and investigative accounting and corporate fraud.

FNCC. A Forensic Nurse Certified Consultant is a registered nurse who can provide valuable testimony or expert evidence leading to a damages calculation in an injury case. The certification is granted by the International Commission on Health Care Certification to qualified RNs who have at least 80 hours of training in forensic science and meet other training requirements.

FSS. A Financial Services Specialist completes six courses given by the American College in such areas as disability income insurance, business insurance, annuities, retirement planning, investment planning, and estate planning.

GBA. The Group Benefits Associate designation is given to those who complete three courses in group health plan design, group benefits management, and health care financing and economics, delivered by the International Foundation of Employee Benefit Plans.

IAR. An Investment Advisor Representative is a lower-level investment advisor operating under the registration of a Registered Investment Advisor (RIA). IARs may be employed by investment firms that are RIAs and may provide many of the same services relating to portfolio management and investment advice.

LUTCF. A Life Underwriter Training Council Fellow must complete six courses through the American College to earn this designation which is jointly conferred by the College and the National Association of Insurance and Financial Advisors. Coursework covers personal financial markets, financial services to women, disability income insurance, business insurance, long-term care insurance, annuities, retirement, and investment planning.

MBC. The Master Business Consultant certification is awarded by the International Management Consultants Certification Board based on educational and experiential credentials. MBCs are required to maintain high ethical standards and complete eight hours of continuing education per year.

MCM. Master Project Manager is a designation of the American Academy of Financial Management awarded to project management specialists who have completed a course in international project management.

MCP. Management Consultant Professional is a designation of the International Management Consultants Certification Board (IMCB), granted upon proof of qualifying education, work experience, and ethical standards.

MFM. Master Financial Manager is a variation of the Registered Financial Specialist (RFS) designation granted by the American Academy of Financial Management. See RFS for further details.

MFP. Master Financial Planner is a designation of the American Academy of Financial Management (AAFM) granted upon proof of qualifying work experience and satisfaction of educational requirements including courses in wealth management. The AAFM also requires proof of academic degrees from accredited or government-sanctioned programs and appropriate professional licenses.

MPM. A Master Project Manager is one who has met the education, training, and examination requirements of the American Academy of Project Management.

PFS. The Personal Financial Specialist designation, granted by the American Institute of CPAs, is conferred upon CPAs who complete a personal financial planning educational program, demonstrate experience in the field, and pass an examination.

PME. The Project Manager E-Business certification is conferred by the International Project Management Commission to recognize professionals who have managed e-business teams and have satisfied the Commission's educational requirements.

PVE. Professional Vocational Evaluator is a designation that qualifies designees to be included in a national registry of vocational evaluators. Inclusion in the registry requires compliance with professional conduct guidelines. PVEs must also have a current Certified Vocational Evaluator certificate or meet other academic or experience requirements.

RBA. Registered Business Analyst is a designation of the International Board of Standards and the American Academy of Project Management granted upon proof of qualifying work experience, educational achievement and ethical compliance. RBAs must satisfy eight hours of continuing education per year.

REBC. Registered Employee Benefits Consultants have completed a five-course program offered by the American College and have otherwise demonstrated experience in the employee benefits field.

RFC. A Registered Financial Consultant can be a CPA, an attorney, a CFA, CFP, CLU, ChFC, EA, or RHU who meets the education, experience, and membership requirements of the International Association of Registered Financial Consultants.

RFG. The designation of Registered Financial Gerontologist is granted by the American Institute of Financial Gerontology after completion of six courses in the field of aging and financial issues. RFGs must pass a comprehensive examination, commit to a code of ethics, and complete a service learning requirement.

RFS. Registered Financial Specialist is a designation of the American Academy of Financial Management (AAFM) granted upon proof of qualifying work experience and satisfaction of necessary educational milestones completed through the Thomas Jefferson School of Law. Coursework covers investment management and compliance, advanced international tax planning, tax treaties, and financial instruments. The AAFM also requires proof of academic degrees from accredited or government-sanctioned programs and appropriate professional licenses.

RHU. Registered Health Underwriters, so designated by the American College, must complete a three-course program dealing with health insurance and must satisfy certain experience and continuing education requirements.

RIA. A Registered Investment Advisor is a person or business entity registered either with the U.S. Securities and Exchange Commission or a state securities agency to provide investment advice for a fee. RIAs manage investment portfolios, design financial plans, and provide ongoing advice to individuals and businesses.

RP. A Registered Paraplanner must complete a Foundations in Financial Planning program administered by the College for Financial Planning. The coursework, which covers financial statements, cash flow, time value of money, equities and debt instruments, tax planning, retirement planning, and insurance products, is followed by a final examination and a three-month internship requirement.

RPA. A Retirement Plans Associate has completed courses in retirement plan design and management and either asset management or personal wealth management, as part of a curriculum administered by the International Foundation of Employee Benefit Plans.

RR. Registered Representatives are associated with broker/dealers and companies that deal securities on behalf of their customers and have passed various licensing examinations that allow them to sell securities. RRs include stockbrokers, account executives, and other general securities representatives.

20.4. Top 25 Rules for Using Financial Experts

After selecting a financial expert, it is important to make efficient and effective use of the expert. Attorneys should dedicate the same amount of time and care to the preparation of financial experts as they do for liability experts. Ultimately, a successfully proved cause of action reaps only the benefits that can be established through competent and admissible evidence establishing the quantum of damages. The following rules should therefore prove helpful in optimizing the use of financial experts.

General Rules

Expert Rule 1. Prediscovery Consultation. Consult with your expert before propounding interrogatories and requests for production of documents. Ask the expert what foundational facts he would like to establish, and think about issuing a request for admissions. If the expert recommends that you obtain records from third-party sources, issue the appropriate subpoenas. Inquire as to what kinds of information would be widely known or widely recognized—for example, the current prime rate, a certain tax rate—and seek stipulations on these matters or ask the court to take judicial notice of these points.

Expert Rule 2. Postdiscovery Analysis. Share deposition transcripts and written answers to interrogatories with your expert as soon as you receive them. Give the expert plenty of time to formulate his opinions. Provide the expert with copies of documents, responses to requests for admissions, and records gathered through subpoenas. Ask him what, if any, additional information would be helpful in formulating his opinions or substantiating his conclusions.

Expert Rule 3. Evaluate Group Behavior. Allow several lawyers and paralegals to meet with your expert. If appropriate and possible, at least two lawyers, or a lawyer and a legal assistant, should meet with the expert simultaneously. Some experts act differently in a group setting and could reveal either positive or negative communication traits and personal demeanor when elevated from a one-on-one meeting to a group meeting. Pompous, overly jocular, confused, or highly moralistic experts could be received adversely by jurors.

Expert Rule 4. Test Response Quality. Gently examine and cross-examine your expert witness as part of the interview process, in order to evaluate the quality of his responses to questioning. Does he stumble? Does he avoid the question or answer an unasked question? Is he misleading or confusing? Is he unnecessarily straitlaced or too casual or insincere? Judges and juries will take great interest in the testimony of a well-spoken, polite, balanced, and informative expert. On the other hand, they may be put off or offended by one who makes rash declarations in a loud, pretentious, or verbose manner.

Expert Rule 5. Testifying from the Report. Work carefully with the expert in the preparation of his expert report. Under most rules of evidence, the expert will be constrained to testify only to those matters, and as to those opinions, set forth within the four corners of his report. Do not allow the expert to prepare the report prematurely, before reviewing all of the necessary discovery materials, and before fully considering the opponent's arguments and positions. Consider how an expert will be cross-examined on the content of his report *before* submitting the report to the opponent. Is there anything else the expert wishes to say in the report that would further elucidate his opinion?

Expert Rule 6. Gather Impeachment Materials. Use your expert witness to help you gather documents and records that will impeach the credibility of any opposing expert, or that will question the reliability of the opposing expert's findings. This may include anything from information about the opposing expert's lack of qualifications to his publication of irrelevant or contrary research. Prior research conducted by the opposing expert may contradict his findings in the present case, and as such, your expert witness may guide you as to leveraging the contradictory findings strategically to your client's advantage.

Expert Rule 7. Explore Qualifications. Consider your expert's curriculum vita in detail. Look beyond the document too, asking about any professional or academic experiences that have been excluded. Are there other, different, or earlier copies of the expert's CV that may be posted on the Internet or otherwise available to the opposing attorney? Ask the expert if all of his degrees were earned from fully accredited universities and colleges, and from fully accredited programs within those schools. Were any degrees earned through online or distance learning programs, and if so, were they grounded in an accredited curriculum run by a physical university or were they obtained through mail-order programs?

Expert Rule 8. Explore Bias and Motivation. Before exposing an expert to a courtroom or to an adversary, be sure that the expert has disclosed all relevant personal and professional activities, memberships, and relationships that may have a bearing on his opinions or that may suggest an interest, a bias, or a predisposition. Be sure to agree, clearly, on the expert's compensation—how much he bills, how much he has been paid—and the fact that the expert is being paid for his time and expertise, but not for his opinion, or for any particular conclusion. If an expert has a long history of testifying for plaintiffs or for defense insurance carriers, the attorney should ferret out the details before deposition and trial and determine how to address these matters.

Expert Rule 9. Identify Treatises and Literature. Ask your expert what learned treatises or professional literature informed his findings in your case. Inquire as to what other treatises or literature the opposing attorney may ask the expert to recognize as authoritative in the field of accounting, economics, or any particular financial specialty as the case may be. Do such authoritative sources contain any principles or conclusions contrary to those of the expert? Conversely, what authoritative treatises or publications would your expert recommend that you utilize as an impeachment tool against the opposing expert witness?

Expert Rule 10. Framing Hypotheticals. The use of hypothetical questions based on a specific set of facts is a common strategy for examining and cross-examining expert witnesses. On cross-examination, an expert can be asked to answer a hypothetical question drawn from a set of facts that has not, in fact, been established but rather has only been presented as a hypothetical. For this reason, it is important for attorney and expert to frame various hypothetical questions that may arise during the course of depositions and trial. Because hypothetical questions are based on a set of facts, it is important to test relevant questions in a variety of permutations, by changing certain facts and asking whether the expert's conclusions would thereby change. Such techniques are frequently employed on cross-examination and ought to be fully fleshed out before trial.

Special Financial Rules

Expert Rule 11. Establish Rates. It is always useful to establish all applicable rates in advance of the expert's testimony, or at the outset of the expert's testimony. So, for example, tax rates, interest rates, discount rates, prime rates, inflation rates, growth rates, consumer price indexes, and other benchmarks should be considered between the expert and the attorney prior to the expert's deposition and prior to trial. If the rate is controversial or subject to challenge, be prepared to defend it with timely exhibits and relevant testimony. If possible, ask the court to take judicial notice of certain published rates, such as exchange rates published and certified by the Federal Reserve, or an interest rate recognized by statute or court rule. If possible, secure stipulations between counsel as to applicable rates.

Expert Rule 12. Clarify Tax Basis. Generally, the expert witness will calculate damages on a pretax basis. Be sure that this point is confirmed with the expert and then explained in his report and his testimony. Where tax consequences are relevant or significant, be prepared to inquire further about the effects of taxation. Ask your expert if an opposing witness or rebuttal expert has not fully addressed tax consequences, and be prepared to cross-examine on this issue, when it is appropriate and useful to do so.

Expert Rule 13. Checklisting Steps Taken and Not Taken. It is common during an expert's deposition for the expert to be questioned as to the steps he took—or the steps he failed (or chose not) to take—in preparing his report and reaching his conclusions. Did he fail to consult with a vocational rehabilitation expert before selecting a time period for calculating the plaintiff's work-related losses? Did he look at only the plaintiff's most recent pay stubs? Did he consider only the last three years' tax returns? Did he consider the management's discussion of operations or the auditor's notes in reading the company's annual report?

In preparing experts for their depositions and their trial testimony, attorneys should ensure that the expert can carefully and comprehensively delineate a checklist of steps taken to support his findings. For example, if an attorney asks an expert witness, "weren't you concerned about the high fundamental volatility of the company from year to year?" and the expert responds affirmatively, the attorney is likely to follow up with a question like this: "Then tell me every step you took to investigate the sources and causes of the volatility." The expert should then be prepared to specify each of the steps, tests, calculations, and inquiries that he made. The absence of any useful step is likely to provide ammunition to the opposing attorney. Thus, the process of *checklisting* steps that were taken to investigate each question is a useful exercise. The process must necessarily inquire into steps not taken, and the expert should be prepared to explain authoritatively why he did not follow a particular step or procedure.

Expert Rule 14. Update Data. Financial data presented at a deposition or a trial should reflect the most up-to-date data available in a given case. Thus, it may be necessary to supplement answers to interrogatories or to amend an expert's report if new data causes the expert to modify his findings or alter his opinions in any respect. Attorneys should beware of the passage of time. A delay in scheduling a trial could mean that a target corporate defendant may have released new annual balance sheets or income statements or published another annual report. Time may alter the census data, production data, worklife expectancy trends, or performance experience that was used to calculate a formula upon which an opinion is based. For attorneys, the passage of time will mean conducting continuing discovery, procuring and disclosing updated documents, tables, and data, and coordinating such efforts with the expert witness.

Expert Rule 15. Ex Ante versus Ex Post Approach. To avoid confusion, the attorney and the financial expert should clarify whether the *ex ante* or the *ex post* method will be applied in any case involving lost profits. The *ex ante* method measures lost profits as of the date of loss, relying only on information known or knowable at that time. The *ex post* method, by contrast, measures damages as of the time of trial, relying on all known information at that time. Knowing which method is applied will clarify how, and to what point, damage calculations are discounted.

Expert Rule 16. Apply Data Mining Techniques. In cases in which large amounts of data are to be analyzed as part of the expert's work, pay special attention to the methods by which the data is collected, extracted, and analyzed. Statistical tests applied to large sets of data can reveal patterns that may prove or disprove an essential fact in a case. Experts skilled in so-called *cluster analysis, anomaly detection,* and other database analysis techniques can be extremely useful in such cases.

Expert Rule 17. Collaborate on Graphical Presentations. Ask your financial expert to work with you to develop persuasive and visually appealing forms of demonstrative evidence. This may include charts, graphs, tables, or formulas. Such graphical presentations remind judges and jurors that there is a science to the expert's work, and that there is a visual logic to mathematics.

Expert Rule 18. Apply Adjustments. What if the interest rate is higher? What if the tax rate is lower? What if the work-life expectancy is greater, or the duration of loss shorter? Ask your expert to explore the outcomes if various rates and contingencies were hypothetically adjusted. By applying such adjustments to the data and the formulas used by your expert, you can test for the extent that your expert's findings are highly dependent on the rates and the data used.

At what point, for example, would a different interest rate make a significant difference in the outcome? How much "wiggle room" do the expert's figures provide? If an adversary can easily invalidate an expert's findings by suggesting that a different tax rate, growth rate, or discount rate applies, then the expert should be prepared to meet this argument.

Expert Rule 19. Confirm GAAP and Other Standards. Accountants and related financial experts commonly follow the Generally Accepted Accounting Principles (GAAP), consisting of dozens of principles, standards, and procedures used in reporting data. GAAP policies include methods and procedures for the calculation and presentation of costs, debt, equity, taxes, revenues, sales, and profits. Confirm whether your expert is following GAAP or any particular widely accepted set of principles and procedures. For example, the International Financial Reporting Standards, adopted by the International Accounting Standards Board, share most, but not all, of the standards and procedures of GAAP. Ask whether your expert has departed from the set of principles or procedures he is following, and if so, why and in what manner. Be prepared to defend and explain the expert's approach.

Expert Rule 20. Establish Causation. Be sure that your expert witness can connect his damage calculations to the events that caused the damages to occur. A decrease in sales must be clearly tied to the proper cause of the decrease, lest the opposing party argue that the decrease was merely coincidental or was the consequence of some other event or circumstance. Test the expert on questions of causation. Explore alternative theories, and develop a line of questioning that convincingly addresses the causation issue.

Expert Rule 21. Independent Data Test. Be prepared to question the independence of the data gathered or used by the expert. Third-party data sources should be evaluated: Are their data collection methods objective? Unbiased? Independent of external funding influences? Many reliable data sources can be found on government websites and third-party industry providers. Be sure you've identified the data sources and inquired about their independence.

Expert Rule 22. Fixed and Variable Expenses. Fixed expenses do not change with an increase or decrease in sales. Such fixed expenses as rent and insurance are consistent from period to period, regardless of production. Variable expenses, however, vary with the volume of sales. Thus, the variable cost of raw materials, supplies, shipping and delivery costs, and sales commissions will ebb and flow with the level of sales.

Be sure, however, that your expert is prepared to address those expense categories that do not fall squarely or exclusively in one category or the other. Indeed, some kinds of expenses, such as electricity or water usage could be classified as both fixed and variable expenses. A business entity could have a fixed utility cost for electrical usage while a part of the monthly electric bill varies based on usage, as a result of increased machine costs due to higher sales volume. An expert should be prepared to discuss hybrid expense categories and to explain and defend why and how such expenses are treated in calculating of damages.

Expert Rule 23. Daubert/Frye Standard. Does the expert's scientific approach or mathematical methodology satisfy the test for scientific validity, reliability, and recognized acceptance as required by *Daubert v. Merrill Dow Pharmaceuticals*, *Frye v. United States,* and their progeny? As discussed in Section 18.6 below, the expertise proffered by the expert, the formulas he applies, and the methodology employed must meet the standards pertaining to statistical reliability and margins of error. Ask the expert whether his methods have been tested, peer reviewed, defined by a known rate of error, and widely accepted by other experts in the field.

Expert Rule 24. Hire a Consulting Expert. If the case is substantial and the circumstances justify the investment, hire a consulting expert to review and challenge the work of your financial expert. A behind-the-scenes consulting expert can retrace each of the calculations made by your financial expert, can challenge and test his assumptions, and can question results obtained through shortcuts or inappropriate rules of thumb. This level of oversight may not be necessary in every case, but when appropriate, it may avoid an embarrassing mathematical error or prevent an undetected opportunity for impeachment.

Expert Rule 25. Don't Forget the Basic Rules. Be sure that your expert adheres to the Ten Basic Rules discussed in Chapter 2 of this book. While an expert would be expected to have mastered the basic rules of calculating formulas, the attorney should always revisit the rules in evaluating the expert's work. Are the expert's assumptions clear? Are they defensible? Is his data reliable and verifiable? Has he considered the hidden or the missing numbers? A review of the basic rules will provide a greater sense of security in the process.

20.5. Objections to Expert Testimony

Once the decision is made to engage the services of an expert witness, an attorney should prepare to meet every potential objection to the expert's qualifications, sources of data, methodology, scientific validity, and evidentiary foundation. Federal Rule of Evidence 702 sets the framework for the admissibility of expert testimony:

> If scientific, technical, or other specialized knowledge will assist the trier of fact to understand the evidence or to determine

> a fact in issue, a witness qualified as an expert by knowledge, skill, experience, training, or education, may testify thereto in the form of an opinion or otherwise, if (1) the testimony is based upon sufficient facts or data, (2) the testimony is the product of reliable principles and methods, and (3) the witness has applied the principles and methods reliably to the facts of the case.

Effective December 1, 2011, absent contrary congressional action, Rule 702 was scheduled to be amended to read as follows:

> A witness who is qualified as an expert by knowledge, skill, experience, training, or education may testify in the form of an opinion or otherwise if:
>
> **(a)** the expert's scientific, technical, or other specialized knowledge will help the trier of fact to understand the evidence or to determine a fact in issue;
> **(b)** the testimony is based on sufficient facts or data;
> **(c)** the testimony is the product of reliable principles and methods; and
> **(d)** the expert has reliably applied the principles and methods to the facts of the case.

The amended rule will clarify the court's gatekeeper role in testing the reliability and validity of the expert's methods and the level of knowledge or credentials required to serve as a forensic financial expert.

Qualifications

Objections to an expert's qualifications can be avoided at the outset by carefully choosing an expert who is suitably qualified in a specialty that is particularly relevant to the facts at issue. Federal Rule 702, and similar state evidence rules, do not impose specific educational or experience requirements. In fact, a wide variety of "skilled" persons, not typically classified as experts, such as bankers, landowners, and restaurant owners may qualify to testify on questions of valuation.[1]

---

[1] *See, e.g.,* Soo Line Railway Co. v. Fruehauf Corp., 547 F. 2d 1365 (8th Cir. 1977); Knuppel v. American Insurance Co., 269 F. 2d 163 (7th Cir. 1959).

On the other hand, not every highly educated or professionally credentialed witness will automatically qualify to testify on the question of damages or valuation. Thus, an orthopedic surgeon was held not to be qualified to render an expert opinion on future damages for the misappropriation of trade secrets in developing an anterior lumbar plating system.[2] Similarly, a consulting engineer with a degree in mechanical engineering and 30 years of experience was found unqualified to testify as an expert as to damages in a misrepresentation case.[3]

In fact, eminently qualified economists who would be considered experts in their own subspecialties could be denied expert status in court if their testimony purports to provide an opinion on financial or damages questions outside the scope of their expertise. One economist, for example, was not qualified as an expert to testify in a malicious prosecution suit that the plaintiff's damages were proximately caused by the criminal prosecution.[4] A planning consultant with a master's degree in urban economic planning was likewise disqualified in his proffer to testify that only three commercially feasible sites were available in a particular city for adult uses under a challenged zoning ordinance.[5]

Because Rule 702 provides no absolute guidelines for the qualifications of an expert, and because every case calls for different specific areas of expertise, the burden falls on the attorney to exercise the highest degree of oversight in investigating the qualifications of the expert witness. The attorney should exert every effort to match the qualifications of the expert to the facts of the case and to qualify the expert specifically in a field that has been directly tied to the issues in dispute.

Data, Methods, and Science

The relevance of an expert's testimony alone will not make his testimony admissible. The testimony must be based on reliable and verifiable data, and the expert must apply generally accepted standards and sound scientific techniques for analyzing the data. A qualified expert

---

[2]Kozak v. Medtronic, Inc., 512 F. Supp. 2d 913 (S.D. Tex. 2007).

[3]Wartsila NSD North America, Inc. v. Hill Intern., Inc., 299 F. Supp. 2d 400 (D.N.J. 2003).

[4]Bass v. Spitz, 522 F. Supp. 1343 (E.D. Mich. 1981).

[5]15192 Thirteen Mile Road, Inc. v. City of Warren, 626 F. Supp. 803 (E.D. Mich. 1985).

could still find his testimony excluded where his methodology is flawed,[6] even with such seemingly simple calculations as present value[7] and future value.[8]

Generally accepted accounting principles and widely known financial formulas are routinely recognized by the courts and are unlikely to present any challenges as to methodology or scientific validity. Yet innovative or unnecessarily complicated approaches to data interpretation and to damage calculations may raise red flags. An opposing party may object that a particular methodology lacks a sound scientific basis or that it is not widely accepted or recognized in the field of accounting, actuarial science, statistics, or otherwise, as the case may be.[9] So, for example, the court rejected evidence of damages based on lost profits in one case where the methodology applied was found not to be in regular use for predicting future profits, was not peer reviewed, had no uniform usage in any known industry, and was capable of manipulation to achieve virtually any desired result.[10]

Even a widely recognized method of calculating damages can be challenged as unreliable or invalid if it is based on unrealistic assumptions[11] or projections of future trends that are speculative or conjectural.[12] Experts should also be counseled to avoid coining their own terms, or unique usages of existing terms. One such expert's testimony that a debtor was in a "zone of insolvency" at the time of an alleged fraudulent transfer was held unreliable, and therefore inadmissible, because the so-called "zone" could not be tested, and the expert had never seen the term in an article or treatise related to valuations and had not personally seen his peers use the term in other valuations.[13]

---

[6]MicroStrategy, Inc. v. Business Objects, S.A., 429 F. 3d 1344 (Fed. Cir. 2005).

[7]Diesel Machinery, Inc. v. B.R. Lee Industries, Inc., 418 F. 3d 820 (8th Cir. 2005).

[8]Nebraska Plastics, Inc. v. Holland Colors Americas, Inc., 408 F. 3d 410 (8th Cir. 2005).

[9]For a further discussion of the *Daubert/Frye* tests for admitting testimony about a scientific test or technique, see Section 18.6 below.

[10]LifeWise Master Funding v. Teelbank, 374 F. 3d 917 (10th Cir. 2004).

[11]Shatkin v. McDonnell Douglas Corp., 727 F. 2d 202 (2d Cir. 1984).

[12]Johnson v. Serra, 521 F. 2d 1289 (8th Cir. 1975), on remand, 458 F. Supp. 297.

[13]Kipperman v. Onex Corp., 411 B.R. 805 (N.D. Ga. 2009).

Laying a Foundation

An expert cannot testify in the form of an opinion without first providing a factual basis for his opinion. For example, if a financial expert was asked to testify whether he believed a certain course of conduct by a corporate defendant would have been profitable, he could neither answer in the affirmative nor in the negative without first testifying as to the facts upon which he based his conclusion. In such a scenario, the attorney must first lay a careful structure and comprehensible foundation. The expert in this case might be asked what data or financial reports he reviewed as part of his investigation. What portion of the reports were of particular interest or concern to him, and why? The expert could then explain how he gathered and verified information about the corporation's annual revenue from sales, what adjustments he made and why, and what costs and expense categories were then considered.

Attorneys commonly use a variety of techniques to lay a factual foundation. These include asking the expert to identify a series of reports, statements, or raw data and to testify about such exhibits; asking the expert to examine a series of facts already admitted into evidence and to respond to hypothetical questions about those facts; or asking the expert to draw on his own personal knowledge.

Particularly in the case of financial experts, it is important to discuss the kinds of data that contributed to the expert's conclusions and why; the method and integrity of the data-gathering method and any sifting process the expert employed to isolate the most useful or relevant data; the facts of the case that prompted him to seek certain kinds of data or to exclude other kinds of data from his analysis; and the formulas or other methods that were applied to form opinions about the issues in dispute.

An objection based on a lack of foundation is a double-edged sword. Where an opposing party raises this objection, it will ordinarily prompt the attorney conducting direct examination of his expert to step back and state a series of foundational questions—a process that may ultimately buttress the expert's findings.

Because experts are permitted to respond to hypothetical questions, there is no requirement that an expert testify only with respect to facts that are in evidence. Still, an opposing party may object to testimony based on facts not in evidence. Thus, if a hypothetical question misrepresents the facts of the case, or introduces new facts that are not alleged or perhaps not plausible, it would be improper to ask the expert to form opinions about such scenarios. This is not to say that an attorney cannot test the waters with the expert, by proposing hypothetical situations in which the facts are more or less favorable to one party or the other. The more strained or doubtful the scenarios, however, the more likely they will be met with an objection that the hypothetical is based on facts not in evidence.

20.6. Scientific Validity and Reliability

Any use of forensic experts at trial must be considered in relation to the court's gatekeeping responsibility. The fact that an accountant or an economist is an expert in his field is not enough to guarantee the admissibility of the proffered testimony and opinions. The methods and techniques applied by the expert must also be relevant and reliable. Moreover, the gatekeeper role of the judge is not merely to prevent so-called *junk science* from coming into evidence. Judges must apply their discretion to all kinds of experts today, not only scientific experts. In fact, Federal Rule of Evidence 702 permits "scientific, technical or *other specialized knowledge*" to be admitted if it will assist the trier of fact to understand the issues or to determine the facts in issue. The broad scope of the rule imposes a correspondingly broad discretion on judges to exclude unreliable evidence from any specialized field.

The judicial debate and legal scholarship over the admissibility of scientific or other specialized expert evidence is extensive. The leading modern precedent, *Daubert v. Merrill Dow Pharmaceuticals,*[14] introduced a four-pronged test that clarified prior law.[15] In *Daubert,* the U.S. Supreme Court held that a court should consider the following four factors:

---

[14]509 U.S. 579, 113 S. Ct. 2786 (1993).

[15]Under an earlier test laid out in *Frye v. United States,* 54 App. D.C. 46, 293 F. 1013 (1923), expert opinions based on scientific theories or techniques that were generally accepted in the scientific community were admissible. This allowed novel scientific evidence to be admitted if the evidence was generally accepted by other experts in the same field. Evidence Rule 702, however, refocused the court on whether the scientific theories or techniques were reliable or trustworthy, not simply if they were generally accepted. *Daubert* now imposes a requirement to take all of these factors into consideration.

1. Whether the espoused theory or technique in question has been or can be tested.
2. Whether the espoused theory or technique has been subjected to peer review and publication.
3. Whether the espoused theory or technique has a known rate of error, and whether there exist standards to control the operation of the technique.
4. Whether the espoused theory or technique has been widely accepted among peers.

In 1999, the U.S. Supreme Court revisited the question of the court's gatekeeping obligation, holding that the *Daubert* factors apply to *all expert testimony,* not only to "scientific" testimony. In *Kumho Tire Company, Ltd. v. Carmichael,*[16] the Court noted that the *Daubert*-driven inquiry into relevance and reliability extends to those kinds of experts who would offer "technical or other specialized knowledge" as those words are envisioned in Federal Evidence Rule 702. Thus, forensic financial experts of the various kinds and specialties discussed in this chapter could all find themselves subject to the *Daubert* factors.

While *Daubert, Kumho,* and various Circuit Court cases define the landscape in federal court, there still remains considerable inconsistency at the state level. The Alaska Supreme Court, for example, has rejected the rule of *Kumho,* holding that the *Daubert* factors apply only to "scientific" testimony rather than to all expert testimony.[17] A number of states have expressly retained the earlier *Frye* standard. Other states have sidestepped *Kumho,* choosing instead to rely only on their own more narrowly construed evidence rules.[18] In fact, attempts to codify the *Daubert* factors in state statutes have not always been successful, with the Arizona Supreme Court notably declaring one such statute unconstitutional as overstepping the separation of powers and

[16]526 U.S. 137, 119 S. Ct. 1167, 143 L.Ed.2d 238 (1999).

[17]Marron v. Stromstad, 123 P. 3d 992, 1006-08 (Alaska 2005).

[18]*See, e.g.,* Logerquist v. McVey, 196 Ariz. 470, 481, 1 P. 3d 113, 124 (2000) (noting Ariz. R. Evid. 702). Other states that have rejected *Kumho* include North Dakota, Maryland, Wisconsin, and Minnesota.

unlawfully invading the court's authority to control the admissibility of expert testimony under its own analytical framework.[19]

Attorneys who use financial experts to establish damages should also consider the likely reception those experts will receive in various administrative tribunals. While expert testimony has been subjected to great scrutiny under *Daubert, Kumho*, and their progeny in both the federal and state courts, it has not been so scrutinized by regulatory authorities, boards, commissions, and administrative law judges. For example, *Daubert* and *Kumho* have been declared inapplicable in Social Security disability cases,[20] in Environmental Appeals Board cases,[21] and other administrative actions. Still other federal agencies have applied *Daubert* and *Kumho* in administrative proceedings while allowing vigorous cross-examination of the witnesses.[22] The intellectual debate continues to unfold, with proponents claiming there should be a "regulatory *Daubert*" standard, if even only through an informal rulemaking procedure[23] and opponents charging that such a standard would introduce an unwieldy paradigm shift into the administrative law system.

Attorneys should therefore consider the forum, the jurisdiction, and the local law governing the admissibility of expert testimony. For better or for worse, *Daubert's* requirements can be easily exploited by litigants, leading to mini-trials, prolonged discovery, and prohibitive costs.

---

[19]Lear v. Fields, 226 Ariz. 226, 245 P. 3d 911 (Ariz. App. Div. 2, 2011), invalidating A.R.S. § 12-2203 in favor of Ariz. R. Evid. 702. *See also* Ariz. Const. Art. 3; Art. 6, § 5(5).

[20]*See, e.g.,* Bayliss v. Barnhart, 427 F. 3d 1211 (9th Cir. 2005); Taylor v. Astrue, 2011 WL 976777 (C.D. Cal. 2011).

[21]*See, e.g.,* In re Solutia, Inc., 2001 WL 1549338 (E.P.A. 2001). *But see* In re Lobsters, Inc., 2001 WL 1632538 (N.O.A.A. 2001).

[22]*See, e.g.,* In the Matter of Daniel Chapter One, 2009 WL 964219 (Federal Trade Commission, 2009), in particular the Order Denying Respondents' Motion In Limine to Preclude Complaint Counsel from Introducing at Trial the Testimony of Dr. Denis R. Miller.

[23]J. Tavener Holland, *Regulatory Daubert: A Panacea for the Endangered Species Act's "Best Available Science" Mandate?,* 39 McGeorge L. Rev. 299 (2008); Raul, Alan Charles and Julie Zampa Dwyer, *Regulatory Daubert: A Proposal to Enhance Judicial Review of Agency Science by Incorporating Daubert Principles into Administrative Law,* 66-AUT Law & Comtemp. Probs. 7 (Autumn 2003).

Daubert, Kumho, and Financial Experts

In the federal courts, the *Daubert* factors have been frequently cited in exclusionary orders barring or limiting the testimony of financial experts. In some cases, the *Daubert* factors have been applied to invalidate a formula, a mathematical rule of thumb, or a statistical technique used to calculate damages.

This was the case in *Uniloc USA, Inc. v. Microsoft Corp.*,[24] in which the U.S. Court of Appeals for the Federal Circuit abolished the so-called 25% rule used in patent law to calculate a reasonable royalty for purposes of determining infringement damages.[25] Under the 25% Rule, patent infringers were said hypothetically to owe a royalty rate equivalent to 25% of their expected profits for the product that incorporates the patent, because this is what they would pay in the form of a royalty to license the patent had they entered into negotiations to do so. The court held that this rule was a fundamentally flawed tool for determining a baseline royalty rate in a hypothetical negotiation in a patent licensing case because it fails to meet the *Daubert* standard for admissibility.

Case law also suggests that the testimony of financial experts with respect to causation may also fail if the causal links are not reliably and verifiably demonstrated in accordance with *Daubert* and *Kumho.* Several rulings by the U.S. District Court for the Northern District of Oklahoma in the *Williams Securities Litigation,* subsequently affirmed by the Tenth Circuit,[26] present a case in point. The plaintiff subclass in the *Williams* case filed fraud claims under various sections of the Securities Exchange Act, on behalf of the subsidiary, Williams Communications Group (WCG).

After WCG filed for bankruptcy and its stock plummeted to 6 cents per share, the subclass retained an expert witness to offer opinion testimony regarding how the decline in the price of the WCG stock was attributable to the alleged misrepresentations, which allegedly caused WCG's stock to fall. The expert witness offered two alternative

---

[24] 632 F. 3d 1292 (Fed. Cir. 2011).

[25] For a further discussion of the 25% rule and reasonable royalties, see Section 17.7.

[26] In re Williams Securities Litigation—WCG Subclass, 558 F. 3d 1130 (10th Cir. 2009).

theories. Under the first theory, labeled the "leakage theory," the expert attributed nearly all of WCG's inflated value to fraud and claimed that almost the entire decline in stock price was a result of the alleged truth gradually leaking into the marketplace.

In an alternative scenario, the expert claimed that WCG's stock price declined after a delay in its earnings report, an announcement to the public that WCG may default on paying promissory notes, a public announcement that WCG was considering bankruptcy, and WCG's actual filing for bankruptcy.

The district court in the WCG case held that the expert's leakage theory "failed to differentiate between losses rooted in causes cognizable under loss causation doctrine, on one hand, and, on the other hand, losses attributable to industry-specific stresses, the meltdown in the telecommunications sector, and other negative developments unrelated to the alleged fraud." The district court also found that the expert's loss causation theory premised on corrective disclosures made by the company was unreliable.[27]

If a moral can be drawn from the Tenth Circuit's holdings in this case, it is that financial experts who go beyond calculating damages, and who are asked to opine about causation, must be prepared to demonstrate that particular losses are causally connected to particular acts or events established by the evidence. Such experts must ultimately be prepared to exclude other causative factors—an exercise that may require additional calculations and additional efforts by the attorney and the expert to prove that the expert's methodology is valid and fail-safe.

---

[27]*See also* Dura Pharmaceuticals, Inc. v. Broudo, 544 U.S. 336, 342, 125 S. Ct. 1627, 161 L.Ed.2d 577 (2005), in which the U.S. Supreme Court noted that "an inflated purchase price will not itself constitute or proximately cause the relevant economic loss."

Mortality Tables

Historical Mortality Tables and Other Rate Tables
Compiled by the Society of Actuaries
http://mort.soa.org/

IRS Actuarial Tables for valuing annuities, life estates, remainders and reversions
http://www.irs.gov/retirement-plans/actuaries-tables

National Vital Statistics System operated by Centers for Disease Control and Prevention
http://www.cdc.gov/nchs/nvss/index.htm

Pension Benefit Guaranty Corporation ERISA Mortality Tables
http://www.pbgc.gov/prac/interest/erisa-mortality-tables.html

Period Life Table by Social Security Administration
http://www.ssa.gov/oact/STATS/table4c6.html

Specialized Mortality Tables from actuary.com
http://www.actuary.com/actuarial-science/actuarial-tables-actuary.htm

Day of the Year Tables

Day	Jan	Feb	Mar	Apr	May	Jun	Jul	Aug	Sep	Oct	Nov	Dec
1	001	032	060	091	121	152	182	213	244	274	305	335
2	002	033	061	092	122	153	183	214	245	275	306	336
3	003	034	062	093	123	154	184	215	246	276	307	337
4	004	035	063	094	124	155	185	216	247	277	308	338
5	005	036	064	095	125	156	186	217	248	278	309	339
6	006	037	065	096	126	157	187	218	249	279	310	340
7	007	038	066	097	127	158	188	219	250	280	311	341
8	008	039	067	098	128	159	189	220	251	281	312	342
9	009	040	068	099	129	160	190	221	252	282	313	343
10	010	041	069	100	130	161	191	222	253	283	314	344
11	011	042	070	101	131	162	192	223	254	284	315	345
12	012	043	071	102	132	163	193	224	255	285	316	346
13	013	044	072	103	133	164	194	225	256	286	317	347
14	014	045	073	104	134	165	195	226	257	287	318	348
15	015	046	074	105	135	166	196	227	258	288	319	349
16	016	047	075	106	136	167	197	228	259	289	320	350
17	017	048	076	107	137	168	198	229	260	290	321	351
18	018	049	077	108	138	169	199	230	261	291	322	352
19	019	050	078	109	139	170	200	231	262	292	323	353
20	020	051	079	110	140	171	201	232	263	293	324	354
21	021	052	080	111	141	172	202	233	264	294	325	355
22	022	053	081	112	142	173	203	234	265	295	326	356
23	023	054	082	113	143	174	204	235	266	296	327	357
24	024	055	083	114	144	175	205	236	267	297	328	358
25	025	056	084	115	145	176	206	237	268	298	329	359
26	026	057	085	116	146	177	207	238	269	299	330	360
27	027	058	086	117	147	178	208	239	270	300	331	361
28	028	059	087	118	148	179	209	240	271	301	332	362
29	029		088	119	149	180	210	241	272	302	333	363
30	030		089	120	150	181	211	242	273	303	334	364
31	031		090		151		212	243		304		365

For Leap Years Only

If a year can be divided by 4 or 400 without remainder, it is a leap year.
If a year can be divided by 100 without remainder it is a common year.
The next year that is divisible by both 100 and 4 will be the year 2100.
The next year that is divisible by 400 will be the year 2400.

Day	Jan	Feb	Mar	Apr	May	Jun	Jul	Aug	Sep	Oct	Nov	Dec
1	001	032	061	092	122	153	183	214	245	275	306	336
2	002	033	062	093	123	154	184	215	246	276	307	337
3	003	034	063	094	124	155	185	216	247	277	308	338
4	004	035	064	095	125	156	186	217	248	278	309	339
5	005	036	065	096	126	157	187	218	249	279	310	340
6	006	037	066	097	127	158	188	219	250	280	311	341
7	007	038	067	098	128	159	189	220	251	281	312	342
8	008	039	068	099	129	160	190	221	252	282	313	343
9	009	040	069	100	130	161	191	222	253	283	314	344
10	010	041	070	101	131	162	192	223	254	284	315	345
11	011	042	071	102	132	163	193	224	255	285	316	346
12	012	043	072	103	133	164	194	225	256	286	317	347
13	013	044	073	104	134	165	195	226	257	287	318	348
14	014	045	074	105	135	166	196	227	258	288	319	349
15	015	046	075	106	136	167	197	228	259	289	320	350
16	016	047	076	107	137	168	198	229	260	290	321	351
17	017	048	077	108	138	169	199	230	261	291	322	352
18	018	049	078	109	139	170	200	231	262	292	323	353
19	019	050	079	110	140	171	201	232	263	293	324	354
20	020	051	080	111	141	172	202	233	264	294	325	355
21	021	052	081	112	142	173	203	234	265	295	326	356
22	022	053	082	113	143	174	204	235	266	296	327	357
23	023	054	083	114	144	175	205	236	267	297	328	358
24	024	055	084	115	145	176	206	237	268	298	329	359
25	025	056	085	116	146	177	207	238	269	299	330	360
26	026	057	086	117	147	178	208	239	270	300	331	361
27	027	058	087	118	148	179	209	240	271	301	332	362
28	028	059	088	119	149	180	210	241	272	302	333	363
29	029	060	089	120	150	181	211	242	273	303	334	364
30	030		090	121	151	182	212	243	274	304	335	365
31	031		091		152		213	244		305		366

Source: NASA Goddard Earth Sciences Data and Information Services Center

Index

A

Abandoned Shipwreck Act (ASA), 534
Abstract recovery, 386
Accelerated entry damages, 434–36
Accounting methods, changes in, 13
Accounts payable turnover (APT), 173–74
Accounts receivable turnover (ART), 171–73
Accreditation Council for Business Schools and Programs (ACBSP), 576
Acid-test ratio, 164–66, 501
Actual cash value, 502–3
Actual damages plus profits, 468–71
  cost-of-production method, 469–70
  number-of-products method, 470–71
  sales revenue method, 471
Actual period of estrangement, 50
Addition, high-speed, 47–49
  rounding and reversing, 50–52
Adjusted gross income (AGI), 518–19
Adjustments, applying, 600
Admiralty law, 531–52
  damages
    available, 536–39
    betterment based on useful life extension, 540–41
    calculating, 539–52
    factors, applying, 547–52
    for general maritime damages, 538–39
    for injured seamen, 536–38
    for other maritime workers, 538–39
    payable on maritime salvage claim, 545–52
    for physical injury to seaman, 541–45
    property damage claim, 539–40
    six-factor Blackwall test, 546
    ten-factor Salvage Treaty test, 546–47
  legal framework for, 531–36
    Abandoned Shipwreck Act (ASA), 534
    Carriage of Goods by Sea Act (COGSA), 535–36
    Death on the High Seas Act (DOHSA), 531–32
    Jones Act, 532–33
    Longshore Harbor and Workers Compensation Act (LHWCA), 532, 538
    Maritime Transportation Security Act, 534
    Ocean Shipping Reform Act (OSRA), 534–35
    Oil Pollution Act (OPA), 535
    Outer Continental Shelf Lands Act (OCSLA), 533
    Wreck Act, 535
  scope, 529–31
Advice, loss of, 222–23
Advisory Circulars (ACs), 552, 556–57

Age, in determining pain and suffering, 231, 232
Age Discrimination in Employment Act (ADEA), 314
  liquidated damages and, 331–32
  punitive damages and, 335
Airworthiness Directives (ADs), 552, 556–57
Alaska Rule (wage increase/discount rate), 200–201
Alimony and spousal support, 486–89
  discounted cash flows, 487–88
  limited term alimony (present value of annuity), 488–89
  permanent alimony (perpetuities), 488
Alternative result—either event occurring, 129–30
Altman, Edward I., 399, 412, 414
American Express Corp., annual report of, 27
American Factfinder, 242
Americans with Disabilities Act (ADA), 335, 530
American Time Use Surveys, BLS, 221
Amortization schedules, 185
Analytical approach, 439–40
Annual consumption or maintenance expense (AME), 567–68
Annual growth factors, 277–78
Annual reports
  as internal source of information, 27, 239
Annuity, present value (PV) of, 93–94
Anomaly detection, 600
Arithmetic mean *versus* geometric mean, 107–11
Asset approaches, 36
Asset-based valuation method, 312
Assets
  calculating, 161–62
  marital, division of, 479–86
  reassigning, 494–95
  valuation and, 312
Asset turnover ratio, 410
Asset utilization ratio, 410
Association to Advance Collegiate Schools of Business (AACSB), 576
Assumptions and formula-building, 10–11
Attachments, 26–29
Attorneys' fees, 468
Audits, 260
Average shareholders' equity (ASE), 275
Aviation law, 552–69
  damages
    available, 558–62
    aviation death claim, 565–69
    baggage loss, 564–65
    calculating, 562–69
    destruction of cargo, 562–64
    domestic regime, 560–62
    international regime, 558–60
  legal framework for aviation cases, 552–58 (*See also* Title 14, Code of Federal Regulations; Title 49, United States Code, Subtitle VII)
    Advisory Circulars (ACs), 552, 556–57
    Airworthiness Directives (ADs), 552, 556–57
    Montreal Convention, 557–59, 563–65
    Notices to Airmen (NOTAMS), 552, 556–57
    Temporary Flight Restrictions (TFRs), 552, 556–57
  scope, 529–31

B

Back pay, 321–27
  back-pay period, adjusting, 324–25
  base salary, 321–24
  fringe benefits, 325–26
  other adjustments, 326
  taxes on, 327
Baggage loss, 564–65
Balance sheet, 243–49
  Boeing Corp., 244–45
  book value per share of stock (BVPS), 247
  business damages and, 243–49
  calculations, 243
  common sizing, 248, 253
  current asset turnover (CAT), 246
  current ratio, 247–48
  debt-to-equity ratio (D/E), 247
  financial ratios, 161–62
  liabilities, 244–45
  off-balance sheet liabilities, 33–34
  partnerships and, 245
  price-to-book ratio (P/B), 246–47
  return on assets (ROA), 246
  Shareholders' Equity, 245–46
Bankruptcy ratios, 399–401
Bankruptcy risk, 399–421
  bankruptcy ratios, 399–401
  cash flow (CF) ratios, 414–21
    cash flow adequacy ratio (CFAR), 419–21
    cash-flow-to-debt ratio, 415–17
    operating cash flow to capital expenditures, 417–18
    operating cash flow to dividends, 418–19
  earnings before income tax to total assets (EBIT-to-TA), 407–8
  equity-to-debt ratio, 408–10
  retained earnings to total assets ratio (RE-to-TA), 404–7
  sales-to-total-assets ratio, 410–11
  working capital to total assets, 402–4
  Z-score bankruptcy prediction formula, 412–14
Barnes & Noble, Inc., debt-to-equity ratio (D/E) of, 160
Base salary
  adjusting, 322–24
  determining, 321–22
Basic earning power ratio, 407, 408
Beaulieu v. Elliot, 200
Beginning shareholders' equity, 276
Benchmarking fractions, 70–71
Benefit-cost analysis, 383–84
Benefit-cost ratio (BCR)
  calculating, 177–79
  for restoration project, 383–84
Beta calculation, 16
Betterment based on useful life extension, 540–41
Bias, exploring, 597
"Big bath" technique, 19
Black-Scholes option-pricing model, 212–13
Blackwall test, 546
Blurring, 467
Book value (BV), 147–48
Book value per share of stock (BVPS)
  balance sheet and, 247
  calculating, 147–48
  price-to-book ratio (P/B), 168
Break-even analysis, 516–18
Breakeven formula, 111–14
  price, determining, 113–14
  profit, breaking even with, 112–13
Build-up method (BUM), 304–5
Bundled sales, 428
Bundled service contracts, 429
Bureau of Economic Analysis (BEA), 217

Bureau of Labor Statistics (BLS)
American Time Use Surveys, 221
reports on employee benefits, 210
tables of employer costs per hour for fringe benefits, 566–67
work expectancy, 195
Burn rate formula, 257–58
Business damages, 235–312
business ratios, devising your own specific, 295–301
earnings per share (EPS), 276–80
financial statements, 243–62
balance sheet, 243–49
cash flow statement, 254–59
income statement, 249–54
information not included in, 259–62
formula, determining, 235–38
fraud and irregularities, 20–21
information sources, 238–43
liquidity *versus* indebtedness, 290–92
net worth, 272–74
price-to-earnings ratio (P/E), 280–85
professional practices and small businesses, 301–12
profit margins, 292–95
gross profit margin (GPM), 293
net profit margin (NPM), 293–95
rates of return (ROR), 285–90
return on assets (ROA), 288–89
return on average assets (ROAA), 289
return on average equity (ROAE), 288
return on common equity (ROCE), 287
return on equity (ROE), 287
return on operating assets (ROOA), 289
SEC-required forms
Form 8-Q, 270–72
Form 10-K, 262–68
Form 10-Q, 268–70
shareholders' equity, 274–76
Business ratios, devising your own specific, 295–301
"But for" test, 426

C

Capitalization of earnings method, 303–9
Capitalization rate (cap rate), 176–77
Cargo, destruction of, 562–64
Carriage of Goods by Sea Act (COGSA), 535–36
Case Information Statement (New Jersey), 28, 29, 492, 498
Case value, estimating, 204–5
Cash flow adequacy ratio (CFAR), 419–21
Cash flow coverage ratio (CFC), 258–59
Cash flow method, 140–41
Cash flow (CF) ratios, 414–21
cash flow adequacy ratio (CFAR), 419–21
cash-flow-to-debt ratio, 415–17
operating cash flow to capital expenditures, 417–18
operating cash flow to dividends, 418–19
Cash flow statement, 254–59
burn rate and, 257–58
business damages and, 254–59
cash flow coverage ratio (CFC), 258–59
financing activities, 255
free cash flow and, 257–58
investing activities, 255
operating cash flow ratio (OCF), 259
operations activities, 255

Cash-flow-to-debt ratio, 415–17
Cash flow-to-interest expense ratio, 401
Casting out nines, 65–67
Causation, establishing, 601
Census Bureau, 100, 241, 242, 512
Central tendency, 96–102
  choosing between, 102
  mean, 96–99
    arithmetic mean *versus* geometric mean, 107–11
  median, 99–100
  mode, 100–101
Certifications, of experts, 578–95
Certifications and designations, 578–95
Chamber of Commerce's annual benefits survey, 210
Change, risk of, 13–15
Change in value (CV), 377–78
Charting restoration costs, 379–81
Checklisting steps, 599
Child labor provisions of FLSA, 313–14
Civil Rights Act of 1964, 334
Civil Rights Act of 1991, 327, 334
Cluster analysis, 600
Code of Federal Regulations (C.F.R.). *See* Title 14, Code of Federal Regulations; Title 49, United States Code, Subtitle VII
College for Financial Planning, 578
Combination result—both events occurring, 128–29
Combined losses, 431–33
Common shareholders, BVPS and, 147–48, 247
Common sizing
  balance sheets and, 248
  income statements, 253
Common stock
  in book value per share of stock (BVPS), 147–48, 168, 247
  on cash flow statement, 256
  in earnings per share (EPS), 155, 157, 250
  in equity-to-debt ratio, 409
  in net worth, 273
  in P/E ratio, 280
  in price-to-book (P/B) ratio, 148
Companionship, loss of, 222–23
Comparables
  P/E ratio and, 281
  trademarks and, 453–55
Comparison methodology, 376
Complement
  finding, 46–47
  in high-speed multiplication, 53–54
Compound annual growth rate (CAGR)
  calculating, 138–40
  capitalization of earnings method, 307
Compounding, monthly
  future value (FV), 84
  present value (PV), 88–89
Compound interest, 117–19
Comprehensive Environmental Response, Compensation, and Liability Act (CERCLA), 373, 375
Consulting expert, hiring, 602
Consumer Expenditure Surveys (CES), 217
Contingent liabilities, 33–34
Contingent valuation method (CVM), 393–94
Convoyed products, 428
"Cookie jar reserves," 19
Copyright Act, 468, 471–73
Copyrights
  actual damages plus profits, 468–71
    cost-of-production method, 469–70

number-of-products method, 470–71
sales revenue method, 471
infringer's accounting methods, 474–77
full absorption costing approach, 474–75
variable costing, 475–77
punitive damages, 473–74
statutory damages, 468, 471–73
Cost- and time-estimating relationships (CERs and TERs), 377
Cost approach, 348–51
Cost-estimating relationships (CERs), 377
Cost of goods sold (COGS)
in full absorption costing, 474
in gross profit margin (GPM) ratio, 293, 334
on income statements, 249, 253
in inventory turnover, 169–71
in net profit margin (NPM) ratio, 294
Cost-of-production method, 469–70
Cost savings, 467
Costs of environmental damages, determining, 375–77
comparison methodology, 376
cost- and time-estimating relationships (CERs and TERs), 377
factor methodology, 376
probability methodologies, 376
standard time data methodology, 376
unit methodology, 376
Counsel, loss of, 222–23
Creative accounting, 30–33
improper recognition of expenses, 32–33
improper recognition of revenue, 31–32
Credibility, in determining pain and suffering, 231, 232
Credit and investing rating services, 42
Cross-check using indicators, 25
Cross-multiplication, 63–64
Cumulative profitability, 404
Cure, for injured seaman, 537, 542
Current asset turnover (CAT)
on balance sheet, 246
calculating, 174
Current liabilities, 245
Current ratio
on balance sheet, 247–48
calculating, 175–76
liquidity measures and, 291
Current reports, 270–72
Customs and Border Patrol, 534

D

Daily maintenance rate (DMR), 542–43
Damage reducers, 215–18
personal consumption, estimating, 215–17
taxes, estimating, 218
Damages experts, 571–611
certifications and designations, 578–95
educational credentials, 573–78
formulas and, 37–39
objections to testimony of, 602–7
scientific validity and reliability, 607–11
theory of damages and, 37–38
top 25 rules for using, 595–602
when to retain, 571–73
Data
independent data test, 601
industry, 242
on Internet, free, 39–43
updating, 599
using recent, 25–26
Data mining techniques, 600

Daubert v. Merrill Dow Pharmaceuticals, 602, 610–11
Day of the year tables, 614–15
Death on the High Seas Act (DOHSA), 531–32
Debt, reassigning, 494
Debt service coverage ratio (DSCR), 365–67
Debt-to-asset ratio, 491–95
  reassigning assets, 494–95
  reassigning debt, 494
Debt-to-equity ratio (D/E)
  on balance sheet, 247
  Barnes & Noble, Inc., 160
  calculating, 159–61
  Microsoft Corp., 160, 162
Debt-to-worth (DTW) ratio, 292
Dependent events, 131–33
Designations, of experts, 578–95
Devising specific business ratios, 295–301
Dilution, 467
Direct income capitalization approach, 351–57
  applying formula, 356–57
  market capitalization rate, 353–55
  net operating income (NOI), 352–53
Disbenefits, 178–79
Discounted cash flow (DCF) approach, 357–61, 446–48
  alimony and spousal support, 487–88
  for calculating damages, 359–61
  trademarks, 446–48
Discounted future earnings method, 311–12
Discount rate
  in capitalization of earnings method, 304–5
  change in, 193
  in internal rate of return (IRR), 149
  validity of, 192–93
Discovery, value of, 217
Disgorgement, 465–66
Dividend, 56
Dividend yield, 162–63, 284
Division, high-speed, 56–60
Divisor, 56
Divorce. *See* Family law formulas
Doctor of Business Administration (DBA), 575–76
Doctor of Philosophy (Ph.D.), 575
Doctor treatment, in determining pain and suffering, 231, 233
Dollar Value of a Day, 221
Domestic exchanges, 41
Double counting, avoiding, 211
Doubling and halving techniques
  in high-speed division, 59–60
  in high-speed multiplication, 54–55
Doubling money, calculating time for, 181
Due diligence, 9–10

E

Earned surplus, 404
Earnings, change in, 193
Earnings, lost. *See* Lost earnings
Earnings and consumption myths, 34–35
Earnings before income tax to total assets (EBIT-to-TA), 407–8
Earnings per share (EPS), 155–57, 276–80
  in business damages, 276–80
  calculating, 155–57
  income statements and, 250–51
Earnings to price (E/P) ratio, 177
Earnings yield, 163–64
Economic circumstances, 237
Educational credentials, 573–78

Effective gross income (EGI), 352
Effective interest rate, 123–24
Emotional distress, 225–29
  general damages, 227–29
  pain and suffering distinguished from, 229–30
  special damages, 226–27
Employment. *See also* Employment law damages
  in determining pain and suffering, 231
  federal employment statutes, 314–16
  probability of, 196–97
Employment Cost Index, 323
Employment law damages, 313–41
  back pay, 321–27
  front pay, 316–21
  liquidated damages, 330–34
  nonpecuniary losses, 327–30
  prejudgment interest, 339–41
  punitive damages, 334–39
  statutory damages framework, 313
  timing issues, 16–17
Entire market rule, 428
Environmental damages, 373–98
  change in value (CV), 377–78
  contingent valuation method (CVM), 393–94
  hedonic pricing method, 389–90
  replacement costs, 384–89
  restoration costs, 378–84
  timing issues, 16
  total economic value (TEV), 394–98
  travel cost method, 391–93
  valuation methods, 373–77
  value after damage (VAD), 377–78
  value before damage (VBD), 377–78
EPS Growth Rate (EPSGR), 277–80
Equal Employment Opportunity Commission (EEOC), 314
Equal Pay Act (EPA), 323
Equity risk premium (ERP), 304
Equity-to-debt ratio, 408–10
Estimation models, 455–68
  attorneys' fees, 468
  blurring, 467
  cost savings, 467
  dilution, 467
  disgorgement, 465–66
  expected profit margin, 466
  5% rule, 465
  loss of goodwill, 467
  Monte Carlo simulation, 466
  orderly disposal value, 466
  for personal consumption, 215–17
  premium pricing method, 457–58
  product sales volume, 467
  profit split methods, 455–57
    excess earnings rate method, 455–56
    residual earnings rate method, 456–57
  proportionate value method, 463–64
  return on assets employed (ROAE), 460–63
  scale comparison method, 459–60
  specific statutory damage ranges, 466–67
  statutory damages, 466–67
  subtraction method, 463
  tarnishment, 467
  treble damages, 468
  25% rule, 464
  unjust enrichment, 467
Estimation techniques, 69–73
Eviction loss (EL) formula, 364–65
Ex ante method, 600
Excess earnings method, 309–11
Excess earnings rate method, 455–56
Excludable employment time (EET), 543–44, 545
Excludable hospital time (EHT), 543–44, 545

Executory contracts, 34
Exemplary damages, 335
Expected profit margin, 466
Expected rate of return (ERR), 141–42
Expenses
fixed and variable, 601
improper recognition of, 32–33
Expenses before interest and taxes (EBIT), 253–54
Experts and formulas, 37–39
Expert testimony. *See also* Damages experts
data, methods, and science, 604–5
laying foundation, 606–7
objections to, 602–7
qualifications, 603–4
Exponential moving averages (EMA), 105–7
Ex post method, 600
Extended useful life (EUL), 540–41
External sources of information, 240–43
ExxonMobil Corp., annual report of, 27

F

Factor methodology, 376
Fair Employment and Housing Act (FEHA), 316
Fair Labor Standards Act (FLSA), 314
base salary adjustments, 323
child labor provisions, 313–14
liquidated damages and, 330–34
punitive damages and, 335
Family law formulas, 479–527
break-even analysis, 516–18
Case Information Statement (New Jersey), 28, 29, 492, 498
fraud and irregularities, 20–21
gross and net analysis, 518–24
adjusted gross income (AGI), 518–19
net savings, 521–22
net worth, 522–24
taxable income, 520–21
pressing *vs.* patient liabilities, 526–27
ratio analysis, 491–502
debt-to-asset ratio, 491–95
liquid assets-to-current liabilities, 501–2
liquid assets to take-home pay ratio, 495–98
take-home pay to debt-service ratio, 498–501
time value calculations, 479–502
alimony and spousal support, 486–89
interest, assessing, 490–91
marital assets, division of, 479–86
timing issues, 16
valuation formulas, 502–16
actual cash value, 502–3
home affordability tests, 503–14
life insurance, adequacy of, 514–16
Wilcox's Prediction Formula, 524–26
Faulty trend-spotting, 25–26
Federal Aviation Administration (FAA), NOTAMS, 552, 556–57
Federal Employees Liability Act (FELA), 533
Federal employment statutes, 314–16
Federal Income Contributions Act (FICA) contributions, 214
Federal Reserve, 242–43
Final drill-down, 444
Final maintenance award (FMA), 543–44
Financial experts. *See* Damages experts
Financial news sources, 42–43

Financial ratios, 155–79. *See also* *Other types of ratios*
  accounts payable turnover (APT), 173–74
  accounts receivable turnover (ART), 171–73
  balance sheet calculations, 161–62
  benefit-cost ratio (BCR), 177–79
  capitalization rate (cap rate), 176–77
  current asset turnover (CAT), 174
  current ratio, 175–76
  debt-to-equity ratio (D/E), 159–61
  devising specific business ratios, 295–301
  dividend yield, 162–63
  earnings per share (EPS), 155–57
  earnings yield, 163–64
  interest coverage ratio, 166–68
  inventory turnover, 169–71
  price-to-book ratio (P/B), 168–69
  price-to-earnings ratio (P/E), 157–59
  quick ratio, 164–66
Financial statements, 243–62
  balance sheet, 243–49
  cash flow statement, 254–59
  income statement, 249–54
  information not included in, 259–62
5% rule, 465
Five times earnings valuation method (5E), 35–36
Fixed expenses, 601
Flight Data Center (FDC), 552
Footnotes and attachments, 26–29
Foreign exchanges, 41
Forensic experts. *See* Damages experts
Form 8-K, 263, 270–72
Form 8-Q, 270–72
Form 10-K, 262–68
Form 10-Q, 268–70
Formula approach, 309–11
Formulas. *See also* specific formulas
  arithmetic mean *versus* geometric mean, 107–11
  breakeven formula, 111–14
    price, determining, 113–14
    profit, breaking even with, 112–13
  business damages and, 235–38
  central tendency, 96–102
    choosing between, 102
    mean, 96–99
    median, 99–100
    mode, 100–101
  eviction loss (EL) formula, 364–65
  experts and, 37–39
  future value (FV), 83–84
  how to use, 3–5
  lost sales, 429–30
  moving averages, 102–7
    exponential, 105–7
    as predictors, 104–5
  net present value (NPV), 89–93
  perpetuities, present value of, 94–96
  present value (PV), 87–89
    of annuity, 93–94
    monthly compounding, 88–89
    of perpetuity, 95–96
  property damage loss (PDL) formula, 362–65
  quick rental loss (QRL) formula, 361–62
  reasons for using, 1–3
  rules for effective use of, 9–21
    assumptions, 10–11
    due diligence, 9–10
    formula value *versus* settlement value, 18
    fraud and irregularities, 20–21
    hidden and missing numbers, 19–20

money moves, 17–18
reliability and verifiability, 12
risk of change, 13–15
show me the money first, 21–22
timing issues, 15–17
strategies and myths, 23–43
creative accounting, 30–33
data on Internet, free, 39–43
earnings and consumption myths, 34–35
experts and formulas, 37–39
faulty trend-spotting, 25–26
footnotes and attachments, 26–29
off-balance sheet liabilities, 33–34
past performance and future results, 23–25
shortcuts and rules of thumb, 35–37
volatility and smoothing techniques, 29–30
time value of money, 81–82
for trials, 7
uneven cash flow, future value of, 85–87
when to use, 5–7
Formula value *versus* settlement value, 18
Forward multiples valuation method, 36
Forward P/E ratio, 281–82
Found, award for, 537, 538
401(k) plans, 206
Fractions, benchmarking, 70–71
Fraud and irregularities, 20–21
Free cash flow (FCF), 257–58, 416
Fringe benefits, lost. *See* Lost fringe benefits
Fringe rate, 208
Front pay, 316–21
Frye v. United States, 602
Full absorption costing approach, 474–75
Fully diluted earnings per share, 157
Future earnings
in capitalization of earnings method, 303–4
loss, 190–94
Future lost profits, 433–34
Future profits *versus* past losses, 37
Future results, 23–25
Future value (FV), 83–84
business damages and, 285
formula for, 83–84
future earnings loss, 191
marital assets, division of, 484–86
of marital assets, 484–86
monthly compounding, 84

G

General damages
for emotional distress, 227–29
maritime, 538–39
Generally Accepted Accounting Principles (GAAP), 600–601
Geometric mean
annual growth factors and, 277–78
arithmetic mean *versus,* 107–11
calculating, 108–9
when to use, 109–11
Georgia-Pacific Corp. v. U.S. Plywood Corp., 436, 438–39
GFI Brokers, LLC v. Santana, 330
Goodwill
of business, 301
loss of, 467
Government financial websites, 39–40
Greene v. Texeira, 201
Gross and net analysis, 518–24
adjusted gross income (AGI), 518–19
net savings, 521–22
net worth, 522–24
taxable income, 520–21

Gross income multiple test, 503–5
Gross income percentage test, 505
Gross potential income (GPI), 352
Gross profit margin (GPM), 293
Gross rent multiplier (GRM), 370–71
Group behavior, evaluating, 596
Growth rate and capitalization of earnings method, 305–8

H

Harvard University's fiscal year fringe rates, 210
Health insurance, 206–7
Hedonic damages, 223–25
Hedonic pricing method, 389–90
Hidden and missing numbers, 19–20
High-value patterns, moderating over time, 26
Home affordability tests, 503–14
- gross income multiple test, 503–5
- gross income percentage test, 505
- Housing Affordability Index (HAI), 510–13
- PITI tests, 506–9
- price-to-rent ratio, 513–14
- residual income test, 509–10
- take-home pay test, 505–6

Hospital treatment, in determining pain and suffering, 231, 233
Household services, loss of, 219–22
Housing Affordability Index (HAI), 510–13
Housing and Urban Development (HUD), 513
Hovering hundreds, 64–65
Hypotheticals, framing, 598

I

Ibbotson Associates, 304, 305
Impeachment materials, gathering, 597
Income, in determining pain and suffering, 231, 232
Income loss formulas, 365
- debt service coverage ratio (DSCR), 365–67
- gross rent multiplier (GRM), 370–71
- return on investment (ROI), 368–70

Income method, 446
Income statement, 249–54
- business damages and, 249–54
- common sizing, 253
- cost of goods sold (COGS), 249, 253
- earnings per share (EPS), 250–51
- expenses before interest and taxes (EBIT), 253–54
- interest coverage ratio, 253–54
- marketing expenses and, 253
- price-to-earnings ratio (P/E), 252

Incremental income approach, 427–28
Indebtedness, liquidity *versus,* 290–92
Independent data test, 601
Individual retirement accounts (IRAs), 206
Industry data, 242
Inflation, future earnings loss and, 193
Information, sources of, 238–43
Infringer's accounting methods, 474–77
In re. See Name of party
Intellectual property damages, 423–77. *See also* Copyrights; Patents; Trademarks
- estimation models, 455–68
- infringer's accounting methods, 474–77
- lost profits, 423–36

royalties, 436–44
statutory damage schemes, 468–74
valuation methods, 444–55
Interest, assessing, 490–91
Interest, calculating, 115–24
compound interest, 117–19
effective interest rate, 123–24
family law cases, 490–91
nominal interest rate, 120–22
periodic interest rate, 122–23
principal, rate, and time, 119–20
real interest rate, 120–22
Rule of 78, 184–87
simple interest, 115–17
Interest coverage ratio
calculating, 166–68
income statements and, 253–54
Internal growth rate (IG), 405, 406
Internal rate of return (IRR), 148–51
Internal sources of information, 238–40
International Assembly for Collegiate Business Education (IACBE), 576
International Carrier Bond, 534
International Convention on Salvage 1989, 546–47
International Monetary Fund (IMF), 558–59
Internet, free data on, 39–43
credit and investing rating services, 42
domestic exchanges, 41
financial news sources, 42–43
foreign exchanges, 41
government financial websites, 39–40
investor websites, 40–41
wage and salary data, 42
Inventory methods, changes in, 13
Inventory turnover, 169–71
Investor websites, 40–41
Itemized present value approach, 207–8
Item 103 of Regulations S-K, 264

J

Jones Act, 532–33
Jones & Laughlin Steel Corp. v. Pfeifer, 200–201
Journals as source of information, 239
Jury selection, 132

K

Kraft Foods, Inc., annual report of, 239–40
Kumho Tire Co. v. Carmichael, 610–11

L

Labor Department, 243, 323
Labor force participation, probability of, 196
Lanham Act, 445, 468
Left-to-right logic, 49
Legal events precipitating loss, 235
Leverage measures, 292
Liabilities
on balance sheet, 244–45
contingent, 33–34
current, 245
liquid assets-to-current, 501–2
long-term, 245, 416
noncurrent, 416
off-balance sheet, 33–34
pressing *vs.* patient, 526–27
Life insurance, adequacy of, 514–16
Life-Participation-Employment (LPE) approach, 195
Limited term alimony (present value of annuity), 488–89
Liquid assets-to-current liabilities, 501–2
Liquid assets to take-home pay ratio, 495–98

Liquidated damages, 330–34
  ADEA and, 331–32
  amount of, controlling, 331–32
  award of, attacking, 332–34
Liquidity measures, 291
Liquidity *versus* indebtedness, 290–92
Literature, 597–98
Living, probability of, 195
Loans, 186
Loan-to-value ratio (LTV), 355
Longshore Harbor and Workers Compensation Act (LHWCA), 532, 538
Long-term liabilities, 245, 416
Loss of goodwill, 467
Lost earnings, 189–205
  basic formulas, 189–90
  case value, estimating, 204–5
  future earnings loss, 190–94
  offset approaches, 200–204
  work expectancy, 194–99
Lost fringe benefits, 205–15
  back pay and, 325–26
  BLS tables of employer costs per hour for, 566–67
  Bureau of Labor Statistics' reports on employee benefits, 210
  calculating, 205–11
  Social Security benefits, 214–15
  stock options, 211–13
  U.S. Chamber of Commerce's annual benefits survey, 210
Lost profits, 423–36
  accelerated entry damages, 434–36
  combined losses, 431–33
  conceptual framework, 423–26
  future lost profits, 433–34
  lost sales and. *See* Lost sales
  measuring, 425
  price erosion, 430–31
Lost sales, 426–30
  incremental income approach, 427–28
  other losses, capturing, 428–29
  shortcut formulas, 429–30

M

Maintenance, for injured seaman, 537, 543
Major Memory System, 73–77
Marital assets, division of, 479–86
  future value (FV), 484–86
  net-net-net present value, 483–84
  net present value (NPV), 482–83
  present value (PV), 480–81
Maritime law. *See* Admiralty law
Maritime Transportation Security Act, 534
Market approach, 36–37, 453–54
Market capitalization rate (cap rate), 353–55
Market comparables method, 453–55
Market Data Center, 242
Marketing expenses, 249
Martin, Gerald D., 204
Master of Accountancy (MAc or MAcc), 577
Master of Business Administration (MBA), 576
Master of Science (MS), 577
Matched pair analysis, 345
Math problems, solving, 45–79
  addition, high-speed, 47–49
  complement, finding, 46–47
  division, high-speed, 56–60
  estimation techniques, 69–73
    benchmarking fractions, 70–71
    estimating decimals, 71
    estimating square roots, 71–73
    rounding numbers, 69–70

memorization strategies, 73–79
Major Memory System, 73–77
mnemonic peg systems, 77–79
multiplication, high-speed, 52–55
complements, 53–54
doubling and halving techniques, 54–55
multiple zeros, 54
numbers ending in 5, 55
rounding up, 53
percentage power, 67–69
rapid squaring, 60–62
rounding and reversing, 50–52
shortcutting and double-checking, 62–67
casting out nines, 65–67
cross-multiplication, 63–64
hovering hundreds, 64–65
reverse subtraction, 62–63
subtraction, high-speed, 49–50
Maximum medical cure, 537
Maximum medical improvement (MMI), 542, 544, 545
Mean
arithmetic *versus* geometric, 107–11
formula for, 96–99
Median, 99–100
Medical cost/discount rate offset, 201
Medical treatment, in determining pain and suffering, 231, 233
Memorization strategies, 73–79
Major Memory System, 73–77
mnemonic peg systems, 77–79
Mental health, in determining pain and suffering, 231, 233
MGM Resorts International, 143–44
Microsoft Corp.
debt-to-equity ratio (D/E), 160, 162
total assets, 162
Uniloc USA, Inc. v. Microsoft Corp., 610
Mnemonic peg systems, 77–79
Number Rhyme System, 77–78
Number Shape System, 79
Mode, 100–101
Money, movement of, 17–18
Monte Carlo simulation, 466
Monthly compounding
future value (FV), 84
present value (PV), 88–89
Montreal Convention, 557–59, 563–65
Mortality tables, 613
Motivation, exploring, 597
Moving averages, 102–7
exponential, 105–7
as predictors, 104–5
Multiple event probability, 127–30
alternative result—either event occurring, 129–30
combination result—both events occurring, 128–29
Multiples method, 312
Multiplication, high-speed, 52–55
complements, 53–54
doubling and halving techniques, 54–55
multiple zeros, 54
numbers ending in 5, 55
rounding up, 53
Multipliers for determining pain and suffering, 230–33
Mutually exclusive events, 133–34

N

National Association of Realtors (NAR), 510, 513
National Technical Information Service (NTIS), 195
Natural Resource Damage Assessments (NRDAs), 375

Net discount rate (NDR), 193, 203–4
Net-net-net present value, 483–84
Net operating income (NOI), 352–53
Net present value (NPV)
  alternatives, choosing between, 92–93
  environmental damages and, 382–83
  formula, 89–93
  marital assets, division of, 482–83
Net profit margin (NPM), 293–95
Net replacement value (NRV), 386–89
Net savings, 521–22
Net terminal value (NTV)
  calculating, 151–53
  trademarks and, 448–50
Net worth (NW)
  business damages and, 272–74
  calculating, 146
  family law cases, 522–24
Nominal interest rate, 120–22, 491
Noncurrent liabilities, 416
Nonpecuniary losses, 327–30
Nonuse value (NV), 394–95
Norfolk and Western Railway Co. v. Liepelt, 218
Normalized earnings, 309
North American Industry Classification System (NAICS), 241–42
Notices to Airmen (NOTAMS), 552, 556–57
Number-of-products method, 470–71
Number Rhyme System, 77–78
Numbers
  change in, risk of, 13–15
  hidden and missing, 19–20
  reversing, 50–52
  rounding, 69–70
    in high speed addition and subtraction, 50–52
    in high-speed multiplication, 53
    in rapid squaring, 61–62
Number Shape System, 79
Numerical rules, 181–87
  Rule of 69.3, 183–84
  Rule of 70, 182–83
  Rule of 72, 181–82
  Rule of 78, 184–87
  Rule of 114, 181–82
  Rule of 144, 182

O

Obligor, 486–87
Ocean Shipping Reform Act (OSRA), 534–35
Off-balance sheet liabilities, 33–34
Offset approaches, 200–204
  Alaska Rule (wage increase/discount rate), 200–201
  medical cost/discount rate offset, 201
  net discount rate (NDR), 203–4
  partial offsets, 202–3
  tax-for-benefits method, 202
  tax-for-tax offset method, 201–2
Oil Pollution Act (OPA), 373, 535
Operating cash flow (OCF)
  bankruptcy risk and, 414–21
  business damages and, 254–59
  to capital expenditures, 417–18
  to dividends, 418–19
Operating expenses, 352
Orderly disposal value, 466
Outer Continental Shelf Lands Act (OCSLA), 533
Overpricing, 281
Owner benefit valuation, 312

P

Pain and suffering, 229–33
  determinants of, 231–32
  emotional distress distinguished from, 229–30

multipliers for determining, 230–33
postimpact, 561, 568
predeath, 568
preimpact, 561
sample scales, 232, 233
Paired sales analysis, 345
Panduit Corp. v. Stahlin Brothers Fibre Works, Inc., 426
Panduit test, 426–27
Partial offsets, 202–3
Partnerships, balance sheets and, 245
Past losses *versus* future profits, 37
Past performance and future results, 23–25
Patents
lost profits, 423–36
accelerated entry damages, 434–36
combined losses, 431–33
conceptual framework, 423–26
future lost profits, 433–34
lost sales, 426–30
measuring, 425
price erosion, 430–31
royalties, 436–44
analytical approach, 439–40
final drill-down, 444
reasonable royalty, 436–39
royalties per unit (RPU), 444
weighted average cost of capital (WACC), 440–44
Payment ability, verifying, 21–22
Payor spouse, 486–87
P/E. *See* Price-to-earnings ratio (P/E)
Percentage-of-earnings approach, 208–10
Percentage power, 67–69
Periodic interest rate, 122–23
Permanent alimony (perpetuities), 488
Permanent partial disability (PPD), 537
Permanent total disability (PTD), 537
Perpetuity
growing, 95–96
permanent alimony, 488
present value (PV) of, 94–96, 488
Perpetuity method, 152–53
Personal consumption, estimating, 215–17
discovery, value of, 217
methods of, 216–17
Personal injury and wrongful death damages, 189–233
damage reducers, 215–18
emotional distress, 225–29
hedonic damages, 223–25
losses
advice, counsel, and companionship, 222–23
earnings, 189–205
fringe benefits, 205–15
household services, 219–22
pain and suffering, 229–33
PetSmart, Inc., 145
PITI tests, 506–9
Polinsky, A. Mitchell, 336–38
Postdiscovery analysis, 596
Postimpact pain and suffering, 561, 568
Potential gross income (PGI), 352
Pre-allision remaining useful life (RUL), 541
Predeath pain and suffering, 568
Predictors, moving averages as, 104–5
Prediscovery consultation, 595–96
Preimpact pain and suffering, 561
Prejudgment interest, 339–41
Premium pricing method, 457–58
Present value (PV), 87–89, 381–82
of annuity, 93–94
business damages and, 285
environmental damages and, 381–82
formula, 87–89

future earnings loss and, 192
marital assets, division of, 480–81
of marital assets, 480–81
monthly compounding, 88–89
of perpetuity, 94–96, 488
Pressing *vs.* patient liabilities, 526–27
Price, breakeven formula and, 113–14
Price, determining, 113–14
Price-earnings-growth ratio (PEG), 282–83
Price elasticity of demand, 431
Price erosion, 430–31
Price-to-book ratio (P/B), 148
on balance sheet, 246–47
calculating, 168–69
Price-to-earnings ratio (P/E), 157–59, 280–85
business damages and, 280–85
calculating, 157–59
capitalization rate, 177
comparables, 281
as decision-making tool, 159
forward P/E ratio, 281–82
income statements and, 252
overpricing and underpricing, 281
price-earnings-growth ratio (PEG), 282–83
price-to-earnings-to-growth-and-yield ratio (PEGY), 283–85
Price-to-earnings-to-growth-and-yield ratio (PEGY), 283–85
Price-to-rent ratio, 513–14
Pricing of stock, 281
Principal, in calculating interest, 119–20
Probability
of employment, 196–97
of labor force participation, 196
of living, 195
Probability, determining, 125–34
dependent events, 131–33
multiple event probability, 127–30
alternative result—either event occurring, 129–30
combination result—both events occurring, 128–29
mutually exclusive events, 133–34
relative frequency, 126–27
single event probability, 125–27
relative frequency, 126–27
Probability methodologies, 376
Product sales volume, 467
Professional practices and small businesses, 301–12
asset-based valuation method, 312
business damages and, 301–12
capitalization of earnings method, 303–9
discounted future earnings method, 311–12
excess earnings method, 309–11
multiples method, 312
owner benefit valuation, 312
Profit, breaking even with, 112–13
Profit margins, 292–95
gross profit margin (GPM), 293
net profit margin (NPM), 293–95
Profits, lost. *See* Lost profits
Profit split methods, 455–57
Property, plant, and equipment (PP&E), 418, 420, 461–62
Property damage loss (PDL) formula, 362–65
Property value formula, 356–57
Proportionate value method, 463–64
Puerto Rico, Commonwealth of v. The SS Zoe Colocotroni, 384–85
Punitive damages
ADA and, 335
ADEA and, 335
amount of, 334–35
calculating, 335–39

copyrights and, 473–74
Title VII actions and, 334–35

Q

Quadrupling, 181–82
Qualifications, exploring, 597
Quick ratio
calculating, 164–66
liquidity measures and, 501
Quick rental loss (QRL) formula, 361–62
Quotient, 56

R

Rapid squaring, 60–62
round and revise, 61–62
squaring numbers that end in 5, 62
25-and-50 method, 60–61
Rate
in calculating interest, 119–20
establishing, 598
Rates of return (ROR), 135–53, 285–90
basic calculation, 135–36
book value (BV), 147–48
book value per share of stock (BVPS), 147–48
business damages and, 285–90
cash flow method, 140–41
compound annual growth rate (CAGR), 138–40
expected rate of return (ERR), 141–42
internal rate of return (IRR), 148–51
net terminal value (NTV), 151–53
net worth (NW), 146
return on assets (ROA), 144–46, 288–89
return on average assets (ROAA), 289
return on average equity (ROAE), 288
return on common equity (ROCE), 287
return on equity (ROE), 143–44, 287
return on investment (ROI), 136–38
return on operating assets (ROOA), 289
simple annualized return on investment, 138
terminal value (TV), 151–53
Ratio analysis, 491–502
debt-to-asset ratio, 491–95
liquid assets-to-current liabilities, 501–2
liquid assets to take-home pay ratio, 495–98
take-home pay to debt-service ratio, 498–501
Ratios. *See* Financial ratios
Real estate damages, 343–71
cause and origin of claims, 343–44
cost approach, 348–51
direct income capitalization approach, 351–57
discounted cash flow (DCF) approach, 357–61
income loss formulas, 365
debt service coverage ratio (DSCR), 365–67
gross rent multiplier (GRM), 370–71
return on investment (ROI), 368–70
rental loss formulas, 361–65
sales comparison approach, 344–48
Real interest rate, 120–22
Reasonable royalty, 436–39
Recoverable repair costs (RRC), 540–41
Relative frequency, 126–27

Reliability and verifiability, 12
Remainder, 56
Rental loss formulas, 361–65
  eviction loss (EL) formula, 364–65
  property damage loss (PDL) formula, 362–65
  quick rental loss (QRL) formula, 361–62
Repair costs, 363, 505, 540–41
Repetitive spikes, 25
Replacement cost method
  environmental damages and, 384–89
  net replacement value (NRV), 386–89
  trademarks and, 450–53
Residual earnings rate method, 456–57
Residual income test, 509–10
Response quality, testing, 596
Restoration costs, 378–84
  benefit-cost analysis, applying, 383–84
  charting, 379–81
  net present value (NPV), applying, 382–83
  present value (PV), determining, 381–82
Retained earnings to total assets ratio (RE-to-TA), 404–7
Retirement programs, 205, 206, 208, 313
Return on assets (ROA)
  balance sheets and, 288–89
  business damages and, 406–7
  calculating, 144–46
  PetSmart, Inc., 145
Return on assets employed (ROAE), 460–63
Return on average assets (ROAA), 289
Return on average equity (ROAE), 288
Return on common equity (ROCE), 287
Return on equity (ROE)
  business damages and, 287–88
  calculating, 143–44
  MGM Resorts International, 143–44
Return on investment (ROI)
  calculating, 136–38
  real estate damages and, 368–70
Return on operating assets (ROOA), 289
Revenue, improper recognition of, 31–32
Reverse engineering, 59
Reverse subtraction, 62–63
Reversing numbers, 50–52
Risk-free rate of return, 304
Risk of change, 13–15
Rite-Hite Corp. v. Kelley, 428
Rounding numbers, 69–70
  in high speed addition and subtraction, 50–52
  in high-speed multiplication, 53
  in rapid squaring, 61–62
Royalties, 436–44
  analytical approach, 439–40
  final drill-down, 444
  reasonable royalty, 436–39
  royalties per unit (RPU), 444
  weighted average cost of capital (WACC), 440–44
Rule 702, 603–4
Rule of 69.3, 183–84
Rule of 70, 182–83
Rule of 72, 181–82
Rule of 78, 184–87
Rule of 114, 181–82
Rule of 144, 182

Rules for using formulas effectively, 9–21
- assumptions, 10–11
- due diligence, 9–10
- formula value *versus* settlement value, 18
- fraud and irregularities, 20–21
- hidden and missing numbers, 19–20
- money moves, 17–18
- reliability and verifiability, 12
- risk of change, 13–15
- show me the money first, 21–22
- timing issues, 15–17

S

Safe rate (SR), 304
Sales, lost. *See* Lost sales
Sales comparison approach, 344–48
Sales revenue method, 471
Sales-to-total-assets ratio, 410–11
Salvage Treaty test, 546–47
Scale comparison method, 459–60
Seamen, damages for injured, 536–38, 541–45
Securities and Exchange Commission (SEC), forms required by, 262–72
Security deposit (SD), 362–63, 365
Selling costs, general, and administrative (SG&A), 474–75
Setoffs, 200, 218
Settlement value, formula value *versus,* 18
Share capital, 275
Shareholders' equity, 274–76
- average shareholders' equity (ASE), 275
- on balance sheet, 245
- beginning shareholders' equity, 276
- business damages and, 274–76
- in return on equity (ROE), 143

Shavell, Steven, 336–38
Shipping Act of 1984, 534
Shortcuts and rules of thumb, 35–37
Shortcutting and double-checking, 62–67
- casting out nines, 65–67
- cross-multiplication, 63–64
- hovering hundreds, 64–65
- reverse subtraction, 62–63

Simple annualized return on investment, 138
Simple interest, 115–17
Single event probability, 125–27
Six-factor Blackwall test, 546
Small businesses. *See* Professional practices and small businesses
Small-size risk premium (SRP), 305
Smoothing techniques, 29–30
Social Security benefits, 214–15
Social Security Disability (SSD) benefits, 215
Somatoform disorders, 228
Sorenson, Philip E., 385
Special damages, 226–27
Special drawing rights (SDRs), 558–60
Specialty degrees, other, 577–78
Specialty doctorates, 576
Specific company risk premium (SCRP), 305
Specific statutory damage ranges, 466–67
Spousal support. *See* Alimony and spousal support
Square roots, estimating, 71–73
SS Zoe Colocotroni case, 386
Stable growth model, 153, 450
Standard time data methodology, 376

Starbucks, annual report of, 27
State Farm Mutual Automobile Insurance Co. v. Campbell, 336
Statutory damages
  copyrights and, 468, 471–73
  employment law, 313
  framework, 313
  range of amounts, 466–67
  top 40 federal statutes, 314–16
  trademarks and, 445
Statutory damage schemes, 468–74
  actual damages plus profits, 468–71
  punitive damages, 473–74
  statutory damages, 471–73
Stock, pricing of, 281
Stock options, 211–13
Strategies and myths, 23–43
  creative accounting, 30–33
  data on Internet, free, 39–43
  earnings and consumption myths, 34–35
  experts and formulas, 37–39
  faulty trend-spotting, 25–26
  footnotes and attachments, 26–29
  off-balance sheet liabilities, 33–34
  past and future, 23–25
  shortcuts and rules of thumb, 35–37
  volatility and smoothing techniques, 29–30
Subpoenas, 10, 596
Substitution, principle of, 345, 348
Subtraction, high-speed, 49–50
Subtraction method, 463
Superfund law, 373, 375

T

Take-home pay test, 505–6
Take-home pay to debt-service ratio, 498–501
  modifying support, 500
  reducing debt service, 500–501
Tangible book value, 147
Tarnishment, 467
Taxable income, 520–21
Tax basis, clarifying, 598
Taxes
  on back pay, 327
  estimating for damage reduction, 218
  jury instructions related to, 219
Tax-for-benefits method, 202
Tax-for-tax offset method, 201–2
Temporary Flight Restrictions (TFRs), 552, 556–57
Temporary partial disability (TPD), 537
Temporary total disability (TTD), 537
Ten Basic Rules, 9–22, 602
  assumptions and formula-building, 10–11
  due diligence, 9–10
  formula value *versus* settlement value, 18
  fraud and irregularities, 20–21
  hidden and missing numbers, 19–20
  money, movement of, 17–18
  payment ability, verifying, 21–22
  reliability and verifiability, 12
  risk of change, 13–15
  timing issues, 15–17
10-factor Salvage Treaty test, 546–47
Terminal value (TV), 151–53, 448–50
  basic formula, 151–52, 448–49
  perpetuity method, 152–53
  stable growth model, 153, 450
Testifying from report, 596–97
Theory of damages, 37–38
Time, in calculating interest, 119–20

Time-estimating relationships (TERs), 377
Times interest earned ratio, 401
Time value calculations, 479–502
  alimony and spousal support, 486–89
  interest, assessing, 490–91
  marital assets, division of, 479–86
Time value of money, 81–82
Timing issues, 15–17
Title 14, Code of Federal Regulations
  Subchapter F (small unmanned aircraft systems and drones), 554–55
  Subchapter G (air carrier certification and operations), 552–54
Title 49, United States Code, Subtitle VII
  Part A, Subpart I, Chapter 401 (general provisions), 555
  Part A, Subpart III, Chapter 448 (unmanned aircraft systems), 555
  Part A, Subpart III, Chapter 449 (security), 556
  Part B, Chapter 471, Subchapter I (airport improvements), 555–56
Title VII actions
  back pay, 323
  front pay, 316–17
  nonpecuniary losses, 327, 329
  prejudgment interest and, 339–41
  punitive damages and, 334–35
Top 40 federal statutes, 314–16
Total economic value (TEV), 394–98
Total replacement and repair costs (TRC), 540–41
Trademarks
  estimation models, 455–68
    attorneys' fees, 468
    blurring, 467
    cost savings, 467
    dilution, 467
    disgorgement, 465–66
    expected profit margin, 466
    5% rule, 465
    loss of goodwill, 467
    Monte Carlo simulation, 466
    orderly disposal value, 466
    premium pricing method, 457–58
    product sales volume, 467
    profit split methods, 455–57
    proportionate value method, 463–64
    return on assets employed (ROAE), 460–63
    scale comparison method, 459–60
    specific statutory damage ranges, 466–67
    statutory damages, 445
    subtraction method, 463
    tarnishment, 467
    treble damages, 468
    25% rule, 464
    unjust enrichment, 467
  valuation methods, 444–55
    discounted cash flow (DCF) approach, 446–48
    market comparables method, 453–55
    net terminal value (NTV) approach, 448–50
    overview, 444–45
    replacement cost method, 450–53
Travel cost method, 391–93
Treasury Department, 243
Treasury shares, 275

Treatises, 597–98
Treble damages, 468
Trend spotting, faulty, 25–26
Trials, use of formulas at, 7
Tripling, 181–82
25-and-50 method, 60–61
25% rule, 464, 610

U

Underpricing, 281
Unearned wages, for injured seaman, 537, 542
Uneven cash flow, future value of, 85–87
Uniloc USA, Inc. v. Microsoft Corp., 610
Unimodal display, 101
Unit methodology, 376
Unjust enrichment, 467
Unseaworthiness, 537
Unused benefits, avoiding, 211
U.S. Department of ___. *See Name of department*
Use value (UV), 394–95

V

ValCALC methodology, 461
Valuation formulas, 502–16
  actual cash value, 502–3
  home affordability tests, 503–14
  life insurance, adequacy of, 514–16
Valuation methods
  asset approaches, 36
  costs, determining, 375–77
  discounted cash flow (DCF) approach, 446–48
  environmental damages and, 373–77
  five times earnings, 35–36
  forward multiples, 36
  market approaches, 36–37
  market comparables method, 453–55
  Natural Resource Damage Assessments (NRDAs), 375
  net terminal value (NTV) approach, 448–50
  overview, 444–45
  replacement cost method, 450–53
  trademarks and, 444–55
    discounted cash flow (DCF) approach, 446–48
    market comparables method, 453–55
    net terminal value (NTV) approach, 448–50
    overview, 444–45
    replacement cost method, 450–53
Value after damage (VAD), 377–78
Value before damage (VBD), 377–78
Variable costing, 475–77
Variable expenses, 601
Verifiability, 12
Vesting period, 212
Volatility, 29–30

W

Wage and salary data, 42
Wage increase/discount rate (Alaska Rule), 200–201
Wall Street Journal Prime Rate, 243
Weighted average cost of capital (WACC), 440–44
Wilcox's Prediction Formula, 524–26
Williams Securities Litigation, 610–11
Witness quality, in determining pain and suffering, 231
Work expectancy, 194–99
  in aviation, 567
  Bureau of Labor Statistics and, 195

- future earnings loss and, 194–99
- labor force participation, probability of, 196
- Life-Participation-Employment (LPE) approach, 195
- probability of employment, 196–97
- probability of labor force participation, 196
- probability of living, 195
- work life expectancy tables, 198–99

Working capital (WC), 291
Working capital to total assets, 402–4
Work life expectancy. *See* Work expectancy
Wreck Act, 535
Wrongful death damages. *See* Personal injury and wrongful death damages

Y

Yield curve, 24, 243

Z

Zeros, multiplying, 54
Zone of insolvency, 605
Z-score bankruptcy prediction formula, 412–14

About the Author

Mark S. Guralnick is a trial lawyer, a law professor, and an author of numerous books and articles in various legal specialties. He has practiced extensively in the fields of civil litigation, family law, and criminal defense.

He is admitted to practice in Massachusetts, New York, New Jersey, Pennsylvania, Maryland, Florida, Michigan, Kentucky, the District of Columbia, and the Commonwealth of the Northern Mariana Islands. He is also admitted as a solicitor of England, Wales, and Scotland. Based primarily in New Jersey, he maintains offices throughout the United States.

Mr. Guralnick has also taught law, political science, business, and media courses at Rutgers University, Ramapo College, the University of Denver, the Pennsylvania State University, and other schools. He has authored books in a variety of practice specialties ranging from employment law to interstate child custody litigation.

A graduate of Columbia University, London Business School, Bennington College, and other schools, Mr. Guralnick holds two MBAs, a Ph.D. in political science, an LLM in international law, a JD degree, and master's degrees in public administration and in fine arts. Among his various leadership positions and appointments, he has served on the Board of Governors of the American Board of Professional Liability Attorneys and as chairman of the International Law Section of the New Jersey State Bar Association.